Beverly Heckart is professor emerita of history at Central Washington University, Ellensburg where she taught German, European and World History for four decades. She has resided intermittently in France and Germany for ten years and has previously published works on French and German urban history.

For
Dietrich Gerhard
Jack Hexter
Purveyors of Professional Principles and Practices

Beverly Heckart

DRESDEN: PORTRAIT OF A CITY

AUSTIN MACAULEY PUBLISHERS®
LONDON * CAMBRIDGE * NEW YORK * SHARJAH

Copyright © Beverly Heckart 2025

All rights reserved. No part of this publication may be reproduced, distributed, or transmitted in any form or by any means, including photocopying, recording, or other electronic or mechanical methods, without the prior written permission of the publisher, except in the case of brief quotations embodied in critical reviews and certain other non-commercial uses permitted by copyright law. For permission requests, write to the publisher.

Any person who commits any unauthorized act in relation to this publication may be liable to criminal prosecution and civil claims for damages.

The story, experiences, and words are the author's alone.

Ordering Information
Quantity sales: Special discounts are available on quantity purchases by corporations, associations, and others. For details, contact the publisher at the address below.

Publisher's Cataloging-in-Publication data
Heckart, Beverly
Dresden: Portrait of a City

ISBN 9798889108948 (Paperback)
ISBN 9798889108955 (Hardback)
ISBN 9798889108962 (ePub e-book)

Library of Congress Control Number: 2024902857

www.austinmacauley.com/us

First Published 2025
Austin Macauley Publishers LLC
40 Wall Street, 33rd Floor, Suite 3302
New York, NY 10005
USA

mail-usa@austinmacauley.com
+1 (646) 5125767

Table of Contents

Prologue In the Beginning   13

I. Dresden Becomes "Dresden"   19
- *The Elector Moritz*   19
- *August I: Building upon the Foundation*   21
- *Dresden and Protestant Saxony*   25

II. The Noble City: Downs and Ups   30
- *The Thirty Years' War*   30
- *Creating the Baroque City*   32
- *Building for the Baroque*   36
- *A Party of Princes*   37

III. The Era of August the Strong   40
- *The Baroque City*   40
- *Baroque Architecture*   43
- *The Zwinger*   44
- *The Elbe as Grand Canal*   47
- *The Neustadt*   48
- *The City Grows*   49
- *Pageantry*   50
- *The Economy*   53
- *Gold and Gems*   55
- *The Green Vaults*   56

White Gold	*57*
The Royal Art Collection	*58*
Dresden's Splendor	*59*
The Court Church	*60*
The Finest Music in Europe	*61*
Theater	*63*
Count Brühl	*63*
Expanding the Royal Collections	*64*
Saxon Rococo	*66*
IV. Dresden Copes with Distress	**68**
Dresden in the Eighteenth-Century World War	*68*
Dresden Copes with Defeat	*71*
Economic Development	*73*
Social Change at the Theater	*75*
Eighteenth-Century Amusements	*77*
Nature	*78*
Club Life	*80*
Dresden's Lower Classes	*82*
V. The French Wars	**84**
The Battle of Dresden	*87*
Dresden Demoted, Saxony Diminished	*90*
VI. Revolutionary Dresden	**91**
Peace Returns	*91*
Reorganizing Dresden	*93*
Forceful Revolution	*94*
Dresden Receives New Life	*99*
Toward the Industrial City	*101*

Steam	*103*
Carl Gustav Carus	*105*
Old Treasures in a New Setting	*105*
Outstanding Artists	*109*
Revolutionary Music	*112*
The Non-Revolutionary Theater	*117*
Revolution Again	*120*
VII. Industrial Dresden	**129**
An Industrial Hub	*130*
Integration into United Germany	*132*
Cameras	*134*
Machinery	*135*
Shopping	*136*
Dresden Expands	*138*
Education	*141*
Government	*143*
VIII. The Middle-Class City	**145**
Music	*145*
Theater	*147*
Art	*150*
Middle-Class Leisure	*154*
The Spa at Weisser Hirsch	*156*
Municipal Improvement	*157*
Reform	*158*
The "Bird Shoot (Vogelschiessen)"	*163*
Hellerau	*165*
World War I	*170*

IX. The Weimar Republic   **180**

   A Period of Unrest   *180*

   The Quest for Stability   *185*

   The Crisis of 1923   *186*

   Republican Dresden   *191*

   Modern High Culture   *193*

   Dresden at Leisure   *196*

   Freshening Up the Architecture   *199*

X. Dresden in the Third Reich   **202**

   The Great Depression   *202*

   The National Socialists Revive Dresden   *206*

   Dresden Churches   *212*

   Everyday Life   *215*

   Sport   *218*

   Theater and Art   *219*

   Circus Sarrasani   *221*

   Other Entertainments   *224*

   Racial Hygiene   *226*

   War on the Horizon   *227*

XI. The Jews of Dresden   **229**

   Early Settlement in the Middle Ages   *229*

   The Early Modern Period   *230*

   Jewish Emancipation in Dresden   *234*

   Assimilation   *239*

   Eastern Jews   *241*

   Anti-Semitism   *242*

   Dresden Jews in the Weimar Republic   *244*

Exclusion	*246*
Crystal Night	*254*
Death	*256*
XII. Shrove Tuesday-Ash Wednesday, 1945	**260**
The Industrial City as a Target	*260*
Bombs Fall on Dresden	*264*
Destruction	*265*
Aftermath	*271*
XIII. The Socialist City	**275**
War's End	*275*
Soviet Normalcy	*276*
The Socialist Unity Party and the Division of Germany	*281*
The Socialist Economy	*284*
The Crisis of the 1950s	*286*
Renewed Repression	*293*
XIV. Post-War Elbflorence	**295**
Early Post-war Developments	*295*
A Birthday Celebration	*295*
Art	*296*
Music	*298*
Rudolf Mauersberger	*299*
Theater	*304*
Sports	*305*
XV. Rebuilding the "City So Deserted…"	**312**
Ruins	*312*
Housing for Ordinary Dresdners	*317*
A New Shopping Street	*318*

Jewish Revival	*319*
XVI. Dresden's Post-war Economy: Herald of the Future	**323**
Old Business	*323*
Dresden Enters the Digital Age	*326*
Microelectronics	*327*
The Technical College/University	*328*
Education as Economic Magnet	*332*
Dresden's Unicorn	*334*
XVII. On the Way to Revolution	**337**
The Local Leadership Changes	*337*
Discontent	*340*
Gorbachev and the Soviet Union	*342*
XVIII. "Velvet Revolution"	**348**
The End of the GDR	*353*
XIX. Reunified	**359**
The Economy	*360*
A New Image for Old Patterns	*365*
Jewish Life after 1990	*369*
More Reminders of the Past	*371*
Updating the Infrastructure	*377*
The Kulturpalast	*379*
Epilogue Dresden's Place in the World	**382**
Acknowledgements	**385**
Select Bibliography	**386**
Notes	**390**

Prologue
In the Beginning

In 1969, Kurt Vonnegut's *Slaughterhouse Five* made Dresden an international icon of war's destruction. A film based on the book appeared in United States' cinemas in 1972 and subsequently provided material for a stage play. People who otherwise knew nothing about the city learned from the book about the ruinous firestorm it suffered from English and American bombings at the end of World War II. The trauma of the bombing's gruesome aftermath yielded a Dresden narrative that portrays the city as a uniquely innocent, peaceful jewel of architecture, art, and music, wantonly destroyed by bombs.

Vonnegut paid tribute to this narrative when his major character, Billy Pilgrim, views the city as the most beautiful he has ever seen. And Pilgrim underscores the wantonness by describing the aftermath as a collection of "corpse mines." He is haunted by his memory of the devastation. Throughout the book Billy is aware that Dresden is a major German city. But he is unaware of the city's long history and political significance. Nor does he take into account the Dresdners' sense of singularity grounded in the city's geography and architecture.[1]

This portrait explores those features of Dresden's experience that created its distinctive, self-confident personality. It accounts for its achievement and victories as well as its mistakes and defeats. Dresden's role as the capital city of the Saxon state insured the persistence of its wealth and importance within Germany from the Renaissance until the present day. Its staunch Lutheran faith made it the leader of German Protestants and prompted the construction of their most prominent church. Dresden's beautiful urban architecture, lauded by Vonnegut's fictional Pilgrim and real-life Europeans alike, became the backdrop for the cultivation of fine art, the performance of dramatic music, the introduction of modern dance and the enjoyment of impressive theater. Those are the highlights. Within the portrait's shadows reside the military defeats and occupations of the city throughout the more than six centuries of its life.

Novelist and native son Uwe Tellkamp, in his novel *The Tower*, repeatedly recites the refrain: "In Dresden, where the muses nest, the sweet sickness of yesteryear rests." After World War II, Tellkamp contends, Dresdners bathed in the memory of the once-splendorous city so savagely destroyed. Its citizens longed to restore the city's role as a cultural beacon, even as its socialist government stressed its historical stature as an industrial/scientific center and strove to create working-class contentment. Tellkamp's novel takes the pulse of the city as it embarked on the peaceful revolution of 1989 that dissolved the socialist regime. This portrait depicts the dramatic scenes of that event. It also illustrates how the paradoxes of Dresden's past continue to inspire and to bedevil its contemporary existence.[2]

* * *

In summer, 2017, I crossed the River Elbe in a Dresden tram with a class of young school children enjoying an extra-curricular outing. Boys and girls alike called out a friendly "hallo, Elbe", as if the river were a familiar pet that they encounter on daily walks through their neighborhoods. And the Elbe is, in the years without a flood, a friendly river. Whole families walk, cycle and sun-bathe on the paths and meadows that line its banks. These meadows also serve as sites of special celebrations and annual festivals. Dresden without the Elbe is unimaginable.

Rising in the Sudeten Mountains east of Prague, the river makes its way through the peaks of Czech Republic toward the gentle slopes of the Ore Mountains and a canyon of sandstone known as Saxon Switzerland before entering a wide valley just south of Dresden. Steep hills protect the valley both north and south without secluding it from the outside world. The Elbe has flowed here for thousands of years and has created a terrain attractive to ancient fishers and farmers and comforting for modern urban dwellers.[3]

During the Roman Empire and early Middle Ages, only a collection of small villages occupied the site of Dresden, where the river meanders into an S-shape. From the sixth century C.E., a Slavic group, the Sorbs, tilled the rich soil of the forested hills and fluvial marshes or plied the river for fish. Flowing into the valley from both south and north were—and still are—several brooks and a larger tributary, the Weisseritz. When German settlers from the West arrived in the tenth century C.E., they found, on both sides of the Elbe, the Drezdany—people of the swampy forest—at the site of contemporary Dresden. On the right bank of the Elbe lived a village of Slavic fishermen. On the left bank the westerners, either in the late tenth or early eleventh century, established a modest Church of Our Lady—the Frauenkirche.

The Frauenkirche was a mission church within the new, medieval German Reich, known as the Holy Roman Empire, established just as the Germans recovered from an onslaught of invasions and plunder by neighboring peoples. The new empire intended to spread Christianity throughout its domains. The settlements of Drezdany—Slavs and Germans—answered to the imperially appointed bishops and counts of the Meissen March. After 1089, the Wettin family and its successor state of Saxony ruled the March for over 800 years.

At this spot on the upper Elbe, there was a ford over the river that had been used by long-distance merchants for centuries. The ford meant that east-west trade traveling through the area linked up with a north-south route, making the villages a transportation node. At some point, a ferry replaced the ford. Convoys of German merchants established themselves semi-permanently at this hub and founded the small church of St. Nicholas, patron of merchants everywhere. This intersection at the Elbe became more important with the discovery of silver in the Ore Mountains south of Dresden in 1168. The silver mines increased the trade that passed through the settlement on its way to the main east-west route through central Germany, the via regia. At the end of the twelfth century, the mercantile settlers decided to build a bridge to increase the security of their shipments. Archaeologists have determined that the original builders used stone, possibly erecting the first stone bridge, now the Augustus Bridge, over the Elbe. Here a small fort, first established by the regional lord, anchored the bridgehead on the south bank of the Elbe, which the Wettins later expanded into a sizable castle.

By the time the town was first mentioned in the written record in 1206, it was well-enough established to serve as the scene of an arbitration in a land dispute. In the early years of the thirteenth century, Dresden, the village, became a chartered city with its own political and economic rights. Historians note that the city was so logically laid out that professionals had probably helped plan it. This merchants' civitas surrounded itself with a protective wall that roughly encircled the area that today encompasses the palace complex and the Altmarkt (Old Marketplace). Within this wall, the Franciscan brothers founded, in the mid-thirteenth century, a cloister and a church.[4]

This settlement on the Elbe had experienced a prosperous beginning, but there was not much to distinguish it from other towns emerging from the Dark Ages. This status changed when the Meissen Margrave, Heinrich the Illustrious, made Dresden his principal residence, and his wife Constance brought to the city in 1234, as part of her dowry, a splinter accepted as a remnant of Christ's Cross. This relic, exhibited in St. Nicholas, drew so many pilgrims to Dresden that a chapel was added to display it. Soon pilgrims dropped the name of St. Nicholas and referred to the Church of the Holy Cross. Eventually, the Bishop of Meissen consecrated the old Nikolaikirche as the Kreuzkirche.

As pilgrims helped the city to flourish, one of Dresden's most enduring institutions established itself: the Kreuzschule and its choir. This Latin school originated as a complement to the parish, and its choir was charged with singing for Sunday, Holy Day and Vesper services, for marriages, funerals, morality plays and for the pilgrims' worship. Choirboys accompanied priests on their rounds to the sick, and they sang at the plethora of church services funded by wealthy donors. In the late fourteenth century, the parish school became a city school, financed by the city council. Instructors were now mostly laymen. The school nevertheless occupied a building next to the church, and the choristers' duties were still religious. It admitted rich and poor alike, and non-Dresdners also attended.[5]

At the end of the fourteenth century, Dresden was still a small city catering to and dominated by merchants. No member of the Wettin family resided there permanently after the death of Heinrich the Illustrious in 1288. It was only after the Wettins had increased both their territory and their power that Dresden became attractive as a permanent residence. In 1404, the family absorbed lands directly southeast of Dresden. Twenty years later, the German emperor Sigismund bestowed on the Meissen Margraves the duchy of Saxe-Wittenberg when its ducal line died out. The Wettins now became Saxon dukes and, according to German law, one of the powerful Electors of the German emperor. An Elector of the Holy Roman Empire enjoyed prestige and influence over other princes as well as opportunities for increasing his family's wealth.

The Wettin territory now extended through the whole of the Elbe River basin from the Ore Mountains in the south to the Havel lakes in the north. In addition to this large expanse came the riches associated with the silver mines in the south. But it was not only silver that contributed to Wettin wealth. Miners dug out a host of minerals—tin, copper, coal, iron—and precious stones.

In 1464, the Wettin brothers, Ernst and Albrecht, jointly inherited the Saxon duchy and moved their principal residence from Meissen to Dresden. Dresden's location enjoyed certain advantages for supplying a princely court. Not only did it sit astride established land routes, the river itself was a highway for shipping a host of products. Rich farmland as well as hunting preserves lay close to the town. There were also enough artisans to meet the basic needs of the court, though elegant clothes in this early period came from the richer city of Leipzig. In order to accommodate both their families and honor their princely obligations, the brothers transformed the castle into a structure akin to a palace. They called their new quarters the Court Depot, indicating that the business of government had become sophisticated enough to warrant the careful storage of records.

In this late medieval period, Dresden functioned as the capital of a united Saxony for only twenty years. At the beginning of the 1480s, the brothers, through inheritance, added the western Thuringian lands to the Saxon ones, and Dresden's eastern German location made administration of the enlarged territory difficult. Thus, the brothers decided in 1485 to divide their extensive legacy. Ernst took southern Thuringia, Wittenberg with its environs, and the title of Saxon Elector, while Albrecht, remaining as Saxon duke, chose northern Thuringia and the old Meissen March including Dresden and Leipzig. The two agreed to share the wealth of the Ore Mountains. This so-called Division of Leipzig separated the Wettin family into two principal branches: the Ernestine and the Albertine. It was the latter line that determined the fortunes of Dresden.

Albrecht, who continued to regard the city as his capital, spent very little time there. Instead, he served in the armies of the German emperor and became governor of Friesland. His son Georg administered the Albertine lands on the upper Elbe and inherited the Dukedom when Albrecht died.[6]

In 1491, Dresden suffered its first episode of destruction. Fire was the culprit. Reconstruction resulted in relieving some of the overcrowding inside the walls, and new buildings were now required to rest upon a stone base and to install tile roofs. Subsequent rulers introduced more regulations to inhibit the spread of fire in the crowded city. During this time, Duke Georg enlarged the space surrounded by the city walls and, for the first time, included the Frauenkirche within the fortification. Expanding the area within the walls led to the creation of the Neumarkt or New Market square that became closely identified with the church. The Duke also attached to the castle the large Georg Gate leading from the town to the bridge, a structure that continues to exist into the twenty-first century. His innovative bent did not, however, extend to religion. He opposed the Protestant Reformation and insisted upon the continued practice of Catholicism within Saxony. Only when he died in 1539 did his brother Heinrich install Lutheranism as the established religion of the Saxon Duchy, making Dresden a staunchly Lutheran city.[7]

When Heinrich's son, Moritz, became Duke of Saxony in 1541, he inherited a city that was a small residence on the Elbe. Its core had already taken the shape familiar to us in the twenty-first century. Landmarks existed that continue to guide our way through the inner city: the Kreuzkirche and Altmarkt, the Frauenkirche and Neumarkt, the Palace. Still, Dresden was only one of a myriad of princely residences strewn across the German empire.

In 1504, the ducal secretary, Hieronymus Emser, described Dresden as "that miserable little city".[8] Only in the course of the sixteenth century did the process begin that made Dresden one of the most important cities of Germany.

I. Dresden Becomes "Dresden"

The Elector Moritz

How did Dresden appear to Moritz and his court when he became Saxon Duke in 1541? In mid-town, the Kreuzkirche, shorn of its relic by the Reformation, served as the city's parish church. In the Altmarkt local farmers from the villages surrounding the city brought their wares to sell at the weekly markets, and it was here that the annual fairs, drawing vendors and buyers from the region and beyond, were held. This large square, with the Kreuzkirche adjoining it to the southeast, was the scene of religious processions and secular festivals. It hosted shows by traveling troupes of actors and other performers. Perched inside the northern part of the square was a large building that served as city hall.

The city did not enjoy much commercial importance. Its merchants and craftsmen mainly served local needs. Its narrow lanes could not accommodate large wagons, so only the long east-west and north-south thoroughfares were paved with stones. Until the mid-sixteenth century, farmers and their barns still existed within the old city walls. A lack of basic hygiene contributed to repeated outbreaks of plague. In 1539, plague almost eliminated the residents of the Scheffelgasse, one of the lanes that led from the city's western gate to the Altmarkt. During these episodes, the authorities banned sales of fruit, the drinking of beer and wine in large groups, and all celebrations. They also ordered the city's poorest residents, who were dependent on alms and not in a position to protest, to care for the sick, with the result that they too soon became infected.

In the preceding half-century, however, Duke Georg had not only enlarged both the palace and the fortified city. He presided over an economic boom occasioned by new techniques in silver mining, and the revenues of the princely house increased. By the 1520s, the humanist Petrus Schade described

Dresden as a "handsome little town". At this promising site, Moritz at first remained merely a duke from an eastern German province.[9]

He was, nevertheless, ambitious. In the religious war between the Catholic German emperor, Charles V, and the Protestant Schmalkaldic League, Moritz, a Protestant himself, wagered that his fortunes lay in an alliance with the emperor against his cousin, the Saxon Elector, whom he thoroughly disliked. He even invaded his cousin's territory and took him prisoner, encouraging the retreat of the now leaderless Protestant princes. For his help in defeating the Schmalkaldic League, the emperor elevated Moritz to the title and function of Imperial Elector. Taken away from his cousin were not only the Electoral title, function and status, but significant territories and a stake in the lucrative silver and other mines of the Ore Mountains.

Electoral Saxony now stretched from the Bohemian border in the south to Wittenberg in the north and from the Unstrut River in the west to the Elbe in the east. Moritz emerged as one of the richest and most powerful German princes. His gamble in the Schmalkaldic War had paid off. The Duke's elevation to Elector of the German emperor provided the means to mold Dresden into a princely residence.[10]

European and German princes were now building in the new Renaissance style, and Moritz determined to do the same. He traveled to northern Italy in search of new ideas and talent. In rebuilding the city's fortifications, he adopted the new Italian technique of surrounding the city with earthworks as well as walls. In order to place his castle in the center of the fortified area, as the new style dictated, he included the old settlement just across the river to the north, an area known then as Old Dresden.

One local chronicler has described Old Dresden as the "Cinderella" of the two linked settlements. During the late Middle Ages, "new" Dresden's economic expansion so benefited its twin across the river that a former Saxon duke had incorporated it as a city, giving it a city council, the right to hold commercial fairs, and to establish and regulate craft guilds. Only then did Old Dresden build the parish church of the Three Kings, establish a market square, and acquire the protection of earthworks and moat.

This shield did not prevent Moritz's cousin from occupying the town during the Schmalkaldic War and using it as a stage for lobbing cannonballs over the river into "new" Dresden. Defense of the Elbe's southern bank was thus a compelling reason for canceling the city status of Old Dresden. In order to persuade Old Dresden's city councilors of this necessity, Moritz imprisoned them until they acquiesced to his plans.[11]

His family's residence, where he was expected to entertain German nobles in grand style, needed attention. The old edifice, though an improvement on the medieval fortification, was not appropriate for his new position. Moritz wanted a real palace, not an improved castle. First he doubled the structure's size by expanding it toward the west. The old castle keep was raised into what became the Hausmann's Tower, and it was placed in the middle of an extended north wing where it housed a loggia or Altan, colorfully decorated al secco, where the Elector's family and distinguished guests could watch games and festivities in the enclosed palace courtyard. The exterior walls of the palace bore black, gray and white sgraffito These glyphs portrayed scenes from the Old and New Testaments and proclaimed Moritz's firm Protestant faith.[12]

It was this Protestant faith, now tolerated by the German emperor who had made peace with the Protestants, that led to Moritz's death. A rogue Protestant prince, Albrecht Alcibiades, refused to join with his peers in reconciling with the emperor and seized territories in violation of the peace. Unless he were brought to heel, the recognition of Protestantism by the Catholic emperor was in danger. Moritz thus joined in battle against Alcibiades in order to protect the Lutheran faith. At the battle of Sievershausen in 1553, Moritz was fatally wounded.

Attached to the bastion at the far eastern corner of Dresden's contemporary Brühl Terrace, is a monument that reconstructs the sixteenth century commemoration of Moritz passing his Electoral sword to his brother, August. This sculpture emphasizes Moritz's strong Christian beliefs. Hovering above the scene are the figures of the Trinity: God the Father embracing the globe; Jesus holding the cross; and the Holy Spirit incarnated as a fluttering dove. Moritz not only made Dresden a Renaissance city projecting Saxon power, he established it as a center of Lutheranism for the entire German realm.[13]

August I: Building upon the Foundation

Moritz had no children, so his brother August inherited Electoral Saxony. After beating back designs on his inheritance by Saxony's southern neighbor and attempts by his cousins, the Ernestine Wettins, to regain the Elector's title and territories, August succeeded in sustaining Saxon wealth and power for the rest of his life. At the same time, his administration provided both stability and impetus for Dresden's economic development.

During the previous century, the government of Saxony had become more and more complex. Previously, princes, including those of Meissen and Saxony, had been peripatetic, holding court and governing from a variety of towns within their jurisdictions. Government officials and written records of governmental actions traveled with them. Officials and records had already proliferated during the fifteenth and early sixteenth centuries, and the Dresden Depot became their permanent home. August's intense interest in bolstering the Saxon economy meant promoting the textile industry as well as mining in the Ore Mountains. Because wood was essential for outfitting mines, the Electoral government carefully supervised the replanting of forests that supplied the lumber. August personally oversaw the operation of his estates and sought to increase their profits. His wife Anna cultivated and sold the products of her gardens. One historian avers that August behaved more like an early capitalist entrepreneur than like a nobleman averse to profiteering.[14]

As his government intervened more and more in various Saxon enterprises, August expanded and improved governmental functions. As he streamlined Saxon government, he unleashed a building boom inside Dresden. Already in 1556, a new mint appeared to the east of the palace. An armory was completed in 1563, and a shot tower rose up in 1567. In that same year, August dedicated a chancellery building to accommodate an expanding bureaucracy and its records. In subsequent years a hunting lodge, the Jägerhof, appeared on the north side of the Elbe. Later, the court pharmacy was established on the south side of the palace.[15]

The Elector's court and the modernizing Saxon government came to dominate Dresden's physiognomy, economy and urban function. Aristocratic and bourgeois officeholders came to town to serve the Elector and his court, and their presence enhanced the town as a princely residence. Mansions lined its narrow lanes. Class differences became more visible. Cultural occupations like musicians, dancers, painters and sculptors joined the populace. Domestic servants proliferated. Formerly self-regulating artisan guilds were subject to pressure from the court to admit newcomers without the requisite qualifying procedures. Dresden's urban independence gave way to increasing domination by the Elector, his court, and his officials.[16]

August, following in his brother's footsteps, tried to sanitize the city in line with a vision of a stately residence. Animals, manure, and farmers' carts were banned from the intra-mural area; farmers moved to the villages surrounding the city, but remaining within the city's legal jurisdiction. Channels were built into the streets to carry off the streams of waste water that inhabitants threw into the city's lanes. Clean water piped from the river Weisseritz, as well as from springs and creeks in the vicinity, supplied fountains distributed throughout the city. Despite these improvements, it was difficult to keep the city clean. Inhabitants continued to throw all sorts of rubbish into the narrow lanes and streets. Dresden, the princely residence, was still a work in progress.[17]

At the end of August's reign, the imposing Electoral Stables began to rise on the Neumarkt. The stables not only housed the Elector's horses and equestrian equipment, they accommodated court festivals and provided storage for their paraphernalia. To provide a proper setting for his noble guests, August covered the floors of four rooms in the stables' upper story with marble tiles and lined its walls with ornamented credenzas.

The Electoral Stables and August's other new buildings belonged to a royal quarter crowded against the bridge and banks of the Elbe. Though the court reserved many of its activities for its own members, the compact size of Dresden and the urban location of the palace complex meant that the city's inhabitants not only supplied the court with both necessities and luxuries, they were influenced by courtly tastes. In the mid-sixteenth century, the Rathaus on the Altmarkt was remodeled in the new Renaissance style, clearly imitating the Elector's Palace.[18]

It was August's enthusiasm for the Renaissance that led to his appointment of Giovanni Maria Nosseni as court sculptor and painter in 1575. At the time, August wanted someone who could cut and polish the semi-precious stones of the Ore Mountains into objects of display. Nosseni was a comparatively young man who hailed from an Italian family of sculptors. At first he was put to work seeking out, cutting, and polishing rich rock for constructing the Elector's various projects. One of his prized accomplishments can still be seen in the mountain town of Freiberg, where August honored his brother Moritz with a large funerary monument in the city's cathedral. Nosseni also designed the Long Gallery that connected the Electoral Stables, now the Johanneum, with the palace.[19]

Chief among Nosseni's tasks was the design and execution of court festivals. In the days before regular schedules of theater, concerts, movies, radio and television, home-grown entertainments were a welcome distraction from the routine of everyday life. Throughout the Middle Ages, the celebration of church holidays provided some respite. Aristocrats entertained one another with frequent jousts and tournaments. Cities and towns held local festivals, often in tandem with annual fairs, where commerce and pleasure were intertwined. In Dresden, even after the court and the town adopted the Protestant Reformation, they celebrated Catholic Carnival with gusto. Nobles and commoners alike used marriages, baptisms and birthdays as occasions for celebrations and entertainments.

When the Elector August borrowed Renaissance innovations in art and architecture, he also adopted the Italian practice of "inventions" for court festivals. Inventions or dramatic tableaux were embedded in the elaborate processions that acted as preludes or accompaniments to the traditional knightly tournaments. They usually revolved around a theme based on Greek mythology, on ancient history, or allegory. Music, scenery, equipment and costumes all had to be specially devised to heighten an invention's dramatic effect. Eventually the inventions became the dominant attraction of the tournaments.

During his lifetime, Nosseni lent an Italian flair to the city's processions, and throughout Germany his "Dresden style" served as a model for other princely courts.[20] The Dresden style relied on a "primitive folksiness (naïve Volkstümlichkeit)" exemplified in a series of processions created for a week-long carnival celebration in 1609. The Elector had invited his now reconciled Ernestine cousins to join the revelry. The festivities included sixty-five competitive Ringrennen or tilts, a game in which horseback riders or charioteers aimed spears at rings hung on posts. Winners were those riders who managed to drive their spears through the rings.

An invention preceded each of the sixty-five tilts and demonstrated Nosseni's creativity. An "African" invention began with twelve heralds on horseback, riding three abreast. Accessories to their black attire were blue, red, and yellow scarves, feathers and staffs. Behind them cantered a group of brown "Africans" wearing large, bright blue coned hats with feathers streaming from their necks, hips and knees. Twenty-one trumpeters and two drummers accompanied by a group of banner-waving equestrians followed. Then came the pièce de resistance: a large float drawn by two decorated elephants. Surmounting the float's decorated base was a pyramid-like edifice upon which sat an "African" armed with bow, arrows and sword. Surrounding him at a lower level were six more compatriots playing stringed instruments. On the float's four corners were live "monkeys", each gazing at himself in a mirror. The invention closed with six flag wavers and an "African" leading a white horse and bearing Mercury's caduceus (a winged staff encircled by two snakes) in his left hand.

Even participants in the tilt that followed were colorfully costumed and choreographed. The Elector appeared dressed in a bright green sailor's garb and carried a rudder in one hand. His horse's head was decorated with goose wings, and on the saddle hung a butter churn with a group of Fastnacht pretzels. Other Saxon nobles followed: one depicting Saturn with scythe and hour-glass; two others in blonde wigs clothed in women's dresses with glittering wings—one in silver to represent the moon, the other in gold to symbolize the sun.[21]

Here was no need for knowledge of Greek mythology or ancient history. Aristocrats and commoners alike could enjoy the colors of the costumes, the sound of triangles, lyres and horns, and the familiar symbols of everyday life. Nosseni operated as a master "inventor" for over forty-five years at the Dresden court, serving four different Saxon Electors.

Not only did he dominate the artistry of the court, Nosseni helped to raise the prestige of his Wettin employers throughout Germany. The electors had no objection to lending him out to other princes to design inventions. His artistry redounded to their renown. One of the last structures to be built according to a design by Nosseni was the pavilion, known as the Lusthaus and later lost to an explosion, on the Elbe bastion that now forms part of the Brühl Terrace. Nosseni and the Elector Christian I, who commissioned the Lusthaus, were the first to perceive how the bastion and terrace could open up the city's view of the Elbe Valley.[22]

Dresden and Protestant Saxony

To an extent that exceeds the fervor of twenty-first century religionists, sixteenth-century Saxony bathed in denominational orthodoxy and controversy. Although Albertine Saxony had not introduced Lutheranism officially until 1539, individual parishes had begun its practice in their Sunday services and theological teaching even before that date. Though the

Reformation significantly ruptured the organization and finances of the Catholic Church, there was a surprising continuity. The Sunday service continued to use the pattern and the Latin of the Roman Catholic mass. Gospels, however, were now read in German. The pastor most likely remained the same, having shifted from Catholicism to Lutheranism almost effortlessly. Some holy days, such as the Ascension of Mary and Saint John the Baptist, continued to be observed. German hymns were only gradually introduced into church services. The Dresden Hymnal was not published until the beginning of the seventeenth century.

Above all, Lutheranism replaced the emphasis on the sacraments with attention to the sermon, the primary focus of the religious service. In order to catch the early sermon on Sundays and Holy Days, Dresdners had to arrive by seven in the morning. There was another sermon at noon. The church was an important part of people's lives, marking marriages, births, baptisms, confirmations, and funerals. In an age when printed public communications were almost non-existent, important governmental measures were read out in church, and they continued to be announced there into the nineteenth century.[23]

In the sixteenth century, the most prominent Lutheran after Luther's death was Philipp Melanchthon. He acted as Protestantism's St. Paul, defining orthodoxy and setting up schools. To maintain reformist harmony, he was flexible about both principles and practice. His followers, the Philippists, took a relaxed approach to the upstart Calvinists, who differed from Lutherans on doctrinal and organizational grounds. Philippists also reacted cavalierly to those Lutherans who complained that the "First Reformation" had not yet created "true" Christians. These Gnesio—or "authentic"—Lutherans desired a "Second Reformation". Apart from the doctrinal differences, there was a political issue.

The Peace of Augsburg in 1555, between the Catholic German emperor and the Protestant princes, had provided toleration only for Catholics and Lutherans. Calvinists received no consideration. Nevertheless, Calvinism won support from several German princes, and they wanted release from what they considered to be Catholic domination within the imperial Diet. They would thus be in a better position to alter taxation, currency regulation, imperial procedures, and the administration of imperial justice, all of which were covered by the Augsburg Peace.

For some time, the Saxon Electors were contented Philippists. Philippist theologians held sway at the University of Wittenberg, and the Elector August appointed a Philippist, Georg Cracow, as his chief minister. He also engaged the Philippist Caspar Peucer as his personal physician. There were even two court preachers, one a strict Lutheran and the other a Philippist. Within the German Diet, the Elector opposed the Calvinists' desire for recognition.[24]

After the death of Melanchthon in 1560, the situation within Lutheranism changed. Calvinists increasingly insisted that the Catholic emperor officially recognize their faith as equal to Lutheranism. Their stance particularly threatened the Gnesio-Lutherans. They claimed that their principles and practices derived directly from Luther and represented the only true Protestant orthodoxy.

The Elector August experienced increasing pressure from the Gnesio-Lutherans to disavow the Philippists and their toleration of Calvinist theology. August's wife, the Electress Anna, on whom he frequently relied for advice, favored the Gnesio-Lutherans. In the early 1570s, the Philippist superintendent of the Lutherans in Pirna, a city just south of Dresden, wrote to the Philippist court preacher, Christian Schütz, claiming that August's reliance on his wife constituted a gynocracy. This view was generally shared by higher Saxon officials. The letter fell into the hands of Georg Listhenius, the Gnesio-Lutheran court preacher, who passed it on to August. Stung by the Philippist lack of respect for his leadership as Imperial Elector and guardian of German Lutherans, the Elector's reaction was angry and swift.

The Philippist prime minister, Georg Cracow, was dismissed, arrested and died after torture. Also dismissed and arrested were Christian Schütz, the Philippist court preacher, and Caspar Peucer, the Elector's physician. At Wittenberg, the Philippist theological faculty lost their posts and dispersed to other universities.[25]

August now decided to exercise his leadership of German Lutherans by supporting a clear definition of the faith. He commissioned several Gnesio-Lutherans to devise the Book of Concord, issued in 1577. While the Book of Concord rejected the most radical Gnesio-Lutheran views, it also clearly demarcated Lutherans from Philippists and Calvinists. Church services eschewed the more Roman elements of the Mass as well as the austere practices of the Calvinists. Between 1577 and 1580, August won over most

Lutheran princes and German nobles to the Book of Concord, and their pastors swore to uphold it.[26]

Such was the situation when August died in 1586. His son, Christian I, succeeded him. Nicolas Krell, already a government official under August, became Christian's most trusted advisor. Supported by Krell, Christian shifted his sympathies to the Philippists and Calvinists. Krell's influence was responsible for Christian's abandonment of support for the German emperor. It also led him to rely heavily on his Calvinist brother-in-law, Johann Casimir of the Palatinate. At home, Christian and Krell ignored the constitutional requirement to consult with the Saxon nobles on governmental matters, a practice that they resented.

In religious matters, Krell as prime minister no longer required pastors to support the Concord Formula. Men sympathetic to Calvinism were appointed to important state and church posts. A new catechism, a new prayer book, a new hymnal, and even a new version of the Bible, were issued. All these changes unsettled parishioners as well as clergy. Simple folk were alarmed by the elimination of the exorcism rite that accompanied baptism, an age-old practice that pre-dated the Reformation. In a time when infant mortality was high, it was understandable that parents wanted to protect their children. Never mind that Calvinist and Lutheran theologians alike considered the exorcism ritual to be a superstitious relic.[27]

As opposition to Krell and his policies mounted, Christian I suddenly died in 1591. His heir was the eight-year old Christian II. Under the regency of the boy's cousin, Duke Friedrich Wilhelm of Saxe-Weimar, Krell was arrested and imprisoned at the Königstein Fortress, close to the Saxon-Bohemian border. His imprisonment lasted for ten years without any serious charge being brought against him. Finally, in 1601 at the end of the regency, an imperial court of appeal sentenced him to die for 'disturbing the peace and unity of the Fatherland.' Inscribed upon the double-edged sword that decapitated Krell were the Latin words "Cave Calvinista"—"Calvinist, Beware!"

Christian II did not attend the beheading held next to the electoral stables, but his pious Lutheran mother, Sophie, who is believed to have engineered the death sentence, took a front-row seat. During the next decade, Sophie helped to restore, for Lutheran services, the former church of the Franciscan monastery. For more than half a century after the Reformation closed the abbey, the church had functioned first as an armory and later as a storehouse for the city's reserves of grain and other items. The restoration continued for almost a decade. Though the church was consecrated to Saint Sophia, its name is also associated with the ex-Electress Sophie who rejoiced at Krell's execution. The co-mingling of religious and political affairs was not unusual at the time. In order to assure the authority of the prince and the loyalty of his subjects, both needed to worship the same God in the same way. This issue had long bedeviled Dresdners and other Europeans. It would not be resolved for another half-century.[28]

Krell's execution marked the end of the sixteenth century in Dresden. By then, the city had changed from a provincial town to a fully-fledged capital city hosting a princely court and a governmental bureaucracy. The transformation was both blessing and curse for the Dresdners. The former autonomy of the citizens to decide their own fate gradually had given way to domination by the Prince Elector and his court. The presence of the court and the growing functions of government attracted an increasingly diverse population—those who worked in transportation, in construction, in education and culture, in administration, and in the military. Incomes increased, but so did inequality. The economic gap was most pronounced between those living inside the walls and those villagers living directly outside. Their inhabitants supplied Dresdners with needed commodities, and they were considered to be legal urban residents.

The city now held its own among other prominent German cities: Munich, Heidelberg, Prague, Vienna. It was not only the seat of the Saxon government, but the political, economic, social, cultural and glowing Renaissance capital envisioned by the Elector Moritz.[29]

II. The Noble City: Downs and Ups

The Elector August's regime, despite political tensions, encompassed a period of peace and prosperity within Saxony and its capital city, Dresden. This relative tranquility extended into the Electorates of his son and grandson. Under his second grandson, Johann Georg I, international and German events shattered the calm.

The Thirty Years' War

During the seventeenth century's first decade, political and religious disagreements resulted in the formation of two armed alliances: the German Protestant Union and the Catholic League. In the midst of increasing tensions between the two groups, Protestant Bohemian nobles revolted against the Catholic German emperor who managed to defeat them. Nevertheless, this local war soon radiated outward from Bohemia and enmeshed not only Germans but their neighbors, particularly the Protestant Swedes.[30]

During the early stages of the conflict, Saxony maintained formal neutrality. Dresden suffered mainly from the burden posed by emigrés from Bohemia, some of whom tried to help. Two different Bohemian, Lutheran congregations donated a total of 12,000 Gulden to compensate the Elector's government for the increasing cost of supplying food for the city. In order to preserve stocks for the city's inhabitants, the Dresden city council forbade the export of grain.

Saxon neutrality was ignored by both sides. The German emperor's forces repeatedly plundered Saxon territory, causing the Swedes to intervene. Initially successful, the Swedish king, Gustavus Adolphus, was killed in the Battle of Lützen in 1632. Thereafter, the Saxons forsook the Protestants and signed the Peace of Prague in 1635. In return for its support, the Catholic Emperor awarded Saxony the neighboring territories of Upper and Lower Lusatia.[31]

This success brought on more tribulation. For the next decade, Dresden suffered all the problems of a capital city in a state at war. Saxon troops were quartered on the city's population, and quartering was an expensive affair for householders. A captain was entitled to six meals a day in addition to cheese, bread and beer. A lieutenant required four meals a day; lower officers had to be content with three. Simple recruits could expect only bread and meat. Soldiers were expected to pay homeowners for meals, but the latter were responsible for donating butter, honey, salt, wood, coal and feed for animals. Both sides felt aggrieved; householders could not afford the added expense, and soldiers were often not paid and threatened to resort to plunder.

The city became severely overcrowded. It was full of soldiers and refugees from all corners of Germany. People flocked to Dresden to escape those parts of Saxony occupied by Swedish forces, to escape fighting in neighboring German states and to avoid re-Catholicization of territories reconquered by the German emperor. The supply of foodstuffs and other necessities was inadequate. Sanitation suffered; plague was a constant menace. The Swedish army twice threatened Dresden and put the surrounding villages to the torch. Their residents joined the crowd inside the walls. Only in 1645 did Saxony conclude an armistice with the Swedes that cleared most, but not all, of their troops from the principality.[32]

Three years later, the Peace of Westphalia ended this Thirty Years' War and altered both political and religious arrangements throughout Germany. The Peace deprived the imperial electors, including Saxon ones, of their former pre-eminence within the empire. All German princes lost the right to impose their religion on their subjects; henceforth all Germans, except those directly subject to the German emperor in Austria and Bohemia, would be able to choose the religion of their choice: Catholicism, Lutheranism, Calvinism. All German princes, no matter how minor, were now free to conclude military alliances with any state of their choosing, even with non-German neighbors.[33]

Despite the Peace of Westphalia, Saxons were free of the Swedes only after they paid an indemnity. At last, in 1650, Saxons were able to celebrate a Day of Peace and Thanks. In Dresden, church bells summoned the grateful to worship. The local garrison fired three salvos. Cattle, brought inside the walls to secure the city's provisions, now returned to the surrounding villages that sought to repair the war's damages.[34]

The revival of the economy was one of Dresden's first priorities. The Elector forgave the back taxes of any householder who returned to the city. He waived the costly contributions of eligible new members to the local guilds, thereby enticing returning soldiers to join them and bolster the local economy. Johann Georg was heavily indebted, not only to bankers and other wealthy lenders, but also to those Dresdner tradesmen who had supplied the court during the war. Eventually new industries replenished the Elector's coffers and restored the payments from the court that funded everyone else. The new wealth meant that Dresden would return to its leading role among German cities.[35]

Creating the Baroque City

Johann Georg II, who succeeded his father in 1656, can be credited with beginning Dresden's transition from the Renaissance to the Baroque city. In contrast to his father, whom many regarded as an incompetent beer-boozer, Johann Georg II cultivated the arts. He used them to demonstrate the premier position of Saxony among German states. As the capital city, Dresden became its showcase.[36]

Foremost among the arts during his electorate was music. The new prince could build on an exemplary musical tradition established already by the Elector Moritz in the preceding century. Moritz had founded the choir for the Court Church in 1548 to provide music for services. A year later he engaged instrumentalists from Italy and charged them with accompanying the choir during services and supplying secular background music for court dinners, much as today we listen to the radio or a recording during our family meals. It was understood that this new orchestra would provide music for important court functions, such as marriages and funerals, and for tournaments and other festivals. Given the scope of the work, it was advantageous that many of the musicians were composers. After Moritz's death, his brother, August, continued to support both choir and orchestra.[37]

When Johann Georg I became Elector in 1611, he wanted to dissolve the court orchestra. But the music lover and privy councilor Christoph von Loss saved the orchestra and saw to the appointment of two distinguished musicians. Michael Praetorius was engaged in 1614 to supply festive music for Johann Georg in the dramatic, harmonizing—Baroque—Italian style, a preference the noble Wettins supported.[38]

In 1615, Heinrich Schütz, the most esteemed German composer of the seventeenth century, was engaged as court organist and director of church music. He later became director of the court orchestra and music teacher of the Elector's heir. He impressed both Loss and Johann Georg I because he had studied in Venice with Giovanni Gabrieli and, like Praetorius, could be counted on to compose in the Italian style. In 1629, Schütz persuaded the Elector to send him back to Italy to become acquainted with the musical innovations of the preceding decade. During this sojourn, he took lessons from Claudio Monteverdi, now credited with the invention of Italian opera. Schütz unfortunately returned to Dresden just as the Thirty Years' War began to burden the Elector's treasury.

Both he and his musicians suffered from low salaries and, sometimes, no salary at all. Until his own resources ran dry, Schütz frequently paid the musicians himself. When the disruptions of war became intolerable, he fled to Denmark, home of Johann Georg I's mother, where he could compose in peace and quiet. The years from 1633–35, from 1637–38 and again from 1642–44 were periods of marauding Imperial or Swedish soldiers and overcrowding in Dresden. Since many other musicians also fled the city, Schütz could not be accused of dereliction of duty. There was hardly anyone left to direct.

Today, we are mainly familiar with Schütz's religious music. But it was part of his official duties to compose secular music as well. One of his better-known works is *Dafne,* often mistakenly identified as the first German opera. Another is *Orpheus und Euridyce,* composed for the marriage of Johann Georg I's son to Magdalena of Brandenburg-Bayreuth. These pieces were "singing ballets" (*Singspiele*), a form adopted from the French court that accompanied dancing with dialogue, recitatives, duets and choruses.

When Johann Georg II became Elector, he merged his own princely orchestra with the official court orchestra. By that time, Schütz was seventy-one years old and eager for retirement. The new Elector allowed him to take up residence in Weissenfels, the town of his childhood, but Schütz continued to write both religious and secular music for the Dresden court until he became too infirm to do so. He died, aged 87, in 1672.[39]

Johann Georg II, himself a composer of church music, imported Italian musicians who brought with them the newest works from the peninsula. It was during his electorate that the first castrato, Giovanni Angelini Bontempi, appeared on the Dresden stage. A composer as well as singer, Bontempi wrote the first truly Italian opera performed in Dresden, 1662; *Il Paride* was based on the story of Paris, the mythological prince who seduced the beautiful Helen and unleashed the Trojan War.[40]

In order to accommodate all the musical forms enjoyed by the court, the Elector built the first opera house in the city. This new theater, attached to the southwestern wall of the palace in 1667, was the fourth to appear in the German-speaking world. It was supposedly the largest in seventeenth-century Germany and could accommodate not only the members of the court but also representatives of the non-noble public. With its Italian musicians and new opera house, the Dresden court made the city a renowned musical center. The Dresden performances helped to introduce the Italian Baroque music into Germany, a style that penetrated other activities as well.[41]

Imitating other sixteenth-century princes, the Elector August, Moritz's brother, was one of the first Germans to create a Dresden *Kunstkammer* or Chamber of Curiosities in 1560. For him, the *Kunstkammer* was a public collection intended to bolster Saxony's economic vitality. Initially, the largest collection consisted of tools used by various Saxon artisans: cabinet-makers, locksmiths, gardeners, turners, gunsmiths, surgeons. Tools and scientific instruments were lent out to workmen throughout the electorate. Work spaces for artisans were scattered throughout the exhibition rooms on the palace's top floor. The Elector August was himself an experienced turner of ivory, and many tools reflected the carving industry. Geodesy was well-represented with maps, charts, and designs relating to water-power.

Included in the collection were games, musical instruments, clocks, hourglasses, precious and semi-precious stones, sea shells, paintings and sculpture. Books, many theological, were not neglected; the Elector's agents bought them at the annual Leipzig Fair. Courtiers and merchants doing business outside Saxony shopped for the collections. The first inventory of the *Kunstkammer* occurred toward the end of August's rule. After his death, the Electors concentrated less on industrial, scientific, and theological materials and leaned more toward antiquities, curiosities, painting and the applied arts. After the sculptor Nosseni's death, Johann Georg I bought up his paintings and designs.

By this time, the Wettin collection already possessed several impressive paintings by the Cranach atelier in Wittenberg; Lucas Cranach the Elder painted the stunning wedding portraits of Duke Heinrich and his wife

Katherine. When Heinrich introduced the Reformation into Dresden and Albertine Saxony, he turned to Cranach to help him create the appropriate imagery. In 1551, Cranach the Younger received the commission to paint the Hercules scenes in the Great Room of the new palace.

It can be argued, however, that Johann Georg II's electorate represents the transition from the old-fashioned chamber of curiosities to collectors' more modern attention to the fine arts. By the mid-seventeenth century, the collection had expanded to eight rooms in the palace, each devoted to one category. The Elector began to give his permission to public groups—princes, diplomats, merchants, scholars, goldsmiths—to view the collection. Some members of Dresden's middle class entertained their wedding parties by taking them to visit the eight rooms, and inn-keepers organized viewings for their guests. By the end of the seventeenth century, as many as 800 people were visiting the galleries annually. At the time, this opening of a private collection to the public reflected a practice of a limited number of other European notables.

Meanwhile, the Wettins had amassed a large amount of armor and weaponry that they housed in the Electoral Stables. They also displayed portraits of their ancestors in the upper story of the Long Gallery linking the stables with the Georg Gate. A coin collection graced the Council Room. Valuables such as jewels, decorative artworks, and gold pieces were stored in the basement of the palace's west wing. Covered with stone arches and painted green, these rooms eventually became the famous Green Vaults (Grünes Gewölbe). Added to these items were the costumes used for the inventions of court celebrations.[42]

In 1658, Johann Georg II appointed Wolf Caspar von Klengel, engineer-architect and public works director, as administrator of the *Kunstkammer*. During the next decade, Klengel bought up over 1000 items, including antiquities that he acquired during trips to Greece and Italy. He also began to weed and organize the collections. His groupings made it easier for guests to digest the displays. Klengel favored painting and sculpture and was also attracted to the work of goldsmiths. In 1671, the mathematician Tobias Beutel compiled a description of the collection in both Latin and German for the benefit of guests. Although the collections retained many of the scientific and artisanal features of the old *Kunstkammer,* the fine arts received increasing attention.

Building for the Baroque

Klengel not only shifted the balance of the art collection. He introduced Dresden to Baroque architecture. Like Baroque music, Baroque architecture featured a dramatic and monumental use of structural elements and ornaments: doubled columns and pilasters, complex curves and scrolls, repetitive figures, symmetrical patterns. This new style favored show as well as substance. Dresden gained fame not only for its Italian opera, but for its theatrical comedies, its ballet, knightly tournaments, and processions. These festivities and the people they attracted required specialized spaces. In 1669, a ballroom was built on a site to the west of the palace. A riding hall/shooting gallery, which could double as the city's largest party venue, appeared next door in 1678. At the same time, Johann Georg II refurbished the palace inside and out and raised the height of the Hausmann Tower, ensuring that its Baroque cap would be visible both near and far.[43]

The opera house, the ballroom, and the riding hall have long since disappeared. What remains is the Great Garden (Grosser Garten), a large park to the east of downtown Dresden. Residents had long planted flower and kitchen gardens just outside the city walls. The Elector and his family did the same. Apart from their practical use, these gardens were a way of escaping the confines of the fortified city. After the Thirty Years' War, as everyone fled the claustrophobic narrow lanes of the city intra-muros, gardens proliferated in a wreath around the ramparts.

In 1676, Johann Georg II decided to establish a great extra-mural garden where he could hold princely parties. He appropriated land from the villagers of Strehlen, Striesen and Gruna—all to the east of the city—in order to lay out an urban forest in the Baroque style. In the middle of a large square of land he situated a summer palace, decorated with garlands, blossoms and drapery, all in stone. Two avenues—north-south and east-west—intersected at the palace. The original square was later reduced to a rectangle, and the trees that surrounded it gave way to hedges laid out in French Baroque symmetry. Over the centuries, the Great Garden advanced from being a playground for aristocrats and became an open scene of recreation for all the city's citizens. The city has retained this expanse of 445 acres, and bicyclists, joggers, pedestrians still enjoy its open spaces, its wooded paths, its fountains and ponds, its flower beds, its sculptures and its strategically scattered benches. In time, it made sense for this spacious Baroque park to encompass the zoo and the botanical garden.[44]

A Party of Princes

The Baroque pomp of the late seventeenth century was designed to demonstrate Electoral Saxony's political importance within the German empire. But the most spectacular show focused on Johann Georg II's pre-eminence within the Wettin family. In 1678, he staged "A Most Illustrious Meeting of Princely Brothers and Brothers-in-Law."

According to the invitation to his brothers, made at the end of 1677, Johann Georg intended the reunion to celebrate the completion of the riding hall/shooting gallery built on the site of the present-day Zwinger. Additionally, he thought it necessary for the brothers to meet and plan for the future peace of Saxony and its people. None of the brothers was getting any younger, and the division of lands and jurisdictions made upon the death of their father, two decades previously, needed to be confirmed for their heirs.

Since the meeting would bring hundreds of people to Dresden—the families and the staffs of the Albertine princes—, planning to provide lodging and food for both people and horses was thorough. At the end of January, the three visiting princes arrived in Johann Georg II's Electoral lands and progressed to towns close enough to Dresden to easily launch a grand entry into the city on the morning of 1 February 1678. Prince Moritz of Saxe-Zeitz, the youngest brother, was the least pretentious of the lot. He entered the city through the Wilsdruffer Gate in a short procession to the center of town. The main event of the day was the elaborate cavalcade that began at the Meissen Gate in Old Dresden, progressed across the bridge to the Neumarkt, where it defiled past the electoral stable and then paraded up the Moritz Strasse to the Kreuzgasse, to the Altmarkt and then down the Schlossgasse to the palace. It was a lively show for the Dresdners.

Riding at the head of the parade, decked out in Saxon green with silver trim, were the courtiers responsible for the shooting parties that would punctuate the month-long festivities. Following were the Elector's troops and their officers, the household courtiers who would serve the princes' entourages, and various officials of the Saxon state, buttressed by drums and trumpets decorated with red flags. Members of the government followed in their yellow and black livery.

Toward the middle of the march were inserted the courtiers of the visiting princes. As befit the drama of the occasion, the brothers Johann Georg, Prince August and Duke Christian, all rode together toward the end of the procession in an open coach drawn by six gray horses. There followed the four sons of Prince August, then the brothers' wives, and lastly the two daughters of Duke Christian. Troops of the Elector brought up the rear. The Elector's heir awaited the arrival of the brothers in the palace courtyard, where they were received with great fanfare.

Now began a month of festivities. The first day, a Sunday, began with a church service at 7:30 in the morning; subsequent Sundays adhered to this pattern. On weekdays, races or target shoots occupied the mornings, followed by a midday dinner. In the late afternoons and evenings, a ballet-opera or a serialized play, a seventeenth-century version of Masterpiece Theater, entertained the visitors. On three afternoons, the men amused their families and staffs by participating in a wild animal chase in the palace courtyard.

On several evenings, there were dances performed in elaborate costumes and masks. One half-day was given over to a performance of the Kingdom masquerade where the high aristocracy chose their roles by lot and then paraded through the palace representing the cast of characters in a royal court. On two different days, the whole company celebrated the marriages of two of their gentlemen-and-ladies-in-waiting. The sheer plethora of events was a marvel of planning and organization. There were only two or three days set aside for people to rest, but there surely must have been individuals who opted out of attending every single race, procession, tilt, shoot or theatrical performance.

We know the illustrious details of the meeting because a close advisor to the Elector and later mayor of Dresden, Gabriel Tzschimmer, produced a folio of text and copper engravings to commemorate the event. Tzschimmer recorded the total activities of each day and added an appendix that narrated the stories of the plays performed and the allegories presented. The engravings depicted the procession preceding the Diana race on February 11, two days before Ash Wednesday. Tzschimmer not only illustrated the different segments of the parade, he developed a series of street scenes giving future generations a picture of the late seventeenth-century city. Attached houses, mostly of stuccoed stone, reached four stories high, many with Renaissance gables and oriels entered through arched gateways. The bastion on the Elbe's left bank towered high over the bridge and turned the town away from the river. The famous Canaletto view of Dresden's skyline was still a half-century away.

The frenzied activities of the family reunion continued through the day of February 28. On March 1, everyone abruptly departed. At some point, the brothers must have conferred with one another about current and future concerns, but the only high-level conference that Tzschimmer recorded was the visit of an envoy from Denmark, then engaged in a war with Sweden, who huddled for one afternoon with Johann Georg and advisors. Everyone else continued to party throughout the days and evenings. The illustrious meeting exemplified the Baroque character of princely and courtly life: the bigger the splash of hospitality, knightly activity, dramatic performances, both in the streets and in the theater, the greater the esteem accorded the ruler and his family. Never mind that Johann Georg's lifestyle and Dresden's luster in 1678 relied on subsidies, ensuring Saxon neutrality in the Franco-Dutch War, from the French King Louis XIV.[45]

Two years later, Johann Georg II was dead. Neither of his two immediate successors, son Johann Georg III and grandson, Johann Georg IV, lived long enough to make a mark either on Dresden or on Saxony. It was his second grandson, Friedrich August, the brother of Johann Georg IV, a man who had never expected to inherit the Electoral title, who continued the work of decorating Dresden.

III. The Era of August the Strong

When I walk or ride across the Augustus Bridge from the Palace Square to Old Dresden, now the Neustadt (New City), the figure of the Golden Rider looms into view. It sits on a high pedestal that calls attention to a large, vigorous man astride a rearing horse. The entire figure is covered in gold gilt. The horseman is the Elector Friedrich August, who chose the design of his own memorial statue[46] and, in the course of his lifetime, caused the creation of landmarks vital to Dresden's sense of place and the objects of every tourist visit. The splendor of Dresden owes much to the work of the man who came to be called August the Strong.

The Baroque City

Born in 1670, Friedrich August prepared for a career as a soldier and diplomat. The engineer-architect and public works director Wolf Caspar von Klengel taught him mathematics, drawing, fortification and military science. To turn him into a proper gentleman, the court chamberlain taught him foreign languages, and the orchestra conductor gave him musical instruction. As a youth, he traveled first to his mother's birthplace in Denmark and then took a grand tour that included Paris, Madrid, Lisbon, Florence, Venice, and Vienna. In all these cities, he frequented the resident courts and became acquainted with the future rulers of his day. He also learned the rituals of courtly culture and the practices of diplomacy.

When his older brother, Johann Georg IV, died suddenly of smallpox in 1694, Friedrich August became Elector. His principal minister, Count Jacob Heinrich von Flemming, after serving him for more than two decades, described him as a knowledgeable man who, when young, had ample energy for further study. At the same time, he frequently made grandiose plans that could not be fulfilled. As a youth, he possessed phenomenal strength, hence the moniker of "the Strong". Among other feats, he reportedly could break horseshoes with his bare hands.[47]

His abiding addictions were ambition and pleasure combined with an appetite for spectacle and status. At his very first carnival as Elector, he portrayed himself at one event as the Roman god, Mercury, symbol of prosperity and well-being. Two years later he appeared in a carnival procession as Alexander the Great. At another event, he imitated a Turkish sultan leading an elite unit of janissaries. August wanted to make himself as visible a ruler as the French sun-king, Louis XIV. For that he needed a kingdom.[48]

When the throne of Poland became vacant in 1697, Saxon Elector Friedrich August I decided to pursue it. Neither a Pole nor a conqueror, he could only hope to become Polish king through election by the magnates in the Polish Diet. Once elected, August would need to attend to the nobles' needs and desires. The Polish connection would also entangle him in the wars of Russia with the Ottoman and Swedish empires. More than military or economic advantage for Saxony, visibility and prestige for Friedrich August were the major benefits of the Polish crown.

One of the requirements for the job was a conversion to Catholicism. The announcement of his conversion shocked his subjects, but it should have come as no surprise. Neither his father nor his brother were pious Lutherans, and some of his socially prominent subjects often left church before the Sunday sermon. For some decades, Saxon Catholics had worshipped in the embassies of foreign, Catholic states. To reassure his rattled subjects, Friedrich August promised to protect their practice of Lutheranism and, despite his conversion, he retained as Saxon Elector the traditional post of leading the Protestant faction within the German empire. The increased toleration of Roman Catholicism now benefited Dresden's Calvinists.[49]

Since seeking refuge in Saxony during the Thirty Years' War, Calvinists had no official permission to practice their religion, and, as Protestants, they were subject to regulation by Lutheran authorities. Lutheran clergy were charged with giving them Communion. After the French government rescinded its toleration of Calvinism in 1685, several French families came to Dresden and, in concert with those descended from the Bohemians of the Thirty Years' War, started to hold private Sunday services. They even appointed a pastor. Although Lutheran leaders insisted they could gather only for prayer meetings. Friedrich August and his government did nothing to stop them, and Calvinists continued to worship without including a sermon in their services until officially granted toleration at the end of the eighteenth century.

Friedrich August's promise to respect his subjects' Lutheranism worked to his advantage. In 1697, he needed considerable funds with which to bribe the Polish nobles into voting for him as King. Some of this money eventually came from a grant by the reassured Lutherans in the Saxon Diet.[50] Other sums were borrowed from a Jewish financier from Halberstadt, Berend Lehmann, about whom we'll hear later. The bribes were successful, and as King of Poland, Friedrich August was absent from Dresden for long periods of time.

Nevertheless, he managed to convey his wishes for the city through the governors he left behind. Like other European rulers, August the Strong assured that Dresden reflected his power and aspirations.[51] Previous electors had already intervened in the city's governance to assure its health and safety. In 1660, in an effort to prevent fire, an ever-present danger within the city's walls, the Electoral officials decreed that roofs be covered in ceramic tiles. High structures were banned because they shut out light and air for other residents. In 1677, the Saxon Inspector of Military and Civilian Structures was made responsible for approving all new buildings within the city walls.

In the year in which he assumed the Electoral title, Friedrich August ordered an inventory of all houses in Dresden. It uncovered 200 wooden structures remaining within the city. Henceforth, all builders were forbidden to construct anything of wood or even to repair a wooden edifice. The clunky wood scaffolding over the city's wells was replaced with new, wrought-iron staves.

Viewing the city as the center of a princely landscape, Friedrich August gave Count Flemming the authority to supersede city government when necessary, and he issued the city's first comprehensive building regulations in 1708. Anyone constructing anything within the walls had to submit a draft plan to Electoral authorities for approval. According to the regulations, stone houses had to be covered in a light-colored stucco. A new superintendent of public works, Count August Christoph von Wackerbarth, issued additional regulations in 1720.

Because these requirements influenced construction in Dresden for many decades, it is worth exploring them in detail. The plans of 1720 required builders to consider the relationship of a new structure to neighboring houses and to the street. On wide city streets and squares, houses of three stories and a mezzanine could be erected. On smaller lanes, one of the three stories had to be lower than normal height. Attic garrets could no longer exist, and stone stairs had to go all the way up to the roof. More than two centuries later, this latter regulation helped to save lives. Lastly, though the color of stucco could not be dark, it also could not be too bright—an indication, perhaps, that some builders in the preceding twelve years had indulged in unorthodox colors.

As a follow-up to these intra-mural regulations, in 1736, three years after Friedrich August's death, the villages of the extra-mural suburbs were finally subjected to the same building regulations as the city intra-muros. These rules created a uniform image as Dresden expanded during the next two centuries. The uniform image was increasingly Baroque. Facades bore such decorative elements as stone busts, draperies, shells, vine leaves, blossoms, and fruits. Windows were symmetrically spaced along the street facade, and stone walls and pilasters divided it both horizontally and vertically. At the top of the house, mansard roofs appeared. These elements applied to noble and non-noble alike.

Up until this time, most Saxon aristocrats who worked either for the government or the court lived much like their bourgeois fellows. They even rented residential quarters from non-noble owners. Now they began to build large palaces that distinguished them from their non-aristocratic neighbors. Of these elegant residences, some survived World War II and were lovingly restored or even rebuilt when the necessary funds became available.

Baroque Architecture

As the city became an aesthetic backdrop to the Elector's court, Friedrich August intensified his efforts to create a royal landscape. Already in 1694, he had envisioned a square for "celebrations" to the west of the palace and south of the riding hall. This vision merged, after a fire in 1701 destroyed the palace's east wing, with plans to enlarge the palace and to build an orangery. The Elector-King, like other German princes of his era, dreamed of creating a second, smaller Versailles in his capital city. Yet neither finances nor space were available for such an ambitious undertaking. The palace remained relatively small and continued to be integrated into the urban fabric, similar to the structure that we see today.

The interaction between the city and the court affected Dresden's urban design. For centuries, city hall had occupied a conspicuous spot within the square of the Altmarkt. It was the site of city elections, of official communications and of the district court. The surrounding square, however, was also appropriated from time to time by the Elector for his entertainments, including jousting tournaments. City hall cluttered up the free field desired for these activities, and beginning with Moritz in the sixteenth century, the electors sought to remove it. The city council resisted these entreaties until Friedrich August threatened to have his soldiers destroy it. Faced with this ultimatum, city government finally yielded and moved city hall to a corner in the western row of buildings surrounding the square. Now the Elector insisted that the building adjacent to city hall alter its facade to give the corner a dignified appearance.[52]

The Zwinger

The razing of city hall occurred in time for the visit of the Elector's Danish cousins and military allies in 1709. Now Friedrich August needed even more space for entertainment—for jousting, for processions, for games, and other amusements. The site just west of the palace was an almost obvious choice. Here was property owned by the Elector, adjacent to the city's western wall, occupied by the so-called Zwinger garden, and by Johann Georg II's riding and shooting halls, which could be and were easily demolished.

Hurriedly a group of wooden buildings was thrown up for the entertainment of the Danish royal family. Once it departed, attention returned to the envisioned orangery and, after several years, a group of stone buildings—today's French and Mathematic-Physical Science Pavilions—were erected to protect orange trees during the winter. The architectural and sculptural masterpiece of this group flanking the city's old earthworks to the west was—and still is—the Wall Pavilion. The Long Gallery and the Crown Gate built on top of the bastion that ran along the city's southern moat, parallel to the Elbe, were added to complete the architectural composition. This group of buildings became the Zwinger, identifying it as the original defensive space between the old inner and outer walls.

By that time, another royal visit was pending, this one more important than that of the Danes. Friedrich August's heir was affianced to Maria Josepha, the daughter of the German emperor. The wedding festivities, planned for a month in 1719, needed space for all the scheduled events. At this point, the Elector decided to erect, on the city side toward the palace, a group of structures that mirrored the Wall Pavilion and its wings. These were not quite finished by the time of the wedding, but the Zwinger square, as we know it today, had taken shape. Originally, the side toward the Elbe was free of any building and, for the wedding, a grandstand filled the gap. Four years later, a short stone wall closed up the square.

The nineteenth-century art historian, Robert Dohme, claimed that the Zwinger pavilions exhibit "the greatest extent of ornamental treasure that Western art has achieved." For Carl Carus, a nineteenth-century polymath and personal physician to the Saxon ruler, the Zwinger conjured up romantic dreams. Hans Christian Andersen called it a visual echo chamber. More recently, Harald Marx, the lifelong curator of Dresden's art, deemed it to be the "key…to the beauty and special character of Dresden."

The architect for the Zwinger was Matthäus Daniel Pöppelmann, a Westphalian of humble birth, who had arrived in Dresden in 1680 and had found employment in the state public works department (Bauamt). Slowly he worked his way up from draftsman and, in 1705, Friedrich August recognized his talent and engaged him for many major projects. In 1710, the Elector sent him to Prague, to Vienna and to Rome to gather ideas for the construction of a new palace. While in Vienna, Pöppelmann became acquainted with Bernhard Fischer von Erlach, noted for devising the Baroque Imperial Style. In Rome, he came face to face with the works of the innovative architect Francesco Borromini and the prolific Lorenzo Bernini, creator of St. Peter's square.

In 1715, Friedrich August sent Pöppelmann on another trip, this time to Paris. By then, he had become, for all practical purposes, the director of state buildings and works. Yet a recent biographer cautions us to remember that Pöppelmann was always a member of a team, that the designs attributed to him probably contain elements of others' ideas. Nevertheless, the Zwinger is Pöppelmann's masterpiece. In this architectural complex are combined the elements of the Imperial style with a refreshing rococo lightness. This delicacy could have been inspired by the style of Rosalbe Carriera, a Venetian portrait painter favored by Friedrich August. Hans Christian Andersen was right to conjure up the Zwinger as an echo chamber. The duplication of the Wall Pavilion with the Glockenspiel (City) Pavilion, the symmetrical repetition of galleries, arches, columns and pilasters, niches, cascades and fountains, evoke a soothing visual mood surprising for a structural group that is, in reality, ponderous.

It is not only Pöppelmann's architecture that creates the mood. Adorning the arches, the columns, the balustrades and the niches are sculpted figures drawn from mythology and nature. The person to credit with these adornments is the sculptor Balthaser Permoser. Slightly older than Pöppelmann, Permoser hailed from Bavaria and had worked in both Salzburg and Vienna before traveling to Italy where he pursued his craft as carver for fourteen years, primarily in Florence at the court of the Medici. His Italian carvings in wood and ivory are delicate and lively and reveal an emotional sensitivity to his subject matter, whether secular or religious.

By 1689, when the Elector Johann Georg III appointed him as court sculptor, he already possessed a solid reputation. After his arrival in Dresden, he went promptly to work making statuary for the Great Garden. Later, Permoser consulted with Pöppelmann on the plans for the Zwinger as they developed between 1711 and 1718. Viewing the features of the Zwinger, one cannot escape the feeling that it was Permoser who gave Pöppelmann tips about what and whom to see on his first Italian trip, an experience that informed his later designs.

Permoser's figures for the Zwinger bear a resemblance to pieces he had already sculpted while in Rome almost thirty years before. The carousing satyr busts adorning the pilasters of the Wall Pavilion are Permoser's work. Atop the Pavilion's dome, the Saxon Hercules, bearing the burden of earth's orb, is the signed work of Permoser. Even earlier are the figures of Ceres and Vulkan that decorate the lower niches of the Crown Gate. In the Bath of the Nymphs, one can find his depictions of joyful maidens going to and from the pools.

Permoser was in his sixties when work on the Zwinger began, and even had he been a younger man, it was impossible for him to carve all the decorative figures required. Members of his atelier produced some of the characters; others were the work of skilled independent Saxons. A walk through the Zwinger reminds us that Dresden was home to a colony of extraordinary artists during the first third of the eighteenth century.

The artists who worked on the Zwinger were responsible for modeling in stone the symbols of Friedrich August's stature within the German political world. The Zwinger was his Hesperides; the golden apples were the Polish crown and Saxon riches. Gathered together to support this stature were gods and goddesses from Greek mythology, wise men like Saul and Solon from the ancient world, forces of nature such as the four winds of the compass. Offering respite from the rigors of ruling were legendary nymphs, the fruits of the vine, the floral beauty of gardens and meadows. Quite apart from the King-Elector's cultural-political message, the Zwinger's carvings are a riotous celebration of the natural world. They were a fitting reflection of a ruler who delighted in wine, women and song.[53]

The Elbe as Grand Canal

If the Zwinger satisfied Friedrich August's desire to emulate Versailles and Vienna, other projects worked toward achieving another vision. He imagined the Elbe as Dresden's Grand Canal, where Electoral palaces would line the banks like pearls on a string. In 1717, he bought, from his prime minister, Count Flemming, the current Japanese Palace—then the Holland Palace—on the right bank of the Elbe in Old Dresden. Upriver from Dresden, at Pillnitz, also on the right bank of the Elbe, there already existed a small summer palace. In 1721, this building was remodeled, and two separate pavilions were added on each side. These functioned as apartments for guests at garden parties. In 1722, an imposing cascade of stairs to the river was constructed where guests would alight from barques. Downriver from Dresden, Count Flemming built, between 1724 and 1726, the Übigau Palace, which was then acquired by Friedrich August in 1726.

Other architectural and landscaping achievements added to Dresden's Baroque character. In 1705, the east wing of the current Taschenberg Palace had been built for Friedrich August's mistress, the Countess Cosel. Far to the city's southeast, property that formerly comprised the manor and village of Grosssedlitz, the King/Elector completed a small palace with orangery and garden in the Baroque style.[54]

He also turned his attention to the medieval Frauenkirche, located on the Neumarkt. Long a mausoleum, composer Heinrich Schütz's remains lay there. The church had become structurally unsound, and Friedrich August wanted to open up vistas to the north, south and east of the site. The party responsible for improving the site was Dresden's city government, and eventually August persuaded the city council to tear down the old church and rebuild.

Once that occurred, it was the city's architect, George Bähr, who drew up the plans for the new church. At the same time, the state superintendent of buildings, Count Wackerbarth, who answered to Friedrich August, closely tracked the design and its execution. He gave Bähr's plans to the court architect, Johann Christoph Knöffel, who contributed suggestions for improvement. Bähr's recent designs for round churches in a neighboring village and in Ore Mountain towns appealed to the King-Elector, because a round church suited the cramped site and opened up the desired views. Furthermore, Bähr intended to crown the structure with a cupola. The cornerstone was laid in 1726. Construction proceeded beyond the term of Friedrich August's life, and the first service was held the year after his death. Even then, the church was not completely finished until 1743. Then and now, its grand dome soars above the river, reminiscent of Santa Maria della Salute in Venice. There are many prominent Protestant churches in Germany, but Dresden's Frauenkirche is "the most splendid and stately Protestant architecture" in the country.[55]

The Neustadt

As with the Frauenkirche, Friedrich August took the initiative in replacing another structure that was the city's responsibility. The bridge over the Elbe, more than 500 years old by the early eighteenth century, could not accommodate the growing traffic caused by Dresden's political and economic development, and, battered by many Elbe floods, it was increasingly unsafe. Because the city council would not finance the replacement, the Elector used his own funds and engaged Pöppelmann to design it. In a short sixteen months, between 1728 and 1730, the bridge was raised, widened and strengthened. The new crossing accommodated two lanes of wagon traffic, and sidewalks served pedestrians. Wrought-iron railings studded with lamps topped the span's arches. It was not only trade that improved. The bridge became a popular promenade that more closely united the city's two sides. Bernardo Bellotto, called Canaletto, painted this bridge into his famous portrait of Dresden's eighteenth-century silhouette.[56]

On the right bank of the Elbe, Friedrich August inspired the completion of a new city. What was then called Old Dresden had burned down in 1685.[57] Almost immediately, Wolf Caspar von Klengel, the Elector's chief architect at the time, drew up a plan for reconstruction, but despite a collection taken up among the left-bank's citizens to help those who were burned out, rebuilding was slow. Friedrich August determined to remedy the situation. He wanted aristocrats and a rich bourgeoisie to populate the new city, and throughout his reign, he offered tax incentives to encourage them to build there. These measures met with some success.

The Hauptstrasse (High Street) led from the Elbe bridge to the Black Gate, now the site of Albertplatz. After his purchase of the Holland Palace, Friedrich August converted it into a Japanese Palace and had a boulevard of linden trees laid out to match up with the palace's middle axis. This became the Königsstrasse (King's Street) and is, still today, a wide and elegant avenue leading to the Albertplatz. To assure that the size of the street's houses did not overwhelm the palace, they could not be more than three stories high.

Eventually, the Elector saw to it that a finishing school for aristocratic boys was located in Old Dresden and that the area to the east of the bridge was reserved for army barracks. After his death, a Blockhaus, destined to shelter the police watch for Old Dresden, was placed at the northern end of the bridge marking the entry to the market square and Hauptstrasse. To finish off the rehabilitation of the old settlement, Friedrich August erected a social hall for state administrators in Meissen Lane. A year before his death, the new city building code rechristened Old Dresden into the "The King's New City", shortened by later generations to the Neustadt.[58]

The City Grows

As an ever-sprawling metropolis, Dresden has, over the years, annexed most of its neighboring villages. One might say that this process started with Friedrich August I. Ever since the thirteenth century, ten settlements ringing the city fell under its legal jurisdiction. By the sixteenth century, they had developed into dependent suburbs rather than separate villages. Yet they remained outside the walls and, as we have seen during the Thirty Years' War, had been sacrificed to the enemy. They were largely populated by the city's lower classes, though aristocrats also acquired estates within their boundaries.

In 1710, Friedrich August enclosed all these suburbs within a wooden palisade that stretched in an arc around them and the walled city. At certain access points, his government stationed agents to collect the general consumption taxes, imposed seven years before, on all goods entering Dresden. These funds gave the Elector a source of revenue that was not dependent on approval by the Saxon Diet. They also meant that the city gates no longer enjoyed full control over everyday entrance and exit of the city. The palisade that connected the collection points incorporated the suburbs into the city's space.

In addition to the older suburbs, there was a new settlement to the west of the city established by Johann Georg II on the Electoral estate of the Ostra Preserve, once the ducal hunting grounds. It was supposed to encourage new workshops and manufactories and bolster the city's economy. Up until Friedrich August's accession to the Electoral title, this new settlement had not lived up to its potential. Even though the area was platted and tax incentives offered to settlers, in 1720 there were only eighteen houses in the area. Several of these belonged to nobles and rich citizens who had built summer houses there.

In 1728, Friedrich August purchased three parcels and named the suburb Friedrichstadt in honor of his son, the heir to the Electoral title. During the next several years, the new suburb began to flourish. After Friedrich August's death, the population was large enough to justify a weekly market, and the streets were paved. Roman Catholics, a minority in Dresden, were encouraged to settle in the Friedrichstadt, and soon it boasted a Catholic school, a Catholic hospital, and a Catholic cemetery.[59]

Pageantry

The princely landscape of Dresden envisioned by Friedrich August formed the setting for his extravagant festivals. We've already seen that the celebration of carnival was a Saxon tradition and that a century before, the sculptor Nosseni had devised elaborate inventions for the amusement of the court and its guests. The seventeenth-century electors, as Johann Georg II's "Illustrious Meeting" attests, continued the practice. Now, Friedrich August carried this tradition to new heights in order to project his own power and prestige—in Dresden, in Saxony, in Germany, and in Europe. Visits of foreign monarchs or advantageous marriages served as occasions for large and endless parties. In 1718 Baron Johann Michael von Loen, a publicist visiting August's court, remembered continuous "masquerades, of heroes, of love stories, errant knights, adventures, dances, hunts, shoots, pastoral plays, war and peace parades, ceremonies, slapstick, lovely curios, in short, everything [wa]s a game..."[60]

It would be repetitious to recount all the fêtes held at Friedrich August's court, but for pure pageantry, let's turn to the month of events celebrating the marriage of the future Elector Friedrich August II to the Habsburg archduchess Maria Josefa in September 1719, the occasion for which the Zwinger formed the backdrop. For the Wettins, this marriage signaled their entry into the exclusive circle of princes suitable for election to German emperor.

Preparations for the celebration began two years before the event. Since his model was the French king and court, Friedrich August preferred French theater. The Habsburg bride's family, the groom, and most of Germany's noble music lovers favored Italian opera. Therefore in 1717, the Elector, while maintaining his own French troupe, hired one of the best and most modern Italian opera companies of the time, that of Antonio Lotti. The company included a composer, a librettist, an architect for the sets, as well as singers and instrumentalists.

At the same time, work began on a new opera house next to the Zwinger. To project the power and pleasure represented by the festivities of 1719, Friedrich August assigned Pöppelmann the task of constructing a stone edifice to accommodate the large number of guests who would view operas and plays during the month of wedding celebrations. This 2000-seat theater was placed just outside the Zwinger's southeast corner. Foreigners had to be hired to do the job, and they worked at a furious pace. Despite a strike called by the workers because one of them was beaten by an overseer, the house was completed in February 1719, six months in advance of the wedding festivities. Outside the Zwinger's northeast corner, an interim, half-timbered ballhouse was built, clearly intended as a temporary structure.

By that time, over 1000 guests from outside Saxony had signaled their intention to attend the celebrations. To this number should be added a crowd of local guests. The theme for the month was the Seven Planets, the sum of those then known.

The festivities began with a reception of the young couple at the Saxon-Bohemian border, after which they traveled by barque to Dresden, where they participated in a four-hour long procession that ended at the Dresden Palace. Several thousand soldiers and citizens' militiamen, dressed in new red and gray uniforms, were called out to keep order along the way. Participants included one section of workers from the Saxon post office, a group of hunting and forestry officials; another comprised members of the Saxon Diet. Groomsmen led 124 richly decorated, riderless horses. Tournament jousters, dressed in old German habits with feathered hats and halberds, were accompanied by hunting horns and trumpeters. Flags waved around them. Next, seventy carriages, each pulled by six horses, carried Saxon aristocrats. There followed nine carriages of Saxon state ministers. Polish servants, Polish horses and the Elector's Polish bodyguard walked and rode behind more riderless horses.

The bridegroom then rode into view surrounded by his Swiss guard. Finally, Maria Josefa's bridal coach brought up the rear surrounded by twenty-five Moors from Portugal, imported especially for the occasion. Her coach, decorated in gold and silver, was drawn by eight horses and accompanied by a Swiss guard. Behind the archduchess's coach rode members of the Austrian court, her ladies-in-waiting and an Hungarian bodyguard.

On the morrow, a second church wedding was performed, the first having occurred in Vienna. This was followed by a banquet served on gold plates. In the days following the wedding, a dance was held in the newly remodeled Great Room of the palace. The opera "Giove (Jupiter) in Argo" was performed in the open air at the Holland/Japanese Palace, capped off by a fireworks display. On another day, a tournament honoring the god Mars, including both mounted and unmounted jousters, competed on the Altmarkt.

A Jupiter Festival of the Four Elements inaugurated the Zwinger and featured a carousel. Carousels were colorful competitions among groups of aristocrats astride horses or settled in chariots. In 1719, each group of contestants represented an Element—earth, fire, water, air—and each division's costumes and banners corresponded with its Element. These groups participated in choreographed processions and races that attempted to hit, with a lance, a target called a quintan, a wooden figure or pole attached to a shield.

Later in the month, a Diana Festival featuring a hunt for water fowl took place at the Elbe bridge. Next, a Fair of the Nations in the Zwinger was an elaborate imitation of an annual city fair. On another day, a Venus celebration in the Great Garden allowed ladies of the court, accompanied in their chariots by two cavaliers, to throw darts through hanging rings. This ladies' race was a Dresden specialty, and chariots received points for the darts that went through the ring. There was also a host of performances in the new opera house designed to keep the guests entertained on every single day of the fête.

Even though some of these events were supposedly closed to the public, the tight space between palace and town meant that there was plenty to be seen from neighboring houses and roofs. Indeed, the city's tradesmen and artisans probably supplied materials and labor for the races and carousels, and on occasion they could be called upon to be supporting extras for the main aristocratic actors. For instance, on September 20, the Mercury Festival in the Zwinger was officially open to the public. Since it included an imitation weekly market, Dresden merchants were invited to sell their wares, and sixty stalls made merchandise available to aristocrats and commoners alike.

The grand finale of the marriage festivities was held to the south of Dresden in the Plauen Valley of the Weisseritz. It had long been a peculiarity of Dresden festivals to highlight the long history of coal mining and iron working in Saxony. This Festival of Saturn was no exception. First a temple to Saturn was blasted into the rock of the Plauen glen and illuminated with hundreds of miners' lamps. One thousand miners and iron workers in twenty-four different costumes, specially made for the event, paraded before the guests. Floats depicted the miners' mountainous landscape: a blow-hole bubbling with water, the replica of a mine, a model blast furnace, a coin-stamping machine. There were various demonstrations of the manufacturing processes involved in iron-making. Guests received programs providing all the details of the technology displayed in the parade. The evening ended with a banquet in Saturn's temple and a fireworks display of the then known planets circling around the crowned monogram of Friedrich August—AR (Augustus Rex=King August).

Events like the wedding festivities of 1719 occurred within an urban landscape dressed up for the occasion. Special shrubbery was placed in the Great Garden and its pond cleaned. The palace, the bridge, aristocratic and bourgeois mansions were illuminated at night. Wine flowed from specially constructed fountains along the city's streets and lanes. By day, the populace walked among grandstands, shooting galleries, temporary pavilions and temples. Musicians, jesters, soldiers and craftsmen were sucked into building the temporary structures and performing or supporting the events. This month of festivities may have cost as much as 25,000 Taler.[61]

The Economy

Compare this sum with the worth of a Dresden shoemaker, accumulated over a lifetime of work: 2500 Taler. Upon his death, this man's tools were valued at less than one Taler. The tools of gold and silver workers, nail makers, and mechanics could be worth only as much as 100 Taler. Outright poverty also existed. Those who could find no work, or were disabled, depended on alms distributed by the municipal authorities.⁶² Or they resorted to begging. An investigation by the city council revealed that many beggars came into the city on market day to sell small lots of firewood, resin, sawdust and other goods but didn't make very much money. They went begging once the market ended. Other beggars were army veterans, or their families, who had received insufficient severance pay when released from service. This circumstance makes perverse the gulf between the thousands spent on a month's worth of parties and the plight of ordinary Saxons.

The Wettin family's wealth, allowing for spending on elaborate fêtes, was first and foremost based on the mines in the Ore Mountains. Silver continued to be mined; and the electors collected fees for access to the mineral rights. Coal and iron lodes made iron-making a profitable industry. The electors owned some mines and smelters outright and collected the profits from their products. Also mined in the Ore Mountains were several valuable stones: marble, alabaster, amethyst, agate, garnet and topaz. In the course of the seventeenth century, a flourishing Saxon textile industry had grown up. Saxons were known throughout Germany for the production of luxury goods. Trade flourished at the annual international fair in Leipzig, and that city was rich and complex enough to establish a stock exchange at the end of the seventeenth century. Even though Friedrich August's dynastic ambitions were costly and led to Saxony's expensive involvement in the Great Northern War, a conflict involving Russia and its allies against Sweden, the state and its ruling family were rich.

This wealth invigorated Dresden. At the beginning of the eighteenth century, the city's economy expanded. Improvements in public infrastructure facilitated exchanges with other regions, and the end of a tariff war with Prussia removed another barrier to trade. Two coaches per week carried mail, packages, passengers and freight between Dresden and Leipzig. Postal stations increased under Friedrich August, and his government regulated postal traffic and made sure that guest houses provided decent food and clean accommodations for both humans and horses. Within Dresden, the city council instituted a sedan chair service that functioned like modern taxis.

The city had developed a lively river trade in flax with the city of Hamburg, and local flax merchants became very rich. Exports were large enough to persuade several English firms to establish themselves in the city. Since the

Saxon Elector was also king of Poland, Dresden supplied materials for buildings in Poland and imported salt and candle wax in return.

Three miles outside the city, the village of Laubegast, perched on the banks of the Elbe, developed a lively cottage industry making thread that was popular in northern Germany. In other surrounding villages, hundreds of women and girls earned a living by finishing underwear in muslin and batiste, embroidering in silk, gold, and silver, or making goods from straw. Another cottage industry was the *pointe de Dresde,* a needle-pointed lace used by both men and women in handkerchiefs, ribbons, sleeve cuffs, or other decorative clothing.

The chief benefit to Dresden from the Elector's court came from the expanding state apparatus and the web of international contacts established by Friedrich August. Moreover, the Saxon Diet met every six years and brought 500 people to town—people who had to be housed, fed, and entertained. As the city's population increased, bakers, butchers, and grocers did a thriving business. Permanently established within the city were retailers of various quotidian wares. Added to these were the stall keepers and hucksters who flocked to the weekly markets on both sides of the Elbe.

Those who were well-to-do could afford luxury items made by skilled craftsmen. They migrated to the city to take advantage of the increased demand for stylish modes of dress and luxury items: Wig-makers, silk embroiderers, hat-makers, feather decorators, silver and goldsmiths.

Gold and Gems

The most prominent goldsmith in the city was Johann Melchior Dinglinger whose "Durbar at Delhi on the birthday of the Great Mogul Aurangzeb"—the powerful ruler of the seventeenth-century Mughal empire—must count among the masterpieces of world art. Dinglinger hailed from Biberach on the river Riss in what is today the state of Baden-Wurttemberg. His father was a cutler, and the youth became acquainted at an early age with all the techniques associated with smithery. When he was sixteen, he became apprenticed to a goldsmith in the neighboring city of Ulm.[63]

No one is completely sure where Dinglinger went after he finished his apprenticeship, but by 1692, he had arrived in Dresden and was already crafting small items for the then prince Friedrich August. He soon joined the local goldsmith's guild and remained active in that organization until the end of his life. In 1696, he married the daughter of a prosperous local goldsmith, and the following year, he bought his father-in-law's commodious house in the Grosse Frauengasse. In that same year, he became a voting citizen of the city and a court jeweler. Later, he purchased a vineyard near the village of Loschwitz, a popular summer refuge for well-to-do Dresdners.

During the 1690s, Dinglinger's younger brothers occasionally joined him to work on special projects. Finally, in 1704, unwilling to live in Biberach during the disruptions caused by the War of the Spanish Succession, they both settled permanently in Dresden. Georg Friedrich was an emailleur, and Georg Christoph was another goldsmith. The three brothers formed an intimate partnership, and it is difficult to imagine Johann Melchior's oeuvre without their participation. The Dinglinger family also maintained ties with a host of other artists in the city, among them Balthaser Permoser.

Friedrich August had a weakness for *objets de vertu*. One of the early objects of Dinglinger's collaboration with Permoser was the Diana Goblet, a work of art that reflected the popularity of the shell and hunting goblets of the early eighteenth century. The eye is immediately drawn to the beautifully carved Roman goddess Diana resting beside her bath in a large calcedony shell. Hanging over the whorl against which Diana rests is a red enameled baldachin beneath a large suspended pearl. Surrounding the chaste Diana are silver dolphins spewing water into the shell of her bath. Garlands on the back of her throne are studded with diamonds. The rest of the highly decorative piece suggests Diana's role as goddess of the hunt and her revenge on the hunter Actaeon for discovering her naked after her bath. The mythical Diana turned him into a stag, and he was killed by his own dogs. Beneath the shell holding Diana's bath, Dinglinger and Permoser rendered both stag and dogs in gold and colored enamel. An eighteenth-century observer would have delighted in the many details of this Baroque work of art. Dinglinger and his brothers fashioned a host of other useful and decorative articles, both for the Elector and other clients.

The Green Vaults

Diana after her bath now reclines in the Green Vaults of the palace, thronged by tourists. The original vaults of impenetrable construction, with green paint accenting the bases and capitols of the columns, housed the Saxon state treasury—cash, jewels, precious art works and important documents—

and could be entered only through the Elector's apartments. When August the Strong dissolved the old-fashioned *Kunstkammer* of the sixteenth century, he gave Pöppelmann the job of designing a space for displaying his valuable artistic objects. Other artists supplied the interior decoration.[64]

Four of the rooms featured mirrored walls and posts that intensified the displays of silver and gold objects as well as precious stones. A fifth room was lined with glass walls that contrasted strongly with the black velvet to which precious jewels were pinned. A sixth room boasted marble panels, and the oak panels of the seventh room provided a fitting background for small bronzes. When completed in 1729, these rooms welcomed visitors from near and far. Dresdners claim that they represented the first museum in the world to display decorative arts. They have continued to do so for the last three centuries.

White Gold

During this period, the industrial breakthrough that occurred in Dresden was the European discovery of how to make fine porcelain. In the fourteenth century, Marco Polo first brought Chinese porcelain to Europe, and once the Portuguese and Dutch established trade routes to Asia, they conducted a robust trade in this commodity. For decades, Europeans experimented with recipes for making porcelain, and Friedrich August was an avid collector of the "white gold". But he also supported any effort that promised to increase his wealth.

For over 100 years, the Saxon Electors had maintained an alchemist's laboratory. The goal was to produce gold for the ruler's treasury. That was also Friedrich August's intent when he brought Johann Friedrich Böttger, a self-styled transformer of base metal to gold, to Dresden, placed him under arrest, and set him up in a laboratory.

The Baron Ehrenfried von Tschirnhaus became Böttger's supervisor. Tschirnhaus was a polymath who had studied mathematics, medicine and natural science at the University of Leiden. He had conducted experiments with members of the English Royal Society and had worked with Christian Huygens, the founder of modern physics, in Paris. In 1675, Tschirnhaus began to experiment with potter's clay to fire primitive porcelain. At this early stage, he thought that porcelain was a kind of glass. His early trials led to the establishment, under Electoral auspices, of a glass making and polishing manufactory in Dresden. He also invented a high temperature oven capable of producing a hard, double-fired brick. In the course of his work, Tschirnhaus traveled to Holland and France to visit firms in Delft and St. Cloud that were also experimenting with porcelain fabrication.

It is tempting to assume that Tschirnhaus, the sophisticated scientist, realized the futility of trying to make gold from base metals and channeled Böttger's efforts into experimenting with the manufacture of porcelain. Maybe not. According to the noted contemporary potter, Edmund de Waal, Böttger and Tschirnhaus stumbled on the recipe for porcelain as a side effect of developing bricks that could best withstand the high temperatures associated with alchemy. In 1706, they combined red clay with quartz and got...red porcelain. One year later, they had succeeded in producing the "white gold" that could be molded, painted, gilded and sold both at home and abroad for very tidy sums. This white porcelain consisted of kaolin, alabaster and quartz, all materials found on Saxon soil. Within two years, Böttger had also solved the problem of how to glaze these wares. The Elector set up a porcelain factory, first at Dresden and then at the neighboring city of Meissen, and the first "China" made in Europe went on sale in 1713.

Over the centuries since then, the credit for inventing European porcelain has gone to Böttger. Recently, scholars have concluded that discovering the process for making the product was the result of teamwork among Böttger, Tschirnhaus, Pabst von Ohain—an expert in mineralogy—and a Dr. Bartholomai, naturalist, who determined the optimal mixture of soils for obtaining hard-paste porcelain.[65]

The Royal Art Collection

The symbiosis between the Saxon Elector and the arts had a long Dresden history. Remember the Wettins' association with the elder and younger Cranachs, with August's establishment of a *Kunstkammer,* and the seventeenth century electors' additions to the collection, with increasing attention to the fine arts. After he became Elector, Friedrich August augmented the collection. Adding to his holdings was not the principal task confronting him. There were also issues of categorization and display that arose from the more modern practices being adopted in Italian and French museums. As a young prince, Friedrich August had visited these foreign institutions, and now he began to apply their principles to his own holdings.[66]

After two decades of experimentation, the old *Kunstkammer* was abandoned, and the outlines of Dresden's modern gallery structure emerged.

In part, they were based on a scholarly inventory ordered by Friedrich August in 1722. The Green Vaults, remodeled by Pöppelmann, housed the precious jewelry, carvings, and gold and silver *objets de vertu* on the ground floor of the palace. The porcelain collection went to the first floor of the Holland/Japanese Palace that was still used as an entertainment center.

Paintings collected by his predecessors and by Friedrich August himself were assigned to the remodeled Electoral Stable, but some were also dispersed among the Elector's various palaces. Between 1717 and 1733, he acquired three separate collections of ancient sculptures that came to be housed in the Great Garden's peripheral pavilions. Eventually, other parts of the collections went to the Zwinger. Books went to the electoral library. Public visits to the collections were expanded in exchange for visitors' donations to the Electoral treasury.

One of August the Strong's recent biographers estimates that his most lasting legacy was the creation of Dresden as a magnet attracting art lovers of all kinds to the city. It is hard to imagine this Elbe metropole as it exists today without the embellishments of Friedrich August and the treasures they protect. When he died in 1733, he left behind a son, Friedrich August II, also elected King of Poland, whom he had not prepared to rule but to whom he bequeathed a similar interest in the arts. The son's prime minister, Count Heinrich von Brühl, governed in place of the Elector/King and used the arts to bolster the status of Dresden.[67]

Dresden's Splendor

The progression from August the Strong to the more diffident Friedrich August II occurred as Dresden approached the apex of its political, economic and cultural powers. Bernardo Bellotto, called Canaletto, captured on canvas the city as it existed in the mid-eighteenth century. In his famous "View of Dresden from the Right Bank of the Elbe", Canaletto placed Pöppelmann's bridge in the center of his *vedute* just as the Elbe loops from south to north, a visual flow that dramatizes the vista of Dresden's skyline. With his *camera obscura* Canaletto captured a cityscape that continues, even with changes in details, to influence our impressions of the town.

In this prospect a new palace fronts the river on the left bank, behind the bridge. Erected by Count Brühl, the massive structure perches just at the edge of the old riverine rampart, converted into a private terrace. To the east of this palace, the Count was only beginning to turn into gardens the three plots of land, including the Virgin Bastion, that the new Elector had gifted him. Behind Brühl's palace rises the stately Baroque dome of the newly completed Frauenkirche, and off in the distance the old spire of the Kreuzkirche balances the more prominent Hausmann tower to the west. Dominating the Elbe bank is the gleaming sandstone of the Catholic Court Church, conceived by the old ruler and implemented by the new. It became the last significant Baroque structure to be built in Dresden.

The Court Church

After he converted to Catholicism, August the Strong, well aware of the Lutheran sensibilities of his subjects, had originally avoided outward displays of his new faith, and the palace chapel continued to hold Protestant services. He and other Catholics associated with the court worshipped almost clandestinely. It was only in 1707 that the empty, seventeenth-century theater was converted into a church. Her biographer reports that August the Strong's mistress, the Countess Cosel, disliked traversing the terrain of the Catholics on her way from the Taschenberg mansion to Protestant Sunday services in the palace chapel.[68] Finally, in the 1730s, Friedrich August I and then his successor Friedrich August II quietly made plans for a Catholic Court Church (Hofkirche).

In 1737, the architect Gaetano Chiaveri transferred from Warsaw, where he worked for the King, to Dresden to preside over the construction of the church. The model was the Palace Chapel in Versailles. In order to locate the church next to the Electoral Palace, it was necessary to breach the fortifications on the Elbe, to destroy both the wall and the old Elbe gate and to level the river bank. These changes created the Palace Square at the southern end of the bridge. In the foreground, Canaletto's painting depicts the broken stones of the old wall and, behind them, the scaffolding of the unfinished church tower.

The construction of the church extended from 1739 until 1754. Already in place by the time Canaletto painted his view from the Elbe were the seventy-eight statues of saints, all designed by Lorenzo Mattielli, ringing the atticae of the lower and upper parts of the nave. The platform created by the differing widths of the lower and upper nave was planned as the stage for processions, such as those on Corpus Christi. According to Dresden city regulations, processions could only occur on church property, and all around the new Court

Church lay forbidden public squares and streets. Adjoining the processional platform was a raised space that could accommodate seats for spectators. The pulpit carved by Permoser already at the beginning of the century was moved from the old theater/church to the new Court Church, and the last organ constructed by the famed Gottfried Silbermann rang out from the balcony opposite the altar.

A by-product of the Court Church was the creation of the little Italian village to the west of the church. Consisting of modest dwellings erected by Italian stone cutters, it eventually provided lodging for servants of the court, artists, composers like Carl Maria von Weber and even the odd aristocrat. Within the tree-lined village, small neighborhood pubs established themselves and became the favorite haunts of visitors to the theater and the opera.

The siting of the new Court Church and the Italian village opened up the city to the riverfront in a way that August the Strong had envisioned. Leveling the old northern bastion and wall now oriented Dresden toward the water aesthetically and socially. This partial abandonment of the old bulwarks demonstrated their uselessness in the face of the improved military technology of the eighteenth century. We shall soon see how vulnerable Dresden had become to a determined enemy.[69]

The Finest Music in Europe

Even before Friedrich August II became Elector with his penchant for Italian opera, the court orchestra had attained a very high quality. Now it became the best in Europe. The composer and flautist, Johann Quantz, who played with the orchestra for twenty-five years, claimed never to have heard more "artful performance[s]". The French philosophe (and musician) Jean-Jacques Rousseau, writing more than a decade after Quantz had departed, judged it to be a "most balanced" ensemble that achieved the "most complete" musical achievement.[70]

In 1734, Johann Adolf Hasse signed a contract as court orchestra director. Hasse hailed from Bergedorf, a small town near Hamburg, where his father was organist at the Lutheran church. As a youth, he went to Italy, studied with Alessandro Scarlatti, and was a celebrated Italian composer even before he arrived in Dresden. While in Italy, he married the famous Italian soprano Faustina Bordoni, who also signed on as the leading court singer. As a composer and director, Hasse knew how to appeal to both his courtier audiences and the Dresden bourgeoisie that was now welcome at the Court Opera where performances were the musicals of the eighteenth century. His usual operatic themes, enticing audiences then as now, were love, hate, heroism, conflict, victory, defeat and sorrow.

The production of his "Solimano", written for the carnival of 1753, provides insight into his appeal. It featured dancers, dwarves, real elephants, horses, and camels. The final scene was set in an illuminated Turkish camp on the Tigris, and scenes of Babylon formed the background for a river filled with ships. This opera, like all his others, would have been written with careful attention to the abilities of the singers and musicians, another characteristic that explains Hasse's popularity.

The musicians that he worked with were first-rate. The best-known today are probably Quantz and the concert master, violinist Johann Pisendel. Two other composers who played under his direction were Jan Dismas Zelenka on the bass viol and Giovanni Alberto Ristori, cembalo. Hasse and Pisendel were responsible for enhancing the musical experience of their listeners. Pisendel was known as a strict task-master, and performances were well-rehearsed. In addition, tuning occurred in a room separate from the concert hall, making the first tones heard by the audience more powerful.

Hasse rearranged the orchestra to create a split-sound effect. Baroque string players usually sat in a semi-circle at the front of the orchestra, with woodwinds and horns behind them. Hasse shifted the strings to the right and the woodwinds to the left. Violinists played with their backs to the audience. The bass viols were distributed throughout the pit, and trumpets and drums sat in two side loges. The bassoons, now liberated from their former role as a comedic instrument, also sat with their backs to the audience and played an octave below the violins. The conductor did not necessarily stand in front of the musicians; he could also situate himself in their midst, which would explain why violins and bassoons would turn their backs on the audience.

The Hasses were friends of the Bach family in Leipzig, and Johann Sebastian frequently visited Dresden. He gave a number of concerts on Dresden church organs. Between 1733 and 1746, his son Wilhelm Friedemann was organist at the Sophienkirche, providing an extra impetus to visit the city.

In the eighteenth century, Hasse's popularity was hardly equaled. Today, barely anyone has heard of him. Unfortunately, his sense of musical evolution was limited. He failed to keep up with the changes occurring in other places, alterations that led to the classicism of the late eighteenth century and the romanticism of the next.

The court opera was not the only musical attraction in town. Dresden's churches had long presented concerts. After the completion of the Court Church in 1754, interest in these concerts increased. The high point of church music occurred during Holy Week, but church concerts occurred all year long. From 1755 to 1785, the director of the Kreuzkirche choir was a student of J. S. Bach, Gottfried August Homilius. His responsibilities extended to the Frauenkirche and to the Sophienkirche. Modern recordings of his compositions testify to the appeal of his music to Dresdners in the Old Regime and to contemporary listeners.[71]

Theater

Although the court opera bolstered the Elector's stature within Germany, it also taxed his finances, particularly after the Saxon participation and defeat in the First Silesian War (King George's War in the Western hemisphere). To relieve the burden on the Elector's treasury, the court opera transferred to a small wooden opera house operated under concession by the Mingotti Brothers in the Zwinger courtyard.

In a move unusual in the eighteenth century, this small court opera began to sell tickets to its performances, supplying funds available for the ensemble. Aristocratic courtiers, who had been obliged to supply the captive audience for Italian court opera, were no longer the primary listeners. In order to appeal to the new bourgeois audience, German Singspiel now formed part of the normal repertoire. After the Mingottis' wooden theater burned down in 1748, court opera eventually returned to the large stone theater next to the Zwinger's City Pavilion, and Dresden's bourgeoisie continued to join the aristocracy at performances.[72]

Count Brühl

While Friedrich August II's support helps to account for the high musical quality of the court opera and orchestra, other accomplishments of his Electoral regime, like the theater, should in large part be credited to Count Heinrich von Brühl, his principal minister after 1738. A recent biographer speculates that his enjoyment of theater was responsible for attracting at least three well-known companies of actors to make regular stops in Dresden. Brühl functioned as a "vice-elector". Because Friedrich August II shunned the responsibilities of governing and lacked the forceful personality of his father, Brühl frequently represented the Saxon state to visiting statesmen and princes, not only at the chancellery in his capacity as prime minister, but also at entertainments in his city palace. His palace on the riverfront terrace was decorated lavishly in the Saxon rococo style and contained both a large dining hall and a ballroom.

The complex of buildings in Brühl's Garden also included a library that matched the quality of the Elector's. When Brühl died, the electoral library merged his collection of 62,000 items with its own, and scholars were welcome to access their riches. This library, which now exists as the Saxon State and University Library, had begun at the same time as the *Kunstkammer*, had appropriated the libraries of the abbeys and convents dissolved at the time of the Reformation and purchased the libraries of private individuals. Just before acquiring Count Brühl's works, the electoral library added the collection of Count Heinrich von Bünau, a significant scholarly accumulation that included flyers from the Thirty Years' War.[73]

Expanding the Royal Collections

Brühl's Garden also included his own private art gallery. As the Elector's Director of Collections, he shared with his prince an interest in painting and sculpture. Friedrich August II, having spent eight years in Italy and France as a young man, had become a genuine connoisseur. He and Brühl had agents stationed in Italy, France and Holland with instructions to seek out the best collections available for purchase.

Already in 1741–2, the Elector had bought 715 paintings from various European owners, including the very valuable Wallenstein Collection. In 1745, he then purchased, from the Duke of Modena, 100 paintings of Italian, German and Flemish artists, including several Correggios. Another coup was the purchase of the Habsburg collection in Prague in 1748/49. Six years later, he acquired Raphael's Sistine Madonna from the monks at the San Sisto abbey in Piacenza. Once the paintings arrived, it was necessary to restore them and to provide a uniform system of gilt frames. It was this purchase, restoration and framing that prompted the remodeling of the electoral stable into a first-class museum.

The upper two stories of the stable were collapsed into one tall chamber, and rooms were combined to form two interlocking U-shaped galleries, grouped around an inner court. The curator-artists decided to hang the entire surface of the gallery's inner walls, top to bottom, with paintings, and this system itself became a work of art. Acquisitions after 1745 prompted a new hanging in 1754, one that lasted into the next century. The inner gallery was devoted exclusively to Italian painters. The outer gallery became the home of paintings from north of the Alps. To invite comparisons among schools and themes, paintings were hung in pairs, as was the practice of the time.

Visitors agreed that this arrangement inspired conversation, clarity, and awe. Wolfgang von Goethe, Germany's equivalent of Shakespeare, remembered the "ecstasy" that arose during his visit to the gallery. Christian von Mechel, the Swiss engraver and art dealer, thought the arrangement created connoisseurs. Wilhelm von Humboldt, the philosopher who founded Berlin's first university, used the paintings to develop a "concept of an individualist ideal." For the Romantic poet, Friedrich von Schlegel, the display explained the relationships among the paintings and developed an appreciation of each individual work. Eventually, catalogs were printed both for engravings and paintings, and paintings were numbered to help visitors find them.[74]

Count Brühl's secretary, Carl Heinrich von Heinecken, both of whose parents were artists, had supervised the purchases. He wanted the gallery to act as an "école publique". It was now taken for granted that the gallery was open to the public on a regular basis, six visitors at a time led by the gallery inspector. There was no admission fee, but viewers were expected to donate a gratuity. Heinecken wanted the paintings to guide the aesthetic judgment of visitors and inspire them toward the good life. Indeed, during the mid-eighteenth century, the gallery influenced the art of Dresden painters whose own works were displayed in the electoral palaces.

At the time, aesthetic judgment was considered to be absolute. Tastes were supposed to conform to the neo-classical style of the mid-eighteenth century. The young Johann Winckelmann, then working in Bünau's library at Nöthnitz manor, frequently came to Dresden to view its ancient statues. These visits helped to prepare his *Thoughts on the Imitation of Greek Works in Painting and Sculpture.* Influenced by this book, Friedrich August II granted Winckelmann 200 Talers to pursue his studies in Rome. Winckelmann's influence on the Elector led to the sale of works from the Dresden collections that did not fit into the neo-classical mold.

As visual drama, paintings attract the most attention from the viewing public, but the Dresden collections, then and now, included engravings, coins, sculpture and firearms. Heinecken, as director of the engravings collection, avidly expanded the holdings, including works by Martin Schongauer and Albrecht Dürer. The Elector's penchant for display enticed the best German engravers to Dresden where they found steady work and good pay. The coin, firearms, and sculpture collections all increased. To pay for some of the acquisitions, porcelain and paintings were sold. Already in 1756, Heinecken auctioned off over 100 old German paintings, including works by both the elder and younger Cranachs. Later in 1765, Baroque paintings were put on the market in Amsterdam. Over the decades, the Dresden gallery has not only acquired art, it has divested itself of works of equal value.[75]

Saxon Rococo

It was Johann Christof Knöffel, Friedrich August II's chief architect, who designed the re-model of the electoral stable into the Electoral Paintings Gallery. Art historians credit him with introducing Dresden's stylistic change from the ornate Baroque to the graceful rococo. At the time of August the Strong's death, a new regulation encouraged builders to pursue fewer carvings and sculptural effects on a structure's exterior. Some of the public buildings to which Knöffel applied this dramatic decorative style, such as the Rathaus on the Altmarkt, disappeared in the bombing of 1945. Citizens can still view the rococo style in the gardens of Grosssedlitz to Dresden's east, on the Kurländer Palace across the square from the Albertinum, and on the Cosel Palace at the Neumarkt. Knöffel did most of his work on buildings outside of Dresden, on urban mansions for aristocrats in the Elector's employ and for Count Brühl. It was he who envisioned how to turn toward the river the platform that is now the "balcony of Europe": the Brühl Terrace.[76]

By the mid-eighteenth century, Dresden counted as one of Europe's artistic centers. At least, one urban patriot has deemed it the "Republic of the Learned and the Artistic". Johann Winckelmann, the archaeologist and art critic, called Dresden the "German Athens". Figures like Count Francesco Algarotti, diplomat and art connoisseur, and the painters Anton Mengs, Giovanni Canaletto, Anton Graff, and Giovanni Casanova, brother of the famous libertine, as well as others, all inhabited or visited Dresden often. In music, there was Johann Hasse and his wife Faustina. "Travelers of experience and taste liked to come to Dresden, and they stayed for long periods of time. They prized the pretty, clean streets, the good restaurants, the cultivated atmosphere, the well-ordered [art] collections, the broad river, the soothing landscape…" The city basked in a climax of Saxon splendor.[77]

IV. Dresden Copes with Distress

Dresden in the Eighteenth-Century World War

The Saxon splendor of the mid-eighteenth century soon faded. The Elector's reaction to events in Europe exposed Saxony and, ultimately, Dresden to foreign invasion. In 1740, the German emperor and Austrian ruler died without a male heir. This situation had been foreseen, and arrangements made to circumvent the German Salic Law that restricted princely inheritance to males. The plan allowed the ruler's daughter, Maria Theresa, to ascend to the throne of the Austrian empire that overlapped with the German one. The sensitivity of the situation provided the opportunity for the new Prussian king, Friedrich II, later called the Great, to achieve the goals of his most recent forbears and increase his state's power and territory. He allied himself with England and attacked the Austrians, seeking to gain the Austrian province of Silesia, a territory to which Prussia had distant claims.

For two centuries, the Albertine Wettins had maintained friendly relations with the Austrian Habsburgs, to whom they owed the Electoral title and their influence within Germany. Moreover, they hoped to gain a land bridge to the kingdom in Poland by acquiring, peacefully, the northern part of Silesia. In pursuit of this goal, they now see-sawed back and forth between the two sides. First, the Saxons allied themselves with Austria in the War of the Austrian Succession (in the Western Hemisphere King George's War).

When that strategy failed, the Saxons switched to the Prussians, who took Silesia in 1742 without offering anything to the Saxons. Back again to the Austrians. This renewed alliance brought upon them a Prussian march through Saxony, a resounding defeat in 1745, and the military occupation of Dresden. The Peace of Dresden committed the Saxons to pay the Prussians an indemnity of one million Talers. The war continued, without the Saxons, for three more years when the Austrians ceded Silesia by treaty to the Prussians.[78]

Between 1748 and 1756, the Austrians rebuilt their armies and effected a "diplomatic revolution", healing a centuries-old hostility with France and forging an alliance with it. This new alliance led to another war. Friedrich II, seeking to forestall an attack by Austria, France and Saxony to wrest Silesia away from him, attacked Saxony in 1756. This time, the king had Saxony clearly in his sights, and his troops acted accordingly. They treated the state like a Prussian province. They quartered soldiers on the populace and impressed Saxon youth into the Prussian army. They seized the Saxon treasury, and Dresden's Frauenkirche was commandeered for the church services of the Prussian military.

The Saxon Elector Friedrich August II and his minister Count Heinrich von Brühl fled to Poland, where Friedrich August, like his father, was king. Prussian King Friedrich took up residence in Dresden, first in a palace just outside the walls, and then in the Brühl palace on the riverfront. When Dresden's city council refused to swear an oath of allegiance to him, he threw the councilors in jail and threatened to destroy their homes. After two days, they gave in. Friedrich's short-term goal was to force the Saxons to pay for his war; his long-term goal was the elimination of Saxon rivalry with Prussia for power within Germany.

Dresden was caught in the cross-hairs of two opposing armies. On the one hand were the Prussian occupiers of the city; on the other were the Austrians, seeking to dislodge their enemy. In November 1758, the Austrians besieged the occupied city and, in response, the Prussians burned the suburbs immediate to the east and west of the walls. Fifteen hundred Dresdners lost their homes. In order to spare the city further destruction, the Austrians lifted the siege.[79]

In the course of 1759, Friedrich withdrew most of his troops from Saxony, leaving light forces behind to occupy Dresden and other towns. In August 1759, the Austrians renewed their siege and forced the Prussians out of Dresden by cutting off the water supply piped in from the Weisseritz and other sources. Inexplicably, they allowed the Prussians to leave with their guns and ammunition as well as Saxon gold and silver. The Prussians thus remained in a good position to contest the new Austrian occupation. Dresdners now had to provide for the Austrian soldiers quartered on them, sometimes fifty men to a house. Malnutrition and disease became the citizens' lot.

Skirmishing between Austrians and Prussians took place in the vicinity of Dresden throughout 1759–60. Before the Prussians left the city, Friedrich II ordered the destruction of Brühl's new rococo Belvedere on the Virgin Bastion, completed a short eight years before. This damage was but a prelude to the Prussian siege and bombardment that began on Sunday, 13 July 1760, while Dresdners attended church.[80]

Christian Heinrich Schreyer, a young boy living in the eastern part of the city, has described the attack. Rather than targeting the city's walls, the Prussians lobbed their artillery over the walls at inner-city habitations. During the bombardments, both Austrian soldiers and local citizens plundered damaged and non-damaged houses alike. Residents protected themselves as best they could, and in at least one case, a businessman living in Schreyer's apartment house threw a looter into the neighboring Kaitz Brook. Soon low-flying cannon balls tore bricks away from the house's exterior and landed in the courtyard. Schreyer's family fled just before the house collapsed on July 17.

First they joined others at the palace in the Great Garden, but when Prussian soldiers stationed there chased them away, they went east to the village of Strehlen to stay with a friend of Schreyer's father. As they made their way to the village, they could see the massive burning tower of the Kreuzkirche. They heard the loud bang caused by the tower's partial collapse and witnessed the church burning throughout the night of July 19.

For a long time, the tower had been considered a part of Dresden's defenses with two cannons lodged on its upper-most platform. Over the years, these cannons were used primarily to give the occasional salute. But the Prussians considered them a serious threat and aimed at the tower. The Kreuzkirche was not the only one hit and burned. Further to the south, the Annenkirche, established two centuries before in honor of the Electress Anna, was burned by fire. Clothiers' Hall, on the Neumarkt, where fairs, markets and theatrical performances occurred, was also damaged.

Before the Prussians withdrew on July 22, they had destroyed half the city: 416 houses between the Altmarkt and the Neumarkt lay in ruins; large sections of the elegant quarters in the Rampisch Lane and Moritz Street were damaged; 374 houses in the suburbs burned out. In the course of the war, the population of Dresden dropped by over forty per cent.[81] After the bombardment, an unknown writer declared:

Dresden no longer completely exist[ed]. Its loveliest and best [lay] in ashes. Its largest palaces and streets, where art and splendor fought with one another for first place, [were] piles of stone... The richest inhabitants had become poor; what fire had left behind, plunder had finished off... Whoever ha[d] previously seen this capital in its ornament and flourish, and view[ed] it now, has no longer a human heart if he... w[ould] not be moved to sorrowful tears... by its current deplorable situation.[82]

As Prussia's glory triumphed over Saxon splendor, how would Dresden recover?

Dresden Copes with Defeat

After the bombardment of Dresden in 1760, the Seven Years' War (in the Western Hemisphere the French and Indian War) dragged on for three more years. The Peace of Hubertusburg in February 1763 left Saxony defeated but intact. Friedrich August II returned from Poland with Minister Brühl at the end of April and expected to restore the pre-war regime. Instead, he died suddenly on October 5 and was followed in death by Brühl three weeks later. His successor, Friedrich Christian, ruled only until December 17, the day on which he died. His son, Elector Friedrich August III was only 13 years old, and his uncle Xaver became regent.[83]

Even before the Seven Years' War began, Saxony had experienced financial difficulties. August the Strong bequeathed to his son a moderate debt. The War of the Austrian Succession had increased the sums owed; Friedrich August II and Brühl's spending added to the indebtedness. The military expenditures of the Seven Years' War and the depredations wrought by the Prussian and Austrian occupations had driven Saxony to the brink of bankruptcy.

The regent and his ministers found it necessary to institute a Spartan administration. Hasse, the court orchestra's director, was fired, along with his wife, in October 1763. By the end of the decade, there was no longer a court theater in Dresden. Instead, performances occurred in private theaters that received court subsidies. In 1765, the Wettins gave up all claims to the Polish throne. The remaining Saxon administration was modernized and streamlined according to eighteenth-century principles of good government.[84]

For the next fifty years, Dresden failed to recoup entirely the population losses suffered during the Seven Year's War. Both large and small houses remained in ruins during the 1770s and 1780s; bats and lizards resided in the rubble. Children played on the ravaged lots. The Zwinger, which the Prussians had used as an ammunition dump and woodpile, was slowly restored between 1783 and 1794. The Brühl Terrace remained desolate.[85]

Whereas some of the principal churches were rebuilt within a decade, the city's iconic Kreuzkirche did not return to its parish for another thirty years. Its fate illuminates the way that the Elector's government could undercut the city's jurisdiction and sheds light on the politics of restoration in Dresden. Initially the responsibility for rebuilding the church belonged to the city council, and it engaged an architect, Johann Georg Schmiedt. The city and church broke ground in 1764. Schmiedt had intended to use the heavily damaged old tower for the restored church, but that was not possible. Instead, the Saxon regent intervened, insisting that he be allowed to choose from several designs for the tower. These designs were not completed until 1767, and a new tower was chosen by the state government's superintendent of buildings, Christian Friedrich Exner. Exner demanded changes in Schmiedt's original plan for the church, and reconstructed sections were dismantled.

Throughout 1768, the municipal council protested this usurpation of its authority, and finally, in 1769, Elector Friedrich August III, freed from his uncle's regency, effected a compromise. Schmiedt's plan for the church would be adopted for the nave, but Exner's tower would prevail. Primarily, the Elector did not want the church's tower to rise above the Hausmann's spire at the palace. Though his plan for the nave was accepted, Schmiedt withdrew from work on the church, and responsibility for the restoration passed to a new architect, Christian Heinrich Eigenwillig. By 1775, construction had progressed to the roofline.

Then a new dilemma arose. How should the roof look? Should it be flat or pitched? Both the city council and the Elector's government opted for a flat roof, and the government's architect, Gottlob August Hölzer, assumed supervisory authority. His plans for the church's exterior were only approved by the Elector in 1781, but approval for the interior's design was delayed until 1783. It took another nine years before reconstruction was complete.[86]

The delays experienced in the rebuilding of the Kreuzkirche reflected a situation that frequently arises for heavily damaged cities. Even before the

Seven Years' War ended, Saxons had established a Restoration Commission with the idea of recovering from the disastrous economic situation created by the war. For Dresdners, that also meant recovering what they had lost from the Prussian bombardment. Tax exemptions were extended to those who began reconstruction immediately. Essentially, city structures and streets retained their former shapes. Ornamentation was less frequent than previously, and building heights rose to five stories, but it was the Baroque city that was restored, and the regulations of the early eighteenth century were carried out more stringently than before.

Certain changes were inescapable. The old city guard-house on the Neumarkt and the Neustadt's city hall were not rebuilt, opening up aesthetically pleasing urban vistas. The Elector also added a west wing to the Taschenberg Palace, thus creating the architectural symmetry that exists today. Because the meeting house of the Saxon Diet had also been destroyed, the Elector offered it the property of the former Minister von Flemming. The Diet's new home, the Landhaus, designed for the property by the court architect, Friedrich August Krubsacius, turned out to be a mixture of the old rococo and the new classical style. Its northern façade sported massive Doric columns. Its interior double staircase was reminiscent of earlier aristocratic mansions.[87]

At the end of the 1770s, the lawyer and historian Benjamin Gottfried Weinart described Dresden's recovery from the Seven Years' War. For a while after the war, he wrote, the earth around Dresden was infertile, and the city had to import foodstuffs from Bohemia and the lower Elbe. Yet he considered the recovery complete by the time that he wrote. City streets, he said, were neither too narrow nor too broad. Above all they were clean, and the paving improved. The city's air was unpolluted, kept pure by the flowing waters of the Elbe. Its residents were "decent,… well-mannered,… hard-working,… [and] persevering." Though the townsfolk were thrifty, their households were usually well-appointed. While neither men nor women were particularly good-looking, they offered a hospitality, he said, that was unusually generous for Saxony.[88]

Economic Development

While Weinart praised the city's craftsmen, particularly the makers of musical instruments, he complained that commerce and industry were weak. In his view, there were too many regulations and taxes. He could have added that a large number of Dresdners made their livings by catering to the court or working for the Saxon government. In this same period, the Saxon state created an Office for the Promotion of Industry and Trade; new industries sprang up in the Friedrichstadt: a gunpowder mill on the Weisseritz, a cannon-boring factory, a laundry bleaching establishment, several glove factories and a manufactory for cloth to be used in interior decorating.[89] Some of these were short-lived but testified to the ongoing attempts to broaden the city's economic base. There were other developments almost unnoticed at the time that would benefit the city's economy in the long run.

Up until the wars of the mid-eighteenth century, medical care had occurred at home or in institutions for the poor and indigent. Universities at Leipzig and Wittenberg trained medical doctors, but their activities were not regulated by the Saxon state. Even though electors had made stabs at providing and regulating medical knowledge and delivery, not much had actually been achieved. The War of the Austrian Succession, 1740–1748, marked a turning point.

The Saxon government now established, in Dresden, a *collegium medico-chirugicum* for the training of surgeons. They were to gain book knowledge as well as hands-on practice, primarily with soldiers, but also with civilians. Twenty years later, doctors were required to learn anatomy, chemistry, physics and pharmacy at the *collegium*. Before being allowed to practice, they had to pass a test and receive a license. In 1768, the government established a *collegium sanitatis* to advise it about hygienic measures. Added to the Medical-Surgery Collegium, was a school for midwifery.[90]

It is easy to forget that Saxony still harbored a large agricultural population, and a veterinary school opened in Dresden that continued to exist in the city for almost 150 years. Other educational institutions followed. After Saxony introduced compulsory schooling for every child in 1773, a normal school began training teachers for Dresden and its region. The contribution of these institutions to the city's prosperity should not be underrated. Economically speaking, schools import consumers and export graduates. They also contribute the expertise of their faculties and students to a city's economy.[91]

In this regard, perhaps no establishment of the late eighteenth century was more important than that of the Dresden art academy. For more than three-quarters of a century, a painting school had existed in Dresden, supported by the state. The chief painter of August the Strong, Louis de Silvestre, had directed the school, and his son succeeded him. This Academy of Painting differed from others of the time in that its students were no longer treated as regulated craftsmen, but as independent, non-regulated artists.

At the end of the Seven Years' War, leaning on models established by the French Académie Royale and the Viennese Academy for Architecture, Painting and Sculpture, the Saxon government decided to expand this institution's functions. The old painting school became an Academy of Fine Arts, offering courses in sculpture, architecture, and copper etching as well as painting.[92] This institution, over the years, has attracted artists of both national and international fame, and its exhibitions and students continue to enrich urban life.

Social Change at the Theater

The development of Dresden's drama, separate from opera, illustrated the city's increasing recovery from the war. Throughout the sixteenth and seventeenth centuries, the court and the city's populace were exposed to sporadic theatrical performances. The court engaged, for short periods of time, traveling troupes of actors from England, Italy and France. Plays were performed in special rooms of the palace until the construction of the first theater in 1667. Thereafter, the theater's large size permitted the free admission of middle-class residents so long as they dressed and behaved appropriately.

Only at the end of the seventeenth century did the court engage companies of German-speaking actors. One of the first to receive a patent as the Electoral Company of Comedians (Actors) came from north Germany under the leadership of Johannes Velten. The patent not only permitted the troupe to perform at the Dresden court; it extended blanket permission to present plays at the Leipzig fair and at all places in Electoral Saxony.

Such permission, of course, was always contingent on the company's ability to persuade municipal authorities to grant or lease them space or to subsidize their performances. Cities had long supported theatrical performances of various entertainments in market squares or other municipal locations. In Dresden the city supported performances of acrobats, freak displays, harlequin and puppetry shows as well as plays in the market squares and in the Clothiers' Halls on both banks of the Elbe. On the river's left bank, there was a large room in the upper story of the Clothiers' Hall that held between 600 and 1000 spectators. In the first half of the eighteenth century, one of the most talented German actresses, Friderike Karoline Neuber, and her company performed for the Dresdners.

In the early eighteenth century, so many companies visited Dresden for longer periods of time that it was difficult to find sufficient performance halls. Sometimes the hall of the Zinzendorf garden in the Pirnaische suburb, just outside the eastern wall, hosted performances. At other times, troupes played in the various taverns of Dresden and its outskirts. Beginning in the 1740s, Johann Kirsch's ensemble began to visit Dresden in the winter of every year, and in the summer it moved to the Augustusbad in Radeberg, a spa close to the Neustadt frequented by courtiers and commoners alike. In 1747, a permanent theater was built on the Brühl Terrace, and by mid-century, ten stages were available to troupes traveling to Dresden. In addition, a gallery to seat the nobility was added to the Clothiers' Hall on the Neumarkt. In 1756, there followed a complete renovation of the room into a permanent theater that was destroyed by Prussian bombardment a short time later. By this time, the Italian actor and impresario, Pietro Moretti, had built a wooden theater on the site of the current Theaterplatz. He later cast the structure in stone. Moretti staged performances of German comedies and pantomimes and offered subscriptions to four months of plays.

During the Seven Years' War, regular theater seasons ceased. Only in 1777 did the Elector's court begin long-term subsidies to the theater, now operated by Pasquale Bondini, in Moretti's old stone building. This new company experienced some success, and the theater's capacity was enlarged in 1783 from 350 to 814. Bondini's troupe lasted until 1789 when Franz Seconda supplanted it. This group performed there three nights a week until 1813.

The subsidies to Bondini and Seconda covered only one-quarter of the theater's expenses, so both impresarios had to rely on box-office receipts in order to break even. Revenue therefore depended on pleasing a Dresden public that was not interested in the heavy drama produced by the great playwrights of the era: Lessing, Goethe, and Schiller. Instead, audiences flocked to a large variety of light comedies à la August von Kotzebue and August Iffland. Occasionally Shakespeare's comedies appeared on the playbill.

Between 1777 and 1813, only 282 serious plays were presented, while 389 lighter works entertained Dresdners. Because of the small market, the same play could not be presented on consecutive evenings. For example, in 1786–87, fifty-seven different plays were staged. Only six played more than once, and none played more than twice. One cannot help but think that these evening entertainments were akin to the TV sit-coms of contemporary America.[93]

The yen for evening entertainment was also satisfied by unofficial theaters in suburban taverns. There it was traveling troupes who offered dramatic fare, and the quality was usually not very good. If the tavern were full on any given night, waiters had no compunction about walking across the stage in mid-scene to serve their customers. These suburban theaters were usually shut down once the city's authorities discovered them.

Puppet theater was also popular. The large Zimmermann family performed in a room of the old court pharmacy. As the family grew in number and age, father Zimmermann began to alternate the puppets with other kinds of shows, many of which attracted respectable people. But for the most part, the place filled with "gutter snipes". When these folk became disorderly, Zimmermann would call out for order from the stage.

One night during a performance of *Charles XII*, someone in the gallery used a peashooter against the king lying on his death bed. Zimmermann rose up, ordered the curtain closed, leaped into the room, and tried to catch and punish the perpetrator. In vain. The culprit had either fled or had hidden himself away from his pursuer.[94]

Eighteenth-Century Amusements

Theater was not the only diversion open to the people of Dresden. Since the beginning of the eighteenth century, shows increasingly available to all Germans visited the city. The population had monies to spare, and the city's location at the junction of north-south and east-west trade routes attracted traveling entertainers. It was easy to combine a stop in Dresden with one in Leipzig.

Acrobats, particularly tight-rope walkers, had long sought out the city in the warmer months of the year. Circus riders were popular after the Seven Years' War. It was not only the lower classes who visited such shows. Aristocrats and army officers particularly appreciated the skills of horsemanship involved in standing astride two trotting horses while balancing a child on the acrobat's head. Another popular diversion was the animal show. Initially, trained dogs and horses were the main attractions. Gradually other trained animals such as seals, monkeys, stags, canaries, even elephants appeared. These creatures could variously recognize colors, do arithmetic, drink wine, play hand-organs, or drive carriages.

Wax-figure shows were a good way to represent prominent personalities in an age when illustrations did not circulate freely, either in magazines or newspapers. In the last third of the eighteenth century, the collections usually consisted of more than 100 individuals, contemporary kings, emperors, scholars and generals. Famous Greeks and Romans of the ancient era were also included. Some even portrayed noted robbers and bandits. A few depicted Biblical scenes.

After the Seven Years' War, an increasingly scientific mentality sparked interest in menageries and nature collections. These served as substitutes for a non-existent urban zoo. In 1781, a collection of 150 live foreign birds attracted spectators. Two years later, it was an insect collection that appealed to a paying public. In 1807, and again in 1812, Joseph Drete displayed a collection of living animals. Commoners flocked to these exhibits, and the court requested special viewings in the palace. The scientific spirit accounts for the increasing popularity of the Laterna Magica. These shows depicted views of other cities and landscapes. Scientific experiments in chemistry and physics also attracted upper-class audiences.

Reflecting the same mentality were shows of automaten. Already in 1732, the organ builder Prock Lard entertained Dresdners with a room where human figures, curtains and other items moved mechanically. By 1772, these efforts had become more sophisticated. Marc Antoine Delolme, the court mechanic in Brunswick-Lüneberg, brought a mechanical female musician, a sooth-saying East Indian king, and a canary to town. A theater with automated puppets, accompanied by music and optical effects, also existed.[95]

Nature

Such commercial entertainments were not the only past-times for eighteenth-century Dresdners. Both aristocrats and commoners discovered the medicinal and social benefits of taking the waters. The Augustus spa near Radeberg, northeast of the city, opened in 1719. It could be reached easily from town, offered weekly and monthly accommodations and amenities such as newspapers, magazines, a billiard table. dancing, and gambling. Theater performances enticed lovers of drama and, in the summer, music lovers enjoyed occasional concerts. After 1781, nature lovers could combine a visit to the spa with walks in the well-known Brühl landscape garden next door. Though commoners would have found an extended stay expensive, the spa's day prices were reasonable. Much later in the century, another spa opened in the neighboring town of Tharandt where Dresdners flocked on Sundays.[96]

Toward the end of the century, families began to rent cottages outside the city. They particularly appreciated the opportunity to escape the confines of the crowded, walled city and enjoy the surrounding countryside. On the right bank of the Elbe, the villages of both Lössnitz and Loschwitz, to the west and east of Dresden respectively, with their vineyards and views of the Elbe, drew city folk during the summer. In the north, the Elbe hills rising just outside the walls of the Neustadt appealed to those who needed to go to work in the morning and return in the evening. The valley of the Weisseritz to the south of Dresden offered overnight accommodations at various price levels.[97]

Friedrich Schulze has described his own and his classmates' passion for insect collecting during the 1780s. The respected entomologist and military staff councilor Romanus and his friend, court physician Dr. Heise, both insect collectors, would take their young sons to the Plauen Valley on Sundays to hunt for bugs. They sometimes invited Schulze to join them. While the fathers relaxed in the restaurant of the Hegenreuter House, the lads clambered over the rocks with nets and boxes seeking caterpillars, butterflies and insects. At the end of the day, fathers and sons enjoyed a supper of trout à la Hegenreuter.[98]

During the eighteenth century, Sunday visits to beer gardens on the outskirts of town became commonplace. Young people of both sexes used the gardens as meeting and mixing sites, and parents encouraged such outings because the gardens provided the desired social control. In the Weisseritz Valley, the Reisewitzen, the Turkish, the Pöppelmann and the Feldschlösschen Gardens were all very popular. On the east side of town, an enticing promenade was located in the Zinzendorf Garden.

Another attractive spot was the large Great Garden. Originally intended for use by the Electoral Court, it was gradually appropriated by the general public. Almost from the beginning, the court gardener, the gatekeeper and the peacock guards all sold tax-free beer to visitors. The crowds who came for beer also played cards, bowled, and smoked. From time to time, the court attempted to limit the Great Garden's use by the public. In vain.[99]

Dresdners also discovered the Elbe as a source of relaxation. In mid-century, Carl Christian Linke opened a spa and amusement park on the right bank of the Elbe: the Linkesches Bad. For a long while, it was one of the most popular of Dresden's diversions. Linke also opened a river bath just beneath the bluffs supporting his spa. His impetus was the German discovery that a full-body, as opposed to a sponge, bath, was healthy for everyone. Because the Saxon government banned swimming in the Elbe to prevent drownings, there was no swimming at Linke's, and the river site closed in 1771. Little more than a decade later, August Andreoli opened a medicinal bath on the banks of the Elbe just outside the Neustadt's walls. Once again, this bath offered no swimming but was nonetheless popular. Despite the government's ban on bathing or swimming in the Elbe, people did so anyway, often in the buff, leading to complaints about public decency. Thus the ban was lifted, and the first Elbe swimming establishment opened on the left bank of the Elbe in 1788.[100]

Club Life

A less active leisure activity was reading. One middle-class chronicler of Dresden life claimed that everyone read materials ranging from historical works to novels. At the end of the eighteenth century, there were three prominent bookstores in the city. There was also a private lending library run by a former soldier who catered to the lower and middle classes. In 1795, Johann Christoph Arnold established a long-lived book store and library that briefly expanded to include a book club. If one can judge from Arnold's experience, book clubs that included a subscription price did not do well in Dresden. Those with means had their own libraries, and they shared with their friends. The Electoral Library, moved from the Zwinger to the Japanese Palace in the 1780s, was open to the public and competed with the book club.[101]

Not all clubs struggled to survive. There was a plethora of cultural organizations supported by monthly dues. These groups, to which whole families belonged, staged plays, concerts, dances, target practices and other kinds of amusement. After events, members of the group usually sat down to supper together. Some of these groups had club houses.

The Societät, originally an exclusive club for aristocrats that eventually admitted commoners as the renamed Ressource, operated a theater in the Hofmann House in the Neustadt's Hauptstrasse. In addition to a public that paid for single performances, the theater was sustained by a group of subscribers who came every three weeks to see a new play. After the play, subscribers would adjourn to a restaurant or member's house to enjoy a group supper. This same group rented a vineyard to the east of the city on the banks of the Elbe where it gathered on summer Sundays. There they ate the midday meal together and staged the occasional play *al fresco*, often written by a member of the group. In the cooler days of autumn, they retired to the vineyard's cottage to dance. Often, members of the group spent the whole weekend at the vineyard. The Ressource, for the benefit of its members, subscribed to German and foreign newspapers and magazines.[102]

More rarefied than the social clubs were the salons established at the end of the eighteenth century. One of the more famous was that of Christian Gottlieb Körner who came to Dresden as a church official in 1786 and later became judge at the Court of Appeals. Accompanying Körner were his wife and her sister, Dora Stock, a portrait painter. In 1791, their son, who became the poet and playwright Theodor Körner, was born. Inspired by the young Friedrich Schiller's plays, Christian struck up a friendship, and Schiller completed *Don Carlos* at the Körner's summer cottage in Loschwitz. Visitors of different political and cultural persuasions were welcome at the Körner home, and the family hosted both literary and musical evenings for a wide circle of friends. Later, the Körners left Dresden for Prussia, where Christian promised himself a more challenging and prosperous career.[103]

The art academy's Professor Seidelmann and his wife, a Venetian, presided over another salon with tact and sophistication. Rich and poor were welcome to enjoy their evenings of art and music. The court secretary, Ludwig Emanuel Ernst, and his wife Charlotte, a sister of the famous Schlegel brothers, hosted art and literary evenings at their home. A visitor could frequently meet one or both of the brothers there as well as a variety of professors from the art academy, including the Swiss portrait painter Anton Graff.

Schiller and others found the Dresden cultural climate too philistine for their tastes. For them, the court was too exclusive and the populace in general too low-brow.[104] But Dresdners, both aristocrats and commoners, enjoyed a variety of entertainments, ranging from the cultivated to the comic.

Dresden's Lower Classes

Many people in the lower classes faced a struggling existence. Christian Heinrich Schreyer grew up in straitened economic circumstances. His father, born in 1715, had migrated to the city from the village of Grossröhrsdorf, northeast of Dresden, had become a mason and married the daughter of a Bohemian immigrant who conducted a sewing school. After she died in 1757, the father cared for the young boy alone and locked him into the apartment if he had to work at night. This practice almost became fatal when their apartment house was shelled by the Prussians in 1758, and a fire broke out. Only when the neighbors made lots of noise did the young boy wake up, but then it was impossible for him to leave the locked apartment. Fortunately, the house did not burn down.

Soon thereafter, a fellow mason found a new wife for Schreyer's father, and to accommodate her work as a weaver of straw goods, they moved to an apartment just outside the eastern city walls. The bombardment of 1760 chased them first to Strehlen, then south to Kaitz, and finally further south to the village of Kreischa. During the time they spent in Kreischa, Schreyer's father stayed the week in Dresden, where there was plenty of work for masons, and traveled south to his family on weekends. There was a well-established pattern of such commuters to and from the city.

Schreyer described his father's life as a hard one that he tried to overcome with good food and plenty of sleep. Nevertheless, his body was often wracked by a hacking cough caused by the fine particles of dust thrown up by the stones with which he worked. He died peacefully in his sleep at an early age in 1767.

Schreyer's stepmother, still weaving straw, tried to keep their apartment, now in the shadow of the palace, by taking in a boarder, and Schreyer and his stepmother then occupied a single room. Since the sixteen-year-old boy disliked being cooped up all day with his stepmother, he took to the streets. Subsequently, he was sent to live with an uncle near the Annenkirche where he attended classes at the church school. Despite this humble background, Schreyer went on to become a composer of church music, a teacher and pastor at a church in Ortrand, a small town north of Dresden.[105]

When Gustav Nieritz's grandfather, a sergeant in the Saxon army, died in 1770, his widow made a living as a cleaning lady and washerwoman. Her daughter was sent as a seamstress to other people's houses as soon as she finished primary school. Her five-year-old son, Gustav's father, augmented the family finances by collecting flies for frogkeepers; he also gathered and crushed plum and peach seeds that the middle classes of the time mixed with coffee. Gustav himself, a descendant of this persevering family, became a famous author of children's books in the nineteenth century.

Johann Kaspar Riesbeck, a journalist and political commentator of the late eighteenth century, observed that, in comparison to the capitals of other German states, like Munich, the gap between rich and poor was not cavernous. He noted that the Dresdners, both the middle and the lower classes, dressed very fashionably. During his stay in Dresden, he boarded with a watchmaker whose two daughters dressed up and had their hair done daily. The family, he said, ate very little in the evening. In comparison to South Germany, he deemed the Dresdners' cuisine to be frugal, even in the "most elegant houses".[106]

Schreyer's and Nieritz's experiences, Riesbeck's observations, and the sharing of amusements within a tight urban space, point to a generally tolerant atmosphere within the city. This circumstance plus the distance between Dresden and Paris might explain why the city's inhabitants hardly reacted to the revolution that shook Europe in the summer of 1789.

V. The French Wars

The news of revolution in France quickly reached Dresden in July, 1789. There was very little interest in the events. Life continued much as it had before. Only in September, 1790 did large groups of peasants revolting against taxes, judicial abuses and aristocratic hunting privileges echo events in France by entering the city in an attempt to gain the support of urban proletarians. These efforts came to naught. In July 1791, the revolutionary Benjamin Geissler planned to lead a group of peasants to kidnap the Elector and lead him on a march from Pillnitz to Dresden in imitation of the Parisian capture of Louis XVI at Versailles. The Saxon government foiled Geissler's plan by closing the city gates, canceling the annual summer fair, and placing the army on alert.

More serious, though not revolutionary in nature, was the strike of the journeymen tailors three years later. The strike broke out spontaneously when a journeyman officially complained to the city council about a master tailor who had treated him unfairly. Although the council reprimanded the master and made him pay damages, one city councilor insulted the journeyman in the process. In response, 3000 journeymen from twenty guilds struck the city. Expressing solidarity with the tailors were shoemakers, locksmiths, blacksmiths, masons, butchers, bakers, brewers and others who all quit work on July 26. Provisioning of the city collapsed.

In response, the government sent troops to arrest the 300 residents of the journeymen tailors' hostel, set up cannons at the watch on the Neumarkt, and unleashed both infantry and cavalry on the 3000 sympathetic strikers. At the same time, the government convened a commission to hear the journeymen's grievances. Calm returned to the city and remained that way for the next decade.[107]

It was aristocratic solidarity that led the Elector to host the famous meeting at Pillnitz Palace that launched the European coalition against the French revolutionaries in 1792. Only when the French declared war on the German empire and invaded the Rhineland did Saxony commit troops to the coalition. When Prussia made peace with the French in 1795 and guaranteed the neutrality of northern Germany for the next ten years, the Saxons withdrew from the war and remained at peace until 1806.

Once the guaranteed neutrality lapsed, the Saxons joined the Prussians in declaring war on the French, now ruled by the Emperor Napoleon. On 14 October 1806, the two sides met on a Thuringian plateau outside the university town of Jena. There the Saxons, together with the Prussians, suffered a decisive drubbing, and many Saxon soldiers were taken prisoner. In the days following the battle, Dresden was tense with apprehension, fearing a French invasion.

When news circulated that the Elector planned to abandon the city, people thronged through the streets and crowded into restaurants and bars. In Schwanz's coffee house in the Schlossgasse, all sorts of political opinions could be heard from natives and strangers alike. When Elector Friedrich August III ultimately decided to remain in town, the throngs gravitated toward the palace. Dresdners breathed sighs of relief when they learned that the Elector had accepted Napoleon's invitation to change sides.

Saxony now entered into an alliance with Napoleon's France and joined the Rhenish Confederation, the puppet state created after Napoleon dissolved the old German empire. Saxons were forced to pay an indemnity of seven million Talers. In return, the Elector acquired the title of the Duke of Warsaw. Last, but not least, Napoleon elevated Elector Friedrich August III to King of Saxony, a title that he and his heirs enjoyed for the next century.[108]

During the next decade, while Saxony was allied with Napoleonic France, Dresdners and other Saxons were subject to a French governor, to intermittent occupations by French troops, to the recruitment of Saxon soldiers for French armies, and to the quartering of soldiers on the population. At various times, French troops quartered with the Körner family broke pottery and stole pillows. Presumably, other Dresdners suffered similar pilfering.

In 1807, after concluding the Peace of Tilsit with Russia, Napoleon briefly visited Dresden. People came from near and far to catch a glimpse of Europe's chief warrior, and he entertained himself by visiting the Paintings Gallery. In 1809, Dresden was contested for several months between the Austrians and the French. First one army and then the other occupied the city. When French forces eventually pushed out the Austrians, a short Te Deum, a service of thankful praise, rang out in Dresden's churches.[109]

Thereafter, calm prevailed until Napoleon collected the Grande Armée for the invasion of Russia in 1812. In the spring of that year, Napoleon met in Dresden with the King of Prussia and the Austrian sovereign, both allied with him for the time being. This meeting of the three rulers created an occasion for urban festivities. Bells pealed, cannons fired, parades defiled. At night hundreds of oil lamps lit the city. Napoleon, with headquarters at the royal palace, rode through the city frequently and, as before, Dresdners and Saxons scampered to catch a glimpse of him. The portrait painter, Gerhard von Kügelgen, having seized every opportunity to view the emperor, eventually painted his likeness. When high mass was held in the Court Church on May 24, with Napoleon in the Saxon king's prayer pew, the church overflowed with "worshippers".[110]

Once the armies had departed for Russia, the city became very quiet. Christian Körner's sister-in-law, Dora Stock, reported that it felt as if everyone had gone on vacation to the countryside. And then, suddenly, the reverses of the Grande Armée made Dresden a center of battle. Briefly, in the night of 14 December 1812, Napoleon rode into Dresden by sled and stayed the night, unheralded. His tattered army stumbled into town, hungry, wounded and determined to stay. It became apparent that the city would be contested between the French and their opponents. As the Russians beat back the French and advanced westward, they signed a treaty with Prussia in February 1813, which not only provided for mutual military assistance but foresaw the incorporation of Saxony, a French ally, into Prussia. When the Russian Czar Alexander I entered Breslau, a day's march from Dresden, King Friedrich August left the city bound for Prague. The depleted Saxon army continued to fight alongside the French.[111]

Russian Cossacks soon appeared at the Weisser Hirsch, then a small settlement of truck gardeners and vintners surrounding a popular restaurant overlooking the Elbe. Fighting between the two sides had filled Dresden with soldiers, either wounded or sick with typhus. The citizenry feared an outbreak of plague. Marie von Kügelgen, Gerhard's wife, sprayed the rooms of her family's apartment with vinegar every day in an attempt to keep the germs at bay. Since the French had blocked the northern or Black Gate (today's Albertplatz) into the Neustadt and had requisitioned all barges and boats on the Elbe in order to assure their retreat, it became more and more difficult to provision the city with milk, fresh butter, and eggs.

When it became known that the city's French commandant was preparing to breach the bridge uniting the two sides of the city, Dresdners attempted to stop this action, ultimately to no avail. On the day of the breach, after a night filled with the noise of French troop movements, those who lived near the bridge were told to open all windows and douse all stove fires at six in the morning. At 8:30 a.m., the breach exploded, with much of the force directed toward the water. In the night of March 26/27, French troops evacuated the city. The occupying Russians and Prussians soon reunited the two sides of the city with a pontoon bridge at Blasewitz, a village east of Dresden. Their stay was short.[112]

The Battle of Dresden

Napoleon managed to recruit a new army during the spring of 1813, and at the beginning of May, he defeated the combined Russian/Prussian forces at the Battle of Lützen. Despite some disgruntlement, Dresdners in mid-May welcomed Napoleon back into the city with bells, thundering cannon, an honor guard and shouts for long life. To facilitate their own movements, the French now restored the stone bridge in the middle of the city. Napoleon made Dresden his headquarters and ensconced himself in the Friedrichstadt at the Marcolini Palace, now a municipal hospital. Almost the entire French army was stationed in Saxony, and large portions camped on the Ostra Preserve, the court's medieval hunting grounds. To honor the French and to amuse the populace, there were illuminations, fireworks, royal visits, and celebratory church masses throughout the last half of May.[113]

All these festivities had their negative side. The young Ludwig Richter, later a famed painter and book illustrator, did not go to school, and his father could find no work. Soldiers were quartered in both rooms of their two-room flat. Ludwig's father had wanted to spare the quartering on two widows who lived in an upstairs apartment, so he had accepted extra soldiers. The city also became a huge field hospital for French soldiers wounded in the battles outside the city. In the streets, soldiers roamed the town, sometimes assaulting young women and men. The price of bread escalated, and city government began doling out two loaves a day for Dresden families. Gardens sprang up inside the walls.[114]

Meanwhile, Napoleon and his Saxon allies maneuvered to gain an advantage. But on May 26, the Austrian foreign minister, Count Klemens von

Metternich, famously refused to support French imperialism in Europe, implying that Austria would henceforth fight on the side of Napoleon's enemies. In response, Napoleon requested and received a six-week ceasefire that extended from June 5 to August 10. Both sides used this period to beef up their armies. In Dresden, Napoleon celebrated his birthday (August 15) early with a banquet for his troops and fireworks and cannonades for the citizenry.

When the ceasefire ended, the Austrians declared war on the French and joined forces with the Russians and Prussians. Napoleon and his army left the city toward the east in pursuit of their opponents, leaving a substantial force behind. In two weeks' time, Dresdners saw the enemies' campfires on the southern hills and braced themselves for an invasion. Napoleon, meanwhile, force-marched his men back to Dresden. On August 26, he attacked.

Ludwig Richter, his father and their neighbors went to the attic of their apartment house, situated on a rise above the Elbe, to watch the battle that raged to the east and south around the villages of Strehlen, Blasewitz, and Räcknitz as well as the Great Garden. The artillery was so close to the city that several cannon balls fell on neighboring roofs, and one grenade landed in the annex to their apartment house. When the group retreated to the cellar, listening anxiously to the battle, one of their fellow tenants—a widow—dug out a battle of cherry liqueur, and nervousness receded. Other Dresdners watched the battle from the earthworks surrounding the Zwinger and from the Brühl Garden next to the Virgin Bastion. Businesses closed at noon to allow their proprietors and employees to watch the fighting. In the evening, the city filled up with troops and carts carrying the wounded. Fighting continued on August 27 until Napoleon and the French prevailed.[115]

After this battle, prisoners of war were brought inside the city and lodged in the churches, in the Brühl Garden, and in the taverns. The Frauenkirche became an ammunition dump. Wounded soldiers, who had found their way back into the city, lay uncared for in the streets next to dying horses. Families from the burned and plundered suburbs surrounding the city wandered into the Neustadt, seeking refuge. Their harvest lay ruined and scattered about their fields. Outside the city, dead soldiers lay, stripped naked, sundered by their wounds and trampled by horses and wagons, and they became spectacles for Dresdners who wandered the battlefield, seeking cheap thrills. Some thrills had occurred even before the battle. One Dresden doctor reported a marked increase of venereal disease among women on whom soldiers had been quartered. Such occurred, he claimed, even in the "best of families".[116]

The month of September 1813 saw skirmishes in which both sides suffered victories and losses. Slowly but surely, however, those allied against Napoleon encircled his armies. When the Prussians crossed the Elbe, to the north of Dresden, planning to encircle the French army, Napoleon left the city, leaving behind 35,000 French troops and 1000 officials.

The Russians then began a siege that lasted five weeks. Not only were the Dresdners starved for food and fuel, but measles and typhus struck many wounded soldiers and civilians. Cater-cornered to the Richters' apartment house was a military hospital where Ludwig and his father could watch the naked corpses thrown out of second-and third-story windows onto wagons filled to the top. As horses died in the streets, French soldiers cut off their meat to cook and to eat. Because the Russian blockade stopped the import of flour, bakers closed their shops.

At the end of October, urban authorities took an inventory of the supplies remaining within the city. Families were told to register their provisions with the authorities. With the city completely cut off from its hinterland, people crowded into taverns and coffee houses to hear the news and to keep warm. Among the clientele was the young E.T.A. Hoffmann, author of the future *Tales*, who was music director for the Moretti theater where performances continued straight through the siege.[117]

After the victory of Napoleon's opponents in the Battle of Nations near Leipzig, October 16–19, the French retreated toward the west. The Saxon king, Friedrich August I, was captured in Leipzig and became a prisoner of war in Prussia, where he was joined by his family. The Saxon army now changed sides and fought against Napoleon. Finally, on November 11, the French army in Dresden capitulated to the Russians whose troops marched in on November 17. It was the Russian commander of the city, Prince Nikolai Gregorievich Repnin-Wolkonski who was responsible for some enduring urban features.

During his brief administration, he caused the steps leading from the Schlossplatz (Palace Square) to the Brühl Terrace to be built according to a plan devised by Dresden architects three years before. Now the Terrace truly became Europe's balcony, enhancing the vision of the Elbe as a Grand Canal. As a sop to the citizenry, the Great Garden was officially opened to the public. Its variety of restaurants offered food as well as drink, and ice skaters glided across the pond in winter. The Russians also combined the separate establishments of court orchestra, opera and playhouse into one single state theater, and the art collections, evacuated to the Königstein, a Saxon fortress far to the south, were returned to the city and again made available for visits by the public. Lastly, the Russians officially accepted the three public swimming sites that had located on the Elbe during the last three decades. People could also swim in the river at non-official sites so long as a fisherman was present, and the activity could not be seen from the city.[118]

Dresden Demoted, Saxony Diminished

In November 1814, the leaders of the victorious powers and their entourages gathered in Vienna to finalize peace with the French and to reconstruct the political geography of Europe. As this massive Congress of Vienna opened, Prussian troops replaced the Russians as the occupying power in Dresden. Ever since the mid-eighteenth century, Prussia had harbored designs on Saxon territory. At the end of the Seven Years' War, it was the Austrians who had prevented Prussian annexation of Saxony. Now, however, the active alliance of Saxony with Napoleon provided a strong reason for its incorporation into the Prussian state. King Friedrich August was a prisoner in Berlin and was excluded from the negotiations in Vienna. Dresdners debated the matter zealously. Some, like the painter Gerhard von Kügelgen, thought absorption by Prussia would be better than a rump Saxony. Those who favored an independent Saxony paraded through the streets displaying pictures of the king and wearing cocardes of the Saxon green and white colors in their hats.[119]

At Vienna, the Austrian prime minister Count Metternich and the English foreign minister, Lord Castlereagh, were determined to maintain a balance of power in Europe. That meant preventing excessive Russian influence in Western Europe and the containment of Prussian power. To attain these goals, the statesmen at Vienna decided that the Saxon state would continue to exist, but they forced the king to sign away two-thirds of his former realm to the Prussians. Only then, in June 1815, was he allowed to return to Dresden. How would he and the city adjust their fortunes?[120]

VI. Revolutionary Dresden

Peace Returns

During the three decades following the Peace of Vienna, Dresden experienced revolutionary changes that created the modern city. But first, Dresdners greeted the returning king with fanfare on 7 June 1815. At the suburban village of Zschachwitz, several miles to the southeast and across the river from Pillnitz Palace, a celebratory arch, from which hung a large crown of flowers, welcomed the monarch home. School children greeted him with song. Prince Putjatin, an eccentric whose house lay nearby, swung by a rope in the crown and saluted the king with a cheer and a shower of roses.

Once the king had advanced to the city walls, a patriotic arch bedecked with flags and the royal coats of arms flanked the eastern gate. Greeting him at the gate were the city council and the neighborhood watchmen, clergymen, the judges and staff of the city courts, the guilds and various choirs. The celebrations lasted for several days. It was easy to forget that Dresden, during the last several decades, had lost almost one-fifth of its inhabitants and that the peace of 1815 had reduced the Saxon state to political insignificance.[121]

The city now began to experience a major change in its physiognomy: the destruction of the city walls. The Seven Years' War had already demonstrated that the walls, moat and earthworks no longer provided protection against modern artillery. Even before that, the walls had begun to act as impediments to urban integration. At the turn of the seventeenth century, almost 39% of Dresdners lived in the suburbs outside the walls; by 1755, over half the city's inhabitants resided beyond the walls. The best way to bind together intra-and extra-mural Dresden was to level the walls.

The newly elevated King Friedrich August I had taken the initiative by ordering the dismantling of the ramparts in 1809. Dismantling soon began. By 1812, large portions of the crumbling fortifications had been removed. But as war threatened the city with fighting and invasion in 1813, this process stopped, and portions of the earthworks were even rebuilt to keep the approaching armies at bay. Yet the armies of both sides had little difficulty entering the city. During the Battle of Dresden in August 1813, the town was spared because the real fighting occurred outside the fortifications.

Only in 1817 did dismantling resume. It continued until the last earthwork was removed in 1831. What remained of the old fortifications were the stone platform supporting the Brühl Terrace and the earthworks behind the Zwinger, both of which still exist. Other German cities that leveled their walls built wide boulevards along the old traces and made them into small green belts. In Dresden, the "ring" was not so lavish because the land where both earthworks and wall resided was sold to private owners in order to increase the state's revenues. A citizens' committee provided landscaping for the newly exposed earth, and its efforts contributed to Dresden's image as a garden city.[122]

When Gustav Klemm, later chief librarian at the Royal Library, visited Dresden as a young man in 1821, he found it in ragged shape. As he approached the city from the south, the roadway was pitted with potholes. On the site of the deserted Wilsdrufferplatz (later Postplatz) were mounds of debris. Both the Scheffelgasse leading to the Altmarkt and the Schlossgasse, the southern approach to the palace, were gloomy passages. West of the palace, in the Italian village behind the "old" Moretti theater, was a clutter of ladders, scaffolding and carts. To him, the theater looked more like a weapons depot than a "temple of the arts".

Close by, the Zwinger presented a "picture of decay" from October to May. Statues and other ornaments were 'damaged, dirty, and in the open fountains of the former nymphs' bath lay years of old foliage.' In its towers were jackdaw and pigeon nests. Behind the Zwinger, the city had just begun to dismantle the walls, and the stones were carelessly strewn about, harboring polecats and martens. To the east of the Zwinger, the Taschenberg palace was hemmed in by the court pharmacy, a neighborhood bakery and shed-like habitations. The latter also encroached on the elegant Landhaus and on several mansions in the Moritzstrasse—once the swankiest street in Dresden.

Apart from the area around the Japanese Palace and the Hauptstrasse, the Neustadt was also neglected. On the Bautzenerstrasse, gardens surrounded small cottages, but otherwise it was the "Sand" that predominated—dune-like, wind-eroded deposits from the glaciers of the early Stone Age—dotted by thinly-rooted trees. On this expanse, the state had located the small industrial area of the New Annex (later the Antonstadt) and the firing range for the army's artillery. For Klemm only the banks of the Elbe in front of the royal palace, the Court Church, the Frauenkirche and the Japanese Palace were presentable.[123]

Another visitor in 1822, the Baron Karl von Voss, governor of the young, mentally feeble duke of Anhalt-Bernburg, was not nearly so critical, but in a letter to his wife, he admitted to finding the city's dust, ankle deep and splattered on pedestrians by passing carriages and horses, to be almost unbearable. Voss, his charge, and their entourage were housed in a pleasant apartment near the Kreuzkirche, where they could hear the pealing of the bells on the hour. They could walk to the Brühl Terrace from their residence and found "streams" of people enjoying the shade of the linden trees and, in the evening, taking advantage of the new lanterns to stay up late.

Voss agreed with Klemm that the Japanese Palace was one of Dresden's assets. He and the young duke received permission to borrow books from the Royal Library housed there, and its large, bright rooms as well as its sizable collections impressed him. They also enjoyed a visit to the eighteen subterranean vaults of the palace, where the valuable royal porcelain collection was displayed. Klemm's and Voss's accounts from the 1820s reveal a city in transition. Despite its flaws, the city continued to attract visitors, as Voss and his charge testified.[124]

Reorganizing Dresden

As the city's walls slowly tumbled down, both court and city authorities soon realized that they needed to take action to prevent hasty, speculative construction. The king particularly wanted to preserve the view of the Loschwitz Heights across the Elbe from the hills of the south. In the 1820s, he decreed a building ban on the land between the Pirnaische toll house and the Great Garden, the area known then and now as the Pirnaische suburb. Not until 1858 was this land platted for construction.[125]

Dresden was no stranger to urban planning. After the fires of the late fifteenth and seventeenth centuries, both the city and the Elector had regulated rebuilding. During the eighteenth century, August the Strong had issued decrees that enhanced both urban shape and safety. Honoring this history, a municipal planning commission (Stadtbaupolizeikollegium) was created in

1825 and issued detailed regulations in 1827. To assure the city's welfare, the commission paid strict attention to "ornamentation". Building plans had to be submitted to the proper authorities, and the height of buildings would be determined by the width of the streets; a minimum of two and a maximum of five stories were allowed in the Altstadt.

Newly plotted lots in the Neustadt would be free-standing; only three stories would be allowed, and pitched roofs would prevail. There would be no mansard roofs. Everywhere in the city, free-standing houses had to be parallel and perpendicular to the street. There could be no skewed arrangement on the lots. A palette guided contractors in the choice of colors for the stuccoed houses, stucco prescribed by law. Fences would be made of iron. Also, no industry would be permitted in new residential areas. Although these regulations were amended twice during the nineteenth century, there was no major change until 1905. These building regulations of 1827 helped Dresden to avoid some of the dismal construction experienced by other German cities during the industrialization of the late nineteenth century.[126]

Once the walls' demolition ended, the state planning director, Gottlob Friedrich Thormeyer, laid out narrow boulevards that stretched in an arc around the city. He punctuated the boulevards with the Pirnaischer Platz in the east—site of the old Pirnaischer Gate—the Antonsplatz in the south—where gardens created a small park in mid-city—and the Wilsdrufferplatz (now Postplatz) in the west, site of the old Wilsdruffer Gate, where seven city streets still meet. The state decreed that only gardens and garden pavilions could occupy the privately owned land where the fortifications once stood.[127]

In the Neustadt, planning was easier because more land remained in the state's hands. Here the chief challenge was to integrate the New Annex, laid out and populated in the mid-eighteenth century, with the area south of the Black Gate. Thormeyer met this challenge, in a last gasp of the Baroque, by planning and constructing a star square—today the Albertplatz—at which a total of twelve streets converge. All these streets were rimmed with trees.[128]

Forceful Revolution

As the razing of the walls, the reorganization of the inner city, and the integration of the inner city with the suburbs progressed, Dresden as well as the rest of Saxony experienced an economic recession. The downturn in the economy, with its shortages of food and other commodities, coincided with a growing liberal atmosphere throughout Germany. In contrast to other German states where the French Revolution and Napoleon had inspired reforms, Saxon politics had remained unchanged.

State government was still in the hands of the king and the privileged Saxon nobility. The law that determined Dresden's city government was the same as that enacted in 1517. The size of the city council had been reduced in the course of the eighteenth century, and city councilors selected their successors—behind closed doors. In 1828, the Austrian journalist Moritz Saphir, when asked what he planned to do in the event of an imminent global collapse, sarcastically announced that he 'would take off for Dresden, where that event, like so many others, would not occur for another thirty years.'[129]

Influential circles, however, were well aware of the need for change. In private conversations, in hotels, restaurants, clubs, and suburban pubs, people complained of excessive taxation and deteriorating social conditions. Dresden's middle classes resented their lack of power and favored policies that would lead to economic improvement. When King Friedrich August I died in 1827, he was succeeded by his seventy-two-year old brother Anton, whose chief advisor was a nobleman opposed to all political reform, Count Detlev von Einsiedel. He ensured that Saxony's constitution, favoring the aristocracy and dating back to the sixteenth century, remained firmly in place. Tensions rose in Saxony and in its major cities when the Saxon Diet met and disbanded during the spring of 1830 without passing even minor reforms.

The first intimation of serious public protest occurred on 25 June 1830, the 300th anniversary of the Lutheran Augsburg Confession, a symbol of challenge to authority. In very Protestant Dresden, this event was heralded already at four in the morning as churches began ringing their bells. Trumpets sounded from the Kreuzkirche tower and from the Rathaus in the Neustadt. At 8 a.m., processions began in the churches. By that time, some citizens had apparently begun to imbibe their celebration, and the police and National Guardsmen were around to keep order.

In the evening, both the Kreuzkirche tower and the Frauenkirche cupola were brightly lighted. On the Altmarkt, the merchant Gleisberg displayed likenesses of Luther and Melanchthon. The inner city was full of people, and quite a few noticed that Dresden's Rathaus remained dark; there was no hint of city government's participation in the festivities. Some people suspected that the patrician city councilors were thus insulting the middle-class

Gleisberg. That sentiment did not hinder the crowd from throwing stones at the upper-story windows of a violinist playing "A Mighty Fortress is Our God" in Gleisberg's house. Police came to restore order, and the crowd went off to the Neustadt to honor Pastor Moritz Schmaltz, the rector of the Three Kings' Church, whose anti-Catholic sermons contributed to his popularity. As celebrations and disturbances continued for the next two days, tensions within the city rose. Saxon army units patrolled the streets.[130]

Even though these disturbances died down, a general dissatisfaction remained, and printed placards urging rebellion could be found on street corners throughout the city. At the beginning of August, news reached Saxony of the successful revolutions in both France and Belgium, increasing the desire for fundamental changes at home. A month later, Dresdners learned that police action against a noisy charivari of young journeymen in neighboring Leipzig had led to several days of rioting. The chief targets of the rioters were the police, but master craftsmen also called for tax reductions and an end to awarding city contracts to non-local builders. The disturbances were only quelled by 1000 soldiers, hastily sent from Dresden to Leipzig, and by the establishment of a royal investigating commission to receive and remedy complaints.

On the day that complaints were aired in Leipzig, Thursday, September 9, young Dresdners attending an evening concert by an army band in the Great Garden demanded to hear the Marseillaise, which they then caused to be played repeatedly. In the suburbs, crowds gathered spontaneously and began marching, without any pre-arranged plan, through the inner city's streets. One group broke all the public lanterns in the Schlossgasse while shouting "Long live the Leipziger!" and "Long live freedom!"

On the Marktplatz, a large crowd of journeymen, day laborers and students gathered in front of the Rathaus. Faced with closed doors, they found ladders, climbed to the second-story balcony, forced their way in through broken windows, and began throwing out papers and furniture. Groups in the Marktplatz, using wood dismantled from market stalls, then set fire to the Rathaus effects. Subsequently, the rioters stormed police headquarters around the corner in the Scheffelgasse and tossed papers, furniture and uniforms, into the Marktplatz fires. Bells rang out from the churches to summon firemen, and troops were sent from the Neustadt barracks to quell the riot. The troops had no orders to shoot, but two journeymen died from bayonet wounds. Eventually, the crowd forced the small military contingent to retreat across the bridge to its barracks.[131]

The government's response was immediate. On September 10, King Anton established a new Communal Guard of citizens to keep order with weapons issued from the royal armory. By September 13, the conservative Count Einsiedel had resigned as prime minister, and his place was taken by the reformist Baron Bernhard von Lindenau. The king's new cabinet persuaded him to set up a Commission to hear all grievances, not just those aired by rioting Leipzigers and Dresdners. The Commission was chaired by the Crown Prince Friedrich August, who also became co-regent with Anton. Petitioners to the Commission urged that the government grant more political rights to Saxon subjects.

As one of the first steps toward reform, direct elections were held on October 31 for a municipal representative assembly. Subsequent laws passed by the state Diet gave this assembly the responsibility for electing the mayor and other city administrators. They also gave the assembly the power of deciding the city's budget. Eventually, the city's courts became separate from and independent of city council, holding out the promise that arbitrary notables would no longer impose their whims on the populace. Since voting rights were granted only to property owners paying a tax of twelve Taler annually, just four percent of the city's populace could vote for assemblymen. Yet the new law and the elections of 1830 were still considered an improvement on the previous regime.[132]

The concessions of October did not entirely end the disturbances. At the beginning of December 1830, the government announced the dissolution of the old National Guard, a force established during the Napoleonic Wars to protect the city when the military was absent. Guardsmen received salaries and could count on additional fees for performing as watchmen and for executing urban contracts. They could also count on receiving tips for their services from grateful citizens. Once the Napoleonic Wars ended, the Guard did not disband, and over the decades it became radicalized. During the September riots, the Guard had done nothing to quell the disturbances, and some Guardsmen had even joined the rioters. With dissolution, National Guardsmen would lose both income and social status.

On December 4, upon hearing the order for dissolution from their commander, the young troops shouted "No!" They soon marched out of control through the Wilsdruffergasse and the Schlossgasse to the Neumarkt, singing the Marseillaise all the while. They then proceeded across the bridge to the Neustadt and struck the colors of the Guard flag in the Neustadt Guard-House.[133]

In the evening, an assembly met in the Neustadt and founded the Bürgerverein (Citizens' Association) to advocate for the re-establishment of the National Guard. This Bürgerverein decided to meet regularly at the coffee house Kreutz in the Altstadt. By the beginning of the new year, it claimed to have 2000 members. As the Saxon Diet was called back into session to discuss reforms, two new men joined the Bürgerverein: the lawyer Bernard Mossdorf and the noodle manufacturer Anton Bertholdy.

Under their leadership, the Bürgerverein devised a radical program that called for a constitutional monarchy in Saxony, an all-powerful single-chamber Diet or legislature, a bill of rights, and the dissolution of the aristocracy. Reflecting the nationalist movement of Young Germans of the time, the club also called for the several German states, including Saxony, to unite under a strong central government. Most alarmingly, it called for a Communal Guard that would not shed citizens' blood, and it threatened to achieve its goals "through pokes with the butt-end of a gun."[134]

These demands occurred against a background of renewed riots of craftsmen in Dresden's suburbs in February and March 1831. In mid-March, unemployed men who had been given jobs on public works projects protested the dismissals of some of their co-workers. There was also an attempt to raid the powder magazine in the city's center. In response, the government doubled the size of the Communal Guard and ended the furloughs of soldiers in the capital city's garrison. It also moved troops from other cities into Dresden.[135]

In April 1831, members of the Bürgerverein began a noisy campaign in Dresden's streets during the evening hours. Lanterns got broken, and riots repeated the previous autumn's events. It became impossible for the Communal Guard, led by Prince Johann, nephew of the king, to keep order. When he commanded his men to withdraw from a demonstration in front of Clothiers' Hall, the mob followed them with "shouts, curses, and whistles". The regular army was called out to restore calm.[136]

From the Lindenau government's point of view, it was necessary to stifle the agitation in order to convince the conservative aristocrats and privileged gentry in the Saxon Diet to vote for reforms that would end the Saxon feudal regime and steer the state toward a modern political system. The conservatives' votes were necessary to counter those of reactionary nobles who rejected any reforms at all. Thus, Lindenau could not show sympathy for the radical demands of the Bürgerverein.

In mid-April 1831, he banned the Bürgerverein. The prohibition only provoked further disturbances. When the government arrested both Mossdorf and Bertholdy and imprisoned them in Dresden's Rathaus, their supporters liberated them on April 17. The government countered with a full military alert, with the arrest of the Bürgerverein's entire executive committee, and with the decisive quelling of an uprising in the Wilsdruffer suburb. Mossdorf and Bertholdy were sentenced to fifteen years in the Königstein Fortress prison, and ten others went to jail for extended terms. The Communal Guard was purged of 1600 men who had proven to be unreliable against the Bürgerverein's supporters. Otherwise, the government took a "mild" approach to the offenders and got on with the business of reform.[137]

In autumn 1831, a new constitution created a Saxon legislature of two houses. In the upper house, the aristocracy would enjoy a two-thirds majority. Projected in the lower house were twenty large landowners, twenty-five representatives of Saxon cities, twenty-five peasant representatives, and five representatives of commerce and industry. Election was indirect. The new Diet had the power to approve, but not to initiate, both the budget and new legislation. In order to reject a governmental measure, either both houses had to agree, or two-thirds of one house had to be in favor of rejection. Thus, the reformers had shifted the political ground only slightly, but at least one historian of the 1830 revolution thinks that they punctured the medieval mentality and prepared the way for a modern Saxony.[138]

Dresden Receives New Life

In Dresden, it seemed as if a new era had dawned. The year of the new Saxon constitution was also the year when the city's de-fortification became complete. The novelist and native Dresdner, Friedrich Schulze, described the "metamorphosis" that Dresden experienced with the razing of the walls. By the 1830s, the previous, "medieval gloominess" had given way to "cheerfulness" [Heiterkeit]. The shacks that had once stood next to mansions, the burned-out lots covered with weeds left over from the Seven Years' War, the dirty, pitted streets, had all disappeared. New, wider sidewalks of granite or sandstone, made walking easier in good and bad weather. Roof water no longer dripped on pedestrians during rain storms but was directed through downspouts into the street.

In the Neustadt, "tasteful" housing developments had transformed the old thinly populated Bautzenerstrasse and the Antonstadt. The latter, annexed to the city in 1835, had acquired sufficient businesses to serve the needs of the neighborhood. In the Altstadt, market halls began to sell a range of products not previously available. To these were added new retail businesses on the ground floors of the buildings on the Altmarkt, the Schlossgasse, the Wilsdruffergasse, and the Pirnaischegasse. The Post Office, moved to the Wilsdrufferplatz, increased the city's amenities and gave its name to the square.

Both the Brühl and Japanese Palace gardens were planted with flowers in every season of the year. A hillock situated in the Japanese Palace garden provided good views of the Elbe and of the vineyards in the northwest. In the Great Garden, new sculptures appeared, and swans populated the pond. Meadows and woods now invited Dresdners to "pleasant walks" lined by benches in the shade. At the Great Garden's restored palace, both garden shows and concerts enhanced the ambience. There were lots of opportunities for refreshment and conviviality. In spring and summer, crowds of Dresdners carried picnic baskets for an evening supper in the park. According to Schulze, this large park, once descended into "wilderness", had been restored to a "work of art".[139]

In the 1830s, the young Louis Lesser frequented the park with his pals where they heard concerts in the early weekday mornings, on Sunday afternoons and during summer evenings. Several restaurants in the park offered him, his friends and his parents refreshment. One resident considered the Great Garden the best place to become acquainted with the better sort of Dresdners: polite, good-natured, happy to indulge in small pleasures. On any beautiful day, one could find them walking in the park at noon as if it were a *corso*. Even the best people, he said, deserted the inner-city musicales in summer for the outdoor fare of the Great Garden. The riff-raff somehow knew to stay away, even though no police or barriers excluded them.[140]

Evening activities, particularly, were made possible by the city's illumination. Various sections of the city had been progressively lighted by lanterns beginning in 1705. The lights were attached either to house facades or hung on wooden poles in the streets. After Napoleon's wars, the king announced the need for up-grading the old oil lamps with gas lighting throughout the city. Not much was done before 1828 when one of the city's most active entrepreneurs, Rudolf Blochmann, established the municipal gas works and began installing the necessary pipe and lights, two decades after London. The illumination, depending on the time of year, began at two in the afternoon and ended at three-thirty in the morning.[141] By the 1830s, Dresden had become a city that was bright and open for all its inhabitants.

Toward the Industrial City

In this early half of the nineteenth century, it was still possible to think of Dresden as the Baroque city shaped by the princely court and capital of a reduced, German state. Dresden's economy was oriented toward the royal government. Craftsmen predominated: tailors, shoemakers, jewelers, carpenters, piano builders, wallpaper printers, paint-mixers, and playing card manufacturers. Primarily these craftsmen worked alone; there were few large shops or factories. Nevertheless, the existence of scientific instrument makers pointed toward the future.[142]

Already in 1815, there was one establishment using an improvised steam-powered machine to extract from dye-woods the colors used in the textile trade. During the next decade, other businesses began using small steam engines for their manufacturing processes: a mill for grinding animal bones to be used as fertilizer; a factory for making wood veneers.[143]

The longest-lived of all these early industries was the firm of Jordan and Timaeus that processed chicory coffee, chocolate and cocoa, as well as spices. Otto Rueger and Hartwig and Vogel joined later in the century. Complementary enterprises, like Friedrich Reiche's, manufacturing tin forms and packing cans, helped to make the city one of Germany's prime chocolate-producing centers. By the late nineteenth century, the city boasted twenty-eight chocolate-making firms and their related industries, employing 10,000 workers. The Association of German Chocolate Manufacturers was founded in Dresden in 1879.[144] Joining the early chocalatiers in the specialty trade was Dr. Adolph Struve who had devised a method for processing mineral water that competed well with the authentic variety. In 1820, Dr. Struve even opened a mineral water "garden" that was wildly popular with native Dresdners and which Voss visited during his stay in the city.[145]

Another firm offering libation was the Societäts brewery. Almost two decades after Struve opened his garden, the Societäts club decided to build a large structure housing both a brewery and a pub on the grounds of the old Waldschlösschen, a hunting lodge originally built by the former courtier, Count Marcolini, for his Scottish wife on the eastern edge of the Neustadt. A rowdy crowd turned up in late March 1838 to celebrate the opening. They left behind hat brims, neckties, torn sleeve cuffs, half an undershirt, a variety of caps, and several pieces of cloth. It took a while for more sober folk, particularly women, to patronize the brewery and imbibe the proffered drink.[146]

Other industrial attractions also existed. Voss dropped in on F.K. Kaufmann and Son, a small shop making mechanical musical instruments such as music boxes and clocks. In the 1820s, the Calberla sugar refinery located on the Elbe bastion closest to the palace. The refinery lasted into the late 1830s when it closed due to stiff competition from the Dresdner Sugar Refining Company.[147]

Continental businessmen during this period felt the full competitive force of the English industrial revolution. They knew they needed to adopt new technology and new products. In the 1820s, several groups of states, including Saxony and its neighbors, initiated customs unions allowing them to distribute goods throughout Germany more cheaply and efficiently. In Dresden the need for industrial expertise and innovation also led businessmen, in cooperation with the Saxon state, to open, in 1828, the Technical Education Institute. The Institute would prepare young men to become technicians and engineers and would help Saxony compete with England's increasing industrial prowess.[148] According to Friedrich Schulze, who worked for the state's Commercial Commission, it was the school's good fortune that Wilhelm Lohrmann, a trained architect and surveyor, became its first director.

Lohrmann had worked for the Saxon Surveyors' Institute and functioned as the chief supervisor for the Zwinger's Mathematics-Physics Salon, that part of the royal collections devoted to scientific instruments. While serving as the first director of the Technical Institute, he performed many of the surveys necessary for introducing the railroad into Saxony. Lohrmann died of typhus at the very young age of forty-four in 1840.

Two other men furthered the cause of the Technical Institute. The first was Rudolf Blochmann, who had trained as a mechanic in Dresden and then went on to study mathematics. As a young man, he had worked with the optical glassmaker, Josef Fraunhofer. In Dresden after the Napoleonic Wars, he opened a shop that made precision measuring instruments. In the same year that he introduced gas lighting to Dresden in 1828, Blochmann became supervisor of the mechanical workshop at the Technical Institute. In the 1840s, he devised a machine for boring stone and was thus able to supply Dresden with a complete system of lithic canalization. Blochmann lived a long and fruitful life, devoting himself in his later years to his business interests. He died in 1871 at the ripe age of eighty-seven.[149]

The other individual determining the destiny of the Technical Institute was Johann Andreas Schubert. Son of a day-laborer in southwestern Saxony, he grew up in Leipzig and became a pupil at the St. Thomas Preparatory School. At the age of fourteen, he entered Dresden's Royal Art Academy, studied architecture and served as an intern in Blochmann's workshop. In 1832, he became a professor at the Technical Institute and, eventually, its director.

In 1834, he helped to establish the Dresdner Industrial Association that sponsored educational lectures and brought students from the Technical Institute into contact with the heads of industrial firms. One of his most beautiful achievements is the design for the Goeltsch Valley rail trestle in southern Saxony. Today, it is the oldest and largest brick trestle in the world, and the German Federal Railroad sends trains daily across its expanse. Through his textbooks and consultations with firms in machine building and construction, he is credited with training the first generation of Saxon engineers.[150]

Steam

In 1836, Schubert became a partner in the Elbe Steamship Company that launched the first two steamboats on the upper Elbe. These vessels were not well-suited for a river that was unregulated and silted up. At Dresden, it was 150 meters wide and one meter deep. The boats never completely coped with the river's shallow depth, but they were popular for ferrying people on Sunday excursions. Dresdners usually walked out to the village of Wachwitz where they refreshed themselves at the restaurant Zur Presse before continuing on to the park at Pillnitz, the royal family's summer residence, opened to the public after the Napoleonic Wars. At the end of the day, they took the steamship back to the city. Others used the ship to travel as far south as the small city of Wehlen on the northern edge of Saxon Switzerland.

During the drought of 1842, the ships heading back to Dresden sometimes got stuck in shallow water. If one happened to be stranded at Anton's, a popular restaurant near the village of Blasewitz, it was possible to reach Dresden on foot. But if the ships could not progress beyond Pirna, some eleven miles south of Dresden, the passengers had to wait until Monday morning and return to the capital with the sausage delivery wagon. It was in this year, perhaps as a result of the drought, that all German states on the Elbe, including Saxony, began dredging the river.[151] In any event, the Steamship Company's white fleet continues to exist to the present day. It offers a variety of excursions, one as far as the border town of Decin in the Czech Republic.

The steam locomotive soon joined the steam ship, an event that created huge excitement in Dresden. This first long-distance line in Germany, between Dresden and Leipzig, was built in stages. In July 1838, when the first section to Kötzschenbroda was opened on the line's eastern end, the railroad's directors sold hundreds of tickets to an enthusiastic public during the first week of operation.

With the launch of the complete line on 8 April 1839, elaborate ceremonies occurred. On the eve of the trip, a dinner was served in the rooms of the elite Harmonie Society. The next morning King Friedrich August II and his brother, Prince Johann, gathered with their families and Saxon notables to make the trip to Leipzig. The royal coach was decorated with garlands and flowers. As the train pulled out of the station, there was a cannonade and shouts from a large crowd. The royal family returned to Dresden in the early evening. On this trip, the Saxonia, the first German-built steam locomotive, produced in Schubert's Machine Building Workshops at Übigau, pulled the cars behind two English locomotives.[152]

During the next half-century, the railway network available to the city expanded, and a separate freight station was built in the Friedrichstadt. The polymath, Carl Gustav Carus, personal physician to the king, observed that the railroad, "came forth like Hercules in his cradle, already strangling snakes, and with giant steps, carved out a place for itself on all sides." At the beginning, he said, it was "wonderfully new and stirred up a multitude of promises…" By the time that Carus wrote these words in his memoirs, the state had acquired ownership of the Royal Saxon Railways, and Dresden had become a major transportation hub.[153]

Carl Gustav Carus

Carus, then a young man of twenty-five, arrived in Dresden in 1814 to become the director of the maternity hospital and to serve as professor of gynecology at the Royal Saxon Surgical-Medical Academy. Established to overcome the shortage of doctors in the army and in the rural villages of Saxony, its clinics were soon treating urban patients. Carus made a splash almost immediately by officially opening the Academy with a celebratory lecture and exhibiting his painting at the art exhibition of 1816. During the next four years he published two books relating to medical practice, all the while teaching, presiding over a daily clinic and making himself available both day and night for women in labor.

Soon, aristocratic and upper-class families engaged him as their physician and recommended him to the king who appointed him as personal physician in 1826. Accepting this prestigious appointment meant giving up his professorship and the supervision of the maternity hospital. At the same time, he kept his private practice of upper-class patients. He continued to write books on medicine and the philosophy of nature and to paint for the rest of his life. The historian and novelist, Ricarda Huch, judged him to have "preserved a noble moderation in thought and life" with a 'superb strength of style, a far-reaching understanding, [and] a fine, logical, consequential intellect…' Meanwhile, the Surgical-Medical Academy continued to thrive.[154]

Old Treasures in a New Setting

As Dresden and Saxony recovered economically from the losses at the Congress of Vienna and modernized politically, they sought to regain their former "fame and respect". Count Heinrich von Vitzthum, Friedrich August I's superintendent of the art collections and later director of the State Theater, argued, along with other advisors, that the best route to an esteemed position led through activating the arts as well as the sciences.

The influential philosopher, Johann Gottfried Herder, had already claimed such a strategy for the city in his short-lived periodical *Adrastea* at the beginning of the nineteenth-century. He praised the Saxon rulers of the previous century for establishing a "school of civility" that spawned an Elbflorenz "with treasures of the art world." He likened Dresden to the Olympia of classical Greece and its artists as heir to the Italian Renaissance.[155]

The art exhibition of 1816, where Carus displayed his painting, revealed that Dresden still prized the fine arts, and an expanding number of visitors to the city valued its collections. The Baron von Voss and his young charge from Anhalt made sure to visit all the galleries open to the public. They frequently found a crowd of artists and amateurs making copies of the paintings. Once, they encountered the English Duke of Cumberland stopping off to view the gallery on his way to take the waters at Carlsbad. On his last visit to the gallery at the height of summer, Voss lamented the museum personnel's careless handling of the paintings.

He also made sure to visit the gypsum copies of ancient statues from Italy and Spain. These had been acquired in 1784 and were opened to the public ten years later. Voss had to laugh when the guard at the gallery showed him a gypsum leaf that had to hang over certain parts of the statues when ladies visited the gallery. Voss's comment: "There was so much else to see, that the ladies really had no need to view *anything more.*" [Emphasis in the original.]

Voss's whole party spent four hours during one afternoon in mid-May touring the "rich" collection of armor and weapons. Wooden horses were used to give the viewer an idea of how the medieval armor once appeared. Another attraction was the natural history collection that included petrified wood and precious stones, stuffed animals and an arrangement of birds' eggs and nests. Most impressive was the royal monopoly over the "lake clams" from the Elster River that formed pearls of "oriental" size. The curator of the copper etchings collection, open to the public every morning of the week, showed several folios to Voss and his party. Hanging on the walls were two Gobelin tapestries.

Last, but not least, Voss made an appointment for his party to visit the Green Vaults, a venue that still allowed only six to visit at any one time. The experience with these *objets de vertu* altered his previous disdain for such luxuries. He was so entranced by this "fairy's den" that, in a letter to his wife, he described the contents of each of the eight rooms, all lined, he said, with columns and mirrors. Voss was so impressed by Dinglinger's Court of Delhi on the Birthday of the Great Mogul that he could not resist telling his wife that the goldsmith had received 85,000 Taler for it. Then and now, Dinglinger's artistry is exhilarating.[156]

Dresden's collections not only attracted viewers, they also attracted creators. In 1805, the portrait painter, Gerhard von Kügelgen, had arrived with his family from Russia, having chosen Dresden as a residence because at the time it was known as a haven for artists. He frequently visited the Paintings Gallery to make copies and to receive inspiration. Though he was never completely able to abandon portrait painting as a source of income, Kügelgen used Dresden as a base for preparing large canvases depicting mythic and historical events.

Kügelgen lived with his family in the Neustadt's Hauptstrasse in a house named "God's Blessing" and kept a studio in Loschwitz. On the moonlit evening of 27 March 1820, God's blessing did not help Kügelgen escape a murderous robber as he made his way home from his studio. His oldest son, Wilhelm, and a policeman with his dog, found him the next morning lying face down in a field close to the Linckesches Bad on the Bautzenerstrasse.[157]

Kügelgen was both mentor and friend to one of the most famous German artists of that day and this: Caspar David Friedrich. Friedrich hailed from Pomerania and received his early training at Copenhagen's Academy of Art. In 1798, he came to live in Dresden, traveling frequently to the north and south in order to paint the natural surroundings that he believed were divine emanations. His career as an artist took off in 1805 when he exhibited his drawings at a competition in Weimar organized by the literary celebrity and statesman, Johann Wolfgang von Goethe. He gained an international reputation, selling his works in Bohemia, Prussia and Russia.

In 1818, he received both Saxon citizenship and membership in the Saxon Academy of Art with a stipend of 150 Taler a year. But he had to wait until 1824 before receiving an appointment to teach landscape painting to the Academy's students. By that time, his popularity had begun to wane, and he increasingly withdrew from public life. Because he was shy and awkward, it was mostly the charity of friends that kept him and his family alive. Gerhard von Kügelgen's death, thought his son, triggered Friedrich's decline. His friend was no longer around to send him the "strangers" who commissioned his paintings.[158]

Carl Carus also considered Friedrich a friend. He used to accompany Friedrich on his morning and evening walks. Carus accepted that Friedrich was a "loner, both socially and artistically", and, in the late 1820s, noted his increasing distrustfulness. Friedrich suffered from periodic bouts of depression and began to abuse his wife. Once, he tried to commit suicide. After he suffered a stroke in 1835, which left his arms and hands too weak to work at oil painting, Carus tried to help but was rebuffed. For him, the earlier friendship was lost.

Today, Friedrich's works can be found all over Germany and as far afield as Russia, Scandinavia and Switzerland. The Dresden Paintings Gallery possesses several of his works, but admirers of Friedrich do not usually associate him with Dresden.[159]

That is not because the Dresdners particularly neglected him. The new Saxon Art Society paid attention to his work. This society was conceived during the celebrations that Dresdners held on the 300th anniversary of Albert Dürer's death. The Nazarene painter Carl Peschel suggested to J. G. von Quandt that Saxony and Dresden needed such an organization. Baron von Quandt, the heir of a wealthy merchant family, was the owner of a "rich" collection of engravings, particularly those of Schongauer and Dürer. Von Quandt liked Peschel's suggestion and shared the idea with the speaker at the Dürer banquet, Karl August Böttiger, the rector of the Dresden Knight's Academy, a private school for aristocrats, and the superintendent of the Museum of Antiquities. As a well-connected person, Böttiger was just the man to launch a new organization.

6 April 1828 became the birthday of the Saxon Art Society. It proposed to interest a large audience in various kinds of artistic works and to create a market for them. Almost immediately after its founding, it attracted seventy members. Goethe became an honorary member, and the Saxon king gave it a subsidy of 500 Taler. In the decade following its founding, it claimed to have spent 46,000 Taler on art works. In addition, it maintained contact with art societies in other parts of Germany. In 1835, when Carus became its chairman, the bylaws changed to allow the Society to present works by all German artists, not just Saxon ones.[160]

In 1836, it sponsored an exhibition of works by the Düsseldorf School, a group of Romantic painters who, like the Hudson River painters of the same era, devoted themselves to *plein-air* painting and favored a subtle palette. In Dresden, the exhibition of 1836 on the Brühl Terrace was a huge success. Many visitors were particularly attracted to Eduard Bendemann's "Jeremiah in the Ruins of Jerusalem". Two years later, the Academy of Art lured Bendemann away from Düsseldorf, and he remained in Dresden for the next two decades. He left to become director of Düsseldorf's Academy.[161]

Outstanding Artists

By the time that the Art Society called attention to the Düsseldorf School and its painters, Dresden's Art Academy had already appointed to its faculty three of the most famous figures of the German art world. Though these three are not well-known in the United States, in Germany they are household names. The first to begin instruction was Ludwig Richter, born in the Friedrichstadt across the street from the Marcolini Palace. Richter's father was a successful engraver who eventually taught drawing at the Academy. When the young Ludwig left school at the age of twelve, he became an apprentice to his father. While working hard in his father's shop, he began taking classes at the Academy. In 1823 at the age of twenty, taking advantage of a generous scholarship from the bookseller Arnold, he went off to study in Rome and remained there for three years.

After he returned in 1826, he taught at the Art Academy's branch in Meissen and worked principally as a landscape painter. He also became his father's successor at the Academy. In the 1830s, he began to cut wood blocks for illustrating books—fairy tales, folios, song books. These illustrations made him the best-known German artist of his age. Several of the books that he illustrated can be accessed through the Internet (https://commons.wikipedia.org/wiki/Category: Ludwig-Richter). When he died in 1884, he received a state funeral at Dresden's New Catholic Cemetery in the Friedrichstadt.[162]

Some years after Richter began teaching at the Academy, he was joined by another native Saxon, the young, but experienced, sculptor Ernst Rietschel. Born in Pulsnitz, just fourteen miles northeast of Dresden, Rietschel studied drawing at the Art Academy and then went to work in a sculptor's shop. In 1826, Count Einsiedel found him a position in the atelier of Christian Daniel Rauch, at that time the most famous sculptor in Germany. In 1830, Rietschel spent a year in Rome. There he learned that, at the tender age of twenty-six, he had been chosen to create the memorial statue of King Friedrich August I. Two years later he accepted a professorship at the Art Academy. Anyone familiar with the Lessing statue in Braunschweig, with the Goethe-Schiller Memorial at the National Theater in Weimar, or the huge Luther Memorial in Worms will be immediately acquainted with Rietschel's work. For most of his life, Rietschel suffered from an inflammation of the lungs, and he died at the age of fifty-seven. The small town of Pulsnitz honors him with a statue on the Marktplatz.[163]

The one artist to arrive in Dresden during this period who enjoys international fame is Gottfried Semper. Many people are aware that he was the architect for the famous Opera House, whose restoration and reopening was a widely-reported event in 1985. This theater exhibits all the characteristics of Semper's neo-Renaissance style, a fashion he helped to introduce into the Germany of his time.

Semper was born into a wealthy Hamburg family in 1803. For a year, he studied mathematics in Göttingen, but in 1826 he drifted off to Paris to study with the noted French sculptor Christian Gau. Between 1830 and 1833, he traveled widely in Italy and Greece. When the architecture chair at the Academy of Art fell vacant in 1833, the Dresdners were in a quandary because their first choice, the Prussian Karl Schinkel, turned them down. Schinkel recommended Semper. At first the Dresdners were reluctant to appoint to the Academy such a young and relatively unknown figure, but Gau recommended him highly, and the Hamburg businessman Johann Wulsten praised his "manly appearance, charm with the ladies and good manners." What may not have been mentioned were his "enormous energy", "indomitable will", and his ability "to bring instant excitement…to any social gathering, with his peculiar habit of contradicting everyone flatly."

Semper began as professor of architecture at the Academy of Art in 1834. His duties entailed far more than teaching. Almost immediately he was caught up in various projects within the city. Working together with Ernst Rietschel and Andreas Schubert for the celebration of King Anton's eightieth birthday in 1835, he designed and supervised several temporary, polychrome structures on the city's squares and bridges. Also for Rietschel, he designed the pedestal for the statue of King Friedrich August I, now lodged on the Schlossplatz.

At the same time, he was called upon to design an appropriate architectural backdrop for the display of antiquities in seven rooms of the Japanese Palace. He chose a different, vibrant color for each room. Greek ornaments served as the background for Greek sculptures. Pompeiian themes accompanied Roman sculptures. These ideas all relied on sketches he had made during his journeys to Greece and Italy as a young man. Such artistic liveliness caused a sensation when the renovated rooms were unveiled.

Another project of the mid-1830s was a new Materni Hospital on Freibergerplatz next to the Annenkirche. His dealings with the trustees revealed the contentious side of Semper's personality. He adamantly refused to make any alteration to his original design, and, as a fee, he demanded two per cent of construction costs, rather than the one per cent the building committee wanted to pay. In the end, the committee paid him the two per cent rather than engage in endless quarrels with a determined man.[164]

One result of the 1830 Revolution was a rationalization of Saxon finances, and funds became available for projects that had been long delayed. One of these was a new Dresden Opera House. Both of the previous opera houses were now dedicated to purposes other than music and drama, and by the beginning of the nineteenth century only the old Moretti theater served the court and the public. Between 1800 and Semper's arrival in Dresden, various plans had been discussed and architects engaged. Nothing had been done, either because the designs were too expensive, or they didn't suit Dresden's purposes. The city now commissioned Semper to submit plans for a new theater in the center of an area that became known as Theaterplatz. The cornerstone for the new theater was laid in 1839, and it opened in 1841 with a performance of Goethe's *Torquato Tasso*.

The building was monumentally neo-Renaissance in style. It echoed the Zwinger's line of arches by threading them around a circular building and filling the niches with statues, some designed by Rietschel: Goethe, Schiller, Gluck, Mozart, Molière, Shakespeare, Sophocles and Euripides. Architectural innovations included the union of different building components usually separated from one another: a round auditorium flanked by rectangular carriage houses; a square stage house behind the auditorium. Gas lights illuminated the sumptuous interior. Semper's structure harmonized with its Zwinger neighbor,[165]

The second delayed project made possible by the reorganized Saxon finances was the Paintings Gallery. Since the early eighteenth century, the paintings collected by the Wettiner had found a home in the old Electoral Stable. Though artfully arranged and visited from near and far, they could not be protected against fire, dampness, dirt, and street vibrations at that location. The inability to heat the building also meant that the gallery regularly closed for the winter.

Plans to relocate the Gallery dated back to the late eighteenth century. After the Revolution of 1830, the royal art collection theoretically remained the property of the royal house, but as a state treasure, it was managed and maintained by the Saxon government. After 1830, the Lindenau administration sold a large and highly valuable part of the original collection. The remaining holdings that were not paintings were carefully distributed between the Zwinger and the Green Vaults.

With the economic upswing of the early 1840s, the Saxon Diet decided to undertake the construction of a new gallery. Its chosen site was the gap between the eastern and western arms of the Zwinger. For Semper, that location demanded even more architectural sensitivity than the Opera House. Contemporary visitors to the Zwinger must conclude that Semper mastered the challenge of integrating the Paintings Gallery with its Baroque surroundings. The rectangular structure was neo-Renaissance in style but devised with a simplicity that enhances the exuberance of Permoser's sculptures. The arched windows and balustrades on the courtyard side deftly blend in with those of the Zwinger's pavilions. The Gallery's central dome echoes the raised roofs of the neighboring structures. On the facade facing the Opera House, triangular pediments and decorated pilasters adorn the arched windows to provide architectural interest. Construction on the Gallery began in 1847 and was completed in 1854.[166]

Public commissions were not the only ones that Semper fulfilled during this period. In 1839, the Villa Rosa, a residence for the banker, Martin Wilhelm Oppenheim, was added to the new structures in the Neustadt. This house became the model for German villa architecture in the nineteenth century. Destroyed by the bombing of 1945, it was not restored.[167] In the 1840s, Semper was a busy professional who also led a vigorous social and political life. One man with whom he had frequent contact was the German composer destined to become even more famous than he.

Revolutionary Music

Dresden was and is a town where music not only adds spice to life, it nurtures the community. The Electoral orchestra had existed since the sixteenth century alongside the municipal musicians and the choirs of the Kreuzschule. The latter, by Electoral decree, roamed the medieval city three times a week at three in the afternoon singing German songs and collecting donations. These street choirs continued into the nineteenth century and were supported, not only by donations, but by the school and the city. The English music historian and composer, Charles Burney, reporting on his visit to Dresden, described how the better citizens paid to have the choirs sing in front of their homes and at their family celebrations.[168]

During the Napoleonic Wars. the court organist, Anton Dreyssig, founded a choir of both male and female voices. This Dreyssigsche Singakademie lasted for over one hundred years. Rehearsals occurred once a week, and members paid annual dues to cover the costs of music and a rehearsal hall. Wilhelm von Kügelgen auditioned for this group in 1819; he had to sing a scale and identify a musical interval. At that time, the chorus contained about 50 singers with a repertoire devoted principally to religious music. The Akademie gave "half-public" concerts in the old post office building in the Pirnaische Strasse. Wilhelm took his father, Gerhard, to a performance of Mozart's Requiem there.[169] In the course of the nineteenth century, many more choral societies followed.

At the beginning of the nineteenth century, the dominant style of the Royal Opera in the Moretti theater remained Italian. This Italian style, foreign to middle-class Dresdners whose patronage for the opera was financially necessary, failed to raise sufficient operating revenues. Accordingly, the director of theaters, Count Vitzthum, decided, in 1817, to introduce a German opera department in tandem with the Italian one. To manage and direct the German style, Vitzthum appointed the noted pianist, composer and opera director in Prague, Carl Maria von Weber.

Although he shared the orchestra with the Italian department, Weber had full responsibility for hiring a troupe of German singers. It was he who brought the famed German soprano of the early nineteenth-century, Wilhelmine Schroeder-Devrient, to Dresden. Some of Weber's most well-known works were composed there. Carl von Voss, visiting the city in 1822, twice saw *Der Freischütz* performed in mid-June. That summer, he also attended three performances of the play *Preziosa*, for which Weber wrote the music.

Weber's son Max has left us a charming glimpse of his father's routine. Because both Weber and his wife Caroline were very sociable, their home on the Altmarkt became a popular place to visit. Carl often brought guests, unannounced, home to dinner at noon. The couple liked to entertain small circles of friends where they would perform together—he at the piano, she with her voice—and young dancers often twirled to Weber's music. Both spouses were early risers, and Weber liked to dispose of practical matters in the morning. After the noonday dinner, he took a short nap, drank some coffee and sometimes took a walk around the remaining city walls. In the afternoons and evenings, if he did not direct a performance, Weber devoted himself to composing.

After performances, he liked to relax at Chiappone's restaurant in the Schlossgasse. This was a haven for the city's artistic and intellectual circles and offered up sophisticated fare: Verona salami, truffle sausage, smoked salmon, tropical fruits, Perigord pâtés, caviar, large blocks of cheese. Weber knew how to have a good time, and his "humorous foolishness" brought out the same quality in others. A good conversationalist, he did not seek to dominate the discussion but engaged in a "bright and mellow" give and take.[170]

Before Weber's death from tuberculosis in London in 1826, where he had gone to direct the premiere of *Oberon*, the young Richard Wagner made Weber's acquaintance by virtue of his stepfather's and sisters' association with the state theater. Weber visited Wagner's family a few times, and Wagner could remember an excursion of the theater troupe to Loschwitz where Weber acted as cook.

Wagner's family had moved from Leipzig to Dresden to accommodate his stepfather's appointment to the theater. After the stepfather died in 1821, Wagner attended the Kreuzschule for a few years before the family returned to Leipzig where Wagner eventually became a pupil at the St. Thomas Preparatory School. His uncle Adolph, a philologist, took the boy under his wing and gave him access to his copious library. Wagner studied music at the University of Leipzig and took private lessons in composition. In 1833, he began to earn his living as a music director at various theaters in Germany and in the Russian empire, composing all the while, but because of his profligacy was obliged to keep moving one step ahead of his creditors. In 1840, he and his first wife, Minna, landed in Paris where he barely supported them both by writing musical treatises for magazines and performing at part-time musical jobs. During this Parisian sojourn, he composed the operas *Rienzi* and the *Flying Dutchman*.

Even though he had moved away from the city, Wagner still had contacts in Dresden. His sister Ottilie lived with her husband, Hermann Brockhaus, in a villa near the Great Garden. He also had ties to Wilhelmina Schroeder-

Devrient and to the associate director of the theater, Karl Winkler (also known as the publicist Theodor Hell). From his childhood, he was acquainted with the musical director of the theater, Karl Gottlob Reissiger, the successor to Carl Maria von Weber. Thinking he could count on the good will of these old friends, Wagner offered his *Rienzi* to the Dresden opera in order to re-establish himself in Germany. He hoped that the popular Dresden tenor, Joseph Tichatschek, would sing the opera's title role. It took a year for the shrewd intendant of the Royal Theater, Baron Wolf von Lüttichau, to decide that *Rienzi* would have its premiere in Dresden. Wagner immediately moved back to the city, even though he was not scheduled to have any part in the premiere or subsequent performances. On opening night, he received several curtain calls, and the opera fulfilled his hopes of making a splash in Germany. After the sixth performance, he was invited to direct the opera himself. At the beginning of 1843, the *Flying Dutchman* also premiered in Dresden, but it was not well received by the audience. Nevertheless, shortly after the premiere, Wagner became an orchestra director at the state theater, gaining "social prestige, a salary and life tenure."[171]

For the next six years, he operated in tandem with Reissiger. One of Wagner's associates once complained that Reissiger had the "Saxon gift of obstruction", putting off the performance of Wagner's operas, including the premiere of *Tannhäuser* in 1845, as long as possible. Wagner was not easy to work with. The dramaturg, Karl Gutzkow, thought that he did not get along well with Lüttichau and that the court perhaps disapproved of him.

It was no secret that he found the orchestra pit in the new Semper Opera House too small and wanted to remove the first row of seats to provide more depth. He also wanted to replace the players' old armchairs with stools and the wooden music stands with iron rods on iron feet. These, he thought, would reflect rather than absorb sound. Wagner wanted to turn the players around so that their backs no longer faced the audience. This change would direct the sound outward. And last, but not least, he wanted to expand the size of the orchestra and break it into small groups, when necessary, in order to fulfill its many duties more expertly. During Wagner's stay in Dresden, the funds necessary for such expansion did not exist.[172]

From today's point of view, there is no question that the orchestra was overworked. It not only performed large and small operas, but farces, ballets, vaudevilles, stage music, celebrations of various kinds, and two Sunday services at the Court Church. These performances required rehearsals. In addition, the royal orchestra performed the music for the well-attended and celebrated Palm Sunday concerts. These began in 1826 after the king eliminated the traditional Good Friday oratorio. Originally, only oratorios were performed, but other genres later appeared on the program. The Dreyssigsche Singakademie provided the voices; sometimes the choir of the Kreuzschule joined in. In 1826, there was a presentation of Haydn's *Creation* and in 1828, there was Händel's *Judas Makkabaeus*. In 1833, Dresdners heard Bach's *St. Matthew Passion*. Ten years later, Felix Mendelssohn conducted his own *St. Paul Oratorio*.[173]

The tickets sold for the Palm Sunday concerts benefited the orchestra's widows' and orphans' fund. In 1846, when Wagner wanted to introduce Beethoven's Ninth Symphony, the concert committee feared that, since Dresdners did not like the symphony, not much money would be raised. To awaken the interest of the public, Wagner wrote short advance notices for the town's newspaper, the *Dresdner Anzeiger,* and he explained the work to its readers. This tactic worked. According to Wagner, the funds raised in 1846 were substantial, and he repeated the Ninth Symphony for the next three Palm Sundays.[174]

This episode reveals that Wagner's own work load was heavy. There were other events for which he was expected to provide incidental music or extended scores. In 1844, he wrote the music, borrowing themes from *Euryanthe*, for the ceremony attending the return from London to Dresden of Carl Maria von Weber's remains. *Tannhäuser* premiered in 1845, and he wrote the operas *Lohengrin* and *Die Meistersinger von Nürnberg* during this time. For a short while, he took over the direction of the men's Glee Club and wrote music for it on one occasion. Somehow he also found time to study German mythology and philosophy.[175]

Dresdners of the 1840s realized that with Wagner's music they were hearing something new. Carl Carus described divisions within both the musicians' group and the public. The old school favored Gluck's *Armida, Iphigenia, Alceste,* all also directed by Wagner. The new school preferred *Rienzi*, the *Flying Dutchman, Tannhäuser*. A competition between the two sides developed, each trying to produce something "extraordinary". The beneficiary of this duel was the opera-going public. Carus himself judged

Tannhäuser to be a skillful composition but "tendentious". He dubbed it a "romantic rococo".[176]

Wagner remarked in his memoirs that giving music lessons in Dresden was a very lucrative enterprise. He could have been thinking of Friedrich Wieck, who came to Dresden in 1844 as a private teacher of musical instruments and of voice. Because there were so many wealthy families in town for whom making music was *de rigueur*, Wieck made so much money that he turned down offers of appointment to both the Leipzig and the Dresden conservatories. He taught the noted pianist and conductor of the late nineteenth century, Hans von Bülow, and his future son-in-law, Robert Schumann. Wieck's daughter, Clara, became a successful concert pianist under his tutelage.

Carus and his wife had invited Clara Wieck and her father to several of their musical soirées in 1830. The then nine-year old behaved, he said, like any other child until she sat down at the piano, where she became an accomplished performer. In 1844, Clara Wieck and Robert Schumann, now married, moved from Leipzig to Dresden in the hopes of improving Robert's health. After the move, Schumann missed the musical life of Leipzig and organized concerts that emphasized the works of the classical Viennese composers. In order to give Robert's music a hearing, Clara, in 1845, played her husband's "A Minor Concerto" and some of his other compositions in a special concert.

The next year, Schumann himself began to hold matinées at his residence in the Cosel Palace, and Clara often performed for private gatherings with the royal orchestra's concert master. In 1850, Schumann hoped to become Wagner's successor as co-director, with Reissiger, of the royal orchestra, but he failed to secure the position. Thus he and Clara decamped to Düsseldorf where he became the director of the Municipal Orchestra. During his residence in Dresden, Schumann composed one-third of his total oeuvre.[177]

The Non-Revolutionary Theater

Attending Schumann's farewell party was Eduard Devrient. Devrient had arrived in Dresden in 1844 as director of the Royal Theater. He had been appointed to that position by a gentleman who is often overshadowed by the many famous personalities who were his appointees and associates: Baron Wolf von Lüttichau. He had earned the loyalty of King Friedrich August I when he accompanied him as a prisoner at the end of the Napoleonic Wars. In

1824, the king appointed him as general director for both the musical and the non-musical sections of the Royal Theater. He remained in that position for the next thirty-eight years. Many of those who worked with him credit his firmness and integrity in dealing with temperamental personalities and with tactful mediation between them and the king. It helped that he married a woman of culture and tact, Ida von Lüttichau, née von Knobelsdorff, an old noble family in Prussian service. It was Lüttichau who appointed both Wilhelmina Schroeder-Devrient and Richard Wagner to the musical department of the theater.[178]

It was also he who appointed Ludwig Tieck as dramaturg in 1825. Tieck loomed large in the Romantic movement of the first half of nineteenth-century Germany. By the time he took up residence in Dresden, he had published several long novels, short stories, fairy tales, plays, and translations of Shakespeare and Cervantes' *Don Quixote*. He was well-known in both France and England. After he settled in Dresden with his family on the Altmarkt, he began a series of dramatic readings that captivated an intimate circle of the city's intellectual world. Tieck was talented enough to give each character in the play or novel he was reading his or her own tone of voice and mannerisms.[179]

Even before Tieck took over as dramaturg, the Royal Theater, pleasing a variety of audiences, had managed a respectable roster of plays. When Carl von Voss visited in the early 1820s, he saw Kleist's *Prince von Homburg* and *Käthchen von Heilbronn*, Euripides *Medea*, Schiller's *Braut von Messina*, all within two months' time. He and his party also visited the theater at the Linckesches Bad, then under the Royal Theater's administration, to take in lighter fare, even one farce. These alternated with performances of Rossini's, Mozart's and Weber's operas, as well as others that have not stood the test of time.[180]

As dramaturg, Tieck helped to choose the dramas performed, and he rehearsed the actors to assure that they accurately interpreted the drama. During his tenure at the theater, he favored Shakespeare's plays, particularly those translated by his daughter, Dorothea, and by his friends, August Wilhelm Schlegel and Count Wolf von Baudissin. It was Tieck who inspired one of the first performances of Goethe's *Faust* upon the occasion of the great man's eightieth birthday. The sailing was not always smooth. Tieck's tastes were intellectually impeccable, but Dresden theater-goers wanted to be entertained more than uplifted. Eventually he left the choice of comedies to the theater's director and concentrated on suggesting more serious fare. In 1841, Tieck left Dresden for Berlin, where the Prussian king had offered him a position.[181]

Only in 1844 did Lüttichau settle on Eduard Devrient as theater director. Devrient belonged to a theatrical family that spanned three generations. He began his career as a singer and performed the role of Jesus in Mendelssohn's revival of Bach's *St. Matthew Passion.* Two years thereafter, a grave illness as well as an abuse of his vocal chords led to the loss of his singing voice, and Eduard became an actor at the Prussian Royal Theater. As actor, director and author, Devrient wanted to raise the standard of theater in Germany and favored, like Tieck, a natural style of declamation and gesturing. He also disliked the way that rulers and aristocrats disdained an equal association with their "servant" actors and agitated for an improvement in their social status.

A zealous diarist, he has given us a glimpse of the theatrical offerings of the 1840s. In 1844, he noted that June heat had hindered attendance at Lessing's *Nathan the Wise.* Molière's *Tartuffe* aroused only a lukewarm reception. For *Julius Ceasar,* he had to combine some scenes for lack of "personnel to meet the complete Shakespearean specifications." Sophocles' *Antigone* did not engage the audience's attention. Both in 1844 and 1845, Lüttichau wanted to remove scenes from productions that might anger or disturb the king and the court. These were references to the church, to popular disturbances, to insults of royalty and nobility. At the end of 1845, the theater's balance sheet revealed a deficit that caused Lüttichau to rearrange the program for the coming year, so as to make as much money as possible. Emil Devrient, who had played at the theater for thirteen years before his brother arrived, claimed that Dresden audiences did not appreciate "poetic masters", and he didn't want his brother to be "painted with Tieck's brush".[182]

In any event, Emil did not have to fear a revolution à la Tieck. In 1846, Eduard resigned his position as director of the Royal Theater because he and Emil did not share the same dramatic values. Eduard wanted to develop the theater as an ensemble, but Emil wanted to be the star of the show. In contrast to his brother, Emil also espoused the idealized approach to acting that stressed exaggerated declamation and gestures. A contemporary described the "great" Emil as the theater's "invisible" leader who had a great appeal for audiences in general and for "women" in particular. He also liked the light comedies that his brother Eduard disdained.

After resigning as director of the theater, Eduard did not leave Dresden but continued to act, to give dramatic readings, and to work on his *History of German Theatrical Art*. In June 1848, almost the entire Devrient family featured in a performance of Friedrich Schiller's *Wallenstein:* Eduard, Emil, their brother Karl, and Karl's son, Fritz. Later, Eduard became director of the new state theater in Karlsruhe, and Emil did not retire from the Dresden stage for another twenty-two years.[183]

Revolution Again

The appointments of Wagner and Devrient exhibited a modestly liberal approach to culture on the part of the king and court, but during the 1840s two different trends emerged. In the Saxon Diet were conservatives who advocated press censorship, a ban on political organizations and a cautious approach to reform that caused the more progressive von Lindenau to resign as Saxon minister in 1842. Steering in the other direction was a simmering desire on the part of Dresdners—reflecting currents both in Saxony and Germany—for more control over civic affairs. A number of middle-class circles promoted the ideals of the 1830 revolution. These met in coffee houses on the Brühl Terrace or in private homes. A particularly famous group that included Semper and Wagner met at Engel's Restaurant on the Postplatz. Wagner even called for a bourgeois-democratic orchestra rather than a royal one. In 1840, a Workers' Society was founded. The reformist Gymnastic Society established itself in 1844. There followed, in 1845, a German-Catholic Club working for a church that was not subservient to the pope in Rome.[184]

Material tribulations of the last half of the decade intensified the mood for change. In 1845, the Elbe at Dresden flooded so strongly that the section of bridge supporting the century-old crucifix washed away. A pontoon bridge over the Elbe and a ferry service temporarily linked the two halves of the city. The floods not only inundated urban dwellers, they washed out the newly planted fields abutting the river in rural Saxony. The harvest of 1846 was poor and contributed to shortages of grain and potatoes that caused staple prices to rise so strongly for the next two years that the government distributed grain from army reserves. Philanthropic societies organized poor relief throughout the city. Gustav Nieritz, then teaching at a school for poor children, remembered that his pupils' bread became blacker and blacker, and he found fewer and fewer buttered slices left behind in the school desks.[185]

Into this mix of hardship and desire for change came the news of the French revolution in February 1848. It did not take long for calls for reform to be heard in Dresden and other Saxon cities. Democrats gathered at the Hotel de Pologne where they drew up a petition demanding the dismissal of the state's conservative government, a guarantee of civil rights and new elections to the Diet by universal manhood suffrage. King Friedrich August II reacted swiftly. Press censorship ended on March 9, and on 13 March 1848, he dismissed the conservative state ministry under Baron Julius von Könneritz and installed the liberal Karl Hermann Braun as leading minister.[186]

Already on March 22, the city celebrated the cause of German unity and Saxon constitutionalism with parades, illuminations, and a show of revolutionary colors—black, red, gold—next to the green and white of Saxony. Even the politically moderate Carus family hurriedly stitched together one of the new flags to wave in the evening celebrations. People began to wear black, red and gold cockades on their hats. These national colors expressed the popular desire to end the loose confederation of states that had replaced the old empire. Germans now wanted the tighter union exemplified by Great Britain and France.[187]

Though united in support of a tight German federation, the revolutionary forces divided into two factions. One large group followed the lead of the Leipzig democrats into the Patriotic Union (*Vaterlandsverein*). By the end of April 1848, 1000 Dresdners had joined as members. They included journeymen, day laborers, soldiers as well as lawyers, teachers, doctors, and radical city assemblymen. Among them was Hermann Köchly, a teacher at the Kreuzschule and tutor to the children of the king's brother, Prince Johann, and August Röckel, an assistant director of the court orchestra. Some of these men were republicans, and their chief goals were a democratic suffrage and a citizens' militia.[188]

Moderates from the city's assembly of representatives founded the German Union (*Bürgerverein*). Government officials, conservative intellectuals, army officers and master craftsmen were attracted to this group. It wanted reform but preferred to remain within a constitutional monarchy. Eduard Devrient joined this Union and became a member of its executive committee. In May, indirect elections sent two moderates from the Dresden region to the revolutionary all-German Frankfurt Assembly; Friedrich Hensel, a justice of the peace from Kamenz represented the Neustadt and Professor Franz Wigard, the Altstadt. Shortly after these elections, the Saxon Diet convened in Dresden to devise a new state constitution and electoral law. Its deliberations proceeded parallel to those in Frankfurt where delegates wrestled with devising a national constitution.[189]

These thrusts toward reform ended in autumn, when conservative royal authority was restored in the leading states of Austria and Prussia in October and November 1848. When the reactionary government in Austria executed Robert Blum in Vienna, it caused great consternation within the ranks of Dresden democrats. As a liberal democrat, Blum was a popular figure all over Germany. He resided in Leipzig with his family where he made a living as a book seller; he also functioned as a journalist and commentator. A member of Leipzig's city assembly, it was Blum who inspired the establishment of Patriotic Unions in Saxon cities.

In May 1848, Leipzig sent him as a regular member to the Frankfurt Assembly seeking to construct a strong, liberal-democratic Germany. In Frankfurt, he associated with the moderate left. When, in the fall, a working-class rebellion against resurgent conservatism broke out in Vienna, he traveled to the city to lend moral support to the workers. He stayed as a rebel commander during the firefights of the last week of October. Despite his immunity as a member of the Frankfurt Assembly and the intervention of the Saxon government on his behalf, the Austrians executed him on November 9.[190]

Nine days later, the Dresden Patriotic Union organized a giant memorial service in the Frauenkirche. Church bells rang throughout the city. A long procession that included members of the Communal Guard wended its way from the Altmarkt to the Neumarkt. The crowd was so large that only one-third could fit into a church that was filled to bursting. The Saxon artillery supplied a chorus for the service. Three members of the state government were in attendance, and a pastor and a deacon read the obituary and eulogy. Eduard Devrient sat with Gottfried Semper, but he noted in his diary that no one else from the German Union was present, and there were not many people from the "educated" classes. There was evidence of mounting bitterness against repressive aristocracy and princes. At the end of the service, the congregation sang two verses of "A Mighty Fortress is our God".[191]

During the uprisings of 1848 in the larger German cities of Vienna and Berlin, Dresden had been comparatively calm. The citizens' Communal Guard had little difficulty in quelling a potential riot in mid-March. The Diet's investigation of workers' conditions had been interrupted by calls for violence, and throughout the spring, summer and fall there had been fifteen to twenty raids by artisans on factories. In general, however, the king maintained a good relationship with the Communal Guard and with the Saxon assembly. Celebrations of the Saxon constitution of 1830 were held as usual in the fall. Carl Carus remembered that Dresden life proceeded as usual. People went to work, to the theater, to art exhibitions and rejoiced in every beautiful summer day.[192]

In July 1848, the Patriotic Union had protested the liberal government's withdrawal of a draft electoral law and had submitted a petition for the introduction of democratic government. But only after it was clear that the revolution had failed both in Vienna and Berlin, was there evidence of gathering unrest. The execution of Blum intensified the resentment of the radicals. By this time, refugees from Vienna had filtered into Dresden, among them the Russian anarchist socialist, Michael Bakunin, whose stance as a revolutionary was already well-known. Political clubs began to collect weapons just in case they needed them, and the Gymnastic Society openly solicited monetary contributions for the purchase of guns.[193]

In this atmosphere, Dresdners, along with other Saxons, went to the polls to elect a legislature at the beginning of December 1848. Citizens, many of whom voted for the first time, returned a democratic majority. Soon after this new, radical legislature convened in mid-January 1849, its majority demanded an immediate guarantee of civil liberties. The king, however, refused to honor this demand until other German states had done the same, and the ministry agreed with him. Rather than remain in office with a truculent legislature, the ministry decided to resign. In its place, the king appointed a cabinet of civil servants under Gustav Friedrich Held. This group took office just as the National Assembly completed its deliberations in Frankfurt.[194]

At the beginning of April 1849, the Frankfurt representatives turned to Prussia's King Friedrich William IV and asked him to be emperor of a tightly organized, democratic Germany. Initially the king dithered by claiming that only ruling princes could determine the head of a unified state. When twenty-eight German states, yielding to popular pressure, subsequently accepted the Frankfurt Constitution, Friedrich William refused to be emperor unless the National Assembly made changes. This, it refused to do.[195]

During this period of waiting, the Saxon legislature pressured both the ministry and the king to join the twenty-eight. It refused to approve the state budget until Saxony accepted the Frankfurt Constitution. Assemblymen and king had come to a stand-off. At the end of April, on the day after the Prussian king definitely rejected the Frankfurt Constitution, King Friedrich August II dissolved the Saxon legislature. In the wake of the dissolution and the public protests that followed, three members of the Held cabinet resigned, leaving only the most conservative members in office.

In the first three days of May, there were numerous attempts to persuade the king to accept the Frankfurt Constitution—by both houses of the legislature, by the moderate German Union, by the Dresden city council and assembly, by the Communal Guard. For all of them, the king had the same answer: Acceptance of the Frankfurt Constitution was not in the best interests of Saxony. During the first days of May, Dresden's streets filled with people, and their mood was surly. Carus reported that coaches belonging to aristocrats could hardly drive through the streets without being attacked or obstructed.[196]

On May 3, Hermann Schöne, then a twelve-year-old boy and later a popular actor, was moving among the groups of grown-ups thronging the streets, trying to hear as much of the conversation as possible. Wall posters announced the various deputations to the king and warned of a military intervention by Prussia. Already there was talk of building barricades against the Prussian "foreigners". Suddenly, an older gentleman from his neighborhood grabbed Schöne by the shoulder and told him to go home to midday dinner. On his way home, he thought it was strange that his neighbors from the Friedrichstadt were making their way across the Weisseritz into the Altstadt; usually these suburban residents stayed at home. After dinner, his mother cautioned him to play close to the house. In mid-afternoon, he and his mates heard a cannon fired in the city. The residents of the Friedrichstadt rushed excitedly into the street, and owners of weapons headed for the inner city.[197]

A throng had stormed the royal armory, now the Albertinum, demanding weapons. In repelling the stone-throwing crowd, an artillerist had fired a cannon and killed twenty people. At 5:30 p.m., a journeyman began to sound the tocsin from the Frauenkirche. At the royal palace, an angry mob threw cobblestones at the palace windows. Barricades appeared before nightfall, and drain covers in the middle of streets were removed to obstruct a maneuvering military. At the Dresden Rathaus, a provisional government was declared. During the night of May 3–4, shots and drum beats punctuated the nocturnal calm.[198]

Very early in the morning of May 4, the king, his wife, his ministers and a small contingent of the court crossed the bridge to the Neustadt and embarked on a ship that carried them south to the Königstein. They left the city secure in the knowledge that Prussian troops were on their way to aid the Saxon military in quelling the rebellion. The king's departure only emboldened the revolutionaries. They asked the Saxon commandant for a 24-hour ceasefire, which was granted and allowed both sides to consolidate their positions: the supporters of the Frankfurt Constitution in the Altstadt, with a provisional, revolutionary government in city hall; the royal military in the Neustadt, the palace, the armory, and the Zwinger.[199]

On May 5, dawn broke on a beautiful spring day, with trees in full bloom. After the truce ended in the morning, the Saxon Lieutenant General von Schirnding opened fire from the Zwinger. For the next four days of fighting, people remembered the incessant ringing of the tocsin from the churches of the inner city, raising a din that could be heard far into the Dresden suburbs. Against the well-armed soldiers, the rebels fought back with any weapons they had been able to gather and by lighting small fires. Barricaded streets sought to halt the advancing troops.

Even though the Communal Guard had been asked to defend the revolutionaries, many simply hid out at home, as did the Carus boys, or, in Eduard Devrient's case, they banded together to protect their own neighborhoods against the revolutionary "mob". The residents of the Friedrichstadt, the locus of revolutionary fervor, also sought to protect their quarters against military incursions. Already on the first day of fighting, the revolutionaries lost significant ground as the Saxon and Prussian military took the Brühl Palace on the Terrace, the treasury building, the Frauenkirche and the Zwinger earthworks.[200]

In their desperation, the revolutionaries followed the suggestion of the anarchist, Michael Bakunin, to set fire, on May 6, to the opera house on the southeast corner of the Zwinger—the one built by Pöppelmann for the marriage of August the Strong's son to an Austrian archduchess. The blaze destroyed both the theater and the Zwinger's Glockenspiel Pavilion. Smoke rose over the city and could be seen across the Elbe by Nieritz in the Antonstadt and by Carus in the eastern suburbs. Carus also heard the salvos that cleared the Neumarkt on this cloudy, rainy Sunday.[201]

By May 7, the noose tightened round the revolutionaries. Saxon and Prussian troops not only spread out from the Neumarkt to the Altstadt, breaking through house walls to circumvent the barricades, they also took both the Sophienkirche close to the palace and a large house south of the Zwinger that provided an advantageous eyrie for sharpshooters. For their part, revolutionaries broke through house walls to carve out paths for themselves from the Friedrichstadt to the Altstadt.

Young Hermann Schöne may have used this route to attain the Postplatz, where he went to view the most famous of the barricades, the Angel, (Engel) engineered by Gottfried Semper, which reached as high as the surrounding houses' second stories. Windows were stuffed with stone and mattresses into which were carved small slits through which to shoot the enemy. While there, he observed reapers, armed with their scythes, who had come from rural areas to support the revolutionary Dresdners. Among them he spied his German teacher, who, he was afraid, might call on him for help. He quickly strode home to avoid getting sucked into the fight.[202]

As the fighting intensified, Eduard Devrient and his family first took refuge in their cellar with mattresses stuffed against the windows to keep out stray bullets, but in the late evening of May 8, they decided to leave the city by train and seek safety in neighboring Pirna. The train conductor described his city as overflowing, and he offered to lodge the Devrients in his living room. That night they slept on beds laid atop straw.[203]

Back in Dresden, the revolt's leaders began to desert the rank and file and to make their way out of the city, including Bakunin, Wagner and Semper. By 10 a.m. on May 9, the rebellion had been fully quelled. When Devrient returned from Pirna, he found Prussian troops at the Dresden station and white sheets hanging from the gallery of the Kreuzkirche. He also seemed surprised to find that his house had not been plundered during the retreat.[204]

The inner city, on the other hand, was ravaged: plots blackened by fire, buildings punctured with thousands of bullet holes, structures damaged by cannon balls, half-destroyed barricades, streets with missing cobblestones. Stretcher bearers carried the wounded through the lanes. The Painting Gallery's director, Julius Schnorr von Carolsfeld, found eighty-three holes in the paintings of the three rooms of the Stable that faced the Neumarkt. Soldiers had occupied the gallery to flush out the revolutionaries in the square.[205]

By this time, the "white terror" of the military had already begun. Many prisoners were brutally mistreated. One of the Prussian generals admitted that fifty captured revolutionaries were dumped into the Elbe from the Augustus Bridge and shot when they tried to swim to safety. In the converted Frauenkirche, many prisoners were beaten, and at least one confused soul was bludgeoned to death. Marauding soldiers entered peaceful streets and homes and shot the inhabitants dead. One group of unarmed men was thrown out of a fourth story window so forcefully that they bounced off the walls of houses across the narrow lane.[206]

The victorious government declared martial law, forbade the formation of political clubs, and reintroduced press censorship. The king did not return to Dresden until July 5, and Prussian troops stayed in the city, quartered on the population, until July 18. Over 800 people were detained until August 1849. Of these, 236 were sentenced to long prison terms; death sentences were eventually commuted to life in prison. Warrants were issued for the arrest of some of the escaped revolutionaries such as Wagner and Semper. Until the 1860s, neither one of these men could return to Germany without risking detention. Bakunin was caught and deported to Russia. The revolution's denouement was an outbreak of cholera, particularly in the restaurants and hotels of the city, and the government canceled the annual summer shooting match with its attendant carnival to prevent the epidemic's spread.[207]

How can we explain the outbreak of revolution in Dresden in May 1849, several months after the defeat of revolution in Prussia and most of Germany. The evidence suggests that democratic ideals were widespread throughout the population, though moderates held sway during the elections to the Frankfurt Assembly. In December, the elections to the Saxon legislature, where universal manhood suffrage determined the outcome, returned a majority of radical representatives. Given its conciliatory behavior through 1848 and even into the opening months of 1849, it seems that the Saxon Royal House and government initially sought to calm the situation but eventually failed.

Analyses of the social backgrounds of the detained revolutionaries after May 9 also suggest that the economic downturn of the 1840s and the loss of jobs and social status accompanying the early stages of Saxon industrialization had caused widespread dissatisfaction. Artists and intellectuals like Wagner had their own complaints with what they considered to be a rigid adherence to the status quo.

Even a man as realistic as Eduard Devrient resented the treatment he received from the status-conscious Saxon court and aristocrats. After the revolution, he placed flowers on a mass grave of revolutionaries in the city's western suburbs. Carl Carus sent food and drink to the revolutionaries holed up in the orphanage close to his home. Gustav Nieritz, who did not sympathize with the revolutionaries, thought that the rebellion resulted from a collapse of trust in the economy and in the government.[208]

What seems to have lit the torch of rebellion was the rumor that the king had requested the help of Prussian troops to compensate for the fact that a large contingent of the Saxon army had left Saxony at the end of March to fight with the Prussians against the Danes in Schleswig-Holstein. Nieritz thought that the government could have brought the situation under control, after the fatalities at the armory, if it had made the effort to maintain order and stop the building of barricades on the evening of May 3. Semper's biographer blames King Friedrich August II for leaving the city on March 4, an act that closed the door, he says, on any hope for negotiations between the king and the revolutionaries.[209] Whatever the case, the failed revolution of 1848 marked a turning point for Dresden, for Saxony and the rest of Germany. It meant that the German states would not unify under a liberal-democratic constitution but under a more authoritarian regime.

VII. Industrial Dresden

In the years after 1849, Dresden lost its pre-revolutionary luster as a leading center of the arts. While some of its revolutionary artists were forced to flee, others left because of lost opportunities. The city now transformed itself into a major industrial hub. As before, the Elbe remained an important commercial corridor, and the elimination, in 1861, of most tolls on the river enhanced the city's position as a port.[210]

Other government intervention helped the city to prosper. Already in 1851, the Marienbrücke (Queen Mary Bridge), downstream from the Augustus Bridge, began to carry rail freight, wagons, and pedestrians across the Elbe. Between the 1860s and 1890s, the railroad's freight depot and marshaling yards were developed in the Friedrichstadt, where they remain to the present day. This infrastructural expansion helped to make Dresden an important entrepôt for goods destined for northern and eastern Europe.[211]

In 1861, the Saxon Industrial Code eliminated the old guild regulations. This measure set the scene for a more competitive economy. It encouraged labor to move out of small artisanal shops and into larger enterprises. It also lifted the restrictions hindering non-Dresdners from locating businesses within the city and its suburbs. Furthermore, the highly skilled labor force, inherited from the old artisanal regime, meant that Dresden was well placed to attract the technologically advanced industries of the day. Toward the end of the 1860s, changes to the Saxon electoral law encouraged the representatives of business and industry to run for political office and to foster an entrepreneurial climate. In the two decades following the mid-century revolution, Dresden's population almost doubled. Its emerging businesses testify to the diversity of the city's industrial economy.[212]

An Industrial Hub

Even before 1848, the bituminous coalfields to the south of the city helped to develop heavy industry in the region. Coal began to be mined south of the city in the Plauen basin already in the sixteenth century. During and after the Napoleonic Wars, the increasing scarcity of wood promoted coal as an alternative fuel. The Saxon government bought up mines in the area, and private companies received government subsidies. The use of the steam engine to pump water from the mines increased their viability.

The most entrepreneurial of the private mine owners was Carl Friedrich August Krebss, Baron Dathe von Burghk, who acquired the mines of the Burgker estate in 1819. He then purchased an iron hammer mill on the Weisseritz and later established furnaces for melting iron and casting steel. To make use of these products, he bought a machine tool factory as well. Little more than a decade after the mid-century revolution, the mines of the Plauen Valley employed over 4000 workers and produced almost 500,000 tons of coal. They continued to be worked until the 1930s, when they closed due to decreasing yields.[213]

Related to the activity of the Plauen mines was the firm of Friedrich Siemens Industrial Furnace Construction. Friedrich, a brother of the famous Werner, had developed, during his sojourn in England, the Siemens-Martin open-hearth process for making steel. When he moved back to Germany, he took the process with him to Dresden, where, in the 1850s, he established a firm for making Siemens-Martin furnaces. He eventually acquired the glass bottling plant established by his brother Hans in the neighboring village of Löbtau. At one point, the Siemens Glass Works produced two million bottles a month. This enterprise continued operations under various guises, into the twentieth century.[214]

More typical of Dresden were the light industries that built on historic activities and introduced new ones. Destined to become an important element in Dresden's industrialization was the Plauen Royal Mill, dating back to the late Middle Ages, which was leased to Gottlieb Traugott Bienert in 1852. Bienert came from a long line of millers and maintained a successful bakery in Dresden-Neustadt. Even though only a leaseholder, Bienert's modernization of the decrepit Royal Mill in Plauen exemplified his generation of entrepreneurs. As he expanded the mill, he invested in the most modern technology. He was not afraid to risk his own and his family's monies in building up the firm. Eventually this gamble paid off when he was able to buy the mill outright from the Saxon state in 1872. At the end of the nineteenth century, the Bienert family parlayed the firm's success into constructing a large harbor on the Elbe, where imported grain could be shipped via rail directly to the Plauen works.[215]

One innovative sector was landscaping. Encouraged by the building boom of the first half of the century, a number of nurseries, following the tradition of the court landscaper, established themselves in the city. Exemplary in this commercial branch was the Seidel family, whose business activities eventually spanned a period of almost 150 years. After humble beginnings at the end of the Napoleonic Wars, the firm moved in 1860 to sixteen and one-half acres in Striesen, where Traugott Seidel specialized in camellias, rhododendrons and azaleas. He helped to organize the first International Garden Show, held in Dresden in 1887. By that time, a well-established landscaping school, supported by the Saxon government, was attracting over 100 students annually. By the end of the nineteenth century, the city sheltered more than 300 nurseries, making it a center for landscaping in Germany and in Europe.[216]

As Traugott Seidel expanded his landscaping firm, Clemens Müller founded the first sewing-machine factory in Europe. By 1867, his firm produced 11,000 machines annually. During the next year, a second firm joined Müller's. Both factories adopted the technology used by I.M. Singer in the United States. Even though the numbers of machines sold by firms in other German cities eventually eclipsed those of Dresden, the city long remained a center of sewing machine manufacture. In the late nineteenth century, both firms diversified into making typewriters.[217]

One stop frequented by contemporary tourists to Dresden is Pfund's Dairy in the Neustadt. There the visitor can admire the decorative tiles of Villeroy and Boch. This ceramics firm established a Dresden affiliate soon after mid-century in order to better supply the markets of northern and eastern Europe. It eventually branched out into producing earthenware tiles and supplying advice about interior decoration to retail shops like Pfund's. The dairy has provided the model for the contemporary café at the Villeroy and Boch museum at Mettlach (Saarland).[218]

Anyone traveling back and forth on trams # 6 and 11 between the Neustadt and the Altstadt is struck, soon after crossing the Elbe, by an edifice completely foreign to the inner city's Baroque monuments: the Yenidze. It once belonged to the cigarette firm of Carl Hugo Zeitz and is modeled on the Egyptian Mamelukes' mosques in Cairo. Dresden had long been involved in the distribution of Balkan tobacco. It was thus a natural location for the Compagnie LaFerme when it moved its cigarette factory from St. Petersburg in 1862. This foundation spawned others. By the late nineteenth century, twenty-seven Dresden firms supplied almost a third of the cigarettes smoked in Germany. Some of these companies were small, but others became large enough to employ 4000 workers. Cigarette making gave rise to the manufacture of a host of associated products: cigarette-making machines, cigarette paper and cartons, cigarette advertising. The Yenidze is no longer a working factory and has been renovated into offices; but it remains a comforting landmark for residents and a striking attraction for visitors.[219]

Integration into United Germany

The city's prosperity not only depended on the introduction of new industries and technologies, but also on political developments within the wider German community. Since the 1830s, Saxony had participated in the all-German customs union that facilitated trade and transportation throughout Germany and, wittingly or unwittingly, accepted Prussian economic leadership in Germany. As Prussia determined to unify Germany under its political leadership and exclude its Austrian rival from any German union, the Saxon government attempted to salvage one last shred of its sovereignty.

As deteriorating Austro-Prussian relations led to war between the two in summer 1866, Saxony allied with Austria. In response, Prussian troops crossed the Saxon border on June 18, occupied the state and appointed a Prussian governor. During this occupation, Prussian authorities requisitioned horses, wagons and medical supplies. They dismissed Dresden's police chief, imported Prussian laborers to build earthworks south of the city, and cut trees in the Great Garden. Prussian troops did not leave Dresden until the beginning of July 1867. Once victorious in the Seven Weeks' War, they threatened to swallow up Saxony. Only the insistence of the Austrian ruler saved the Saxon state. Nevertheless, it was forced to join the newly formed, Prussian-dominated North German Confederation, its independence severely curtailed. Prussian behavior so alienated the populace that Saxon proponents of a unified Germany had a hard time generating enthusiasm for the national cause.[220]

Only during the war of unification against the French in 1870–71 did Saxons warm up to the unity of the new German Empire. When the Saxon army returned victorious from the campaign against the French in July 1871, Dresden was decorated with flowers, flags, and tapestries. As troops lined up along the route from the Great Garden to the Bohemian Station (now the Main Rail Station), young girls bedecked them and their guns with laurel wreaths.

Bells pealed at noon as the parade down the Prager Strasse honored the troops and their leader, Crown Prince Albert. After pausing at the Neumarkt to hear a victory poem and gather more laurel wreaths, the soldiers marched across the Augustus Bridge to pass review on the Bautzenerplatz (now Albertplatz) in front of King Johann and the royal family gathered on a tribune. In the afternoon, the troops banqueted, at city expense, on the Elbe meadows beneath the Waldschlösschen brewery.[221]

In the years after German unification, Dresden became more nationalistic and more militarized. As the second largest garrison city in Germany, the military was a constant presence, both economically and socially. The King, like the German emperor and other imperial officials, wore a military uniform to functions that had a purely civilian character. Ernst Venus, then a young civil servant and later administrative director of Dresden county, called his friends' attention to the royal penchant for uniforms and how that differed from the Hessian duke's civilian attire. His friends simply shrugged.[222]

Dresdners, like other Germans, religiously celebrated Sedan Day, the date of the decisive victory over the French in 1870. In the morning, they attended church services and concerts. During the afternoon, gymnastic societies and glee clubs held forth on the Elbe meadows. In 1898, an Association for Fatherland Games took over the formal organization of these activities. Added to the games were speeches, torchlight parades and processions of veterans' organizations.[223]

National identities did not completely supplant regional ones. In 1889, the Wettins celebrated their 800th year as rulers of Saxon territory. Among other festivities, they staged a parade through Dresden, advertising the event as a "Spectacle of the Multi-faceted Cultural and Material Achievements" of their subjects. They could no longer expect Dresdners or Saxons merely to revere them as elevated personages; cooperation between royals and citizenry had become the order of the day.[224]

The wealth of the city and of the kingdom depended on the efforts of the Saxons gathered in the streets to view the parade. Dresden was now a major industrial center. In 1875, there were 1100 factories in the metropolitan region employing a total of 25,000 workers. Yet most businesses remained small or medium-sized. One-third were owned by craftsmen working alone. Another third employed five or fewer workers. This was a diversified economy that paved the way for the industrial success of the late nineteenth century.[225]

Cameras

Already in 1839, Friedrich Wilhelm and Carl Heinrich Enzmann founded the first German camera company in Dresden. Their most significant contribution to the industry was the diminution of photographic plates that enabled them to reduce the size of their cameras. But the time had not yet come for "everyman" to buy a camera, and the Enzmanns soon closed their shop. A resumption of camera making in Dresden had to await the arrival in 1887 of Richard Hüttig who moved from Berlin in order to escape its stiff competition. That move proved propitious not only for him but for Dresden. Hüttig's firm developed and distributed some of the first German-made, single-lens reflex cameras.

The most successful camera maker in the city, at least for a few decades, opened for business in 1889: Heinrich Ernemann. Ernemann was primarily a salesman who relied on his partner, Wilhelm Matthias, for expertise in camera building. For the next thirty-seven years, the Ernemann Works flourished. It made cameras for the common man and also produced movie cameras and projectors. Together with Hermann Krone, a well-known photographer, Ernemann succeeded in making photography a major subject at the Technical Institute. By the first decade of the twentieth century, Ernemann was the largest German producer of photographic, cinematic and optical equipment. The old Ernemann Works is still one of the most impressive buildings in the city and now houses the Dresden Technical Collections.

As a center of the photographic industry, Dresden's camera manufacturers constituted a crowd. When the world-wide recession occurred at the beginning of the twentieth century, Hüttig, particularly, felt the slump. In order to make itself more competitive on the world market, his company merged with the camera branch of Carl Zeiss (Jena) and camera firm Dr. Krügener (Frankfurt am Main) to become the International Camera Corporation (ICA). In addition to cameras and their accessories, the ICA also produced slide and movie projectors. On the eve of World War I, the ICA was the largest photographic firm in Europe.[226]

Machinery

A camera is a type of machine, and in the realm of machine makers, Dresden was an important player on the German scene. In mid-century, Carl Friedrich Kühnscherf opened a locksmith shop in the Wilsdruffer Gasse, specializing in wrought-iron gates, fences and other items. After German unification in 1871, the firm branched out into elevators. One of its better-known products required cooperation with a foundry established by the court blacksmiths in 1874. The founders, Dietrich Kelle and Adolf Hildebrandt, began to build bridges, machines and steel edifices. A particular specialty was stage machinery. At the Paris Exposition of 1889, Kelle and Hildebrandt exhibited several of their products including a wrought-iron gallery now attached to Hildebrandt's former villa in Radebeul and listed on Germany's historic register. The firm also built a tower for one of Kühnscherf's elevators that still operates in Bad Schandau, a town south of Dresden close to the Czech border. This elevator shaft supplied the model for the steel tower featured in the 2014 film, "The Grand Budapest Hotel".[227]

As improvements in technology altered the structures of German and European industry, Dresden's entrepreneurs kept pace. In 1888, Oskar Kummer established a factory for making electric motors. Six years later, Kummer employed 2000 workers and had set up branches all over Germany. This new technology led to the city's first municipal generating plant in 1895 and to its first communal heating plant in 1900. Because it was located behind the Semper Opera, the latter was decked out in neo-Baroque architecture. These developments did not help Kummer. He expanded too quickly into projects that were not profitable, and in 1901 he went bankrupt.

In 1903, Kummer's firm re-established itself under new ownership and became one of Dresden's most successful businesses. The Saxon Works (Sachsenwerke) made transformers, circuits, motors and generators. It not only took advantage of the new technology's possibilities, it helped to expand the use of electricity throughout Germany. Eventually the Saxon Works branched out into electronic consumer goods.[228]

It was not the only Dresden industry associated with the consumption of articles in daily use. Already in the 1870s, Carl Eschebach, a sheet-metal worker, began to make household goods. As Dresden's industry attracted more and more workers from other German regions. Eschebach supplied them with iceboxes, oven shields, bathtubs, toilets and sinks. Already in the 1880s, the firm produced enamel tableware and medical supplies. Eschebach's products were sold all over Europe, and by 1900, he was one of the richest men in the city. His stately villa on Albertplatz, now the headquarters of the Dresdner Volksbank, attests to his wealth. When Eschebach died in 1905, his firm employed 2000 workers. These continued to manufacture household goods right up until the firm, no longer operating in his name, closed in 2004.[229]

As the German standard of living improved, businesses that satisfied expanding consumer tastes multiplied. In 1881, Otto Weber moved his factory from Berlin to make pressed cakes of Chinese tea and roasted figs, then used as a coffee substitute, in the town of Radebeul, one of Dresden's economic satellites. Weber sold large amounts of tea to the German army and developed a thriving export business for his coffee extracts. A related firm, Seelig and Hille, set itself up in 1882 in a shop selling tea and pots from China and Japan. Six years later, this firm became the Theekanne, a brand that continues to exist today. Further ventures into foodstuffs were malt and waffles. To meet the expansion of industry, bureaucracy and literacy, an ink and paint firm established itself in another of the city's satellite villages.

The boom of the late nineteenth century also stimulated the tourist industry, now an important component of Dresden's economy. Between 1899 and 1909, the number of visitors to the city increased from 321,428 to 433,308, and these sums do not include day tourists who never registered in an hotel. Many tourists purchased the picture post cards of Stengel and Company, which also printed packaging labels for customers as close as Germany and Austria and as far afield as the United States.[230]

Shopping

The products of these various establishments found their way into Dresden's expanding retail sector. Even before the city's walls had been completely razed, a small indoor market arose on Antonsplatz, a space made available by the demolition of the wall. In the 1850s, a department store bearing the French name, *Au petit Bazar*, appeared on the Neumarkt.[231]

The working-class citizens of Dresden supplemented these retail opportunities with their own grocery cooperatives. The first appeared in 1882 in the suburb of Pieschen. This former village had grown into a full-blown industrial district where factories offered employment to hundreds of workers. Pieschen's cooperative soon joined other local groups to serve all of metropolitan Dresden. As the cooperative movement spread throughout Germany, Dresdners were prominent in its leadership. A person can still shop the cooperative Konsum's grocery stores scattered throughout the city.[232]

One can also encounter, either in a Konsum store or local drugstore, an Odol mouthwash. This product gained world-wide recognition in the period before World War I and continues to be a popular German product. The entrepreneur behind this success was Karl August Lingner. Born in Magdeburg, he apprenticed himself as a salesman and, after two years in Paris, he settled in Dresden in 1885. At first, he worked for the Dresdner Bicycle and Sewing Machine Factory and distinguished himself by writing short, catchy ads. After a short stint selling notions, Lingner bought a recipe for mouth wash and patented the rinse that he called Odol.

On his way to establishing his brand, Lingner first had to convince the German authorities that his mouthwash could be sold in the new *Drogerien* springing up in growing cities. Drogerien can be translated as drug stores, but they sell no prescription medicines. Instead, they concentrate on products for body care and for cleaning houses and offices. Once Lingner secured the right to sell Odol in drug stores and combined it with a clever advertising campaign, he was well on his way to making Odol a household word and his fortune a large one. The Italian composer Giacomo Puccini, who visited Lingner in Dresden, even wrote an "An Ode to Odol". It didn't hurt that Lingner launched his new product just as the science of bacteria and viruses seized the popular imagination and made necessities out of cleaning products of all kinds. In addition to Odol, the Lingner works developed a disinfecting machine and a sterilizing soap.

Karl August used his fortune to improve the city. He joined with associates to open, in 1898, the first infant clinic in the world and helped to reduce infant mortality in Dresden. Two years later, he founded an Institute for Dental Hygiene. In 1911, he organized the first International Hygiene Exhibition in Dresden and marked the proceeds for the construction of a National Hygiene Museum. Dresdners can still enjoy his legacy by visiting the museum. When

Lingner died of cancer in 1916, a comparatively young, unmarried and childless man, he left his money to philanthropic societies in Dresden. Odol is now made and sold by an affiliate of the large pharmaceutical outfit of Glaxo/Smith/Kline.[233]

Dresden Expands

On the eve of World War I, Dresden was the fifth largest city in Germany, and its metropolis covered more than 100 square miles. Within this conglomeration small businesses, spread out over fifty different economic sectors, continued to dominate. Even though the city seemed still to grow into its landscape, the transition from small city to metropolis had not been easy.[234]

As we have seen, in the early nineteenth century, the Saxon state, prodded by the monarchy, took steps to assure that Dresden retained its residential character even as it industrialized and expanded. The building ordinances and decrees of the 1820s and 1830s were designed to avoid planning mistakes. There was a concerted effort to preserve the panorama of the city as seen from the open spaces along the banks of the Elbe.

To the south of the city center, a large number of villas dotted the periphery of the Great Garden. The village of Blasewitz, to the east, also hosted a number of urban villas. Across the river, in the village of Loschwitz, an elegant neighborhood emerged. Nevertheless, in both the city assembly and the Saxon legislature, industrialists and land speculators applied intense pressure to provide for denser, more profitable development.

Although there was, after 1826, a construction ban for the area of the Johannstadt, one-third of a mile from the old eastern city wall, it left out the Blumenstrasse, a street that ran parallel to the river and had traditionally harbored industrial activities. As a result, the Saxon state's building authority designated it as an industrial zone in 1853 against the wishes of the Dresden city government. For the next several decades, a tug of war occurred between those who favored industrial development along the Blumenstrasse and those who insisted that the district conform to the city's residential character. In the last part of the nineteenth century, the area became a factory district, and businesses expanded into the courtyards and second floors of the existing buildings.

Only on the eve of World War I did the area revert to residential structures. As technology forced businesses to grow larger, spaces in the Johannstadt were no longer suitable for industrial activities, and well-paid, skilled workers appropriated the buildings for their dwellings. There were even some upper middle-class families who built villas on vacant lots. The city also acquired ownership of the Elbe's banks, where it created a large recreational area.[235]

There were other areas where industry found it convenient to locate. On the right bank of the Elbe, the Leipzigerstrasse was favored because of its proximity to the Neustädter rail station. In his autobiography, the satirist Erich Kästner described how his uncles, whose business was horse trading, marched their newly-purchased horses from the station to stables in the nearby Antonstadt where there was a mixture of industry, residences and open spaces.

Along the Weisseritz, long the site of industry, the Albert rail line from the Elbe to the neighboring town of Tharandt, laid down in the 1850s to take coal from the Plauen Valley to Dresden, attracted new factories. Cement, glass, chemical and machine building firms established there, and it became a significant industrialized zone. In this case again, the Saxon state overrode the objections of city government. This old industrial neighborhood became the most unhealthy one in the city.[236]

As economic growth attracted more people to the city, there was increasing pressure on the housing stock. Already at the end of the 1860s, residential building lots, previously designated for single-family dwellings, switched to the denser construction of apartment houses. This happened in parts of the South Suburb (Südvorstadt), in the Johannstadt, and in the Antonstadt on the right bank of the Elbe. At the end of the nineteenth century, the Saxon state developed the huge army garrison called the Albertstadt. This area, adjacent to the Neustadt, stretched from north of the Neustädter Station to the Waldschlösschen and contained an arsenal, drill fields, rifle ranges, horse stables for the cavalry, an industrial park, barracks for the recruits and officers' quarters. It was a densely packed area, and Dresdners dubbed it "Kasernopolis (barracks' city)".[237]

As the population of the city grew from 177,000 in 1875 to almost 277,000 in 1890, both individual families and businesses gravitated toward the surrounding villages where space could accommodate them and rents were cheaper. That meant that the population of surrounding villages grew exponentially. For instance, the village of Pieschen, directly west of the Neustadt, experienced an increase of 617% from 1871 to 1890; on the Elbe's left bank, the villages of Löbtau and Cotta, south and west of the huge railroad marshaling yards, experienced increases of 420% and 478% respectively. To the east, the suburb of Striesen grew together with the Johannstadt and became a working-class neighborhood, while the village of Strehlen, to its south, attracted the upper middle class of Dresden, who could travel to the city by streetcar after 1882. Even King Albert built a villa for his family there.

The city began to locate some facilities in these outlying villages. In both Trachenberge and Mickten, on the Elbe's right bank, the city established streetcar barns for its public transport system. It was not surprising therefore that, beginning in 1892, the city started to annex those villages most tightly tied to its economy and social structure. The municipality could use the income from wealthy villages like Strehlen to pay for the infrastructure necessary to support the industries and social services of less prosperous areas like Pieschen, a strictly working-class neighborhood. Strehlen and Striesen were the first to be annexed. Pieschen and Trachenberge followed in 1897. In 1902–3, a grand total of twelve nearby communes were added to the city. Two more followed before the outbreak of World War I. By 1910, Dresden officially contained 550,000 people.[238]

New infrastructure facilitated the city's expansion. Along the north-south axis, the city, already in the 1850s, had bought up the properties that extended the old Seestrasse southward to the soon-to-be famous Prager Strasse. In the 1870s, it punched through a street connecting the old city center with the industrializing Friedrichstadt, and by 1880, it had extended two streets in the east from the city center through to the Johannstadt. In the city center itself, a thoroughfare from west to east extended the Wilsdrufferstrasse to the eastern ring street. To accommodate the increasing traffic to and fro across the Elbe, the city built three new bridges: the Albert Bridge in 1875; the Blue Wonder, so named for its painted color and new technology, in 1893 between Blasewitz and Loschwitz, both outlying villages at the time; and the Carola Bridge in 1895.

Traffic was not the only concern. Even before German unification, Dresden had created a modern system of storm water drainage. Between 1870 and 1914, the city built new water works on the Elbe just outside the city limits in the villages of Loschwitz and Tolkewitz and established a gas works at Reick, southeast of the city. In 1909, it set up a sewage treatment plant at Kaditz, another village northwest of the city.[239]

Water was a continual threat; the Elbe flooded at regular intervals, and the problem was compounded by its tributary, the Weisseritz, fed by the same mountain waters and in a position to inundate the city center, including the Zwinger. The first extreme flood recorded occurred in 1501. There was a damaging flood in 1845, and yet another in 1862. After the flood of 1890, the city set about trying to prevent future damage. Beginning in 1891, a new bed was dug for the Weisseritz, diverting it west by almost three miles to join the Elbe downstream from the city center. The dirt from the new stream bed was used to shore up the banks on the left side of the Elbe, which were then regulated to chase the water downstream onto the right bank meadows that were left exposed to the water.[240]

Education

On another level, the elementary school system was expanded to include industrial and commercial schools. Fewer schools now taught more children. A teacher-training institute opened close to the city center, and the city built seven new high schools that equipped students to enter university. Churches opened parochial schools for Catholics.

The Kreuzschule, considered by some as the most prestigious in the city, experienced changes. Already at the beginning of the nineteenth century, the school had become a gymnasium, introducing a modern curriculum and providing its graduating students with an entrée to university. Private lessons ceased, tuition was raised, and teachers received an increase in salary. The choir introduced contemporary music, and concerts became regular events. In 1866, the school moved to a new, neo-Gothic building on what is now Georgplatz. In this same year, the traditional street singing, deemed to be inappropriately old-fashioned, also ceased.[241]

In the realm of educational facilities, there were three that significantly influenced the constructed physiognomy of the city. The Technical Institute had started life in the old Royal Stable on Neumarkt; in mid-century it moved to the Antonsplatz on the city ring street; in the 1870s it transferred to the Bismarckplatz just behind the Bohemian railway station. Meanwhile, it had upgraded from a mere institute to a Technical College that awarded master's degrees and certified instructors for secondary schools. By this time, everyone realized that the quarters on Bismarckplatz were too small, and the lack of space was adversely affecting the institution's academic reputation.

Thus, at the end of the 1890s, the new College moved south to a location on the George Bähr Strasse. Professors developed close relationships with Saxon and German industry, and hundreds of students flocked to Dresden to study. These students came not only from Germany, but from Russia, Austria, Scandinavia and other countries. Meanwhile, the facility developed a liberal arts component—literature, foreign languages, and history—all the while retaining the name of a *technical* institution. At the turn of the century, it received the right to offer the doctorate and to award honorary degrees. The first industrialist to receive an honorary degree was Friedrich Siemens.[242]

An even older institution than the Technical College also received a new home at the end of the nineteenth century. The Art Academy was the oldest of the "universities" in Dresden. Begun at the end of the seventeenth century as a drawing and painting school just down the lane from the Kreuzkirche, it moved in the mid-eighteenth century to the Fürstenberg Palace on the rampart that later became the Brühl Terrace. As the Royal Academy of Art, it soon moved again into Count Brühl's library where it remained for a century.

At the end of the nineteenth century, the Academy razed its old quarters and commissioned Constantin Lipsius, then a faculty member, to construct an enlarged, neo-classical campus on the Brühl Terrace. Lipsius' design excited controversy. Critics found the building too large for the location and out of tune with the neo-Renaissance styles that were familiar to Dresdners. There are still Dresdners and others who consider the pleated glass dome, dubbed the "lemon reamer" by the populace, to be unwelcome competition with the Frauenkirche. Atop this dome stood, and still stands, the gilded goddess Fama, proclaiming the glory and honor of the artists below.[243]

The last of the higher education facilities to be built before World War I was the Royal Saxon Applied Arts School. Split off from the Technical College when it moved to the Bismarckplatz in 1875, the school was modeled on similar institutions in Berlin and Leipzig, and they all foreshadowed the German *Werkbund* and *Bauhaus*. The school's goal was to train artisans who could endow industrially produced articles with aesthetic appeal. At the beginning of the twentieth century, the Dresden Applied Arts School constructed an enlarged campus in the Johannstadt that encompassed instructional facilities, a museum, and the conserved auditorium of the old Brühl Palace, razed to accommodate new quarters for the Saxon legislature. Created in two stages, with designs by two different architects, the buildings reflected both the neo-Renaissance and the Art Nouveau movements. Some of the school's students, like Otto Dix and Lea Grundig, moved on to the Art Academy downtown once they completed the applied arts' curriculum.[244]

Government

Schools were not the only institutions bursting at the seams as industrialization contributed to Dresden's growth. Today's visitor to Dresden can't miss two very large buildings on the right bank of the Elbe. It is not surprising that the first of these to be completed was the Finance Ministry in 1896. Revenues and expenses are every government's pre-occupations. The adjacent Saxon State Government Building, topped by a gilded crown, followed in 1906. These two structures and the new quarters for the Saxon legislature, adjacent to the palace, employed the neo-Baroque style. Paul Wallot, architect for Berlin's Reichstag, was engaged to design new quarters for the Saxon Diet. Lodged on a sensitive spot, this building appropriately merged new with old architecture.

The last important administrative building to rise in the center city was the New Rathaus. For centuries, city hall had governed the city from the Altmarkt, either from a building situated within the square or from a structure along its edge. Now, the city's growth and a variety of liberal reforms made a new facility necessary. By 1910, a neo-classical Rathaus stood completed on the Moritzring (now Dr. Külz Ring) just down the lane from the Altmarkt and the Kreuzkirche.[245]

The man responsible for many public buildings constructed before World War I was Hans Erlwein. Contemporaries have testified to a self-confidence bordering on arrogance but also to considerable diplomatic skill when dealing with politicians, developers, and neighborhoods. Erlwein arrived to be city planner in Dresden in 1905. During the next nine years, he designed over fifty buildings. A member of the *Werkbund* (Association of Craftsmen), he strove to make his structures aesthetically appealing by fitting them into the size and style of their surrounding neighborhoods. While acknowledging the necessity of using industrial building methods, he eschewed super-modern designs.

This tendency characterizes his most famous achievement, the Dresden Slaughterhouse, a grouping of modest neo-Baroque buildings, where Kurt Vonnegut, together with his fellow prisoners of war, sat out the city's bombing by British and American forces in February 1945. The Dresden Fair now uses the rehabilitated structures of the Slaughterhouse. Also designed by Erlwein, soon after he arrived in the city, is a landmark known to almost all Dresdners: the small, domed temple-like structure that covers the artesian well at Albertplatz.[246]

VIII. The Middle-Class City

In 1889, when the Wettin family celebrated its 800th year as Saxon rulers, Dresden still reflected the glow of a princely residence. Now the educated middle class joined the court in projecting the city's reputation. It began to set the city's cultural and political tone.

Music

The loss of artistic talent that followed the mid-century revolution created an hiatus on the city's musical scene. Contemporaries do not mention any stellar musical occasions at the court opera and theater in the years following the revolution. In 1862, Baron Lüttichau ended thirty-seven years as superintendent of the court theater. He could no longer count on Richard Wagner as composer and conductor, and Henriette Schroeder-Devrient had also left Dresden.

Seven years later, the Semper Opera burned down. The theater critic, Friedrich Kummer, whose grandfather and father were musicians in the court orchestra, was four years old at the time. He remembered standing on a small hill in Strehlen, watching the "black smoke" of the fire rising above the city, while tears streamed down his mother's face. Informed by telegraph, King Johann rushed in from Pillnitz. He was relieved to discover that no one had died in the fire. The Saxon military had to clear spectators from the Zwinger ramparts, from the Brühl Terrace and from the Augustus Bridge to ensure their safety.

Given the high premium placed by Dresdners and the Saxon government on music and the arts, it was a foregone conclusion that the Semper Opera should be almost immediately rebuilt. By this time, Gottfried Semper had been granted amnesty for his previous revolutionary activities, but he was unwilling to participate in the prescribed competition for the new opera's design. As the

German-speaking world's most renowned architect, he refused to vie with anyone else for the commission. Local and national voices supported him. King Johann and the government gave in to popular opinion. Planning began in 1870; ground was broken in 1871; Semper's son Manfred supervised the construction that was finally complete in 1878. Even though this second Semper Opera resembled the first, it was actually a new design, incorporating the architect's leading concepts: architecture as theater, as information and, as utility.[247]

By the time the new opera house was inaugurated, the Dresden opera had acquired a new orchestra director who polished the city's musical reputation for over forty years: Ernst Schuch. Schuch hailed from Graz, Austria. Already as a child, he performed publicly on both the violin and the piano. As a young man, he gave up the study of law to become a professional musician. By the time he arrived in Dresden, he had accumulated experience in a number of German orchestras. Schuch had a penchant for Italian opera, and he introduced the famous Italian composers of the nineteenth century to Dresden audiences: Giuseppe Verdi, Giacomo Puccini, Ruggiero Leoncavallo, Pietro Mascagni. Nor did he neglect Wagner, now a celebrated German composer. But Schuch's great achievement was his introduction of Richard Strauss to Dresden and to the world.[248]

Strauss was the son of a horn player at the Munich court opera and, like Schuch, a child prodigy. As a teen, he composed serious orchestral works and directed them for German audiences in Dresden and other places. At the end of the century, he turned his attention to opera. His early work, *Feuersnot* (In Need of Fires), premiered in Dresden in 1901. Between then and the beginning of World War I, Dresden audiences heard the first performances of *Salome* (1905), *Elektra* (1909), and the rollicking *Rosenkavalier* (1911). *Der Rosenkavalier* was such a sensation that special trains brought ticket-holders from Berlin and other cities to Dresden for the performances.

Schuch, however, did not confine himself to opera. Under his direction, the court orchestra offered, in addition to the Palm Sunday concerts, two other benefit performances: on Ash Wednesday and, in the autumn, on the Day of Prayer and Repentance. He continued the six subscription concerts that had begun in mid-century and added six more with virtuoso artists. As with the modern Italians, he included in his symphonic programs contemporary Germans like Johannes Brahms, Anton Bruckner, Gustav Mahler and Max

Reger. His own stellar reputation attracted to Dresden some of the best singers and instrumentalists of the time. For his contributions to the musical world, the Habsburg ruler ennobled him in 1897.[249]

The court orchestra under von Schuch deserved the respect shown it at the end of the nineteenth century, but it was not the city's only musical attraction. For centuries, the City Musicians, paid by the municipal government, had provided accompaniment for Dresden's four principal churches, for the boys' choir of the Kreuzkirche, for the Singakademie, for municipal celebrations and open-air concerts in summer, and incidental music for coffee houses, hotels and restaurants. City Musicians had to be proficient on at least two instruments: wind and string. During the first two-thirds of the nineteenth century, their numbers grew from twelve to forty.

In 1870, the *Gewerbeverein* (Commercial Association) erected a large building on the Ostraallee and included a concert hall, the *Gewerbehaussaal*. At this time, the City Musicians took the name of *Gewerbehausorchester* and offered symphony concerts in the large auditorium on Thursdays and Saturdays. On Sundays, they bowed to the popular taste for lighter fare. During the summer, the Gewerbehausorchester gave open-air concerts in the Great Garden, at the Schillerschlösschen in Blasewitz, and, until 1888, at the Hotel de Saxe on Neumarkt. These musicians not only enjoyed local renown but built up an international reputation by touring abroad; in 1909, they traveled as far as north America.[250]

A plethora of choirs also provided musical entertainment. Offering serious fare was the boys' choir at the Kreuzkirche that performed, among other religious compositions, Bach's Saints John and Matthew Passions as well as the *B Minor Mass*, the *Christmas Oratorio*, and the *Magnificat*. The most famous men's choir in Saxony was the Dresdner *Liedertafel* (Song Banquet) that toured Germany, Switzerland, Austria, Sweden and Norway in the period between German unification and World War I. Women finally joined the men in 1906. Not to be forgotten were also the numerous workers' glee clubs that operated under the auspices of the Social Democratic Party. In the period prior to World War I, Dresden was a musical mecca.[251]

Theater

For most of its history, the court theater had presented both operas and plays. In fact, music remained a vital part of drama into the nineteenth century.

After Schuch arrived in Dresden in 1872, he slowly expanded the number of operas performed during the week. In 1873, operas were held four times a week; after 1896, the court orchestra and singers offered operas daily. This meant that non-musical theater could no longer count on using the Semper Opera and needed its own performing space.[252]

Ernst Venus, later executive of Dresden county, remembers that the "whole atmosphere in Dresden" during his boyhood "was turned to the world of the stage". The establishment that lasted the longest was the Albert Theater on Bautzenerplatz (now Albertplatz). Native Dresdner Erich Kästner, poet, cabarettist, and author of children's books, recorded in his memoirs what a treat it was for him as a boy when his mother, finished with her daily work as a hairdresser, hustled him out the door of their apartment on the Königsbrückerstrasse for an entertaining evening down the street at the Albert Theater.

Originally built by the Neustadt's Beautification Society, it was leased by the court theater in 1873 and gave 386 performances during that year. Intended to present only spoken drama, this institution catered to a different crowd than the opera on Theaterplatz. Dresdners could purchase subscriptions or buy single tickets. A visit was memorable for a working-class lad like Kästner. The auditorium was decked out in colors of gold and white, accentuating the gas illumination. The King finally bought the theater in 1895, and at that time, the Albert Theater, offering only spoken drama, was the only one in town that did so.

For a long time, Dresden audiences favored potpourri performances of several small comedies. Classical plays, particularly Shakespeare's, were offered over and over again. According to Friedrich Kummer, the dramatic standard left a lot to be desired. Leading actors did not rehearse with the full cast, and sometimes understudies performed without any rehearsal at all. Sets often did not match the action, and lighting was erratic. A turning point finally occurred when the famous Meiningen Theater chose Dresden for one of its guest productions in 1876.

The Meiningen Ensemble is often credited with modernizing the German theater. Encouraged by the Duke of Meiningen in his small principality during the previous decade, its reforms derived from the English Shakespeare revival under the actor-director Charles Kean. The Meiningen Theater stressed a troupe's possession of a strong director who imposed his interpretations on the members of the cast. These actors adopted a natural rather than a declamatory style. Costumes and sets had to be historically accurate. Critics at the time were particularly impressed by the ensemble's artfully staged mob scenes. These techniques were similar to those that Eduard Devrient had wanted to employ before he was forced to bow to the more star-centered productions of his brother Emil. The Meiningen Ensemble performed in Dresden six times between 1876 and 1887. By the time of the last Meiningen visit, the Dresdners had adopted many of its practices.

At that last appearance, the ensemble staged Henrik Ibsen's *Ghosts*. The next day, the Saxon censors forbade it; the substitution was Shakespeare's *As You Like It*. This censorship was typical of Dresden at that time. Modern plays either offended the moral sensibilities of the elite or were too complex to satisfy the pedestrian taste of the audience. Only little by little did plays by nineteenth-century playwrights like Heinrich Kleist, Franz Grillparzer, Christian Hebbel, Otto Ludwig, Henrik Ibsen and Gerhart Hauptmann catch on. The man who was most responsible for making the dramatic backwater of Dresden into an exemplar of the avant garde was Nicolas von Seebach, intendant of the court theater(s) beginning in 1894.

Count Seebach was not an artistic individual, but he was open to new ideas, and, as an independently wealthy man, he was little influenced by other people's opinions. He had traveled widely, was well connected to the royal family, and tended to appoint good directors and performers and then let them do their jobs. During his tenure as intendant, Dresden became one of two leading court theaters in Germany. While more literary Dresdners relished the new trends, the theater still had to make money, so Seebach could never completely forsake the pot-boilers that delighted the greater part of local audiences.

The emergence of Dresden as a theater town inspired Mayor Otto Beutler to found a Theater Building Society in 1908 with the goal of erecting a Royal Playhouse to act as a counterpart to the Royal Opera. The municipality helped by donating a site across the Ostraallee from the Zwinger's Long Gallery, and in 1913, the new Playhouse gave its first performances. Across the river, the Albert Theater devolved into private management.

Children's theater matched that of the adults. There was a puppet theater at the Waldschlösschen brewery, and the Dresden People's Cooperative operated two theaters. There was a nature theater on the Dresden public heath that gave three afternoon performances a week—fairy tales, comedies, farces, folklore. Another on the Ostraallee staged standard plays for children and adults alike. In the suburb of Strehlen, the Hotel Duttler offered variety shows in the garden during the summer. The future founder of Dresden's Circus Sarrasani, Hans Stosch, performed there in 1899.[253]

Art

Theater was not the only realm where Dresdners experienced new ideas. Both the Royal Art Academy and the Royal Art Collections were sources of urban pride. Already in 1855, the royal art collection had moved into the new gallery next to the Zwinger designed by Gottfried Semper during the preceding decade. Visitors to the new gallery could now view the paintings in full natural brightness due to the building's skylights. Central heating allowed the collection to be exhibited during the winter. Indeed, central heating finally made other facets of the royal collection available to the public.

In the 1870s, the Paintings Gallery on the Neumarkt was remodeled for the porcelain collection and for an historical museum. A decade later, the sculpture collection and the state archives moved into the old arsenal, rechristened the Albertinum. By the turn of the century, the Saxon court and state administered ten museums. Now presiding over each collection was a director with appropriate academic credentials to make sure it was properly maintained and expanded.

Beginning in the 1880s, these directors responded to the new artistic developments emerging during the last part of the century, and they attempted to introduce them to a Dresden public whose aesthetic outlook was very conservative. Karl Woermann, an art historian who became director of the Paintings Gallery in 1882, complained in his memoirs that he had to work with a Gallery Commission whose members were neither painters nor trained conservators but who had to approve all his purchases and restorations before the responsible ministry consented to pay for them. Up until 1891, the Culture Ministry appropriated the museum's funds, at which time, the Finance Ministry took over the job. Final approval for purchases was given by the King.

Woermann reported that the Gallery Commission had recommended purchases by some mid-century painters but not by prominent German artists like Adolph Menzel and Franz von Lenbach. French and German impressionists were slow to catch on. In 1893, the Gallery Commission sent

Woermann and two others, an architect and an art professor, to an exhibition in Berlin where they were allowed to purchase paintings independently of the commissioners. The three decided on paintings by the German Symbolist Max Klinger and the Norwegian Impressionist Christian Krogh.

When these paintings were hung in the Semper Gallery, a group of old-guard artists protested and published their criticisms in popular national magazines. The Saxon Diet even considered a vote of no-confidence in the gallery's director. These groups were finally forced to back down when the art critics of two local newspapers, along with forty-three local painters and sculptors, supported the purchases. Given the philistine climate, painters with national and international reputations hesitated to show their works at the annual Dresden Art Exhibition, and Woermann, who was tasked by a local foundation with purchasing only exhibited works, feared encumbering the collection with a lot of mediocrity.

Nevertheless, Woermann persisted in acquiring new styles for the Semper Gallery, and the directors of other collections succeeded as well. The director of the sculpture collection, Georg Treu, personally bought original plaster casts from August Rodin, and Max Lehrs acquired etchings directly from James Whistler and Henri Toulouse-Lautrec. In 1898, Käthe Kollwitz's "Weavers" was denied the Gold Medal at the Berlin Art Exhibition, by express wish of the German Kaiser. So Lehrs arranged for her to receive it at Dresden. During his lifetime, he amassed for the Dresden museums the largest German collection of Kollwitz's oeuvre. He early recognized photography as an art form and collected selected works for Dresden.[254]

Dresden artists matched the boldness of the curators. In painting, in sculpture and architecture, young men and women seceded from the traditional styles and techniques and imitated French *plein-air* impressionists. One group coalesced in the 1890s in the village of Goppeln, south of Dresden. Eventually, this Secession merged with a group of young architects who called themselves The Guild.[255]

In the last two decades before World War I, the city attracted a number of innovative personalities. Cornelius Gurlitt arrived in Dresden in 1872 as designer for an architectural firm and began writing books about the city's prominent structures. In 1879, he became assistant at the new Museum for the Applied Arts. His work on the history of architecture and art, most specifically his esteem for the Baroque, led to a professorship and eventually the directorship of the Technical College. Gurlitt has remained a renowned art historian who laid a base for many different fields of art history. Teaching next to him at the college for a short period of time was Fritz Schumacher, architect and urban planner, who instructed his students in interior design and later associated with the German *Werkbund* (Association of Craftsmen), forerunner of the Bauhaus.[256]

It was the Impressionist Gotthardt Kuehl who revived Dresden's reputation as an art center. In the mid-1890s, he became professor at the Academy of Art and made Dresden's art exhibitions his forte, both in the new exhibition rooms of the academy and at the newly constructed Exhibition Palace on the edge of the Great Garden. In 1899, Lukas Cranach was featured at the annual German exhibition. Four years later, the illustrator Ludwig Richter starred in a Saxon Exhibition. In 1906, Dresdners were treated to a show of works by Edvard Munch. In addition to exhibits at the Academy of Art and the city's Exhibition Palace, the Saxon Art Society also held shows, and two private galleries, Art Salon Emil Richter and Gallery Ernst Arnold, displayed and sold modern art. In 1905–06, these two establishments cooperated in bringing to the city the works of Vincent Van Gogh. They also featured paintings by other post-Impressionists.[257]

The rich environment that arose at the turn of the century inspired a group of young men to found a movement that was later hailed as the birth of German Expressionism. These students at the Technical College are still well-known today: Erich Heckel, Ludwig Kirchner, Karl Schmidt-Rottluff, and Fritz Bleyl. Others, such as Max Pechstein and Emil Nolde, joined them. They named their group *Die Brücke* (The Bridge).

Artistic influences for Die Brücke started with classes at Dresden's museums. At the college, the young men learned drafting in Fritz Schumacher's classes. Lukas Cranach attracted them as a bridge between the medieval and the Renaissance periods, and they identified with his reputation not only as a German, but as a Saxon artist. Seeking to imbue their work with Saxon techniques, the Brücke artists imitated medieval wood-cuts directly or adapted their rough style.

Rembrandt must be counted as an inspiration, modulated through Julius Langbehn's book, *Rembrandt as Educator*. Modern historians consider Langbehn to be a forerunner of German fascism, but at the beginning of the twentieth century, his depiction of Rembrandt appealed to artists in the up-and-coming German Empire. For Langbehn, Rembrandt was a painter of the common folk, a truly Germanic artist, and reliance on his approach could "bridge" the gap between the incomplete man of the nineteenth century and the completely integrated, creative one of the twentieth. Cornelius Gurlitt was friendly with Langbehn and, as one of the mentors of Die Brücke, had probably introduced the group to Langbehn's work.

At the same time, members of Die Brücke were exposed to artistic developments in both France and England. Schumacher certainly introduced them to the British Arts and Crafts Movement. Publications like Julius Meier-Graefe's *Evolution of Modern Art* put them in touch with contemporary French developments: the Post-Impressionists, the Symbolists, the Fauvists, and the early Cubists. Die Brücke's manifesto of 1906 declared its intention of supporting anyone among the younger generation expressing his own, individualistic vision of life.

In 1910, the Dresden Museum for Ethnology reopened and reinforced yet another inspiration for Die Bruecke: Asian, Oceanic and African art. Kirchner had early become interested in Asian art, and Heckel had absorbed an appreciation for East Indian forms from his teacher, Wilhelm Kreis. At the Ethnological Museum, the Palau beams particularly attracted the young artists. Palau was a village in Micronesia where men lived together in a club house, visited their families only as guests, and entertained young girls from neighboring hamlets. The beams represented, in stylized form, fully aroused and fertile males. A chief of Palau had given them to the German traveler Karl Semper who, in turn, passed them on to the museum.

Palau's art spoke to Die Brücke's desire to live an harmonious, communal life rather than to endure the urban isolation of industrial Germany. Members kept a communal studio with furnishings made by the artists and where they, their friends, their neighbors and their models came and went. In 1909, they began to visit, during the summer, the small lakes in the region around Moritzburg Castle, northwest of Dresden, where they bathed nude, played games, and painted in relaxed fashion among the trees. A particular favorite was the Dippelsdorf Pond where a thick screen of reeds shielded their playground along the water from prying eyes. Kirchner's painting, "The Bathers", records one of their outings to the pond.

However Bohemian their values and lifestyle, the members of Die Brücke wanted and needed to sell paintings, and they displayed their works whenever and wherever they had an opportunity. Their works did not appeal to Dresdners. Beginning in 1906, they presented them at the Leuchtenberg factory in Löbtau because the Saxon Art Society denied them space at its annual art exhibition in the center of town. They ultimately mounted 150 shows in suburban Löbtau, at the Richter Gallery in the Pragerstrasse, and in the Arnold Gallery in the Schlossstrasse. In 1909, the critic Richard Stiller, writing in the *Dresden Anzeiger*, advised Die Brücke artists "to pursue a definite and artistic goal, instead of flirting in a half-barbaric, half-refined manner" with the French modernists. Such criticisms of modern art were common among German conservatives before World War I.

In 1908, Max Pechstein moved to Berlin where he found commercial success for his works and a more tolerant artistic climate. Yet he returned during the summer to join his friends' gamboling in the ponds around Moritzburg. Finally in 1911, Kirchner, Heckel and Schmidt-Rotluff decided to join Pechstein in the German capital in order to expand their fortunes. They held their final exhibition as a group in Berlin in 1912, after which they each went their separate ways. Even though the city's shabby reception of Die Bruecke discouraged its artists from remaining in town, it was Dresden that provided the cradle for the movement of German Expressionism.[258]

Middle-Class Leisure

Die Brücke's social life seemed rough and tumble in comparison with the more refined pleasures of the city's middle class. A variety of cafés served coffee and pastries, and the Brühl Terrace remained the place to see and be seen. Restaurants such as the Bärenschänke, the Ratskeller in the New Rathaus, or the Italian Village on the Theaterplatz attracted those seeking good bourgeois cooking. After 1895, the Luisenhof in Loschwitz, located on the bluffs above the Elbe, provided for lively outings. Middle-class Dresdners also liked to entertain at home. Musical evenings were especially popular. The most musical of all the city's private homes belonged to Baron von Kaskel, principal investor in the Dresdner Bank and a local philanthropist. But other citizens shone as well. Woermann once attended a recital by Franz Liszt at the home of the poet Adolf Stern. He also enjoyed the company of Johannes Brahms at a dinner party given by one of Dresden's businessmen. The future Saxon Minister Willibalt Apelt remembered sitting, as a child, in a corner at home listening to his mother playing the piano and singing with friends.[259]

Private occasions could also be the scene of lush entertainment and cultural enrichment. On 4 July 1914, Woermann celebrated his seventieth birthday, a "biblical age" as he put it, with a day of festivities. Military music played in the background as his out-of-town guests joined him and his family at breakfast. His friends and acquaintances from the museums, from the civil service and from local clubs enjoyed snacks between eleven and three. The banquet at six in the evening served fifty-four people who subsequently filed out to the illuminated garden for a performance of Goethe's *Moody Lover* and a short play written by Woermann as a youth. The evening ended indoors with a "picture show" about his life.[260]

If middle-class Dresdners were not keeping company at home, they could interact with one another in a burgeoning club life. By 1900, there were over 1000 clubs catering to a variety of interests. The Inner Mission Society's house on the Zinzendorfstrasse offered a large auditorium and several small meeting rooms for this plethora of organizations. Clubs tended to group not only around interests, but also around social classes. Not until the turn of the century did middle-class organizations admit women and Jews.

Dresden's social world, according to Woermann, was highly stratified. At the top, the court circle included the royal family and the old aristocracy. Below them were the groups of higher military officers, civilian officials and jurists who served the government. A separate group consisted of directors of cultural institutions and the professors at the Technical College, the artists of the Art Academy, and the musicians and actors of the royal theaters. Factory owners, bankers and rich businessmen formed yet another group. There was even a circle comprising retirees who had migrated to the city from the rest of Germany. Woermann claimed that Dresden was a town of "the shame-faced rich", whose taxes contributed even more to Saxon state coffers than did those of Leipzig, its more commercial neighbor to the north.

The clubs these people joined had either a literary or an artistic cast. The Literary Society held lectures on a variety of topics relating to German and non-German literature, to history, art, religion, philosophy and travel. The Tuesday Society was a scholarly group of civil servants and officers. The membership belonged to the older generation, and the dominant taste was old-fashioned. Eventually, the Tuesday Society split into two, due to a misunderstanding within the leadership, and the dissenting half became the "Fourteen". These included younger writers, scholars, artists, poets and actors.

The orchestra conductor, von Schuch, as well as Woermann, were among the "Fourteen". Woermann also helped to found the "Symposion", a group of poets that met weekly. It offered readings and lectures on an irregular basis.[261]

In the years before World War I, Dresden's middle class participated in a host of nationalistic movements. Among the most popular were the German Colonial Society, the Eastern Marches Club, and the German Naval Club. The Dresden chapter of the Pan-German League, a national organization dedicated to supporting German culture throughout the world and expanding German power in Europe, influenced other organizations by "infiltrating" them. It also helped to elect deputies to the national and state legislatures and to the city assemblies and councils. Local members of all these organizations sat on the board of Dresden's Club for Patriotic Festivities that, beginning in summer 1898, organized an annual celebration of the Empire with sports events, parades, and commemorations. Among prominent members of the board was the Odol industrialist Karl Lingner.

Otto Beutler, Dresden's mayor from 1895–1915, was an ardent supporter of the official celebrations of the Battle of Sedan that led to German unification, and he frequently acted as speaker, sponsor or honorary guest at functions of nationalist, conservative, and monarchical groups. These activities reflected the dominant political climate of middle-class Dresdners. Between 1888 and 1911, the Emperor Wilhelm II visited Dresden nineteen times.[262]

The Spa at Weisser Hirsch

The Kaiser was not the only aristocrat to visit Dresden. The resort at the Weisser Hirsch, originally a locale on the edge of the Dresden forest, attracted both German and European royalty, nobility and the upper middle class. In 1888, medical doctor and naturopath Johann Heinrich Lahmann took over the site of an earlier bankrupted facility. He arrived from Chemnitz where he had served a year as manager of a similar institution. This local area had been named a climatic health spa, and its inhabitants had formed a Beautification Society.

The sanatorium that Lahmann established specialized in treating chronic and short-term conditions like diabetes, overweight, gout, arthritis, rheumatism, wounds and fractures. No tubercular patients or individuals with venereal diseases were accepted. Lahmann healed without medications; he applied hydrotherapy, open-air treatment, a vegetarian diet, and exercise. An able businessman as well as medical doctor, Lahmann easily expanded his sanatorium into a complete resort.

He installed bathing rooms, open-air huts, massaging rooms, gymnastic equipment and clinics, walking paths in the forest, tennis courts, a bowling alley, a library, an outdoor concert area with stage, and a café. Many patients brought their children with them, so child care was also provided. In case the sanatorium/resort did not provide enough recreation, after 1899, patients could take the streetcar into downtown Dresden.

This expansive facility provided work for 300 people, from cook to medical doctors. It also led to increased residential development that merged Weisser Hirsch with Upper Loschwitz. One entrepreneur built an elegant hotel to serve those who came for treatment or visited at the sanatorium.

Municipal Improvement

City government also attended to Dresdners' health. The city had introduced its own training academy for doctors and instituted its first general municipal hospital in the mid-nineteenth century. The practical experience that the Medical Academy offered aspiring doctors became a state-wide measure in mid-century, and finally, at the beginning of the twentieth century, the German state made internships in clinics obligatory. Already the government in Berlin had made medical care almost universal in the 1880s by introducing mandatory sickness insurance for German workers and partially subsidizing the premiums. Thus the market for medical care had expanded exponentially.

Responding to this stimulus, a private doctor opened a polyclinic for poor children that was soon joined by Lingner's privately-supported infants' hospital. The demand for its services was so great that the municipality soon took over its operation. The royal family also established a polyclinic for women. Operating parallel to these efforts were establishments, both private and public, for training nurses.

The flu epidemic of 1889–90 revealed that Dresden's one municipal hospital in the Friedrichstadt, even when helped by the private hospitals in town, was not sufficient to serve its growing population. This realization triggered the decision of Dresden's city council to establish a second municipal hospital in the Johannstadt. After three years of construction, the new hospital's campus opened in 1901. Even today the ambition of that initiative stuns the observer. There were originally seventeen Art Nouveau pavilions on twelve and a third acres, creating a park-like setting that was easily accessible to patients. The pavilions, each dedicated to a separate medical problem, were connected with one another through underground passages. A central furnace supplied both heat and hot water to all buildings. Extra frills included a gymnasium in the bathing pavilion and a separate chapel. The Johannstadt hospital has served the city well for over one hundred years.[263]

Reform

While providing a municipal hospital testified to middle-class concerns for the health and safety of all Dresdners, it is difficult to know how committed was the middle class to significant political and social reform before World War I. Some contemporaries claimed it was almost non-existent. What cannot be disputed is the degree of political engagement practiced by Dresden's workers. As the city industrialized during the last half of the nineteenth century, it acquired a growing working class consisting primarily of skilled and semi-skilled laborers who intended to improve their working, living, cultural and political conditions.

At the end of the reactionary 1850s, political activism had revived, and middle-class national liberals took the lead in agitating for a united and parliamentary Germany. The working class, while desiring unity, was divided. A significant group shared the liberal opposition to a unity dominated by the illiberal state of Prussia. Another group favored Prussian leadership and principally advocated state intervention to address working-class economic and social interests.

The six weeks' war of 1866, between Prussia and Austria, led inexorably to German unity under Prussia without, however, providing for a liberal state where parliament determined policy. As soon as this conclusion became clear, working-class leaders August Bebel and Wilhelm Liebknecht, founded the Saxon People's Party that fought the first election campaign of the newly unified state in opposition to the dominance of illiberal Prussia. In 1868, they emphasized their working-class sympathies by piloting the party into the International Workingmen's Association, better known as the First Socialist International. The People's Party then renamed itself the Social Democratic German Workers' Party in 1869.

This foundation in and of itself was not radical. The process that eventually turned these Social Democrats into political pariahs was the leadership's unpopular, anti-nationalist rhetoric. German unity was popular among wide strata of the German populace, and Social Democratic leaders' refusal to support Prussia's premier position in the unified Germany seemed unpatriotic. What's more, they even opposed the war with France, characterized by the Prussians as defensive, that completed German unity. And they glorified the insurrectionist, working-class program of the Paris Commune that refused to accept the German victory.

Working-class groups made themselves visible in the new German Empire's assembly—the Reichstag—by supporting trade unions, advocating a reduction in the workday, and calling for better enforcement of factory laws. Even when harassed and imprisoned by conservative governments, they relentlessly campaigned for seats in the Reichstag. In the 1874 elections, they increased their representation from one to ten seats. In 1875, the groups for and against Prussia amalgamated into what eventually became the Social Democratic Party of Germany, the SPD. During this period of growth, Social Democracy was closely identified with Saxony, one of Germany's pioneering industrial states. In 1877, Dresden elected the SPD leader, August Bebel, to the Reichstag. By the end of the century, Social Democrats had captured both of Dresden's national electoral districts. By the beginning of World War I, the SPD was the largest party in the Saxon state.

Connected to the party were a plethora of clubs for hikers, cyclists, choruses, card-players, women, rabbit owners, emergency rescuers, and many others. Some of these organizations built their own clubhouses. Both the trade unions and the Socialist party opened workers' libraries that proliferated in the city's working-class quarters. This growth justified the acquisition of a *Volkshaus* at the beginning of the twentieth century where the trade unions, the SPD, and the party-affiliated Association for People's Education and Art had their offices. The Volkshaus also sheltered journeymen who came to Dresden seeking work, and it provided a respectable venue, as opposed to the neighborhood pub, for events that included women and children.[264]

Associated with the SPD were the trade unions. In 1906, there were over 72,000 organized workers in the city. They agitated and struck for higher wages and shorter working days. Even though Dresden's working class was associated with the labor aristocracy, hardship still existed. At the end of the century, seventy percent of Dresden households had a monthly income of only ninety marks, considered to be almost subsistence level. Infant mortality in working-class neighborhoods was high. And even if a child survived the first years of life, his or her youthful years could be harsh. In 1898, 5800 schoolchildren needed to work in order to assure the family's survival, and children's wages helped to pay the obligatory elementary school fees. After the turn of the century, inflation of food and consumer goods' prices reduced the standard of living. Strikes multiplied.

In the period of intense industrialization, the city had developed an affordable housing shortage, and between 1885 and 1900, housing costs had increased by forty per cent. In 1900, forty per cent of workers' families enjoyed the use of only one room in their apartments. It was not unusual for them to rent out rooms—thereby creating sub-tenants—in order to make ends meet. Erich Kästner's parents rented the largest bedroom in their apartment to primary school teachers who had a powerful influence on the young boy's life. His mother also worked at home, first as a corset maker, and later as a hairdresser.[265]

Whatever the rhetoric or the agitation, the Dresden working class was not insurrectionist. Historians for the party emphasize that the local leaders favored an evolution toward social democracy. Party members in Dresden, in contrast to strict, atheistic Marxists, went to church, and the young Herbert Wehner, later a prominent West German politician, sang in the choir of his neighborhood's Church of the Redeemer. Nevertheless, party and trade-union leaders were harassed by both the Saxon and the national governments.

The anti-socialist attitude permeated bourgeois society. In the 1880s especially, Social Democrats could expect house searches, confiscations of mail, arrests and prison terms because of their political activity. August Kaden, both a local and a national leader, was blacklisted by employers. In the 1890s, the military, barracked nearby, boycotted his cigar shop in the Neustadt. Eventually, he established the publishing company that printed the SPD newspaper for the entire state of Saxony. Other local leaders had similar experiences. Saxon elites were unable to countenance the new force that had risen up within the city and state.[266]

German governmental structures encouraged the frustration of SPD success. At the highest level was the Imperial government in Berlin possessing a Reichstag (legislature) elected by universal manhood suffrage. But each state in the Empire determined its own governmental practices, and each included a Diet (legislature), usually of two chambers, selected by its own unique suffrage. All male citizens could vote in Reichstag elections, but laws in the constituent states varied. At neither the national nor the state level was any minister accountable to the Reichstag or Diet. The emperor and the states' princes were responsible for appointing and dismissing ministers who were usually drawn from the conservative aristocracy. At the local level—cities, towns, villages—yet another unique structure prevailed—council and assembly—and was elected by yet another unique suffrage. Local elites were the most powerful but could be overruled by state laws and ministers.

In nineteenth-century Saxony, the state suffrage of 1831 had remained in force until 1868 when, under the influence of the constitutional reforms that accompanied the unification of Germany, the Saxon diet passed a new law governing state elections. Although not as liberal as the national universal, direct suffrage, this new legislation allowed male citizens, aged twenty-five and older, who paid at least three marks in taxes per year, to vote directly for their representatives to the Saxon legislature. One man, one vote. In 1877, the Social Democrats elected their first representative to the Diet. Twenty years later this representation had increased to fifteen.

Saxon Conservatives feared that the SPD would eventually swamp the Diet. After all, by this time, the party occupied half the Saxon seats in the national Reichstag. In 1897, the Conservative party, representing aristocrats and rural areas, the National Liberal proponents of business, and the left liberal Progressives jointly passed a new, restrictive election law. Saxon citizens were now divided into three classes according to taxes paid, and each class voted for electors who, in turn, selected the legislative representatives. The system was structured so that those who paid the most taxes elected more representatives than those who paid fewer. Over eighty per cent of Saxon voters fell into the third class, the one with proportionately the fewest representatives. At the next election in 1901, the SPD won not a single seat in the Diet. Even the middle-class Progressives' mandates shrank from eight to two.[267]

The situation of the Dresden city government was similar. There the election law in force since 1874 restricted the vote to those males aged twenty-five and over, who possessed good character, Saxon citizenship and residence in Dresden. For this latter condition, citizens were divided into long-term—ten years or more—, who were entitled to half the seats in the assembly, and short-term—at least two years—residents, who were entitled to the other half. City assemblymen were elected for three years on a rotating basis; each year one-third of the assembly was up for election. Independent master craftsmen and the Homeowners' Association, with 4000 members, supported the Conservatives and anti-Semites—with their own political party—and dominated a city council, elected by assemblymen, that administered the city. The suffrage law of 1874 was so restrictive and the political situation so hidebound that the SPD did not even bother running any candidates for the city assembly until 1900.[268]

In that year, the SPD began to "storm" Dresden politics. In 1903, the party captured 22 out of the 23 Saxon seats in the national Reichstag, and Germans began to dub Saxony the "Red Kingdom". In that same year, the Saxon Court of Appeals deemed sub-tenants to be economically independent according to the terms of the election laws and thus eligible to vote in local elections. By this time, for a variety of reasons, middle-class National Liberals had abandoned their alliance with the Saxon Conservatives, and they, together with the SPD, encouraged sub-tenants to vote.

In response to this threat to the existing order, city government's Conservative majority changed the election law in 1905. Not only were voters divided into long-term and short-term residents, they were further subdivided into twenty different occupational groups, with the more wealthy groups receiving a disproportionately high number of assemblymen. Despite this chicanery, the SPD won six seats in the election of 1906 and fourteen seats in the election of 1908. In the communal elections of 1909, the party captured forty-six per cent of Dresdners' votes. Considerable portions of the middle-class voted for the Social Democrats out of protest against a suffrage that excluded even them from power. Nevertheless, the large percentage of votes for the SPD did not translate into the same percentage of the assembly's seats. Even though Socialists worked well with other assemblymen, Conservative property owners continued to dominate Dresden city government until the end of World War I.[269]

At the state level, mass demonstrations, some of which turned violent, convinced both the King and the middle class of the need to change the law of 1896 governing elections to the Diet. In 1906, the king appointed a new state minister of the interior with the understanding that he would draft a new election law. Finally in 1909, the Diet passed a plural suffrage that divided the state into forty-three urban and forty-eight rural districts. The vote was now direct; but it was still not equal. Voters received between one and four votes, depending on their income, their property and their education. Every voter over fifty received two votes automatically. Despite a reform that was heavily loaded in favor of Conservatives, the SPD won fifty-four per cent of the vote, gaining twenty-five seats in a legislature of ninety-one.[270]

Ernst Venus reported that as a young lawyer working in Saxony's Interior Ministry, he was sent to a workshop in Cologne dealing with economic and social issues. When he returned, he proposed to hold educational sessions for young lawyers training to be civil servants. The ministry accepted his suggestion, but it was only Conservatives and National Liberals who were admitted to the classes. At that time, those civil servants interested in social policy were deemed to be "pink", even "reddish". In part, the ultra-conservative approach to reform helps to explain the difficult situation that developed in Saxony after World War I.[271]

The "Bird Shoot (Vogelschiessen)"

There was one municipal event that brought the different social classes together at the same time in the same place. This was the popular festival called the "Bird Shoot" that occurred in summer on the meadows lining the Elbe. Dresden was not the only German city to celebrate a "Bird Shoot", but it was attractive both to the city's residents and to people in the region. The festival harked back to the Middle Ages when citizens were responsible for the city's defense and practiced shooting—first with a crossbow and later with a musket—on a regular basis. As there was then no standing army to fall back on, these practice sessions were vitally necessary.

In time, the crossbow practices evolved to include the shooting of wooden birds mounted on poles and marked by a circle that served as the target. Annual contests among the armed citizenry arose around these bird shoots, and sharpshooter societies formed to organize the competitions. Whoever won the competition became the sharpshooter king for the next year.

By the sixteenth century, the modern facets of the "Bird Shoot" had appeared. The banquets that followed the competitions became so elaborate that the city council tried to limit the amount expended on them. By this time too, the sharpshooter king enjoyed certain perquisites. He was freed from standing watch, he could use a small parcel of land on the Commons, and he received free brewing privileges. Accompanying the shooting competitions were rustic entertainments: dancing, jousting, pole climbing, cockshies (missiles thrown at a target). Clowns and musicians enlivened the scene.

During the next century, a long parade opened the Bird Shoot, and hawkers' stalls appeared among the rustic entertainments.

Bird Shoots were held only sporadically during the seventeenth century, and the city council wanted to do away with them entirely. They were no longer militarily necessary, and they entailed a great expenditure from city coffers. It was August the Strong who insisted on continuing the contests. The city council managed in 1700 to escape the expense by foisting off organization and financing on the Sharpshooter Society which, by this time, hardly included any commoners.[272]

The Society had become aristocratic and subject to the manipulation of the Saxon ruler. The Elector (later King) and the royal family belonged to the Society, and it set aside a separate tent for the King at every Bird Shoot up to 1914. Participants in the shoot were also mainly aristocrats and gentry: members of the royal family, diplomats, military officers, court officials, and some clergymen. At the same time, the entertainments expanded to include all the attractions of a modern carnival: picture shows, stage skits, the eighteenth-century equivalents of the merry-go-round and the Ferris wheel, stalls selling food and drink, gymnastic contests, races among young men and women. Artisans opened up stands where they offered their goods for sale.

The main function of the Shoot was no longer the competition but the social integration of Dresden's inhabitants. It was one of the ways in which Dresdners, by focusing on the Shoot's tradition, asserted their unique urban identity. During the course of the nineteenth century, the royal family gradually withdrew from the Shoot, and often, its tent was occupied by a court functionary. The middle-class element came more and more to the fore, even though the contestants in the traditional competition remained aristocratic.

The Shoot was popular. Crowds came from miles around. By the beginning of the nineteenth century, they had become so numerous that the police recommended that the aisles of the carnival be widened and improved. Soon, women and children's competitive shoots were introduced. In 1888, a contemporary complained that the whole entertainment, thanks to railroads and steamboats, had shifted from being a local affair to resembling an "international swarm". The early evening hours used to be "respectable", and the "wild quarter" of gambling stalls, theater, carnival rides, peep shows and hurdy-gurdies—the haunts of the lower classes—was relatively tame. This agreeable atmosphere, he said, had been ruined—by beer. By this time, the

Shoot, as the largest amusement in all of Saxony, had been transferred from the meadows close to town to much broader, improved spaces to the east, fitted out with electricity, paved pathways, and storm drains. The Bird Shoot's functions now encompassed the whole kingdom and not just its capital city.[273]

Hellerau

At the beginning of the twentieth century, a migrant entrepreneur made a less flamboyant attempt at social integration than the Bird Shoot. The migrant's name was Karl Schmidt, later becoming Karl Schmidt-Hellerau to distinguish him from Die Brücke's Schmidt-Rotluff. In some ways, his project reflects the challenges and responses that Dresden experienced in the two decades prior to World War I.

Born in 1873 to a poor weaver of Zchopau in the Ore Mountains, Schmidt apprenticed himself as a teenager to a cabinet-maker in his hometown. His training complete, he set out on his "wander years", at that time obligatory for German journeymen. His travels eventually took him to London, where industrial conditions and new ideas significantly influenced his life. After his English sojourn, he returned to Berlin where he worked for the Prussian Court cabinet-maker and took classes at the Applied Arts School.

In 1896, he landed in Dresden, attracted perhaps by the city's economic boom and its artistic flair. At that time, the city was an acknowledged leader of the architectural and applied arts. Its Technical College, its Art Academy and its Applied Arts School and Museum attracted some of the best German talent. Periodicals and organizations promoting the arts either located in Dresden or used its Exhibition Palace.

At first Schmidt worked at a small shop on the fringes of downtown and then for a cabinet-maker in Pillnitz, site of the King's summer palace. In 1898, he acquired a partner to help him finance his own Dresdner Workshops for Arts and Crafts. The business throve. By 1902, it had grown from two to over 250 employees and had moved from a small shop in a river-side village east of Dresden to a series of workrooms in the working-class suburb of Striesen.[274]

When Schmidt established his own furniture workshops at the end of the nineteenth century, the international Arts and Crafts Movement, dedicated to infusing the decorative arts with the modern principles of simplicity, solid craftsmanship and artistry, had been growing for almost fifty years. Essentially, the movement represented a rebellion against the ornamental, historic styles then prevalent in furniture and other household goods. Dresden's Applied Arts School, established in 1865, was part of this development. During Schmidt's stay in England, he probably became acquainted with the Arts and Crafts Movement's principles of social reform and artistic design.

The year before he opened his furniture factory, he had visited the International Art Exhibition, held in Dresden, and had immersed himself in the Art Nouveau rooms created by Henry van de Velde, the father of modern design. Once he owned and managed his own business, Schmidt engaged artists to design the furniture for his workshops and paid them royalties on each of their pieces sold. He also began to exhibit his furniture at local and international art exhibitions. His was the only Saxon firm invited to display its wares at the International Art Exhibition in Paris in 1900; and in 1902, his company contributed to another international exhibition in Turin. Along with other German firms, he also exhibited at the World Fairs in St. Louis and Brussels.[275]

Schmidt's furniture won prizes and attracted the attention of German artists and reformers. In 1902, he began his long association with the Munich architect Richard Riemerschmid, whose sister he later married. The following year, he met the Prussian civil servant and architect Hermann Muthesius, newly returned from a stint with the German embassy in London and an avid proponent of the Arts and Crafts principles. By 1904, he had become acquainted with the social reformer and politician Friedrich Naumann and his Adlatus, Theodor Heuss, later the first president of the German Federal Republic. Through his contacts in Munich, Schmidt became acquainted with Karl Bertsch, an entrepreneur with a business similar to his own, and in 1907, they merged their two firms. All these individuals shared Schmidt's ideals of providing a better life, including consumer products, for the working classes.[276]

In the year of the merger, this group, along with other artists and manufacturers, founded the German *Werkbund* in Munich. The goal of the Werkbund, like that of the English Arts and Crafts Movement, was to "reforge the links between designer and producer, between art and industry" that had been "...broken by industrialization." Fritz Schumacher, mentor of Die Brücke, gave the keynote address at this initial meeting. The Werkbund, a forerunner of the Bauhaus, proposed a unique German style that emphasized simplicity, unity of form and function, and reasonable prices. The first headquarters of this new organization resided at Schmidt's German Workshops.[277]

As Schmidt's sales increased, he needed more space for his factory. At the same time, he wanted to establish a model community that would avoid the ills of an industrially booming Dresden that, like other cities, was experiencing overcrowding and air pollution. For this new community he drew on concepts propagated by the new German Garden City Society which, in its turn, had borrowed ideas from the English garden city movement.

His friends in the Werkbund encouraged his plans, and in 1907 Schmidt crisscrossed the Dresden countryside on his bicycle seeking properties that would accommodate his dreams without breaking his bank. He finally found this land on the territory of the communes Rähnitz and Klotsche on the Heller, the hill to Dresden's north, inspiring the name of Schmidt's new community: Hellerau. He quickly acquired approval of his plans from the communes' mayors and persuaded 140 landowners to sell him a total of 336 acres. In 1908, he chartered the non-profit Garden City Hellerau Society, an umbrella organization, and a Cooperative Building Society to help finance construction of workers' cottages.[278]

The Hellerau Society planned to hold the land in trust to prevent the speculation that drove up rents in the rest of the district and to rent out small workers' houses. Middle-class villas would rest on long-leased land. This new community was supposed to provide affordable housing for the workshops' employees and accommodate a variety of social groups. Schmidt wanted neither a proletarian nor a bourgeois ghetto.

He engaged his associate Riemerschmid to plat the town, to design the new factory and to devise plans for the first affordable workers' homes. Muthesius and other architects contributed blueprints for additional structures in the complex. All the homes included the modern conveniences of the time: tap water, electricity, laundry facilities. By 1914, Hellerau had a population of 2000, but only a third of inhabitants was employed by the workshops. For some workers, the rents were still too high, and others did not want to leave the urban neighborhoods where they felt at home. Instead, the new community became an attractive place for the "new middle class"—white-collar employees in a variety of businesses and organizations.[279]

The first executive director of the Hellerau Society was Wolf Dohrn. As the second son of a prominent, wealthy family, Dohrn was closely associated with social reformer Friedrich Naumann and with many of the artists who were members of the Werkbund. He was particularly attracted to projects that innovated social and aesthetic reforms. In 1909, he and Karl Schmidt attended in Dresden a performance of Emile Jacques-Dalcroze's eurhythmic dances.

Jacques-Dalcroze was an instructor at the Geneva Music Conservatory and developed musical gymnastics as a pedagogic technique for training the ear to hear differing musical rhythms. His methods are still used in today's public schools. Both Schmidt and Dohrn were impressed by Dalcroze's success and invited him to establish a school at Hellerau. Attracted by the ability to design his own performing spaces, Jacques-Dalcroze accepted. The result was the Educational Institute for Rhythmic Gymnastics, lodged in a building that came to be called the *Festspielhaus* (Festival Hall) designed by the young Heinrich Tessenow, who later became famous as architect Albert Speer's mentor.

Tessenow's stark, modernistic exterior enclosed a large space of white cloth walls and ceiling, behind which were 3000 light bulbs arranged in sections that could be controlled separately to bathe the audience in brilliant or muted light depending on the desired mood. Dalcroze and Tessenow dispensed with a stage that would separate audiences from performers, so that the two participants, the active presenters and the passive observers, could constitute one, single production. Surrounding the performance space were other rooms to be used for instruction, for practice and for administration. The Festival Hall fronted on a large square edged along its three other sides by lodgings for both students and faculty. The school quickly attracted students from all over the world.

The first School Festival was held in 1912 and was so well advertised that the international literati descended on Hellerau to become acquainted with Dalcroze's innovative techniques. A second School Festival in summer 1913, offered a professional eurhythmic performance of Gluck's *Orpheus and Eurydice*. In October of that same year, the German premier of Paul Claudel's *Tidings Brought to Mary* attracted such literary celebrities as Rainier Rilke, George Bernard Shaw, Franz Kafka and Franz Werfel. The *Tidings*' German translator, Jakob Hegner, a friend of Dohrn's, had recently settled himself and his publishing business in Hellerau.

There can be no doubt that the eurhythmic school and the Festival Hall put Hellerau on the map and helped to attract a variety of avant-garde artists to the garden city. Though Schmidt encouraged the initial invitation to Dalcroze, he was much more cautious than Dohrn. He envisioned a modest, wooden structure for the school until it could establish itself financially. It was, after all, Schmidt's money that was initially committed to the enterprise. Both he and Riemerschmid thought the Tessenow design much too grandiose for their utopian community.

On the other hand, Dohrn was so determined to achieve an ideal marriage between art and social reform that he circumvented Schmidt's objections and persuaded the other members of the supervising board to approve the project. He also put up 300,000 marks of his own money to assure its construction. In the end, Festival Hall and associated buildings cost a total of 1.75 million marks, almost six times the original capital of the Garden City Hellerau Corporation. In protest, both Schmidt and Riemerschmid resigned from the corporation's board. Dohrn died in a skiing accident in 1914. Dalcroze, a Swiss citizen, became *persona non grata* in Germany after he signed a public letter protesting the German bombardment of Rheims cathedral at the beginning of World War I. His school in Hellerau closed and never reopened. The Festival Hall and its complex developed into a white elephant. Yet Schmidt's Hellerau Corporation continued to own the building into the 1930s.[280]

Hellerau became a mythical place, Germany's first and only real garden city, an ideal community in which living, working, learning and entertaining would combine into a work of human harmony. It never became what its founders wanted it to be. Even before 1914, the Corporation and the Cooperative experienced financial difficulties and social tensions.[281] World War I unleashed destructive currents unforeseen when Hellerau was founded. Today, the city of Dresden sells the Festival Hall as a tourist attraction, and the new owners of the workshops continue to nourish art, music and fine workmanship, but they have abandoned the idea of supplying the masses with solid, reasonably-priced consumer goods. Hellerau is still a desirable place to live, but it is not utopia.

Dresden was a city caught between its reputation as the "Florence of the Elbe" and the socio-economic tensions accompanying industrialization. Its upper and middle classes supported old and new music, its youth experimented with modern arts, its working classes, proud and innovative in their own right, insisted on being included in the common weal. In 1914, modern Dresden was the fifth largest city in the German Reich. But it, like the German state, could not resolve the tensions between old and new.

World War I

On 1 January 1914, Semper gallery director Woermann, now retired, posed a crucial question for the coming year. "Will it bring us war or peace?" he wrote. "All around us the storm clouds are gathering. May a fresh wind scatter them. We are staggering thoughtlessly into uncertainty."[282] Uncertainty became certainty eight months later.

When war broke out at the beginning of August 1914, Dresdners flocked to the colors enthusiastically. The response to the mobilization was so great that families were forced to take in military men for whom there was no room in the barracks. Woermanns willingly boarded young relatives who had to report for duty in Dresden. They also had eight Silesian soldiers quartered on them. Willi Apelt remembers that his family needed to provide room and board for five soldiers. His mother cleared out one room, laid down straw and gave each one a pillow and a blanket. Men sang as they marched to the rails that would carry them to war, while their families wept at their departure.

During the month of August, Dresdners rejoiced at every victory over enemies they were sure the Germans could defeat. When French Lorraine fell, bells rang out all over the city, and the streets sported colorful flags and banners. People sang in the streets, and citizens decorated the Bismarck monument just south of the main rail station with wreaths and flowers. At the end of August, when the Boy Scout troop of the Lucas Church presented the colors, both Pastor Kessler and Cornelius Gurlitt urged the boys to volunteer usefully during the conflict. A few days later, Dresdners hung out flags to celebrate General Hindenburg's victory against the Russians at Tannenberg. On Sedan Day, September 2, as the German armies prepared to take Paris, a victory "fever" pulsed through the city.

Thereafter, as the German government's war reports fell silent, Dresdners marked the retreat on the Western front. Paris had not fallen. Perhaps the boys would not be home for Christmas after all. Yet no one gave up hope of winning the war. Additional municipal celebrations followed, until the last great victory observed came when Bucharest capitulated in December 1916. By that time, social tensions were exacerbated by worsening material shortages.[283]

During the early years of the war, the city kept up appearances. Both cultural and sporting events continued as before, even though both were affected by the mass conscription of men. The streets and squares of the city were quieter during the day, and at night, street lights burned "more thriftily".

Meals became more modest in solidarity with the many fighting men who were hardly enjoying good, bourgeois cooking. Altruism apart, there was also a shortage of foodstuffs due to the British blockade of German ports and to the loss of imports from continental enemies like Russia and France. Bread rationing began in 1915, followed by meat rationing a year later. In the course of 1916, shortages appeared among many of the goods previously considered necessary for everyday life. At the same time, Dresden industry, heavily dependent on consumer spending, export markets, and a steady supply of raw materials, suffered a steep decline. Some of the city's private firms went bankrupt; others quietly closed.

The wartime shortages plus the borrowing binge of the national government contributed to an ever-escalating inflation. Price controls, which attempted to combat this evil, simply led to the emergence of both gray (semi-legal) and black (illegal) markets. The standard of living of white-collar employees, civil servants, and workers declined. Only energetic Dresdners who went to the countryside were able to buy eggs—at very high prices. During the winter of 1917, potatoes were so scarce that clever housewives devised tasty dishes using turnips. People lost weight, and tailors experienced a boom.

Outright poverty and hunger posed serious problems for the city. By the end of 1917, the municipality was receiving 63,000 applications of support for 95,000 individuals. That was almost one-fifth of Dresden's pre-war population. City government bought up fruit, vegetables, and grain in the countryside and collected animal bones in order to produce fat. In 1918, the number of soup kitchens operating in the city increased to 274, serving 170,000 meals daily. The municipality also had to find clothes for those individuals unable to work.[284]

Dresdners not only helped those affected by the shortage of food and other materials, they also cared for wounded soldiers. Retired museum director Woermann and his wife nursed young officers in their home for weeks and months at a time. Only as provisions became ever more scarce in the middle of the war, did middle-class families cease this volunteer activity.

Volunteers succored the troops who passed through the main Dresden rail stations. Initially carried out with private funds, the municipality soon supported this effort financially. Dresden's women "manned" the stations night and day, helped by the local Boy Scouts. Cooking took place at the station kitchens, at the women's homes and at the Hotel Europäischer Hof, a block away from the main station. The owner, Rudolf Sendig, volunteered this service to the war effort. Mill owners Theodor and Erwin Bienert donated the bread consumed at both stations.

At the main station, meals were served upstairs in a large hall, and guards stood at the doors to make sure that only soldiers gained entry. Dresdners arranged both Christmas and New Year's celebrations for soldiers passing through town. Pastors, helped by laymen, added an appropriate spiritual dimension. Many of the soldiers unburdened themselves to Frau Woermann, who was in charge of the volunteer effort at the main station. Occasionally, the former gallery director visited the main station to mix with the troops and boost their spirits. Frau Woermann, on the brink of exhaustion, remained "on duty" at the main station until war's end finally provided rest.[285]

Even as Dresden's middle class continued loyally to support the war effort, its working class, materially hardest hit by the war, began to question its necessity. In 1914, the Social Democrats, persuaded that the conflict was defensive, had joined the various committees involved in the war effort. By 1915, however, the party faced increasing censorship and restraints on its ability to hold rallies and assemblies. It was also clear that the German government had now embraced the imperialistic goal of dominating Europe, both politically and economically. Social Democrats did not sanction this policy. They were particularly rankled by the government's refusal to accept responsibility for the care of fallen soldiers' wives and children. The party insisted that the Saxon state should directly assume this burden. Instead, it set up a private foundation to which the state and the communes made contributions.

As food shortages increased, the Saxon Foodstuffs Agency failed to control speculators in grain and to adequately regulate the rationing system. In summer 1916, protests broke out all over Saxony, including Dresden. As winter arrived, seven thousand people, mostly women, gathered before the Saxon Ministry of the Interior to complain about the shortage of food. Finally, when the extreme scarcity of potatoes and bread gave way to the turnip winter of 1917, the state invited a Social Democrat to join the Food Agency.

By this time, the Saxon government had discovered that it lacked sufficient police to contain the developing unrest. After the Russian Revolution of March 1917, there was also a fear that the few troops that might be mustered against rioting workers would simply prove to be as unreliable as Russian soldiers when confronted by hungry protestors. In April 1917, a wave of strikes flooded Saxon cities. In Dresden this wave was comparatively small, but massive strikes in neighboring Leipzig led the government to make state-wide economic concessions: higher wages, higher bread rations, shorter work weeks. By this time, the national Social Democrats had split into two different organizations: the Majority who continued to support the war; and those Independents who wanted to end hostilities through negotiations.[286]

The leaders of Russia's Bolshevik Revolution in November 1917 called for peace on the basis of the pre-war status quo and thereby bolstered similar demands within Germany. Philip Scheidemann, a leading Social Democrat, spoke in Dresden in mid-November and favored peace, but he cautioned his listeners against a Bolshevik government. Bolshevik methods, he said, were not suitable for Germany. At the same time, Frau Woermann reported that soldiers passing through the main rail station were talking openly about making peace in the trenches. This sentiment was echoed in louder and "wilder" tones throughout the coming year.[287]

At the beginning of 1918, Saxon support for the war effort was severely tested. The official meat ration represented 31% of the pre-war level; for butter it was 22%; for flour, 52%. Only potatoes, at 70% of the pre-war level, were in comparatively good supply. Inflation was so rampant that real wages had declined to 25% of the pre-war level. At least one observer thought that Saxon conditions were the worst in all of Germany. As representatives of the national government negotiated the Peace of Brest-Litovsk with Vladimir Lenin's new Russian government, numerous strikes hit the city and its environs in January and February 1918. These protested the poor economic conditions and called for an end to the war in both east and west.

Increasingly, Dresden's workers insisted on a negotiated peace. In September, 20,000 people, again mostly women, attended a protest rally. As new recruits were called up in fall 1918, mutiny occurred as they marched to the Neustadt station accompanied by a crowd of anti-war civilians. Most of the recruits either left the train or claimed they were sick. They refused to ride off to war.[288]

Events at the national level re-enforced the Dresdners' actions. At the end of September, the German military conceded the loss of the war and insisted that a new government in Berlin sue for peace with the Western allies. Long overdue political reform was also on the agenda. On October 3, Social Democrats entered a national government for the first time. Two weeks later, in Dresden, Social Democrats joined the Saxon government, still under the leadership of the Conservative Count Christoph Vitzthum. Only on October 28, when the Reichstag passed a law instituting parliamentary government all over Germany did Vitzthum resign in favor of the National Liberal Rudolf Heinze. He possessed the confidence of both the left liberals and the Social Democrats and was expected to make Saxony's government conform to that of the Reich. National events soon made these plans moot.[289]

In the midst of the ceasefire negotiations with the Western allies at the end of October, the German naval leadership ordered the fleet to launch forays against the English in the Channel to support the beleaguered army still fighting in France. Believing this effort to be futile, sailors in Wilhelmshaven refused to fire up the ships' boilers. Within days, the mutiny spread to all North German ports.

The most significant for future developments was the country's main naval base at Kiel. There, on the evening of November 4, an assembly of sailors and soldiers formed a revolutionary council and drew up the Kiel Resolutions calling for the end of the war and the freedom of speech and press. These sailors, while hissing their red flags over German ships, wanted no part of a Bolshevik regime. They simply wanted the fighting to cease. Soldiers in Dresden shared their goals and, in a rally, adopted the Kiel Resolutions.

Real revolution arrived in Dresden on November 8. Pilots stationed in the Grossenhain garrison to the north released flyers from their planes calling for support of the Kiel sailors. Mass demonstrations filled the Altmarkt. Soldiers from the Albertstadt barracks established control over the city. They freed military prisoners and occupied the main railway station. The next day, Dresden's workers left their factories and gathered in the city center where radical Independent Socialists rallied them.[290]

In the course of November 9 and 10, Saxon Socialists declared a republic and formed a revolutionary Soldiers and Workers' Council in the capital city. Sunday, November 10, was a rainy day, but that did not deter civilian Dresdners, joined by an overwhelming number of soldiers, from crowding the city's streets. Shops were closed. So were the doors of the main train station. Guards no longer stood at the closed gates of the palace, and a red flag unfurled on the palace's Hausmann Tower. Members of the Soldiers' and Workers'

Council roamed the streets determined to maintain order. Nevertheless, officers were fair game; they were stopped in their tracks and stripped of their stripes. In one incident, Friedrich Salzburg stood on the front platform of a streetcar when a group of young revolutionaries attempted to storm the tram, tear off his officer's insignia, and break his sword. Observing the intent, the conductor quickly closed the platform's door and drove away so fast that the revolutionaries could not keep up.

Within the next week, the Soldiers' and Workers' Council set up a provisional Saxon government consisting of six Socialists: three from the moderate Majority and three from the more radical Independents. The related group of Spartacists would soon divorce themselves from Social Democrats and become the German Communist Party.[291] On November 13, King Friedrich August III abdicated the throne of Saxony. He had left Dresden four days before. By the time Rudolf Heinze, representing the Saxon government, arrived at his new residence to seek his "unavoidable" abdication, both the kings of Bavaria and Prussia, the latter also as German emperor, had relinquished their thrones. The King laid his head on a table across his folded arms and remained silent for a long time. Perhaps he recalled the 829 years of his family's suzerainty of Saxony. Finally, he lifted his head and quietly signed the abdication document.[292]

August the Strong, Saxon Elector and Polish King

Canaletto Prospect, 1748   Canaletto, Ruins of Kreuzkirche Tower, 1765

Satyrs, entrance to Wall Pavillion, Zwinger, 1930
SLUB/Deutsche Fotothek, Walter Möbius

Carl Gustav Carus as a young man ©

Semper Synagogue

Rabbi Frankel

Engel Barricade, 1849
Kupferstich Kabinet/Staatliche Kunstsammlung Dresden

Ludwig Richter, Hansel and Gretel ⓒ

Ernemann Tower, 1949
SLUB Deutsche Fotothek/ unknown photographer

Festival Hall, Hellerau, 1915
SLUB Deutsche Fotothek/unknown photographer

Ludwig Kirchner's Bathers at Moritzburg
Tate Gallery London

Ilgen Arena, George Arnhold Swimming Pool, 1933
SLUB Deutsche Fotothek/Walter Hahn

IX. The Weimar Republic

A Period of Unrest

In the last weeks of 1918, the capital city of Dresden found itself in the midst of a Saxon state on the verge of civil war. The conditions facing the new government were overwhelming. The state as a whole had suffered over 200,000 thousand dead and over 300,000 wounded. Forty thousand men were prisoners of war. As the British continued to blockade the coast of Germany until it signed a peace treaty, thousands suffered from malnutrition. Both grain and potato supplies were low due to reductions in acreage, fertilizer, and seed during the war. There was practically no meat available. At the end of 1918, the Saxon Foodstuffs Agency estimated that it had enough reserves to last only eight days. Food was so scarce that lawyer Friedrich Salzburg was asked to defend a former soldier who, in a band of six others, robbed grocery stores at night. The new government finally formed a Free Corps of decommissioned army officers and citizen volunteers that patrolled the streets in order to prevent burglaries of stores and residences.

The medical system had broken down completely, and the mortality rate, particularly that of infants, increased. Divorces, especially among couples who had hastily married during the war, became so frequent that the Dresden superior court had to double the number of public defenders to help those too poor to engage a lawyer. According to Karl Woermann, social life for the upper class also changed due to the shortage of food. Instead of the elaborate dinners served before the war, people now resorted to afternoon or evening tea. That was just as well, as the lack of domestic help meant that upper-and-middle-class women now did a host of household chores themselves. Due to a lack of construction, there was also a housing shortage. Woermann and his wife, now living on a government pension, took in boarders. This measure not only provided housing for others, it augmented their income as inflation, begun during the war, became rampant.

Industrial production was in a state of collapse due to a shortage of raw materials and to the wartime closure of one-third of small and medium-sized Saxon businesses. Industrial exports, due to the English blockade and civil war in Russia, also did not quickly resume their pre-war levels. Returning from the fronts were thousands of Saxons expecting to resume their old jobs. Almost immediately, the new government introduced aid for the unemployed in order to avoid marauding "bands of workless soldiers". These efforts were not completely successful.[293]

At the beginning of 1919, there were bread riots and plundering within Dresden. On 8 January 1919, a large demonstration of the unemployed gathered in front of the Rathaus, and nervous watchmen almost fired on the demonstrators. Four days later, incited by the local Communist leader, Otto Rühle, a crowd marched off to the offices of the Dresdner *Volkszeitung* (People's News), the press organ of the ruling Social Democratic Party. The demonstrators believed the rumor that anti-Communist flyers, distributed to soldiers of the Dresden garrison, had been printed on the newspaper's presses. This scene was highly reminiscent of events occurring almost simultaneously in Berlin, where Communists rebelled against the provisional government in that city's newspaper district. The revolt in Berlin was only painfully quelled by the action of Free Corps units.

In Dresden therefore, watchmen at the *Volkszeitung* were wary of the approaching crowd. They stopped the marchers with a hail of bullets, killing twelve people and wounding fifty. Rühle and other Communists were arrested and sent to the Königstein, the southern Saxon castle that had served for centuries as the prison for dissenters and revolutionaries. The provisional government declared martial law throughout Dresden, banned Communist rallies and made participating in demonstrations a punishable offense. When the Independent Socialists in the government demanded the release of Rühle and the formation of an investigating committee, the three Majority Socialists refused. The Independents therefore left the government in protest against what they saw as the increasing arbitrariness of their Socialist partners.[294]

Elections both to the Saxon Diet and to the Dresden city assembly did little to stop the unrest. On 2 February 1919, Saxon voters chose a new People's Assembly. Since the Majority Socialists gained 41.6% of the vote and the

Independents 16.3%, it was assumed that the two socialist parties together would form a coalition government. That proved to be impossible as the two, given the disagreements of the preceding three months, could not reach compromise on the issues. The next most logical partners were the left-wing liberals with 22.9% of the vote. Yet the Majority Socialists decided not to ally with a non-socialist party and formed a minority government instead. Even the middle-class parties voted for this new government. Only in July 1919, when they needed to pass a workable budget, did the Social Democrats invite the left liberals to join them in running the Saxon state.

During the revolutionary months, it was the Socialists who played the most active roles. But the bourgeois parties that had previously dominated Saxon politics were not inactive. They too had formed councils and subsequently had given their pre-war groupings new names. The old Conservatives became German Nationals, and the former Progressives transformed themselves into the German Democrats. The old National Liberal party relabeled itself the German People's Party. In any case, neither the German Nationals, with 4.9% of the vote, nor the People's Party, with 14.3%, did well in the state elections.[295]

Middle-class parties fared better in the elections to the city assembly on February 9. On that day, Dresdners elected forty-three Socialists, both moderate and radical, and forty-one non-Socialists. In any case, the mayor, right-wing liberal Bernhard Blüher, remained the same. In June 1918, the city council had elected him mayor for life, and the Social Democrats had no intention of breaking the contract. In that period's communal system, the mayor acted like a city manager and could be elected for periods longer than the regular election cycle. If the parties that elected him lost their majority, he continued to serve until the contractual term expired. Blüher served as Dresden's mayor and manager for the next twelve years, championing enlightened social policies as well as economic growth.[296]

Conditions within the city after the elections of February 1919 remained unsettled. Dresden could not escape the cascading political currents of the national scene. In early spring, a protest rally turned particularly violent. On April 12, the Communists organized at the War Ministry a demonstration of war wounded and medics from Dresden's military hospital. The War Ministry was then located in the Blockhaus on the Neustadt's end of the Augustus Bridge. The rallying men were protesting a decrease, determined by the national government in Berlin, in their wages, salaries and pensions. The Communist Max Frenzel and a sixteen-member committee wanted to negotiate this issue with the Saxon War Minister, Gustav Neuring.

Neuring refused to discuss the issue and ordered active-duty soldiers to barricade the ministry. Determined protestors, nevertheless, gained entry to the Blockhaus through a light shaft. They disarmed the security guard, and the demonstrators stormed the building, captured Neuring, and threw him off the bridge into the Elbe. When he tried to rescue himself by climbing onto the river bank, the protestors shot and killed him. The demonstrators remained in the ministry until darkness fell. Frenzel and his group finally negotiated an agreement with government representatives: 1) Neuring's murder would be punished; 2) The Saxon government would demand that the national government help the war-wounded and their caregivers.

At the same time, the state government declared martial law in Dresden and extended it to all of Saxony the next day. It also asked the national government to send troops to help it keep order. Those troops arrived on April 15. They were soon joined by bands of Free Corps. On April 23, the national government added its own declaration of martial law to that of the Saxons and banned the traditional May Day celebrations. For a short period of time, the Independent Socialists, with their stronghold in the neighboring city of Leipzig, threatened a general strike. Even though this strike was called off, the German army did not vacate Saxony until mid-June 1919.[297]

Both the state and national governments were nervous about Communist-inspired demonstrations. On the day of Neuring's murder, a Communist Republic was declared in neighboring Bavaria, hostages taken, and at the end of April, eight of the captives were executed. Regular army troops and Free Corps only managed to end the Bavarian Communist Republic with a "white terror" in mid-May.[298]

After Neuring's murder, life in Dresden returned to relative calm. The former gallery director, Woermann, remembered in his memoirs that Dresdners were spared the vandalism, plunder and street fighting that continued to disturb the peace of many other cities. During these waning days of summer, the nation received its new Weimar Constitution, so-called because of its creation in the small southern city of Weimar whence the National Assembly had gathered to escape the violent political strife of Berlin.[299]

The Versailles Treaty, making peace with the World War's victors, came into force at the beginning of 1920. That meant that Germany was required to assume the responsibility for causing World War I and for paying the damages that the war had inflicted on the combatants. It also meant that a four-million-man army would be reduced, almost overnight, to 100,000 men. Last, but not least, Germany lost territory to France in the west and Poland in the east. Many Germans, including Dresdners, rejected these conditions because they had difficulty accepting their loss of the war. The old imperial government had kept them in the dark about the setbacks suffered during the last two years of hostilities, and no enemy soldiers had set foot on German soil. The military establishment broadcast the idea that it had been stabbed in the back by striking workers and pacifist political parties at home. The national government's order to disband two notoriously right-wing Free Corps units led to armed insurrection.

On 13 March 1920, a group of Free Corps stationed near Berlin marched on the city intending to restore the old regime with a new, right-wing government under the leadership of the nationalist conservative Wolfgang Kapp. The whole episode has gone down in history as the Kapp Putsch. In response, the moderate republican government called for a general strike that effectively shut down all transit in and out of the national capital. Then it fled to Dresden where it thought it could count on the support of the military and Free Corps units under General George Maercker. This hope was mistaken. General Maercker instead appeared at the Saxon War Ministry flying the red, white and black flag of the old monarchical regime. He also issued an order against the general strike.

The national government moved on to the more welcoming city of Stuttgart, and the Saxons were left to deal with the Putsch itself. While the government of Majority Socialists and Democrats dithered, neither the Saxon army nor the Saxon civil service supported the Putsch. Eventually, the Socialists and the trade unions settled on a large protest strike for March 15, a Monday.

During the night of March 14, Free Corps units supporting the Putsch occupied the main post office. When a crowd of strikers gathered on the Postplatz in the morning, they demanded the opening of the gates, and the putschists gave in without a fight. Thereafter a group of strikers occupied the post office and set up two machine guns at the entrance. At 2 p.m., the army, with the approval of the Saxon government, rattled onto the Theaterplatz with two armored cars, occupied the Zwinger and from there proceeded to attack the strikers in the post office with machine guns. Though the workers fired back, they could not prevail against the army, and they cleared the premises at 7 p.m. The army then cordoned off the area with barbed wire. This encounter left fifty-nine workers dead and 200 wounded. Only six soldiers of the regular army were killed.[300]

The Quest for Stability

Though there was considerable violence during and after the Putsch of 1920 in other Saxon cities, calm once again returned to Dresden. Nevertheless, events and attitudes at the national and state levels could not help but affect the city. The Kapp Putsch had revealed at least two conditions critical for the nascent democracy in Germany, in Saxony and in Dresden. First, the army took an ambivalent stance vis-à-vis the Republic and the working class that supported it. And secondly, there was no evidence that Communist activists had staged the post office's occupation. Yet the moderate Socialists that governed both Germany and Saxony were so wary of leftist movements that they were willing to sanction military measures against defenders of the republic. On March 16, the national government in Berlin raised General Alfred Müller, who had led the army's attack on the Dresden post office, to Commander in Saxony, with headquarters in Dresden. The Saxon government did not protest this appointment. Consequently, popular dissatisfaction with the Saxon government's stance was so great that the moderate Socialist Minister-President George Gradnauer resigned in April. His resignation did not change the orientation of the Saxon government. Wilhelm Buck, another moderate Socialist, replaced Gradnauer.[301]

The next two years were characterized in Germany by an ever-growing assertiveness on the political right, both at the national and the local levels. Already in 1919, the Independent Socialists Kurt Eisner and Hugo Haase were assassinated by violent right-wingers. In 1921, it was the turn of the Catholic Centrist Matthias Erzberger, who had signed the armistice ending World War I and, as Finance Minister, had introduced a significant tax reform two years before. In 1922, right-wing extremists assassinated the Jewish Foreign Minister Walter Rathenau who had advocated an acceptance of the Versailles Treaty in order to create a climate that would persuade the Western allies to renegotiate some of its more offensive provisions. Rathenau's murder was so shocking that it led the Centrist Prime Minister, Joseph Wirth, to warn his republican countrymen that "the enemy [stood] on the right", not on the left.[302]

In Saxony, the moderate Socialist government encountered opposition from both left and right. In spring 1922, the state government declared both May 1, the traditional European "Labor Day", and November 9, the anniversary of the republic's establishment, to be legal holidays. The middle-class, anti-Republican parties were so incensed about these holidays that they joined the Communists in helping to dissolve the legislature. This collusion of the radical left and the radical right against the moderate center later became common practice in German interwar politics.

Also in 1922, contrary to the hope of the right-wing parties, the Saxon elections returned a majority that stood even further to the left than the previous one. Ten assemblymen represented the Saxon Communists. The moderate Socialist Wilhelm Buck again became minister-president, receiving the votes of the reunited Socialists as well as the Communists. His government did not last long. On 30 January 1923, the Communists and the middle-class parties, together again, voted no-confidence in his government. In March, another Socialist, Eric Zeigner, became minister-president just as Germany faced another crisis.[303]

The Crisis of 1923

In the early 1920s, the German government had resisted paying the reparations demanded by the World War's victors. In response, the French occupied the Ruhr coal district in January 1923, intending to allocate to themselves and other Allies the mined coal as payment for the damages Germany had inflicted on them during World War I. In retaliation, the German government called for "passive resistance"—zero cooperation with the French—on the part of the coal miners and all government officials in the district. The French then sent in their own miners and administrators to collect what was due them, generating a Ruhr crisis.

These actions not only worsened German-French relations, they created havoc in the German economy. During World War I, inflation had already caused severe problems, and once the war was over, little was done to reverse it. Instead, the German government printed money to cover reparations payments and its social obligations to the citizenry. As the value of the mark declined relative to other currencies, foreigners with strong currencies—principally the dollar and the Swiss franc—could buy German goods at bargain basement prices. Thus they flocked to Germany, including Dresden, to take advantage of the situation.

Inflation had been steadily creeping up, and during the Ruhr crisis, given the French seizure of vital coal, it exploded. Prices changed so rapidly in the course of a day that businesses started to pay wages and salaries daily instead of weekly or monthly. Individuals withdrawing money from the banks appeared with large wicker baskets, allowing them to transport the piles of bills that they needed. People on fixed incomes, pensioners like the Woermanns, simply could not maintain their old standards of living. Modest middle-class savings were lost, because banks canceled the accounts, claiming that it cost more to sustain and administer these accounts than they were worth. Landlords and creditors found they could not raise rents and interest to match the rate of inflation. In short, the inflation affected prices in all realms of life.[304]

Before the war, streetcars in Dresden cost 10 pfennigs a ride; in November 1923 the same ride cost 100 billion marks. In April 1923, a loaf of bread cost 750 marks; in September the price was 2 million. A quart of milk then cost 3 million. Salzburg and one of his associates kept track of the financial markets, and when a depreciation of the mark was projected, they went out and bought everything they could before their existing horde of marks was worth less. Once, they intended to buy pears at a grocery. Just as they got ready to pay, the stallkeeper's wife hung up her telephone, reported a 100% depreciation and promptly doubled the price of the pears. Eventually, the effects of inflation on business and industry led to layoffs and gathering unemployment. By the fall of 1923, 22% of the German unemployed were Saxons, and 60% of Dresdners suffered from partial or full unemployment. This situation fed discontent on both the left and the right.[305]

Throughout the year, Saxon Minister-President Zeigner advocated the end of passive resistance and the pursuit of a "policy of fulfillment", whereby the French would be assured of punctual reparations payments required by the Versailles Treaty and would therefore end their occupation of the Ruhr district. He and his fellow Social Democrats also enacted policies, such as price control committees, that would mitigate the effects of inflation on the Saxon working class. Yet their efforts were not effective enough to prevent riots from occurring in Dresden in May and early June 1923.

Meanwhile, events abroad impacted the political climate in Germany, including Saxony. After months of right-wing violence, in the preceding October, Fascists, with the help of the army, had assumed control of the Italian government. Much of the Italian Fascist violence resembled that in neighboring Bavaria, where a right-wing government had held sway ever since the end of the local Soviet Republic in 1919. Right-wing groups had proliferated, among them the National Socialist Party and its militia, the S.A. (Sturmabteilung—Stormtroopers). These right-wing militias, supported by the army, spilled over the border into southern Saxony and attacked leftists of all stripes. At the end of July 1923, the Communists held a peaceful anti-Fascist rally in Dresden, which thousands attended.

The Zeigner government now supported the creation of Communist militias. These left-wing groups were supposed to be unarmed, and Zeigner's government knew that they were capable neither of mounting full-scale rebellion nor of a serious challenge to the army. For its part, the army in Saxony, though also aware of their weakness, was wary of the Communist militias and stepped up its support for right-wing groups. It signaled in other ways its disdain for the democratic republic.[306]

By late summer 1923, even nationalistic Germans knew that passive resistance in the Ruhr had failed to chase out the French and that some accommodation with their old enemy would have to be found. On August 13, a broadly-based government, with Gustav Stresemann as Chancellor, formed in Berlin. The national Social Democrats joined this coalition. One month later, on September 26, the Stresemann government ended passive resistance and, fearing widespread opposition to this act, declared a state of emergency all over Germany.

The Bavarian right wing strongly opposed the end of passive resistance. When the national Army Minister Otto Gessler applied the state of emergency to Bavaria and forbade the publication of the rabidly critical National Socialist newspaper, the army commander in that state, Otto von Lossow, refused to carry out the minister's orders and placed his division at the disposal of the Bavarian right-wing government.

The German army's commander in Berlin refused to send another division into Bavaria to carry out the government's wishes. He further challenged the legitimacy of Stresemann's government by claiming that it did not enjoy the support either of the German people or the army, and he strongly hinted that the army should be given full powers at the national level. In the face of the army's stance, Stresemann's government feared a successful uprising of right-wing groups all over the nation.[307]

In Saxony, the exact opposite occurred. Left-wing violence had been escalating throughout the year. In the south, Communist militias battled with the right-wing Bavarians spilling over the border. Workers stole crops from farmers, and employers complained that they were harassed and intimidated by their workers. At the beginning of September, the Communist militias held a mass meeting in Dresden, attended by 8000 people. The Saxon middle class and farmers truly feared a Communist uprising.

Thus, when the national state of emergency was proclaimed, General Müller in Saxony was given full powers to implement it, even though the decree allowed the several German states to appoint their own commissioners, and Minister-President Zeigner insisted that a civilian in the state's Interior Ministry be given the responsibility. When the national government ignored his protests, he reorganized his cabinet to include two Communists and appointed the head of the German Communist Party as director of his staff. Even if they were too weak to carry out a revolution, the Communists could use these positions to influence existing governments. Zeigner's appointments thus led to a firestorm on the part of the right-wing, middle-class parties that supported the army's subsequent actions in Saxony.[308]

General Müller proceeded to ban all Communist newspapers, to dissolve the left-wing militias, to dismiss the price-control committees, to assume control of the Saxon police, and to execute a military occupation of all Saxony. The army in Berlin sent additional units to Saxony to support General Müller. Middle-class Dresdners greeted the army's imposition of order by showering flowers on the soldiers. Stresemann's government in Berlin demanded that Zeigner dismiss the Communist members of his cabinet, arguing that their inclusion violated the constitutional provision requiring office holders to support the republic.

Stresemann also demanded Zeigner's resignation as minister-president. When the latter refused, the army, on October 29, occupied Saxon governmental offices in Dresden, including those of the Saxon Diet. The Chancellor appointed Rudolf Heinze as governor of the state, deposing Zeigner. These actions occurred with the help of tanks and machine guns. In two towns immediately south of Dresden and in the Ore Mountains, workers fought back against the military occupation, which opened fire on the resisters.[309]

Saxon Social Democrats, meanwhile, had refrained from inciting armed opposition to the national government, though both they and the trade unions worried that the continued rightward political trend would undermine the economic benefits they had gained from the 1918 revolution. Even the Communist leadership refrained from urging armed resistance to the military. The workers' conflicts with the army's occupation were "wild" events. For most of October, however, the Saxon Socialists had supported Zeigner and refused to let him resign.

On October 31, two days after Heinze stepped in as commissar, moderate Socialists in the legislature intervened to rescue the situation. They formed a new government with left-wing liberals in the Democratic Party, excluded the Communists from the cabinet, and elected the moderate Socialist Alfred Fellisch as Saxon Minister-President. Even the German People's Party, representing Saxon businessmen, supported Fellisch. The state of emergency and the military occupation, however, lasted until February 1924. By that time, the political pendulum in both Dresden and Saxony had swung ever rightward. In the state legislature, the Social Democrats entered into a coalition with middle-class liberals. Elections held at the beginning of 1924 in Dresden returned a middle-class majority to the city's assembly.[310]

Historians agree that the events of 1923 cast a shadow over republican democracy in the state of Saxony and in Germany as a whole. Zeigner, some say, was the pawn sacrificed to the army to prevent its alliance with the radical right. In Bavaria on November 9, when the National Socialist Stormtroopers (SA) attempted their march on Berlin to install a right-wing government, the army did not prevent the Bavarian police from stopping them. That made the army's action in defense of right-wing elements in Saxony all the more galling.

The use of the army in Saxony in 1923 embittered the Social Democrats and alienated many of their working-class members. At the end of November 1923, they introduced a vote of no-confidence against Stresemann to protest the lack of stringent measures against the right-wing government in Bavaria, a government that was, arguably, more unconstitutional than the last Zeigner cabinet. The rank and file of Saxon Socialists formally labeled as unconstitutional the military measures of 1923, and increasingly expected their leaders to refuse cooperation with middle-class parties.[311]

Republican Dresden

Even though the events following the Kapp Putsch heavily impacted Dresden, urban government under Blüher continued to do the best it could to further the city's welfare. As the capital of Saxony, Dresden continued to host the legislative Diet and various state agencies. To these were added branches of the central German government: the treasury, the railroad, the post office, the labor department, the army, and others. These offices attracted people to Dresden who paid taxes that compensated the city for the loss of some of its revenues to the government in Berlin, the result of tax reforms in the early 1920s. Already in 1921, the city had annexed twenty-two peripheral villages which included the prosperous eastern suburbs of Blasewitz, Loschwitz and Weisser Hirsch. At one fell swoop, the city's population increased by almost 100,000 people.[312]

During the early interwar period, Dresden experienced tugs in two directions. On the one hand, many firms that closed during the war never reopened. Mergers of small into larger firms reflected the twentieth-century trend toward consolidation. For instance, before the war, 127 cigarette factories had called Dresden home. After the war, these were reduced to forty-two. In 1925, three of the most important ones signed a cartel agreement with the expanding Reemtsma firm to regulate prices and profits. Reemtsma, by this time, had already mechanized large parts of its production, resulting in a massive loss of jobs.

This interwar consolidation and rationalization of production meant that unemployment became a permanent problem for the city. At the same time, Dresden found itself geographically much more peripheral to the European economy than previously. The German loss of Posen to the newly independent Poland and the splintering of the old Austrian empire, due to the treaties concluded at Versailles, adversely affected the exports on which Dresden's economy depended.

On the other hand, Dresden now became part of a large economic conurbation that stretched along both sides of the Elbe from Meissen in the west to Pirna on the east, from Tharandt in the south to Radeberg in the north. Some of the consumer goods industries, long established in the city, continued to flourish: chocolates, condiments, pharmaceuticals, sewing machines, lace and other textiles. Measuring instruments and metallurgy also continued to do well. The manufacturers of electrical products, Koch and Sterzel as well as the

Saxon Works, found an expanded market for their goods as electrification throughout the world increased during the interwar period.[313]

There were already numerous, well-established camera manufacturers in Dresden. After World War I, technological improvements made photography increasingly popular, and competition became stiff world-wide. Challenging the Dresdner firms were Leitz in Wetzlar, which manufactured the Leica, and Eastman in Rochester, New York, with its handy Kodak brownie. Thus, in 1926, International Camera joined two others to form one of the world's best-known firms, Zeiss-Ikon. It was the Zeiss Foundation that instigated the merger, and the overriding goal of the newly merged firm was to make it more competitive on German and European markets. The stakes were high. Not only did the reflex camera and 35mm film make photography available to anybody capable of focusing a lens and clicking a shutter, but cinema, already available before the war, steadily grew into an entertainment medium appealing to Everyman. It too needed cameras and film, both of which were manufactured by Zeiss-Ikon, dominating two-thirds of the German market.[314]

Taking advantage of the increasing appeal of new technologies was also the firm Radio H. Mende, founded in Dresden in 1923. Mende quickly became one of the largest German manufacturers of radios and remained a known European brand for decades. Dresdners recognized, quite early in its development, the importance of the airplane for commercial purposes. The first airport opened before World War I on city property in Kaditz on the Elbe's right bank. Beginning in 1921, there were regular flights to Bremen and Hamburg, and the next year, state government formed the Saxon Airport Company. The airport was soon moved to a site on the Heller ridge, where it remained for only eight years, finally moving to a site in Klotsche, where it remains, significantly expanded, to this day. For a short period of time in the 1920s, the Junkers all-metal civilian aircraft, at that time an innovation, was manufactured in Dresden.[315]

The city, as the capital of Saxony, was no longer just a governmental town, catering to aristocrats and bureaucrats. By the 1920s, it depended on the manufacture and sale of goods and services to an expanding market. Sixty percent of the region's industrial workers were employed in large firms. And there were thirty establishments that gave work to over 1000 people. For instance, over 4000 employees toiled for Zeiss-Ikon after the merger of 1926. Yet the overwhelming number of firms in the conurbation were small: 95% of the total. The metropolitan area's economy was dichotomous. On the one hand were industries at the cutting edge of new technology, employing thousands of workers. On the other hand were hundreds of small firms exposed to the cruel winds of economic fortune, and these were located in the traditional sectors of clothing and foodstuffs. In any case, both large and small firms were tied to consumer spending and export markets.[316]

Modern High Culture

As Dresden's industrial role became increasingly important, the city did not abandon its historically cultural pretensions. As soon as the dust had settled on the post-war revolutionary events, the city and the Saxon state, now performing the functions of the old royal house, appointed a new General Director of State Theaters: Alfred Reucker. Formerly the director of the United City Theaters in Zurich, he came to Dresden with a host of experience and hired first-rate personalities to oversee both the theater and the opera.

When Reucker arrived in Dresden, Paul Wiecke had already been selected as theater director in 1920. Wiecke had long been associated with Dresden's state theater as an actor, having been wooed away from Weimar in 1895. He was particularly well-known for his performances in classical plays by Shakespeare, Goethe and Schiller. According to Karl Woermann, Dresden remained among the foremost German theaters during the Weimar Republic, and Wiecke, during the early 1920s, introduced expressionist and other modern plays to the Dresden stage.[317]

Wiecke's counterpart in the field of music was Fritz Busch. When Busch took over as conductor of the State Orchestra 1921, he was thirty years old and already respected among his peers. The next year he became director of the State Opera. He continued the pre-war practice of staging the premieres of Richard Strauss' operas. Dresden audiences greeted the first staging of *Intermezzo* in 1924 and of *The Egyptian Helena* in 1928. Bolstering this indulgence of romantic music was a Verdi Renaissance introduced after the writer Franz Werfel aroused interest in the composer with *Verdi: Novel of the Opera*, published in the mid-1920s. But Busch not only catered to Dresden traditionalists, he included in his programs works by modern composers such as Paul Hindemith, Kurt Weill, Bela Bartok, Leos Janacek, and Sergei Prokoviev. Keeping up with other modern developments, he began taking the State Orchestra on tour and recording its performances.

Henny Wolf, born and raised in Dresden as the daughter of a movie theater owner in the Neustadt, has described the allure of the theater and the opera for her parents, who had subscriptions for both houses. On the night of a performance, a hairdresser came to the house to style her mother's hair and to give her a manicure. Then, her mother, dressed in a fashionable, long evening dress, took a taxi with her father to the theater restaurant or to the Ratskeller where they dined before attending the evening's performance. At Christmas, Henny was treated to a matinee performance of a fairy tale at the state theater.

On the right bank of the Elbe, the Albert Theater kept up a lively competition with its more prestigious neighbors downtown. The repertoire ranged from Shakespearean dramas to Bernard Shaw and Frank Wedekind. During the 1925–26 season, it performed Carl Zuckmayer's then controversial *The Happy Vineyard,* and six years later his humorous critique of German militarism, *The Captain of Köpenick*. Just as controversial, in 1929 the Albert Theater staged Bert Brecht's *Three Penny Opera*, a satire about the capitalist economy. In 1931, it reached out to children with performances of Erich Kästner's *Emil and the Detective*. The performances on the Albertplatz remained popular and affordable straight through the Weimar Republic.[318]

Alongside the opera, the orchestra and the theater, there was dance. The more traditional ballet schools were joined by the new form of modern dance. Once World War I ended, one of Jacques-Dalcroze's students, Mary Wigman, opened a school in the Neustadt. By this time, she had toured a number of German cities, where her expressionism had been received enthusiastically. Throughout the 1920s, Wigman's recitals inspired a following among aficionados of free dancers not only in Germany and Europe, but also in the United States. The Saxon government considered her artistry important enough to grant her school, which attracted numerous students from around the world, a state subsidy.

The other significant free dancer in Germany, Gret Palucca, also established a school in Dresden. Palucca originally trained as a ballerina and was a student at the State Opera when she saw Wigman dance in recital in 1920 and was immediately converted. Between then and 1924, she studied under Wigman in Dresden and became a member of the ensemble. After that, she struck out on her own with solo recitals and, in 1925, she opened her own Dresden Dance Conservatory. Like Wigman, Palucca enjoyed an international reputation. Unlike Wigman's brooding motion, Palucca's dancing was exuberant, punctuated by her talent for high jumps.[319]

For six years in the 1920s, Palucca was married to the Dresden industrialist Fritz Bienert. At his mother's house, she associated with the modern artists of the interwar period. Ida Bienert was a force in her own right. In Plauen, a suburb of Dresden where she and her husband were at home, she opened the first independent and free, public lending library in Saxony. During the interwar period, modern artists were frequent guests. She also circulated in the group of the Dresden Secession, founded in 1919 by the Expressionists Conrad Felixmüller and Hugo Zehder. This circle held its first exhibition in Emil Richter's gallery shortly after its formation. One of the honorary members of the group was Oscar Kokoschka.[320]

By 1919, Kokoschka had already established himself as a portrait painter in Vienna and as a creator of rural and urban scenes. The noted art dealer Paul Cassirer had contracted with him to supply his gallery with one painting a year. Kokoschka arrived in Dresden as a convalescent from war wounds at the Weisser Hirsch's spa. In 1919, he secured a seven-year contract as professor at the Dresden Academy of Art, a position he had sought for several years. For the next four years, he painted several scenes of the Elbe and its bridges and threw himself into teaching at the academy.

A clue to his personality and attitudes occurred in 1920 when he wrote an open letter to his fellow citizens requesting that they not hold military practice in front of the Zwinger gallery. During the Kapp Putsch, a Rubens had been seriously damaged in a cross-fire of the combatants. For their part, the Dresdners labeled him, because of his lifestyle, as that "crazy" artist. In 1923, he asked for a two-year leave of absence from the academy and, though he returned to Dresden sporadically thereafter, he never really resumed his duties as professor. In 1927, the academy did not renew his appointment. Instead, it signed a contract with Otto Dix.[321]

At the time of his appointment, Dix was no stranger to the city. Before World War I, he had studied at the city's School of Applied Arts and had begun to experiment with several forms of modern art: post-impressionism, expressionism, cubism and futurism. He volunteered for the army in 1914 and saw service on both the eastern and western fronts, leaving the army as a sergeant. His experience as a soldier made a deep impression on Dix and, for the next decade, he depicted some of the most brutal scenes of the conflict.

Dix returned to Dresden after the war to study at the Academy of Fine Arts and acquired a rent-free studio at the former building of the Technical College on Antonsplatz. During this early post-war period, he was a founding member of Dresden's Secession 1919, and in Berlin he participated, in 1920, in the First International Dadaist Exhibition. In 1922, Dix exchanged his studio on Antonsplatz for other rent-free accommodations in Düsseldorf, and thereafter made a name for himself in the Rhineland, in Berlin, and in Munich. In 1927, the Dresden Academy of Fine Arts wooed him back. Along with his teaching duties, he produced two memorable large canvases: "Metropolis" and "War". The centerpiece of the "War" triptych was a reworking of "The Trench", an expression of the violence of trench warfare. In 1930, the prestigious Prussian Academy of Arts made Dix a member.[322]

Continuing to function as a cultural capital during the first decade of the Weimar Republic, Dresden's municipal Exhibition Palace next to the Great Garden staged an International Art Exhibition in 1926. Like its pre-war predecessor, although cultural conservatives disliked the trend, it showcased contemporary art, both local and international, and reinforced Dresden's artistic reputation, At the same time, the city, both government and citizens, wanted the rest of the world to know that Dresden was an industrial and scholarly center as well.

For instance, the exhibition of 1926 was the fourth Annual Show of German Labor. These yearly events featured different aspects of Dresden life: sports and games; residential developments; scientific progress. In 1928, the Technological City was the theme of the show, and a sphere-shaped structure was built next to the exhibition grounds to demonstrate advances in the building trades and professions.[323]

Dresden at Leisure

For those who either had no money or no time or even inclination to visit the opera, the stage, the museums, there was the new medium of cinema. Readers of Victor Klemperer's memoirs and diaries know that he and his wife were avid consumers of the movies. These had arrived in Dresden in 1904 with a demonstration film, and in 1906 the fully-fledged Campanetto Theater had opened in the Freibergerstrasse. By 1909, the Olympia Theater enlivened the Altmarkt. Movie houses, lodged in second stories and back rooms, continued to be built during World War I, and the pace accelerated in the 1920s. The

Schauburg in the Neustadt, constructed in 1926, was the first free-standing cinema and, at a busy intersection north of Albertplatz, still projects movies there today. By 1930, there were twenty-nine movie theaters in Dresden.

Movies became such an important part of everyday life that working-class children devised a variety of ways to earn the price of a ticket. Some collected water fleas for which there was apparently a market; others distributed advertising flyers; a few worked as models at the Art Academy; and the more energetic chased balls at the tennis courts or polished boots at the army barracks.[324]

Gymnastics, broadly defined, were another mode of relaxation. Such activities for the general population appeared in Dresden in the first half of the nineteenth century. Young men not only swam in the Elbe, as did Louis Lesser and his friends, they also participated in athletics. In the last third of the century clubs for a diversity of sports—hiking, cycling, swimming, mountain climbing, skiing—proliferated. The city council allowed the clubs to use both city and school properties for their activities. In 1885, Dresden had hosted the sixth all-German Gymnastic Competition. Local contests at first were held on the Elbe meadows just east of the Albert Bridge. Later, they took place in the Ilgen Arena.

For the benefit of the whole population, the Hermann Ilgen Foundation financed the construction of a stadium just west of the Great Garden to host the annual show of sports and games in 1923. At the time, this was a first-class soccer field and running track. Pharmacist Hermann Ilgen had made his money concocting and selling rat poison in the outlying village of Kötschenbroda. After he moved to Dresden, he expanded his fortune by speculating in real estate in both Dresden and Leipzig. The Ilgen stadium accommodated 10,000 marchers and 24,000 places for spectators.

Wolfgang Mischnick, later a prominent West German politician, recalled how all the high schools in the Dresden region held a Sport Festival there at the end of the academic year. Pupils marched through the city to the Arena, and then the competition began: foot races, long jumps, shot puts. They even played rounders, a game similar to American baseball.

Only toward the end of the nineteenth century did separate sports clubs emerge that strove to best one another in competitions. These included swimming clubs, motivating the construction of swimming pools, and a horse racing association that laid out a race track behind the Great Garden. The Bike

Racing Association embraced the Odol manufacturer Lingner, the director of the local branch of the Deutsche Bank, and Heinrich Arnhold, a prominent private banker. In preparation for the European championship races in 1910, the association built the cycling track in Reick, which became known as the best course for speed in all of Germany.

Today, the Ilgen Arena is the home of the soccer team: Dynamo Dresden. Soccer, called football by Germans and other Europeans, was and still is the rage among Dresdners of all ages. Boys played soccer in the streets and empty lots. Dresden's high schools fought to become local soccer champions; and businesses sponsored local amateur teams. After 1919, the professional Dresden Sport Club (DSC) team played at the stadium it built at the Ostra Preserve. This stadium was unusual for the time in having grandstands for spectators fronting both sides of the playing field. For those spectators who either couldn't or wouldn't pay the price of admission, the cashiers closed down the ticket offices thirty minutes before the end of the game and admitted them free of charge.

From its founding to the end of the Weimar Republic, the DSC's soccer team was at the top of its form. Between 1908 and 1933, it won five Middle German Championships. It also regularly supplied players for the national team that competed in international games. In 1930, a contest between Germany and Hungary, played in Dresden, became legendary in the city's history. At the end of the game, the Germans came from behind, 3:0, to defeat the Hungarians, 5:3. The win was partially attributed to Dresdner fans "whipping up" the Germans to victory. Afterward, the national soccer league scheduled difficult competitions against other countries in Dresden in the hope that the local fans would cheer the Germans on to success.

But it was not only the DSC that claimed the loyalty of the populace. It was the game itself. The *Dresdner Anzeiger*, with a sports editor first hired after World War I, wrote at the end of the decade that soccer "trumps over all games", that whoever viewed "the masses...pass the time" Sunday after Sunday watching soccer, "had to be amazed at the attraction exerted by this popular sport."[325]

The youth of Dresden could also entertain themselves by the more traditional hiking in the forest to the northeast of town—the Dresdner Heide—or in the countryside to the south. Wolfgang Mischnick's uncle Richard belonged to a gymnastics club that owned a hut in Saxon Switzerland, the area of Elbe sandstone highlands southeast of Dresden containing intriguing rock formations. On the weekend, both male and female members would travel to the village of Rathen by train or boat and then hike to the hut where they would climb a mountain or work out on gymnastic equipment. Parents acted as chaperones and supervisors for youths and children.[326]

Freshening Up the Architecture

The opportunities for vigorous exercise and outdoor enjoyment fit in with the municipal government's mission of creating a healthy city. At the top of the list was the creation of affordable, modern housing. The city's industrialization had been so swift that the population overwhelmed the market's ability to provide healthy living quarters. Windows faced inner courtyards and didn't provide much ventilation. Apartments were small, dark, and damp. Tuberculosis, pneumonia and anemia were frequent physical ailments. Depression and alcoholism plagued certain segments of the working-class population.

At the very beginning of the Weimar Republic, the city government's financial situation did not allow it to solve the housing shortage directly. Instead, it resorted to indirect manipulation. It conducted a survey of available space and tried to match demand with supply. The survey had revealed a need for small abodes. Thus, large apartments were divided into small ones, and condemned apartments were reopened. For a while, the municipality banned immigration into the city and strongly encouraged villa owners, like the Woermanns, to rent out their empty rooms. Vacant industrial buildings were converted to residential use, and barrack shelters, to be used as flats, were constructed.

Housing cooperatives and housing development corporations began, in the mid-1920s, to build single-family homes in the outlying suburbs. At the German Workshops in Hellerau, Karl Schmidt designed wooden houses whose sections could be made in the factory and later assembled at a building site. At the end of the 1920s, large apartment buildings began to appear. Two of these, in Trachau and in Gruna, adopted the modernistic designs of the New Sobriety (*Neue Sachlichkeit*) and are now listed on Germany's equivalent of the national register.

The city planner, Paul Wolf, encouraged a high building density, so that land would be left over for the platting of allotment gardens. In Germany, these date back to the mid-nineteenth century and have functioned differently from the community gardens developed in North America. Each family fences off its small piece of ground, and then erects a small garden house where it can spend a day or a weekend in the fresh air growing flowers and vegetables as it pleases. By 1925, there were 199 allotment clubs in Dresden with 13,960 members. Some of these organizations built club houses and laid out playing fields to enhance the recreation of the gardens.[327]

As the city's financial situation improved from the mid-to-late twenties, it turned its attention to providing more sports fields, swimming pools, schools, homes for the elderly and even a student dormitory. In Pieschen and Löbtau, the homeless shelters, built already before World War I, were expanded. In 1930, the Johannstadt hospital was transformed into a full-scale medical facility with a children's clinic and a nursing school.

One of the novelties of the interwar period was the "skyscraper". City planner Wolf and his staff were not opposed to tall buildings in Dresden. They just didn't want them in the old city center where their height would spoil the profile of the city as seen from the Elbe or from the Neustadt. In 1930, the Reichsbank was allowed to build a tall structure on the city center's periphery behind the Kurländer Palace, and the State Revenue Office constructed a large building behind the opera. The old bank building has been redesigned, and the Revenue Office has given way to another modern structure.

On Albertplatz stands an eleven-story building that towers over the square. Originally occupied by the Saxon State Bank, it was badly damaged during World War II but revived to house Dresden's Metropolitan Transportation Administration. When I began work on this book in 2009, it was an empty, derelict structure badly in need of rehabilitation—an eyesore. It was subsequently acquired by private enterprise, and today houses an inner-city shopping mall.

Although there was, of necessity, much attention paid to the living conditions of Dresden's inhabitants, the older structures were not neglected. The Wackerbarth Palace, in the course of its restoration, regained its old gray-red stucco, and the Cosel Palace, once the home of noted citizens, received its coat of yellow paint. Rehabilitation of the Japanese Palace, home of the Saxon State Library for over 100 years, began in 1925 and took ten years to complete. Semper's wall paintings of the early nineteenth century, based on the frescoes of ancient Pompeii, were discovered on the ground floor and restored.[328]

Throughout the Weimar Republic, the Social Democrats were the largest party in Dresden's communal assembly, even though they lost their majority in the election of 1924. As the list of the city's accomplishments attests, they worked well with the moderately liberal Mayor for life, Bernhard Blüher. In 1930, Blüher refused, as leader of the People's Party caucus, to support a National Socialist as president of the Saxon legislature. His party's criticism of this stance was so aggressive that he felt he had no choice but to resign all his political posts, including the mayoralty. His successor in Dresden was Wilhelm Külz.[329]

During the brief period of the Weimar Republic, Dresdners sought to return to the patterns of pre-war life and to meet the challenges of the times. They even regained the city's strength as an industrial center and European cultural magnet. But Germany's lurches from crisis to crisis had created obstacles difficult for Dresdners and other Germans to surmount.

X. Dresden in the Third Reich

The Great Depression

In 1931, Mayor Wilhelm Külz could look back on a distinguished career in municipal service in southern Saxony, and later in the small northern principality of Schaumburg-Lippe. For a short period of time before World War I, he served as Commissioner of Local Government in the German colony of Southwest Africa, now Namibia. After four years in the army during the war, he joined the middle-class Democratic Party. For ten years, beginning in 1922, he was a member of the Reichstag. Simultaneously, he became, in the crisis year of 1923, a member of Dresden's governing council, responsible for municipal finances. Later, in 1926, he served as Germany's Minister of the Interior. In 1930, he was appointed the Federal Commissioner for International Exhibitions in the new Hygiene Museum.[330]

As mayor of Dresden, he needed all the wisdom that this experience bestowed. The Great Depression, unleashed in 1929, had a devastating impact on a Dresden economy that was heavily dependent on consumer spending and exports. In 1929 alone, almost 700 local firms closed their doors. In July 1930, the unemployed and the casually employed numbered 56,000 or 17% of the work force; three years later, this same category had risen to 100,000. In construction, wages fell by 26%; in the metal industry, they declined by 19%. In 1930, the German General Electricity Company in Berlin bought the Saxon Works, one of the city's major independent enterprises, in order to rescue it from financial ruin. Over 700 properties had to be auctioned off because owners could no longer meet their mortgage payments or pay their taxes. In 1931, in order to reduce expenditures, the Saxon legislature cut the number of required school hours, reduced spending on school lunches and laid off 200 teachers throughout the state, some of them in Dresden. The central German government also reduced social security payments to the elderly and disabled.[331]

The harsh economic climate radicalized a population that had already manifested signs of distress throughout the preceding decade. Some Germans, looking back on this period, have focused on the growing strength of the Communists. Their representation, both in the Dresden city assembly and the Saxon legislature, rose between 1929 and 1932. The leader of the German Communist Party, Ernst Thälmann, even appeared at a mass meeting in Dresden during the Depression.

But the most significant radicalization occurred among the middle classes, particularly in Saxony, where businesses tended to be small and resentment of trade unions, big business, government regulation and taxation became ever greater. By the early 1930s, large sections of Saxon businessmen had become hostile to the German republic. Increasingly, they deserted the old liberal middle-class parties in favor of the new and energetic National Socialists.

Even though the municipality pursued a progressive socio-economic policy during the 1920s, no one can ignore that Dresden society harbored a significant population of right-wing radicals who could not make their peace with the republic. The National Conservatives, who had dominated Dresden politics before World War I, combated liberal and social-democratic policies introduced at both local and national levels. Dresden was also one of the largest garrison cities in Germany, and its officers had suffered from the humiliation of the Versailles Treaty and the reduction of the army's size. They were not inclined to tolerate liberal views.[332]

In January 1924, a crowd of nationalistic conservatives and populists whose tickets to the state theater had been bought and distributed by the National Socialist Martin Mutschmann, later Saxon governor, so severely disrupted a performance of Ernst Toller's pacifist play, *Hinkemann*, that it was quickly discontinued. Some of the demonstrators even shouted, "Drive out the Jews". In the same year, the noted art critic and director of the Municipal Museum, Paul Ferdinand Schmidt, was forced into retirement because his purchases, favoring the new Expressionism and other modern genres, displeased a conservative segment of city government. Again in 1924, armed right-wing groups of the Fatherland Association marched through the city. Herbert Wehner described in his memoirs how his socialist youth group protested the march and caused a street fight. In 1926, civil servants in the

Dresden county government as well as major Dresden newspapers endorsed the attempt of Hermann Ehrhardt, an instigator of the Kapp Putsch, to capture a nationalist, anti-republican majority in the Saxon legislature.[333]

Dresden could not escape its immersion in the greater Saxon sea. In 1929, the Saxon legislature, expressing its twist toward the right, eliminated the state holiday celebrating the birth of the Weimar Republic. In the elections of 1929, the National Socialists gained 15% of the Saxon vote and, because of increasing political fragmentation, were in a position to influence the shape of the Saxon government. In 1930, the Nationalist Club, an umbrella organization of right-wing groups, invited Hitler to speak to them in Dresden. Two years later, the local National Socialists held a rally at the cycling race track in the suburb of Reick where Adolf Hitler again spoke to the crowd.[334]

At the end of 1930, the American film based on Erich Maria Remarque's *All Quiet on the Western Front*, a pacifist German's portrayal of life in the trenches of World War I, began showing in German cinemas. National Socialist Stormtroopers unleashed demonstrations and riots against the film. Ostensibly concerned about "public security", the Saxon government asked the national censor to ban its distribution. Moreover, the Saxon Interior Minister refused to provide police protection for movie houses that showed it. After the national censor had banned the film, the National Socialists in the Saxon legislature introduced a successful motion to prevent school libraries from purchasing the book and schools from including it in the curriculum. The legislature's action went so far as to prohibit school libraries from purchasing any book that "demeaned the German army and falsified German history."

The national Social Democrats managed to achieve a revision of the nation's cinema legislation, so that films banned by the censor could still be shown to special groups. The working-class parties and the trade unions all over Germany took advantage of this revision. In Dresden, the local branch of the trade-union federation showed the film daily.[335]

In order to understand the success of National Socialism in Saxony in general and Dresden in particular, it's necessary to take the Saxon economy and demographic into account. By the beginning of the Weimar Republic, Saxony was the most densely populated of all the German states and proportionately the most industrialized. Industries were mostly small-scale and dependent on exports. During World War I, the Saxon economy suffered major losses and, after the war ended, there was no period of economic stability. For most of the years between 1923 and 1929, Saxony's unemployment rate exceeded that of the rest of Germany.

Politics in Saxony were already polarized before World War I. A truly democratic suffrage was introduced only in 1909 after massive street demonstrations, instigated by the Social Democrats, and the insistence of the king led to suffrage reform. The Revolution of 1918 and the events that followed only intensified this polarization. Once the Social Democrats gained control of the government, they introduced a host of reforms in political processes and socio-economic policy that the middle-class viewed with hostility. Even before the Communists were invited into the Saxon government in 1923, large middle-class blocs considered the reforms of the early Weimar Republic to be bolshevist.

Once the political and economic situation stabilized at the end of 1923, a Saxon Grand Coalition formed from the Social Democrats to the right-wing liberals. But in the face of rising conservatism, the Social Democrats, internally fragmented, could offer little resistance to the coalition's reversal of reforms implemented in the early years of the Weimar Republic.[336]

By spring of 1929, the Great Depression had already arrived in Saxony. In the legislative elections in May, the National Socialists became the kingmakers in the legislature, and their votes helped to replace the former Social Democratic minister-president with Wilhelm Bünger of the German People's Party. Bünger remained in charge of the Saxon government for only a short time. Because of his support for the Young Plan, which implicitly accepted the Versailles Treaty while achieving a reduction of the reparations imposed on Germany, the National Socialists introduced a vote of no-confidence against him that was supported by the National Conservatives, by the Social Democrats and the Communists.

The Communist vote expressed that party's extreme hostility to bourgeois parties in general. But the vote of the Social Democrats merits explanation. It revealed the almost suicidal alienation from middle-class politics that seized the rank and file after the national government's intervention in Saxony in 1923. This hostility would soon carry over to the national level with fatal consequences for German democracy.

In any event, Walter Schiek, former head of the Saxon State Revenue Office and member of the German People's Party, replaced Bünger as minister-president. Schiek's government consisted almost entirely of bureaucrats with no party affiliation. As an elected entity, it lasted exactly one week until a vote of no-confidence, once again supported by the National Socialists, the Social Democrats and the Communists, attempted to unseat him. It proved impossible, however, to form a new government that could not be toppled by a vote of no-confidence, so Schiek and his bureaucrats continued to run the Saxon government until the National Socialists removed him in March 1933.[337]

The National Socialists Revive Dresden

The National Socialist Party arrived in Saxony in 1921. The party's initial program, devised the year before, already advertised its primary nationalistic goals: the "union of all Germans"; the exclusion of Jews from German citizenry; the "abolition" of the Versailles Treaty; the acquisition of land for the "sustenance" of the German people. Social policies included the disbanding of large businesses and favoritism of small business. Its greatest appeal for the following decade lay in southwest Saxony where industrialization had caused the greatest dislocation of the middle class and where support for German expansion during World War I and Saxon anti-Semitism were strong. Rallies attracted thousands in the Saxon south. But within Germany as a whole, the Saxon National Socialists' main achievement was the build-up of a large youth organization. Even though the party won two seats in the Saxon legislative elections of 1926, it remained politically isolated.[338]

In Dresden, the party hardly made a dent before the 1930s. One analyst estimates that in the entire region comprising Dresden and Leipzig, there were only 600 card-carrying National Socialists at the beginning of the Great Depression. The events of the succeeding years changed this picture. Not only did economic conditions radicalize large segments of the population, the frequent elections inflamed their mood. There were Saxon legislative elections and Dresden municipal elections in 1929; Saxon legislative elections in June 1930; elections to the Reichstag in September 1930. In April 1932, there was a referendum to decide whether to dissolve the Saxon legislature. Elections were occasions for all parties, particularly the National Socialists, to spout their promises of a change for the better: a chicken in every pot, a return to old values, and a restoration of German prestige.[339]

The campaigning paid off. By 1931, the Dresden National Socialists had thirty-two party cells within the city. In March 1932, 25% of Dresden's voters selected Adolf Hitler in the first round of the presidential elections. A month later, when the run-off election for president occurred, almost 34% of the Dresden district voted for Hitler. That was a sizable slice of the city's electorate. The National Socialists attracted 38% of Dresden district's voters in the Reichstag elections of July 1932. In November 1932, there were both national and municipal elections. Thirty-three per cent of the Dresden-Bautzen district elected National Socialists to the Reichstag, and a week later 30% of Dresdners selected National Socialists for the city assembly.

An analysis of the July 1932 Reichstag elections indicates three trends. Those areas of the city with a high middle-class demographic voted most strongly for the National Socialists. At the same time, in some areas of National Socialist strength, a combination of Social Democratic and Communist voters—the "Reds"—beat the "Browns". Some former Social Democrats and Communists also switched parties, but in general the left-wing vote held steady. It was simply divided. The two leftist parties refused to have anything to do with one another; the Communists considered the Social Democrats to be little better than the National Socialists.[340]

At the end of January 1933, Adolf Hitler became Chancellor of all of Germany, appointed by the physically and mentally frail president of the Republic, Paul von Hindenburg. One month thereafter the Reichstag in Berlin caught fire, and the National Socialists blamed the burning on the Communists. This event provided the new government with the excuse for declaring a state of emergency that allowed it to suspend all civil liberties. In elections, held on 5 March 1933 to legitimize Hitler's leadership, almost 44% of the Dresden district voted for the National Socialists. But these elections were not really free. The emergency decree, which should be seen as the basis for the Nazi dictatorship, allowed Hitler's government to ban the Communist Party outright and to arrest its leaders. It also formed the basis for the harassment of the Social Democrats and the trade unions in order to suppress the remaining left-wing votes. Such was the scene all over Germany, not just in Dresden. Indeed, the Dresden district remained one of the two best Social Democratic strongholds in Saxony.[341]

Once Hitler's government gained full control, National Socialists lost no time synchronizing Dresden's institutions to their values and policies. To underscore their intent to dominate municipal life, groups of National Socialist Stormtroopers marched through Dresden's streets. Pedestrians had to be very careful about their public reaction to these displays. If they smiled condescendingly or neglected to tip their hats to the marchers, they could find themselves beaten at best or arrested at worst. On March 10, state government formally passed into the hands of the National Socialist Manfred Killinger, who was named Reich Commissar for Saxony, the equivalent of governor. By that time, specific institutions and individuals had already experienced oppression by the new regime.[342]

Social Democrats and their supporting trade unions were, in addition to the Communists, initially the principal scapegoats of the National Socialists. On March 8, Stormtroopers occupied the headquarters of the local trade-union federation. Even though the Dresdner *Volkszeitung*, the local Social Democratic newspaper, had by this time ceased to publish, the brown-shirts wanted to wipe out all traces of the organization. At the paper's headquarters on Wettiner Platz, they dragged all the files and the entire inventory—dailies, weeklies, monthlies, brochures, flyers, books—into the square and set the mass of paper on fire. The editor, Max Sachs, was arrested and sent north to the Sachsenhausen concentration camp where he died in 1935. In a related action, the publisher and editor of the liberal *Dresdner Neueste Nachrichten (Dresden's Latest News)*, the converted Jew Julius Ferdinand Wolff, resigned so as to spare the newspaper from National Socialist predation. Eventually, the local National Socialist newspaper, the *Freiheitskampf (Freedom's Fight)*, moved into the *Volkszeitung*'s offices on Wettiner Platz and appropriated the Socialists' presses and other machinery.[343]

In addition to their journalistic activities, the Social Democrats had controlled a vast establishment of workers' gymnastic, sports and cultural clubs. These groups reached far more people than the formal party organization. Moreover, they had supported the Eiserne Front (Iron Front), an armed group of democratic organizations prepared to fight against the National Socialist Stormtroopers, themselves armed and supported by the German army. For the National Socialists, the Social Democratic clubs posed a potent threat to their own organizations.

Stormtroopers occupied the headquarters of the Workers' Gymnastic and Sports League in early March. Thereafter, the league's sports facilities were closed to its members, and the league itself was banned. To prevent socialist infiltration of other groups, the league's members were barred from middle-class clubs. The Socialist Workers' Youth and its coming-of-age ceremonies were forbidden. Even the People's Theater Club was deemed a threat to the regime. The traditional working-class May Day celebrations were canceled, and two days later, the huge trade-union federation associated with the Social Democrats was dissolved.[344]

After the National Socialists had assumed power, they demanded the dismissal of Socialists, Jews, and other anti-Fascists from the city's administration. Külz refused. They also hissed the swastika flag on the east side of the Rathaus. Külz ordered it removed. He was subsequently suspended on March 14 and formally dismissed from office. During the same week as his suspension, both Communist and Social Democratic members of the city assembly were removed from their positions. All other municipal assemblymen and councilors then joined the National Socialist Party. These deputies elected Ernst Zörner, a National Socialist from Braunschweig, as the head of city government. Two years later, the city council ceased to meet.[345]

For a while, a detention center in the basement of the former Dresdner *Volkszeitung* funneled political opponents to the concentration camp closest to Dresden, Burg Hohnstein. This castle, before the National Socialists came to power, was a large and comfortable youth hostel in Saxon Switzerland. As a concentration camp, it now received former Saxon government ministers and legislators, city councilors and assemblymen, even ordinary people who dared to criticize the regime. Torture was common, and forty people were murdered outright. Before Hohnstein was closed in summer 1934, 5,600 individuals had passed through. During the early stages of the National Socialist regime, one-sixth of all German concentration camps were located in Saxony and primarily counted working-class activists among their inmates.[346]

Left-wing activists were not the only targets of the brown mob. One of the institutions affected was the State Opera Company. On 7 March 1933, Fritz Busch was scheduled to direct a performance of *Rigoletto*. Busch had many Jewish friends and associates and refused to dismiss any Jews from the orchestra and the opera's ensemble. Dresden's Nazis thus proceeded to stage an event very similar to the Hinkemann scandal nine years before. They made sure that they occupied the front-row seats in the Semper Opera, and as Busch prepared to direct, they rioted, shouting "Out with Busch". Busch had to leave the pult and allow his assistant to conduct the performance. In a subsequent public poll of the ensemble, not a single member spoke up for Busch. He was forced to resign, and he eventually left Germany. At the state theater, the Jewish director, his actress wife and two actors were all fired. Two years later, the premiere of Richard Strauss' *Die Schweigsame Frau (The Silent Woman)* closed after only three performances; the libretto had been written by the Jewish Stefan Zweig.

On the Brühl Terrace, Otto Dix was the first at the Academy of Fine Arts to be relieved of his professorship. Others also lost their positions. In September 1933, the new director of the academy, blessed by the city's assembly, organized an exhibition in Dresden's Rathaus entitled "Reflections of a Decadent Art". Included were works by Dix, Ludwig Kirchner, Paul Klee, Max Beckmann, Marc Chagall, Lionel Feininger, Wassily Kandinsky, Conrad Felixmüller, Karl Schmidt-Rottluff and other representatives of modern art, all gathered from museums located in Dresden. This show was one of the first of its kind in Germany and prefigured the famous "Degenerate Art Exhibition" in Munich four years later. This later exhibition was organized by Adolf Ziegler, President of the National Chamber for the Visual Arts, at Hitler's behest and affected all museums, galleries, and collections in Germany. Dresden lost fifty-seven works from the Paintings Gallery and numerous holdings from the Etchings Collection. Otto Dix's famous painting of "The Trench", depicting the horrors of World War I, was last seen in this exhibition; it was destroyed sometime afterward. Today we can only grasp a sense of its power through photographs and a subsequent version in the triptych "War".[347]

Further to the city's south, students at the Technical College erected an advertising pillar on campus where Jewish professors were publicly shamed. Eventually thirty-two Jews lost their positions, and Gentile professors of the progressive stripe were also denounced and fired. At the beginning of May, the thoroughly Nazified student government at the Technical College, imitating similar events all over the nation, staged a torchlight parade to the Bismarck monument in the neighborhood of Räcknitz and set fire to a pile of books by authors banned by the new regime because of their politics, their Jewishness or their cultural progressivism. Authors included Karl Marx, Heinrich Mann, Erich Kästner, Karl Maria Remarque, Kurt Tucholsky, and the noted theater critic Alfred Kerr. During the burning, the students sang the National Socialist Horst Wessel anthem and delivered several Sieg Heils to Hitler.[348]

Reich Commissar Killinger's political base rested on the Saxon Stormtroopers with headquarters in Dresden. Born at Nossen, about thirty miles west of Dresden, he fought during World War I in the Imperial Navy. At the time of the post-war Revolution, he joined the right-wing Ehrhardt Brigade and participated in the Kapp Putsch of 1920. Thereafter he moved to Munich where he took over the military arm of the right-wing Organization Consul (O.C.) that was responsible for the assassinations of Finance Minister Matthias Erzberger and Foreign Minister Walter Rathenau. By 1923, he had moved to Dresden where he eventually joined the National Socialist Stormtroopers, served in the Saxon legislature as leader of the party's caucus, and as a Reichstag deputy. Killinger functioned as Saxon chief of government until 1934, when he and his close associates were arrested during Hitler's purge of the Stormtroopers, known as the "Night of the Long Knives". The fiercely anti-Semitic Martin Mutschmann replaced him.[349]

Mutschmann dominated Dresden and Saxon life for the next eleven years. He had grown up in Saxony's southwestern city of Plauen/Vogtland (not to be confused with the Dresden suburb of Plauen) where he founded his own lace-making firm in 1907. The firm suffered from the loss of supplies and markets during World War I and from a decline in demand for lace. By the time it closed its doors at the beginning of the Great Depression, Mutschmann was a leading National Socialist, having joined the party in 1922 and cultivated ties to Adolf Hitler. By the mid-1920s, he had emerged as the Saxon party leader and jealously guarded his power. At the beginning of the Third Reich, the only person standing between him and absolute power in Saxony was Manfred Killinger.

In an attempt to secure his own position as Saxon leader, he took a group of Stormtroopers from Plauen/Vogtland to Dresden on 9 March 1933, intending to dissolve the legislature and demonstrate National Socialist strength. Even though the legislature's session for that day had been canceled due to the tense situation in the city and state, Mutschmann and his men entered the building on the Brühl Terrace, tracked down several delegates and beat them. His men also attacked a Jewish journalist whom they found in the building. He was spared brutal treatment only because Killinger ordered his own band of Stormtroopers to stop the attack. Up until Killinger's arrest in June 1934, Mutschmann's brutality was restrained.[350]

Once Killinger no longer exercised the position of Saxon executive, Mutschmann moved fast to unite in his own hands the leadership of both party and state. His office on the Brühl Terrace became responsible for all personnel decisions in the Saxon civil service. He took charge of the former labor, welfare, and finance ministries, going so far as to incorporate the Forest Service into his own personal party bureaucracy. Within the Third Reich, this union of party and state was unusual; other states kept the two institutions separate. Mutschmann, however, made Saxony his own National Socialist fief.

Only the national government's expansion of power during World War II undermined Mutschmann's ambitions. By that time, he was consoling himself with the enjoyment of his commodious villa next to the Great Garden and a princely hunting lodge in the Tharandt Forest south of Dresden. He also acquired foods that were either in short supply for Dresden's population or had long vanished from groceries and restaurants in the city. The former Dresden county executive, Ernst Venus, described him as "a brutal human being, primitive, lacking refinement or higher interests."[351]

Dresden Churches

Until the end of World War I, German churches were official state institutions, nominally headed by the ruling family and supported by state governments. After the postwar revolution, Socialists sought to disestablish state churches, but governments still provided financial support, and clergymen decided theological questions. As they had with other institutions, National Socialists infiltrated Protestant churches, and in 1931, they formed a group of "German Christians" with the goal of capturing the leadership of the various state churches.

In Saxony, they seized the opportunity to do so when the state's bishop died in June 1933. The Saxon National Socialist Minister of the Interior, responsible for supervising church affairs, proceeded to appoint the German Christian, Friedrich Coch, as interim bishop. Upon assuming office, Coch arbitrarily replaced pastors and church leaders with clergy who agreed with his politics and theology. This German Christian group then succeeded in winning a majority of positions in the state synod when official elections were held in July 1933. The synod then made Coch's interim status permanent.[352]

Although Dresden's Protestant pastors, following a national pattern, were originally sympathetic toward the National Socialist government, because they welcomed its national renewal and promise of political stability, signs of disagreement arose soon. The cause was the so-called Aryan paragraph, originally contained in the law for the Restoration of the Professional Civil Service and adopted by the Protestant church in late summer 1933. The paragraph stated that clergy of Jewish descent could no longer serve their congregations. And soon, even if he was simply married to someone of Jewish descent, a pastor was de-frocked. By the end of 1933, Coch's synod was actively propagating, within the Saxon Lutheran Church, the "blood and soil" ideology of National Socialism that denied the importance of the Old Testament for Christian belief and favored removing all Jewishness from the Bible.

Concerned about this perversion of Christian orthodoxy, a small group began regular meetings to plan for the assembly of 400 pastors and their wives that founded the local Pastors' Emergency League in December 1933 at Dresden's Zionskirche. The associated lay organization established itself at the same time with a large gathering in the neighboring Jacobikirche. These measures echoed the initiatives of churches in Berlin and throughout Germany. Originally, the Emergency League sought to help pastors of Jewish descent, but with the Barmen Declaration of May 1934 they established the German Confessing Church. The Confessors claimed to be the true Evangelicals and protested the interference of the state in ecclesiastical affairs. In other words, they explicitly refused to honor the authority of German Christians over German Protestants.[353]

The leading light of Dresden's Confessing Church was Hugo Hahn, pastor at the Frauenkirche and a member of the Saxon church's administration. In his memoirs, Hahn freely admitted that before 1933, he did not patronize Jewish businesses. Because of his own precarious position, he could not offer any "practical" help to Dresden's Jewish community after 1933. Already in January 1934, several members of Dresden's Emergency League were arrested for protesting the German Christians' rejection of the Old Testament. Though they were soon released, the Confessing Church's pastors continued to be harassed by the regime even though they stressed that their main opponents were German Christians, not all National Socialists.

In Dresden and in Germany as a whole, most Protestant pastors preferred to remain in the "middle", neither joining with the German Christians nor with the Confessing Church. Between 1935 and 1937 in Saxony, a truce prevailed among the three sides, and they cooperated in governing the church. But in 1937, the German Christians, supported by the central government, barred the representatives of the other two factions from their offices in the Saxon church consistory, ending the cooperation.[354]

Defying this move of the German Christians, Hahn began to appoint pastors to vacant posts without informing the German Christian authorities. Congregations supported the Confessors, but the German Christians fought back by suspending the new appointees, by surveilling them in their churches and homes, and by arresting them outright. On Septuagesima Sunday, 1938, in preparation for the season of Lent, the Confessing Church called on pastors to read from the pulpit a proclamation based on First Corinthians 5: 23–27. This text contended that "Confessors" pursued an imperishable prize—the blessings of the gospel—whereas ordinary others chased corruptible laurel wreaths. The implication was quite clear; Confessors were incorruptible, German Christians were not. All Confessing pastors read the proclamation, and 150 of "middle" pastors joined them. But the majority of the "middle" refused to proclaim.

Two days after Septuagesima, Hahn was relieved as the Frauenkirche's pastor. He was arrested by the Gestapo, interrogated, and asked to name the authors and readers of the proclamation. After interrogation, Hahn waited in an ante-room where several silent police officers were working. Only one was witting enough to remark that in contrast to the Gestapo (secret state police), the ordinary police had a much easier job. They were only responsible for "real" criminals. It didn't take long for the Gestapo to decide that Hahn was an undesirable Saxon. He was expelled from the state in May 1938. His parishioners at the Frauenkirche had to take their leave of him on the platform of the rail station in Görlitz, seventy miles to the east of Dresden.[355]

In Saxony, as in Germany as a whole, the Confessing Church as an organization never took a public stand against the persecution of the Jews. According to Friedrich Delekat, Professor of Religion at the Technical College after 1929, Saxon Protestants, including Dresdners, remained loyal to the National Socialists. It was their opponents who regarded and treated them as resistants. There were some Confessing pastors who were not just indifferent to the Jewish question, they were openly anti-Semitic. Hugo Hahn lived out the war in Wurttemberg and returned to Dresden in 1945.[356]

Catholics in Dresden experienced a different kind of turmoil. Until 1945 they were a small minority within the city and thus particularly vulnerable to harsh treatment. For the most part, Dresden Catholics were first subjected to Nazism when the regime banned Catholic clubs, except for charities, in 1935. Eventually even Catholic soup kitchens were supplanted by National Socialist ones. The regime closed all Catholic elementary schools between 1936 and 1938. In that latter year, Catholic religion teachers in the remaining schools were forbidden to teach the Old Testament. In 1939, the regime closed the city's only Catholic high school. Among German Catholic dioceses, Meissen, to which Dresden belonged, experienced the most clergy in concentration camps.[357]

Everyday Life

Given the National Socialists' iron grip on Dresden, how did life in the city unfold? One of the most noticeable effects of synchronization was the increased membership in the National Socialist Party. Wolfgang Mischnick's father, encouraged by his Nazified brother, joined the party in order to assure that his young son could attend the schools of his choice and receive the professional training that he desired. Others, such as civil servants, were similarly motivated by economic considerations.[358]

Another development associated with National Socialist rule was the end of unemployment. In January 1933, the city had registered 80,000 unemployed persons; by September 1934, this number had been cut by 40%. One way to cut male unemployment was to discourage women from entering the work force. Some were fired, others asked to resign, and still others encouraged to marry. In March 1934, there was a mass wedding of sixty-seven couples in the Frauenkirche; the brides had given up their jobs in the Leo Works where Chlorodont tooth paste was made. By marrying, they were promised help in creating "authentic German homes". Throughout this year, mass weddings occurred in four of the city center's churches. The problem of unemployment slowly disappeared.

Victor Klemperer reported meeting a deliriously happy young man in the Prager Strasse in fall 1936 who couldn't resist calling out to him: 'I have work—the first in three years—at Renner's [the largest department store in the city]—they pay well—for four weeks!' Other young men found jobs at Dresden's camera firms where the single-lens reflex camera experienced a marked success with consumers. Between 1933 and 1937, there was a complete transformation of the Elbe's right bank into a nature refuge from the

Waldschlösschen to the Queen Mary Bridge. This project involved massive new landscaping as well as the construction of several small buildings.[359]

In the suburb of Trachau, building resumed in 1934 on one of the most famous affordable housing settlements of the interwar years. Architecturally modern during the Weimar Republic, its designs were reworked in a more traditional direction—pitched roofs—in 1934. This large community of apartment buildings, mixed with detached cottages, figured prominently in the novelist and scriptwriter Helga Schütz's *Mädchenrätsel (A Young Girl's Dilemma)*. The brutal bombs of World War II did not reach Trachau, and Schütz and her family found refuge there after the war.

But Trachau was not the only building site offering work and shelter to Dresden's residents. In accordance with a long-term plan to modernize the city center, demolitions of some very old houses began in the area to the east of the Altmarkt, and larger buildings took their place. For the National Socialists, this area was a thorn in the side; it sheltered a host of Social Democrats and Communists. The new rents were so high that the apartments were considered to be unaffordable, and the former non-conforming population was permanently displaced.[360]

The last building sites were famous structures that contributed heavily to Dresden's tourist industry. Ongoing from 1924 until the beginning of the 1940s was the restoration of the Zwinger. When removal of paint on the Zwinger's exterior sculptures uncovered extensive damage to the sandstone, work began on the repair and restoration of the stone sculptures. Along with the rehabilitation of the pavilions, the Nymphs' Bath, severely overgrown and cracked, was also made new. When the exterior work ended in 1936, the city turned to repainting the frescoes on the interior's ceilings. The Zwinger project was not completed until the beginning of the 1940s.

The renovation of the Frauenkirche had also begun before 1933. Because of its historic and artistic value, and hence a source of tourist revenue, the rehabilitation of the Church of Our Lady was an ongoing saga. The damaged sandstone was repaired, as were the wooden galleries encircling the dome. At that time, the city's engineers noted that the eight pillars supporting the dome were over-stressed. They were secured. That work uncovered sections of the original Baroque paintings, and the city decided to restore those as well. The church then seized the opportunity to augment the Silbermann organ that dated back to the time of J.S. Bach. The alterations and the expansion of the organ were not completed until 1942. All were destroyed in the Shrove Tuesday/Ash Wednesday bombings three years later.[361]

Contributing to Dresden's economy, especially after the Third Reich's rearmament began, was the city's role as a military hub. Before World War I, the Saxon government had created a large military complex just north of the Neustadt. This Albertstadt, named after the then-reigning Saxon king, was not incorporated into the Dresden municipality but was controlled by a separate administration. It contained barracks, supply depots, workshops, firing ranges, drill fields, a hospital, a military court building, a prison, a cadet training school, an arsenal and a church.

Containing enough space to accommodate 20,000 soldiers and civilians, it was the largest and most modern military facility in Germany. Even before the National Socialists took power, five thousand soldiers were already stationed in the Albertstadt. Universal conscription of men into the armed services, announced in March 1935, increased this number and relieved unemployment. Rearmament benefited the city's numerous war industries. Linked to rearmament was the building of a new airport in the town of Klotzsche, later annexed into Dresden. The related construction of Autobahn sections from Dresden to the small town of Wilsdruff and from Klotzsche to Weixdorf village meant work for Dresdners.

Klotzsche hosted a variety of institutions important for the regime: the training school for officers of the air force, the air force communications school, the school for anti-aircraft units. In 1934, the only Saxon National Political Training Institution (NAPOLA School) moved into a former, liberal arts boarding school. The NAPOLA School was one of several scattered across Germany and functioned like a military academy. Its goal was the inculcation of National Socialism into young men destined to be future leaders in the Third Reich.[362]

In general, the National Socialists sought to attract German youth by appealing to its desire for camaraderie and ritual. Decades later, Dresdners who were forced to belong to the Hitler Youth remembered excursions followed by campfires, treasure hunts, fights between cowboys and Indians. Chapter meetings buzzed with various activities. Youth also participated in marches accompanied by thrilling musical fanfare. In Coschütz, a summer solstice ceremony took place on the Heidenschanze (Devil's Eyrie) high over the

Weisseritz. These dramatic activities hooked the loyalty of many youth to the regime.

Not all young people fell for the National Socialist line. Some sought to express their individuality by flying the green and white Saxon flag; others raised the old imperial flag on which there was nary a swastika. A few were even bolder. Some boys wore their hair long, behaved rudely in public, sang forbidden jazz and boycotted service in the Hitler Youth.[363]

Sport

Although heavily controlled by the National Socialists, sport was another outlet for youth, either by participating themselves or by cheering for local teams and athletes. The regime sought to win international acclaim by hosting and performing well in the Olympic Games of 1936. Recruitment and training of outstanding athletes had begun two years before and led to gold medals for three Dresdners, in rowing, in running and in gymnastics.[364]

During the Third Reich, the most famous German athlete hailed from Dresden: Rudolf Harbig. Born in the suburb of Wilder Mann in 1913, he helped his team to place third in the 400-meter relay race in the Olympic Games of 1936. Harbig went on to become the European champion in the 800-meter race in 1938. In July 1939, he set a world record in an 800-meter race against Italy, and a short month thereafter, he won the world record in the 400-meter race in Frankfurt/Main. Two years later, he set another world record in Dresden for the 1000-meter race. None of these feats was superseded until after World War II, where Harbig lost his life as a parachutist on the eastern front.

Harbig was associated with the Dresdner Sport Club (DSC). During the Third Reich, there were two soccer players who captured the loyalty of fans. The first was Richard Hofmann who joined the DSC in 1928. "King Richard" was chosen to participate in the national A-Team twenty-five times between 1927 and 1932. Between 1932 and 1936, he was a record-breaking player for the German Soccer League. During the early years of World War II, he twice led the Dresden team to German championships. The local commander, Lieutenant General Karl Mehnert, was a member of the Dresdner Sport Club and contributed to the local morale by sparing its players' deployment to the front.

Richard Hofmann was not the only member of the team who avoided service in the army. At the beginning of the 1930s, Helmut Schön joined the

DSC. In 1937, he was selected for the winning German team in the World Cup's qualifying game against Sweden. During the war, he helped the DSC to win the German national championship in four different years. Schön's claim to fame, however, did not reside solely in Dresden. After World War II, Schön moved to West Germany and, in 1964, became the manager of the Federal Republic's all-star soccer team. Until his retirement twelve years later, he led Germany in 1966 to second place in the World Cup competition and to third-place in 1970. Finally, his German team captured the European championship in 1972 and took first place in the World Cup in 1974. By that time, his old Dresden team had been supplanted by the new Dynamo Dresden.[365]

Theater and Art

For Dresdners of all stripes, before and after the National Socialists came to power, there was the theater. During the Third Reich, the city enjoyed the most theater seats of any in Germany. There was the State Opera, the State Theater, the Albert Theater (after 1937 Theater of the People), the Central Theater concentrating on operettas and musical reviews, and the House of Comedy. There were also several smaller theaters. Already in 1933, the Dresden State Opera was considered a first-class company within the nation.

Even though the Nazis used the theater to promote their ideology, one-third of the Dresden State Theater's program was devoted to the German classics, one-third to new plays and one-third to popular comedies. The most popular classical plays were *Faust, Iphigenia, Minna von Barnhelm,* and *Prince Frederick von Homburg.* Shakespeare's plays were frequently on the playbill. Another popular German dramatist was Gerhart Hauptmann, whose eightieth birthday was the occasion for a big celebration at the Theater.[366]

One of the highpoints of Dresden's State Theater was Hitler's attendance at the Festival of 1934. Previously this occasion had acted as the annual assembly of German stage producers and had attracted several thousand people from all over the nation. In this year, the Ministry of Propaganda decided to use the festival to broadcast Joseph Goebbels' cultural agenda. All art, theater included, should bond with German Aryans; non-Aryans, Communists and modernists should be removed from cultural life. The festival also ran concurrently with Dresden's Exhibition of Degenerate Art in the Rathaus.

Hitler decided to attend the festival at the last minute. That short notice did not prevent the visit from becoming a high-powered propaganda event. Hitler arrived in a motorcade along a highway decorated with forests of swastika banners. Accompanying him were War Minister Werner Blomberg, Propaganda Minister Joseph Goebbels, SS leader Sepp Dietrich and other prominent National Socialists. An honor guard of boys from the Hitler Youth and girls of the League of German Maidens lined the highway. Saxon Governor Mutschmann met the motorcade at the city limits, and almost 60,000 Stormtroopers and SS men lined the streets into the city center. Hitler stayed at the Hotel Bellevue just next to the State Opera.

During his stay of three days, Hitler saw performances of Wagner's *Tristan and Isolde* and Dietrich Eckhardt's adaptation of Ibsen's *Peer Gynt*. He also met with Richard Strauss, the favorite composer of Dresdners at the time. But his sojourn in the city was not limited to cultural activities. Mutschmann held a Grand Tattoo of the Stormtroopers at his villa in the Comeniusstrasse, and Hitler inspected the Army's Infantry School in the Albertstadt. In addition, he opened the exhibition of the German League of Military Graves and visited with war wounded from the Great War. Last, but not least, he sauntered through the exhibition of Degenerate Art in the Rathaus. Everywhere he went he was showered with gifts from parading Dresdners and the enthusiasm of cheering crowds.

This festival of 1934 was not the only occasion for which Hitler visited Dresden. In the course of the Third Reich, he came to the city often to attend operas by Richard Stauss. But the cheering crowds of the National Theater Festival stayed home. Eventually he confined himself to his room in the Hotel Bellevue and walked across the street to the opera without fanfare.[367]

The other pole of high-brow culture continued to be art. Even though the regime had deprived Dresden of works by modern artists, there were still meaningful exhibitions in the city during the Third Reich. In 1933, the city museum mounted "Richard Wagner in Dresden", a show attended by 100,000 people. In that same year, the 200th anniversary of the death of Elector Friedrich August I was commemorated in the palace with "August the Strong and his Era". Those who attended re-discovered the beauty of the Baroque style, and those who wandered over to the Semper Paintings Gallery could delight in works from the early eighteenth century. Later in the 1930s, the gallery mounted shows celebrating the art of Lucas Cranach the Elder, Anton Graff, and Ludwig Richter.[368]

Circus Sarrasani

Families seeking lighter fare could enjoy the Circus Sarrasani whenever it played in town. The moving spirit behind this circus was Hans Stosch. Born in Prussian Posen (now Poznan, Poland), he ran away from home at fifteen and joined a local traveling troupe. Quickly he worked his way up from stall sweeper to performer. Eventually, he borrowed the name "Sarrasani" from the French writer Honoré de Balzac and struck out on his own, contracting as a clown with a variety of circus firms. During the 1890s, he expanded to a full-scale ensemble making the rounds of northeastern Germany. In 1901, his group performed at Duttlers, a beer garden in Dresden-Strehlen, and there he found the father he had escaped more than a decade before. Stosch thereafter lived with his father in neighboring Radebeul but continued to travel with his circus. His success was due to a number of innovations: playing the winter in a heated tent, using steam vehicles for transport, hiring a group of American Indians to pose as exotics.

Eventually Stosch decided to adopt one German city as his home base and erect a permanent structure for performances. Dresden was favored because the city fathers wanted to upgrade the Neustadt, and they offered Stosch a property at a discounted price while promising to improve the streets around the building. City government also granted his company a municipal monopoly for the next thirty years. The Dresdner Bank lent Stosch the money to purchase the property, located on the site of the present Carola Platz.

On 12 December 1912, the round, domed circus building of the Circus Sarrasani was dedicated with a procession and a gala performance for the benefit of the Children's Hospital. King Friedrich August III attended with his family as did Mayor Gustav Beutler, Dresden's police commissioner, military officers and prominent citizens. Even after acquiring a permanent home and gaining the support of city and state, Stosch's ensemble continued to travel. When it was on the road, he rented out the building to variety shows, to serious dramas, and once even to the Oberammergau Passion Play.

During World War I, when most of his performers and staff were drafted, Stosch stayed in business by offering public spectacles of animal dressage. Dresdners flocked to his circus, the military praised his performances, and Sarrasani was able to get some of his artists and staff released from military service. Beginning in 1916, shortages made it difficult for him to feed his animals, and he began to sell them off—some to the military—along with some of his technical aids. Locals became used to seeing circus animals hauling coal through Dresden's streets. After the war ended, it became so hard to feed the animals that most of them died—either from outright starvation or being killed by Sarrasani to feed the others. Nevertheless, Stosch still managed to buy livery and tableware from the palace of the fallen monarchy.

In 1921, the Sarrasani circus began traveling again throughout Germany and Europe. Audiences were huge, but profits were low. To escape the post-war inflation, Stosch decided to go on a South American tour. The trip across the Atlantic was financed by the industrialist Hugo Stinnes. While it was on tour, Stinnes died, and his son refused to pay Stosch for the return trip. The Dresden city government, the Dresdner Bank, and the German Foreign Office, all intervened to persuade son Stinnes to ship the circus back over the Atlantic.

During the latter years of the Weimar Republic, the Circus Sarrasani built itself up and continued traveling throughout Europe. It performed in one huge ring, and each skit contained dozens of people. By 1931, however, the circus was once again in trouble. Attendance plummeted, and a fire during a tour in Belgium, probably arson motivated by anti-German sentiment, represented another loss. It became increasingly difficult for Stosch to pay his employees, and in 1932, he cut short a tour to western Germany. At the end of the year, he was reduced to asking Dresdners for donations and the municipal government for a subsidy. He received both.

But once again, Stosch decided to improve his business fortunes by making a tour of South America. He left with his troupe in April 1934, going first to Rio de Janeiro and then to Sao Paulo. There he had several heart attacks and died in September. After his body was shipped back to Germany, the circus mounted a memorial ceremony in the Sarrasani building that attracted hundreds of Dresdners. A small altar surmounted by a cross occupied the ring, and another cross graced the coffin.

While alive, Hans Stosch had not kowtowed to the National Socialist Party. He had refused to join its ranks; he had closed the circus building to use by the Stormtroopers after one of their rallies there became too raucous; he fired a number of Nazi party members when they tried to tell him how to run his business; and he continued to employ Jews in management and other positions after the National Socialists came to power. He even hired a few more for the South American tour.

As in life, so in death. At the memorial ceremony, no prominent National Socialists were present, only the district head of the National League of German Artistes spoke in the name of the national organization. There were no Sieg Heils. Black bunting in the Sarrasani foyer and black bows embossed with gold letters from well-wishers were the only decorations. Circus firemen bore the coffin toward the Dresden Crematorium through the hundreds of mourners gathered outside the building.[369]

Hans Stosch, Jr. did not share his father's coolness toward the National Socialists. He had joined the party already in 1932. Continuing the South American tour after his father's death, Stosch Jr. staged a celebration of Hitler's Chancellorship on that continent. In December 1935, Hans, Jr. brought most of his employees home from South America and mounted "Eighteen World Sensations": in Dresden on Christmas Day: various levels of dressage, including the classical, tigers and elephants, trampolining Brazilian acrobats, clowns, exotic Argentinians and Abyssinians; an orchestra expanded by SS instrumentalists; several other groups such as Billy Jenkins and his eagles. Stosch soon gave up this expensive spectacular and returned to ordinary circus fare. He also abandoned his father's frugal management style. He organized holiday parties for the staff, company trips, more comfortable traveling conditions. And he continued to give work to many half-Jews.

The outbreak of war in 1939 was disruptive. Circus artists and staff were drafted into the armed services. When Hans, Jr. tried to reverse some of the conscription, the government sent him foreign workers to keep him in business. It also became impossible for him to go on tour not only to Western Europe but to Western Germany. He had to fall back on Dresden, other Saxon cities, and areas in the east that had either been annexed or converted into protectorates. At the time of the invasion of the Soviet Union in 1941, the Circus Sarrasani was performing in Slovakia; the tour had to be broken off and returned to Dresden. Two weeks later, Stosch, Jr. died during a circus' guest performance in Berlin; he was 41 years old. His widow, Trude Stosch-Sarrasani, became owner of the business.

Trude was able to keep the circus afloat throughout World War II with help from two knowledgeable men. One was a former acrobat, Gabriel Nemedi, who not only became director of the circus, but Trude Stosch's life partner. He knew the circus inside and out. The other was manager Hans Schlenkrich who, as a boy, had collected food for the animals in World War I and began working for the circus in the 1930s. These three cultivated both the Saxon National Socialists and the military elite in order to sustain operations. They treated the workers well, both Germans and foreigners, obtaining illegal rations and used clothing for them. Thus the circus continued to entertain Dresdners until almost the very end of the war.[370]

Other Entertainments

More mundane amusements continued to exist during the Third Reich. Victor Klemperer and his wife took advantage of bus tours through the Dresden region that included nature, music, coffee and tortes, and a small cabaret show with penetrating jokes. There were also excursions to Saxon Switzerland. After the couple purchased a property in the suburb of Dölzschen, they held a roof-raising party with the roofers and the neighbors. And gardening served as duty and as entertainment.

That pastime helped to explain the popularity of the National Garden Show, held in Dresden from the end of April to the beginning of October 1936. Visitors could purchase individual tickets or a pass for the show's duration. Klemperers were on their way to a traditional asparagus feast at a friend's when they visited the show in June to find it overflowing with people treating it like a city fair, taking advantage of sales and advertising booths.[371]

Other holdovers from earlier times were the shooting matches and the harvest festivals of various clubs and neighborhoods. The Striezel Market, traditionally held before Christmas, continued to offer Saxon wares. This old market, which took its name from the medieval word for stollen, had once stretched from the Altmarkt to the Neumarkt and had included baked goods, other foodstuffs, ribbon makers, linen weavers, lace knitters, and toy craftsmen, even potters and glass blowers. Customers came from miles around to take advantage of the variety of goods and reasonable prices. In 1934, this great market no longer existed in its old form. Instead, the Striezel Market of the 1930s took place in the Stable Close, a courtyard connected to the palace. Like every Christmas market, this one too, though much reduced in size, provided Dresdners with Christmas cheer.[372]

Wolfgang Mischnick has left us an idyllic description of the Christmas holidays in the outer Neustadt. Growing up in Dresden, he lived with his family on Bischofsweg, still today a densely populated area, rich with children. As the holiday season began, the women of the neighborhood would gather with their stollen and other dough in the Däbritz bakery in the Kamenzerstrasse. Apprentices would knead it for them and finish it in the bakery's oven. The baking completed, employees would deliver the bread and cakes to the appropriate residences.

Dresdner Stollen has become a delicacy sold round the Western world, but its origins are humble. The medieval stollen was a bread made from flour, yeast, oil and water consumed during the Advent fast—no meat, fish, eggs— that ended only when the Christmas feast days began. One of the most important changes occurred at the end of the fifteenth century when the Saxon dukes Ernst and Albrecht—after multiple petitions—finally convinced the austere Papacy to allow butter to substitute for scarce Saxon oil, though the loaf continued to remain a relatively dry bread, perhaps harboring a few lonely raisins. As with much else in Dresden's history, it was August the Strong who was responsible for directing the recipe toward a richer loaf. In 1730, for the military exhibition known as the Zeithain Encampment, he ordered eggs and sugar be added to the stollen. In the course of the next three centuries, Dresden's bakers added ingredients.

There is general agreement that only in the twentieth century did the city's stollen acquire the fruits of the modern loaf. In 1991, Dresden bakers founded the Protection Association for Dresden Christstollen, and in 2010, the bread was registered with the European Union as a geographically protected indication, similar to those for French cheeses and wines. Accordingly, only stollen produced by bakeries in the city's metropolitan region and containing the Protection Association's prescribed ingredients can be sold as authentic Dresdner Christstollen. The prescribed ingredients are wheat flour, yeast, whole milk, granulated sugar, candied lemon and orange peel, raisins, both sweet and bitter almonds, lemon zest paste, and stollen spices that include cinnamon and nutmeg. The baked bread must be covered with melted butter and powdered sugar. Like Mischnick's boyhood neighbors, home cooks the world over combine these (and other) ingredients that they allow to "ripen" during Advent.

Mischnick's family first cut the stollen on Christmas Eve, when the Christmas celebration commenced with the family singing Silent Night and opening gifts. Then they all sat down to a supper of wurst and potato salad. On Christmas Day, the traditional meal was roast goose and dumplings. There was a "glorious" party of the extended family on New Year's Eve with lots of singing accompanied by Mischnick's father on the piano. By this time, the stollen had been finished off, and the tree soon followed on Three Kings' Day.[373]

Racial Hygiene

Less cheerful was the attempt to indoctrinate Dresdners with National Socialist racism at the German Hygiene Museum on the old City Commons. This austere building had finally been constructed with Adolf Lingner's funds in 1930, in time to host the Second International Hygiene Exhibition. The exhibition included a section on racial hygiene, that emphasized promoting superior human characteristics and combating inferior ones. Attracting the most notice was the Glass Man, whose transparency and electrical illumination displayed—then and now—the anatomy and physiology of the human body. After the National Socialists took power, the museum became the local headquarters of their race ideology.

Thus, the museum organized traveling shows examining "Blood and Race", "Volk and Race", "Eugenics and Health Care". In 1934, the Saxon State Academy for Race and Health Care became associated with the museum, and four years later, the Medical Continuing Education Academy joined it with responsibility for promoting race hygiene. The museum's reading room received the new title of Science of Race and Inheritance. An SS medical doctor headed up a new section on German Blood that imparted information about the need to weed out and sterilize inferior humans.[374]

In this connection, the museum took school groups on excursions to the asylum for mentally and physically disabled individuals at the Castle Sonnenstein overlooking the town of Pirna, eleven miles south of Dresden. After the beginning of World War II, this institution became the regional euthanizing facility for the kinds of people it had ministered to before the war. Those destined for euthanasia were transported to the facility in vehicles resembling police vans that Pirna residents called the "whisper coach, (*Flüsterkutsche*)", probably because they referred to it in inaudible tones. Families of euthanized individuals received the remains of their relatives in urns after they were killed. These practices, dubbed the T-4 program, were the forerunners of the death camps for Jews that operated during World War II.

Even before war broke out, the women's clinic at the municipal Johannstadt Hospital began, under the direction of SS Dr. Heinrich Eufinger, to sterilize women with congenital illness, defined as mental retardation, schizophrenia, manic-depression, epilepsy, Huntington's chorea, blindness, deafness, alcoholism or severe physical deformation. It is possible to document over 700 women who received such treatment. The Dresden painter Elfriede Lohse-Wächtler, diagnosed with schizophrenia, was sterilized in 1935 and later murdered at Sonnenstein.[375]

War on the Horizon

The beginning of war on 1 September 1939 was no surprise for most Dresdners. After conscription was introduced four years previously, young men disappeared into the armed services. The Saxon Works in the Niedersedlitz suburb began to make parts for radar and other machines. In 1938, the optical factory of Zeiss-Ikon in Striesen had received a contract from the Air ministry to manufacture bomb sights. Dresden became the headquarters of Air District III that supervised the establishment of anti-aircraft batteries for the states of Saxony, Thuringia and southern Prussia. At the time of the Sudeten crisis in 1938, the directors of the Paintings Gallery and the etchings rooms closed their collections to the public and removed their most valuable works to the deep cellar of the Albertinum, the city's former arsenal.[376]

At the end of August 1939, the public mood was subdued. On a visit to the main railroad station on the Sunday before war broke out, Victor Klemperer thought that people looked depressed. His wife noticed that their neighbors in Dölzschen, returning from the local sports center, had abandoned their usual banter, practical jokes, and laughter.

By the end of September, one month after the start of war, shortages of goods, including foodstuffs, had already occurred. Lending libraries removed English-language books from their shelves, and even books translated from English into German were no longer available. To conserve gasoline, private automobiles could no longer ply the streets, and in some cases, they had to be given up to the army. In November, the young Wolfgang Mischnick, who had not yet graduated from high school, was drafted. He received his diploma without taking any of the usual exams. And even though he was later released to study engineering at the Technical College, he was soon called back to the army.[377]

The seriousness of the war situation, the deepening shortages of all goods, and above all the ideological bent of the National Socialist regime, not only caused hardship for the general population, the murders of innocent adults and children, and the sacrifices of young men to the war effort. They also brought with them the intensified abuse of those Dresden Jews who had not emigrated to safer places in the British Empire or the western hemisphere.

XI. The Jews of Dresden

Early Settlement in the Middle Ages

When the Third Reich began in 1933, there were almost 4400 Jews living in Dresden. By the beginning of World War II, only 1,146 Jewish men, women and children remained. By the end of the war, fewer than 100 still resided in the city.[378]

Though they probably arrived with other merchants as medieval trade expanded, we can first document a settlement of Jews in Dresden in the thirteenth century. Either just before or just after the turn of that century, they acquired a site close to the original city wall—the Jewish close or *Judenhof*—where they built a large structure that housed the synagogue, a school, a brewery, a granary and a warehouse. Adjoining the synagogue was the Jews' Lane. The lane was not a ghetto, and Jews owned their own residences. There was a Jewish cemetery just outside the city's southern wall. At this early date, Jews enjoyed the protection of the Wettin counts, and their position and activities were determined by a Jewish Decree issued in the mid-thirteenth century.

They were periodically subjected to harassment and persecution, and at the time of the Black Death they fell victim to mass executions on the Altmarkt. Thereafter, as was the practice across Germany, they were alternately expelled and allowed back into the city until, during the fifteenth century, they lost the protection of the recently elevated Saxon dukes. After 1500, there's no evidence of Jewish settlements in all of Saxony, including Dresden. For the next two centuries, the ruling Wettins, like many other German princes, forbade the settlement of Jews in their principality.[379]

Guiding the Wettins was the common stereotype of Jews: Profits were their principal motives, making them morally unreliable. That many Jews, deprived of permanent roots in German communities, resorted to crime in order to survive only reinforced this judgement. Since Jews were subject to a different legal system than Gentiles and generally lived separately in their own neighborhoods, Christians had little opportunity to experience normal Jewish morality.[380]

The Early Modern Period

Into the seventeenth century, the Wettins continued to forbid the settlement of Jews in their realm. Nevertheless, there is evidence that Jews attended the Leipzig Fairs regularly at the end of that century; and at least one Jew was operating a currency exchange in that city full time. A Jewish presence in Saxony, either permanent or temporary, can be inferred from the fact that in 1682, the Duke/Elector Johann Georg III renewed the ban on permanent Jewish settlements, and in 1692, his son Johann Georg IV issued a decree banning Jewish religious services throughout Saxony.

There's a common understanding in Germany that princes' Jewish policy was often their fiscal policy. And such was the case with August the Strong. As we have seen, August's ambition to become an European king and not just a German Elector, led to his claiming the Polish crown when it became vacant in 1697. That claim necessitated massive infusions of money to bribe the Polish nobles to encourage their vote for him as king. Later, when he became embroiled with Sweden in the Great Northern War, there was a further need for funds. In both these cases, the Jewish banker, Berend Lehmann of Halberstadt, lent Friedrich August some of the necessary sums.

Taking advantage of this indebtedness, Lehmann petitioned the Polish king/Saxon Elector to allow him, his family and servants to reside officially in Dresden and to own property there. August the Strong granted these permissions in 1707 and 1708. Even though Lehmann himself never lived in Dresden permanently, his son, also named Berend, and his brother-in-law, Jonas Meyer, occupied the house and garden of the old post office, located between Neumarkt and the city wall. Eventually this house sheltered a large number of "servant" occupants who added their commodities' trading to the Lehmanns' banking functions. The Gentile city councilors and merchants in Dresden objected so strenuously to the competition posed by this trade in goods that August the Strong finally forbade these activities to Jews in 1728.[381]

Though Gentiles agitated to rid the city and the principality of Jews, their numbers in Dresden slowly increased. There was a considerable influx when

Jews were expelled from Prague in 1745. In an attempt to limit the Jewish population, August the Strong's son imposed a head tax on any Jew over ten years of age staying in the Saxon state either permanently or temporarily. When this measure didn't decrease the population, a new decree limited outright the number of Jews permitted to reside in Saxony and restricted the numbers of their commercial outlets. Also forbidden to Jews, because of pressure from Gentiles, was the right to bury their dead in Dresden. For several decades, corpses had to be taken across the border to Bohemia for burial. This cumbersome practice ended only when, in 1751, Jews received the right to establish a cemetery on the eastern fringe of the Neustadt. This event marks the beginning of a Jewish communal structure in Dresden. It led to a Society for Tending the Sick and to a Burial Brotherhood responsible for washing and burying the dead.

Attempts to limit the numbers of Jews in Dresden (and Saxony as a whole) foundered on the shoals of contemporary events. The Prussian occupation during the Seven Years' War brought Jewish currency dealers and Jewish merchants—sometimes peddlers—to Dresden, and many stayed. In 1746, there were 260 Jews resident in Dresden; at the end of the Seven Years' War in 1763, there were 809, almost a four-fold increase. In this same year, the Elector tried to deport all Jews living in Dresden (or Saxony) without a permit. Those without permits succeeded in evading the decree; the city's Jewish population remained the same.

At mid-century, a custodian had begun to operate on behalf of the Saxon state to assure the proper burial of the dead and to translate Yiddish into German when necessary. In 1772, this custodian became responsible for registering Jewish births, deaths, marriages, emigration, and issuing transit visas. Although the state continued to ban any new Jewish settlement in Dresden, it also recognized the need for regulating the relationships between the state and the Jewish community. In that year, the community was told to elect three elders to act as liaisons with state authorities. Previous to this arrangement, the Jews of Dresden had lived in large households. These groupings had enabled Jews to live illegally in Dresden as servants of the house. In 1772, however, a household was defined as a nuclear family, and the old conglomerations began to break up.

Nevertheless, built into the decree was a measure ensuring the dominance of the Jewish elite. Public worship services were forbidden; only private "prayer rooms" were sanctioned. At the time, there were eight such rooms, seven of which were maintained by wealthy Jewish families, and one, the community prayer room behind the Frauenkirche, was supported by those attending the services. By the beginning of the nineteenth century, the number of prayer rooms had dwindled to four, but their sponsors were still influential members of the Jewish community. To all intents and purposes, these "rooms" resembled and functioned like synagogues. The Aron family's room attached silver ornaments to the Torah housed in the Ark and used silver for the chalice and spice containers. The room was decorated with brass chandeliers and wall sconces, wooden benches, chairs, and a carved lectern. It even boasted galleries for the women attending services.[382]

As much as one-third of the Jewish community, now broken up into individual families, were considered by Dresden's officials to be poor or very poor, and 46% were deemed to be without wealth. These people were prime candidates for discrimination and expulsion. In 1777, one of Dresden's Jewish leaders, Samuel Halberstadt, asked the noted Jewish philosopher and scholar Moses Mendelssohn in Berlin to intervene with the Saxon government to reduce or eliminate the annual poll tax imposed on rich and poor Jews alike. Halberstadt complained that many of Dresden's poor Jews had been expelled for failure to pay the tax and had nowhere else to go. Mendelssohn who, the year before, had received a repayment of the poll tax levied on him during a visit to Dresden, obliged by contacting an advisor to the Elector, who in turn revoked the expulsions.[383]

Moses Mendelssohn played such an outsized role in the emancipation of German Jews, including Dresdners, that he warrants a brief biography. Born in Dessau in 1729 to a Hebrew teacher, he migrated to Berlin, speaking only Yiddish, as a fourteen-year-old, and eked out a living as a scribe. He first taught himself German, then Latin, and later English and French. In 1750, he became a tutor to Isaac Bernard's children, advanced to bookkeeper in Bernard's silk factory, and eventually ascended to manager and partner in the firm.

In the 1750s, Mendelssohn made friends with the playwright Gotthold Lessing and Berlin's Gentile intellectuals. At the end of that decade, he published *Phaedon,* a book read widely throughout Europe. It was an attempt to fit Plato's thought into the eighteenth-century Enlightenment. After a breakdown in health in the 1770s, Mendelssohn vowed to pursue the cause of

Jewish assimilation. To make this task easier for his co-religionists, he translated the Pentateuch and other parts of the Jewish Bible into German.

He also encouraged the translation from English into German of Manasseh ben Israel's *Vindicial Judorum (Vindication of the Jews)*, a tract urging Christian toleration of Jews. Mendelssohn's own book *Jerusalem* emphasized Judaism as a guide for the religious and moral lives of its adherents, and he urged his fellow Jews to "hold fast" to it. But he also counseled them to adapt to the "customs and constitutions" of their residences, while depending on human reason, as opposed to supernatural powers, to guide their thoughts.

The introduction of this Jewish Enlightenment meant not only assimilation to German life but an end to Jewish poverty. Poor Jews needed to be weaned away from the peddling of goods and be allowed to pursue greater occupational choices. Better education for Jews was the way to accomplish this goal. Mendelssohn and others encouraged Jews to break out of the isolation of their Jewish communities, to adopt German rather than Yiddish as their everyday language, to wear contemporary German clothes rather than their medieval black robes, and to practice the secular life of ordinary Germans. Such an Enlightened course required changes within both the Jewish and the Gentile communities. Prominent Gentiles such as Lessing and the historian Christian Wilhelm von Dohm propagated the idea of Jewish emancipation and equal treatment with Christians.[384]

In Dresden, the ideas of the Enlightenment caught on slowly. Saxon Jews began attending Leipzig University at the end of the eighteenth century, and the Elector approved the award of the doctorate to a Jew in 1784. As Dresden Jews formed organizations such as the Burial Insurance Club and the Israelite Women's Club, these groups helped to overcome the former fragmentation of the Jewish community. They took over some of the social functions of the prayer rooms, helping to provide communication and identity among the local Jews. In 1803, the city council approved the appointment of a chief rabbi, and David Wolf Landau arrived to minister to all the prayer rooms. In 1808, the Saxon state, perhaps encouraged by its more socially progressive French ally, proposed a committee chaired by the Jewish supplier of the army, Michael Kaskel, to devise a plan of Jewish emancipation. At that time, the community was still so traditional that it rejected the proposal.

By 1813, it had apparently reconsidered its position, and Jewish elders petitioned the government to grant Jews all the benefits of Gentile citizenship as well as the elimination of the poll tax. Only the poll tax was lifted the following year, not by the Saxon state, but by the victorious Russian occupiers of Dresden and Saxony. At the peace conference in Vienna in 1815, the Saxon representatives, following the wishes of the Gentile population, opposed inserting Jewish emancipation into the constitution of the newly created German Confederation.[385]

Jewish Emancipation in Dresden

Even into the 1820s, many Dresden Jews still spoke Yiddish, attended only Hebrew schools, dressed in the traditional fashion and resisted modernization. At the same time, there were several families that pursued a more secular lifestyle. They sent their children to Dresden's prominent Gentile high school, the Kreuzschule, or to private schools in Saxony or neighboring states. The banker Mendel Schie, whose family was influential in the Jewish community, hosted discussion groups at his home attended by Jews and Christians alike. Another prominent family, the Bondis, entertained at home with games, musical evenings, and plays; they also took liberal advantage of the city's theaters, concerts and museums.[386]

The most outstanding member of the Bondi family was Bernhard Beer. His father Hirsch Beer, from Regensburg, had married a cousin, Clara Bondi, in Dresden. Hirsch had received a traditional Jewish education before becoming a businessman, but in order to promote his business, he had learned German and also a little French. After 1821, he functioned as one of the elders of the Dresden community. Bernhard, his second child, was born in 1801 and received a first-rate, secular education. The young Beer became a private tutor and scholar and eventually received an honorary doctorate from Leipzig University. One can assume that while he was growing up, he regularly attended his family's private prayer room. At the same time, like the Bondi family in general, he vigorously pursued Jewish emancipation. In 1826, he preached the first German sermon in a Dresden prayer room.[387]

Three years later, he established the Mendelssohn Club, considered to be the organizational impetus behind the modernization of Dresden Jews. The Mendelssohn Club grew out of a Bible study group that Beer and other young Jewish men had set up earlier in the decade. This club, founded in honor of Moses Mendelssohn's 100th birthday, vowed to encourage "every useful activity" on the part of Jewish youth and to pursue an "improved view of Jews and Jewishness".

On the idealistic plane, it claimed to further the crafts, the arts, and the scholarship of Jewish youth. On a more practical level, it financed the training of Jewish craftsmen: carpenters, cutlers, shoemakers, tailors and other skilled trades. Many of these young men then parlayed their skills into owning or managing prosperous manufacturing or retail establishments. The club also encouraged young Jews to pursue higher education that would lead to careers in the civil service and the professions.

In addition to "ennobling" Jews' quality of life and their image in the eyes of Gentiles, the club encouraged the modernization of religious practices. The changes in Mendel Schie's prayer room give us an idea of how this goal worked out in practice. While providing a "solemn" and "dignified" atmosphere, Schie introduced regular German sermons, a contemporary Hebrew liturgy, the "confirmation" of youth, and the seating of women with men in the room's main worship space.

Most members of the Mendelssohn Club belonged to the city's Jewish elite: The Schies, the Bondis, the Kaskels, the Meyers, and others. Also, the membership was young. In the early 1830s, the average age was forty-two. The executive committee, with an average age of thirty-two, was even younger. In the early membership lists were twelve Gentiles, including members of the royal family. Given its membership and goals, the Mendelssohn Club easily became the organizational fulcrum for the emancipation desired by both the Jewish community and the Saxon state government.[388]

The club began life at a propitious time. The Revolution of 1830 catapulted Saxony politically out of the traditional into the modern world. During the uprising, Jews had even joined the Communal Guard that protected the new Lindenau government against radicals. Initially, this revolution did not much help the Jewish community. Only Christians received full civil and political rights in the constitution of 1831. Jews continued to experience discrimination. For instance, the first Jewish doctor in Dresden had to establish himself as a "doctor for patching wounds", a status that relegated him to the position of barber. Disabilities were lifted only slowly.

Nevertheless, in 1833 the Saxon legislature charged the Ministry of Religion and Education to "lift" the most "inappropriate" restrictions on Jews. State officials themselves deemed the position of Jews within the kingdom to be unsatisfactory. In response, Bernhard Beer submitted to the government a Plan for the Improvement of the Worship and Schooling of Jews.

During the next few years, the Saxon government and Diet began to follow Beer's recommendations, though some restrictions were still imposed. The Minister of Religion and Education decreed that Jews could now live in Dresden's suburbs, could function as apprentices and journeymen, and were subject to the religious and educational regulation of his ministry. They were now eligible to serve in the military. Jews could now buy property and build a public synagogue. They still did not enjoy full political rights, but the reforms of the 1830s opened to them the doors of normal, civil society.[389]

By this time, most of the Jewish community was Germanized, speaking and dressing like their Gentile contemporaries, and pursuing German leisure activities. If it was still not completely German in economic life, that was because the state restricted Jews from freely choosing their occupations. The best evidence for the embourgeoisement of Jewish life in Dresden comes from the diaries of Louis Lesser.

Lesser was born in 1815. His mother was a member of a respected Dresden family, and his father, a merchant, had migrated to Dresden from the Prussian province of Posen. When Louis was thirteen, his family apprenticed him to the bank of Mendel Schie, and by the time he began his short-lived diary, he was a full-time clerk at the bank. He kept his diary from 1833 until 1837 and recorded the activities of his family and friends. Although there were frequent references to observing the Saturday Sabbath and the High Holy Days, the diary reflected the lives of young, middle-class Germans at that time. Lesser and his friends shared books; they went to coffee shops to play pool; they swam in the Elbe; they played cards. During the summer they attended concerts in the Great Garden. During the winter, Louis led an active social life at the Jewish social club called the Union, where dancing often continued into the early hours of the morning.

At the same time, the diary testified to the social striving of the modernizing generation of Dresden's Jews. Louis wrote his diary in English, because he was taking English lessons when it began. He also tried his hand at French and Italian. For a short time, he and his friends wrote and distributed a small literary magazine, *Akrothinia*. Three of his friends, Bernhard Hirschel, Veit Meyer, and Wolf Landau, attended the Kreuzschule and then went off to university, either in Leipzig or in Berlin. Both Hirschel and Meyer became medical doctors in Dresden. Lesser worked himself up through the ranks of the Schie bank and later became its chief executive officer, due to the lack of any Schie heirs.

The diary reveals that the community took pains not to offend Christian sensibilities. On Sundays and Christian holidays, the bank operated for only a half day, and that included Christmas. The Lesser family went to synagogue on Saturday and observed Jewish holidays, but Louis' attendance was sporadic. When a new chief rabbi arrived in 1836, Louis told his diary that a "new life [was] beginning for the Jews" of Dresden.[390]

The new rabbi was Zacharias Frankel. When the old chief rabbi died, Bernhard Beer had conducted a "campaign" within the community for the appointment of Frankel, and he became the choice of the Saxon Minister for Religion and Education. Frankel was a native of Prague and had received his doctoral degree from the University of Pest (now the Eötvös Loránd University in Budapest). Thereafter he became county rabbi in Leitmeritz and local rabbi in Teplitz, an area in Bohemia bordering the Ore Mountains with close ties to the Jewish community in Dresden.

Frankel preached his sermons in German and advocated modern changes in the synagogue service. The Saxon secret police labeled him "liberal". In his negotiations with the ministry and the community, he drove a hard bargain, insisting on a salary of 700 Taler a year and a 100 Taler subsidy for living quarters in a good neighborhood with at least four rooms and a kitchen. To enable the Jewish community to pay this high price, the ministry agreed to help with a contribution of 170 Taler annually. It was Frankel's intention to modernize the community and make German Jews more bourgeois.

After his arrival in Dresden, plans within the community kept pace with the reforms introduced by the state. Taking advantage of the introduction of compulsory schooling for Jews and their right to set up their own state-sanctioned schools, Rabbi Frankel combined the two existing private, Jewish elementary schools into one. Under Frankel's direction, the community decided to build a common synagogue, and the state supported this decision in 1837 by allowing Jews to form a corporation, to purchase property as a congregation and to hold public worship services. Under pressure from both Beer and Frankel, the private prayer rooms were banned. By the time this legislation passed, the community had already set up a building committee to raise funds for a synagogue, and a property was purchased on the Elbberg along the trace of the old ramparts to the east of the Brühl Terrace.[391]

In 1838, the building committee arranged with Gottfried Semper to design the new place of worship; it also engaged two construction contractors to carry out his plans. In this instance, Semper altered his specifications in order to accommodate the congregation's budget. It had originally envisioned a much grander building than it could afford. His final plan yielded a synagogue in the Byzantine style. Its dome and two towers, surmounted by Stars of David, became part of the city's skyline. In the main room were 300 seats for men and, in the gallery, 200 seats for women. To save money, wood was substituted for stone, both in the dome and in the interior pillars. Finally, the Saxon state provided a contribution of 200 Taler to help defray the final construction cost of 30,000 Taler.

On 8 May 1840, the Royal Theater delayed the beginning of the evening performance to accommodate the synagogue's dedication. Officially present at this event were several Saxon ministers, representatives of the Saxon legislature, high officials of the royal court, the city council and members of the city assembly. With the new building came several small changes in the worship service: choral singing in Hebrew, short prayers and a short sermon in German. Frankel wanted to keep his diverse congregation together, and that meant introducing innovations incrementally in order not to alienate his community's traditionalists. In Germany as a whole, Frankel is seen as the founder of Conservative Judaism, but in Dresden he was considered a modernizer.[392]

With the reforms of the 1830s, culminating in the festive dedication of the synagogue, it seemed as if Dresden Jews had finally gained substantial respectability in Saxon society. But limitations on their full exercise of equality remained. Although Jews could now own property, they were limited to one parcel of land that had to be held for at least ten years. They could freely choose most occupations, but they were subject to a quota in most guilds. Jews could also apply to become citizens in the cities where they resided but could not receive the right to vote or hold office.[393]

The event that established full political equality for Jews in Saxony was the revolution of 1848–49. Jews voted in the elections for the new city assembly in 1848, and Bernhard Hirschel, Louis Lesser's friend, now a medical doctor, was elected assemblyman. Wilhelm Schie, Lesser's employer, was elected as an alternate to the same group. In the following year, Jews gained the right to vote for and to hold office in the Saxon legislature. But they were still restricted to settlement in either Dresden or Leipzig, and they were constrained from marrying Christians. Only after Saxony was incorporated into the new North German Confederation were these constraints lifted. At the same time, it was extremely difficult for any Jew to be appointed to a post in the civil service. A recent chronicler of Jewish emancipation in Germany characterizes the Saxon approach as "retarded". It simply did not keep pace with emancipatory measures in other German states.[394]

Assimilation

During this period of revolutionary upheaval, Jews became more prominent in the economic life of the city. By 1851, Jews had opened several respected shops in the center of town: Joseph Meyer's fabrics; Moritz Meyer's porcelain and bronze; Ludwig Wolf's antiques and *objets de vertu*. Wolf did not limit himself to Dresden; he marketed his valuable wares to the whole region. As the North German Confederation gave way to the united German Empire, most of Dresden's Jews were considered to be middle class. A very high percentage was engaged in the free professions of the law, medicine, or journalism. Many managed enterprises owned either by other Jews or by Gentiles.[395]

This progress toward embourgeoisement was reflected in the congregational life of the Jewish community. In the synagogue, a new liturgy introduced many similarities to the Protestant church services. There were now hymns sung in German, and in 1870, the congregation installed a pipe organ in the gallery, a feature that was absolutely taboo thirty years before. The new Jewish cemetery in the city's Johannstadt also resembled the patterns of its neighbor, the Protestant Trinity Cemetery. Graves were no longer oriented toward the east; flowers and urns proliferated, and a small chapel graced the entrance.[396]

In addition to the Mendelssohn Club, there was a full slate of social and charitable organizations. Dating back to the eighteenth century were the Burial Brotherhood, the Society for the Care of the Sick and the Sickness Insurance Group, the Women's Club, even a Brotherhood Lodge. Others had grown up in the nineteenth century. Just after the mid-century revolution, Wilhelm Schie had bought a house and garden for an old folks' home which he gave to the Henrietta Foundation to administer. The Fraternitas Lodge was established in

1885 and modeled on the B'nai B'rith organization, founded in New York a half-century before. This group supported a day-care center, a workers' canteen and a vacation camp for youth in the neighboring village of Rochwitz. A few Jews also participated in the Gentile clubs of the city, but mostly the life of Dresden's Jews revolved around their work and their synagogue.[397]

Jews in Dresden had been involved in finance and banking since their arrival at the end of the seventeenth century. With the economic uptick of the last half of the nineteenth century, banks in Dresden proliferated, and the city became the most important banking center in central Germany. Already in 1857, Dresden's bankers had established a stock exchange. Of the numerous banks, one-third were Jewish. The most renowned of these banks was the one that evolved into the Dresdner Bank, one of the legendary big four of German commercial and investment banking.

The core of this institution was the Kaskel enterprise that began with the arrival of Jakob Kaskel from Poland in the late eighteenth century. Kaskel parlayed his original mercantile concession into that of court agent. His son, Michael, opened a bank at the end of the eighteenth century. Michael Kaskel continued to be involved in the life of the Jewish community, but his son Carl converted to Christianity in 1844. At the end of the 1860s, he received the noble title of Baron. When the small Kaskel bank experienced difficulties in the early 1870s, the family engaged Eugen Gutmann, a banker and businessman, to rescue it. He advised transforming the private company into a corporation and merging the bank with other prominent players in Frankfurt/Main, Hamburg, Berlin and Leipzig. The result in 1872 was the Dresdner Bank.

Gutmann was a proponent of branch banking and opened the first branch in Berlin in 1881. This move was so successful that in 1884, the Dresdner Bank moved its functioning headquarters to the German capital, retaining its juridical seat in Dresden. By the end of the century, it had the largest branch banking network in the country. It was also actively invested in the burgeoning German consumer cooperatives. The Dresdner Bank survived until its merger with the Commerzbank in 2009.[398]

The other bank of local renown was that of the Arnhold Brothers. The two men had moved from Dessau to Dresden during the 1860s, and their bank was closely associated with the German beer brewing industry. Eventually, the Arnhold Bank branched out into electrical and mechanical engineering. It was responsible for transforming the bankrupt Kummer Works into the locally important Saxon Works at the turn of the century. The Arnholds developed a reputation for being socially conscious. In their banking endeavors, they financed a lot of small and medium-sized businesses. Their workers enjoyed high salaries and knew they could count on the Arnholds during family crises. The brothers established a German Pension Fund for white-collar workers, and later they founded a scholarship for students at the Art Academy. Not surprisingly, the Arnholds were among the seventeen Jewish millionaires within the city at the turn of the century.[399]

Eastern Jews

Just as it seemed that the Jewish community of Dresden had settled into a respected and amicable relationship with its Gentile neighbors, new problems arose. The increasing industrialization and prosperity of the city attracted many migrants, among them Jews from Eastern Europe. By 1910, there were 3,689 Jews within the city, of whom 53 per cent were foreign. Most of these foreigners hailed from Galicia in the Austro-Hungarian monarchy. Initially, many of them were very poor and dependent on help from societies founded by Dresden's Jewish congregation. At the same time, Jews from Russian Poland and from Russia itself opened up cigarette factories in Dresden and prospered.[400]

The Katzenbogen family migrated from Minsk to Dresden in the 1890s in order to escape the Russian pogroms. Although the family's father first worked as a tobacco cutter, he soon started his own small cigarette factory. The family then moved into a "large, comfortable apartment" and kept a samovar heated in the living room; the sideboard was filled all day long with both cold and hot kosher foods. The children's names were Germanized. The Katzenbogens became so integrated that a daughter married an independent Gentile businessman. Not all the Eastern Jews managed the same kind of integration into German society.[401]

Up until this time, the Jews in Dresden had taken care to maintain a unified congregation and had, as we have seen, developed a reformed approach to their existence; they adhered to German bourgeois norms in everyday life while adhering to the religious practices of Judaism, albeit a practice that mimicked their Protestant neighbors. Many Orthodox Jews from the East could not accept this reformed Judaism, and the existing congregation had difficulty assimilating them. The Dresden congregation in 1887 devised a statute that excluded the foreigners from voting and holding office within the congregation. By the beginning of the twentieth century, there were three different Orthodox prayer rooms, all served by the same rabbi who made his living running an antiques store.[402]

Anti-Semitism

The arrival of the Eastern Jews not only caused friction within the Jewish community, it intensified the anti-Semitism that had long been both overt and latent within Saxon society. In 1879, an organized anti-Semitic political movement began with the founding, in Saxony, of the German Reform League by Alexander Pinkert, and two years later a national German Reform Party emerged. Its goals were the exclusion of Jews from German legislatures, including the Reichstag, and from the civil service. In 1882, the first International Anti-Jewish Congress was held in Dresden. Anti-Semitism as an "ideology became firmly anchored in the Dresden bourgeoisie" and dominated municipal politics for over two decades. In a particularly petty instance of discrimination, the Saxon Diet outlawed kosher butchering in the state on the grounds of its cruelty to animals. Instead of slitting the throats of live animals outright, it was necessary, said the legislators, to sedate the animals before killing them. Such sedation ran directly counter to Jewish law and practice. This Saxon law against kosher butchers persisted for several years.[403]

Emil Lehmann, descendant of the Lehmanns who had financed August the Strong's claim to the Polish throne, was one Dresdner who combated the new manifestation of anti-Semitism. Whereas previously, the impetus for discrimination against Jews focused on the differences in religion and lifestyle, in the last part of the nineteenth century, anti-Semitism became racial. Jews were seen as physically and mentally inferior and threatening to Germans; they would undermine the nation if they were not prevented from doing so.

The logic of racial anti-Semitism countered everything Jewish emancipators had worked for since the eighteenth century. It meant that no amount of assimilation would make Jews acceptable within the wider society. Lehmann had attended Dresden's Kreuzschule and studied law in Leipzig. As a lawyer, Jew and patriot, he had served in the city's assembly and been elected to the Saxon Diet in 1875. His *Collected Works* attest to his anxieties over the appearance of this new anti-Semitism. In 1893, Lehman was one of the founding members of the Central League of German Citizens of Jewish Belief. Its goal was to demonstrate the loyalty of Jews to the German Reich and their desire to make positive contributions to German society.[404]

It is tempting to think that Dresdners did not join their fellow Saxons in being the most anti-Semitic state in Germany. Examples from daily life in Dresden suggest otherwise. Friedrich Salzburg, a Jew who was born and raised in Dresden and practiced law in the city until his forced emigration, attended the Kreuzschule in the 1890s. He categorically states that most of the teachers there were anti-Semitic, and two or three blatantly asserted their views in class. When a soccer club was introduced at the school, one of the two Jewish players was elected team president. When he graduated, the team promptly passed a resolution barring any more Jews from becoming members. A similar ban occurred in the school's literature club. Such anti-Semitism was not limited to the Kreuzschule. During the 1890s, Jewish girls and boys were taunted by the young street rabble on their way back and forth to school, and boys frequently found themselves engaged in fights, though Salzburg admits that Gentile friends aided their Jewish comrades.

When Salzburg pursued military service in the Saxon army, it was out of the question for a Jew to become a reserve officer, a position that carried social prestige. Had Salzburg served out his military service in Bavaria, the reserve officer title would have been automatically awarded him. In 1899, the Dresden city council rejected the application of an Austrian Jew for German naturalization. The council made it quite clear that the denial was due to the applicant's Jewishness and, further, that all such applications in the future would also be denied.

When World War I broke out, Salzburg admitted to feeling a certain bitterness toward Germany and Saxony because of discrimination against Jews. He was initially inclined not to join up. Nevertheless he became seized by the war fever of 1914 and said he felt ashamed to walk the streets as an able-bodied civilian. When he finally volunteered for the front, his wife was proud of him. Salzburg's psychology was typical of a general Jewish response to the war. Jews hoped that their participation would finally lead to full equality with Gentiles. And Salzburg's experience was shared by many of his co-religionists. In 1915, he became a commissioned officer and later won the Iron Cross, Second Class and the Iron Cross, First Class. The Iron Cross is roughly equivalent to the U. S. Distinguished Service Cross.

While Salzburg, and over 100,000 other Jews were fighting, dying, and being decorated for valor in World War I, anti-Semites continued their agitation. The reactionary German War Minister decided to bolster their movement by conducting, in 1916, a census of Jews serving in the ranks. The point was to prove that Jews were shirking their military duty and undermining the German nation. The survey completely refuted this assumption, and the results were never published. German Jews felt betrayed.

Nevertheless, this ever-optimistic community thought that it could successfully combat the insidious continuation of anti-Semitism by publicizing their wartime service. The first monument to German Jews killed in the war was erected in Dresden in 1916 in the new Jewish cemetery. Eventually chiseled into the stone were sixty names. Once the war was over, Jews founded the National League of Jewish Front-Line Soldiers. Indeed, the early years of the post-war Republic were characterized by the two faces of the Roman god Janus.[405]

Dresden Jews in the Weimar Republic

The face looking toward the future vindicated those Jews who thought that participation in World War I would usher in full equality. For the first time, practicing Jews were able to find jobs in the Saxon civil service. They also began to serve as jurors and judges. In 1923, Friedrich Salzburg was one of eighteen men elected to the executive committee of the Saxon Bar Association that had significant official powers. Jewish retailers packed downtown Dresden, north and south of the river. Some managed important stores like the branch of Tietz, the largest department store chain in Germany, and the locally owned "Reka" (*Residenz Kaufhaus*). Others opened small stores selling a variety of surplus goods, sometimes referred to by Germans as junk stores. When Central German Radio beamed out a program of synagogue music in April 1929, it seemed as if Jewish life had entered the mainstream. During that same month, a young Yehudi Menuhin played a concert with Fritz Busch, the director of the State Opera.[406]

As before the war, Jews were some of Dresden's most generous philanthropists. During the severe inflation of 1923, the Jewish congregation ran a soup kitchen that fed between 90 and 100 people every day. In 1926, Oscar Schmitz, a textile manufacturer, lent his impressive modern art collection to the International Art Exhibition. This exhibition was the first major one staged in Dresden after World War I and sought to revive Dresden's former prominence in the art world. In the same year, George Arnhold donated to the city a large public swimming pool next to the Ilgen Arena. The Rotary Club, one of the first German chapters, was established in Dresden in 1927 and welcomed Jews into membership. In 1930, Viktor von Klemperer, the Jewish manager of the local Dresdner Bank, was chair of the organization, and the club recruited Salzburg in 1931.[407]

Even in this more liberal context, the problem of Eastern Jews continued to plague both Jewish and Gentile society. During the war, Jews fleeing the fighting on the Eastern front in the Polish territories of the Russian and Austro-Hungarian Empires had migrated to Saxony. Though these migrants had been excluded by the German military from the areas surrounding Dresden, they arrived in the city after the war. Here, they helped to establish their own Orthodox synagogue with their own rabbi in 1920. By the middle of the decade, sixty per cent of Jews in Dresden hailed from foreign countries.

Within the established reformed congregation, the question of Eastern Jews' rights caused a crisis. When, in 1929, the reformed synagogue decided to grant Eastern Jews the right to vote and to hold office within the congregation, more conservative members of the community, who wanted to limit the foreigners influence, opposed this action. In response, someone submitted the resignation of the conservative council members. This rift within the group continued until Yom Kippur—the Day of Atonement—when it was resolved by a compromise.[408]

This split within the Jewish camp revealed the Janus face of the past. The conservative members of the Jewish community were not the only Saxons seeking to limit the number of Jewish foreigners within their midst. Throughout the early years of the Weimar Republic, politicians, bureaucrats and the press conducted an intense discussion about the issue of Eastern Jews. In the economically depressed area of southwestern Saxony, there were repeated attempts to deport Russian Jews deemed harmful to local industry. This was the area that spawned the first National Socialist cell in Saxony in 1921.

The Saxon Interior Ministry, led by a Social Democrat, calmly revoked any local law instituting deportation, claiming that there was absolutely no reason to chase these Jews away. At the same time, Saxon policy regarding naturalization was one of the strictest in Germany. Before they could become citizens, Eastern Jews had to live in Saxony between 25 and 30 years. In Prussia, naturalization could occur after 10 years of residency.

The right-wing party in the legislature, the German National Party, repeatedly brought up the issue of Jews in a variety of assemblies. This party, the successor to the old Conservatives, which had enthusiastically embraced anti-Semitism before World War I, blamed Jews for losing World War I and for importing Bolshevik ideas into Germany. This propaganda went over well with large numbers of the middle and upper classes who had difficulty absorbing the loss of World War I, the punitive Treaty of Versailles, the 180-degree turn in the country's political orientation, and the unsettled economy of the post-war years.[409]

Before the war, under the authoritarian Kaiser, the aristocratic Conservatives and their allies in the military, industry and agriculture had dominated politics. After the war, it was the working-class Social Democrats and the liberal middle class, some of whom were Jews, who determined policy and who passed laws that favored their constituents. As we have seen, during the inflation of 1923, the old political forces were willing to use the army to undermine the duly elected, new political elite. In Saxony, the first head of government after the revolution was a Social Democrat, George Gradnauer. Never mind that he had been baptized a Protestant and pursued conservative policies in a revolutionary situation. He had the Jewish ancestors that conservatives and the radical right abhorred. During the Third Reich, he was sent to the concentration camp of Theresienstadt, survived, but died soon after the end of World War II.[410]

Exclusion

Another example of this racial anti-Semitism occurred in Dresden shortly after the National Socialists and their conservative allies came to power in 1933. Arthur Chitz, born to a Jewish manufacturer in Prague, was the baptized music director of the State Theater. He had lived in Dresden since 1908 and, in addition to his work for the theater, taught at the Saxon State Orchestra school and gave piano and harpsichord recitals. He was forced to retire in April 1933, as were all the Jewish actors and staff at the theater.

At the Technical College, professors who were practicing Jews lost their jobs immediately; within three years, those professors who were not religious or who had converted to Christianity were deprived of their posts. At the

Municipal Utilities Corporation, the two Jewish directors were told to leave. About the same time, several prominent Dresden Jews were arrested by Stormtroopers. In an instance of double threat, the Dresden police, with a contingent of 20 men, appeared at the Salzburg's residence to arrest son Peter, who was suspected of being a Communist and thus an opponent of the new regime. He was allowed to return home only after ten days.[411]

Some of the most pathetic cases involved the reaction of Gentiles to the onslaught of anti-Semitic persecution. The maid of one of the Jewish professors at the Technical College quit and told her employers that they soon would be unable to pay her, and she had an offer of a secure job. At the end of March, the liberal *Dresden's Latest News* (*Dresdner Neueste Nachrichten*) sought to placate the regime by announcing that "Aryans" owned 92.5% of the newspaper and that the Jewish owner of the other 7.5%, the baptized and respected editor Julius Ferdinand Wolff, was resigning.[412]

On the other hand, some Gentiles went out of their way to show solidarity with their Jewish neighbors and associates. On Saturday, April 1, the National Socialists called for a boycott of all Jewish businesses. Salzburg, who enjoyed a large Gentile clientele, did not go to his office. When he arrived there on Monday morning, he found two bouquets of flowers thanking him for his efforts on behalf of two of his Gentile clients. There were apparently other Jews who had shops in the Prager Strasse who chose not to open on that Saturday and not to confront the loitering Stormtroopers carrying signs urging Gentiles not to buy from Jews. The boycott was not successful, neither in Dresden nor in Germany, and was called off after this one day. In another context, the pastors Mensing and Klare extended their sympathy to the Arnhold family because of the anti-Semitic measures directed against them. At dancing class, Gentile mothers insisted that their daughters choose the Jewish Hans-Georg Maron as a dancing partner in a minor show of disagreement with the regime.[413]

The mothers' actions also sought to relieve some of the social isolation that the regime imposed on children and adults alike. Beginning in the summer of 1933, Jewish children could not participate in school sports competitions, theater visits, or vacation retreats in the countryside. They could not attend the weekly school assemblies. Rosemary Salzburg's teacher tried to console her by saying that now she could stay home and sleep another hour on assembly day. Rosemary rode the streetcar to school with a girl in her class, and the latter's mother picked her up after school, rode home with the girls and conversed normally with both of them. One day, his supervisor asked the girl's father, who was a civil servant, if he knew that his wife and daughter associated with a Jewish girl. Civil servants could be fired for associating with Jews.

School teachers were told to discriminate openly against Jewish pupils, and the Saxon Ministry of Religion and Education kept lists of National Socialists willing to give lectures on the Jewish race. At the Annen School, one such lecturer claimed that anyone could differentiate between Jews and "Aryans". Aryans were tall, thin, strong, with an oblong skull, blonde hair and blue eyes; Jews had bowed legs, black eyes and black, frizzy hair. Then the lecturer called a pupil to the front of the room as an example of a model Aryan. The class broke up in laughter and identified the pupil as the son of the Jewish banker Mattersdorf.

At the town's elite public high school, the King Georg Gymnasium, a teacher asked all Jews to stand up. The one who rose had his name, Merzon, declared disgusting and was told that a new wind was blowing through the school. Latin, Greek, and math were "out", and gymnastics and physical fitness were "in". Later, the teacher asked everyone who had received the highest gymnastics grade to stand, and once again, Merzon presented himself, all alone. The one other pupil with the highest grade, a Gentile, had refused to stand in order to embarrass the teacher.

In 1934, Dresden's National Socialist mayor decreed that Jews could no longer use the public baths, the hot mineral springs in the region, and the city's swimming pools. This decree, of course, included the George Arnhold Swimming Pool next to the Ilgen Arena. At that juncture, George's son, Kurt, asked that the pool be given a new name. The city then called the pool after the original holders of the property, but most people continued to use the old one.[414]

It was not only children who were socially stung by the regime's racial restrictions. During the first months of the regime, the Art Society asked Heinrich Arnhold to give up his membership. He and his brothers were excluded from the philanthropic societies to which they had contributed generously: The Public Health Club and the Club for Support of the Needy, the Friends and Supporters of the Technical College. After Heinrich's death in 1935, his widow found she could not receive an official certificate for putting her dog through a rigorous training program; the dog was Jewish.

The Rotary Club also suffered for a variety of reasons. Civil servants, whose membership put their jobs in jeopardy, withdrew. In order to stay afloat, the group decided to dissolve the club to avoid dealing with Rotary headquarters in Chicago and to re-form it on a non-affiliated basis. The new statute excluded all Democrats and all Jews who were not veterans. By 1935, with the passage of the Nuremberg Laws that deprived Jews of German citizenship, even this provision was no longer adequate. The president of the new Rotary privately asked Salzburg to tell the other two Jews—the von Klemperer brothers—that the executive committee wanted them to resign.

At this time, the State Theater fired its Jewish dramaturg, Dr. Karl Wollf. In order to provide him with an income, Friedrich Salzburg's wife decided to establish a lecture series where he could talk about Buddhism. She invited forty paying guests, and Friedrich decided that it would be wise to notify the police by certified letter about this entirely private event. That forced his wife to withdraw the invitations to civil servants so as to spare them any difficulties for attending an assembly with a Jew. Fifteen minutes before the first lecture, a Gestapo official appeared in order to take notes. At the last minute, a National Socialist Stormtrooper also showed up, claiming to represent the party and wanting to know what was "going on". For each of the succeeding lectures, a representative of the police and of the party attended.

Stormtroopers also appeared at the Salzburg residence one morning when no Salzburgs were home and asked the housekeeper, the cook and the maid if they were being treated all right. When the three ladies had no complaints, the party men told them that nice Gentile girls should not be working for Jews. They also urged them to encourage the Salzburgs to leave the country, because they couldn't vouch for what would happen to the family.[415]

On the economic front, the example of the Arnhold family reveals how the regime intimidated Jewish families. At first, the Arnhold family believed that their bank could weather what they considered to be the last in a long line of anti-Semitic persecutions. Ninety percent of employees at the bank were Gentiles, and the National Socialists had appointed an office ombudsman to deal with any complaints. Not only that, the Arnhold Bank was heavily involved in helping to stabilize the German economy, still suffering from the effects of the Great Depression.

Nevertheless, in May 1933, rumors began to circulate that Nazi party leader Mutschmann planned to harass the Arnholds in order to force them out of Germany. Already several companies, in which the bank was invested, had requested that the Arnholds send Gentile representatives to board meetings or else withdraw. Heinrich Arnhold was interrogated about "irregularities" in the business of one of his investments. Several months later, the bank was searched and documents confiscated. State prosecutors questioned Heinrich Arnhold and his brother about their "defrauding" the German General Electric Company when they persuaded it to rescue the Saxon Works from bankruptcy. More and more Saxon firms severed their relationships with the bank. There was increasing pressure on the Arnholds throughout 1934 to sell out to the Saxon State Bank.

In 1935, the Saxon state began prosecuting the Arnholds for foreign-exchange manipulation in dealing with a Bulgarian tobacco merchant. Eventually, the National Business Court found the bank innocent of fraud but fined the business manager for having made a mistake. Hard on the heels of this judgment, Heinrich Arnhold died. He was fifty years old and in good physical condition; one can only conclude that the harassment by the Nazi Saxon state was responsible for his death. Jews and Gentiles alike attended the funeral, as did government informers.

As anti-Semitic agitation intensified, Heinrich's brother decided to sell out. It was the Dresdner Bank that bought up the Arnholds' industrial and business assets in central Germany, leaving the family with the less lucrative holdings. By the time of the sale, the Dresdner Bank was no longer owned by the Kaskels and their associates. In the banking crisis of 1931, the German state had acquired a dominating interest in the bank to prevent it from failing. Thereafter, the National Socialist regime was in a good position to guide the bank's activities. In 1933, the Dresdner had fired its Jewish employees all across Germany, and in 1934 it forced the resignation of the prominent manager of its Dresden branch, Victor von Klemperer von Klemenau. When purchasing the Arnholds' bank, the Dresdner refused to continue the employment of its Jewish employees, so the family gave severance pay to those terminated.

During the next two years, Mutschmann's machinations led to the sale of the remaining private Jewish banks in Dresden. After the arrest of Rudolf Maron in 1936 when he was forced to pay a high price for his release, he decided to liquidate the Bondi and Maron Bank and emigrate. At the time of sale, the regime seized the bank's assets under the pretext of currency exchange fraud. In 1937, the Mattersdorf Bank was also sold.[416]

Other Dresden businesses felt the pressure. Right after the National Socialists took power, Dresden newspapers collectively agreed that they would no longer accept advertisements from Jewish firms. Already in June 1933, the National Socialists forbade Jewish vendors from holding stalls at public markets, both outdoor and indoor. The large department store, Tietz, first advertised that it had been Aryanized and then announced its closure in January 1934. Retailers in the Wilsdrufferstrasse, a busy shopping street, also sold out to Gentiles. The locally owned "Reka", was sold in the mid-1930s. When it held an anniversary sale in 1937, it painted all its entrances with the words, "ARYAN BUSINESS". In 1938, there were still 91 shops in Dresden that had to display signs announcing their Jewishness. By 1939, the indefatigable chronicler of the Third Reich in Dresden, Victor Klemperer, found new Gentile names on all the shops in the Wettinerstrasse, just up the street from the Zwinger.

A similar situation prevailed in Dresden industry. The tobacco firm "Yramos" was one of the few that had escaped Reemtsma's wave of purchases in Dresden and other cities during the Weimar Republic. At the beginning of the Third Reich, it employed 200 workers and hired Jews who could not find employment elsewhere. In 1937, boycotts inspired by the Saxon state forced the Jewish owner, Julius Lewin, to sell the business. The state confiscated the 400,000 RM that Lewin realized from the sale. Also in 1937, Mutschmann demanded that the Jewish director of the Hille Works be fired. The firm tried to circumvent this demand by sending him to Hamburg to direct its Import-Export Office. Mutschmann pursued him even there, and the firm eventually terminated him with a severance payment of 72,000 RM.[417]

Other pressures were initially more subtle. At the beginning of the Third Reich, Friedrich Salzburg was allowed to continue to function as a notary only after his captain during World War I was questioned by the police for two hours. In continental Europe, a notary is a state official who authenticates all legal documents. So, a large portion of Salzburg's livelihood depended on his notarial functions. This relatively tolerant practice ended in 1935 upon orders from the national Justice Ministry.

The Marriage Counseling Service that he had served as a member of the Saxon Bar Association also stopped inviting him to meetings and calling on him for advice. The Dresden branch of the Commerzbank, which had used Salzburg's services for 34 years, terminated its association with him after the passage of the Nuremberg Laws in 1935. By this time, some of his former clients had sought out other lawyers and notaries, because they feared that their cases, represented by a Jewish advocate, would not fare well in court. Finally, in 1936, the National Socialists deemed it dishonorable for party members who were lawyers to represent Jews. Dr. von der Bey, Salzburg's Gentile partner, left the firm for that reason.

In contrast, the Dresdner Bank continued to use Salzburg's services but requested that he not sign his briefs with his Jewish name. The Officers' Association of the Former Royal Saxon Heavy Artillery refused to exclude Salzburg. When someone made the motion to end the membership of Jews, one of the men voting against the motion averred that "if the two Jewish gentlemen were good enough to be our comrades at Verdun and on the Somme," two punishing campaigns of World War I, "then they're good enough to be our comrades now."[418]

Dresden Jews were increasingly thrown back upon themselves. Up until the beginning of the Third Reich, emancipated Jews thought of themselves as Germans and Jews. They did not attend synagogue frequently, but they still considered themselves to be part of the congregation. Now, increasingly they simply became Jews. Some, like the Arnholds, ceased to attend the opera and the theater because of the dismissals of Jewish performers and staff. More began to participate in the synagogue's governing board and in the charitable organizations that it supported. Heinrich Arnhold had joined the newly formed Cultural League of German Jews in an attempt to advertise his stance as German as well as Jew.

Despite National Socialist harassment, the congregation demonstrated unusual optimism. In 1935, it opened an elementary school next to the synagogue, a measure that was beneficial later, when Jews were excluded from Dresden's public schools. At the end of the same year, it dedicated an expansion of the synagogue so that it could accommodate all Dresden's Jews who worshipped during the High Holy Days of Rosh Hashanah and Yom Kippur. In 1936, when the reading rooms of all public libraries, including the State Library in the Japanese Palace, were closed to Jews, the congregation opened an educational center. Proudly it also celebrated the fiftieth anniversary of Rabbi Jakob Winter's tenure in Dresden.[419]

At the same time, it escaped no one that Jews were leaving Dresden and Germany for good. Already in 1933, the congregation had established an

Emigrants' Advisory Board and turned to Heinrich Arnhold for help. He suggested that Dresden's private bankers could advise concerning the sale of property and transfer of assets abroad. Some people, like the composer Paul Aron, simply moved to neighboring countries and returned periodically to Dresden to give concerts, to visit, or for other reasons. Parents, like Arthur Chitz, Friedrich Salzburg and the Arnholds, began to send their children abroad to study or to pursue internships. Finally, they reluctantly decided there was no other choice than emigration for the whole family. Many crossed the border illegally. Others, faced with the regime's onerous emigration tax and other confiscations, emerged poor and embittered.

In 1936, Fanny Silberschein, a member of the synagogue's staff, went home to eat her midday dinner and discovered, through a Gentile neighbor, that during the morning the Gestapo had come looking for her. Fearing that the police would confiscate her passport, Fanny took the train that night to Basel, Switzerland. where her sister lived, carrying only the passport, a hatbox, and 10 RM.

The passage of the Nuremberg Laws in September 1935, removing German citizenship from people of Jewish descent, set the scene for the intensified harassment and persecution that followed. Without citizenship, Jews resided in a legal no-man's land, protected by nothing more than their usefulness to the regime, their reputations, and, possibly, their friends in high places. Earlier, the Jewish congregation had thought it possible to help people plan rationally for emigration: language courses and job training for work in offices, industry or agriculture. By 1936, it was clear that this course had to be abandoned in favor of flight, as quickly and as advantageously as possible.[420]

For those unable or reluctant to flee, life became more and more restricted and threatening. In 1937, the municipal Building Society, that had once made affordable housing available to Jews and Gentiles alike, began to cancel the leases of its Jewish tenants. Similar companies were doing the same. Anyone who was Jewish or related to a Jew and renting municipal property was chased out.

Henny Wolf, whose father was Gentile and whose mother was Jewish, explains that her family had to give up their spacious apartment in the Blasewitz neighborhood. When her father, who owned and ran a movie theater in the Neustadt, could no longer rent the premises, even her paternal grandmother had to abandon her home and move in with her daughter in

Berlin. Henny's father was told that he could keep all his assets if only he would divorce her Jewish mother. He refused. The family's laundress quit under pressure from the regime. At the opposite end of the city in Dölzschen, so did the Klemperer's cleaning lady whose son and daughter stood to lose their jobs if their mother continued to work for Jews.[421]

The beginning of 1938 signaled an escalating attack on Jews. In January, two thousand National Socialists gathered in Dresden's posh neighborhood of the Weisser Hirsch to hear Martin Mutschmann give a "comprehensive settlement of accounts with the Jews". He wanted Germany's high culture freed from the "world plague of Jews". This meeting and speech reverberated throughout Saxony. In Dresden, the Saxon government confiscated the Jewish congregation's treasury and the funds of all its philanthropic organizations. All the city's parks were closed to Jews. Jews now had to carry identity cards bearing the names foisted on them by the state, "Sara" for women and "Israel" for men. Jewish doctors could no longer participate in private health insurance plans and eventually lost their medical certification, more or less depriving them of the right to practice medicine.[422]

Crystal Night

In the midst of these humiliating affronts to Jews in Germany, the Polish government in October 1938 declared that all Poles living abroad for longer than five years, or with a passport that didn't allow them re-entry into Poland, could be denied entry at any time. The German government responded by rounding up all Polish Jews the police could find and transporting them to the German-Polish border where many found themselves stranded. Altogether 724 individuals from the Dresden region were arrested and transported. After a protest by the Polish government, the Germans rescinded the order and took back the Jews affected. Nevertheless, the damage had been done.

On 7 November 1938, Herschel Grynszpan, whose parents had been stranded at the Polish border, shot and killed a staff member of the German embassy in Paris. His death led the National Socialist propaganda minister, Joseph Goebbels, to instigate the S.A. (Stormtroopers) and the S.S. (Security Services) to unleash the famous Crystal Night (*Kristallnacht*) throughout Germany on November 9. As in other German cities, groups of Stormtroopers and other party members rampaged through the streets of Dresden. Using sledge hammers and other tools, they crashed through shop windows, plundered the goods, and tore up the décor. In the middle of the night, individuals arrived at the synagogue, laid down gasoline and ignited it. Built chiefly of wood, the synagogue went up in flames immediately. Only the new annex was spared. Rabbis Jakob Winter and Albert Wolf were arrested, beaten and incarcerated in Buchenwald. With them went scores of the congregation's members.

The next morning, November 10, a flock of secret police appeared at the synagogue's offices that had been spared by the flames. A crowd of National Socialists followed the police. The Gestapo relieved the synagogue's staff of the monies in the safe, of the liturgical silver and of the surviving Torah Rolls. Then they draped prayer shawls over the heads of the male staff, bound children's bibs from the day-care center around their necks and topped them off with smashed top hats. So dressed, the male staff was forced to do gymnastics in the synagogue's offices to the tune of curses and beatings. Afterword, they were positioned at the office windows, so they could be seen by the raucous crowd below, and police fists "rocked" them back and forth as the mob below jeered.[423]

In mid-November, air force commander and plenipotentiary for the war economy, Hermann Goering, decreed that all Jewish businesses had to close, and the property of emigrants and deportees would be confiscated by the state. At the beginning of December, all Jews lost their drivers' licenses, and the librarians at the State Library told Victor Klemperer, former professor of French at the Technical College, that not only was he banned from the reading room, he could no longer borrow books. The Jewish organist of the American church, an English woman married to a German Gentile, had to give up her job because the church was a registered German Foundation. The regime began to confiscate valuables declared on an inventory of wealth required earlier in 1938.[424]

At the beginning of 1939, the Saxon National Socialists mounted a large show in Dresden's Exhibition Palace: "The Eternal Jew". Martin Mutschmann opened the show by telling his fellow Saxons that "the Jew [was] the world's sole troublemaker". To drum up attendance at the exhibition, the party launched propaganda parades through the city with loudspeakers blaring music and participants bearing pictures of crooked figures with long noses, fleshy lips, small foreheads and frizzy hair. They fit the popular caricatures of the "revolting faces" of "cold-blooded, calculating" capitalists. Children, particularly, were entertained. Lea Grundig, a Jewish artist, who twice went to prison for her Communist sympathies, was waiting for the streetcar at Albertplatz when she witnessed one such spectacle. Adults, she said, either stood by passively or turned their backs on the whole troupe. There was 'no protest, just a mute lack of participation…and that consoled me a little bit,' she said.[425]

Death

And then came the war. World War II was deadly for Germany's Jews, and Dresden was no different. Outright robbery had occurred even before war began on 1 September 1939. With the outbreak of war, the regime blocked Victor Klemperer's security account containing gold and conducted a search of his house for valuable rare books for donation to the State Library. At the end of December 1939, Klemperers were told they had to give up their house, built a few years earlier, and that the regime would select the tenants to rent it after Klemperers moved out. In any case, all Jews were being moved out of their old residences into thirty-two Jewish houses where they could be easily monitored. Thereafter, there were frequent searches of the premises, and usually some items belonging to Jews were stolen during the searches.[426]

Jews' lives became more and more regulated and impoverished. Week by week and month by month the regime dreamed up decrees that functioned like pin-pricks on Jewish lives. At the end of December 1939, families were restricted to only one place where they could buy groceries. Eight months later, they were told to shop only between three and four on weekday afternoons and between eleven and twelve on Saturday mornings. Shops were not open on Sundays. By 1942, Jews were forbidden to store foodstuffs, and in one egregious episode at Easter 1942, the Gestapo appeared at a Jewish house and confiscated all the food that the residents had bought to tide them over the holiday, when the shops would not be open for two days. Eventually, Jews were prohibited from eating in restaurants.

Added to these bans was the progressive denial of certain types of rationing coupons to Jews: first chocolate, then clothing, then milk, later eggs and vegetables. Klemperer reported to his diary in mid-1942 that he and his Gentile wife were short of bread, potatoes and coal; her ration cards were not sufficient to provide for both of them. As the war progressed, she took to going to whatever restaurants were serving meals, and he stayed home.

There were other confiscations: woolen goods, furs, metal objects, telephones, radios, all electrical appliances, and bicycles. This latter theft was another attempt on the part of the regime to cause hardship. Beginning in March 1940, Jews were pressed into service in the war industries and other businesses essential to the economy. They were expected to turn up for work on time, just like any other employee. At first, they could take public transportation. Then they were refused rides on buses. After that, they could no longer ride the streetcar—on the outer platform only—unless their workplace was more than seven kilometers (4.2 miles) away from their place of residence. So they rode their bikes. After a while, they could no longer take the street car or ride their bikes, and so they walked.[427]

Henny Wolf worked the late shift at a manufacturing plant, and one midnight a drunk trailed her home, even putting a foot in the door as she turned the key. At that point, her father, who had waited up, called out to her, and the drunk disappeared. For a few weeks thereafter, her father came to fetch her when her shift ended, but he walked more slowly than she, and that made them both more vulnerable to attack. They also worried about leaving her Jewish mother home alone. So, Henny again walked alone.[428]

After September 1941, Jews were marked individuals. In a throwback to the Middle Ages, they all had to wear a yellow star prominently displayed on their coats or apparel. This caused a variety of reactions. Soon after the decree went into effect, one of Klemperer's neighbors was cheerfully greeted by a stranger as she left a shop. When she protested that she didn't know him, he told her that he belonged to a group who were making it a practice to "greet the yellow star", another attempt by well-meaning Gentiles to combat the marginalization of Jews. Once, when Henny Wolf was still riding her bicycle to work, her tire got stuck in the streetcar tracks and she fell. When a young soldier, who came to help, saw the star, he shook his head in sympathy.

Victor Klemperer was reluctant to leave the house, because of the star, and he missed strolling with his wife through the streets. After he was assigned a job, he could no longer avoid the streets, and one night, as he returned home from work, a group of teen-agers on bicycles overtook him, and shouted: 'He'll get a shot in the back of the head... I'll pull the trigger... He'll be hanged on the gallows—stock exchange racketeer...' The reference to the shots suggests that information concerning the killing of Jews in the Polish campaign—a shot in the back of the neck—had filtered down to the civilian population long before these boys' shouts.[429]

Zeiss-Ikon, a pre-war maker of cameras, now manufactured fuses, targeting devices, and anti-aircraft cannons and shrapnel. It created a special munitions factory in Pieschen in 1940/41, the Goehle Works, and employed thousands of workers. Jews were happy to work there, because they thought that this contribution to the war effort was insurance against deportations. At the end of 1942, a concentration camp, the Hellerberg, was established in a gravel pit not far from the army's infantry barracks. Two hundred ninety-three Jews from the Goehle Works were removed from their homes to primitive shelters and tasked with making parts for the Works. They remained there for a little over three months. In January 1943, the regime forbade using Jews in the munitions industry, and in March 1943, they were all transported from the Hellerberg to Auschwitz.

The deportations from Dresden to the East—to Riga, Theresienstadt, and Auschwitz—had begun at the end of January 1942. The first to be taken were the old people living in the Henrietta Home for the Aged, the foundation established a half-century before. News of what occurred in Auschwitz quickly filtered back to Dresden. Already on 16 March 1942, Klemperer recorded that it was rumored to be the worst of the concentration camps. People who arrived there died within a few days. Jews with Gentile spouses felt safe for a time, but as the war and the deportations dragged on, the regime began to attack not only the Jews in a mixed marriage but also their wives and husbands.[430]

Henny Wolf says that the regime at one point planned to draft Gentile men married to Jewish wives into the Organization Todt (responsible for military engineering and construction) for work at the front. The idea was to get the men killed, so that their wives and children could then be deported to the death camps. In any case, by the time the Hellerberg was established, there were only a few hundred Jews left in the city, and many of them had Gentile spouses. By the beginning of 1944, it was clear that the regime had so-called "privileged Jews" in its sights, and it was not clear what would happen to their spouses or their children.

Toward the end of the war, Henny worked at the Bauer cartonnage factory. There were frequent visits by National Socialist officials, and each time, they took someone who was never seen again. The workers lived in constant fear of being the ones taken at the next visit. "The fear," she said, "was indescribable; it quite nearly drove us insane... [I]t was impossible to identify a system in their selections. Nobody knew whose number would be up next day." Worse than hunger, even worse than the star, was the fear.[431]

Throughout 1944, most of the Jews left in Dresden had escaped deportation because they were married to Gentile spouses. Victor Klemperer reported to his diary that those whose spouses had died and whose Christian children were no longer by their sides were beginning to disappear. As Germany's prior victories now turned into defeats, these "privileged" Jews were vulnerable. The first significant air attack on Dresden occurred in October 1944, and Jews were called up along with prisoners of war to clear the rubble in the Wilsdruffer neighborhood. The second attack came in mid-January 1945 when the railroad marshaling yards in the Friedrichstadt were targeted. The Soviets were advancing toward Germany's eastern border. In response to Germany's imminent defeat, the regime now targeted those Jews who still remained in Dresden.[432]

XII. Shrove Tuesday-Ash Wednesday, 1945

The Industrial City as a Target

When World War II began in 1939, Dresden was the sixth largest industrial city in the German Reich. We've already seen that important Dresden firms received subsidies from the state to help them make the transition to armaments production. To the thirty firms involved in munitions at the beginning of the war was added, by 1945, almost the bulk of industry inside the city and in the surrounding region, altogether 240 firms.

Dresden produced a high percentage of the "high-tech" products vital to the war effort: measuring and targeting instruments, communications installations, machine tools, detonators. It also supplied parts for the construction of submarines and torpedoes, for airplanes and for the V rockets that rained down on London in 1944 and 1945. Toward the end of the war, some German firms, particularly in the west, relocated to Dresden in order to escape Allied bombing or to restore capacity lost to the Allied advance. In addition, the headquarters of the armaments inspection for the Dresden region were located in the Neustadt. One historian has stressed that the city was far more than a cultural mecca and healing center for the war wounded.

Due to its involvement in supplying the armed forces, Dresden's economy experienced a boom during World War II. Its chief problem was the labor supply. By the time of the invasion of the Low Countries and France in 1940, the Wehrmacht stopped drafting men aged thirty-one and older in order to assure that sufficient numbers of male workers would remain to supply the armed services with vital materiel. After the attack on the Soviet Union in mid-1941 the regime resorted to forced labor from occupied territories, to prisoners of war, to its persecuted Jews and to Gentile inmates from concentration camps. As many as 20,000 forced laborers, and maybe thousands more, were employed in Dresden industry. It's in this context that the Hellerberg camp was established until the state decreed that Jews could no longer be used in the munitions industry. In one of his diary entries for 1942, Victor Klemperer recorded that the Soviet women who worked at Zeiss-Ikon, manufacturing detonators and precision instruments, received one slice of bread in the morning and one at night with only a thin soup at midday. By contrast, the Jews working in the same establishment at least received a complete midday dinner.[433]

It was not only Dresden's industrial firms that were heavily involved in the war effort. Faculty at the Technical College also contributed to the solution of the armed service's problems. Collaboration between the college and the armed services dated back to World War I. Once that war ended, faculty continued to cultivate relationships with the army, and in 1937 the Institute for Organic Chemistry began to offer instruction in chemical weapons. Others acted as advisors for the building of the autobahn network and for the manufacture of synthetic materials that imitated leather and wool, both related to the war effort. From both the German and the Allied point of view, the most critical was the Technical College's participation in the design and production of missiles.[434]

German interest in rocketry had started as a purely civilian enterprise, but the military became interested in 1929 and established both a research and a testing program for liquid-fuel missiles. When World War II broke out, the missile program had to compete for funding with other weapons systems, and the army began to lean heavily on engineering professors to advance its development. Professors joined the program in order to avoid their own and their assistants' conscription for service on the fighting fronts. Dresden's Technical College was one of two large partners of the army in the Working Group Project Peenemünde, the spit on the Baltic Sea where the instrumentation and propulsion systems for both the V-1 and the V-2 rockets were tested. In 1941, electronics engineer Walter Wolman became the leader of the Dresden center that concentrated on designing the rockets' telemetry and guidance systems.[435]

In addition to its importance as an industrial and engineering center, Dresden was the site of a strategic rail marshaling yard. The major north-south and east-west lines of southeastern Germany met here and distributed the industrial goods of the entire region. The German Railways supported a locomotive depot, a repair shop and a deployment center in Dresden. That meant that during World War II, Dresden's rails ferried troops to and from the front and transported labor from concentration and POW camps to factories producing war materiel.

Because of the rail hub, the English had identified Dresden as a bombing target quite early in the war. They were particularly interested in the Saxon Works as an industrial facility and in the role of the rails in distributing synthetic fuel from the refineries of Ruhland to the north and Brüx to the south. As the city came within range of Allied bombers after 1942, both the English and Americans shot aerial photographs of the whole urban area in preparation for future bombing attacks. The English extensively photographed the airfield and its garrison at Klotzsche, just to the north of the city.[436]

Many Dresdners refused to believe that the city was in any danger of being bombed. One of the more frivolous reasons for this cavalier attitude was the belief that a relative of Churchill's still lived in the city, a holdover from the time when Dresden hosted a sizable English Quarter. Others thought that those English who were acquainted with the city's cultural treasures would simply prevent its bombing. Another group argued that Dresden was known as a recovery center for servicemen wounded at the front. At least three military hospitals existed in the Dresden area.

One circumstance lulling the Dresdners into complacency were the frequent air raids, beginning in 1941, when nothing much happened. When bomber planes entered Germany's southeastern tangent, air defense sounded the alarm. Targets in other cities were bombed, but no planes appeared over Dresden; no bombs dropped. People even stopped going to the cellars when the sirens sounded. This situation lasted well into summer 1944. By that time, the city had become a refuge for Germans fleeing the Soviets approaching from the east. For many of its residents, Dresden was an open city and therefore off limits to Allied bombers. What they neglected to consider was that the Wehrmacht intended to defend the city to the hilt against any invading troops.

National and local authorities were aware that the city was vulnerable. In fall 1943, the national government ordered all cities to designate evacuation routes and bomb shelters. Yet Dresden was not high on the national government's list of priorities and received little support for the construction of bunkers or other facilities to protect the populace in the event of a bombing attack. The city designated the Ostra Preserve, the Great Garden and the Elbe meadows as shelter areas and breached walls beneath row houses so that people could escape from individual cellars, but there was little attempt to tunnel under intersections to allow for unbroken lines of flight.

Large basins were dug on several of the city's major squares to serve as sources of water to put out fires. On the large open space in front of the Semper Opera, today's Theaterplatz, then called Adolf-Hitler-Platz, prisoners built two large pits that were roofed, fortified with cement, covered with grass, and fitted out with air pipes. Götz Bergander, the leading authority on *Dresden in the Air War*, calls them little more than fancy trenches. According to him, they could not withstand a near hit, much less a direct assault.

By fall of 1944, with the Soviet army moving inexorably toward the German border of 1939, many Dresdners were aware that they were ill-protected against bombs. Houses with cellars designated as bomb shelters were marked with chalked circles and arrows bearing the letters "LSR" meaning, in German, air-raid shelter. Citizens joked that the letters actually meant "learn speedily Russian". There was also great resentment of the sturdy bomb shelter that Commissar Mutschmann, thinking it highly likely that the city would be bombed, constructed in his back yard close to the Great Garden. Even the local S.S. protested to Heinrich Himmler, national S.S. director, the expenditure of building this facility. Local school authorities warned parents to send their children away from Dresden, but few did so. The regional air defense authority also distributed circulars urging the public to prepare for a catastrophe, just in case. Some factories organized air-raid watch teams that were supposed to help workers in the event of an attack.

There were only a few secure bunkers within the city. There was a deep cellar under the New Rathaus; the air-raid command post in the cellar of the Albertinum was also well fortified; the command post of the Nazi party's administration in the Lockwitz valley was secure; and the command post of the S.S. in Loschwitz would provide safety for Nazi administrators. In addition there were two business firms secured against bombs: the Goehle Works in Pieschen and the Bramsch Distillery in the Friederichstadt. When the latter shelter was built in 1943, many Dresdners ridiculed the unnecessary expenditure on this facility. In 1945, when it withstood three half-ton bombs that exploded within 75 feet of the distillery, no one was laughing.[437]

At least, one partial protection against air raids was anti-aircraft artillery. Dresden seems never to have enjoyed heavy contingents of anti-aircraft batteries. Pupils from the city's high schools—eighteen- and nineteen-year-olds—and older males manned the guns. In December 1944, as the Soviets bore down on the German border, the anti-aircraft guns were removed from Dresden and other towns nearby to provide fire on the eastern front. At the same time, there was still heavy anti-aircraft protection for the synthetic fuel refineries at Ruhland and Brüx. People were expendable; fuel was not. After New Year's Day 1945, there was no ground fire to hamper any bombers targeting Dresden.[438]

Bombs Fall on Dresden

The first time that bombs fell close to Dresden occurred on 24 August 1944 when the British attacked the Rhenania Assag Mineral Oil Works in Freital just outside the city's southern limits. Although areas within the city were hit, Dresdners chose to believe they were not affected. On October 7, the refinery at Brüx was protected by cloud cover, so the Americans chose Dresden's marshaling rail yards in the Friedrichstadt as a secondary target. Bombs also fell on the area behind the Postplatz, on the Wilsdruffer Quarter, and on the working-class neighborhood of Löbtau. This attack was serious enough to kill 200 people and leave 3000 homeless. Thereafter air-raid warnings occurred, but no bombs fell, so Dresdners were again lulled into complacency.

The morning of January 16 was bitterly cold, and snow lay on gardens and roofs. Just before noon, the sirens sounded, and 400 American bombers swooped over Dresden. The main target was, once again, the rail yards in the Friedrichstadt, but the Hecht Quarter in the western Neustadt also suffered heavy damage. The gas works behind the Neustadt's rail station exploded twenty times. The freight station in the Altstadt was also hit along with working-class neighborhoods in Cotta and Löbtau. During this attack, not only was there no anti-aircraft fire to protect the city, but no fighter planes engaged the bombers. At the end of 1944, the regime had decided to desist from air battles. There simply was not enough fuel to support such operations. This last attack was massive and put the Dresdners on notice that they would now be subject to serious Allied bombing.[439]

By this time, the Soviets had launched the offensive that led into Germany, and they expected the Western allies to prevent Dresden, with its excellent transportation and communication facilities, from becoming the center of a counter-offensive against them. Meanwhile, the regime advised all non-combatants in Breslau, a mere 120 miles east of Dresden, to evacuate the city. Thousands of Breslauers and other Germans fleeing the Soviet advance, trekking west or riding the rails, were passing through Dresden. The city gave them permission to rest, but only for a short time. There was simply not enough food and other commodities to supply both Dresdners and refugees.

The refugees informed the Dresdners of the deteriorating military situation, but there were other sources of news. The army issued a daily news bulletin broadcast during the day through loudspeakers at the major city squares, and many people listened clandestinely both to Radio London and Radio Moscow. For the British, the refugees enhanced the city's value as a bombing target. Not only would their deaths demoralize the civilian population; their presence would also cause the chaos that would hamper military operations. For British Prime Minister Churchill and for the Royal Air Force, Dresden was simply one German city among several possible targets. At the end of January 1945, it appeared on the Allies' priority list of cities to be bombed.[440]

Destruction

Shrove Tuesday in 1945 occurred on 13 February. Although Protestant Dresden did not rival Catholic Rhenish cities in the celebration of carnival, it was traditional for children to dress up in costumes and parade through the city. Even in the midst of war, they did so. The Sarrasani circus also geared up for a large crowd of spectators that evening. Since official decrees had closed all theater and orchestra performances at the end of the previous September, it was one of the few evening entertainments left in town. The regime sanctioned its shows, because they provided the populace with a distraction from the woes of war.

At approximately 9:30 that evening, the first warnings of an air-raid sounded throughout the city and eventually reached a scream. Bombs began to drop over the Altstadt shortly before 10 p.m. In this first raid, 244 bombers of the Royal Air Force unleashed 500 tons of heavier blast bombs and 375 tons of incendiary bombs over the city. Within half an hour, a firestorm—an intense and spreading conflagration creating its own wind system—had developed that could be seen from miles away. This first attack knocked out most of Dresden's electricity, so that the sirens announcing the next raid barely sounded beyond a block of their location, and people were caught off guard. In addition, firemen who had rushed to put out fires caused by the first wave, now found their trucks stranded in burning asphalt.

The second wave of 529 British bombers, carrying 1800 tons of bombs, flew over the city at 1 a.m. and targeted the railroad's marshaling yards. In this second attack, both industrial and residential areas were hit, as were the Catholic and municipal hospitals, the main rail station stuffed with refugees, the Great Garden, and the Elbe meadows. These bombs only intensified the firestorm. Yet the Air Protection Command Post under the Albertinum had managed to call for help from neighboring communities. As day broke on Ash Wednesday, firefighting units from Leipzig, Chemnitz and Halle appeared at the gates of the city. By this time, the fires were so hot that any attempts to extinguish them were like "drops on a hot stone".

At noon on Ash Wednesday, the rail yards were still a visible target, and 316 American B-17s, with a total load of 771 tons of bombs, appeared in a sky that was partly clouded by natural conditions and partly filled with smoke from the firestorm below. In such a situation bombing was more imprecise than usual, and a wide swath of the city was hit, expanding the area covered by fire. While the fires continued to burn, the Americans appeared again the next day, February 15, still aiming for the marshaling yards but once again striking a wide area beneath a sky covered with clouds. Within the space of three days, Dresden had been struck by hundreds of tons of bombs. The city burned for three days; the glow of its fires could be seen from Prague in the south and Halle in the north, scores of miles away.[441]

Survivors of the firestorm have told countless stories about the terrible night of February 13–14. Here, a few will have to bear witness for the rest. Hans Köppe was an eleven-year-old schoolboy who lived in the Kleine Zwingerstrasse, a working-class neighborhood of old wooden homes and outhouses that sheltered many older people. Fathers were serving on the war front; mothers were alone with their children. On Shrove Tuesday, Hans and his buddies celebrated carnival by playing cowboys and Indians, and he had gone almost straight to bed after arriving home later than usual. When the alarm sounded at 9:30, his mother tore her children from their beds and marched them to the cellar. After the all-clear, they found their apartment severely damaged by the bombs' impact, and Frau Köppe decided to get her children to the Elbe. Once in the street, they found their cul de sac closed by rubble on its only open end.

Before panic began to descend into chaos, neighbors formed a long line into the cellar of the quarter's printing shop and followed it to an underground water tunnel. They marched through the tunnel to the Postplatz where they encountered the firestorm. Undeterred, they kept going through the flames of the Zwinger to the river. Hans was carrying one of his two younger sisters on his back. They had wrapped wet cloths around their mouths and had had the presence of mind to carry a pitcher to re-dampen the cloths when necessary. Hans saw dangling tram lines, smoldering autos, and flames illuminating the windows of the Semper Opera and the palace's tower. As terrible as it all was, he remembered the sight as "beautifully macabre (*schaurig-schön*)".[442]

Fire Chief Hans Rumpf and his men were overwhelmed by the firestorm. They could do little to prevent those trying to escape the fires from being sucked into the flames' voracious air shafts, which moved horizontally as well as vertically. Eyewitnesses have described watching people drawn back into the fire they were fleeing and dropping dead from the capture by the flames. Some people who tried to escape the cellars crowded together at the exits so tightly that they couldn't move. They, or others who feared to venture out, literally either steamed to death or suffocated in the heat that penetrated from the fires above. In one cellar, neighbors blocked a steel door to prevent one man from creating an escape hatch. All 200 persons were burned to death by fire approaching from the side opposite the door.[443]

Günther Kannegiesser was fourteen years old on the night of Shrove Tuesday, and he and his pals from the Johannstadt were acting as messengers and helpers for the neighborhood police station. When the all-clear sounded, he guided a group of women pushing baby carriages to the nearby hospital, where they were all surprised by the second raid. When that finally ended, he took the women to the Elbe meadows, and there he fell asleep. As morning dawned, he pushed his way back home and found a totally destroyed building with a fire still burning where the cellar steps began. He called out several times and got no answer. For years afterward, he tried to trace his mother and his two siblings and drew a blank. Five decades later, he received a copy of a letter from a boyhood friend's father who had managed in mid-March 1945 to gain access to the basement of Kannegiesser's apartment house.

According to his account, a month after the firestorm, the cellar space was still stiflingly hot. In the various underground rooms were twenty-nine burned bodies, that were no longer recognizable. From their calm and peaceful posture, it was apparent that they had died from asphyxiation long before the fires had consumed them. They had been afraid to venture out of the cellar into the fires; they had felt safe in the cellar; they had lain down on the ground where the air was better; and there they were poisoned by the low-lying carbon monoxide.[444]

On this same evening, two thousand spectators filled the large room of the Sarrasani Circus on Carolaplatz as the air-raid warning sounded just before the last act. Management had carefully drilled its personnel for such an eventuality. Ushers emptied the auditorium row by row and directed people to the three air-raid shelters underneath the building. When the all-clear sounded at 11 p.m., people were released from the shelters and sent out to the enveloping flames and any homes not caught in the firestorm. In the interlude between the all-clear and the second raid, neighboring residents sought refuge in the Sarrasani shelters even though hay and straw had begun to burn and the offices above the main entrance had been hit by a bomb. Trudi Stosch managed to send the circus' valuable Lippizaner horses to the Elbe.

In the second raid, when the circus building itself caught fire, so did the air-raid shelter. There had not been time to return the animals released after the all-clear to their cages and pens, and now some of them were injured. Circus personnel, who tried to save both the wounded and the non-wounded, did not succeed. Tigers suffocated; horses and other animals were bleeding. The Lippizaner sent to the Elbe were killed with their trainers by the bombs of the second raid. Some circus animals survived the second bombing raid, and afterward, they were taken to an estate in Saxon Switzerland. Surviving in the circus ruins was Wally the Hippopotamus who was watered by volunteers until the Red Army arrived in May. Soviet officers then shipped Wally off to the Leningrad Zoo.[445]

The second air-raid of February 13–14 wiped out Dresden's Zoo on the edge of the Great Garden. Several animal houses caught fire; the director and the staff tried to free the animals from their cages. They had orders to shoot animals that were particularly dangerous to humans, but several of them escaped. Lions sought shelter along with humans under the Great Garden's trees. Rhesus monkeys took up quarters in the branches. People lay on the ground with hands pressed over their eyes, and bears simply stepped over them. One touching story may be apocryphal. On the morning after the raids, one Dresdner was awakened by scraping and scratching at her front door. She opened to find a large, brown bear with a monkey on his shoulders holding out his scorched paws in a plea for help.[446]

Some of the worst tragedies occurred at the two main rail stations. Pupils at the Three Kings' School in the Neustadt had dedicated themselves to caring for the wounded shipped to Dresden from the fighting front and the refugees streaming into both stations from the east. In the night of February 13–14, those who had taken the night shift all lost their lives. At the main rail station on Wienerplatz, hundreds had crowded into its basement, thinking it to be a safe shelter. In the end, hundreds became trapped there, where they were asphyxiated.[447]

Kurt Vonnegut and his fellow POWs in the Slaughterhouse Five were not the only Americans to experience the raids. Living high above the city at Weisser Hirsch, the Noble family felt the impact of the bombs from the cellar of their house, to which they had retreated when the first sirens sounded. Charles Noble, a German who had emigrated to the U. S., had exchanged his own photo finishing business in Detroit for Benno Thorsch's camera factory in Dresden in 1937. Thorsch was escaping the increasing torment of Germany's Jewish population. When war broke out in 1939, the U. S. Embassy assured the Nobles that the U. S. would never enter the war, so that their property was safe. Their camera company employed hundreds of people and exported most of its products to the U. S.

When the U. S. entered the war in 1941, the Nobles were prevented from departing for the U. S. and found themselves under a barrage of restrictions. They could not leave Dresden; at any one time they could not carry more than 50 RM on the streets; certain streets and streetcar lines were prescribed for travel to their factory in Niedersedlitz; they could only shop at grocery stores selected for them by the regime. Nevertheless, they managed to continue to sell their wares to the U. S. by shipping them via the neutral countries of Sweden and Switzerland.

Both Charles and his son, John, had arrived home from their factory late on the evening of February 13. The Swiss border had closed, and they had to arrange to move a whole shipment from the factory to their home at Weisser Hirsch. The alarm sounded as they got ready to eat dinner, and they trooped off to the cellar. Once they emerged from the shelter, they found that the bombs' shock waves had broken all the windows in the house. At 1 a.m. they heard the second warning only very faintly, but they managed once again to retreat to the cellar. Once that attack ended, they found burning embers blowing in through the windows. Fearing fire, each family member was assigned a room in which to keep watch.

At 6 a.m. on February 14, Charles and John rode their bicycles toward the city in an attempt to reach their factory. At Körnerplatz in Loschwitz, just on the right bank of the Blue Wonder bridge, they could no longer ride the cycles, but they managed to walk to the factory. They found the building untouched except for a few broken windows, but they determined to secure their most important files: the account books and the camera designs. These they loaded onto a large tricycle and were preparing to leave when the Americans' daytime raid began. To save the files, they pushed the cycle into a culvert under the Bismarckstrasse until the raid was over. Once back at Weisser Hirsch, they found the house full of acquaintances and employees who had been bombed out of their homes. For the next several weeks, they cooked and kept warm with an old stove in the kitchen that used gas and coal.[448]

The bombing raids of Shrove Tuesday and Ash Wednesday spelled destruction and death for large parts of Dresden and thousands of its citizens. Jews were not spared; but some used the chaos created by the bombing to escape their Jewish plight and to survive until the end of the war.

On Tuesday, 13 February 1945, Victor Klemperer had spent the day notifying other Jews that they would be "evacuated" on Friday. Henny Wolf and her mother were among those who received such an order. With grim gallows humor, Henny's Gentile father had remarked that only a "massive attack on Dresden" could save the family. Barring such an event, they decided that the women would tear off their stars and go into hiding. The confusion that followed the bombing of Shrove Tuesday made hiding much easier.

During the first attack, their house was hit, and when they emerged from the cellar, Henny and her mother tore off their stars. The second attack caught them on the city streets, but they managed to take shelter in a nearby basement. They were spared suffocation, because Henny's father decided that the family needed air and shepherded them toward the Elbe meadows, where they lived out the third attack at noon on February 14 by lying flat on the ground. Eventually, they found an abandoned apartment in Blasewitz. Neither Henny nor her mother left this shelter until war's end on May 8. Henny claimed that the Gestapo was still looking for Jews in the days after the bombing. To keep the family alive, Henny's father went out almost daily to find food.

A special irony of their situation was the Stormtrooper and his family who moved in next door. This Nazi never reported the Wolfs, even though he had to know that he was living next to Jews. On the evening of May 7, just before the Soviets occupied the city, the Stormtrooper got drunk and burned his uniform. In the de-Nazification process that followed, Henny's father refused to report the man, because, he said, he didn't want to deprive the neighbor's two children of their father.

On the evening of February 13, Klemperer and his wife rode out the first attack in the cellar of their residence in the Jew house on the old synagogue's site. After the second attack in the early morning of Ash Wednesday, he and his wife became separated for a while, but they both finally ended up by the bastion of the Brühl Terrace where a medic treated their irritated eyes. After that, they found refuge in the cellar of the Albertinum. As the headquarters of air defense, it was basically untouched by the bombing. Electric light from a separate generator continued to burn, and late in the night, the authorities distributed sandwiches. By this time, Victor had removed his yellow star and could no longer be identified by strangers as Jewish. On the morning of February 15, trucks transported the survivors in the Albertinum to the intact airfield at Klotzsche.

When they later learned that they would be evacuated from Klotzsche and settled in nearby towns, they decided to move to the village of Piskowitz, northeast of Dresden, where they received a warm welcome from their former cleaning lady. After a short stay there, they set out for southern Germany and experienced the end of the war in Bavaria. Finally, at the end of May, they decided it was safe to return to Dresden. On May 26, they set out on foot from Munich and reached Dresden, after traveling almost 300 miles, on June 10.[449]

Aftermath

In their absence, Dresden continued to suffer the vicissitudes of war. On March 2, the city was twice bombed again. These attacks stretched out over eight and one-half miles along the Elbe and included the southern suburbs as well as the suburban palace of Pillnitz. On April 17, another raid targeted the city's rail facilities with the primary goal of severing the link between Berlin and Prague. Because the fighting front was not very far away, there was at least a defensive flak that attempted to protect the city.[450]

The question arises whether the bombings of Dresden, and most particularly the controversial raids of February 13–15, hampered the German war effort and assisted the Allies toward their ultimate victory. To the extent that the bombings had targeted rail traffic in all directions, the raids made little difference. Within days, a single track was opened for freight traffic, and within two weeks two tracks were available. Even though the rail system lacked telephone service, and many workers were missing, shipments occurred on a regular basis. Only after the "precision" bombing of April 17 was Dresden eliminated as an important hub of the German rail system. The Wehrmacht quickly recovered from the loss of its communications center in the Taschenberg Palace by establishing a new facility at the edge of the city at a fruit pressing plant. The central post office followed suit. Streets necessary for military vehicles were quickly cleared of rubble, and work on building the city's defenses against the approaching Soviets went forward. In mid-March, anti-tank barriers appeared on the city's bridges.

More serious was the effect on industrial war production. Forty-one firms important for military production were affected by the February raids, and at least half of them were heavily damaged. Some of these reported that they could not resume work, while others indicated they could start production again within a few weeks. The firm most seriously affected by the bombing was Zeiss-Ikon, producer of firing mechanisms and sighting devices for a range of weapons. Prominent Dresden employers, including Zeiss-Ikon, reported that substantial parts of their work forces, in some cases more than three-quarters, simply did not show up. Either they were dead, wounded or clearing away rubble in their neighborhoods. The English historian, Frederick Taylor, estimates that industrial damage would have been much greater if the British had targeted the suburbs where manufacturing plants were located. Instead, the residential city was hit the hardest. It was the loss of life that resulted from that decision that Dresdners have not been able to forget.[451]

The evidence of the human toll was all around. Calls for help brought rescue crews from neighboring towns before noon on Ash Wednesday. Soldiers from the barracks in the Neustadt began work on digging out cellars in the afternoon. Sometimes they found people who were trapped but still alive; more frequently they found those who had suffocated to death. Prisoners of war, like Kurt Vonnegut and his fellow Americans, were also sent to clear the cellars. The dead were very visible at the main rail station where refugees awaiting departing trains sought shelter in the basement. Hundreds died of asphyxiation. Götz Bergander, then eighteen years old, remembers walking through the city with his younger brother on February 16 and seeing hundreds of the piled-up casualties. They also encountered women's and children's shoes that had stuck in the melting asphalt; a person could only imagine what had happened to their owners. Within ten days, 10,000 bodies had been recovered, registered and, when possible, identified before their burial in the Cemetery on the Heath (Heidefriedhof) north of town.

Even so, authorities feared the spread of disease from the presence of those still not collected and buried. They thus gathered the dead of the inner city on the Altmarkt and burned them. The burning continued for almost two weeks, each fire consuming 500 bodies. Altogether 6,865 corpses were reduced to ash in the middle of the city. Even though the square was sealed off to the public, Dresdners still saw the piles of bodies, and photos continue to remind them of the February raids.[452]

Ever since the end of World War II, Dresdners have set aside February 13 as a day of remembrance. The ceremonies associated with the memory are dedicated to the prevention of war and a striving for peace, a sense of the solidarity with all mankind. At the same time, the shock of the bombings led to a long discussion about how many actually died in the February raids.

Early estimates by German experts familiar with the bombing of other German cities placed the loss of life at about 25,000. Yet it suited Nazi propagandists to assert that 200,000 had died, among them many refugees fleeing the advancing Soviet troops. This number, or an even larger one, corresponded with the memories of many surviving Dresdners.

Nevertheless, even at the height of the Cold War when an inflated figure would have highlighted the inhumane capitalists of Britain and the United States, two administrators of Communist Dresden, in their accounts of the city's history, scaled the casualties back to 35,000. Documents discovered in West German archives in the mid-1960s placed the figure at 25,000. Many Dresdners continued to cling to the higher numbers.

In an effort to finally put the matter to rest, the Dresden city council in 2004 created an Historical Commission to examine all the evidence relating to the numbers of people who died in the February raids. This commission gathered information for several years and issued a final report in 2010. It concluded that the maximum number of dead did not exceed 25,000. Historians are obligated to accept this judgement. Laymen are not.

Many Dresdners—other Germans and foreigners—simply cannot accept it. The historian/journalist Götz Bergander, himself a survivor, argues that the city's ordinary residents, who never expected to be bombed, overnight lost not only family and friends but their most meaningful urban environment. Human memories almost always include the places where the memory was formed. Losing the city's landmarks and neighborhoods meant that Dresdners suffered a mental amputation, perhaps even more traumatic than losing an arm or a leg.[453]

The bombing of Dresden has become part of the larger discussion about the effectiveness of bombing civilian populations. Certainly, the carpet bombing that the British resorted to did not hinder the war effort in the short term, nor did it lead to a recognized dampening of civilian morale. On the other hand, the damages that bombing inflicted meant that German resources had to be deflected away from the fighting fronts toward repairs and relocations of streets, public utilities, hospitals, schools, homes. Technical innovation became impossible. Indeed, the laboratories of Zeiss-Ikon were wiped out in the February raids. Bombing eventually also exhausted the civilian population, gradually reducing its effectiveness as laborers and citizens.

For Bergander, the bombings brought home to the civilian population, including Dresdners, that World War II was definitely lost. In contrast to Germans after World War I, few, if any, would entertain the idea of a home front "stabbing" the fighting front in the back. The bombings helped to shorten the war. He quotes the familiar adage uttered by many Germans: "Better an end with horror, than a horror without end." How would Dresdners cope with war's horrible end?[454]

XIII. The Socialist City

War's End

On April 17, the last raid on Dresden occurred when the Americans bombed the railway's freight yards and weakened the eastern front. By this time, only a narrow German corridor from Berlin to Prague existed between the Allied armies approaching from both east and west. The sound of artillery, now only thirty miles away, accompanied the Dresdners night and day. Both the German army and the city's Nazi administrators were determined to hold the city, and Soviet officers prepared for a hard fight.

The city became a fortress. On April 21, every man, woman and youth over fourteen was ordered to appear daily, including Sunday, at designated places with pickaxes or hoes, shovels or spades. Anti-tank trenches ringed the city. On April 26, the day after American and Red Armies met at the Elbe, just north of Dresden, S.S. Pioneers blew up the autobahn bridges west of Dresden. Final desperate measures included the drafting of untrained sixteen- and seventeen-year-olds as well as older men to fight seasoned Soviet soldiers.

In the end, reason prevailed. On May 6, the day after the fall of Berlin, commander Baron von Gilsa received the order to retreat toward the Ore Mountains. As the army retreated, S.S. units blew up the remaining Elbe bridges, all except the Blue Wonder. To save this final link between the northern and southern parts of the city, a group of Dresdners cut the demolition wires during the night of May 5–6. Soviet troops marched over the bridge on their way to the city's center on May 8. As war ended, Dresdners were in danger of being plundered by their neighbors, being shot by fanatical Nazis for helping Jews, and/or for undermining the war effort.[455]

With the arrival of the Soviets, danger continued from another direction. The rapes of German women by Soviet soldiers are common knowledge. Groups of soldiers gang-raped women while their fellows-in-arms stood watch. Neighborhoods attempted to protect themselves by hiding women in secluded places and by banging pots together when they saw Soviet troops approaching. For Dresden, no statistics exist for the numbers of women raped or for those who developed venereal disease as a result.[456]

Looting continued, both by Soviet soldiers, who were poorly fed, and by the German population. The food supply was critical. Bombing had destroyed the municipal granaries, and the Red Army eliminated the system of tapping neighborhood warehouses and army reserves. Not until mid-May did the Soviet army distribute thousands of tons of potatoes, meat and other foodstuffs. It also continued food rationing, establishing a base line for all adults. Workers doing hard labor and those tending the sick and wounded received more than those who worked less strenuous jobs or were idle altogether.[457]

The harvest of 1945 was understandably poor, and in September 1945, the Soviets expropriated large estates all over their zone of occupation, causing a further decrease in agricultural production and distribution. In addition, the victorious Allies had ceded the eastern provinces of Prussia to Poland. This meant that grain, previously imported into Saxony from large estates in the former German northeast, was no longer available in pre-war or wartime amounts. Problems with the food supply continued for several years.

The summer and winter of 1945 represented the city's nadir. In comparison to its pre-war size, the population—due to flights of both Jews and Gentiles, to war deaths, to wartime evacuations—had almost halved. The death rate had more than doubled; infant mortality was high. Though the Soviets restored both electricity and water systems in mid-May, many Dresdners continued to draw water from public wells. There was no garbage or trash pick-up; the sewer system did not function. The city stank. Rats and flies spread disease. Come winter, typhus and tuberculosis plagued the city. Children developed rickets and suffered from recurring colds. The elderly were prone to frequent illness. Hands and feet froze. Because so many had to share beds, the incidence of gonorrhea increased. Due to malnutrition, mothers had difficulty nursing their babies. In order to survive, many women resorted to prostitution. Young people simply avoided getting married.[458]

Soviet Normalcy

Although the victorious Allies had made some provision for managing Germany at the Yalta Conference before the end of the war, some details were only decided at the Potsdam Conference during the summer following defeat. All agreed that the Allies would divide Germany into zones of occupation, but in principle they would treat it as a single unit. Germany's capital was also divided into four sectors of occupation, but since the city was located within the larger Soviet zone, the French, the British and the Americans there depended on Soviet good will for access to their occupations of Berlin. Each occupier was to be responsible for administering its zone, but they agreed on common policies of de-militarization, de-Nazification and democratization. Each occupier was also entitled to take war reparations from Germany in the form of industrial equipment and forced labor. Dresden found itself in the Soviet occupation zone, and the city's important factories were dismantled almost immediately.

Dresdners needed desperately to re-establish everyday life on as normal a basis as possible. They were used to going to work, and the city's economy had functioned up to the end of the war as regularly as the bombings allowed. Once the occupation began, experience was mixed. The Soviets dismantled important factories at Koch and Sterzel, at the Saxon Works, at Radio Mende, at the Brückner Turbine Factory. They stripped these businesses to the bone and then blocked further production in order to make sure they had taken everything of value.

Because the Red Army had sent the municipal generators off to the Soviet Union, manufacturing in other plants was hindered by a shortage of electricity. Production quotas set both for capital and consumer goods—cameras, shoes, electrical insulation, protheses, surveying instruments, piston rings, frying pans, etc.—could often not be met because of the dismantling. Because the Soviets seized buses, cars, trucks, locomotives and railroad tracks in the two weeks following the capitulation, distribution of food and other necessities of life became difficult. It's been estimated that in the ten months following the end of the war, the Soviets took out of Dresden industrial material worth 100 million marks. Adding to the economic disorder was the closing of banks and the freezing of accounts at the end of May. Both the municipality and private businesses then found it difficult to pay their employees and others entitled to funds.

Despite the disruptions, business rebounded. It was surprising that the official unemployment rate at the end of 1945 was only 7.4%. These were mostly women pushed out of jobs by men returning from the war. Able males found jobs in construction, in sectors that supplied the occupiers, in the clothing and foodstuff industries, and in smaller manufacturing firms less affected by the dismantling. Already before the end of 1945, the large firm of Zeiss-Ikon returned to the civilian production of its consumer-oriented thirty-five-millimeter camera, developed just before the outbreak of war.[459]

The overall responsibility for life in Dresden rested with the Red Army. If the commanding officers opposed a measure, it didn't happen. They, however, preferred to work through German administrators. Officially, a new mayor, Rudolph Friedrichs, a left-wing Social Democrat and former civil servant, began exercising power on 12 May 1945. In July, he became minister-president of the newly formed Saxon state government, and former judge Johannes Müller took over as his successor, presiding over a city council installed just a few days after Soviet occupation began. The Soviets insisted on the formation of new political parties, with a view to advertising their democratic credentials. In reality, the real drivers of political life were those Communists returning from their wartime exile in the Soviet Union.

In this initial period, the most important of these men in Dresden was Hermann Matern, a former trade-union functionary. After escaping imprisonment by the National Socialists in 1933, he made his way to Moscow where he spent the war. Matern saw to it that a Saxon Communist Party was officially instituted according to the strong, central leadership desired by Moscow. At the end of June, the Social Democrats, many of whom desired to make common cause with the Communists, were forced to establish their own party. Middle-class parties soon followed suit; the Liberal Democrats officially registered as a party on August 15 and the Christian Democrats a week later.

The representatives of these parties soon discovered there was to be no independent, possibly dissenting, action. They were pressured into cooperating with one another in a governing bloc on a city council that consisted of six Communists, two Social Democrats and two from the other two parties. The middle-class Christian and Liberal Democrats were not treated as equal partners in the bloc, and their members were not appointed to posts in the municipal administration.

Ultimately, it was the Communist Walter Weidauer who became the most important person on the city council and in the governance of Dresden. He had joined the German Communist Party as a young man, had actively resisted the National Socialists, and had spent the last four years of the war in prison. When

Judge Müller succeeded Friedrichs, Weidauer became his deputy, and he took charge of all personnel matters for the city. By the end of summer 1945, he had insured that Communists dominated the leadership positions within the city's civil service, and in 1946 he became Dresden's mayor.[460]

As it took control of Dresden, the Red Army arrested National Socialist leaders and members of the army. Even those old men and boys who had been conscripted to defend Dresden in the final hours of the war, many against their will, could be imprisoned. As the political new broom established a Communist monopoly at the highest municipal level, de-Nazification and de-militarization were imperative. National Socialists at the neighborhood level were set to work clearing rubble, repairing bridges, railway tracks and other infrastructure.

In the neighborhoods, anti-Fascist committees reconstituted the old resident registration files and distributed a questionnaire to flush out former National Socialist Party members. They then set up a file that was used to carry out arrests among the general population. Families were not told what their relatives were charged with and where they were being held. It was difficult to know whether the offense was membership in the National Socialist Party, a recent act that disturbed the Communists, or normal criminal behavior. As had happened under the Hitler regime, some people settled personal grudges by falsely accusing their neighbors or co-workers of some irregularity. Communist Party members also used the arrests to get rid of people they disliked.

Cleansing city administration of National Socialism became a high priority. By late summer, Saxon state government had determined that all National Socialists could be dismissed from public service. By the end of 1945, over 4000 of Dresden's municipal employees had lost their jobs. Most of the people who replaced them were either Communists, Social Democrats or politically unaffiliated. More draconian were the measures taken to deprive National Socialists of their property. Almost immediately, Soviet occupiers had confiscated the property of the National Socialist Party and its related organizations. Also seized was the private property of leading National Socialists.

In the course of the summer, the city government began to investigate business owners and managers and, if necessary, to replace them with anti-Fascists. The appropriate office could also revoke business licenses and appoint trustees of confiscated properties. In September 1945, a new Chamber of Commerce and Industry was established consisting of employers, trade unionists and city officials, a composition that clearly signaled its existence as a municipal body, not an autonomous organization. The Communist Party got busy reorganizing works councils, co-management committees dating back to the Weimar Republic, that could be used to pressure owners and managers to adopt Communist practices.

As these official measures occurred, National Socialists were pressured by Communists to evacuate their apartments, and these were promptly distributed to fellow Communists. Thomas Widera claims that the Communist Party used the shadows cast by the official umbrella of occupation to transfer all kinds of wealth—businesses, money, furnishings—both to the party and to its individual members. Though Dresdners at first had wished to "punish" National Socialists for bringing about the destruction of the city and causing their post-war hardships, they soon experienced a change of heart as they watched individuals unfairly treated by the Soviet occupation and its German allies.[461]

As political life resumed, police, whose ranks were being rapidly filled with Communists, created a special unit to deal with political crimes and misdemeanors. This division started surveillance of rallies held by various organizations throughout the city. It also sent agents to report on theater performances, movies, cabaret acts, sports events and other forms of entertainment. By sharing this information with the Soviet army, the police were able to manipulate the occupation authorities to benefit German Communists. Often, the police exceeded the expectations of the Soviet occupiers. For instance, a Soviet officer once stopped, as fascistic, the public denunciation of a female black marketer in foodstuffs. The German district leader told the officer that black marketeering sabotaged the city's reconstruction, and the woman was released to the police as a criminal.

In the case of the many unemployed young Dresdners, the Soviets wanted them to help clear rubble and rebuild the city. Youth did not want to do this work for the poor pay offered. So the police solved this problem by arresting youth and other idlers and placing them in work camps. Living beside the youth were female prostitutes rounded up because Soviet officers considered them guilty of increasing venereal disease among the occupying troops. Germans in charge of the work camps tried to prevent soldiers from invading the camps in search of women and avoided sending women to work for the Soviets as much as possible. Outside the camps, women continued to be at risk of sexual assault from the occupying forces.

By late summer 1945, the persistent insecurity, the shortage of food, the spike in infant mortality, the dismantling and unfair treatment of minor National Socialists all caused Dresdners to be critical of the Soviet occupation and the activities of the Communist Party. When Mayor Müller reflected this disenchantment by stopping the confiscations of property belonging to former National Socialists and charging the Soviets with neglecting the health and welfare of the city, the Saxon state government removed him as mayor in October 1945. When Karl Albrecht, the Social Democratic deputy mayor in charge of the food supply, also publicly criticized Soviet policies in Dresden, the Saxon state government arrested him and arranged for a successor.[462]

Both the Soviet authorities and their German Communist allies were alarmed at the expressions of discontent and of the growing popularity of the Social Democrats. Due to their professional expertise, Social Democrats increasingly filled vacancies in the city's bureaucracy. Social Democrats were particularly successful in recruiting young people as party members. Together with the other non-Communist parties, they had persuaded the Soviets to give their members positions on various official commissions in numbers that equaled those of the Communists. On factory floors, Social Democrats dominated the trade unions. Even when the Soviet Commandant decreed the dissolution of the old unions and the creation of new ones, Social Democrats still captured two-thirds of the new leadership positions. Whereas they had warmly welcomed the Communist Party immediately after the war, by fall 1945, Social Democrats were no longer eager to make common cause.[463]

The Socialist Unity Party and the Division of Germany

At party rallies and trade-union conferences, Social Democratic rank and file were pressured to endorse a merger. Those who opposed this action were prevented from speaking. Press reports, released by the Communist Party, alleged a groundswell of agitation favoring unity. When the Social Democratic newspaper, the *People's Voice (Volksstimme)*, urged a test vote on the issue, the Soviets confiscated that day's issue.

Dresden's Social Democrats refused to cooperate with the rush to merge with the Communists. And they continued to recruit members to their own party. Even when the Dresden leadership, pressured by Soviet officers, finally consented to unity, the rank and file at first refused to vote for union at the local party conference. Soviet officers, present in uniform and in civilian dress, did not daunt them. One of Dresden's historians claims that only after a "tumultuous session" did the vote for unity at the local level finally occur. During the third week in April, Dresden's delegates in Berlin helped to create the Socialist Unity Party (SED—*Sozialistische Einheitspartei Deutschlands*) in the Soviet occupation zone.[464]

Those who feared increasing repression did not need to look far to find it. During the campaigns preceding municipal and state legislative elections in September and October 1946, the SED tried to prevent the emergence of any real opposition. The Soviet occupiers helped the new party by forbidding posters, flyers, and publications of the non-Communist parties. In some cases, they forbade assemblies outright.

When rallies were allowed, police observers attended. At a Liberal Democratic rally presided over by youth leader Wolfgang Mischnick, a Soviet officer abruptly closed the meeting when Mischnick criticized the Communists. His fellow Liberals were so afraid that he would be arrested that they accompanied him home. On another occasion, they told him to disappear from a rally through a window, because there was a rumor that Soviet authorities were on the way to detain him.

During the municipal election campaign, Mischnick was so annoyed by the aggressive tactics of the Communists that he circulated a parody: "When early morn' the sun ascends/And evening when it sets/And when it shines in bright brocade/That's what the SED has made." Later, during the campaign for the Saxon legislature, the Communists mounted an illuminated advertisement on the prominent, high-rise building at the transportation hub of Albertplatz: "Down with Liberalism". This sign was sensational because electricity was in very short supply. But as Mischnick observed, the Communists permitted themselves to do anything.

Despite vigorous campaigning, the Communist SED failed to gain a majority of seats on the city council. Dresden women had cast 54% of their vote for the bourgeois parties. Nevertheless, when it came time to elect a mayor at the beginning of October, the Soviets withdrew their support from the former

Socialist Gustav Leissner, because he had questioned their policies. Instead they engineered a bloc vote of all parties for the Communist Walter Weidauer. Joining him in the urban cabinet were seven SED members out of a total of fourteen. For the next forty-three years, the Communist SED dominated Dresden's city government.[465]

Once the Communists had consolidated their power in the municipal assembly, they strove to rid themselves of irritants in everyday life. At the end of 1946, communization measures, in the guise of de-Nazification, intensified. The Soviets decreed an investigation of all workers in government service and in several factories, intending to remove from political and economic life all those who potentially and actually opposed the new regime. Owners lost their businesses; managers lost their positions; workers became unemployed. At the same time, the secret police forces were strengthened. Arrests at the beginning of 1947 increased 500%. Social Democrats, now ostensibly united with Communists in the SED, were targeted as well as members of the Christian and Liberal Democrats.

Evidence of growing opposition to the Communist regime grew. Several Dresden groups maintained contacts with the "Eastern Offices" of West German political parties. Joachim Petzold was just a schoolboy when he frequented a bar on Alaunplatz where a chess club gathered regularly. There he heard "passionate" expressions of dissatisfaction. Some courageous souls even called for the re-establishment of the Social Democratic Party. Youthful movie goers greeted the propaganda films that preceded the features with foot stomping and catcalls. Police then started to patrol the cinemas. Because Mischnick opposed the foundation of the Communist Free German Youth, the Soviets banned him from writing or speaking publicly. The ban meant that he lost his job with the Liberal Democratic Party. Finally, after an interrogation by the Soviet secret police and the fear of an eventual arrest, Mischnick hopped a train to East Berlin and, easily possible in those days, crossed the border to the West.[466]

In 1948, as currency reform in the West, among other developments, moved it further away from the East, Soviet authorities decided to hold a referendum in their occupation zone concerning German unity. The vote occurred on the eve of the Soviets' blockading the access of Western allies and their supplies into Berlin and the westerners' responding airlift. The strangeness of this referendum was that no polling places existed. Instead, people were asked to sign lists in businesses, in the streets, in other public places, at the entrances of their apartment buildings. There was thus no secret ballot, and a lot of pressure could be applied to signers of the list. Shortly thereafter, the Soviet occupiers postponed municipal elections.

Instead, in 1949 they prepared for a People's Congress elected on the basis of unity lists, ballots that lumped all parties together in a single bloc. Thus there was no opposition. Although a majority of Dresdners voted for the lists, their vote lay below the East German average. The city harbored only tepid support for the German Democratic Republic (GDR) established by the Congress. Once this new state existed, the party of unified Socialists and Communists— the SED—assumed the functions of the Soviet Military Administration. Increasingly, power was centralized in Berlin, and local autonomy diminished. In 1950, the Saxon Justice Ministry disappeared, and its functions devolved to the Saxon Minister-President. In July 1952, the central SED government in Berlin abolished the former federal states in East Germany. Saxon government ceased to exist. In its place, three administrative districts were created, each containing about two million people who were easier to control than the united Saxon population. Dresden and its environs comprised one of the three districts. Despite the dissolution of Saxon government, other Saxon institutions continued to exist, such as the Institute for Historic Preservation *(Institut für Denkmalpflege)* and the Saxon State Library *(Sächsische Landesbibliothek).*[467]

The Socialist Economy

When the Saxon state dissolved and Dresden's active role as state capital ended, the restructuring of its economy to match Communist and Soviet principles progressed substantially. Regardless of ownership, the Soviet occupiers had taken control of the larger factories. In June 1945, Mayor Friedrichs had confiscated all properties within the German military's industrial park north of the Neustadt. As expropriations of private properties occurred, several prominent firms moved their operations westward. Odol, maker of mouthwash, moved to Düsseldorf. One of the world's best manufacturers of radios, Mende, moved to Bremen and became Nordmende. Later Max Baldeweg took his small camera firm to Bunde in Westphalia. They left behind the functional shells of their former firms.

By the time the Socialist Unity Party emerged, the Soviets and their German Communist allies had decided to set the scene for further seizures of large private properties. The device selected was a People's Referendum, scheduled for June 1946. Throughout the months of May and June, police patrolled the streets of Dresden to prevent any "agitation" against the referendum. Apartment house communities and youth and children's groups were sucked into supporting the "yes" campaign. The Soviets now promised an end to the dismantling of industry. They flooded the stores with all sorts of provisions previously in short supply. On the eve of the vote, the Communists held torchlight parades in some city neighborhoods to encourage a "yes" vote. On the day of the vote, June 30, they mobilized a host of volunteers to take people to the polls, and choruses gathered at apartment buildings chanting in favor of a 'yes' vote.

Ultimately, 78 per cent of Saxons voted for the confiscations. Sixty-one large Dresden firms became Soviet-owned corporations, including Zeiss-Ikon (cameras), Seidel and Naumann (sewing machines and typewriters) and Universelle (cigarette machines). In the greater Dresden area, 176 companies were eventually converted into cooperatives, called People's Own Enterprises (*Volkseigene Betriebe* or VEBs). Many of those Dresdners who voted "yes" did so because they feared that a "no" vote would lead to further repression.[468]

In 1948, the pace of transforming private firms into VEBs picked up. Some firms that had been destroyed or dismantled earlier were re-established. They all became the basis for Dresden's economy during the next forty years. The camera industry remained strong, with some firms retaining private ownership into the 1950s.

For Dresdners, it was most important that the city's economy continued to provide jobs and sustenance for their families. As the city maintained its strength in the electrical, machine-building, camera and condiments industries, many continued to be employed in the plants where they had always worked. In Hellerau, the German Workshops converted to civilian production and found a new niche in the manufacture of inexpensive furniture for the hundreds of new dwellings. In other sectors, production returned to the pre-war level by 1950, and 100,000 found employment in the construction industry. Added to these continuing strengths was the graphics industry; the Saxon News (*Sächsische Zeitung*) became one of the largest news organizations in East Germany. As East Germany embarked on an independent existence, Dresden revived.[469]

The Crisis of the 1950s

In comparison to other areas of East Germany, the city experienced a relatively light flight of population to the west. Given how essential much of its industry was to the GDR's economy, workers were relatively well-paid and provided for. Nevertheless, tensions accumulating throughout East Germany affected Dresden. The first was the transition to a centrally planned economy. The first Five-Year Plan for the GDR's economy began in 1951 and led to chronic disruptions in the manufacturing process. Workers also saw their formerly independent organizations converted into instruments of the SED that brooked little dissent. Their right to strike existed mostly in theory. Those with close ties to the Evangelical Church suffered from mounting intimidation of its clergy. Its youth group, Young Parish (*Junge Gemeinde*), endured increasing harassment before being made illegal, a process hauntingly portrayed in Uwe Johnson's novella, *Ingrid Babendeerde*.

In the middle of 1952, the SED's leadership, puffed up with the ideological certainty that came with the new state, made a series of decisions that resulted in heightening dissatisfaction. First, it announced the creation of a Barracked People's Police that was a prelude to the formation of a standing army. To pay for this militarization, it increased its exports to the Soviet Union, which already received a large portion of the GDR's production. Further funds were found by cutting social security and welfare payments and introducing higher property and income taxes.

At a party conference in July 1952, party leaders decided it was time to construct a socialist Germany along Soviet lines. That meant a rapid development of heavy industry, a decline in the manufacture of consumer goods, the confiscation of small businesses, and the pursuit of agricultural collectivization. The result was the wholesale abandonment of many farms, giving rise to shortages of meat, fat, fruits and vegetables, and finally price increases at the beginning of 1953.[470]

As the standard of living declined, unrest grew. Wildcat strikes became more frequent, and protest rallies occurred in many factories. When the death of Stalin in March 1953 seemed to open a window to political relaxation, the East German leaders asked the Soviets for help. The Soviets were willing to waive the Germans' export and reparations obligations, but that was simply not enough. Rather than mitigate the situation through a slower pace of socialist construction, the SED stubbornly pressed forward.

In late May 1953, it raised production quotas by ten per cent and sent the signal that worker welfare was not a high priority. The increase in the quotas constituted a ten per cent decrease in wages at a time of inflated prices and additional taxation. By this time, the new Soviet leadership had become alarmed by the rising tensions in East Germany. At the beginning of June, it summoned the SED leadership to Moscow and bluntly demanded that it postpone the development of a Soviet-style economy.

As a result, a New Course was announced on 9 June 1953. The SED publicly declared that its previous policy had been mistaken. Agricultural collectivization ceased; price and tax increases were rolled back; confiscated small businesses returned to private owners; harassment of the churches ended. This abrupt about-face took the lower echelons of SED leaders by surprise. People in the street were "incredulous".[471]

Rightly so, it seemed. Left untouched by the New Course were the elevated production quotas with their accompanying wage decreases. That was no oversight. On June 16, the trade-union paper, the *Tribune*, declared that the new quotas were "correct" and irreversible. Incensed construction workers on a model project on Berlin's Stalinallee laid down their tools and marched first to trade-union headquarters and then to the seat of the Council of Ministers where they chanted their demands to meet with the East German leadership. In the early afternoon, the minister for heavy industry emerged from the government building to announce the rollback of production quotas. This announcement was so poorly worded that trucks broadcasting the news throughout the city were not believed. Instead the strikers of June 16 called for a general strike the next day.

On this same June 16, a group of thirty Dresdners from the Saxon Works had traveled to Berlin to consult with the workers on the Stalinallee and to learn from them new methods of construction. Instead, they learned that the construction workers' strike had not resulted in any arrests. As they appeared for the early shift of the Saxon Works on June 17, they shared their knowledge with their comrades.[472]

The Saxon Works were now Soviet-owned and still one of the largest firms in the city, employing almost 5500 people making electrical appliances. A tense atmosphere existed within the factory. The Soviet and the German managements did not get along with one another, and the German management did not agree with the SED party representatives assigned to the plant. Workers on the factory floor frequently found themselves caught in the cross-currents generated by the leadership.

The Saxon Works' employees enjoyed higher than average wages, but they had no interest in the Stakhanovite competition promoted by the SED, and did not enjoy the bonuses sometimes awarded workers in other firms. It was also irritating that hours were cut when deliveries of needed materials did not arrive at the beginning of the month, only to be compensated by overtime when the materials showed up at the end of the month. The threatened increase in production quotas simply added to the accumulating grievances. When the SED representative in the factory responded over the firm's loudspeaker to signs of unrest on June 17 by defending the projected quotas, the workers' rage exploded.

After the mid-morning break, the production crews did not go back to work. Instead they gathered in the factory's courtyard. Already, some people were expressing anger not only at the increased work norms but also at the East German government. Between 10 and 11 a.m., several hundred workers marched out the factory gates singing Germany's traditional national hymn and the Internationale, the Communist anthem. One group of workers simply withdrew from the fray and went home. A second group took the train south to Heidenau to urge workers there to go on strike too. Another group started to march toward the inner city, picking up workers from factories along the way.

Their chants and their hand-made signs revealed that the demonstration was much more than discontent with the increased production quotas. "Down with the [Soviet Occupation] zone", shouted some groups. Others demanded "…free elections". One of the more colorful chants was a rhyme: "Goatee, paunch, and eyeglasses/Were not chosen by the masses." The goatee was Walter Ulbricht's, first secretary of the SED and primary power in East Germany. President Wilhelm Pieck sported the paunch. The eyeglasses belonged to Otto Grotewohl, prime minister, former Social Democrat and now considered to be a puppet of the SED. Signs made clear that the workers wanted these three top government leaders to resign. Other placards demanding German unity made clear that many workers did not accept the division of Germany by the victorious powers.[473]

Some Saxon Works' laborers stayed behind and headed for the neighboring cooperative for Equipment of Mining and Heavy Industry (*Sächsischer Brücken und Stahlhochbau*), locally known as ABUS, which produced reparations for the Soviet Union. After the visitors had broken down the factory gate and attacked several of the plant's officials, a group of workers from both firms marched off toward the city. Other ABUS workers followed the suggestion of the trade-union leadership and gathered in the assembly line's workshop to discuss whether or not to join the protest. One of the firm's bookkeepers, Wilhelm Grothaus, took charge of the gathering and persuaded it to approve demands that included a new government chosen by free and secret elections and an improvement in the GDR's standard of living. The ABUS workers then formed a committee, with Grothaus as chair, that eventually compiled a resolution for presentation to the government.

Grothaus hailed originally from Westphalia where he was born into a working-class family. As a youth, he held a series of white-collar jobs and joined the Social Democratic Party after World War I. Between 1926 and 1934, he worked for organizations that encouraged affordable housing for the working class. In 1934, the National Socialist authorities expelled him and his wife from Berlin, and they migrated to Dresden where he found work as a bookkeeper. During World War II, he became active in a resistance group, was betrayed to the Gestapo by a fellow resistant and ended up in the prison for political criminals on Dresden's Münchner Platz. The bombs of February 13–14 enabled him to flee the prison and escape trial and execution.

After the war, he joined the SED and occupied a series of posts in the Saxon state administration until the flight to the west of Agriculture Minister Reinhard Uhle, for whom Grothaus was working at the time. Tarred with the brush of his boss's disloyalty, he was banned from serving in any public post for the ensuing two years. He then turned to ABUS for whom he had briefly worked before World War II, when it was still a private firm, and afterward. By 1953, he had earned a reputation within the firm for defending workers' welfare. He also possessed the knowledge, the skills and the experience necessary for leading—and controlling—a mass movement. Much later, in an interview with West German radio, he confessed that he knew all along that an uprising could never succeed, but he wanted to demonstrate to the world how a workers' state treated its people.[474]

Meanwhile the Saxon Works' management had invited a member of the government to speak to the workers, and Otto Buchwitz appeared there at 2 p.m. Buchwitz was a former trade-union functionary and Social Democrat. During the Weimar Republic, he had represented Lower Silesia in both the

Prussian state legislature and in the Reichstag. As a member of the armed militias opposed to the National Socialists, he escaped to Denmark in 1933. When the Germans occupied that country in 1940, he was arrested and spent the rest of the war in prison. After the war, he helped to re-establish the Social Democratic Party in the Soviet occupation zone but ardently supported the merger of Socialists and Communists in 1946. Thereafter he became one of the new party's top leaders and, in 1953, was a member of the national People's Congress.

Management clearly counted on Buchwitz's background to conciliate the strikers. It was mistaken. When the workers from the Saxon Works, from ABUS and other neighboring firms gathered to listen to Buchwitz's speech, they were not conciliatory. Although they listened quietly at first, they soon began to hoot at Buchwitz's claims that their strike strengthened the positions of West German Chancellor Adenauer and the Americans. When he encouraged them to go back to work until their demands were presented to the East German government, he was greeted with howls of disagreement.

Grothaus then took the floor, reported on the work of the ABUS committee and urged the Saxon Works' laborers to form their own committee with similar demands. Buchwitz met with this committee and agreed to present its wishes to the government in Berlin, but he refused to cast his lot with the strikers. By this time, the assembled workers decided to march toward the city center, even though Buchwitz informed them that the government had already declared a state of emergency. Demonstrators, he warned, risked confrontation with the police and the "occupation forces". The strikers simply laughed at him.[475]

Meanwhile, authorities in central Dresden were coping with the arriving strikers. Warned by Berlin authorities during the night of June 16–17, local Soviet forces and German police had prepared for trouble. Soviet infantry units in the Dresden garrison had deployed on city streets and squares by mid-morning. Tanks were stationed on the main thoroughfares. Security details surrounded the post office, the telegraph office, the railroad stations, the state bank, police headquarters, and the SED party headquarters. Armed motorcycle units drifted through the city.

When the marchers reached the Stübelallee next to the Great Garden in the early afternoon, they simply ignored the police officers informing them of the state of emergency and walked on toward the city center. By 3 p.m. approximately 4000 demonstrators had reached the Theaterplatz and the neighboring Postplatz. Nevertheless, Soviet troops succeeded in clearing the Theaterplatz and, by firing shots in the air, prevented the storming of the telegraph office at the Postplatz.

Back at the Saxon Works, Soviet troops broke up a second wave of marchers, and streetcars stopped traveling to the city center, thereby deterring all but the most determined. In contrast to other cities, Dresden was calm. No buildings or prisons were stormed. The security measures instituted early in the day by the police and Soviet troops contributed to the lack of violence. Soviet troops, though armed, were ordered not to fire on the strikers unless they were fired on first. Some Soviet troops even conversed genially with the demonstrators as they arrived in the city center and just simply let them march on. In a few cases, workers' protests against arrests of their comrades were sufficient to gain their release on the spot. When the German police proposed using fire hoses against the strikers, local Soviet commanders dissuaded them.

Moreover, the ABUS committee fully expected the night and the next morning's shifts to show up for work. Grothaus, after the meeting with Buchwitz at the Saxon Works, returned to the ABUS factory to arrange for its safety during the night. When a demonstrator came back from the inner city to tell him that the demonstration was over, Grothaus went home on the tram. By the time the 9 p.m. curfew took effect, the city was quiet. The streets were empty.[476]

During the night of June 17–18, the local SED, the local security forces and Soviet troops decided to limit access to the inner city except for three access points. Nevertheless, a crowd managed to get through and gathered at the Postplatz on June 18. In contrast to the previous day, troops fired into the crowd and injured three. They cleared the square by the early evening, and the barriers around the inner city were removed. To the southeast of the center city, Soviet troops occupied the Saxon Works as the morning shift arrived, and tanks, armored cars and motorcycle units took up stations in the surrounding area. There, and in other places, police reports indicated that almost 49,000 workers struck—or attempted to strike—some of the largest Dresden factories on June 18. Many of these actions included assemblies within the factories that passed resolutions similar to those drawn up by the ABUS and Saxon Works' laborers the day before. To prevent large-scale demonstrations, Soviet tanks moved up to factory gates and closed them so that workers could not leave.

In the middle of the night of June 17–18, authorities arrested Grothaus and five members of the ABUS strike committee. Two more were picked up during the day of June 18. Dresden's prisons soon filled up, and temporary holding pens for 1500 people were created at the gymnastic center of the Barracked People's Police. The prisoners were held until the beginning of July, and often these inmates were slapped and beaten during interrogations. In one case, guards threatened to shoot those demanding release. The record shows that people arrested and held by Soviet troops were treated better than those guarded by German police.

Dresden's police chief was wary of mass arrests, fearing they would cause more bitterness and unrest. He was not the only one to think so. At the end of June, the GDR's Justice Minister, Max Fechner, became alarmed at the high number of arrests following the mid-month strike action. A former Social Democrat and Prussian state legislator, he was well aware that the GDR constitution gave workers the right to strike. On June 30, he allowed *Neues Deutschland*, the official SED newspaper, to publish an interview where he claimed that only individuals "guilty of a serious crime" on June 17 would be punished. Serious crimes included arson, theft, and murder but not the leadership of a strike.

Retaliation was swift. On July 14, the SED executive committee expelled him from the party and relieved him of his duties as Justice Minister. Thereafter, he was arrested, deprived of sleep, and questioned by the State Security Service. He refused to confess to any crime and would admit only that his interview for *Neues Deutschland* had "damaged the interests" of the GDR's workers. Eventually, GDR courts convicted him of helping "provocateurs" to stage a "Putsch" and sentenced him to eight years in the penitentiary.

Fechner shared his fate with many of his fellow citizens. Throughout the land, the party suggested to the judicial system which prosecutors should try the cases of strike leaders and which judges would hear them. In Dresden, the State Security Service wanted harsher sentences than the district's judges were willing to mete out. Nevertheless, local courts sentenced over 100 people, some to very long periods of incarceration. Wilhelm Grothaus received 15 years for leading a Putsch. Two of his associates on the ABUS committee were sentenced to ten years. Other members were absolved of wrong-doing.[477]

The uprising of June 17 had repercussions for the GDR in both the long and the short term. In the Dresden district, almost 300 SED members resigned from the party, claiming that they no longer agreed with the party's policies. A large number ceased to wear the ubiquitous lapel pins that identified their solidarity with the SED. Others blamed the party's leadership for the crisis of mid-June. At the end of July 1953, the SED's national leadership put an end to the New Course and solidified the position of Walter Ulbricht as leader of East Germany. This high-level meeting also determined that "inconvenient colleagues" in a factory should be fired without notice, that they should be expelled from the party and the trade unions, and be denounced to the authorities.

Local party leaders suggested to co-workers and neighbors that they mete out these punitive measures to undesirables. Since this method appeared to be "democratic", it was difficult for anyone so isolated to defend himself. These exclusions continued into 1954 and meant that many who had escaped imprisonment in July were re-arrested. The best way to save oneself was to flee to West Germany. Yet the records show that Dresdners' flight to the West remained under one per cent in 1953 and 1954. Flights did not increase until 1955 and 1956 when many of those sentenced for their roles in the uprising received amnesties and apparently used them to leave the GDR.[478]

Renewed Repression

The Dresden region continued to cough up cases that revealed ongoing dissatisfaction with the regime. In late 1956, three Dresdners were tried as foreign agents. In 1957, there was a veritable rash of prosecutions for offenses against the GDR. In the small neighboring town of Radeberg, members of a mambo club were brought to trial, ostensibly for dancing the decadent Western jitterbug. At the same time, a farmer was prosecuted for possession of anti-Communist propaganda and for listening to Western radio. In mid-year, a Dresdner was sentenced to ten years' imprisonment for sending letters to West Germany begging for asylum.

Most revealing of all the cases in the late 1950s was that of Fritz Löffler. Löffler was born and raised in Dresden and was intimately associated with its cultural development. A graduate of the King Georg High School, he began to work at the Municipal Museum after receiving his doctorate in Munich. During the 1930s and 1940s, he served Ida Bienert as secretary and, along with her and her son, Fritz, championed modern art. The National Socialists rewarded this support by firing him, without notice, from his job at the museum, and afterward hounded him out of Dresden.

After 1951, Löffler worked for the Saxon Institute of Historic Preservation. He also began to publish biographies of well-known local artists such as Otto Dix and Josef Hegenbarth. He ran afoul of local authorities, particularly the SED Mayor Weidauer, when he aggressively countered, both locally and nationally, city government's plans to raze the ruins of important, historic buildings. In 1955, he first published his classic work, *Das alte Dresden*, that ultimately ran to sixteen editions. It chronicles the evolution of the city's architecture from the Middle Ages to the eve of World War II, with a strong emphasis on its Renaissance and Baroque periods. Two years later, his essay about the history of Dresden's art museum praised Hubert Ermisch's efforts to save the ruins of the Semper Opera from the "pickaxe".

Mayor Weidauer took issue with this "slander" of the new socialist state, and for the next year, he subjected Löffler to showers of political harassment. In June 1958, he forced Löffler to exercise self-criticism, Maoist style, in a meeting of the city council. At the time, Löffler, aged fifty-nine, claimed that the pressure and humiliation caused by the interrogation compromised his health so much that he was uncertain how much longer he could continue to work productively. Even after he retired as mayor in 1961, Weidauer maintained his vendetta against Löffler. Yet Löffler continued to work for the historic preservation agency until his retirement in 1966, and today, his history of Old Dresden is an invaluable resource. It goes without saying that Löffler's real offense, in the eyes of Weidauer and other East German officials, was his defense of a pre-socialist era that they wished to destroy. Weidauer once said that the new regime had no use for churches and Baroque facades.[479]

XIV. Post-War Elbflorence

Early Post-war Developments

Regardless of their distaste for Baroque architecture, Communists like Weidauer desired wholeheartedly to restore Dresden's position as a cultural center, even though that role was increasingly hard to play, given the separation of East Germany, and with it, Dresden, from former patrons in Western Europe. At the Soviet occupier's insistence, an active cultural life resumed already in 1945, even when theaters and concert halls had to be found in makeshift quarters. Beginning in 1946, the city mounted All-German Art Exhibitions, continuing a tradition begun in the previous century. Both East and West Germans contributed artworks to these exhibitions, even in the face of pressure to prevent an all-German event. Contacts with West German artists never ceased, and they continued their relationships with Dresden throughout the life of the GDR.[480]

A Birthday Celebration

In 1956, when the city celebrated its 750th anniversary, it signaled its hope for rekindling its former cultural appeal. The festivities began on June 1 with a Children's Congress. On June 2, the day ended with a concert by the Leningrad Philharmonic Orchestra.

The most prominent event occurred on June 3 when Dresdners welcomed home over 1000 art works to a rebuilt section of the Semper Gallery. The fate of the Dresden collection is part of the city's twentieth-century saga. To protect paintings and other works from Allied air raids during World War II, museum directors had evacuated them to Saxon fortresses, castles, palaces, mine shafts, quarries and tunnels so remotely rural they were not likely to be bombed. Some sites lay west, but others lay to the east of the city.

As the Soviets advanced westward at war's end, directors decided to move works stored in the east toward western locations. On the night of 13 February 1945, some of the works in transit sat in trucks parked within the city. At least, sixty-six paintings were lost in the firestorm. After the Soviets entered Dresden, they quickly pried loose from knowledgeable staff the information needed to locate large parts of the collections, and these were carted off to Moscow and other Soviet cities where they remained until 1955. In that year, the Soviets consented to return most of the confiscated works from Dresden and other cities, after first exhibiting them in Moscow. It was fitting that this homecoming was a celebration of the city's birth. In the succeeding decade, the Soviets returned almost all of the confiscated art, and the city completed the restoration of other museums.

Harald Marx, long the director of the Old Masters' Gallery, has claimed that the art works' return represented the rebirth of Dresden as an international art capital. Had they not been returned, not only would the city have lost precious cultural treasures, it was probable that those facades so disdained by Weidauer would never have been restored, among them the Palace, the Semper Opera, the Frauenkirche. Important institutions would also have disappeared. Florence on the Elbe, almost completely obliterated, would be but a distant memory.[481]

Art

One of those institutions was the All-German Art Exhibition held every five years as well as other public showings of the city's collections. One trait of these occasions was the continuation of the cultural conservatism that had plagued the early twentieth century. In the 1960s and 1970s, exhibits favored traditional subjects and styles. In 1970, the Etchings Department of the State Museum had to remove works by Pablo Picasso, Paul Klee and Robert Rauschenberg from its Dialogue Exhibition. For the GDR state censors, their art was simply too modern.

Undeterred were young artists who experimented with various modern forms. The most famous twentieth-century German artist to study and paint in Dresden, Gerhard Richter, migrated to the West in 1961, but he left behind a group of neo-Expressionists associated with another Dresdner who eventually adopted the name A. R. Penck. In 1965, he and his friends mounted an exhibition of their work in the club house of the German-Soviet Friendship

Society. Another group of avants gardes established itself in the Leonhardi Museum in Loschwitz. These iconoclasts were deemed to be dissidents, and the State Security Service (Stasi) kept them under surveillance. Eventually Penck moved to East Berlin, where he found it convenient to arrange for his and others' works to be shown in the western half of the city. Later, Penck was expelled to West Germany where he painted, sculpted and exhibited there and in non-German cities.

Once a new generation established itself in the mid-1970s, a more diverse, a more modern, and more controversial selection prevailed at the All-German Exhibitions. Hans Modrow, the Dresden district's last SED chairman, claims, a little too apologetically, that the party ceased to influence the exhibitions' content. The opening of each exhibition was a state occasion. The Minister of Culture gave a speech followed by a midday banquet attended by East German leaders. Parallel to these exhibitions, Dresden's city government continued the older urban tradition of hosting several small galleries. They were now state-owned and managed, rather than private, and each catered to a different artistic group.

The official tolerance of modern art that emerged during the later period of the GDR was uneven. Travel to exhibitions in West Germany was restricted. Exhibitions of modern art could still be banned. In 1979, the local authorities closed an exhibition/happening at the Leonhardi Museum because the organizers refused to remove two works by A. R. Penck, *persona non grata* in the GDR.

Three years later, the Stasi, increasingly disturbed by the dissident art displayed at the Leonhardi, framed the hosts of a vernissage by having a petition circulated that protested the GDR's military conscription. This event led to the museum's closure for three years. A well-known art critic who promoted dissident art was watched by the secret police and frequently forbidden to work or to give talks. In 1984, he was arrested and expelled to the West. This technique, of course, was the one that exiled the famous balladeer of Berlin, Wolf Biermann, because his lyrics expressed bitter criticism of the GDR.[482]

If contemporary artists found themselves struggling, the State Art Collections got a new lease on life after the Soviets returned the works they had spirited away at the end of World War II. Relying on these classical works, the State Collections mounted major expositions of Albrecht Dürer and his contemporaries in 1971, of Caspar David Friedrich in 1974, of Peter Paul Rubens in 1977, and of Ferdinand Goya in 1978. The goal of these shows was what it had been for more than a century: to showcase the city as a cultural center and make money to support either the city or the collections.

Classical artists were, however, not the only money-makers. The State Collections also staged exhibits of twentieth-century artists active in Dresden, men like Josef Hegenbarth for drawings and Conrad Felixmüller for Expressionism. In 1976, Dresdners and their visitors were treated to a spectacle of Chagall paintings in the Albertinum. The decade ended with an exhibition that had great appeal for Dresdners: the work of Wilhelm Rudolph, who had assuaged his grief over the bombing of Dresden by sketching the ruins and presenting some of them as prints from wood-cut blocks.

The State Art Collections also traveled. I first became acquainted with the "Splendor of Dresden" at an exhibition in Washington, D. C. in 1978 that displayed many of the intricate *objets de vertu* from the Green Vaults. By that time, major shows had taken Dresden's treasures to Heidelberg, Vienna, Stockholm and Tokyo. Expositions in Mexico City, New Delhi, and major European cities followed the D. C. trip. It was an extravagant—and also lucrative—way of keeping the memory of Dresden alive in the hearts and minds of the rest of the world.

If the State Collections possessed a world-wide appeal, there was another museum that catered to hometown memories: the Institute and Museum for the History of Dresden in the Landhaus. This beautiful example of classical architecture had been restored by 1966, and it began to house the artifacts relating to the city's history. The special shows at Christmas were "much loved", but the propaganda at other times of the year seemed heavy-handed. Only in the 1980s was Communist indoctrination minimized, and Dresdners could soak up the zeitgeist of past eras.[483]

Music

During the celebrations of 1956, the city could not ignore its historic high culture, but it took care to emphasize other aspects of its development. Mayor Weidauer, in a newspaper article, lauded the city as a center of nuclear research and technology, highlighting the nuclear physics laboratory at Dresden-Rossendorf. The city council published a Commemorative Anthology (*Festschrift*) that focused on Dresden as a socialist center. There was a gondola show on the Elbe, a fashion show in the Great Garden. One day was set aside to honor the trade unions. Amid the still visible signs of the city's destruction, a wreath was laid at the ruins of the Frauenkirche, and a commemoration of war dead took place at the Cemetery on the Heath. To mark the close of the anniversary celebrations on June 30, there was a huge folk festival on the Altmarkt, accompanied by a Soviet ensemble and performances by Dresden's well-known Mountain Climber Choir.

The festivities would not have been complete without the music that had so richly embellished Dresden's history. On the evening of the Semper Gallery's reopening, the Grand Theater presented *Der Freischütz*, Carl Maria von Weber's quintessential German opera. Later in the month a whole week honored Heinrich Schütz by featuring performances by the two Dresden orchestras and the Kreuzkirche choir under Rudolf Mauersberger's direction.[484]

Rudolf Mauersberger

Mauersberger is a legendary figure in Dresden's modern history. Born in the Ore Mountains at the end of the nineteenth century, he trained at the Leipzig Conservatory and, by the time he arrived in Dresden at the end of the Weimar Republic, he had a wealth of experience in other cities. In Dresden he was chiefly responsible for training and leading the Kreuzkirche boys' choir, the Kruzianer, that dates back to the fourteenth century.

During the 1930s, he took the boys on tour through Germany and Europe and, twice, to the United States. The tours to foreign countries occurred as late as the 1940s. For local church services, he introduced the singing of the epistle and gospel. At Christmas and Easter, he staged the choir boys as various actors in the Bible's stories. Under his leadership, the choir gave concerts at churches throughout the city and sometimes included secular music in its programs. After the National Socialists came to power, Mauersberger joined the party but resisted its efforts to synchronize the choir with its ideology. He continued to emphasize sacred music and even included works by Jewish composers in his concerts, without mentioning their names in the program.

A former member of the choir, Bodo Seiffert, has described what happened when the boys went on tour to the German-occupied Netherlands in 1944. Dressed in the uniforms of the Hitler Youth, they received a pompous farewell from its local leader at Dresden's main train station. After Mauersberger joined the choir at the Neustadt station, he told the boys to change into civilian clothes. For Seiffert, the choir, during the Third Reich, was a "small, holy island" detached from the politics of the day. It was not so detached that they were spared the sight of bombed-out cities in Holland, nor were they exempted, as the Soviets approached Dresden, from digging trenches designed to stop the enemy's advance.[485]

On the evening of 13 February 1945, Mauersberger tried to make his way from his residence to the Kreuzschule on Georgplatz. The second raid found him on the Commons and, due to his smoke-filled lungs, he never reached his destination. The school was heavily damaged by the bombing, and altogether eleven of the choir's associates died in the raid, either from suffocation, from the bombing at the school or at their homes. Lives and buildings were not all that was lost. The firestorm consumed the choir's musical archive, assembled over hundreds of years.

After the bombing attack of Shrove Tuesday/Ash Wednesday, Mauersberger found refuge in the Ore Mountains where, on Good Friday, 1945, using Jeremiah's Lamentations, he began to write the composition for which he is most famous, "The Hymn of Grief: How Deserted Lies the City…". (*Trauermotette: Wie liegt die Stadt so wüst…*) By that time, he had re-established contact with the Kruzianer so that, once the war was over, he could bring them back to the task of making music. A memorable photograph records the first post-war Vespers held on 4 August 1945 in the ruins of the Kreuzkirche. In front of the altar on which eleven candles burned beside eleven school beanies, Mauersberger led the Kruzianers' memorial to their dead schoolmates.[486]

Kruzianer who performed with the choir have vividly described the travails of the immediate post-war period. The school was able, in the immediate aftermath of war, to convene in the damaged structure on Georgplatz. Rehearsals for the choir took place in the old art classroom. Because of the loss of the archive, music for services and concerts had to be copied out by hand and distributed in unbound sheets to the boys. Mistakes that arose in copying or loose sheets that fell to the floor gave rise, sometimes, to cacophony. In the first years after the war, even intact churches were not heated, so the boys shivered through their performances. Because of power outages, streetcars often could not travel between the Martin's Church, previously ministering to the Dresden garrison, which served as a substitute for the ruined Kreuzkirche, and the school's boarding department or the boys' homes. Then they had to walk the distance to and from the church.

Nevertheless, Mauersberger constructed an ambitious program of concerts. When the boys traveled to village churches in the Dresden region, they usually got fed well, a welcome occasion for young people living in a city with chronic shortages. In 1947, they traveled to Bavaria. The next year, they sang not only for Bavarians, but for churches in neighboring central and northern Germany.[487]

In 1955, the restoration of the Kreuzkirche was completed. It included a Heinrich-Schütz-Chapel financed with funds donated by Mauersberger. In that year also, he launched the Heinrich-Schütz Week, held annually during his lifetime. Performances during that week included not only works by the seventeenth-century Kreuzkirche cantor but those composed by twentieth-century composers. Mauersberger also reinstated one of the church's former traditions with choristers roaming through the city after the Vesper service at Pentecost.[488]

Mauersberger remained the choir's director until the end of his life in 1971. His last decade was not an easy one. The director of the Kreuzschule, a radical Communist, used his position to enforce ideological purity within the school, including the choir's cantor. His meetings with Mauersberger resembled interrogations, and he tried to block talented choirboys from gaining admission to GDR conservatories. The situation became even more antagonistic after six boys defected to the west during the Kruzianers' tour to Austria and Switzerland. Wanting to retire but also to shield the boys, Mauersberger not only conducted the choir at home and abroad but refined the compositions of his earlier period and recorded, with the choir, works by Schütz and other historic composers. It was fitting that the city's anniversary celebration opened with a performance by the Kruzianer. The Kreuzkirche, the school and the choir encapsulated both the achievements and the aspirations of the city.[489]

In the immediate post-war years, the State Opera and its orchestra acted swiftly to maintain continuity. The first post-war opera, *The Marriage of Figaro*, entertained Dresdners already in August 1945. For several years, the Opera performed in a small intact auditorium in the Neustadt until the Grand Theater on the Ostra Allee was rebuilt in 1948. It was there that the regime imposed its ideological tests on the musical world. In 1950, it closed down Carl Orff's *Antigone*, ostensibly because of its Formalism. Never mind that the story glorifies resistance to a tyrannical ruler. At the time, the SED, taking a cue from its Soviet supervisors, charged various artistic measures—art, architecture, theater, music—of Formalism when banning them from public distribution. Formalism, technically, meant the negation of realism, but it was regularly used to combat modern art or anything that the regime associated with the bourgeois culture of the United States, Britain or West Germany.[490]

Despite his association with the bourgeois culture of the past, Dresdners did not forget that Richard Strauss had premiered many of his operas in their city. When the one hundredth anniversary of Strauss' birth rolled around in 1964, the State Opera mounted a whole roster of his work: *Rosenkavalier, Arabella, Salome, Ariadne auf Naxos* and *Cappricio*.[491]

The next year, the Dresden State Orchestra performed Benjamin Britten's *War Requiem* in the Martin Luther Church on February 13, the day when pealing church bells annually commemorated the Shrove Tuesday bombing of 1945. Britten had composed the work three years before to celebrate the dedication of the new Coventry Cathedral, a church that, like the Frauenkirche, had been destroyed by bombs—dropped by the Luftwaffe. This performance in Dresden, Coventry's sister city, represented the East German premiere of Britten's work. On this occasion, Theo Adam, a native Dresdner, sang the leading baritone role.

As a boy, Adam had sung with the Kruzianer and had studied voice privately at the Dresden State Opera. He made his professional debut in Dresden as the bass-baritone in Weber's *Freischütz*. Though he remained a member of the Dresden State Opera for the whole of his career, he quickly developed an international reputation, sang regularly at Bayreuth and the Berlin State Opera, and appeared as a guest in Western Europe and in the United States, including the Metropolitan Opera.

Another Kruzianer who achieved an international reputation was the tenor, Peter Schreier. Appearing in Mozart's *Magic Flute* as a nine-year old, he studied voice at the Dresden Conservatory and at the State Opera's training school. Even while engaged at the Dresden State Opera, he accepted numerous guest appearances in Western Europe, in the United States and in Argentina. From 1970 onward, he combined his singing career with conducting and continued to direct orchestras until the end of his life in 2019.[492]

In the mid-1970s, objections to Formalism belonged to the past, and the Dresden State Opera introduced contemporary music with works by native

Saxons. In 1976, there were two premieres: Rainer Kunad's *Lithuanian Pianos*, dramatizing the novel by Johannes Bobrowski, and Udo Zimmermann's *The Schuhu and the Flying Princesses*, based on a fairy tale by Peter Hacks. Rainer Kunad had briefly studied at the Dresden Conservatory and functioned as director of theatrical music at the State Theater after 1971. He left Dresden for West Germany in 1985. Of the two men, Udo Zimmermann enjoyed the better renown. As a native Dresdner, he sang with the Kruzianer and studied composition at the Dresden Conservatory before completing his musical studies in Berlin. Beginning in 1970, Zimmermann was the dramaturg for the Dresden State Opera and a guest conductor for German orchestras on both sides of the Wall. He also raised his baton in other European cities. In the mid-1980s, he founded the Dresden Center of Contemporary Music and became a prominent promoter of modernistic music.[493]

In the GDR, the days were gone when the state railways attached extra cars to trains from Berlin to Dresden for performances of *Der Rosenkavalier*. Yet the city continued to maintain a high musical standard, not only at the State Orchestra but also at the Philharmonic. For a long time, the Philharmonic existed as a musical stepchild, first fostered by the local Commercial Association that sold it to a private foundation during World War I. Between the two world wars, the orchestra managed to survive with a subsidy from the city and by giving concerts to professional groups and high schools. As soon as World War II ended, a former guest conductor organized a concert in mid-June, even before the State Orchestra's first post-war event. The Philharmonic, in this early period, was not particular about its venues. It played in dance halls, in movie theaters, in factory cafeterias, for all sorts of people. In 1947, it founded the Dresden Musical Summer by performing a series of concerts in the Pillnitz Palace park.

Slowly it became a state institution in demand for working-class festivals, youth concerts, chamber music recitals. Eventually, it received invitations for radio programs, for recording events, for tours inside and outside the GDR. In the 1950s, Kurt Masur, later the renowned director of the Leipzig Gewandhaus orchestra, acted as co-conductor. After the Philharmonic in 1969 acquired its own hall in the new Kulturpalast on the Altmarkt, Masur was briefly its chief director. At that time, the orchestra established its own chorus, and in 1984, it introduced Dresdners to *Porgy and Bess*. It's possible to say that the GDR helped to make the Philharmonic a permanent feature of the city's musical scene.[494]

There was also music provided at Herkuleskeule (Hercules' Club), a cabaret located after 1965 on the inner city's Sternplatz, now in the remodeled Kulturpalast. It is remarkable that this cabaret has maintained itself through thin and thick over more than fifty years. Jazz concerts also became regular occasions during the 1960s, and the Dresden Conservatory even established a jazz department. The greater tolerance for jazz led to the establishment of a Dixieland Festival in 1971. This group of concerts continues into the twenty-first century and partially overlaps with the more ambitious Music Festival in May.

For the city's future as a musical magnet, the establishment of the Music Festival in early summer 1978 was portentous. Orchestras, choirs, other musical ensembles came from as far away as Moscow, Warsaw, Venice and Stuttgart. The organizers even managed to entice Herbert von Karajan and the Berlin Philharmonic to Dresden. This festival also continues into the twenty-first century and offers a rich palette of instrumental and vocal music as well as dance. It takes over the whole city and enlivens towns in the Dresden region with performances.[495]

Theater

By the time the Grand Theater in the Ostraallee had been rebuilt, it had lost to West Germany the well-known stage and film actor Erich Ponto, associated with the Dresden Theater Ensemble since 1914. Immediately after the war, he and others had formed a committee to re-introduce Dresdners to serious drama. He even assumed the position of the theater's general director. By 1947, he was fed up with no longer being able to "act freely" in the repressive political atmosphere of the East. One example was the authorities' refusal to allow Carl Zuckmayer's *Devil's General* to play at the Grand Theater, presumably because of its sympathetic treatment of a Nazi era's army officer. Increasingly, even as German classics and Shakespeare appeared on the playbill, there was an orientation toward Russian drama. Some critics claim that Dresden theater stagnated during the 1950s.

One attempt to recreate Dresden as dramaturgical magnet was the Dresden Theater Festival of 1954. The neighboring ensembles at Meissen and Leipzig came as guests, and the high point was the performance of Bertolt Brecht's

Mother Courage and her Children by the Berliner Ensemble, a troupe that was and still is world famous. Playing the title role in Dresden was Helene Weigel, Brecht's second wife, who had starred in the part when the ensemble was founded after World War II. Expressing the hopes of Dresdners for a restoration of their former renown, Max Seydewitz, then the director of Dresden's Art Collections and a loyal member of the ruling SED, wrote that many West German guests who attended the plays in 1954, when travel between east and west encountered few impediments, anticipated describing to their home towns the excellent performances they had experienced at the Dresden theater. They also intended to return for future festivals, an aspiration possible for only a few more years.

In 1955, Germans celebrated the 150th anniversary of playwright Friedrich Schiller's death, and the Dresden stage performed his *Wallenstein* trilogy and *Maria Stuart*. In that year also, the theater troupe toured West Germany and Czechoslovakia, following a practice established in the pre-war era. During the 1960s, Dresden audiences began to sample plays written by West Germans. And in the 1970s, the ensemble performed works by the radical Peter Hacks, whose ideas found favor in West Germany but displeased East German officials, even though he was an avowed Communist living in East Berlin.[496]

Not until the 1980s did Dresden reclaim its role as a leading dramatic center. The new superintendent of the state theater, Gerhard Wolfram, managed to present plays that were banned in other cities. Modern versions of German classics and controversial contemporary drama attracted large audiences of young Dresdners. In 1987, the Dresden State Theater produced Samuel Beckett's *Waiting for Godot*. A very large crowd showed up on opening night. Accommodating it caused a delay in raising the curtain. Impatient, the audience began to clap a protest. In response, someone in the audience shouted: "You've waited for thirty-five years, so what's wrong with waiting another ten minutes." Little did they expect on that night that they would soon be able to attend almost any theatrical work they wanted.[497]

Sports

Resuming an active sports life was another way of enlivening the town and its environs. In the immediate post-war period, the Soviets understood this need, even though at first they confined competitions to the city and the state. Once the Soviet occupation yielded to the German Democratic Republic, excellence in sport was one way the new regime could distinguish itself, and it recruited youth of both sexes who exhibited athletic promise. Political reliability was a prerequisite for selection. The regime had no desire to be embarrassed by defecting athletes in international contests.[498]

Even though the socialist state encouraged all kinds of sport, soccer retained its popularity. After World War II, Dresdners fielded the Sport Association Friedrichstadt that had taken the place of the dissolved Dresden Sports Club. Its matches regularly attracted 30,000 spectators. In April 1950, it played Zwickau in an East German championship game. When Zwickau won, 5-1, the 60,000 spectators in the Dresdner stadium rioted, causing injury to some of the players. Thereafter, the authorities dissolved the Friedrichstadt team and supplanted it with the squad fielded by the local People's Police. This substitution occasioned flights by all but two of the Friedrichstadt players to West Germany where they were quickly snapped up by professional teams. Those moving west included Helmut Schön, who later gained acclaim as the outstanding manager of the Federal Republic's national team.[499]

In Dresden, the soccer team soon became an instrument of the State Security Ministry (Stasi). Its long-term director, Eric Mielke, was "crazy about soccer" and set up the Sports Association Dynamo. With the help of the Stasi, Dynamo Dresden formed in 1953 and, within three months, won an East German championship. For Mielke, it was important for the GDR's capital to field a first-rate soccer team. He had the Dresden players moved *en masse* to a newly created East Berlin team. This raid on Dresden, at a time when no Wall separated the two parts of Berlin, certainly resulted from a determination to rival West Berlin's teams and to attract spectators to games played by a stellar GDR group. It also reflected East Germany's quest to equal West Germany's capture of the World Cup in 1954. Bolstering East Berlin's fortunes would position its team to compete successfully on the international stage.

Berlin's gain was Dresden's loss. The team lost its place in the GDR's premier league (*Oberliga*) but determined to build back. Progress was slow, but the team persisted. It amply demonstrated its loyalty to Dresden and the GDR in August 1961. When the club traveled, with other Saxon players, to the West German city of Ulm for a "friendly contest", it found itself trapped when the "Wall" was erected during the night of the thirteenth. Yet all of the East German team members returned home on August 14.

Dynamo Dresden finally regained a permanent spot in the leading league in 1968. In that year, Dynamo president Mielke promised that Berlin would no longer raid Dresden for its best players and that the city would gain a Performance Center, a training facility for top athletes destined for both Dresden soccer and international competitions.[500] By this time, Dresden had become good enough to compete for the Europa Cup, and it began to play teams in Scandinavia, the British Isles, and Holland. Throughout the 1970s, it performed well both at home and abroad with the help of Walter Fritzsch, a gifted manager.

In many ways, Fritzsch was a martinet. After every game, team members had to assess their strengths and weaknesses, exposed on videotapes made by Fritzsch. He also frowned on excessive consumption of alcoholic drinks. Some of these traits did not go down well with the players. Most particularly, the team's star member, Hans-Jürgen Kreische, 1973s GDR Player of the Year, resisted the coach's attempts to reduce his boozing. At the same time, Fritzsch didn't have much use for the politicization of sport, and he achieved a reduction of the obligatory political training required by the regime. Once, when the SED's district director, Werner Krolikowski, asked him why he didn't field a particular player, Fritzsch retorted that if Krolikowski could better manage the team, he could take over the job.

Under Fritzsch, Dresden won the East German Master (first among a group of qualified teams) five times during the 1970s, the East German Cup (first among a group of all teams) twice and gained a victory over FC Ponto—one of Portugal's elite teams—and FC Juventus Turin—the equivalent of the Italian national team—in the 1972–3 season. The high point of the decade occurred in 1973 when Dynamo Dresden came up against Munich in the European Cup playoffs.[501]

The prospect of a German-German match was exhilarating. The team would have two chances to show its East German mettle, one in Munich and one in Dresden. Before the game in Munich, the players took a tour of the city and a trip to the local shops. For the return game in Dresden, the Stasi strongly controlled the spectators. Eight thousand tickets were reserved for the region's industrial firms so as to assure a politically correct public. Thousands of ordinary fans lined up all night, fortifying themselves with sleeping bags and garden chairs, hoping to purchase the two tickets allowed them by the regime. Although elaborate preparations occurred at the Hotel Newa, scheduled to host the Bavarians, they ultimately opted to spend the night in Hof, a West German city on the border, with just a short drive to Dresden.

On the day of the Dresden game, the Stasi set up barriers around the Harbig Stadium—the old Ilgen Arena—to prevent anyone without a ticket from approaching the field or the Western buses. The Stasi also packed the stadium with unofficial informers and bugged the room reserved for the Bavarians' use before the game. Leaving little to chance, their pre-game meeting was broadcast directly to the local Stasi headquarters, and their starting strategy was immediately communicated to Fritzsch. The Dresdners lost the first game in Munich, 4-3, and the second game in Dresden ended in a tie, 3-3, meaning that Munich won the match. Nevertheless, exuberant Dresden fans carried their team off the field. Losing the match by only one point was good enough for them.[502]

The Dresden team remained extraordinarily successful during the 1970s, particularly against the Berlin team favored by Mielke. When Dynamo Dresden won the East German championship against East Berlin in 1978, Mielke traveled south to congratulate them but publicly vowed that the Berlin club would do all it could to assure future titles for Berlin and to relegate Dresden to second place. For the next ten years, East Berlin won all the East German championships, and Dresdners continue to suspect that Mielke manipulated this result. Dresden only regained the GDR championship in 1989 and again in 1990.[503]

Dresdners were not alone in suspecting chicanery in favor of the Berlin team. Complaints were widespread. But the rivalry between Dresden and Berlin was intense. Already in 1950, Dresdners suspected that referees had favored Zwickau when it won the GDR championship. Incidents also arose in the 1960s and 1970s. Almost always, it was referees who were supposedly pressured by Mielke.

Complaints about them reached a peak in the mid-1980s, and GDR sports authorities felt enough pressure to launch an investigation of the game in which Dresden, playing against Berlin, won the trade unions' Cup. The inquiry concluded that Dresden had received two-thirds more foul calls than Berlin. A special panel identified ten glaring mistakes by the referees, nine of which disadvantaged Dresden. The offending officials were disciplined. Yet the GDR archives reveal no overt pressure by Mielke. One historian of GDR soccer surmises that referees, knowing that the powerful Stasi director favored the

Berlin team, consciously or unconsciously, gave it preferential treatment. In addition, referees could be influenced by gifts—autos, nice apartments, weekend houses, easy schedules at their places of work—that they received from Stasi headquarters. That offending referees were also Stasi informers might also have played a role.[504]

To what extent can doping account for the winning streaks of both teams in the 1970s and 1980s? Well-known revelations after German unification unveiled the GDR's systematic doping program, planned for and implemented by the regime's highest officials, in international sports contests. Although doping in soccer did not produce the same dramatic effects as in other performance sports like swimming, its victories in international contests could still add to the GDR's luster. There is evidence that performance-enhancing drugs were administered to the GDR's national team already in 1965 and thereafter, whenever an Oberliga team confronted a non-GDR opponent. In 1978, stimulants were given to all Dresden players in the European Cup contest against Belgrade. After his flight to the West during summer 1989, a top player of the 1970s confessed to West Germany's *Bild-Zeitung,* a tabloid, that Dresden's team members were given pills before every international game. And even when the regime's sports officials did not authorize drugs, "wild" doping, encouraged by local officials and agreed to by team members, was practiced by all elite teams. Theoretically, doping in domestic games was banned, but it happened anyway.[505]

Manipulated refereeing and doping aside, there were other possible explanations for Dresden's relative weakness in the 1980s. Star player Kreische resigned from the team in 1977. Fritzsch retired as Dresden's manager in 1978. He ended his career working for the East German Soccer Association, cultivating youthful soccer players and training future managers. The Dresden team continued to consult him, even after it entered a West German league in 1991. There now stands a small obelisk in his memory in the Harbig Stadium.

Prager Strasse, 1930
SLUB Deutsche Fototek/unknown photographer

Prager Strasse, with street cars, 1960
SLUB Deutsche Fototek/Christian Borchert

Prager Strasse, 1970
SLUB Deutsche Fototek/Richard Peter sen.

Dresden Women removing rubble, 1945
SLUB Deutsche Fotothek/Erich Höhne

Bodies awaiting burning, Altmarkt, 1945
Bundesarchiv Bild/Hahn

Neumarkt, 1957
SLUB Deutsche Fotothek/Walter Möbius

New Synagogue, 2009
Marco Mraz

Human chains remembering Dresden's bombing and protesting the Neo-Nazi mourning marches 2010 and 2011
André Schulz

XV. Rebuilding the "City So Deserted…"

Ruins

Dresden's revival of its artistic and sportive reputations occurred even before it restored its famous landmarks and recaptured the cityscape along the banks of the Elbe. While it was impossible to rebuild the city to its pre-war form, Dresden could at least regain the traditional Canaletto prospect. When Dresdners celebrated their city's 750th anniversary, they had not yet removed the signs of destruction. East Germany's head of the ruling party and state, Walter Ulbricht, had inaugurated the reconstruction of the Altmarkt in 1953, but at the time of the celebratory Volksfest, the square was not yet fully enclosed, and it remained partially open until the end of the East German regime.

A photo overlooking the areal of the Neumarkt and its surroundings, taken in the 1950s, reveals an open space planted in grass. Historians claim that it took fifteen years to clear the whole bombed-out area. Today, Dresdners and visitors alike saunter, jog and cycle the path along the river from the Albert Bridge to the Blue Wonder in Blasewitz without realizing that the Elbe meadows to the southeast conceal millions of cubic meters of rubble. Further to the east at Dobritz another heap of debris lies buried. At the western end of the Altstadt, the rubble was used to create a small hill on the Ostra Preserve.

In addition to professional construction crews, scores of women labored in the ruins, salvaging reusable stone and brick and tossing hopelessly broken and charred materials onto carts that were wheeled along tracks to the Elbe meadows. In 1952, the city commissioned and erected a statue, the Rubble Woman (*Trümmerfrau*), on the New City Hall Square to commemorate their work. In the immediate post-war years, men were also drafted to work alongside them. Over the years, many volunteers, both willing and unwilling, toiled away at clearing the rubble. By the time of the city's 750th anniversary, donated time approached 800 hours per year per volunteer.[506]

As the rubble slowly disappeared, the chief issue facing the city was how to rebuild. Should the old city reappear just as it used to be, as so many other municipalities, both East and West, decided? Or should a new, socialist town emerge? This issue generated a controversy that raged for decades among townspeople and sympathetic outsiders. It accounted for the attacks on Fritz Löffler that occurred in the 1950s, and it contributed to the dissatisfaction that ultimately motivated many to turn against a state that claimed to represent their interests. Wisps of it linger in Dresden's written histories and contemporary politics.

Even conservatives understood that the city should not be entirely restored to its pre-war state. Narrow, dark lanes in the city center, held over from the medieval and early modern periods, needed to give way to more hygienic open spaces. Traffic patterns would have to accommodate modes of transportation barely envisioned in previous eras.

At the same time, many Dresdners, led by Herbert Conert, city planner since 1922, wanted to preserve the old city's main outlines, its architectural proportions, its famous landmarks and, above all, its character as a residential city. He anticipated restoring the Zwinger and the Court Church, parts of the old royal palace, the eighteenth-century homes on the Grosse Meissner Strasse in the Neustadt, and the well-known Baroque townscape of the Rampische Strasse just to the east of the Neumarkt. The local office for historic preservation agreed with him.[507]

Wolfgang Mischnick has told an amusing story about the efforts to preserve the Semper Opera in the early post-war period. He and his Liberal Party comrades in the municipal assembly heard a rumor that the local SED intended to demolish the ruins of that iconic building. For German Communists, it was a "remnant of the imperialistic, monarchical mindset". The structure was further tainted because Richard Strauss had conducted the premieres of his operas there and was known to have supported Hitler's early career.

Determined to save the building, Mischnick and three Liberals from the city's Culture Commission descended on the Soviet culture officers living at the Weisser Hirsch. Bolstered with lots of vodka drunk throughout a long night of discussion, they persuaded the Soviets that it would be a "disgrace" to destroy the landmark. Though heavily damaged, it was capable of being rebuilt. Meanwhile, the Theaterplatz had resumed its old function as the rallying point for citizens' demonstrations of all kinds.[508]

Restoring the Zwinger was never in question. Hubert Ermisch, whose thorough restoration had ended only three years before, once again took up the task of re-creating this famous Baroque structure. The damage was so extensive that he had to search for sculptors capable of re-fashioning Pöppelmann's and Permoser's architectural and sculptural ornaments, and he had to hire geologists to tell him where to quarry the stone that was used for the original structure. This work took just as long as the restoration of the pre-war period. Ermisch died in 1951, and the work continued until its completion in 1964.[509]

Next door to the Zwinger, the Court Church began holding services in the southeastern portion of its nave in 1947, and work soon began on the main body of the church. Funds, both from the new East German republic and from Catholics in West Germany, enabled the fully restored church's rededication in the early 1960s. For their part, the Protestants became responsible for rebuilding, by 1955, a number of damaged churches, above all the Kreuzkirche. In addition, the historic Annen Church, on the fringes of the inner city, and the imposing nineteenth-century Christus Church in Strehlen were also restored by that date. The Luther Monument, long a fixture on the Neumarkt, resumed its old location. Max Seydewitz, an official in the ostensibly atheistic Communist regime, proudly listed these rebuilt houses of worship in his post-war history of Dresden.[510]

Seydewitz, with his Social Democratic background, was probably too optimistic about the sentiments and plans of his Communist colleagues in the SED. Even as the German Democratic Republic was born, politicians and architects made no secret of their desire to erase the traces of the former bourgeois eras and build a "democratic" modern city. As the rubble was cleared from Dresden's streets, dynamite leveled ruined shells and facades not only of heavily damaged but also salvageable buildings. The reverberations from the explosions weakened nearby structures that could have conceivably been restored. The Institute for Historic Preservation protested the wide-ranging destruction but lacked the legal means to stop it.

Hans Nadler, the post-war preservation officer, finally resorted to two basic arguments in his attempt to save as much as possible. First, he suggested ways in which restored buildings could be totally or partially used by the new regime. Architects at the Technical College helped him by holding seminars and directing masters' theses devoted to the old buildings. Secondly, he fell back on the affection for the city's skyline inside the Elbe Valley, a sentiment felt by almost everyone associated with Dresden, natives and newcomers alike. He emphasized preserving the inner city's chief artery from the main railroad station to the Albertplatz. That meant saving much of the old urban pattern that surrounded this trace. While it is not entirely true that Nadler preserved the old city intact, his fellow citizens have credited his guile with restoring much of Old Dresden.[511]

Nadler had to work hard to preserve the old urban fabric. The tempo of destruction picked up with the founding of the GDR in 1949. Kurt Leucht, the new director of the city's development office, devised a comprehensive plan that foresaw the elimination of the old city's intimate spatial relationships and the removal of all but seven of thirty-one historic buildings. For all cities, the regime's chief preoccupation was the creation of wide boulevards, called Magistralen in the Soviet style, that would accommodate crowds of Communist marchers converging on central squares large enough to stage huge propagandistic rallies. These central squares would be dominated, again in the Soviet style, by a tower or skyscraper to serve as SED party headquarters or other official functions and symbolize the victory of the new regime.

The national Ministry of Reconstruction in Berlin considered Dresden's Altmarkt the best site for these political purposes, and it wanted the Dresdners to enlarge the square, thereby distorting its old proportions. Even Mayor Weidauer resisted this enlargement, and the city council agreed with him. In the architectural competitions that normally preceded the award of a contract, no architectural firm followed the central government's criteria to the letter.

But as with so much in the GDR, the central government overruled the locals. In response to the Dresdners' refusal to follow the architectural guidelines for the central square, the central government ordered construction to begin in 1953 according to socialist dimensions. The size of the square was doubled and the height of the structures raised. Ultimately, the west and east sides of the square were completed in a faux Baroque style with shops on the ground floor and apartments above. The Wilsdrufferstrasse—then the Ernst Thälmannstrasse—was enlarged, and today, instead of supporting large columns of marching Communists, it facilitates fast east-west traffic through the inner city.[512]

The towering skyscraper never got built. Eventually, in the 1960s, the city opted for the low-rise, modernistic Kulturpalast on its designated site. For many years, the Kulturpalast served as the concert hall for the Dresdner Philharmonic, as a venue for the city's Dixieland Festival instituted in the 1970s, and as a conference center for local and national groups.

The disposition of the Altmarkt set the tone for the rebuilding of the whole city. In the end, even as the forces of restoration and modernization contended with one another, a compromise between old and new emerged. Preservationists grieved the loss of the Albert Theater, where Erich Kästner once attended shows with his mother, the stealthy razing of the ruins of Baroque neighborhoods in the Grosse Meissner and Rampische Streets, and the disappearance of the Palais Oppenheim and Villa Rosa, both designed by Gottfried Semper.[513]

In 1962, the "last ideologically motivated destruction" occurred: the razing of the Sophien Church's ruins cater-cornered to the Zwinger. Built in 1265 to serve the Franciscan monastery, it was converted after the Reformation into a church for the court's Protestants. Two neo-Gothic towers had been added in the nineteenth century. The building was heavily damaged in the bombing raid of February 13, and the Evangelical-Lutheran Church did not want to spend the money to restore it. Clerical authorities gave away the steeple bells and the sculptures that could be salvaged. During the early post-war period, it was the city's administration that preserved the ruins.

Just as the city took steps to raze them, the church changed its mind and protested the destruction. The architectural faculty of the Technical University supported the ruins' preservation and proposed a configuration that would fit the neighborhood. Finally, Walter Ulbricht, head of the GDR state and the SED, decreed that the church's ruins be cleared, and the municipal assembly agreed. Although Dresdners mounted a concerted action, resulting in the Stasi's arrest of several protestors, by the end of the year, the towers no longer existed and the site stood vacant.[514]

At the same time, some important structures were saved during the early phase of reconstruction: the so-called Excise House next to the Japanese Palace, the Palace itself, the Albertinum (once the armory), the Johanneum (the old royal stables), the Jägerhof (formerly the electoral hunting lodge), the Hygiene Museum, even the restaurant called the Italienisches Dörfchen on the Theaterplatz. The current visitor to the electoral/royal palace and the Brühl

Terrace experiences much of the pre-war urban silhouette. During the decade of the 1960s, the Georg Gate to the palace was restored to its original Renaissance style, as was the Stable Close. The palace itself remained a wreck. On the Terrace, the pre-Nazi buildings of the king's second-born son (Sekundogenitur) and the Art Academy also reappeared. And adjacent to the Terrace, west and east, so did the old Saxon diet and the Albertinum, which houses the collection of art from the nineteenth century onward. In mid-town, the classically elegant Landhaus, once the seat of the Saxon Estates, and the New Rathaus, dating from the beginning of the twentieth century, were rehabilitated.[515]

Housing for Ordinary Dresdners

From the authorities' point of view, the city's chief problem was not the preservation of historic buildings, but the provision of housing for all those bombed out on the night of February 13–14. Before the bombardment, Dresden counted 222,000 residences. These existed in the Altstadt and its vicinity as well as in numerous suburbs—former villages—that had been annexed by the city. The residences served a population in 1939 of c. 630,000. By war's end sixty per cent of the residences had been fully destroyed; eighteen thousand had been heavily damaged, and eighty-one thousand lightly damaged. In other words, over half the city's usable shelter needed to be replaced in a wide swath that stretched from Friedrichstadt and Pieschen in the west to Prohlis and Niedersedlitz in the east and from Reick in the south to the Antonstadt in the north. And even though the city's population had declined to a little over 450,000, the shortage was severe.[516]

According to Max Seydewitz, who served as Saxon Minister-President from 1947 to 1952, the city had either repaired, reconstructed or newly built 99,000 residential units. A large residential construction program began in 1949 on the Grunaerstrasse in the Pirnaische neighborhood and then extended to the south city, and to the Plauen Valley. In the late 1950s, a completely new neighborhood, consisting of simple modernistic designs of reinforced concrete, grew up in Striesen.

During the next few decades, the Dresdner authorities continued to construct apartment buildings in the inner city and in the numerous outlying neighborhoods—altogether 60,000 new residences between 1967 and 1982. The program included two new towns: Prohlis in the southeast and Gorbitz in the southwest. The new structures invariably used prefabricated cement elements and were initially attractive to people wanting to escape crowded, deteriorating older housing. As late as 1977, only 25% of Dresden residences enjoyed central heating, and fewer than half (43%) could count on running hot water. After German reunification in 1990, almost all the prefabricated structures and most of the pre-war housing were improved and modernized.

The ongoing residential construction still had to be balanced with the rebuilding of famous landmarks and prestige objects within the city. The building of the Berlin Wall, in 1961, facilitated this balancing act by stopping the drain of brains and labor to the West. During this decade, East Germans experienced their own economic miracle. In city government, Gerhard Schill replaced Weidauer as mayor, and he presided over a decade of growth.[517]

A New Shopping Street

In addition to the Kulturpalast on the Altmarkt, the prominent project during this decade was the restoration of the Prager Strasse. This popular shopping street dated back to the mid-nineteenth century. Initially, it connected the Bohemian rail station to the old inner city, and the individual villas lining the street soon gave way to a variety of wall-to-wall structures. At the insistence of the original landowners, the street's width was limited to fourteen meters, a dimension that proved to be too narrow by the beginning of the twentieth century. When the city's main rail station replaced the old Bohemian one at the same site, the Pragerstrasse linked the station to the Altmarkt and to the arterial that extended all the way to Albertplatz.

The stretch between the station and the Altmarkt was lined with all kinds of commercial establishments. Toward the Altmarkt were department stores and cafés, toward the station were elegant hotels. One of the city's first movie theaters was located in the Prager Strasse, and Richter's avant-garde art gallery mounted *Die Brücke*'s first exhibition at a downtown address. At the beginning of the twentieth century, a printed guide described the street as "…the most glamorous [in the city] because of its art, jewelry, and fashion shops. Here, at every time of day, the elegant world of Dresden promenades. Here, one gazes at an array of luxurious stores; here a crowd of natives and strangers is on parade."

This rich mix disappeared in the bombing of February 13–14, and a bare tract of grass led from the main rail station to the Altmarkt for almost two decades after the war. The city, in conjunction with the national government, had decided not to rebuild any of the former, salvageable structures, to do away with the previous dimensions, and to create a "special realm of experience". Modeled on the Lijnbaan in Rotterdam and the fresh city of Brasilia, the new Prager Strasse's modern, cosmopolitan architecture symbolized the new Germany. The winning design of 1962 created a pedestrian zone that was four times the width of the old street. On the east side, the architects created a "residential array" of 614 small apartments with balconies that overlooked the street. Facing the apartment house on the west side were three large hotel buildings positioned at right angles to the street and connected by low-rise structures for shops. The residential building and the hotels were all twelve stories high.

Thus was the street transformed into a square. To further the illusion, great care was taken to plant whimsical fountains and statuary at strategic spots along the street's trajectory to break up the monotony of the straight line. A particular favorite of the Dresdners was the dandelion fountain that sprayed water into pools through spiky petals arranged on a sphere. The sides of the fountain acted as benches where tired shoppers rested, and young adults met their friends. Along one side of the square was an allée of red horse-chestnut trees. Architects, both East and West, considered the entire ensemble to be an exceptional example of the postwar style. At least one Munich architect considered it to be one of the best-designed municipal spaces of the twentieth century. It took a long time to fill out the Prager Square, and the original concept was never fully achieved. During the 1970s, the GDR placed a higher priority on building housing to satisfy its citizens' demands.[518]

Jewish Revival

Rebuilding the deserted city also meant reviving Dresden's Jewish community. The task of restoring the Jewish congregation fell to a small group of Holocaust survivors: Helmut Aris, Richard Lewinsohn and Leon Löwenkopf. Forty individuals joined this group, and its offices were located on the Bautzener Strasse in the Neustadt, a property that had belonged to the congregation before the war and returned to it during the Soviet occupation. At this early stage, there were several sources of help for Jews.

In September 1945, the new government promised financial welfare to the "Victims of Fascism". Jews turned to this source for old age and disability pensions, medical treatment, lodging, business spaces. At the same time, the Soviets decreed that any individual Jewish wealth or business confiscated by the Nazis would not be returned but would remain confiscated as the people's property. But Dresdners did not just count on the Soviets and the German Communists to help them out. They also, through an intermediary in Berlin, turned to the American Jewish Joint Distribution Committee. The JOINT responded by sending CARE packages to the congregation's leaders for distribution to its members.

Through this assistance, through their own resilience and through Jews arriving from elsewhere to work in the state bureaucracy or the Technical College, the Jewish population swelled to 200 by the end of the 1940s. The Dresden congregation became responsible for the Jews in the surrounding region, and it shared a rabbi with Jewish communities in the neighboring cities of Leipzig and Chemnitz. Signs of the congregation's recovery were the first post-war Bar Mitzva in 1948 and the establishment of a new synagogue next to the Jewish cemetery in the Johannstadt on property owned by the congregation. This house of worship imitated some of the features of the old Semper design, but it remained small and relatively humble throughout the life of the GDR. As a sign of reconciliation, the Saxon government contributed funds for the construction, and Mauersberger led the Kruzianer at the dedication ceremony in 1950.[519]

Even as Dresden Jews celebrated the completion of their new building, storm clouds gathered around them. The Soviet Union had originally supported the creation of the state of Israel and even supplied it with arms during the first Arab-Israeli conflict. It hoped that the large numbers of socialist and Communist Jews would propel the new state into the Soviet orbit. This hope was soon dashed, and the Soviet Union found itself on the defensive, even within its own political sphere.

Josef Stalin, still the paranoid leader of the Soviet bloc, began to fear the influence of Communist nationalists in the various satellite states. In 1949, the Hungarian László Rajk was charged as a Titoist spy—working for the West in opposition to Soviet domination—and executed. In 1952, Rudolf Slánský, the Jewish General Secretary of the Czechoslovak Communist Party, was also charged with Trotskyite Titoism, once again opposition to Soviet Stalinism. He too was executed. In each of these cases, their co-defendants were Jewish, and one of these confessed to spying for the United States. The propaganda campaign that accompanied these trials in the Eastern bloc's press reverberated with anti-Semitic overtones. In East Germany, Paul Merker, a Communist who had spent the war in Mexico, not in the Soviet Union, and harbored strong sympathies for East German Jews, had been suspected of disloyalty for several years and had been deprived of his privileged positions within the SED. During the Slánský trial, he was charged with spying for the United States and with supporting the restitution of Jewish property.

Thus were combined the elements of anti-Titoism, anti-Americanism, and anti-Semitism. The political climate became overtly anti-Semitic. People were publicly labeled as cosmopolitans—a code word for Jewish westerners—as agents of American Jewish finance, as Zionist spies. Denunciations of Jews as disloyal to the regime occurred in Dresden as well as other places. Jews lost their jobs, were expelled from the SED, and were arrested. Leon Löwenkopf, long an advocate of the state's making restitution for Jewish property confiscated by the Nazis, was charged with embezzling funds as the director of the State Bank. After sitting in jail for three months, he was released and rehabilitated in 1950. The anti-Semitism grew more intense as fabricated reports of a Jewish doctors' plot to kill Stalin and other Soviet leaders circulated in 1953. In that year, Löwenkopf and most of the synagogue's executive committee fled to West Germany. During this period the congregation lost thirty per cent of its members. Only Stalin's death in March 1953 ended this overt anti-Semitism.[520]

For many years afterward, Dresden's Jewish community, like many others in the GDR, was figuratively paralyzed. The congregation stayed alive only with financial help from the state. The potentially positive development that followed the discrimination of the early 1950s was the foundation of the East German Association of Jewish Communities, with its headquarters in Dresden. Helmut Aris, a native Dresdner and successor to Löwenkopf as chair of the congregation, helped to establish this group. He became its president from 1962 until his death in 1987. According to one chronicler of Jewish life in the GDR, the association was a captive of the regime and bore no relation to the reality of Jewish life. Congregations stayed small, religious observance lackluster, and Jewish youth agnostic. In Dresden, only sixty-one Jews remained in the congregation when the GDR ended.[521]

Despite the stagnation, there were some signs of Jewish self-confidence and tolerance on the part of city government. In 1968, a ceremony in the

Hygiene Museum memorialized the Crystal Night of thirty years past. When the GDR established closer relations with West Germany after 1972, the regime encouraged general remembrances of Crystal Night. In Dresden, a plaque placed close to the old site of the Semper Synagogue, commemorated the six million Jews killed during the Third Reich.

With the restlessness of the 1980s came a greater relaxation of Jewish life. East German Jews could now travel abroad. Helmut Eschwege, Zionist, historian of Jewish culture and member of the congregation, used this opportunity to visit Israel. The GDR now permitted West German rabbis to minister to Jewish congregations. In 1982, Eschwege and the Protestant pastor Siegfried Reimann organized a study group, called "Encounters with Jews", with the goal of creating a dialogue between Christians and Jews. These "dialogues", held in the Annenkirche on weekends, took the form of lectures about Jewish history, religion, and art. Given by internationally known figures, they attracted sizable audiences.

On 9 November 1988, a host of activities took place throughout the GDR calling attention to the Crystal Night pogrom. In Dresden's city churches, the local study group mounted an exhibition of "Jews in Saxony. Their Lives and Sorrows". The group also affixed a memorial plaque in the Kreuzkirche. At this time, the city's censored press, which published the lectures held in the Annenkirche, carried a series of historical articles about Dresden's Jews. The year before, an extensive investigation had led to the trial and conviction of Henry Schmidt, the director of Jewish Affairs at the Gestapo headquarters in Dresden during World War II. Since the end of the war, he had lived under an assumed name in the neighboring state of Thuringia. For crimes against humanity, he was sentenced to life imprisonment. Despite this enlightened atmosphere, an active, contemporary member of the congregation complained that anti-Semitism in Dresden continued to exist.[522]

XVI. Dresden's Post-war Economy: Herald of the Future

Old Business

After the wave of dismantling by the Soviet occupiers and the nationalizations that accompanied the founding of the East German state, the people's enterprises or VEBs, in size and scope, resembled the old private firms that had contributed to the city's industrialization. Only in the 1960s did this pattern begin to change.

Relying on the stellar, pre-war reputation of German cameras around the world, the VEB Zeiss-Ikon resumed the export of its 35 mm single lens reflex (SLR) apparatus. This machine became known as the Praktika after court cases reserved the use of the Zeiss name to the West German firm. For more than a decade, the VEB Zeiss-Ikon competed with almost a score of other Dresden companies—all VEBs. In the 1960s, the SED state determined that technological innovation and international competition necessitated a merger of all camera manufacturers into the VEB Kamera and Kinowerke Dresden. This Kombinat (corporation) evolved into Pentacon in 1964 and came to employ almost 9000 workers. Throughout the life of the GDR, Pentacon's exports earned hard currency on the world market, including dollars from J. C. Penney. Collectors still prize its products. They may be unaware that the cases for their Praktika cameras were produced, under adverse conditions, by political prisoners at the Cottbus Central Prison, a little over eighty-four miles northeast of Dresden.[523]

Another traditional industry in Dresden was bottling and packaging of all kinds. The best-known corporation was Nagema. The core of this firm was the old Gäbel Machine Factory that was nationalized right after the war. Already in 1948, it was a combination of firms located in the Dresden region and in towns to the north and west. The variety of its functions was astounding.

Nagema made machines for packing cigarettes and caramels, conching machines for chocolate, packing machines for margarine, also for flour and rice. It made roasting and baking appliances for camping and equipment for large kitchens and bakeries. Since the Soviets had taken the firm's equipment as war reparations, the business was forced to buy more sophisticated, new machines. This sophistication led East Germany, Dresden included, to become the packaging center of Eastern Europe.

During the 1960s, Nagema began to cooperate with Dresden's Technical College. The goal was to stimulate both exports and the home market. The cooperation yielded, *inter alia,* a process for making egg-white products, and another for preserving mustard, mayonnaise, and catsup. The firm particularly wanted to satisfy super-market shoppers. Because Nagema depended on engineers, it decided in 1979 to build a research center on the campus of the college, financed out of its own budget and not directed by the central planning agency. The firm's innovations led it to compete successfully in some sectors on the world market, even as far away as the United States.[524]

Another sector that benefited from the assistance of Dresden's Technical College was the electrical machine industry. Well-established before World War I, it had been sucked into armaments manufacture during World War II. After the Soviets occupied Dresden, they lost little time in dismantling the electrical machine factories and carting off their equipment to the Soviet Union. Private firms were quickly nationalized. Koch und Sterzel was transformed into the VEB Transformatoren-und Röntgenwerk Hermann Matern.

Eventually, the regime added factories from Saxon and Thuringian towns to the Dresden firm. Products included elevators, greenhouses, pacemakers, measuring transformers and other instruments. In the early period of the GDR, the company acquired new accommodations that are now listed on the city's register of historic buildings. Located in an industrial park in Kaditz, "monumental" cement pillars rise from the foundation to an entablature that supports a slightly pitched roof of steel. Windows stretch from pillar to pillar and are surrounded by cement frames in different colors. Inside are assembly halls divided by "monolithic" supports of reinforced concrete. The building is truly striking and visible from the banks of the Elbe. During the life of the GDR, this People's Workshop was the largest employer in Dresden.[525]

The second electrical machine building business in Dresden was the Saxon Works. Historically, the firm built large electric motors and generators. In 1920, it acquired the Royal Fireworks Laboratory in Radeberg and began to produce transformers of all kinds as well as consumer appliances such as vacuum cleaners and refrigerators. Like most Dresden industries, the Saxon Works joined the armaments industry during the 1930s and 1940s; the Radeberg works was transformed into a work camp for prisoners of war. Once the war ended, the Soviet occupiers completely dismantled the Radeberg plant and assigned it the job of making radios and televisions. At the end of the 1950s, it was completely separated from the Saxon Works.

The Dresden plant was also dismantled by the Soviets in 1946 and consigned to making consumer goods like electric cooking pots, refrigerators and electric saws. As a corporation under Soviet ownership, its primary market was the Soviet Union. After the strike of 1953, the Soviets returned the ownership of the company to the East German government, and the Saxon Works resumed the manufacture of motors and generators. It eventually became the only fabricator of medium-sized and large electric machinery within the GDR.[526]

One ambitious undertaking of the East German regime originally ended in failure but eventually produced a permanent business for Dresden. When the GDR joined the East European Warsaw Pact in 1955, a manufactory for civilian aircraft was located in Dresden on the site of the former Luftwaffe training school. Despite superior engineering, the planes it produced did not find a market either in the Soviet Union or in the bloc of Eastern European countries, and the enterprise folded in 1961.

Its replacement was the VEB Aerodrome that repaired civilian and military aircraft. As German reunification loomed, the company, already in November 1989, seized the initiative in negotiating an agreement with the Airbus Group. The agreement projected Dresden as an aeronautic hub. In 1991, the company changed its name to the Elbe Aerodrome Workshops, Inc. In the early 1990s, it became the sole maker of fiber-reinforced furnishings for Airbus and later began converting passenger planes into freighters, its primary contemporary business. In 2000, Airbus acquired the Dresden firm, and it maintains aircraft for the corporation.[527]

Dresden Enters the Digital Age

There is no development in Dresden under the SED regime that was more portentous for the future than that of automated computing. Already in the 1950s, Carl Zeiss Jena, the East German company, had developed at least two computer prototypes. Simultaneously, as East German economic planners became aware of the electronics future, they began incorporating into the state's official economic plans monies to develop the industry. At the beginning of the 1960s, the GDR government moved the Zeiss efforts to Dresden, creating a Central Institute for Automation.

At this time, the VEB Electronic Calculating Machines in Karl-Marx-Stadt, now Chemnitz, was developing the first transistorized and programmable digital machines. By 1965, this firm achieved the first Robotron computer allowing for electronic data processing. In 1969, in the wake of a restructuring of the GDR's economy, a new Corporation Robotron was projected for Dresden. Three years later, its headquarters moved into a new, centrally located structure on Dresden's Pirnaischer Platz. A large complex for the firm was also constructed in Dresden-Gruna, several miles to the east.

The Robotron Corporation comprised twenty-one different firms with, ultimately, a work force of 68,000. Included were not only establishments in the Dresden region but those as far afield as Leipzig and Erfurt. Robotron sold not only computers, but also operating systems, software and printers. Added to these new-fashioned products were older ones like typewriters, radios, televisions and measuring instruments. Its markets ranged from business firms throughout the GDR, the Eastern bloc, West Germany and to the United States, and it developed electronic military systems for the Warsaw Pact.

Robotron helped to catapult the GDR to a model of information technology within Eastern Europe. But its membership in that organization's unified system meant that deficiencies in the quality of other states' products could impede East German progress. East German engineers knew their informatics industry limped behind the West. The State Security Agency blamed the GDR's own scientists for this lag, and in 1982 it forced the resignation of Robotron's CEO. The last SED leader of the GDR, Hans Modrow, observed that the real problem was East Germany's isolation from the world market.[528]

Microelectronics

When Robotron moved to central Dresden in 1972, the city was already a center for microelectronics, the field that introduced a revolution in electronic development. A start had been made at the Technical College at the beginning of the twentieth century, when low voltage technology had been pursued in connection with railroad telegraphy and electrical machine building. Engineers employed by the railroad, by Koch und Sterzel, and by the Saxon Works had all graduated from the Technical College. During World War II, as we have seen, the college's professors had developed the steering mechanisms for long-range rockets. Beginning in 1950, the college established a collection of institutes related to electronic instruments and contributed heavily to the GDR's computer industry.

In exploring the development of the computer/electronics industry in Dresden, it is impossible to forget that the city and state operated at a disadvantage. The Soviet occupation forces shipped off to the Soviet Union all the sophisticated scientific instruments and equipment they could find, and for ten years, 1945–1955, prominent East German scientists were transferred to institutes in the Soviet Union working on the atomic bomb and other projects. When they returned in 1955, they assumed professorships in universities and founded research institutes.

In 1961, Werner Hartmann, a professor for Nuclear Physics at the Technical College, founded the institute that eventually became the Dresden Research Center for Microelectronics. In time, Hartmann's institute was recognized as a leader in electronics research throughout the Soviet bloc. In 1988, the research center developed the first one-megabyte memory chip in the GDR, but Hartmann himself was no longer associated with his creation. The Ministry of State Security had dismissed him as the center's director more than ten years before. Because of his critical attitude toward the GDR, he was relegated to a post as staff scientist at a trace metals firm in Freiberg, south of Dresden.[529]

After the creation of the GDR, its scientists had access to Western scientific literature, but eventually the state's shortage of hard currency meant that Western scientific literature was rationed. At the same time, too much consultation of Western periodicals and books was frowned upon by the state. Selected scientists could travel to Western countries for conferences and for visiting professorships, but they were subjected to thorough debriefings when they returned. They also had difficulty acquiring the electronic technology required for their research.

The U.S.S.R had no interest in furthering high technology in the German Democratic Republic, and NATO countries refused to export to any Eastern bloc state, including the GDR, any items related to the alliance's military security, including computing technology. Here, the East German Ministry for State Security was vital for the development of the GDR's computer industry. Sometimes its agents smuggled Western equipment into the GDR so that engineers could pirate the technology. If it was not possible to purchase high technology through non-NATO states, the Stasi resorted to simple spying.

In 1983, the physicist Alfred Zehe, professor at what was now the Technical University, got caught up in a "sting operation" conducted by the FBI. Agents in the East German embassy in Washington, D. C. bought sonar technology information generated by the U. S. Navy. The GDR agents asked Zehe, then a visiting professor in Puebla, Mexico to interpret the documents, which proved to contain outdated knowledge. On the strength of this activity, Zehe was arrested while attending a scientific conference in the United States, was tried and convicted of espionage and sentenced to eight years in prison. He was set free under the terms of a prisoner exchange in 1985.

Zehe's case illustrates yet another occupational hazard of East German scientists. Many were involved in research for the East German army and the Warsaw Pact. In such cases, they could be physically isolated from their colleagues in the same department, so that no military secrets could leak out. For a variety of reasons, they were frequently subjected either to investigations by the State Security Service or to "invitations" to become unofficial informers on their colleagues. Many university professors wanted to avoid participation in military projects, but they were often "forced" to do so. In order to practice the natural sciences, including electronics, in the GDR, individuals truly had to love their subjects. Scientists in Dresden's (and East German) universities, institutes and industries soldiered on despite their relative isolation. Even though the GDR was five to eight years behind developments in the West, their efforts provided the knowledge and the skills necessary for the future.[530]

The Technical College/University

Throughout the history of the GDR, the Technical College participated in the development of the computer industry. Its main contributions were the results of its scientific research and its preparation of engineers in all technical fields. Indeed, it is hard to envision the growth of Robotron or the Center for Microelectronics without the training that their staffs received at the Technical College. Then and now, the Technical College—elevated to university status—defines Dresden as one face of Elbflorence: the visage engaged in training the labor force of a burgeoning high-tech industry.[531]

The bombings of 1945 did extensive damage to the college's campus, and it was the last German institution of higher learning to reopen in fall 1946. The 450 students who showed up for the winter semester worked in laboratories almost completely denuded of equipment by the Soviet occupiers. Some of the college's leading scientists had been drafted to work in the U. S. S. R. The college's library, was non-existent. Its subject catalog had been destroyed, and holdings evacuated during the war had to be reclaimed and rehoused. The library's circulation department did not reopen until April 1947. Almost a decade passed before the complete catalog and the library's valuable collection of patent specifications were once again available.

German anti-Fascists and the Soviet Union heavily controlled which professors returned to teaching. Two-thirds of the former professoriate did not reappear in post-war classrooms. The lack of instructional staff and the concern for ideological conformity also dictated which subjects would be taught. There was only one lecture hall available for three faculties, and the first winter of operation was so cold that professors held classes in their heated homes; the college's buildings were frigid. Three years after the war, both professors and students were still helping to clear away the rubble left by the bombing. Only by 1949 had the college restored most of its damaged buildings. Thereafter it expanded both its physical facilities and its curriculum.[532]

Meanwhile it began to recruit a group of students that had previously barely considered higher education. Preparatory classes for academically under-prepared, working-class youth were established in various localities, and upon the reopening of the college in 1946, over one hundred enrolled. Two years later, the first dormitory for a preparatory school opened its doors. A formal Workers' and Peasants' Faculty was established in 1949. Recruitment of students for this curriculum occurred in schools and factories throughout the state. Its appearance changed the college's political spectrum markedly.

The students who matriculated immediately after the college's post-war reopening were not very friendly toward the SED. In elections to the Student

Council in 1947, only one-third of the winning representatives belonged to the SED. In order to improve this situation, the authorities changed the rules. In addition to the regularly registered students, those in the preparatory classes were also allowed to vote. In 1948, therefore, SED members gained nine out of the fifteen seats available on the Students' Council. In that year, the SED's youth organization, the FDJ (Free German Youth), also established a college branch. It principally operated through dormitory committees to ensure support for the regime. Students began to be arrested for participation in so-called "illegal" groups and for boycotts of political events. By 1952, the elected Student Council had ceased to exist, and its functions passed to the FDJ.[533]

In 1953, a consultant's study of the college claimed that neither professors nor students demonstrated the desired appreciation of the Soviet Union's achievements in science and technology. Nor did they show the proper interest in Marxist-Leninist issues. In an attempt to achieve more ideological purity, college authorities tried to dissuade students from traveling to West Germany, still possible in the 1950s. This dissuasion did not go down well with the students, and in 1957, some of them protested the lack of travel freedom. They were promptly condemned as illegal demonstrators. In 1958, a small group of dissidents formed a National Communist Students' League whose program demanded freedom of speech and assembly as well as a change in economic policy. The members all ended up in prison, charged and convicted of trying to overthrow the government.

It's difficult to know how many students finally fled to West Germany before the building of the Wall. One history of the college claims a peak of student emigration in 1955–6. This pattern conforms with police figures reporting total emigration from Dresden of one to two per cent of the population between 1955 and 1957. The latter figures might contain some students from the college. Those fleeing west from towns outside the Dresden region might have been counted in their home territories.[534]

In any case, throughout the 1950s, the Technical College was expected to contribute to the reconstruction of the city and the state. And it did so. Students and professors alike were drafted as volunteers to bring in the harvest. They also participated in the voluntary National Reconstruction Action that salvaged stones from the rubble of Dresden's ruins. During their vacations, students not only worked on farms, but in the GDR's factories. The various academic departments helped with reconstruction by sharing technical and scientific information. The GDR's economy also benefited from the college's research. Courses of study concentrated on training engineers, and by 1961, over 10,000 students were matriculating annually. The fields of aeronautics, nuclear technology, mechanical and electrical engineering were especially attractive.

The Technical College was very much a part of the city's civic life. In June 1953, the celebration of the Technical Institute's 125th anniversary involved the whole town. There was a procession from the Brühl Terrace to the State Theater, a speech by the vice premier of the GDR, a performance of Beethoven's *Fidelio*. Dresden's Rathaus hosted an exhibition of the college's history. On the last two days of the celebration, there were sporting events and performances by the college's cultural club. The festivities emphasized the link between town and gown.

Periodically, the college showcased the city by hosting international conferences of scholars from around the world. Even though it was mostly scientists and engineers from the Soviet bloc who attended, hundreds of people became acquainted with Dresden in this way. For a short time the college also resumed a Sunday lecture series for the public in cooperation with the URANIA Association, dedicated to popularizing scientific knowledge, that operated in several East German cities.[535]

The college's remarkable building program testifies to its post-war recovery and growth. In the ten years preceding 1961, it added fifteen new buildings, including those at the Chemical Institute in Pirna and the Forestry Institute in Tharandt, to the southeast and south respectively. Over 17,000 students matriculated in that year, including those taking correspondence courses. Finally, the GDR transformed the Technical College into a genuine university (TU) that offered degrees in the liberal arts as well as scientific/engineering studies. The library now also became the central technical library of the East German state.[536]

In the period that followed, the Technical University's cooperation with industrial enterprises intensified. Relationships developed with universities in the West, notably with Great Britain, France, Switzerland and Sweden. As physical expansion occurred, the university acquired and remodeled the old home of the Saxon Higher Regional Court on Münchnerplatz, where so many opponents of the Nazi regime and the Soviet occupation had been tried, incarcerated, and executed. By the late 1970s, the university occupied over 600 acres, including the Forestry School in Tharandt.

Its offerings had also branched out to continuing education courses for those in industry and the professions. Despite increasing pressure from the regime for political conformity from both professors and students, at least one historian maintains that the Technical University managed to preserve significant political independence due to its vital contribution to the economy and army of the GDR.[537]

Education as Economic Magnet

The TU was not the only institution of higher learning in Dresden. To aid in the training of engineers, the regime established the Dresdner Academy for Transportation Systems. To handle the training of teachers, it divorced the old Pedagogical Faculty from the college in 1953 and set up a separate teacher-training establishment. After reunification, these were brought back under the umbrella of the Technical University.[538]

Musical instruction has existed in Dresden for a long time. Not only did the Kreuzschule develop a reputation for training male voices, but the Royal, later the State, orchestra school trained instrumentalists. To these establishments was added, in 1856, a private music school. After an initial period of struggle, it began calling itself a conservatory. During the Third Reich, the Dresden city government assumed control of the conservatory and combined it first with the State Orchestra school and then with the Mary Wigman Dance School. This conservatory's home was completely destroyed in the bombing of 1945. When it reopened in 1946, it became the Academy of Music and Theater and, at the end of the 1950s, was renamed the Carl Maria von Weber Music Academy. It continues to thrive and to maintain close associations with the State Orchestra and the Dresdner Philharmonic.[539]

No exploration of Dresden's institutions of higher learning would be complete without attention to the oldest: the Academy of Art. The bombing of 1945 damaged the distinctive Lipsius Building—the lemon reamer—on the Brühl Terrace. That structure remained in ruins for decades. The academy, when it reopened in 1946, began operations at the School of Applied Arts in the Guntzstrasse. When the first post-war director, Hans Grundig, resigned in 1948, the two schools combined into the Academy of Fine Arts under the leadership of architect and urban planner, Mart Stam.

Stam, heavily influenced by the Bauhaus where he once taught, believed that art should serve architecture. His modernistic ideas for rebuilding Dresden would have eliminated most of the city's landmarks and were rejected by the citizenry, including staunch Communist mayor Weidauer. When Stam proposed to remove the master classes in painting from the academy's course of study, the academy's painters, including Communist Lea Grundig, severely protested. In 1950, he left Dresden for Berlin. Thereafter, the academy's directors conformed to the prevailing artistic and ideological taste.[540]

Of critical importance, both for the city and for the GDR, was the founding in 1954 of the Carl-Gustav-Carus Academy for the training of doctors and other medical personnel. The flight of physicians to the West had led, by the beginning of the 1950s, to shortages that motivated the GDR's government to establish four new medical academies; Dresden initially did not figure as a suggested location. To remedy this oversight, doctors at the municipal hospital in the Johannstadt, working in concert with the city government, undertook to educate the central government in Berlin. They emphasized Dresden's tradition of training doctors, and they gathered materials supporting the city as an appropriate site for a new academy. In addition, they traveled to Berlin to urge the government to substitute Dresden for one of the initially chosen locations.

Their action was successful, and in 1954 the Carl-Gustav-Carus Academy officially opened its doors. Legally, the academy operated like a university, and its course of study emphasized clinical training. Research was not neglected; in 1959 the academy instituted a scholarly periodical to showcase the work of its staff. The Johannstadt's municipal hospital was the original partner of the academy. Eventually it acquired partnerships with independent Dresden institutes of anesthesia, intensive therapy, pharmacology as well as with the Technical University and with Manfred von Ardenne's private research institute at the Weisser Hirsch.

The foundation of the academy, in Dresden and in other cities, never completely resolved the issue of physicians' flight to the West. In the period after the establishment of the Berlin Wall, members of the academy's staff increasingly applied for permission to leave the GDR. There were multiple reasons for dissatisfaction. After 1963, the regime required university professors—in this case the medical faculty—to take courses in Marxism-Leninism at the Technical University. An historian of the academy complains that doctors wasted hundreds of hours subjected to this ideological exercise. At the same time, members of the SED were favored for appointments and promotions. Doctors had to put up with shortages of equipment and medicines, and they resented their isolation from the international medical community.[541]

The institution that helped to preserve this isolation was the Military Academy of the GDR's People's Army, located in Dresden between 1956 and 1990. As a full-fledged university with the ability to grant higher degrees, it occupied the former buildings of the Wehrmacht's Air Force Command Division IV in Strehlen. After reunification, the Federal Republic's armed forces moved in and continue to use the space today.[542]

Dresden's Unicorn

Contributing to the city's economy and related both to the Technical College/University and to the Carus Medical Academy was the Research Institute von Ardenne, the largest private employer among the Warsaw Pact countries. Its founder, director, and honorary professor at the Technical College/University, the Baron Manfred von Ardenne, was already a unique individual before World War II. Born and raised in Hamburg and Berlin, he established himself as a practitioner of applied physics as a teen-ager, leaving high school without a diploma and preferring informal internships with established entrepreneurial engineers instead of a university education. As a twenty-one-year-old, he founded his own research laboratory and pursued developments in radio and television on the one hand and in electron physics on the other, garnering numerous patents useful in German business. He also entered into a close relationship with the director of the German post office that subsidized the laboratory's research.

Ardenne's work with measuring devices for the post office led directly to an association with military intelligence and indirectly to involvement with the German pursuit of an atomic bomb. These contacts made him an attractive recruit for the Soviet Union and, almost immediately after the cessation of World War II's hostilities, Ardenne came to an agreement with the military occupation whereby he would engage in a scholarly cooperation with the Soviet Union in return for the transfer of his entire laboratory directly to a site of his choice. He and his family left Berlin on 21 May 1945. From 1945 until 1955, Ardenne, working from the Black Sea coast of the Georgian Soviet Republic near the city of Sukhumi, contributed to the Soviet Union's development of its thermonuclear bombs.

As his usefulness to the Soviets declined, Ardenne prepared to return to East Germany. He charged his brother-in-law with finding and acquiring properties suitable for a laboratory and a home in Dresden. Once they were found, efforts moved on to appointing suitable scientific staff and locating homes for them. The Soviets aided all these efforts, most particularly persuading the Dresden city government to countenance a privately run research facility within its boundaries. Given these advance preparations, the move of the Research Institute von Ardenne, as it came to be called, occurred easily in March 1955.

No grass grew under Ardenne's feet. Throughout the life of the GDR, the institute sold its discoveries and technological innovations to the nationalized East German industries. These included a multi-chamber electron beam furnace for the refinement of reactive and refractory metals, installations for evaporation coating with thin films, radio polymerization of synthetic materials and, for agriculture, radio sterilization of crop seeds. One new device that appeared already in 1957 was the ingestible transmitter for measuring pressure and pH values in the human gastrointestinal tract.

This development previewed the medical technology that became a primary focus of the institute. One of the most significant technologies was the heart-lung machine used in the GDR's heart centers. Another was the multi-step oxygen therapy attractive in both East and West Germany as well as in Austria and Switzerland. This technique is still in use today. In the early 1970s, the institute's innovations proved so useful to the GDR, that it began regularly to receive state subsidies.

Ardenne's contribution to the GDR resided not only in his technical contributions to industry but also in his civic activities. In the early 1960s, he became president of the Cultural League that served as the umbrella organization for all local cultural activities in the GDR. Concurrently, he became a delegate to the People's Assembly that functioned as East Germany's legislature. According to his official biographer, Ardenne became an "institution" that could help Dresdners solve their problems with the state's authorities. He also kept up contacts with influential people in West Germany.

In 1984, Kurt Körber, Hamburg industrialist and philanthropist, invited Ardenne to attend, in Dresden, a meeting of the Bergedorfer Round Table, an organization that hosts free-wheeling discussions of German, European, and global issues by relevant experts and politicians. That contact led to a friendship between the two men, and Körber later financed the production and distribution of an instrument necessary for Ardenne's multi-step oxygen therapy. The two men had a lot in common. Both were inventors of technology; both were entrepreneurial; Dresden and Hamburg figured prominently in both their lives. Up until the end of World War II, Körber had been technical director for Dresden's Universelle Works, makers of machines for manufacturing cigarettes. Both men knew how to charm politicians into supporting their efforts. And both fostered the establishment of a sister-city relationship between Dresden and Hamburg, a tie that continues to exist.[543]

In the second half of the twentieth century, as Dresden lived out its life in the GDR, the twin facets of its personality—art and industry—became more closely linked. While the city's cultural and scholarly institutions supplied artisans and technicians who nourished both body and spirit, its workshops, large and small, produced commodities needed and coveted by countries in Europe's eastern bloc and even further afield. Because the city's geography prevented it from easily receiving West German radio and television, it once again gained a reputation for backwardness—derided by other East Germans as the "valley of the clueless" (*Tal der Ahnungslosen)*. Dresden nevertheless maintained, in both cultural and economic spheres, its contacts with the world beyond the valley, a world that soon restored the city to its former prominence.

XVII. On the Way to Revolution

The Local Leadership Changes

In 1973, a major change in the Dresden party leadership occurred. The conformist Werner Krolikowski resigned as SED Party Secretary—or chief—of the Dresden District; Hans Modrow took his place. Within the East German party, Modrow was best known for his willingness to criticize the party leadership in Berlin. For the duration of the SED regime, Modrow could rise no higher in the party hierarchy than district secretary, a position that mediated between the central and the local governmental levels.

Modrow has claimed that the Dresdners' rejection of the SED leadership in Berlin was greater than anywhere else in the GDR. As a result, he said, the central government treated Dresdners like step-children. He thus kept as much distance between Dresden and Berlin as he could, but he and the Dresdners could not escape completely the tight control of the East German state. The last SED mayor of Dresden, Wolfgang Berghofer, has testified that Modrow always had the city's best interests at heart and that he circumvented the central leadership as best he could whenever it was necessary to solve a problem.[544]

When Modrow arrived in Dresden, he found in his office a photograph of the model previously developed as the city's plan for the future—the one that many Dresdners considered to be destructive. After a year, he decided that the premises of the model were wrong. Historic Dresden had to be the central idea behind a plan for the future. He had the photograph removed.

After discussion with the city's mayor at the time, Gerhard Schill, the historic preservationist Hans Nadler, and with his own staff, Modrow sanctioned a plan for resuming the reconstruction of historic buildings. First on the list was the Semper Opera, to be rebuilt in its nineteenth-century form with an annex to the west that would contain all the amenities that a twentieth-century theater needed. That was an easy choice; Modrow's predecessor had already agreed to the opera's reconstruction, and the West German government had promised a donation of thirty million marks.

It took a while to execute the whole plan. As the process of rebuilding began in 1976, Dresdners held a Construction Workers' Rally. The State Opera's chorus sang; soloists from the State Orchestra serenaded the public. Gunther Emmerlich, a State Opera singer known for his renditions of tunes from American musicals, was master of ceremonies and soloist. The entire celebration took place in the weed-studded ruins of the old building. Once the weeds were removed and the rubble cleared, the cornerstone for the new Semper Opera was laid in 1977. At that time and in the following year, there were two more celebrations for the construction workers, and then they got on with the job.

The reconstruction took nine years altogether, and finally on 13 February 1985, the Semper Opera was officially ready for song. This day marked the fortieth anniversary of the firestorm, and the city decided to hold a large rally both to commemorate the destruction and to celebrate the renewal. The GDR arranged for television coverage world-wide. Despite the bitter cold, a large crowd gathered on the Theaterplatz. Erich Honecker, leader of state and SED, traveled south from Berlin and spoke of the "torch" that Germany had thrown at the world, only to have it boomerang. Helmut Schmidt, the former West German Chancellor whose government had helped to finance the reconstruction, also attended. That evening, Gunther Emmerlich sang the title role in Carl Maria von Weber's *Freischütz*. The Semper Opera's forty-year silence had ended.

Emmerlich's wife, Anna-Kathrein, experienced the opening in the fourth balcony. She recalled that the State Orchestra struck up the melody of the GDR's anthem, and she so much wanted to sing. For her, the text was doubly meaningful: "Risen up from ruins: Devoted to the future; Let us serve you for the best; one Germany, our Fatherland." At that time, she says, she couldn't even imagine a united Germany. After opening night, the house was sold out for every performance. People came mostly, Emmerlich said, to view the reconstruction. The ensemble sometimes felt that their singing distracted the audience from the architecture.[545]

As the Semper Opera progressed toward completion, Modrow continued to confront the two dilemmas of post-war Dresden: how to rebuild the historic inner city while simultaneously easing the housing shortage. There was only so much money. The rebuilding of the Blockhaus, the eighteenth-century guard-house at the north end of the Augustus Bridge, provides an example of how Modrow circumvented the state's regulations to address a problem.

Once the state had approved the monies for the erection of a number of modern apartment houses in the area, it wanted to raze the Blockhaus and build a neighborhood bar and restaurant, establishments that had served the pre-war residents. It claimed that the state's construction equipment was not designed to work with historic structures. Undeterred, Modrow negotiated a deal with the state railways' district office. He would make a group of the new apartments available to railway employees if he could use the railways' more differentiated equipment to rehabilitate the Blockhaus. His justification was that the Blockhaus would provide a home for the restaurant that the state desired. Once restored, the building became a clubhouse for the German-Soviet Friendship society. The GDR state deemed the whole operation to be illegal but, as Modrow had foreseen, it would not raze a completely new structure.[546]

Almost simultaneously, the issue of the last Baroque structure in the Grosse Meissner Strasse arose. Recall that the ruins of most old buildings in this street had been cleared away by 1950. There was one that remained, and at the beginning of the 1980s, it was threatened. At the beginning of the decade, Erich Honecker visited Japan and sought a construction project to offer Japanese businessmen. GDR planners finally settled on a new hotel for Dresden at the site of the remaining historic building. Although Modrow, along with the citizens of Dresden, wanted to restore the building, the Japanese construction firm, Kajima, did not want to pay for restoring and incorporating it into a modern hotel.

Checkmated, it looked as if Dresden would have to be content with saving whatever historic decorations were still intact and incorporating them into a new structure. The district's historic preservation office persisted in delaying the final destruction by finding ever new salvageable fragments. The mayor procrastinated in issuing the demolition permit. Finally, the stage and screen actress, Anna Katrin Bürger, wrote to Honecker asking him to support the desires of the Dresdners. Her plea succeeded. The Japanese built the modern Hotel Bellevue, and the East German state paid for the reconstruction and incorporation of the old structure into the new building. The hotel opened in 1985.[547]

As plans were firmed up for televising the rally that accompanied the opening of the Semper Opera, authorities noticed that the old royal palace, directly opposite the theater and still in ruins overgrown with weeds, would be visible to any camera revolving around the Theaterplatz. To avoid the embarrassment of revealing this forty-year-old ruin in the inner city, scaffolding was placed all around the palace, creating the appearance of another ambitious building site.

The original post-war plans had foreseen the reconstruction of the palace, but it was not a high priority. Two years after the completion of the Semper Opera, Modrow tried to persuade Honecker and the director of the State Planning Office to make the palace's reconstruction an immediate project. He argued that the specialized equipment used to rebuild the opera should not be allowed to deteriorate. Honecker responded by emphasizing the importance of easing the housing shortage and could not be otherwise persuaded. That meant that the Dresden government continued to work on the palace slowly, without any extra funds, and this job remained unfinished right up until the end of the GDR.[548]

Discontent

Even as Dresdners celebrated the restoration of favored historic structures on both sides of the Elbe, dissatisfaction with the East German regime intensified. Early in the GDR's history, the secret police had steadily kept those known to oppose the regime under surveillance. This watchful eye had discouraged the formation of permanent secular clubs and organizations. Thus, it was primarily the churches that established and maintained civic networks. Already in 1962, they had achieved the introduction of a program called Construction Soldiers (*Bausoldaten*) for conscientious objectors to serving in the East German army. In Dresden, the Lutheran parishes of the Lukas, Resurrection and Zion churches established contacts with the Russian Orthodox Church in 1961. Vatican Council II, with its promise of ecumenism, led Protestant and Catholic parishes to cooperate with one another.

It took almost a decade after the building of the Wall for Protestants to sever their organizational ties to their co-religionists in West Germany, and the financial and personal ties never dissolved. But the formation of the League of Protestant Churches in the GDR and its resolve to work constructively with the atheistic regime facilitated the churches' new freedom. In 1970, the

Ecumenical Study Days of Academic Pastors met in the Annenkirche and continued every year thereafter.

The churches led the peace movement that ran parallel to that in West Germany. Already in 1978, when the GDR introduced military instruction into the common schools' curriculum, it was the Evangelical Student Community that first objected. When one young man refused to attend the classes, his friends wore stickers outlined in red that depicted a tank covered by a great big X.[549]

In 1980, Pastor Christoph Wonneberg and the Peace Circle at Dresden's Weinberg Church recommended a social peace program as an alternative to serving in the army or working as a Construction Soldier. Even though the Saxon Synod did not support this initiative, the idea caught on among youth. In 1980, the Saxon Synod's Youth Pastor, Harald Bretschneider, devised a felt patch to be worn on coats, jackets, sweaters and shirts. The patch bore the outline of the monument donated by the Soviet Union to the United Nations and showed a man beating swords into plowshares. Along the edge of the patch, the Biblical slogan (Isaiah 2:4) encircled the figure. In 1981, numerous young people wore this patch during the ten days leading up to Repent and Pray Day, an annual Protestant observance.

All these measures prepared the ground for the mass peace movement that welled up in 1982. In both Germanies, this movement was a response to NATO's decision, in response to a Soviet modernization on Warsaw Pact territory, to upgrade its arsenal of missiles in Germany. The Wolf's Pelt *(Wolfspelz)*, a youth group influenced by Pastor Wonneberger's movement, had illegal flyers printed and distributed throughout East Germany. They invited others to join them on 13 February 1982 at the ruins of the Frauenkirche. Here, as memorializing church bells pealed, they intended to demonstrate for peace.

The State Security Service soon got wind of this effort and moved to squelch it. The leaders were arrested and abused. It was apparent, however, that the youth could not be controlled, only channeled. Saxon State Bishop Johannes Hempel and Hans Modrow, both desiring to prevent any confrontations with the police, organized a peace forum on February 13 at the Kreuzkirche. Five thousand people gathered in the Altmarkt and then took seats in the church. The forum ended with a candlelit march to the Frauenkirche's ruins. Throughout the evening, both the regular and the secret police waited nearby to spring into action should any violence occur. None did, and the day ended in the spirit of peace. Soon afterward, a Working Community for Peace was established to bring the various Dresden groups together, and the candlelit marches to the Frauenkirche on February 13 became an annual event.[550]

This network reflected the parallel environmental movement that had grown up at the beginning of the 1980s. The Ecological Circle of Dresden Church Districts operated under the protection of the Kreuzkirche and conducted a series of actions to combat the increasing industrial pollution inside East Germany. At the regional church conference of 1983, a banner flew from the Kreuzkirche's tower warning that "Konsum kostet Leben (Consumerism destroys lives)". This local measure drew attention to Dresden's participation in the united East German effort.[551]

Gorbachev and the Soviet Union

It cannot be forgotten that the various dissident movements in the GDR (as well as elsewhere) received a boost when Mikhail Gorbachev became leader of the Soviet Union's Communist Party in 1985 and head of state three years later. He initiated reforms that allowed for more freedom of expression in the political realm and more reliance on market mechanisms in the economy. These measures were well-publicized in the Eastern bloc, and it eventually became apparent that Soviet troops would no longer prop up the Honecker regime. As Gorbachev's actions diverged more and more from the usual Communist pattern, the East German government suppressed the circulation of Soviet news reports within the GDR, but their measures only resulted in the news traveling underground.

In the midst of increasingly visible dissatisfaction, Wolfgang Berghofer arrived in Dresden to take over the mayor's position from Gerhard Schill, whom he describes as "tired and worn out" after twenty-five years of service. What he found in the valley of the Elbe was a "Baroque wreck". The city's administrators had become "resigned" to a situation of shortages. They could not summon up any "visionary fire" even when a lot of money was not necessary. The structural fabric of the city was slowly disintegrating; construction of housing had not kept up with projections.

When he became mayor in 1986, Berghofer confronted a waiting list of 30,000 apartment seekers. Indeed, there were still bomb-damaged buildings in the inner city and the suburbs. Older, pre-war structures were still inhabited but were slowly deteriorating. Berghofer later described the condition of apartment buildings in the Neustadt, dating back to the late nineteenth century, as catastrophic. When plans materialized to destroy these structures, a group of professors at the Technical University saved them by emphasizing their historic value. Yet nothing was done to rehabilitate them, and demolitions of the older fabric continued to occur in working-class neighborhoods. The state planned, someday, to replace these older buildings, which frequently lacked the basic amenities of twentieth-century housing, with prefabricated high-rise apartments.

There were other shortages as well. Water was rationed during certain periods of the day. Electricity sporadically blacked out during the cold season. In the snowy winter of 1986/87, coal was in short supply. Berghofer announced that there would be a two-week school vacation in order to save fuel. Only then did the central government in Berlin arrange to have coal shipped to Dresden. The school vacation did not occur. Other municipal agencies lived with the shortage. The city's transportation system was inadequate. Potholes studded the streets; streetcars and trains ran late. Materials needed for Dresden's industries did not arrive when they were promised, so firms instituted a lot of overtime after late arrivals in order to meet planning goals.

Consumer goods made in Dresden did not show up in Dresden shops. Instead, the planning authorities directed them to Berlin in order to prevent unrest in the capital city that would clearly be visible to the international press. A joke circulated locally and throughout the GDR that a customer asked a shopkeeper if there were *no* T-shirts in the store. Answer: Here there were *no* jeans; next door there were *no* T-shirts. Dresdners frequently traveled to Berlin in order to buy the goods made in their city but not available there.

Like Modrow, Berghofer too circumvented the central planners by appealing directly to East Germany's director of Commercial Procurement, Alexander Schalk-Golodkowski. For decades, he had bought items in Western Germany and Western Europe, as well as other places, that were in short supply in the East. When Berghofer needed a sweeping machine for cleaning Dresden's streets, he obtained one through Schalk-Golodkowski. When the city's administration needed a stronger computer system than was available in the GDR, the Commercial Procurer found one in the West. (9)

As the shortages and deterioration in Dresden progressed, "many people lost their loyalty to the city, and there raged an epidemic of despair." Local SED leaders shared the frustration of the populace, more and more of whom simply wanted to "escape". Some people moved to Berlin where goods were in better supply and the political atmosphere perceived to be more tolerant. Others resorted to private petitions, a measure allowed by the GDR government, to protest onerous conditions and achieve relief. Others just simply gave up and applied for emigration even though these applications were stigmatized and sometimes criminalized.[552]

Still others, emboldened by the Soviet reforms, refused to bow to despair and intensified their protests against the regime. In 1987, the official Olaf Palme Peace March took place and wound its way in the GDR from north to south, eventually ending in Dresden. The march, a cooperation of peace movements in both Germanies and Czechoslovakia, sought to create a nuclear-free zone through Central Europe. For the first time at official marches, participants carried independent placards in addition to the state-approved banners. Party officials tried to keep these dissident posters out of view or removed altogether from the march. But their efforts were in vain.

On 13 February 1988, the anniversary of the firestorm, a group of would-be emigrants demonstrated at the Transportation Museum directly opposite the ruins of the Frauenkirche. Again on Easter Sunday, another group conducted a protest march through the Theaterplatz and over the Augustus Bridge. Later, in July, another such group of prospective emigrants gathered demonstrably at the Kreuzkirche.

Already in April that year, members of the state theater ensemble had sent a letter to the Minister of Culture, Kurt Hager, protesting the removal of *Sputnik,* a Soviet magazine, from newspaper kiosks and subscribers' mailboxes. They also criticized Hager's interview with the West German magazine *Stern* where he claimed that a person doesn't change his wallpaper just because his neighbor does. He was referring, of course, to the Soviet Union's reforms as publicized by *Sputnik*. The actors found his remarks misguided and disorienting.

The Ecumenical Assembly for Peace, Justice and Conservation—a convergence of three critical movements—met in Dresden in both 1988 and 1989. When the organizers invited parishes to submit written suggestions for discussion topics, ten thousand people responded, most with complaints about the GDR's problems. For the first time since the 1950s, the churches became active participants in political dialogues about education, state paternalism, electoral reform, civil rights, and the environment. These conferences helped Protestants and Catholics to converge in ways that determined the political future of East Germany.[553]

As part of the drive to develop a viable microelectronics industry, the GDR needed to produce the purified silicon necessary to fabricate semi-conductors. The basic ingredient for this process was trichlorosilane, a highly flammable liquid. If accidentally released into the atmosphere, it yields chlorine gas, a substance used in World War I with lethal consequences for the combatants. As the uranium mine at Dresden-Gittersee yielded less and less ore, it was apparent that the mine would be abandoned, and other work would have to be found for the miners. For the central planners in Berlin, a silicon producing factory in Gittersee, using trichlorosilane, made perfect sense. Not so, in Dresden.

When local authorities were consulted about this location, they advised against this placement. The possibility of an accident, either through transport by train and truck or through crashing aircraft, was too great in such a densely settled area. When the central planners went ahead with the project anyway, the relevant information was leaked to Pastor Wilfried Weissflog at the Protestant church in Gittersee. As the news about the Silicon Works spread through the Dresden parishes, church members, including Pastor Weissflog, flooded the appropriate authorities in Berlin with petitions protesting the location. Modrow also protested siting the factory in Gittersee, as did the local State Security, mostly because of the inhabitants' furor against it.

In response, the authorities in Berlin decided to put the population under great pressure to accept the plant. They interrogated Pastor Weissflog and his colleague in the neighboring parish of Plauen, Pastor Karl-Ludwig Hoch. SED functionaries spent three weeks in the area trying to convince the residents that no danger would emanate from the plant. Six thousand flyers were distributed, and articles appeared in the local edition of the *Sächsische Zeitung* praising the undertaking. The state promised to apply all the technology necessary to make the Silicon Works super-safe.

When an informational meeting scheduled for the Red Rose restaurant in Gittersee attracted an overflow crowd, the proceedings adjourned to the church where residents let fly all their criticisms of the silicon plant, of the "arbitrariness" of SED officials, and of the general shortages. After this meeting, the Saxon Protestant Synod and the Catholic Diocese of Dresden publicly supported the protests. Clergy were then pressured to prevent church services that condemned the silicon plant. People who submitted protesting petitions were disciplined.

Eventually the magazine of the influential Environmental Library in Berlin told its readers about the events in Dresden. Beginning in June, the Gittersee pastor held regular supplicatory church services against the plant. After one service in the church, the congregants demonstrated up to the gates of the construction site for the works. When West German TV cameras recorded the event, the police did not intervene, but they vowed not to let that happen again.

For the August 6 service, the police gathered in force, armed with fire hoses and rubber truncheons. As the demonstration began in conjunction with the service, they waded into the crowd, seizing the homemade posters, physically attacking the Wolf's Pelt group, battering grandmothers, arresting the protestors. One witness claimed that the police even overturned a man in a wheel chair, leaving him lying in the street. Workers from the SED district offices, who were present to engage in discussion with the demonstrators, complained that the police had intervened before they even had a chance to begin.

The intervention, however, achieved its purpose. *Plein-air* demonstrations against the Gittersee plant ceased, and protest occurred only in church. Clergy continued to voice their opposition to state authorities. Construction of the Gittersee plant stopped only when the East German regime collapsed. After reunification, the site of the uranium mine was rehabilitated and converted into an industrial park where a number of well-known Dresdner firms found a home.[554]

During the fight at Gittersee, conflict occurred elsewhere. In May 1989, communal elections were held all over the GDR. Throughout the life of the socialist republic, the balloting and counting had been arranged so that the so-called bloc parties—the SED leading the puppets—gained almost 100% of the vote. Everyone knew the result was rigged. This time, peace groups in the neighborhoods of the Johannstadt and Leubnitz-Neuostra, as well as the Wolf's Pelt youth, organized observers at the various polling places to detect the fraud. The Saxon State Church lent them support. After the elections, protest demonstrations occurred all over the city when the observers reported that the opposition vote clearly exceeded that admitted by the authorities.

In July, a small group of teenagers staged a protest at the entrance to the Kreuzkirche against the Chinese Communist government's quelling of the student rebellion in Beijing's Tiananmen Square. Throughout East Germany, there was a fear that German dissidents would meet the same fate. The youth at the Kreuzkirche were arrested and each fined up to 1000 GDR marks. The Saxon Protestant Church asked for donations to help pay the fines; the collection amounted to 32,000 marks.[555]

Dresdners were also reaching out to the West. In the mid-1980s, the mayor of Hamburg, Klaus von Dohnanyi, had approached the city with an offer of a closer connection. Linking the cities at either end of the German Elbe was partly a sentimental and partly a political gesture. Originally, the East German government forbade the Dresdners from accepting a close tie with a West German city. In 1987, however, Mayor Berghofer let Hamburg know that Dresden would entertain a sister-city relationship with the great North Sea port, and so it came to pass. As the crisis of the GDR deepened in 1989, sixty Dresdners traveled by Mississippi steamboat to Hamburg to help celebrate its 800th birthday.

Fifteen thousand Hamburg residents visited the steamboat; the Dresdner jazz band, Elbmeadow Rambler, played in the Hamburg Music Hall; and the Dresden Artisans' Chamber mounted a photo exhibit of views along the Elbe. The director of Dresden's Philatelic Society presented to Hamburg a bill of lading that bore a silhouette of both cities connected by the blue ribbon of the Elbe. This work of art daringly depicted no border between the two Germanies, even though no one as yet had even hinted at a reunification. In generous advertisement for the southern city, the Hotel Bellevue prepared a dinner of Saxon specialties for Hamburg's notables.

During the visit, Berghofer encountered the former technical director of the Dresden Universelle firm, Kurt Körber, the noted philanthropist who was closely connected to the Institute von Ardenne. He presented some sage advice for the mayor, artistically drawn on a piece of paper: "Ecological and socially oriented market economy. Only that will solve your problems." Körber was very well informed, and Berghofer must also have shared some of his concerns about Dresden's fate.[556]

XVIII. "Velvet Revolution"

In the first half of 1989, over 18,000 Dresdners legally left for West Germany, braving the regime's malice toward them. Many more prepared to leave in their wake. At least one-quarter of the GDR's applications to emigrate during that period came from Dresden. Most applicants belonged to the age group between eighteen and forty—people in the prime of life whom the GDR could ill afford to lose.

Gorbachev's reforms had not encouraged only East Germans to protest. In other countries of the Eastern bloc, important changes were also occurring. By 1989, the Poles were inching their way toward a true parliamentary democracy. The Hungarians were following suit, and in May, they removed the barbed wire lining the border to Austria.

Hungary was a favored travel destination of East Germans, and hundreds had made reservations to vacation there in the summer of 1989. After the opening to Austria, East Germans who wanted to flee illegally flocked south. Hungarians, honoring their treaty with their socialist comrades, could prevent flight at train stations and highway checkpoints, but it was more difficult to prevent clandestine trekkers through fields and forests adjacent to the border. Some East Germans eschewed this rural route and camped at the West German embassy in Budapest. We now know that an agreement between the West German and Hungarian governments led the latter to allow the East Germans safe passage. When the East German regime then forbade its citizens from traveling to Hungary, their destination became Czechoslovakia, where thousands camped in the West German embassy's compound in Prague.[557]

Soon, this encampment developed a food shortage. Sanitary facilities were overwhelmed, and as summer turned to fall, the thousands who had abandoned almost all their belongings in East Germany, were unprepared for the increasingly chilly weather. Meanwhile television cameras from West Germany and elsewhere recorded the predicament for the rest of the world. To avoid embarrassment, the East German government finally gave way to West German entreaties to let their people go, under the condition that the exit from Prague occur on trains traveling through East German territory. In that case, the East German government could claim it was expelling the emigrants. The rail route chosen ran from Prague to Bavaria through Dresden. One train left during the night of September 30 without much advance publicity, and a few Dresdners managed to hop a ride and wend their way westward as it passed through.[558]

Additional trains of refugees from Prague were scheduled for the coming days, and Western news media provided a lot of advance notice. Saxons along the rail route to Dresden lined the tracks hoping to jump on board. With the same plan in mind, would-be refugees from various points in the GDR flocked to Dresden. On October 3, 2000 people gathered in the main rail station shouting "We want out." Demonstrators threw stones and burned a police car. Police were able to clear the station with water hoses and truncheons, but the crowd remained undaunted.

During the day of October 4, 20,000 demonstrators gathered in the Prager Strasse. Parked in all the surrounding streets were GDR autos from far and wide. The leadership in Berlin had assured the local authorities that it would handle problems from the capital. But that was easier said than done. The crowds shouted "Gorbachev" and "Freedom!" They lashed out at the security forces with bicycle chains. Young people once again threw stones.

In the evening, Modrow called the transport minister in Berlin and asked to have the train for that evening rerouted through a more southerly, less densely populated area where there was a direct border between West Germany and Czechoslovakia. The transport minister informed him that the trains at that moment were located in Bad Schandau, approximately twenty miles to the south, poised to travel to Dresden and could not be rerouted without causing a "catastrophe". Normal train traffic halted. Roads from Bad Schandau were closed to prevent any more influx into Dresden.

About this time, the police chief informed Modrow that his forces were not strong enough to keep the crowd out of the station and allow the trains from Prague to pass through freely. The main fear was that emigrants, many with children, would be hurt by trying to board the moving cars. Finally, army units arrived to reinforce the police. Three overloaded trains passed through Dresden at 1:30 a.m. with no casualties on the tracks or on the platforms. Nevertheless, at the end of the night there was shattered glass everywhere: in the corridors of the station, on the street outside, in the shop windows of the Prager Strasse. Two hundred were arrested. Modrow was relieved that no one had died. A general agreement of all security forces had been reached in advance that no guns would be used.[559]

Demonstrations continued on the days following this violent confrontation. But all sides wanted to avoid further violence. The unofficial Neues Forum, a newly-founded citizens' action group called for a "democratic dialogue" between state authorities and citizens. On both October 5 and 6, Pastor Christof Ziemer at the Kreuzkirche held services where he called for non-violent demonstrations. On the evening of October 6, Dresden's state theater ensemble gathered in front of the curtain and demanded reforms. Their example was imitated throughout the East German state. Also on that date, even as police and military units confronted demonstrators on the Pirnaischer Platz and at the main rail station, arresting 367 people, Modrow and the police began to consider de-escalating the turbulence in the streets with "political measures".[560]

From the vantage point of over a quarter century, it seems bizarre that the GDR leadership staged a grand celebration of the fortieth anniversary of the state's founding on October 7. In Berlin, the Soviet leader Gorbachev arrived to grace the ceremonies. The People's Army paraded in the Karl-Marx-Allee before a viewing stand featuring the SED leaders and visitors from the Eastern bloc. During Gorbachev's visit, he famously warned the East German leadership that "life punishes those who come too late".

In Dresden, both Berghofer and Modrow had been busy during this week of demonstrations preparing for the local celebrations, held not only in Dresden but throughout the GDR. Mayor Berghofer has described the scene in the Dresden Rathaus that took place behind closed curtains on October 7. In the Rathaus ballroom, local leaders and guests from Dresden's sister cities enjoyed a buffet; Modrow gave a speech. Outside, on the Leningrader (now Petersburger) Strasse, thousands marched by, some silently—and some not so silently—on their way to the Prager Strasse. At 8 p.m., someone pulled back the thick curtains of the windows that looked out on the street. Then came the cry: "We are the People! You ought to be ashamed!"[561]

Demonstrations resumed the next day, a Sunday. Thousands marched through the city carrying the lighted candles that had emerged during the week as symbols of non-violence. They matched their steps to shouting choruses of "We're staying here, join us, we want no violence;" and "We are the People!" This was the phrase that came to dominate demonstrations all over East Germany and eventually transform into "We are *One* People!" As the crowd filled up the Prager Strasse north of the rail station, they found themselves surrounded by police and military units.

Instead of resorting to panic, the crowd sat down. Some hummed the *Internationale*—the socialist anthem since the late nineteenth century; others intoned the *Dona nobis pacem* from the Latin mass; a few sang *Thoughts are Free,* dating from the sixteenth-century peasant wars. Again there were sporadic shouts of "No violence!" and "We're staying here!" The police, ordered by Modrow to desist from aggression, urged the crowd to disperse but otherwise applied no force. There was now a stand-off between the security forces and the demonstrators.

Among the latter's ranks were two Catholic chaplains, Frank Richter from the Court Church, now the cathedral, and Andreas Leuschner of St. Josef's, Dresden-Pieschen. In order to end the stand-off, Richter sought out a police officer and asked if Mayor Berghofer would consent to speak with representatives of the demonstrators. The officer agreed to ask. To meet with the mayor, a group of volunteers, later to become the Group of 20, was selected. After being chosen, one of the group's women persuaded the police to withdraw their dogs and lower their shields.

Berghofer had spent the day conferring with his closest local colleagues. By day's end, he had decided to urge the national leadership to institute reforms. As the request from the demonstrators reached him, he sat in his office struggling with the text for his announcement. He had already agreed to speak with the demonstrators when three Protestant clergymen also appeared at the Rathaus to request the same action: Saxon bishop Johannes Hempel, Reinhold Fritz, church assembly member, and Christof Ziemer from the Kreuzkirche. They had no knowledge of Richter's action in the Prager Strasse and had little difficulty in securing from Berghofer an assent to their request.

Berghofer made only two conditions. First, the demonstrators must disperse peaceably that night. He would meet with the demonstrators' committee at the Rathaus at nine the next morning. Secondly, he insisted that the report on the initial discussion be made, not in the unruly streets, but in four principal Dresden churches the next evening. He then dispatched the clergy to the Prager Strasse via police car, blue lights flashing. After Richter and then Ziemer announced the mayor's decision, the crowd started for home within a short period of time. Contacted shortly thereafter, Modrow, who that evening had divided his time between the Semper Opera's production of *Fidelio* and the neighboring police headquarters, gave his blessing to Berghofer's plan. That night, as the stirring prisoners' choral ode to freedom ended, *Fidelio's* audience had spontaneously and silently risen to its feet and "endlessly applauded".[562]

Over a decade later, Pastor Karl-Ludwig Hoch, the long-term pastor in the Plauen Valley, who had supported the Gittersee protests, related how traumatizing these nights of protest could have turned out for his family. Many people feared that the demonstrators, most of them young, would be crushed by the security forces, just as had happened five months before at Beijing's Tiananmen Square. Hoch's younger son had just been ordered to report for military service, and his unit had received the truncheons the soldiers were expected to use against the demonstrators. Hoch's oldest son was standing, and then sitting, with the demonstrators in the Prager Strasse. Had violence erupted, his two young sons could have squared off against one another.

Uwe Tellkamp, in his mammoth novel, *The Tower*, stages a scene that reflects Pastor Hoch's fear. The young hero of the story, a draftee in the Volksarmee, is detailed to a demonstration in the Prager Strasse. There he witnesses a member of the State Security forces beating his mother, a demonstrator. Only his sidekick saves him from acting on his murderous rage by physically restraining him and dragging him toward the rear. An officer relieves him of his duty, secures for him a sedative, and the Volksarmee sends him to live with his older and wiser grandfather. On the turbulent nights of protest, there must have been several such potential situations.[563]

The Dresdners claim that without the unprecedented events of October 8, there could have been no turning point in Leipzig on October 9. Leipzig's Nikolaikirche had long been the scene of Monday prayer services for peace, inspired for all the churches in Saxony by Christoph Wonneberger when he was pastor at Dresden's Weinbergkirche. In 1989, demonstrations for reform of the GDR had begun to follow the Monday prayer meetings, and protestors streamed out of the church and into the Leipziger Ring. Leipzig, in the week before October 9, had also experienced protestors in the streets every evening, countered by police who had made many arrests. Everyone expected a showdown on October 9.

On that evening, Frank Neubert, a member of Dresden's Group of 20, drove to the Nikolaikirche in his East German Trabi, in order to describe the events unfolding in Dresden. He left Leipzig right after his speech to drive back to Dresden to hear the report of the meeting with Berghofer. What he missed was the dramatic stand-down of the security forces in Leipzig. As the 60–70,000 protestors began their march around the Ring, girded for confrontations but determined to remain peaceful, they were astounded that the armed police and military units, stationed along the marchers' route, simply stood and watched them walk by. Finally, the crowd perceived that someone was addressing them through the city's loudspeakers.

The speaker represented a committee of prominent men: Kurt Masur, director of the Gewandhaus Orchestra; Dr. Peter Zimmermann, clergyman; Bernd-Lutz Lange, a local cabarettist; and three local SED leaders who had long favored reform. It was Masur who called for non-violence and announced that the Leipzig SED had called Berlin to ask whether the crowd should be forcedly dispersed. In the meantime, the local police chief had asked the local State Security forces to desist until Berlin called back. It was this decision that led to the stand-down and to the dramatic victory of the marchers in Leipzig.

By this time, the idea of dialogue instead of violence had spread around the GDR. Neues Forum had raised the call, and SED authorities, churches and citizens had heard it. Witness Modrow's desire for political measures to address the demonstrations. On October 7, the birthday of the GDR, aggression by both demonstrators and police in Plauen/Vogtland, a town hard on the East-West German border, had morphed into a peaceful assembly, and the mayor had agreed to a dialogue that began later in the week. Discussions began in Leipzig two weeks after the stand-down of October 9. The crucial breakthrough to dialogue occurred first in Dresden; by the time the other discussions started, the Group of 20 had already met once with Dresden's mayor. Two days thereafter, the SED leadership in Berlin announced a policy of dialogue for the entirety of the GDR.[564]

The End of the GDR

On October 9 in Dresden, discussions between Mayor Berghofer and the Group of 20 had begun. The representatives of the protestors launched their demands: release of the demonstrators arrested during the preceding week, many subjected to severe mistreatment; official recognition of Neues Forum; freedom of press and assembly. When Berghofer called together the Rathaus staff to inform them about the discussions, he found a reformist circle in his own ranks. Why, asked the staff, did the GDR refuse to recognize a loyal group of citizens? Why did the borders remain closed to emigration? Why did the SED not espouse a form of democracy?

Berghofer had a difficult time securing the release of those arrested. When he tried to find out where they were being held, the district prosecutor's office refused to give him information. He finally appealed to Modrow who wrung from the police and the prosecutor's office the concession that they would release all those not responsible for damaging the rail station. At the same time, flyers for Neues Forum were found in the city's streetcars. Resignations from the SED and from the trade unions spiked. There was a new wave of applications for apartments. The state agency responsible for supplying the daily needs of Dresdners reported delivery delays of almost 100 tons of commodities, a circumstance likely due to the emigration of personnel crucial to the supply chain.[565]

Over the next few weeks, dialogue did not occur easily. Initially, Berghofer, supported by Modrow, insisted that he was merely participating in a discussion with a group of private individuals, not with the political movement that the Group of 20 claimed to be. When the Group suggested the formation of citizens' working groups to address specific issues confronting Dresden, Berghofer replied that he could not officially assent to such a plan. He insisted that the Group was merely a church organization and not representative of all Dresdners. It was true that the Group received crucial aid from the church. It originally met to devise strategy in the Catholic Cathedral's offices in the Schwerinerstrasse. Used to dealing with SED authorities, Pastor Ziemer attended meetings of the Group, bolstered its spirit of independence and also counseled compromise when necessary. He had prevailed on the Protestant church's attorney, Steffen Heitmann, to render legal aid to the Group.

It was Ziemer, along with the mayor, who eased continued communication when intransigence on both sides seemed to endanger the dialogue. On October 16, unyielding discussion prolonged the second Rathaus discussion, and a large crowd gathered outside demanding information. This pressure led Berghofer to announce his intention to include members of the Group in committees of the city assembly. In other words, he planned a co-optation. He promised that the press would carry more information on the morrow. This last intention raised shouts of protest from those gathered below. No one trusted the censored GDR press. In order to save the situation, Ziemer intervened by promising the crowd that unfiltered information would be given, once again, in the churches on the following evening.[566]

Those gathered in the churches on the morrow, agreed that the Group of 20 should be recognized as the official representative of Dresdners. Dialogue with the mayor should continue on that basis. In order to prove the Group's legitimacy, Friedrich Boltz, a Group member, borrowing from an action previously used by the environmentalist movement, created the One Mark Initiative. He opened a special bank account to which he urged all citizens, in flyers distributed throughout the city, to deposit one mark as a vote in support of the Group of 20. The action was immediately successful, and by mid-November the account contained 100,000 marks, contributed, arguably, by almost half of all adult Dresdners.

Even before this success, Berghofer had made some concessions. In a special meeting with members of the Group, he agreed to the formation of the independent citizens' groups desired by the Group of 20. They would cooperate with delegates from the city's assembly. The independence of the Group of 20 was assured by allowing it to choose one-half the citizens in these working teams. Each member of the Group would act as a liaison with the committees but would otherwise not participate; the issues to be addressed by the teams, such as economic development, needed expertise that the Group of 20 did not generally possess. Given this progress toward new urban policies, the Group now began cooperation with Neues Forum and other reformist movements, cooperation that eventually led, at the beginning of 1990, to a fully-fledged and extra-legal Democratic Grass Roots Caucus in the city assembly.[567]

The early success of the Group of 20 was not initially geared to German reunification. Dresden's citizens, the Group of 20, other reformist movements like Neues Forum, and most of all Berghofer and Modrow, considered dialogue to be a means of reforming the GDR's system under the continued dominance of the SED. In Dresden, they eagerly applied this method. By now, demonstrations were assuming an almost official character. On October 23, a spontaneous rally occurred on the Theaterplatz that both Berghofer and Modrow attended. The police even set up loudspeakers. A question-and-answer session continued until after 9 p.m., but the sound system was weak, and there was no podium for the speakers. The assembled agreed to meet again three days hence.

On 26 October, 100,000 rallied on the Commons next to the Hygiene Museum. Two microphones were set up, and Dresdners were free to express their fears, their doubts and their hopes. The meeting lasted four hours. Loudspeakers surrounding the field meant that everyone could hear. By this time, it was clear that the SED leadership in Berlin would initiate reforms.[568]

All over the GDR, rallies and demonstrations erupted at the end of October and the beginning of November. In Dresden, the Group of 20 initiated Monday night demonstrations as a means of furthering reform, and it initially cooperated with the mayor and council in staging them. When this cooperation resulted in State Security's monopolizing the vital space around the microphones and using it to interrupt reformist speakers, the Group discontinued the relationship. Modrow, Berghofer and others were allowed to speak at the rallies, but city government was not involved in their planning or execution. In toto, the Group held thirteen demonstrations at the end of 1989 and the beginning of 1990.

During this period, as thousands of East Germans now emigrated in waves through Hungary and Czechoslovakia, demonstrated *en masse* not only in Dresden and Leipzig, but in Berlin and other East German cities, the SED first tried to regain popular support. On October 17, the Politburo removed Erich Honecker as party chief and head of state and replaced him with a younger man, Egon Krenz. His government worked hard to reform the government, both by placing younger people in positions of responsibility and changing laws to meet the escalating demands. The right to travel outside the Eastern bloc and to emigrate was one law to be introduced.

On November 9, the SED chief of the Berlin district, Günter Schabowski, held a press conference to announce the change, implying that emigration was now open for everyone to go everywhere. After West German television reported the news about 7 p.m., the Wall that divided Berlin was swamped. The police, unsure of the situation, opened the checkpoints. And West met East with champagne and flowers. Within the next several days, millions of East Germans visited the West.

It still was not clear that the GDR and the SED regime would cease to exist. When Hans Modrow became prime minister of East Germany on November 13, there was strong support for a separate, German socialist state. This sentiment soon dissipated. When Modrow's government revealed the economic distress of the GDR and appealed to West Germany for help, the SED was discredited. At the beginning of December, the GDR's People's Assembly removed from the state's constitution the clause mandating the SED's dominance of the government. This action then encouraged the occupation of the State Security headquarters in both Dresden and Leipzig; measures to dissolve both local units soon followed. Herbert Wagner, leader of the Group of 20 and later mayor of Dresden, deemed the occupation the crucial turning point in the history of the GDR; thereafter, there could be no return to the previous status quo. On December 16, faced with the loss of power, mass resignations from the membership, and political disgrace, the SED transformed itself into a new grouping: the Party of Democratic Socialism (PDS).

Three days later, West German Chancellor Helmut Kohl traveled to Dresden, where he met with members of the city government. Dresdners greeted him enthusiastically when he spoke at a rally before the Frauenkirche's ruins. Kohl and his entourage also sounded out the Group of 20 about reunification and received positive feedback.

This question had arisen already at the beginning of November when a delegation from Hamburg had visited the city and learned that some reformers were flirting with the idea. Shortly after becoming prime minister, Modrow had floated the idea of a confederative "Contract Community"; Kohl had responded with a program for a gradual approach to unity. East German demonstrators espoused the idea with choruses touting "We are *One* People." At the beginning of January 1990, members of the Group of 20 and other reformist organizations accepted the invitation of the Baden-Wurttemberg government to visit for a week and study how the legal and political arrangements of West Germany could be applied to East Germany.[569]

By the beginning of 1990, the hard work of fighting for reform through dialogue had been accomplished. The last formal discussion between the Group of 20 and Berghofer occurred on 23 January 1990. As the SED dissolved and the central government embraced reform, Berghofer's attention shifted away from Dresden toward the fresh prospect of German unity.

Members of the Group also decided either to join the all-German political parties—CDU, SPD, FDP—that spilled over into the East or to remain loyal to their Eastern reformist movements. At the end of January, one-third of the city assembly's delegates resigned their mandates, and after February 16, the assembly held no formal meeting until the spring. In the elections for the GDR's People's Assembly on March 18, a majority of Dresdners joined with other East Germans and chose to follow the path toward German unification.

The closing act of the Group of 20 occurred a bare two months later when communal elections returned the Christian Democratic Union as the dominant party with Herbert Wagner, spokesman for the Group, as its candidate for mayor. Among the new city assemblymen were nineteen individuals who had participated in the Group. Wagner's governing coalition included almost all parties except the PDS, the inheritor of the old SED. The Group formally dissolved after the elections and donated the remaining 300,000 marks in its treasury to the Protestant Inner Mission.[570] Wagner then embarked on the restorative but difficult adjustment to living and governing in a reunified Germany.

XIX. Reunified

Even before legal unification occurred, East Germans began coming to terms with the moral and material legacies of the GDR. Dissidents insisted that anyone who had acted as a Stasi informant should be disqualified for public service. These unofficial collaborators, who had secretly spied and reported on their friends, colleagues and, in some cases, family members, had, said dissidents, ruined both lives and careers. Since the Stasi files existed almost intact, it would be possible to ferret out such individuals. In summer 1990, the People's Assembly passed a law for such use of the files, and the Unification Treaty of August, 1990, between the two Germanies, incorporated this measure.

Subsequently the reconstituted East German states, including Saxony, established commissions to investigate public officials' possible service as Stasi collaborators. Although originally intended to apply to candidates for political office, the process quickly extended to almost all individuals engaged in public employment and, in some instances, to those employed by private business. The total number of individuals dismissed because of collaboration with the Stasi will probably never be known, but the investigations themselves led to the conclusion that the activity of unofficial Stasi informants was much less than had been feared by citizens of the GDR.

Saxony was known to be one of the strictest states for disqualifying its public servants. One of the public sectors most stringently evaluated was education. In Dresden, 1844 school teachers lost their jobs for collaboration with the Stasi or having close ties with the former SED. At the Technical University, 3000 employees, including professors, were barred from further service. Hardest hit were the social sciences and the humanities, which included the academic disciplines most susceptible to influence by Marxist ideology. Saxony paid a high price for the "blacklisting" of its teachers. More than thirty-three million marks had to be paid for successful challengers' legal fees and for their retroactive salaries.

A Saxon sector that emerged relatively unscathed by "destasification" was the police. Scholars of the process conclude that across the board, throughout the old GDR, a disparity of treatment existed. If a sector, such as education, could be easily supplied with replacements, dismissals of public employees were proportionately larger than in sectors where labor was scarce. In Saxony, there was a severe shortage of policemen across the state, even before 1989. After that date the pool of new recruits was limited. This situation meant that Dresden, as well as other localities, suffered from various levels of unemployment and dislocation.[571]

The Economy

Destasification thus added to the economic consequences of East Germans' revolutionary exhilaration. Freedom to emigrate meant that thousands of people left Dresden and other East German cities to take up jobs and residency in West Germany. Those remaining stopped buying goods produced in East Germany. They anticipated stores filling up with Western goods of supposedly better quality. The same expectation caused customers in eastern European countries to cut orders from former suppliers in Dresden. In order to shore up the eastern economy, the East agreed to economic union with the West, a measure that came into effect, even before formal unification, on 1 July 1990.

People remember this economic union as the currency reform that enabled people to exchange their East German for West German marks, at an overvalued eastern rate of 1:1. Wages, salaries, pensions, rents and prices were all adjusted to conform to the currency exchange. This action immediately lost, drastically, the East German export markets in both East and West; most buyers simply were not able or willing to pay West German prices for eastern goods. Now subject to privatization and a market economy, the former state-owned firms experienced decline, bankruptcy and closure; their employees suffered unemployment, many for the first time in their lives. Dresden's unemployment rate rose to almost twelve percent in 1993 and spiked at sixteen percent in 1997. Thereafter it bounced up and down at a high rate for several years.[572]

Added to "destasification's" effect on the economy was a delay in granting clear titles to property ownership. Early in the unification process, both East and West Germans were aware that "open property questions" needed settlement, and both experienced public pressure for returning "illegally acquired property". For East Germans this issue involved Jewish properties more or less extorted by Gentile purchasers during the Third Reich, properties nationalized by the Soviet occupation of East Germany after World War II, and properties expropriated by the SED state after 1949. Recognizing that the claims were numerous and complex, the Unification Treaty provided not only for restitution but also for "socially acceptable compromise" among rival claimants. For many sites, property ownership remained in limbo for over a decade, and this situation delayed investment in new business needed for East Germany's economic recovery. Eventually, East Germany adapted to a market economy as formerly nationalized firms, now privatized, found their footing, and West German businesses located in Dresden.[573]

One of the first Dresden firms to endure the exposure to a globalized world was Pentacon, the state-owned heir to Dresden's legacy of camera production. The Trustee Agency, formed by vote of the GDR's People's Assembly in summer 1990 to pursue the privatization of East German business, failed to find an owner committed to completely rehabilitating the firm and quickly decided to liquidate it. On 30 June 1991, almost overnight, 3000 workers lost their jobs, while the Joseph Schneider Group from West Germany acquired Pentacon's assets at fire-sale prices. One can still find a Pentacon Corporation in Dresden, but it doesn't make or sell cameras; instead it's a die casting and machining plant that employs 100–200 people.

One firm that fared well after German reunification was the economically successful packing cartel, Nagema. The Trustee Agency disaggregated its various functions into separate, smaller firms, and a packing industry continues to thrive in Dresden. Another successful establishment was the Transformatoren- und-Röntgenwerk, the inheritor of Koch and Sterzel. After a brief ownership by the Siemens Corporation, Highvolt, now associated with the Reinhausen Group, began manufacturing high voltage test equipment in 1995. The firm still resides in Kaditz, its large windows surrounded by cement frames in different colors.

The Saxon Works provide another success story, albeit one that developed slowly. The Works had joined an East German association of electric machine-building companies shortly after World War II, and in 1961 this cluster had coalesced into a trademark group—VEM (Vereinigung Elektromaschinenbaus)—that was registered in the GDR and in several west European countries. Between 1960 and 1990, the West German Wittenbecher agency arranged sales of six million East German VEM products throughout the world. Moving quickly after the peaceful revolution, the Saxon Works transformed itself into a private corporation early in 1990, and in April, it joined the newly formed VEM Propulsion Technology Corporation. Nevertheless between 1990 and 1995, orders from customers fell, and its labor force sank from over 2000 people to 400; the firm struggled to stay alive. Not until 1997 did the Trustee Agency succeed in finding a West German entrepreneur, Adolf Merckle, to acquire the VEM Holding that included the Dresden firm. The Merckle family invested millions in the modernization of the firm, assuring the continued existence of work for 600 Dresdners. In 2017, the Chinese Wang family acquired VEM Holding, thereby raising the prospect of easy access to the large Chinese market.

Nowhere is the economic legacy of the past more apparent than in the field of electronics. The huge Robotron firm, with its ties to the Technical University and research institutes, dissolved in 1990. East German scientists and workers knew that the disappearing GDR lagged behind electronic developments in the west, and this circumstance accounted for the difficult transition that successor firms experienced in the years after reunification. Nevertheless, parts of Robotron were incorporated into West German companies, and some of the firm's enterprising employees founded new ones. In 2000, these businesses formed the Silicon Saxony Association. More than 300 members project the state as a center of the microelectronic, semi-conductor and photovoltaic industry. Many of the association's firms are located in Dresden and its environs. The Technical University, as well as local research institutes, are association members.

The private research Institute von Ardenne did not escape the trauma of transition. It lost its customers in the GDR and the Soviet Union, and the newly unified Germany took its time replacing the former East German subsidies with pan-German ones. Because the institute was a private entity, the Trustee Agency did not take responsibility for its continued existence. Manfred von Ardenne personally took out a loan from the Dresdner Bank to cover severance payments to the 300 employees that the institute had to lay off. Although West Germany's Fraunhofer Institute, a prominent establishment for applied scientific research, took over Ardenne's electron beam and plasma technology research, the family managed to retain control over the remaining operations by forming three separate companies. Most successful was the Von Ardenne Corporation that supplies vacuum coating for a variety of materials. After the years of struggle, the firm finally took off in the mid-1990s by landing several lucrative contracts.

In Hellerau, the German Workshops represent the power of myth to sustain a business. Like the Saxon Works, the German Workshops transformed themselves into a corporation in 1990 and prepared to satisfy demand both East and West for high-quality furniture. They quickly faced disappointment; the expected orders did not appear. As the Trustee Agency began searching for a buyer, four West German businessmen sought new challenges in the east. As they made the round of firms on the agency's list, they visited the workshops on a fine spring day. Though they acknowledged that the firm was burdened with heavy debt, and the industry suffered from oversupply, they were attracted to the firm's structurally sound buildings and its historic value. They also feared that other interested parties either wanted to misuse the company's reputation or to exploit the firm's valuable real estate. In mid-September 1992, the four acquired the German Workshops at 11:50 p.m.—the witching hour.

The new owners wasted no time in confronting their new employees with bad news. On the day after acquiring the firm, the new manager, Fritz Straub, announced impending layoffs and a new orientation—interior fittings from couches to cabinetry to curios—, an idea that a previous manager, a long-term employee of the firm, had also projected. But the promised plan was far removed from the workshops' traditional values. The target was the luxury trade, and the firm would only build on commission. Even though the new owners committed to socially responsible reductions in the work force, the mood among employees was bitter. By and large, the new management kept its promises while working fast to inaugurate the new production regime. By the beginning of 1994, obsolete machinery had been replaced with new equipment, and new customers were lined up.

The contract that mattered most was concluded with the Saxon state. That body, desiring to be the first East German state to complete its new quarters, commissioned an acoustic wall for its legislative plenum. Straub made sure that the workshops' bid was low enough to get the contract. Once the wall was in place, its artfulness announced the viability of the workshops' new course.

At the same time, Straub arranged for struggling Dresden artists to adopt, as rented studios, the empty rooms in the historic buildings' upper stories. And gradually, the new owners committed themselves to restoring those structures to their original polished form.

Decades later, the German Workshops are thriving at supplying interior furnishings for public buildings, for hotels, for mansions and villas, for private aircraft and yachts. In 2006, they completed modernistic office and factory spaces across the road from the old Riemerschmid campus. In 2019, they built a new production facility in a neighboring village. In the workshops' completely restored historic ensemble, a related firm has installed meeting rooms, recital halls, a gallery, two restaurants, and office and artisanal spaces for a variety of tenants. In short, the revived German Workshops benefit from and contribute to the prosperity of Dresden.

The city's official website proudly proclaims a multi-faceted urban economy. Its industry continues to be heavily dependent on the export market. It also demonstrates a strong continuity with its past; not only are the Saxon Works and the Von Ardenne corporation important enterprises, so are Dr. Quendt—baker of the famous Christmas Stollen—and Dr. Doerr, preparer of delicatessen commodities: salads, sauces and remoulades. Mostly medium-sized businesses supply the bulk of employment for Dresden's residents. The tourist industry continues to enliven the service sector as do the multiple conventions attracted to Dresden's fairgrounds, its large and small conference centers and its abundant accommodations. Last, but not least, Dresden is the capital of reinvigorated Saxony, and in 2019 the Saxon state employed almost eight per cent of Dresden's total labor force. At the beginning of 2020, unemployment stood at the healthy rate of 5.3%, a statistic that preceded the coronavirus lockdowns.[574]

Another continuity with the past is the heavy weight of educational establishments. The Technical University has played an important role in boosting the city's, the state's, and the nation's economy. In the wake of the peaceful revolution, the university adopted the academic patterns of West German universities and, in line with other Dresden institutions, restored and modernized its buildings and laboratories. It also continued the process of erecting new facilities both to the east and south of the original campus. New faculties in law, business, philosophy and architecture were added to the older technical functions, and other important institutions attached themselves to the university: the Medical Academy Carl Gustav Carus, the College of Transportation Systems, and the College of Pedagogy Karl Friedrich Wilhelm Wander.

As in West Germany, the prominent national research institutes such as the Fraunhofer and Max Planck Societies arranged partnerships with the university. Responding to the German Republic's initiatives to create world-class institutions of higher learning, the Technical University has been recognized by the German federal government as a "university of excellence", one of only eleven selected schools.

Dresden advertises itself as a "student city". As of 2020, those studying at institutions of higher learning, the TU, the Academy of Fine Arts, and the Music Conservatory, numbered 45,000 or eight per cent of the city's population. They lend to Dresden a vibrant, youthful energy apparent on the streets, in the trams and buses and in the myriad student locales located in the outer Neustadt.[575]

A New Image for Old Patterns

As the city slowly found its economic footing during the 1990s, it returned politically to the conservative orientation that marked its history during the nineteenth century and the late Weimar Republic. In the first free communal elections in 1990, after the collapse of the GDR, the leader of the Committee of 20, Herbert Wagner, now a CDU member, was elected Mayor by the city assembly. In 1994, a new Saxon communal code prompted direct election by the urban populace, and Wagner won once again. Dresdners, as we shall soon see, remained a quarrelsome lot, but despite disagreement within the city assembly, the 2001 elections yielded another conservative, Ingolf Rossberg, member of the FDP. Since then, though others have become mayor, Helma Orosz in 2008 and Dirk Hilbert in 2015, the center-right pattern has prevailed.[576]

Given the neglect and subsequent shabbiness of residential structures prior to 1990 and the availability of Western capital to buy up large swaths of East German land, it was not surprising that Dresden experienced a residential building boom during the 1990s. Almost 5000 single-family homes were built during this decade, particularly on the outlying fringes of the existing city. This boom amounted to a huge process of suburbanization. It resulted in burdening the city with the cost of supplying and maintaining the infrastructure necessary to support the new settlements. It also meant that developers favored the construction of shopping malls on the city's fringes, centers that catered to an expanded car-owning public that lived in the new suburbs. Only when new tax laws favored rehabilitation of old structures as well as the construction of new ones did this suburbanization boom recede.

By 2000, the boom had led to three additional developments. First, in order to generate the revenues necessary to pay the costs of new infrastructure, the city annexed in all directions wide swaths of territory adjoining its borders. Secondly, as the building boom progressed, and many Dresdners moved west for employment, a surplus of housing emerged that contributed to sinking rents all over the city. Even when older concrete-slab structures were rehabilitated, they did not attract tenants, so that the city resorted to razing some of the housing built during the GDR regime. Thirdly, the attention to the urban fringes meant that plots in the inner city that had never recovered from the bombing of 1945 remained undeveloped.[577]

Slowly, at the turn of the millennium, attention returned to the inner city. One of the most successful rehabilitations was the lordly avenue of the Königstrasse where eighteenth-century structures were lovingly restored, and new building was designed to fit into the Baroque neighborhood. Another successful venture occurred in the outer Neustadt, where a large group of late nineteenth-century apartment houses, once associated with the German military's Albertstadt, became habitable once again. In Striesen and Blasewitz, where spacious villas persist, other restorative efforts occurred so successfully that those neighborhoods, now as before, have no difficulty attracting tenants. To the west of the Neustadt the working-class Hecht neighborhood and the old village of Pieschen regained their former livability. Matthias Lerm, one of Dresden's city planners after reunification, points to a modern development in the neighborhood of St. Lucas, a church just south of the main rail station. Here the architects showed the restraint necessary to mold the structures comfortably into the older urban fabric.

There was general agreement that Dresden after 1990, could not return to the old pre-war city. Too much had been destroyed, and post-war generations did not want to abandon the neighborhoods developed during the GDR regime. City planners maintained the inner-city corridor from Albertplatz, the busy transportation hub in the Neustadt, to the Wiener Platz, just outside the main rail station. Three pedestrian zones, established after the war, anchor this corridor. At the northern end lies the Hauptstrasse, rebuilt in the 1970s to echo, in modern cement slab construction, its original eighteenth-century architecture. After crossing the Augustus Bridge, the corridor meets the Schlossstrasse, leading past the restored palace and chancery to the Altmarkt where it links up to the Pragerstrasse. This pedestrian zone remains a shopping and entertainment strip, but its original span of sixty meters was reduced after 1990. Its more intimate urbanity of eighteen meters welcomes workers and tourists arriving in the city by train.

While this corridor preserved for Dresdners a familiar sense of place, most important was the restoration of the famous Canaletto prospect, the city's skyline on the Elbe as viewed from the Japanese Palace. That urban silhouette had changed in the course of the centuries that followed him. One of the first additions was the dome of the Jewish synagogue, added to the east in the mid-nineteenth century. At the beginning of the twentieth century, the Art Academy's exhibition hall—the lemon reamer—and the towers of the New Rathaus and Saxon legislature enriched the scene. Some of these landmarks, both old and new, reappeared during the forty years of the GDR. But other structures remained in ruins. Shortly after reunification, the Hausmann tower—one of the prominent spires of the silhouette—was restored along with earnest work on rehabilitating the palace. Most urgently missing from the panorama was the dome—dramatically exaggerated by Canaletto—of the Frauenkirche.[578]

Immediately after World War II, there was no doubt about restoring this church. Donations flowed in; a lottery was instituted. SED authorities accepted this intention, and city planners devised guidelines for rebuilding the surrounding Neumarkt so that it would maintain the former architectural proportions of church to square. Nevertheless, the ruins remained. For the legal owner of the property, the Saxon Protestant Church, the sheer cost of the undertaking was daunting, and other projects enjoyed a higher priority. Yet for many Dresdners, the dream never died, and a small group remained poised to initiate restoration as soon as the time was ripe.

At the end of the 1980s, that time arrived. When the peaceful revolution occurred in 1989, the team supporting restoration sprang into action. Twenty Dresdners met shortly after the SED's collapse to prepare the well-known "Call from Dresden", issued on 13 February 1990, inviting West Germans, other Europeans, and eventually the world to support the reconstruction of the Frauenkirche.

Concerts benefiting the Frauenkirche began already during the Christmas season of 1989 and never ceased until the church was rebuilt. Volunteers mounted other efforts such as the sale of various items—T-shirts, stationery, glassware—carrying images of the church. Information desks at regional fairs and commercial congresses continually called attention to the project. Tours of the construction site maintained local support once work began. The IBM corporation helped the group to mount an advertising blitz in print and other media. The Dresdner Bank came up with the idea of selling stones to be used in the reconstruction effort. In West Germany, membership groups formed to raise money.

The Dresden Trust in the United Kingdom, nominally headed by the Duke of Kent, pledged to finance the crafting and installation of the golden orb and cross that ultimately crowned the lantern atop the massive dome. In the United States, the German-born Nobel prize winner, Günter Blobel, founded the Friends of Dresden and acquired Henry Arnhold, forced out of Dresden as a Jewish teenager, as one of the society's honorary directors. In Paris, the French established a Frauenkirche Association. In addition to donations, the Rebuilding Society secured financing from the Saxon state, from Dresden city, from the Saxon Protestant Church and ultimately from the Federal Republic. From start to finish, the reconstruction cost 180 million euros, 115 million supplied by donations.

By 1992, a Frauenkirche Foundation had formed to oversee the reconstruction, and work began in earnest in 1993. It was a foregone conclusion that, given the image imprinted in every Dresdner's mind, the church would be rebuilt in its historic form, following George Bähr's blueprints. Modern architects and engineers deviated from his methods when modern technology and materials could help to avoid the chronic cracking in base and pillars caused by the load of the massive stone dome. Adherence to the eighteenth-century plans was so great that stones and other artifacts salvaged from the ruins were used in the reconstruction.

One of the last decisions in the process of reconstruction concerned the church's organ. The venerable Gottfried Silbermann had built the original organ that J. S. Bach once played in recital, and it was regularly used by his student Gottfried Homilius. Although that organ had been altered in the course of the succeeding two centuries, many Dresdners considered it a part of the historic structure. After collecting donations with the promise of restoring the Silbermann organ, the Frauenkirche Foundation changed course at the end of the 1990s and decided to install a more modern instrument. This decision angered a host of parties. Most of the Saxon firms who had planned to bid for the organ-building job withdrew. Prominent European organists issued a "Call *to* Dresden". Saxon "nationalists" were outraged that the only firm willing to build the more modern instrument was Alsatian. The issue was not instrumental quality. It was local patriotism; Silbermann was Saxon, and the replacement of his instrument in the Frauenkirche should also issue from a Saxon firm. Abandoning the Silbermann organ damaged the credibility of the foundation and lost many of the Frauenkirche's supporters. Ultimately, a panel of experts and the Dresden city council supported the foundation, and the "Alsatian" organ now accompanies services and concerts in a Saxon church. Purists might console themselves with the knowledge that Silbermann learned his craft as organ builder in Alsace.

Throughout the course of reconstruction, the Rebuilding Society had hosted services and other events in the finished portions of the church, first in the crypt and then in the unfinished main hall. Progress was so sustained that the reconstructed Frauenkirche was dedicated to great fanfare in 2005. On October 30, the city invited 1700 guests to the inaugural service, including Germany's president and the Duke of Kent. A crowd of 60,000 gathered outside the church and followed the ceremony on a large screen.

In this same year, the exhibition hall and glass dome of the Art Academy replaced the ruins that had kept company with the Frauenkirche throughout the life of the GDR. It too completed the scene for Dresdners who remembered the pre-war city and identified with the silhouette along the Elbe. Left invisible—at least from the river's banks—was the old trace of the synagogue.[579]

Jewish Life after 1990

The reconstruction of the Frauenkirche helped to call attention to Dresden's once vibrant Jewish community. At the time of reunification, Dresden's Jews still worshipped in the small structure next to the Jewish cemetery in the Johannstadt. Meanwhile, their congregation, as well as those in other Saxon cities, was expanding due to Jews arriving from Russia after the Soviet Union's collapse. Dresdners now also enjoyed the support of the West

German Central Council of Jews, with whom they united after 1990. In 1994, the Saxon state also began to support the community financially.

In 1998, for the first time since the 1930s, the Saxon government appointed a state rabbi to be shared among its Jewish congregations. In addition, the first Bar Mitzva in fifty years gave Dresden's Jewish community hope for a sustained future life. By this time, Jewish religious instruction, on a par with Catholics and Protestants, had begun again in Saxon schools, and Dresden's Jews banded together with those in Leipzig and Chemnitz to support a religion instructor, Ruth Röcher. She shouldered the burden of instruction and also arranged extra-curricular activities that appealed to Jewish youth. Among the ranks of the adults, Jewish charitable organizations revived.

Dresden's congregation resumed its leadership role among Jewish communities in East Germany. It was the first after reunification to merge its study group into the West German Society for Christian-Jewish Cooperation. It was also the first East German congregation to join the German-Israeli Society. As its members numbered in the hundreds, it welcomed in 2013, for the first time since the 1930s, its very own rabbi. His successor, Rabbi Akiva Weingartern, in 2020, established a liberal-Hasidic yeshiva open to Dresdners, other Germans and Europeans.

Soon after reunification, Jewish historian Helmut Eschwege helped to form HATIKVA (Hope), a society supporting the pursuit of Jewish history and culture in Saxony. Located next to the city's oldest, existing Jewish cemetery in the Neustadt, the society has organized courses, lectures, concerts, seminars and exhibitions. Its publications have provided some of the best sources for the history of Jews in Dresden.

In the decade after 1990, it became apparent to those inside and outside the congregation that Dresden Jews needed a new synagogue. Pastor Reimann at the Annenkirche, who did so much to remind Dresdners of their ties to German Jewry, pointed out to popular Mayor Wagner that a new synagogue needed as much attention as the Frauenkirche. Reimann won the support of the mayor, of Saxony's minister-president—the equivalent of governor—and a host of others for a new building. After construction began in 2000, Günter Blobel contributed to its construction. Former Jewish residents, invited by the city beginning in the early 1990s to visit and reminisce, also donated funds. Functioning as the collection site was the Frauenkirche.

The new synagogue opened on the Hasenberg, the location of the former Semper structure, on November 9, 2001, the sixty-third anniversary of the old temple's destruction. Its outer wall contains fragments of the Semper building. The golden star of David, rescued and hidden by a fireman on Crystal Night and returned after 1990, graces the entrance. But the new synagogue is a modernist cube reminiscent of ancient Israelite temples. Architecturally, it neither echoes the old neo-Byzantine structure nor the prized Baroque style of the city center. The fortress-like edifice faces, across a courtyard, the glass façade of the communal shelter for a variety of functions—lectures, concerts, committee meetings, administrative offices, school and library. The new synagogue is a very prominent contemporary building in a very prominent place. Only the desire to avoid seeming anti-Semitic muted the severe traditionalist criticisms that usually greet similar architecture.

Susanne Vees-Gulani, a scholar of the German response to the bombings of World War II, views Dresdners' memory of its National Socialist past in a splintered light. She says they focus on their roles as victims, first of the Shrove Tuesday/Ash Wednesday bombings and then of the SED's insensitive reconstruction of the city. They have tended to forget, she says, their participation in the Holocaust. Their selective memory began quite early in the history of the GDR with the creation of the memorial at the Cemetery on the Heath, where so many of the dead were buried after February 13–14. The memorial singles out the concentration camps, the cities that were bombed, including those by the Luftwaffe, and makes heroes out of resistance fighters. But, she says, nowhere does it mention the Holocaust, either in Dresden or elsewhere. After German reunification, Dresdners expended a lot of energy on reclaiming the Frauenkirche. In comparison, they paid less attention to the synagogue.[580]

More Reminders of the Past

Although it is not an official holiday, February 13 has been commemorated every year since 1946. At first, only the church bells pealed at the hour of the first attack. Beginning in 1982, candlelit marches to the church's ruins helped to bolster the GDR's peace movement but also served to remind Dresdners of their city's destruction. It is unclear whether anyone knows how many of the commemorators were neo-Nazis. We do know that neo-Nazism, as an echo of the West German movement, furtively existed in East Germany beginning at the end of the 1960s.

After reunification on 3 October 1990, the movement was no longer furtive. Already on Saturday, 19 October, neo-Nazis held a march in Dresden, waving anti-Semitic banners and overturning autos parked in the streets. Police did nothing to stop the demonstrators. City hall later admitted approving a march billed as a pro-unification rally. Approval was considered wiser than dealing with an illegal demonstration.

Soon, small gatherings of neo-Nazis showed up at the annual ceremonies, at the Frauenkirche ruins and at Dresden's Cemetery on the Heath, for the victims of Allied bombings. There they were tolerated by members of other Dresden organizations. In 1999, the neo-Nazis held their first large-scale "mourning march". For the next ten years, their rallies on February 13 grew ever larger, drawing hundreds from all over Germany, including those who had been pushed out of other towns by anti-fascist governments and organizations. Gradually, the day of "mourning" was preceded by pre-viewing days, where neo-Nazi groups handed out leaflets or staged small acts around town before the main event. In 2009, just as the economic recession was coming to an end, almost 7000 neo-Nazis from all over Europe gathered for the march in Dresden.

Eight years before, newly-elected Mayor Rossberg had tried to mobilize a coalition against the marchers. In the wake of his failure, the anti-fascist forces, consisting of many left-wing radicals and even Antifa, could neither unite nor find a strategy strong enough to attract a crowd capable of thwarting the right-wingers. Finally, in 2009 a host of anti-fascist organizations attempted to stop the neo-Nazi march. Instead, they found themselves blocked by police who were called out to prevent violence erupting between the two groups. The threat of violence was real. Anti-fascist demonstrators reported four assaults by neo-Nazis in the course of the march on Saturday, February 14. A group of forty neo-Nazis at a highway rest stop attacked anti-fascist demonstrators traveling home from Dresden and kicked a trade-unionist so brutally that they fractured his skull. Thus, planning began for a united front of anti-fascists in February, 2010: "Dresden Free of Nazis".

Once again, Dresden police tried to thwart this anti-fascist movement by confiscating its posters, by shutting down its webpage and by attempting to cancel the buses engaged to bring the demonstrators to Dresden. The anti-fascists responded by mobilizing 600 organizations throughout Germany to obstruct the Nazis' march in 2010. City authorities finally decided to take action. They called upon the major political parties—including the dominant CDU—church congregations and other organizations to build a human chain around the city center on February 13. Touted as an act against violence, this human chain eventually attracted over 200,000 people.

Paying little attention to this effort, "Dresden Free of Nazis" planned and executed a series of blockades against the neo-Nazi march. In the Neustadt, 12,000 anti-fascists blocked the streets leading from the train station to the inner city. Amid numerous clashes with the anti-fascists, police eventually closed down the Nazi march due to the threat of violence posed by the blockades.

In 2011, the neo-Nazi mourners brought suit against the Saxon state, claiming that it had violated their constitutional right to freedom of assembly (and demonstration) and had neglected to engage sufficient police forces to protect them from the anti-fascists. The Dresden Administrative Court agreed with the neo-Nazi organizers. When the city, however, attempted to meet its constitutional obligation by combining three petitions into one stationary demonstration on Saturday, February 19, the neo-Nazis took it to court and won once again. Three separate marches had to be approved. The city and the police, determined to prevent violence, relegated the anti-fascist demonstrators to the Neustadt, far across the Elbe from the Nazis in the Altstadt. Police also tried, unsuccessfully, to stop non-Dresdners from entering the city. The threat of violence between the two sides was so strong that the police ended up canceling the Nazi demonstrations.

During the next year, February 13 fell on a Monday, so the police, anticipating blockades by "Dresden Free of Nazis" and another human chain around the inner city, shortened the neo-Nazi march. The insult of the shortened march plus the promise of blockades caused the fascists to call off the big march scheduled for February 19, a Sunday. Again in 2013, a small neo-Nazi march was stopped by thousands of counter-demonstrators. Thereafter, the marchers received reinforcement from another right-wing group.[581]

In October, 2014, Lutz Bachmann, owner of a Dresden ad agency, established PEGIDA (Patriotic Europeans against Islamization of the West). This organization aimed not only to protect Dresden, Germany and Europe from Islamic refugees, but to combat the German government's "political correctness", and its "continual insulting of Germans as Nazis". Modeling themselves on the Monday night demonstrations of the 1980s, Bachmann and his associates claimed to be the true representatives of the German people. Their Monday evening marches through Dresden's inner city began in October, 2014 and continued every week for several years. Although there was an initial spike of 25,000 marchers in January, 2015, their numbers declined thereafter but were seldom less than 2000 and could sometimes ascend to 10,000 or more. PEGIDA was still holding Monday marches in Dresden in 2024.

As PEGIDA sprang to life at the beginning of 2015, a research team at Dresden's Technical University attempted to discern its source of support. The majority of marchers generally came from the Dresden region and considered themselves to be middle class. Most were middle-aged men who enjoyed incomes exceeding the Saxon average. Over seventy per cent said they were dissatisfied with German politics, and only one-third expressed "fundamental reservations" against migrants. For most participants, the PEGIDA marches were expressions of resentments against the political and cultural elites identified with West Germany and the pluralistic United States.[582]

These resentments intensified with the right-ward drift of the newly created Alternative for Germany (AfD). Originally a party that questioned the wisdom of Germany's participation in the Euro and its cooperation with other European economies, the new party shed its politically centrist adherents in 2015 to become a party of fundamentalist Christians with a populist and reactionary character that reminded some political scientists of the 1930s' National Conservatives, the party that invited Adolf Hitler to assume control of the federal government.

The AfD generally supports limits on the number of migrants and banning Muslims from entry into German society. It has even called for appropriate measures to remove the "illegal" contents of the Koran. Björn Höcke, leader of the Thuringian AfD who frequently speaks for the national party, has supported the idea of an authority figure who exhibits the virtues of "valor, wisdom, relentlessness, and severity" in relationships with others. The party's legislators have supported neo-Nazis, and its extreme right wing is especially attractive to some supporters of PEGIDA.

In the federal elections of 2017, the AfD became the first right-wing party to gain seats in the national parliament, and in Saxon state elections it received the largest number of votes. Two years later, it became the second largest party in the legislature and captured votes both from the CDU and the Left Party. Only one of Dresden's legislative districts provided a majority for the AfD; primarily its votes came from the districts bordering Dresden to the East and to the West. In the neighboring state of Thuringia, the AfD became strong enough to help the CDU and the FDP (Free Democratic Party) to elect the new minister-president—governor—of the state. The national leaderships quickly forced the CDU and the FDP to desert the AfD, and the former governor, a member of the Left Party, resumed his old position.

Since 2019 the federal Office for the Protection of the Constitution has investigated the AfD to determine whether its public statements and actions contravene those portions of the German constitution and the criminal code that ban defamation, discrimination, and violence against others on the basis of race, religion, and nationality. It has also placed Höcke and leading members of the AfD right wing under surveillance.

In 2020, on the seventy-fifth anniversary of the bombing of Dresden, Pegida/AfD determined to hold the usual mourning march. In order to provide a counter-narrative, Germany's president, Franz-Walter Steinmeier, traveled to Dresden on the eve of the event to remind Germans of the racism and anti-Semitism that had led to the city's destruction. He contended that the old "dangers" of nationalist hubris and contempt for humanity threatened to poison German public life. Five days later, Dresden's PEGIDA invited Höcke to give a speech to the mourning marchers of Dresden. Addressing a throng of 4000 in front of the Frauenkirche, he railed against the federal government's opposition to him and his party. In 2021, in an electioneering speech, he used a Nazi slogan—Alles für Deutschland (Anything for Germany)—for which public prosecutors later charged him with a violation of German law. The court eventually convicted him of this charge and, in May 2024 fined him €13,000.

The question remains why Dresden's city council, despite the decisions of the Saxon Administrative Courts, did not initially act more aggressively against right-wing organizations. For centuries, local politics have been conservative; the strong resistance to the SED during the life of the GDR must be interpreted in this way. It's helpful to know that even before the emergence of PEGIDA and the AfD, right-wing extremists won seats on the city council, blunting the usual German aversion to neo-Nazis. For instance, in November, 2019, the council voted 30-29 to declare a municipal emergency, identifying an "unacceptable" Nazi problem. The local CDU opposed this resolution, claiming it to be an unnecessary "provocation". Mainstream conservative parties like the CDU and FDP resisted joining with left-wing radicals or even with groups just left of center to counter neo-Nazis. Both parties had lost votes to right-wing groups. Their vulnerabilities testified to a complex approach to the city's past and future.

The coronavirus pandemic presented both city and state with the opportunity to limit right-wing activity and visibility. In 2021, Saxony exempted Dresden from the strict lockdowns imposed by other German states, but it limited public gatherings to 1000 persons and insisted on participants' maintaining a social distance of six feet and wearing masks. During the Shrove Tuesday commemorations, a massive police presence at the main rail station and in the city's streets insisted on observance of the anti-virus measures. In 2021, city government sponsored several small events on the Altmarkt and Neumarkt, and the human chain of commemoration and peace was replaced by a virtual chain. Both neo-Nazi and anti-Nazi demonstrations remained small and peaceful. In 2022, the chain of peace was revived in reduced form to stretch along the Wilsdrufferstrasse between Alt-and Neu-markt. Once again, anti-virus measures prevailed for everyone, and a massive police presence enforced the restrictions and safeguarded the peace between neo-Nazis, who marched in the city center to Wagnerian music, and counter-demonstrators at the Zwinger shouting "Nazis-out".

In both 2023 and 2024, in the absence of anti-virus requirements, the city continued to muster a massive police presence for the Shrove Tuesday events. Its primary task was to assure that both sides could exercise their right to assemble without harassment. That mostly meant protecting right-wing mourning marchers from counter-demonstrators. In both years, police claimed success in keeping order within the city. At the same time, thousands of Dresdners continued to participate in the commemorative human chain.

While a variety of local groups have continued to publicly express their aversion to right-wing attitudes and actions, the vulnerability of mainstream conservative parties became evident just a few months after Shrove Tuesday, 2024. In communal elections on June 9, Dresdners gave the highest percentage of votes, 19.4%, to the AfD, awarding it with 14 seats within the city's assembly of 70. The next highest vote went to the CDU. Nevertheless, during that same year, in expectations. legislative elections on September 1, the city's voters, with an unusually high turnout, overwhelmingly favored the CDU. Uniquely, the Neustadt returned a Green to the state's assembly.[583]

Updating the Infrastructure

While reunification helped to complete the rehabilitation of Dresden's former landmarks and maintain the city's old infrastructure, it also paved the way for some long-planned improvements. The first was the construction of a four-lane highway between Dresden and Prague, two cities with a long history of association. The idea of an expressway linking the two cities initially occurred in 1938 as the Third Reich prepared to end the independence of Czechoslovakia. Spending on World War II swallowed up funds that could have been used on the highway.

After 1990, truck traffic between the two states multiplied along the old-fashioned highways that connected them, and German businessmen pressured the government to relieve the congestion. At the time, it was apparent that Czechoslovakia would soon join the European Union and that truck traffic would only increase as a result. In response, the German government revived the plan of 1938. The new highway would link up at Dresden with the main autobahn across central Germany and stretch across the southern edge of the city to potentially impact some densely populated neighborhoods.

Dresden's mayor and city council repeatedly opposed this route, fearing increased noise and traffic jams along the way but could not persuade the federal government to make changes. Taking matters into their own hands, a number of citizens' groups, including environmentalists, joined with the local CDU in 1995 to introduce a referendum on the plan. Two-thirds of Dresden's voters favored the federal route. In order to spare both neighborhoods and nature preserves, a series of tunnels and bridges, introduced to decrease noise and congestion, spun out construction from 1998 to 2006.[584]

Autobahn 17 to Prague was a straightforward matter and did not disturb the city's historic identity. The construction of a new bridge over the Elbe was more contentious. In the last quarter of the nineteenth century, as Dresden's industrialization boomed, the city had proposed building a bridge at the site where the Elbe meadows are broadest—from the Waldschlösschen brewery to the Johannstadt. For a variety of reasons, this bridge was not achieved at the time, but the idea revived in the 1930s. It was shelved again after World War II began.

Once the war was over, and the city made grand plans to build a new, socialist city, the idea of a bridge across the Elbe meadows at the Waldschlösschen brewery sprang back to life. By 1988, city plans envisioned a four-lane structure, and soon after Dresden joined the Federal Republic, the city council took up the subject of the bridge. A design competition led to the city council's selection of a modest structure, and preparations for construction began in 2000. Pursuit of the Waldschlösschen Bridge ran parallel to the reconstitution of Canaletto's famous Baroque vista. As the restored Frauenkirche neared completion, Dresden's promoters decided to apply for designation as a World Heritage Site under the rubric of a "cultural landscape"—a combination of man-made structures with works of nature. The nomination in 2003 leaned heavily on the architecture of Dresden's inner city, but it also included the unimproved Elbe meadows as part of the plan. The fact that a bridge would eventually cross those meadows was mentioned only in passing. In 2004, UNESCO designated the entire Elbe Valley from the Pillnitz to the Übigau Palaces as a world heritage.

Meanwhile, the bridge's construction had become a contested issue within the city. Many saw the bridge as damaging to the view of the valley from the slopes above the Waldschlösschen. The view of the valley, they claimed, provoked a meditation about the essentials of life, not just about dividends and wealth. Moreover, the bridge's location meant that it would not rid the city of traffic jams or otherwise contribute to the citizens' mobility.

The opposition to the bridge was strong enough that the city once again resorted to a referendum. The choices in 2005 were "bridge" or "no bridge". A large number of Dresden's voters, 67.8%, approved the bridge. Why the International Council on Monuments and Sites (ICOMOS) took up the issue of the bridge after the referendum is unclear; the organization had known about and not opposed the structure when the Dresden Elbe Valley was listed. Nonetheless, in 2006, following ICOMOS' advice, the World Heritage Committee declared the Elbe Valley's designation to be "in danger" and urged all parties to find a "less harmful alternative" to the bridge.

Emboldened by this decision, the local opposition petitioned the Saxon Higher Administrative Court in 2008 to call for a referendum on the alternative of a tunnel, a choice not offered in the first vote. The court denied the petition.

City government continued work on the bridge. As a consequence, at its meeting in 2009, the World Heritage Committee deleted the Dresden Elbe Valley from the list of Heritage Sites. In 2013, the Waldschlösschen Bridge opened to great fanfare.[585]

The Kulturpalast

As was the case for most cities in the GDR, Dresden escaped the construction of a dominant "wedding-cake" tower à la Moscow due to the delay in rebuilding the inner city and to the municipal budget's difficulties in paying for all the structures that needed replacement. When the city finally got around to filling in the northern side of the Altmarkt, Stalin's decorative architecture had gone out of style, and modernistic, industrial construction was preferred—all over the Eastern European bloc. What the city needed in the 1960s was a multi-purpose structure to serve the varied interests of its citizens.

Lacking was a large space that would host both the Philharmonic and the State Orchestras, visiting concerts, shows, and lectures, and a banquet room for local and national organizations. To accommodate these multiple purposes, the architect prescribed an adjustable floor—one that could be swiveled up for concerts, shows and films and be laid out flat for banquets and dances. Such devices were built into assembly spaces in both East and West Germany at the time. Grouped around this festival hall were club rooms, rehearsal spaces, a studio theater and a restaurant. When completed in 1969, it was truly a *Volkshaus*; citizens had volunteered 3700 hours of work during its construction, and students had polished the copper covering of the festival hall that rose above the roofline.

Throughout the years of the GDR, the Kulturpalast created many memories. It opened with two performances of the Bolshoi ballet. Thereafter it presented concerts by Dresden's two well-known orchestras as well as orchestras from cities near and far. Children's and pop music concerts, talent and variety shows educated and diverted the populace. During school vacations, there were special revues for the whole family. Management maintained a special relationship with a West Berlin agency that helped to bring Western performers to Dresden. Although those engaged were paid in East German marks, they were always taken on shopping tours that enabled them to buy good-quality items—like Meissen porcelain—at East German prices.

Though the building had succeeded in keeping all strata of Dresden's population entertained, the Philharmonic was less than satisfied with the acoustics of the festival hall. The orchestra had enjoyed the excellent resonance of the Commercial Association's auditorium before World War II, and it complained continually that the Kulturpalast's auditorium did not replicate that sound. Mayor Wagner promised the Philharmonic that the city would provide a suitable building as soon as funds were available. Indeed, the city planned to raze the palace and build a new concert hall. Due to the building's popularity, this idea soon disappeared. In the first decade of the new millennium the Saxon state's Office for Historic Preservation placed its exterior mural, "The Path of the Red Flag", and the building itself on the historic register.

In 2011, Dresden's city council decided to rehabilitate the *Kulturpalast* and rent it out to the Philharmonic, to the municipal library and to the well-known cabaret, *Herkuleskeule (Hercules' Club)*. The building's exterior would be preserved, and the interior, though rearranged, would use the former fittings in the foyers and new rooms. Since the adjustable floor was slated to disappear, the major interior change would occur in the concert hall. In the town where yesteryear rests, this alteration could not go unchallenged. The original architect, joined by his supporters, took the city to court in an attempt to save the old multi-purpose room and its adjustable floor. They lost. Renovation began in fall, 2013 and finished in summer, 2017.

The finishing touches involved a minor instance of *Ostalgie* (nostalgia for East Germany). The original *Kulturpalast* had sheltered an organ, and many Dresdners, including the Society for the Promotion of the Philharmonic, thought that the rehabilitated structure should include one. Yet the municipality resolutely refused to include an organ in its plans. In response, the Society in Support of the Palace, founded just after reunification, took over the planning, financing and installation of the new instrument. By 2012, the Society had succeeded in persuading the city council to donate 300 thousand euros, but the total still fell short of the amount needed.

Though no longer resident in the city, George Arnhold, grandson of the municipal pool's Jewish donor, had resolutely supported the Philharmonic until his death a few years before. Thus, the Society approached his son, Anthony, who agreed to sponsor a benefit concert in Dresden to raise the funds for the organ. One hundred fifty members of the Arnhold family came from around the world to the concert, and together they donated 450,000 euros.

Despite the indignity and rejection visited upon the family three-quarters of a century before, this gesture proved to be a variation on an old adage: you can remove the family from the city, but you cannot remove the city from the family. Today, the new organ graces the proscenium of the new concert hall. Its inauguration in September 2017 opened a series of new memories in a renovated palast.[586]

These developments underscore Dresdners' multi-faceted approach to their sense of place and cultural identity. They can meet the demands of the modern world with resilience and, in the case of the Kulturpalast, they mix the social democratic experiences of the twentieth century with an older pride in aristocratic artistry.

Epilogue
Dresden's Place in the World

On the occasion of the city's functional 800th birthday, in 2006, the Hygiene Museum mounted an exhibition entitled "Mythos Dresden". It reminded Dresdners that the city has spawned multiple myths—tales that mix reality with imagination to create meaning for both individuals and the collectivity. Some of the exhibition's stories included events narrated in this portrait: August the Strong's creation of the Baroque city; his era's collection of fine art; the establishment in the nineteenth century of a sustaining industrial base; the nineteenth and twentieth centuries' birthing of artistic movements in music, painting, and drama.[587]

A portrait of Dresden resembles the crowded village landscapes painted four centuries ago by the Pierre Breugels, father and son. One needs to focus on each scene to grasp how the multiplicities combine to complete the canvas. For Dresdners and many Germans, the city was and is a town of splendid art collections—a Florence on the Elbe. For music lovers, it's the city that made the Richards Wagner and Strauss famous. For businessmen and bankers, it's the metropolis that emerged in the nineteenth century as producer of tasty confections, popular cameras and precision tools. It continues to thrive as the center of Silicon Saxony. For sports fans, it's a professional soccer team. And for the world as a whole, it's an anti-war memorial.

Yet Dresden is more than its memorable images. Over the centuries, creative, productive, and unique personalities have helped to shape its life and destiny. It's a locality where the inescapable themes of German national history have found an echo—from a cluster of principalities in the early German empire, to a fragmented, weak entity exploited by Napoleon, to the strong, industrialized state that challenged the British Empire in World War I, to the National Socialist marauder of World War II, to the division of defeat.

Approaching the "caesura" of the February bombings, the exhibition of 2006 cast doubt on the myth of the "innocent" city. Dresden, during the Third Reich, was little different from other German towns in its loyalty to the Führer and its persecution of Jews. After defeat in World War II, the city endured fifty years of "socialism", tempered by its citizens' determination to conserve its identity as a cultural magnet. The events of 1989 reinforced the image of the city as peaceable victim. The demonstrators of October 8 sat down, assumed a posture of non-violence, and defused a tense situation with the police.

In contrast to the myths, the curators of 2006 shone a spotlight on "metamorphoses". Dresden is an important industrial and scientific center. Baroque buildings remain in the center of town. But they are surrounded by "socialist concrete blocks", by the blend of Neo-Baroque with Art Nouveau in the reconstructed Rathaus, by the modernist Kulturpalast and New Synagogue, and by the post-war buildings of the Technical University. One need only access the city's official webpage to discover the kaleidoscope of contemporary urban life: Planning for both historic center and far-flung periphery; integrating newcomers, be they German or not; providing adequate child care for working parents; and many other tasks. The cultural realm is not neglected, not only because it's part of the urban identity, but because art for the tourists contributes to the city's prosperity.

At the center of this crowded canvas is the Frauenkirche, first as a German mission church, then as a mausoleum for Dresden's worthy citizens, later replaced as a Lutheran monument with a famous dome. After World War II, the church's ruins nurtured the peace movement of the 1980s. Throughout the history of the GDR, the vision of a restored Frauenkirche, and with it a recovered city, provided a spirit of strength for Dresden's citizens. Once the church was rebuilt, it became a symbol of conciliation with Germany's neighbors, near and far.

Dresden's history will not be razed, but as the passage of time produces new generations, new challenges, new consensus, and new memories, the old myths weaken. They will never completely disappear. Eventually, pealing church bells on the evening of February 13 will be the lasting reminders of a Dresden narrative.

Frauenkirche with black stones salvaged and reused
Dr. Volkmar Rudolf/Tilman 2007

Acknowledgements

Without librarians, both in the United States and in Dresden, this portrait would not have been possible. At a crucial stage in the process, Thomas Dell, at the Brooks Library in Ellensburg, rendered valuable service with professional competence and grace. Over the many years of the portrait's gestation, many friends encouraged me to continue. In its final stages, native Dresdner Christian Schneider, fellow historian Barbara Newman, and Germanophile Charles McGehee read the portrait critically and made useful suggestions for improvements. I take full responsibility for any factual mistakes and other flaws.

Select Bibliography

Arnold, K. P (1993) *Vom Sofakissen zum Städtebau; Die Geschichte der deutschen Werkstätten und der Gartenstadt Hellerau.* Dresden.

Bergander, G. (1995) *Dresden im Luftkreig: Vorgeschichte, Zerstörung, Folgen,* 3. Auflage. Dresden.

Blaschke, K. hrsg. unter mitwirkung von Uwe John (2005) *Von den Anfängen bis zum Ende des Dreissigjährigen Krieges,* Vol. 1, *Geschichte der Stadt Dresden.* Stuttgart.

Clayton, A. and Russell, A. eds. (1999) *Dresden: A City Reborn.* New York.

Czok, K. (1988) *August der Starke und Kursachsen.* München.

Czok, K, hrsg. (1989) *Geschichte Sachsens.* Weimar.

Delau, R. and Sprenger, L. (1998) *Schmidts Erben: Die Deutschen Werkstätten Hellerau.* Dresden.

Dresdner Geschichtsverein, e. V. hrsg. (2002) *Dresden: Die Geschichte der Stadt von den Anfängen bis zur Gegenwart.* Dresden.

Fabian, W. (1972) *Klassenkampf um Sachsen. Ein Stück Geschichte 1918-1930.* Löbau: 1930, reprint Berlin: 1972.

Förster, R. (1984) *Dresden: Geschichte der Stadt in Wort und Bild.* Berlin.

Gross, R. hrsg. unter mitwirkung von Uwe John (2006) *Vom Ende des Dreissigjährigen Krieges bis zur Reichsgründung*, Vol. 2, *Geschichte der Stadt Dresden*. Stuttgart.

Haenel, Erich and Kalkschmidt, Eugen hrsg. (1977) *Das Alte Dresden: Bilder und Dokumentation aus zwei Jahrhunderten.* Leipzig: 1934, reprint Frankfurt/Main: 1977.

Hädecke, W. (2006) *Dresden: Eine Geschichte von Glanz, Katastrophe und Aufbruch,* München.

Hänseroth, T. hrsg. (2003) *Wissenschaft und Technik: Studien zur Geschichte der TU Dresden*, Vol. 2, *175 Jahre TU Dresden*. Köln.

Heidenreich, F. (1995) *Arbeiter Kulturbewegung und Sozialdemokratie in Sachsen vor 1933.* Weimar.

Hermann, K. hrsg. (2014) *Führerschule, Thingplatz, "Judenhaus": Orte und Gebäude der nationalsozialistischen Diktatur in Sachsen.* Dresden.

Jäger, W. and Brebbia, C.A. eds. (2000) *The Revival of Dresden.* Boston.

Kiesewetter, Hubert (1988) *Industrialisierung und Landwirtschaft: Sachsens Stellung im regionalen Industrialisierungsprozess Deutschland im 19. Jahrhundert.* Köln.

Knebel, Victoria (2007) *Preserve and Rebuild: Dresden during the Transformations of 1989-1990.* New York.

Kroll, F. L. ed. (2004) *Die Herrscher Sachsens.* München.

Lässig, Simone (2004) *Jüdische Wege ins Bürgertum: Kulturelles Kapital und sozialer Aufstieg im 19. Jahrhundert.* Göttingen.

Lapp, Benjamin. (1997) *Revolution from the Right: Politics, Class, and the Rise of Nazism in Saxony, 1919-1933.* Boston.

Laudel, H. and Franke, R. hrsg. (1991) *Bauen in Dresden im 19. und 20. Jahrhundert*. Dresden.

Lerm, Matthias. (2000) *Abschied vom alten Dresden: Verluste historischen Bausubstanz nach 1945.* Neuausgabe. Rostock.

Löffler, F. (1989) *Das alte Dresden: Geschichte seiner Bauten*, 9. Auflage. Leipzig.

Paeschke, C-L. and Zimmer, D. (1994) *Dresden: Geschichten einer Stadt.* Berlin.

Pommerin, R. hrsg. (1998) *Dresden unterm Hakenkreuz*. Köln.

Pommerin, R. (2003) *Geschichte der TU Dresden 1828-2003*, Vol. 1, *175 Jahre TU Dresden*. Köln.

Quinger, H. (2011) *Dresden und Umgebung: Geschichte, Kunst, und Kultur der sächsischen Hauptstadt*. Ostfildern.

Retallack, James, ed. (2000) *Saxony in German History: Culture, Society, and Politics, 1930-1933*. Ann Arbor.

Rosseaux, Ulrich (2007) *Freiräume: Unterhaltung, Vergnügen, und Erholung in Dresden, 1694-1830*. Köln.

Starke, H. hrsg. unter mitwirkung von Uwe John (2006) *Von der Reichsgründung bis zur Gegenwart*, Vol. 3, *Geschichte der Stadt Dresden*. Stuttgart.

Szejnmann, C-C. (1999) *Nazism in Central Germany: The Brownshirts in 'Red Saxony.'* New York.

Taylor, F. (2004) *Dresden: Tuesday, February 13, 1945.* New York.

Tellkamp, Uwe (2016) *The Tower: Tales from a Lost Country.* trans. Mike Mitchell. London.

Ulbricht, Gunda und Glöckner, O. hrsg. (2013) *Juden in Sachsen.* Leipzig.

Watanabe-O'Kelly, Helen (2002) *Court Culture in Dresden: From Renaissance to Baroque.* New York.

Widera, Thomas (2004) *Dresden 1945-1948: Politik und Gesellschaft unter sowjetischer Besatzungsherrschaft.* Göttingen.

Notes

Prologue

[1] References to the novel from Kurt Vonnegut, Jr., *Slaughterhouse-Five or The Children's Crusade* (New York: 1971 reprint), 148, 150, 177–81, 186–8, 212–214; https://en.wikipedia.org/wiki/Slaughterhouse-Five, edited 2/13/22, retrieved 2/16/22; www.nytimes.com/2019/03/21/books/kurt-vonnegut-dresden-anniversary.html.

[2] Uwe Tellkamp, *The Tower: Tales from a Lost Country* (London: 2016), passim. The Tower as a "novel of the Wall's fall," https://de.wiki/Uwe Tellkamp, edited 4/23/22, retrieved 5/2/22.

[3] For the Elbe at Dresden, Heinz Jacob, "Die Vor-und frühgeschichtliche Besiedlung der Dresdner Landschaft bis zur Stadtwerdung. Ein Siedlungsgeographisch-archäologischer Überblick," *Geschichte der Stadt Dresden,* Bd. 1 (Stuttgart: 2005), 25–8, 50, hereafter cited as *Geschichte.*

[4] Dresden's early history in Jacob, *Geschichte,* Bd. 1, 48, 53–62; Karlheinz Blaschke, "Die Entstehung der Stadt," *Geschichte.* Bd.1, 89–100; Werner Coblenz, "Ur-und frühgeschichte bis um 600," *Geschichte Sachsens* (Weimar: 1989), 24.

[5] Kreuzkirche, Kreuzschule, Kreuzchor, Alexandra-Katrin Stanislaw-Kemenah, "Kirche, geistliches Leben und Schulwesen im Mittelalter," *Geschichte,* Bd. 1, 205, 235–236; Daniel Hartwig, "Die Kreuzschule im Zeitenwandel," *Der Dresdner Kreuzchor: Geschichte und Gegenwart, Wirkungsstätten und Schule* (Leipzig: 2006), 301–306; Hans John, *Der Dresdner Kreuzchor und seine Kantoren* (Berlin: 1982), 12–14.

⁶ Wettiner acquisition and disposition of Meissen/Saxon lands/relationship to Dresden as residence, Ingo Zimmermann, *Sachsens Markgrafen, Kürfürsten und Könige: Die Wettiner in der meissnisch-sächsischen Geschichte* (Berlin: 1990), 50–63; Norbert Oelsner, "Die Dresdner Burg im Mittelalter," 121–49. Karl-Heinz Blaschke, "Dynastie-Regierung-Schloss," 422–3, Heinrich Magirius, "Architektur und Bildende Künste," 528, all in *Geschichte*, Bd. 1; Brigitte Streich, *Zwischen Reiseherrschaft und Residenzbildung; Der wettinische Hof im späten Mittelalter* (Köln: 1989), 3, 296-3-1, 296–297, 523–529.

⁷ Fire, rebuilding, and Reformation, Jorg Oberste, "Alltag und Lebenswelt im spätmittelalterlichen Dresden," 330–331, Hans-Peter Hasse, "Kirche und Frömmigkeit im 16. und frühen 17. Jahrhundert," 469–71, 477–80, both in *Geschichte*, Bd. 1; Siegfried Hoyer, "Das Herzogtum Sachsen in der Zeit des Frühkapitalismus und der frühbürgerlichen Revolution (1485–1547)," *Geschichte Sachsens*, 205.

⁸ Rudolf Förster, *Dresden: Geschichte der Stadt in Wort und Bild* (Berlin: 1984), 32.

Chapter 1

⁹ Schade quote, Rudolf Förster, *Dresden: Geschichte der Stadt in Wort und Bild* (Berlin: 1984), 32–33, hereafter cited as *Wort/Bild*; George's contributions, see preceding Prologue and Matthias Meinhardt, *Dresden im Wandel: Raum und Bevölkerung der Stadt im Residenzbildungsprozess des 15. Und 16. Jahrhunderts* (Berlin: 2009), 579–580.

¹⁰ Moritz, Ingo Zimmermann, *Sachsens Markgrafen, Kürsten und Könige: Die Wettiner in der meissnisch-sächsischen Geschichte* (Berlin: 1990), 69–71; Siegfried Hoyer, "Das Herzogtum Sachsen in der Zeit des Frühkapitalismus unter der frühbürgerlichen Revolution (1485–1547)," *Geschichte Sachsens* (Weimar: 1989), 199–200; Johannes Herrmann, *Moritz von Sachsen (1521–1553): Landes-Reichs-und Friedensfürst* (Beucha: 2003), 127–29, 138; Italian influence, Förster, 32.

¹¹ Old Dresden, Förster, *Wort/Bild*, 30–32, 90–94; Karlheinz Blaschke, "Wirtschaft und Verfassung" and Alexandra-Katrin Stanislaw-Kemanah, "Kirche, geistliches Leben und Schulwesen im Mittelalter," Eva Papke,

"Festungsbau 1500-1648," and Jörg Oberste, "Alltag und Lebenswelt im Spätmittelalterlichen Dresden," all in *Geschichte der Stadt Dresden,* Bd. I (Stuttgart: 2005), 157–168, 206, 220, 449, 330, hereafter cited as *Geschichte*; Herrmann, 130.

[12] For Palace, Norbert Oelsner "Das Dresdner Residenzschloss in der frühen Neuzeit," *Geschichte,* Bd. I, 432–437; Hermann, 99–100, 130–133.

[13] Moritz' death and monument, "Zweiter Markgrafenkrieg," de. Wikipedia.org, retrieved 8/20/20; Heinrich Magirius, "Architektur und Bildende Künste," *Geschichte.* Bd. I, 533.

[14] Government of Moritz and August, Hermann, 53–55; Karl Czok, "Kurfürst August I von Sachsen (1526–1586)," *Kaiser, König, Kardinal. Deutsche Fürsten 1500–1800* (Leipzig: 1991), 116–121; August as capitalist entrepreneur, Zimmermann, 74.

[15] Government streamlining, Jens Brüning, "August (1553–1586)," *Die Herrscher Sachsens: Markgrafen, Kurfürsten, Könige, 1089–1918* (Munich: 2004), 117, hereafter cited as *Herrscher Sachsens*; building boom, Meinhardt, 114; Magirius, 535–536, Karlheinz Blaschke, "Dynastie-Regierung-Schloss," 424, both in *Geschichte*, Bd. 1.

[16] Dominance of court, Meinhardt, 580–581; Karlheinz Blaschke, "Ratsordnung und Bevölkerung," *Geschichte*, Bd. I, 364.

[17] Förster, *Wort/Bild,* 32–3.

[18] Royal stables and influence, Magirius, *Geschichte*, Bd. I, 537–39, 551.

[19] Walter Mackowsky, *Giovanni Maria Nosseni und die Renaissance in Sachsen* (Berlin: 1904), available through Münchener Digitalierungszentrum; Igor Jenzen, "Handwerkkunst und Kunsthandwerk," *Geschichte*, Bd. I, 600.

[20] Moritz Fürstenau, *Zur Geschichte der Musik und des Theaters am Hofe zu Dresden,* I. Teil (Dresden: 1861), 83–4; introduction of inventions, Machkowsky, 85–7; Friedrich Sieber, *Volk und Volkstümliche Motivik im Festwerk des Barocks: dargestellt an Dresdner Bildquellen* (Berlin: 1960), xii; Dresdner style, Blaschke, *Geschichte*, Bd. 1, 431.

[21] For "primitive folksiness," Sieber, xiii; 1609 inventions, Mackowsky, 88–92.

[22] Mackowsky, 81–84; enhancement of Elector's importance, Jürgen Müller, "Giovanni Maria Nosseni und die Dresdner Kunst zwischen 1580 und 1620,"

Im Fürstlichen Glanz: Der Dresdner Hof um 1600 (Dresden: 2004), 36–7, hereafter cited as *Im fürstlichen Glanz*.

[23] Practices before and after reform, Herrmann, 60, 112–13; Hans-Peter Hasse, "Kirche und Frömmigkeit im 16. und frühen 17. Jahrhundert," *Geschichte,* Bd. I, 475–490; Hans John, *Der Dresdner Kreuzchor und seine Kantoren* (Berlin: 1982), 18–19; 46–47.

[24] Melanchthon's role, "Philip Melanchthon," https://www.conservapedia.com, retrieved 9/1/20; "Philippisten," https://de.wikipedia.org, retrieved 7/2/13; Hasse, *Geschichte,* Bd. I, 500; Peace of Augsburg, Peter H. Wilson, *The Thirty Years' War: Europe's Tragedy* (Cambridge, MA: 2009), 35, 41, 201–203; First and Second Reformation, Henry J. Cohn, "The Territorial Princes in Germany's Second Reformation, 1559–1622," *International Calvinism, 1541–1715* (Oxford:1985), 138–144.

[25] For "gynocracy," Hasse, *Geschichte,* Bd. I, 498; John, 29.

[26] Wilson, 36; Cohn, 145–46; "Konkordienformel," https://de. Wikipedia.org, retrieved 7/2/13,

[27] Krell's measures, Hasse, *Geschichte,* Bd. I, 505–508; John, 30; Wilson, 213–14; Jochen Vötsch, "Kursachen im Reich und in Europa: Dynastie-Politik-Religion," *Im fürstlichen Glanz,* 29; Thomas Niklas, "Christian I. (1586–1591) und Christian II. (1591–1611), *Herrscher Sachsens…* 128–132.

[28] Niklas, 133–136; Sophienkirche, Fritz Löffler, *Das alte Dresden* (Leipzig: 1989), 45; "Sophienkirche," https://de.wikipedia.org. version 8/24/20, retrieved 9/2/20.

[29] Dresden's prominence, Meinhardt, 573–581; Dirk Syndram, "In fürstlichem Glanz," *Im fürstlichen Glanz,* 19.

Chapter II

[30] For general background and progress of Thirty Years' War, S. H. Steinberg, *The Thirty Years War and the Conflict for European Hegemony 1600–1660* (New York: 1966), 31–41, 44–57, 63–73, 76–8.

[31] Reception of Bohemians and economic difficulties, Alexandra-Katrin Stanislaw-Kemenah, "Lebensbedingungen unter den Einfluss des Dreissigjährigen Krieges," *Geschichte der Stadt Dresden,* Bd. 1 (Stuttgart: 2005), 626–33, 639, hereafter cited as *Geschichte;* Siegfried Kube, "Im

Schattenkreis der Residenz. Zu Lebensbedingungen und Lebensweise werktätiger Schichten in Dresden, insbesondere während des 18. Jahrhunderts," *Volksleben zwischen Zunft und Fabrik. Studien zu Kultur und Lebensweise werktätiger Klassen und Schichten während des Übergangs vom Feudalismus zum Kapitalismus (Berlin: 1982), 252–3.*

[32] Quartering and overcrowding, Stanislaw-Kemenah, *Geschichte,* Bd. I, 621–4, 635–6.

[33] Friedrich Reichert, "Turnen, Sport und Spiel in Dresden seit 1844,"*Dresdner Geschichtsbuch* 6 (2000), 79, 138, 147-8, 150-1; Holger Starke, „Die Vereidigung des Dresdner Volkssturms auf der Ilgen Kampfbahn," *Führerschule, Thingplatz, „Judenhaus": Orte und Gebäude der nationalsozialistischen Diktatur in Sachsen* (Dresden: 2014), 291; Wolfgang Mischnick, *Von Dresden nach Bonn: Erlebnisse—jetzt aufgeschrieben* (Stuttgart: 1991), 74-5, 79-80.

[34] Hädecke, 279-80; Mischnick, 61, 79-80; Reichert, 153.

[35] Mischnick, 41.

[36] Kübler, *Geschichtsverein,* 204-6, 220; Kersten Hahn and Ines Marrin, „Die bauliche Entwicklung Dresdens von 1918-1933," *Bauen,* 95, 100-1; Gilbert Lupfer, „Architektur und Stadtplanung," *Geschichte der Stadt Dresden,* Bd. 3, 305, 308-9, hereafter cited as *Geschichte;* Starke, *Geschichte,* Bd. 3, 302; Caris Heidel and Maria Lienert, „Das Stadtkrankenhaus von 1919 bis 1932," *Von Stadtkrankenhaus zum Universitätsklinikum: 100 Jahre Krankenhausgeschichte in Dresden* (Köln: 2001), 90, 94-5.

[37] Lupfer, *Geschichte,* Bd. 3, 311; Heinrich Magirius, „Stadtbild und Denkmalpflege,"
Geschichte, Bd. 3, 322-26; Kübler, *Geschichtsverein,* 209-10.

[38] Lapp, *Revolution,* 133, 202.

[39] For Praetorius and Schütz, Steude, *Geschichte,* Bd. I, 576–8; also Steude, "Zur Musik am sächsischen Hof in Dresden während der Regierung Kurfürst Johann Georgs" and "Heinrich Schütz und der dreissigjährigen Krieg," *Annäherung durch Distanz: Texte zur älteren mitteldeutschen Musik und Musikgeschichte* (Altenburg: 2001), 110–15, 119–126; Hans Joachim Moser, *Heinrich Schütz: A Short Account of his Life and Works* (New York: 1967), 21–96; for "singing ballets," Moritz Fürstenau, *Zur Geschichte der Musik und des Theaters am Hofe zu Dresden,* Teil I (Dresden: 1861), 87–8.

[40] Johann Georg's preference for Italian music, Hecht, *Herrscher*, 157; first Italian opera, Helen Watanabe-O'Kelly, *Court Culture in Dresden: From Renaissance to Baroque* (New York: 2002), 191–2.

[41] Friedrich Kummer, *Dresden und seine Theaterwelt* (Dresden: 1938), 55–8.

[42] History of *Kunstkammer*, Damian Dombrowski, "Dresden_Prag. Italienische Achsen in der zwischenhöfischen Kommunikation," *Elbflorenz: Italienische Präsenz in Dresden 16.-19. Jahrhundert* (Dresden: 2000), 76; Gerald Heres, "Die kurfürstlichen Sammlungen in Renaissance und Frühbarock," *Geschichte*, Bd. I, 562–6, 569–70; Karin Kolb, "Cranach und die Malerei in Dresden im 16. Jahrhundert," *Geschichte*, Bd. I, 584–5, 589–93. Heres, "Von der *Kunstkammer* zum Museumskomplex," *Geschichte*, Bd. II, 251–54; Frank Aurich, "Von der Büchersammlung zur Bibliothek," *Geschichte*, Bd. I, 559–60; Joachim Menzhausen, "Elector Augustus's *Kunstkammer*: an Analysis of the Inventory of 1587," *The Origins of Museums: The Cabinet of Curiosities in Sixteenth and Seventeenth-Century Europe* (Oxford: 1985), 69–75; Hecht, *Herrscher*, 158; Watanabe-O'Kelly, 91–8.

[43] For Klengel and Johann Georg II's construction, "Frühbarocke Bauten in Dresden," https://www.dresden-und-sachsen-de/dresden/geschichte07_fruehbarock, retrieved 9/1/20; Sieglinde Richter-Nickel, "Aufstieg zur Residenzstadt von europäischen Rang (1648–1763," *Dresden: Die Geschichte der Stadt von den Anfängen bis zur Gegenwart* (Dresden: 2002), 68–9.; Anke Fröhlich, "Höfische Festkultur im Augusteischen Dresden," *Geschichte*, Band II, 200.

[44] Gardens versus claustrophobia, Walter Hentschel, *Johann Christoph Knöffel: Der Architekt des sächsischen Rokokos* (Berlin: 1973), 31; Reiner Gross, "Die Stadt in der zweiten Hälfte des 17. Jahrhunderts," *Geschichte*, Bd. II, 40; Great Garden, Walter May, "Städtisches und Landesherrliches Bauen," *Geschichte*, Bd. II, 152–4; for expanse https://en.wikipedia.org/wiki/grosser_garten#:~:text, retrieved 9/11/2020.

[45] Johann Georg II's relationship with the arts and with brothers, Watanabe-O'Kelly, 33–4; Gabriel Tzschirmer, *Die Durchlauchtigste Zusammenkunft/oder Historische Erzehlungen* (Nürnberg: 1680), schedule of events recorded for each day, townscape copper plates from Diana Procession on February 11, planning 4–6, arrival procession 26–37, Danish envoy's visit 207, Kingdom game on

February 18, 233–4, marriages on February 25, 291; for subsidies, Heinrich Theodor Flathe, https://de.wikisource.org/wiki/ADB:Johann_Georg_II.(Kurfürstvon Sachsen), updated 5/1/19, retrieved 9/12/20; townscape analysis, Heinrich Magirius," Architektur und Bildende Künste," *Geschichte*, Bd. I, 552–4.

Chapter III

⁴⁶ Sigfried Asche, *Balthaser Permoser: Leben und Werk* (Berlin: 1978), 53–5.
⁴⁷ Friedrich August's education, Helmut Neuhaus, "Friedrich August I (1694–1733)," *Die Herrscher Sachsens* (Munich: 2004), 176–78, hereafter cited as *Herrscher*; Karl Czok, *August der Starke und Kursachsen* (Munich: 1988), 10–15, 270, hereafter cited as *August*.
⁴⁸ Czok, *August*, 17, 259; Neuhaus, *Herrscher*, 173–4, 190; processional roles, Karl Czok und Reiner Gross, "Das Kurfürstentum, die sächsische-pölnische Union und die Staatsreform (1547–1789)" *Geschichte Sachsens* (Weimar: 1989, 271.
⁴⁹ Czok, *August*, 49; T. Kevorkian, "Piety Confronts Politics: Philip Spener in Dresden, 1686–1691," *German History,* 16:2 (1998), 145–164; Christoph Wetzel, "Kirche und Religion," *Die Geschichte der Stadt Dresden*, Bd. II (Stuttgart: 2006), 105, 113, hereafter cited as *Geschichte*; Helen Watanabe-O'Kelly, *Court Culture in Dresden: From Renaissance to Baroque* (New York: 2002), 196; Reiner Gross, "Vom Dreissigjährigen Krieg zum Siebenjährigen Krieg—Dresden als Zentrum sächsischer Herrschaftsausübung," *Geschichte*, Bd. II, 34.
⁵⁰ Wetzel, *Geschichte*, Bd. II, 106, 133, 139–41.
⁵¹ Regulation, Gross, *Geschichte*, Bd. II, 32–3, 41; Walter May, "Städtisches und Landesherrliches Bauen," *Geschichte*, Bd. II, 155–8, 160, 167–8, 177; Rudolf Förster, *Dresden: Geschichte der Stadt in Wort und Bild* (Berlin:1984), 47–8, 56, hereafter cited as *Wort/Bild*; Sieglinde Richter-Nickel, "Aufsteig zur Residenzstadt von europäischen Rang (1648–1763)," *Dresden: Die Geschichte der Stadt von den Anfängen bis zur Gegenwart* (Dresden: 2002), 90, hereafter cited as *Geschichtsverein*; Fritz Löffler, *Dresden sowie es war* (Düsseldorf: 1979), 25–6; landscape on water, Heidrun Laudel, "Stadt am Fluss," *Geschichte,* Bd. III (Stuttgart: 2006), 317. For princely city planning,

see Wolfgang Braunfels, *Urban Design in Western Europe: Regime and Architecture, 900–1900* (Chicago: 1988), 181, 184–6, 188, 211; also Hartmut Hofrichter, "Die Entwicklung bis zum Ende des Alten Reichs," *Geschichte der Stadt Koblenz: Von den Anfängen bis zum Ende der kurfürstlichen Zeit* (Stuttgart: 1992), Bd. 1, 419–38.

[52] Karlheinz Blaschke, "Dynastie-Regierung-Schloss," *Geschichte*, Bd. I, 424–5; Förster, *Wort/Bild*, 44; Richter-Nickel, *Geschichtsverein*, 80.

[53] Zwinger/its creators, Harald Marx, "Dieses Werk allein musste ihn unsterblich machen," 9–19, 47–8, 53–6, 70–3, 77–8, 89 and Norbert Oelsner/Henning Prinz, "Die Neugestaltung der Repräsentations und Fest-Etage des Dresdner Residenzschlosses unter Leitung Pöppelmanns 1717 bis 1719," 180–4, Michael Kirsten, "Der Dresdner Zwinger," 161–2, 170–4, all in *Matthäus Daniel Pöppelmann: Der Architekt des Dresdner Zwingers* (Münster: 1989–90), hereafter cited as *Pöppelmann;* Fritz Löffler, *Der Zwinger zu Dresden* (Dresden: 1989), 4, 6–7, 12–18, 20, 36–41, hereafter cited as *Zwinger;* Förster, *Wort/Bild*, 58; Pöppelmann in team, Wolfgang Hädecke, *Dresden: Eine Geschichte von Glanz, Katastrophe, und Aufbruch* (Munich: 2006), 66; Asche, 9–14, 17–20, 46–7, 49–50, 53, 55, 61, 79–81, 208.

[54] Elbe as Grand Canal, Laudel, *Geschichte*, Bd. III, 317; Taschenberg Palais, Förster, *Wort/Bild,* 58; palaces on string, May, *Geschichte,* Bd. II, 170; and Walter May, "Das Holländische und das Japanische Palais, *Pöppelmann*, 207, 210.

[55] May, 169–70 and Wetzel, 127–31 in *Geschichte*, Bd. II; Hädecke, 101, Watanabe-O'Kelly, 201–3; quote in Heinz Quinger, *Dresden und Umgebung* (Ostfildern: 2011), 142.

[56] May, *Geschichte* Bd. II, 171; Hagen Bächler, "Die Dresdner Elbbrücke," *Pöppelmann*, 251–2.

[57] For Neustadt, Förster, *Wort/Bild*, 58; Gross, *Geschichte*, Bd. II, 37–9; Richter-Nickel, *Geschichtsverein*, 90–1; Czok, *August.* 182; Fritz Löffler, *Das Alte Dresden* (Leipzig: 1989), 79, 116–7, hereafter cited as *Alte Dresden.*

[58] Gross and May, *Geschichte*, Bd. II, 49–50, 171–4.

[59] Gross, *Geschichte,* Bd. II, 39–40; Ulrich Rosseaux, *Freiräume: Unterhaltung, Vergnügen, und Erholung in Dresden, 1694–1830* (Cologne: 2007), 54.

[60] Quoted in Rosseaux, 73.

⁶¹ Reiner Gross, "Feste und Feierlichkeiten am Hof Augusts des Starken—Wiederspiegelung absolutistischer Machtpolitik," and Kirsten, *Pöppelmann,* 173, 238; Czok, *August,* 205; Förster, *Wort/*Bild, 58–60; Watanabe-O'Kelly, 225–229; Rosseaux, 77–82; Elaine Tierney, "The Festivities of Augustus the Strong," *Baroque, 1620–1800: Style in the Age of Magnificence* (London: 2009) 179; Michael Walter, "Italienische Musikals—Repräsentationskunst der Dresdner Fürstenhochzeit von 1719," *Elbflorenz: Italienische Präsenz in Dresden 16.-19. Jahrhundert* (Dresden: 2000), 177–81, hereafter cited as *Elbflorenz;* Anke Fröhlich, "Höfliche Festkultur im Augusteischen Dresden," *Geschichte,* Bd. II, 200.

⁶² Fröhlich, *Geschichte,* Bd. II, 212; Sieglinde Richter-Nickel, "Handwerk, Manufaktur, Handel," *Geschichte,* Bd. II, 71–5, 77, 79–83, 97–103 and *Geschichtsverein,* 82, 88; Watanabe-O'Kelly, 6–8; Czok, *August,* 67, 126–7, 132, 136; Siegfried Kube, "Im Schattenkreis der Residenz. Zu Lebensbedingungen und Lebensweise werktätiger Schichten in Dresden, insbesondere während des 18. Jahrhunderts," *Volksleben zwischen Zunft und Fabrik: Studien zu Kultur und Lebensweise werktätigen Klassen und Schichten während des Übergangs vom Feudalismus zum Kapitalismus* (Berlin: 1982), 266; Förster, *Wort/Bild,* 46.

⁶³ Dinglinger biographies, Erna von Watzdorf, *Johann Melchior Dinglinger: Der Goldschmied des deutschen Barock* (Berlin: 1962), Bd. I, 15–23, 26, 35–40, 112, 122, 126, Bd. II, 303–4, 317–8; Asche, 70–1.

⁶⁴ Watanabe-O'Kelly, 212–20; Tierney, *Baroque,* 130–32.

⁶⁵ Watanabe-O'Kelly, 109, 115, 117–19, 221–25; Richter-Nickel, *Geschichte,* Bd. II, 91–2; Edmund de Waal, *The White Gold: Journey into an Obsession* (New York: 2015), 157, 178–81, 184–90; also C.M. Quiroz and S. Agathopoulos, "The Discovery of European Porcelain Technology," available arrXiv.org, retrieved 9/21/20.

⁶⁶ Collection development, Gerald Heres, "Von der Kunstkammer zum Museums Komplex," *Geschichte,* Bd. II, 254–9; Gregor Weber, "Die Galerie als Kunstwerk. Die Hängung italienischer Gemälde in der Dresdner Galerie 1754," *Elbflorenz: Italienische Präsenz in Dresden 16.-19. Jahrhundert* (Dresden: 2000), 229, hereafter cited as *Elbflorenz*; Czok, *August,* 267–8; Watanabe-O'Kelly, 219–20; Förster, *Wort/Bild,* 59; Harald Marx, "Painting in Dresden in the Eighteenth Century," *Dresden in the Ages of Splendor and*

Enlightenment: Eighteenth-Century Paintings from the Old Master Picture Gallery (Columbus: 1999), 3, hereafter cited as *Splendor/Enlightenment*.

[67] Views, Heidrun Laudel, "Stadt am Fluss," *Geschichte*, Bd. III (Stuttgart: 2006), 316; Fröhlich, *Geschichte*, Bd. II, 192–3; Walter Fellmann, *Heinrich Graf Brühl: Ein Lebens-und-Zeitbild* (Leipzig: 1990), 61, 71, hereafter cited as *Brühl*.

[68] Gabriele Hoffmann, *Constantia von Cosel und August der Starke: Die Geschichte einer Mätresse* (Köln: 1984), 302.

[69] May, *Geschichte*, Bd. II, 179–81; Hädecke, 105–9; Löffler, *Alte Dresden*, 203–9; Fellmann, *Brühl,* 182–3; Konstanze Rudert, "Lorenzo Mattielli—ein italienescher Bildhauer am Dresdner Hof, *Elbflorenz*, 204.

[70] Wolfgang Hochstein, "Die Dresdner Kapelle unter Johann Adolf Hasse" und "Vorwort," *Der Klang der Sächsischen Staatskapelle Dresden: Kontinuität und Wandelbarkeit eines Phänomens,* (New York: 2001), xvi, 83–89, 94; Manfred Fechner, "Musik im barocken Dresden," *Geschichte,* Bd. II, 224–5; Friedrich Kummer, *Dresden und seine Theaterwelt* (Dresden: 1938), 63; Moritz Fürstenau, *Zur Geschichte der Musik und des Theaters am Hofe zu Dresden*, Bd. II (Dresden: 1862), 275–7; Förster, *Das Alte Dresden: Bilder und Dokumente aus zwei Jahrhunderten* (Leipzig: 1934/Reprint: Frankfurt/Main: 1977), 57, 64.

[71] Dieter Hartwig, "Die Kreuzkantor 1720–1828 von Reinhold bis Agthe," *Der Dresdner Kreuzchor: Geschichte und Gegenwart, Wirkungstätten und Schule* (Leipzig: 2006), 57, 59–60; Fechner, *Geschichte*, Bd. II, 221; Hans John, *Der Dresdner Kreuzchor und seine Kantoren* (Berlin: 1982), 66–7.

[72] Rosseaux, 134–8.

[73] Friedrich August II, Brühl, theater, Fellmann, *Brühl*, 60–1, 71, 173–7, 186; for palace, Löffler, *Alte Dresden*, 241–2; library, Wolfgang Frühauf, "Von der kürfürstlichen Privatbibliothek zur Sächsischen Landesbibliothek," *Von der Liberey zum Bibliothek: 440 Jahre Sächsischen Landesbibliothek* (Dresden: 1990), 15–8, 20.

[74] Marx, 20–3, and Gregor Weber, "The Gallery as Work of Art: The Installation of the Italian Paintings in 1754," *Splendor/Enlightenment* 188–95; Fellmann, *Brühl*, 194–9, 203–6; Weber, *Elbflorenz*, 230–6; Heres, *Geschichte*, Bd. II, 260–2.

[75] Heinecken's biography,

https://en.wikipedia.org/wiki/Carl_Heinrich_von_Heinecken, updated 7/14/20, retrieved 9/24/20; Marx, *Splendor/Enlightenment*, 307, 49–54; Fellman, *Brühl*. 207; Fröhlich, *Geschichte*, Bd. II, 242–3: Günter Jäckel, "Literatur der Goethezeit," *Geschichte,* Bd. II, 431–3 and https://en.wikipedia.org/wiki/Johann_Joachim_Winckelmann.

[76] Decorations, Fellmann, *Brühl*, 126, 161–2; Knöffel, Walter Hentschel and Walter May, *Johann Christoph Knöffel: Der Architekt des sächsischen Rokokos* (Berlin: 1973), particularly 115–116.

[77] Cited in Erich Hänel, "Die Stadt der Vergangenheit," *Alte Dresden:Bilder/Dokumente*, 11.

Chapter IV

[78] Theodor Schieder, *Frederick the Great* (New York: 2000), 93, 95–7, 101, 103; Karl Czok and Reiner Gross, "Das Kürfürstentum, die sächsische-polnische Union und die Staatsreform (1547–1789)," *Geschichte Sachsens* (Weimar: 1989), 283–4.

[79] https://en.wikipedia.org/wiki/Diplomatic_Revolution, retrieved 10/6/2020; Schieder, 121; Czok and Gross, *Geschichte Sachsens*, 286; Reiner Gross, "Vom dreissigjährigen Krieg zum Siebenjährigen Krieg—Dresden als Zentrum kursächsischer Herrschaftsausübung," *Geschichte der Stadt Dresden*, Bd. II (Stuttgart: 2006), 50–1, hereafter cited as *Geschichte;* Carl-Ludwig Paeschke and Dieter Zimmer, *Dresden: Geschichten einer Stadt* (Berlin: 1994), 40.

[80] Gross, 51–3 and Walter May, "Städtisches und Landesherrliches Bauen," 189, *Geschichte*, Bd. II.

[81] Plundering/Schreyer experience, C.H. Schreyer, "Selbstbiographie," *Das Alte Dresden: Bilder und Dokumente aus zwei Jahrhunderten* (Leipzig: 1934) [Reprint Frankfurt/Main: 1977], 34–9, hereafter cited as *Alte Dresden Bilder/Dokumente;* damage, Günter Jäckel, "Im Banne Preussens und Napoleons (1763–1830)," *Dresden: Die Geschichte der Stadt von den Anfängen bis zum Gegenwart* (Dresden: 2002), 102, hereafter cited as *Geschichtsverein*; Walter May, "Städtisches und Landesherrliches Bauen," *Geschichte*, Bd. II, 190; churches, Fritz Löffler, *Das Alte Dresden: Geschichte seiner Bauten* (Leipzig: 1989), 31, 39, hereafter cited as *Alte Dresden*.

[82] Quoted in Jäckel, *Geschichtsverein*, 102

[83] Jäckel, *Geschichtsverein,* 104, 106.

[84] Karl Czok, *August der Starke und Kursachsen* (Munich: 1988), 218, hereafter cited as *August*; Robert Beachy, "The Alchemy of Credit: Saxony's Rétablissement after 1763," *Decades of Reconstruction: Postwar Societies, State-Building, and International Relations from the Seven Years' War to the Cold War* (Cambridge, U.K.: 2017), 143, 145; Reiner Gross, "Zwischen Niedergang und Revolution," *Geschichte,* Bd. II, 329; Jäckel, *Geschichtsverein*, 104, 114–5.

[85] Population, Christian Päschel, "Die Städtische Finanzwesen," *Geschichte*, Bd. I, 365ff.; Friedrich Schulze, *Memoiren* (Bunzlau: 1837), Teil I, 5; Friedrich Kummer, *Dresden und seine Theaterwelt* (Dresden: 1938), 13; Jäckel, *Geschichtsverein*, 108.

[86] Rudolf Förster, *Dresden: Geschichte der Stadt in Wort und Bild* (Berlin: 1984), 68, hereafter cited as *Dresden Wort/Bild*; Walter May, "Städtebauliche Entwicklung," *Geschichte,* Bd. II, 393–6, 402.

[87] Gross, 329 and May, 393–411, *Geschichte*, Bd. II; Fritz Löffler, *Dresden so wie es war* (Düsseldorf: 1979), 30.

[88] B. G. Weinert, "Von Dresden überhaupt," *Alte Dresden Bilder/Dokumente*, 26–8.

[89] Heidrun Wozel, *Der Dresdner Striezelmarkt: Geschichte und Tradition des ältesten deutschen Weihnachtmarktes* (Husum: 2009), 75, hereafter cited as *Striezelmarkt*; Sieglinde Richter-Nickel, "Handwerk, Handel, Manufaktur, und Fabrik," *Geschichte*, Bd. II, 363; Siegfried Kube, "Im Schattenkreis der Residenz. Zu Lebensbedingungen und Lebensweise werktätiger Schichten in Dresden, insbesondere während des 18. Jahrhunderts," *Volksleben zwischen Zunft und Fabrik: Studien zu Kultur und Lebensweise werktätiger Klassen und Schichten während des Übergangs vom Feudalismus zum* Kapitalismus (Berlin: 1982), 264–5, hereafter cited as *Volksleben; * Jäckel, *Geschichtsverein*, 85, 107; Förster, *Dresden Wort/Bild*, 67–8.

[90] Caris-Petra Heidel, "Das medizinische Dresden," *Vom Stadtkrankenhaus zum Universitätsklinikum: 100 Jahre Krankenhausgeschichte in Dresden* (Köln: 2001), 1–5; Jäckel, *Geschichtsverein*, 108.

[91] Jäckel, *Geschichtsverein*, 110; Czok und Gross, *Geschichte Sachsens*, 290.

[92] Anke Fröhlich, "Malerei und Bildhauerkunst," *Geschichte,* Bd. II, 234, 473–5; Harald Marx, "Painting in Dresden in the Eighteenth Century," *Dresden in the Ages of Splendor and Enlightenment: Eighteenth-Century Paintings from the Old Masters Picture Gallery* (Columbus: 1999), 14; Förster, *Dresden Wort/Bild,* 59, 68; Jäckel, *Geschichtsverein,* 115.

[93] Eckkard Simon, "German Medieval Theatre: Tenth Century to 1600," *A History of German Theatre* (New York: 2008), 8–33; Moritz Fürstenau, *Zur Geschichte der Musik und des Theaters am Hofe zu Dresden* (Dresden: 1861–2)/Reprint New York: 1971), Teil I, 67–81; Teil II, 285, 298–9, 307–9, 311, 323, 344–8; Christian Hecht, "Johann Georg II (1656–1680)," *Die Herrscher Sachsens* (Munich: 2004), 156–7; Günter Jäckel, "Hofpoesie und Aufklärung," und "Literatur der Goethezeit," *Geschichte,* Bd. II, 272, 437-9; Ulrich Rosseaux, *Freiräume: Unterhaltung, Vergnügen und Erholung in Dresden, 1694–1830* (Köln: 2007), 98–100, 103–14, 117–29; W. H. Bruford, *Germany in the Eighteenth Century: The Social Background of the Literary Revival* (Cambridge, U.K.: 1952), 323.

[94] Schulze, Teil I, 85, 88–90.

[95] Rosseaux, 172–5, 177–9, 182–3, 191–3, 197, 199, 201, 312–3, 319–22, 327.

[96] Rosseaux, 212–18, 220, 223,

[97] Rosseaux, 225–31.

[98] Schulze, Teil I, 18.

[99] Rosseaux, 234–7.

[100] Rosseaux, 240–1, 251–5; Schulze, Teil I, 78; https://de.wikipedia.org/wiki/Lincke'sches_Bad, retrieved 10/6/20.

[101] Kaspar Riesbeck, "Lichter und Schatten," *Alte Dresden Bilder/Dokumente,* 79; Jäckel, *Geschichte,* Bd. II, 435–6, 440; Schulze, Teil I, 153–6; Brigitte Emmrich, "Wir haben's Recht, ganzungefragt". Zur Rolle anti-feudaler und demokratisch-revolutionäer Lieder und Gedichte des werktätiger Volkes in der Zeit nach der Französischer Revolution…" *Volksleben,* 430–1.

[102] Schulze, Teil I, 71–3, 178.

[103] Jäckel, *Geschichte,* Bd. II, 441–3; Schulze, Teil I, 91–3, 97; Linda Siegel, *Dora Stock, Portrait Painter of the Körner Circle in Dresden (1785–1815)* (Lewiston, N.Y.: 1993), 22, 49, 53 85–6, 100, 108, 119, 121.

[104] Schulze, Teil II, 3–4, 206–8; Kummer, 85.

[105] Kube, *Volksleben,* 259–61, 267–88, 270–1;

https://de.wikipedia.org/wiki/Christian_Heinrich_Schreyer, retrieved 10/6/20.
[106] Kube, *Volksleben*, 278; Rieck, *Alte Dresden Bilder/Dokumente*, 75–6, 79; Heidrun Wozel, "Brauchtum," *Geschichte*, Bd. 2, 516

Chapter V

[107] Reiner Gross, "Zwischen Niedergang und Revolution," *Geschichte der Stadt Dresden* (Stuttgart: 2006), Bd. II, 332–3, hereafter cited as *Geschichte*; Günter Jäckel, "Im Banne Preussens und Napoleons (1763–1830)," *Dresden: Die Geschichte der Stadt von den Anfängen bis zur Gegenwart* (Dresden: 2002), 113, hereafter cited *Geschichtsverein*; Rudolf Förster, *Dresden: Geschichte der Stadt in Wort und Bild* (Berlin: 1984), 71, hereafter cited as *Dresden Wort/Bild*.

[108] Reiner Gross and Karl Czok, "Das Kurfürstentum, die sächsische-polnische Union und die Staatsreform (1547–1789)," *Geschichte Sachsens* (Weimar: 1989), 314 ff.; Friedrich Schulze, *Memoiren* (Bunzlau: 1837), Teil 2, 105–11; Jäckel, *Geschichtsverein*, 20–1; Gross, *Geschichte,* Bd. II, 333–5; Förster, *Dresden Wort/Bild*, 71.

[109] Linda Siegel, *Dora Stock, Portrait Painter of the Körner Circle in Dresden (1785–1815)* (Lewiston, N.Y.: 1993), 91, 93, 446–7; Schulze, Teil 2, 139.

[110] Wilhelm von Kügelgen, *Jugenderinnerungen eines alten Mannes* (Leipzig: 1907), 108, 110–11; Schulze, Teil 2, 214–16; Siegel, 100; Gross, *Geschichte,* Bd. II, 37.

[111] Erich Haenel and Eugen Kalkschmidt, *Das alte Dresden: Bilder und Dokumente aus zwei Jahrhunderten* (Leipzig: 1934) (Reprint Frankfurt/Main: 1977), 137, hereafter cited as *Alte Dresden Bilder/Dokumente*; Gustav Nieritz, *Selbstbiographie* (Leipzig: 1872), 111; Schulze, Teil 2, 217.

[112] Haenel/Kalkschmidt, *Alte Dresden Bilder/Dokumente*, 140, 143–44; Jäckel, *Geschichtsverein*, 123; Schulze, Teil 2, 218–20.

[113] Gross, *Geschichte*, Bd. II, 338; Jäckel, *Geschichtsverein,* 124.

[114] Ludwig Richter, "Die Kriegszeit," *Alte Dresden Bilder/Dokumente*, 155; Förster, *Dresden Wort/Bild*, 77; Kügelgen, 158–9.

[115] Gross, *Geschichte*, Bd. II, 338; Jäckel, *Geschichtsverein*, 124–5; Nieritz, 134; Richter, *Alte Dresden Bilder/Dokumente,* 157–8; Schulze Teil 2, 234.

[116] Jäckel, *Geschichtsverein,* 125; Schulze, Teil 2, 244–6; Nieritz, 165.

[117] Jäckel, *Geschichtsverein*, 125; Richter, *Alte Dresden Bilder/Dokumente*, 30–3; Schulze, Teil 2, 248–9, 251; Förster, *Dresden Wort/Bild*, 77.
[118] Gross, *Geschichte*, Bd. II, 342–3; Schulze, Teil 3, 9–11; Jäckel, *Geschichtsverein*, 126; Förster, *Dresden Wort/Bild*, 78.
[119] Kügelgen, 220.
[120] Gross/Czok, *Geschichte Sachsens*, 322–3; Jäckel, *Geschichtsverein*, 126.

Chapter VI

[121] Wilhelm von Kügelgen, *Jugenderinnerungen eines alten Mannes* (Leipzig: 1907), 221; Reiner Gross, "Zwischen Niedergang und Revolution," *Geschichte der Stadt Dresden* (Stuttgart: 2006), Bd. II, 346, hereafter cited as *Geschichte*.
[122] Siegfried Kube, "Im Schattenkreis der Residenz. Zu Lebensbedingungen und Lebensweise werktätiger Schichten in Dresden, insbesondere während des 18. Jahrhunderts," *Volksleben zwischen Zunft und Fabrik: Studien zu Kultur und Lebensweise werktätiger Klassen und Schichten während des Übergangs vom Feudalismus zum Kapitalismus* (Berlin: 1982), 281, hereafter cited as *Volksleben*; Walter May, "Städtebauliche Entwicklung," *Geschichte*, Bd. II, 404–5; Yair Mintzker, *The Defortification of the German City, 1689–1866* (New York: 2012), 93; Ulrich Rosseaux, *Freiräume, Unterhaltung, Vergnügen und Erholung in Dresden, 1694–1830* (Köln: 2007), 263, 268, 271–2; Thomas Kantschew, *Die Städtebauliche Entwicklung Dresdens im 19. Jahrhundert: Von der Entfestigung bis zur Gründerzeit* (Magisterarbeit, FU Berlin: 1996) Section 3.2.1, www.TOM-CONNECT-de/Staedtebau-DRESDEN/STADT.html, retrieved 10/14/20.
[123] Gustav Klemm, "Vor fünfzig Jahren," *Das Alte Dresden: Bilder und Dokumente aus zwei Jahrhunderten* (Leipzig: 1934) (Reprint Frankfurt/Main: 1977), 239–42, hereafter cited as *Alte Dresden Bilder/Dokumente*.
[124] Carl von Voss, *Eine Reise nach Dresden. Aufzeichnungen des Kammerherrn Carl v. Voss* (Pfullungen: 1986), 26, 81, 112, 120, 186, 194.
[125] Heidrun Laudel, "Architektur und Bauwesen," *Geschichte*, Bd. II, 629.
[126] Laudel, *Geschichte*, Bd. II, 629; May, *Geschichte*, Bd. II, 410–11; Kantschew, Section 4.1; Rosseaux, 267–9. Germans do not count the ground

floor as one of a house's stories. For them the Neustadt was limited to two stories. I have followed American usage and counted the ground floor as a story.

[127] Kantschew, Section 3.2.1.

[128] Rosseaux, 269.

[129] Michael Hammer, *Volksbewegung und Obrigkeiten: Revolution in Sachsen, 1830/31* (Weimar: 1997), 55; Gerhard Schmidt, *Die Staatsreform in Sachsen in der ersten Hälfte des 19. Jahrhunderts: Eine Parallelle zu Steinsche Reformen in Preussen* (Weimar: 1966), 30–3; Roland Zeise, "Die bürgerliche Umwälzung. Zentrum der proletarischen Parteibildung (1830–1871), *Geschichte Sachsens* (Weimar: 1989), 332.

[130] David August Taggesell, *Tagebuch eines Dresdner Bürgers oder Niederschreibung der Erignisse eines jeden Tages, soweit solche vom Jahre 1806 bis 1851 für Dresden und dessen Bewohner von geschichtlichem, gewerblichem oder örtlichem Interesse waren* (Dresden: 1851), 532–3, 535; Reiner Gross, "Dresden im zweiten Drittel des 19. Jahrhunderts—Zentrum des politischem Geschehens im Lande," *Geschichte*. Bd. II, 530; Hammer, *Volksbewegung*, 36–9, 98, 147–9; Zeise, *Geschichte Sachsens,* 335.

[131] Hammer, *Volksbewegung*, 125, 129–32, 134, 137–9, 149–52; "Die September Revolution. Zeitgenössischer Bericht," *Alte Dresden Bilder/Dokumente*, 271–3; Gross, *Geschichte*, Bd. II, 531.

[132] Gross, *Geschichte*, Bd. II, 531–2; Reiner Gross and Ines Werner, "Verfassung und Verwaltung nach Einführung der kommunaler Selbstverwaltung," *Geschichte*, Bd. II, 569; Wilfrid Hahn, "Auf den Weg zur Grossstadt (1830–1871)," *Dresden: Die Geschichte der Stadt von den Anfängen bis zur Gegenwart* (Dresden: 2002), 136, hereafter cited as *Geschichtsverein*; Hubert Kiesewetter, *Industrialisierung und Landwirtschaft: Sachsens Stellung im regionaler Industrialisierungsprozess Deutschlands im 19. Jahrhundert* (Köln: 1988), 105; Rudolf Förster, *Dresden: Geschichte der Stadt in Wort und Bild* (Berlin: 1984), 87, hereafter cited as *Dresden Wort/Bild.*

[133] Gross, *Geschichte*, Bd. II, 534–5; Zeise, *Geschichte Sachsens*, 333; Hammer, *Volksbewegung, 457.*

[134] Hammer, *Volksbewegung*, 458–61; Gross, *Geschichte*, Bd. II, 536.

[135] Hammer, *Volksbewegung*, 461–2.

[136] Carl Gustav Carus, *Lebenserinnerungen und Denkwürdigkeiten* (Neuausgabe Weimar: 1966), Bd. I, 512–3.

[137] Hammer, *Volksbewegung*, 107–8, 462–5; Gross, *Geschichte*, Bd. II, 537–8; Zeise, *Geschichte Sachsens*, 336–7.

[138] Schmidt, 140–2, 171; Hammer, *Volksbewegung*, 110–11; Zeise, *Geschichte Sachsens*, 337.

[139] Friedrich August Schulze, *Memoiren* (Bunzlau: 1837), Teil 3, 105–16; 118–21; "Gesellschaftlicher Naturgenuss um 1830," *Alte Dresden Bilder/ Dokumente*. 279–83; Voss, 75.

[140] Christopher R. Friedrichs, *Jewish Youth in Dresden: The Diary of Louis Lesser, 1833–1837* (Bethesda: 2011), 45, 72–3, 79, 137, 148–9, 176, hereafter cited as *Lesser Diary*.

[141] Rosseaux, 64, 69, 71; Rudolf Forberger, *Die Industrielle Revolution in Sachsen 1800–1861* (Berlin: 1982), Bd. I, 1, 303; www.urban75.org/london/london-gas-lamps-and-gaslighting.html, retrieved 10/14/20.

[142] Kantschew, Section 5.2.1; Kube, *Volksleben*. 268.

[143] Forberger, Bd. I, 1, 248–9.

[144] http://dresden-kompakt.de/thema-familie-freizeit/suesse-geheimnisse-oder-wie-die-schokolade-nach-Dresden-kam; http://de.wikipedia.org/wiki/Friedrich_Anton_Reiche, both retrieved 7/31/2014; Forberger, Bd. I, 2; Hahn, *Geschichtsverein*, 138, 158.

[145] Voss, 314; Forberger, Bd. I, 2.

[146] Karl Otto Bucher, "Jugenderinnerungen eines alten Sachsen," *Alte Dresden Bilder/Dokumente*, 286.

[147] Voss, 314; Sieglinde Richter-Nickel, "Handwerk, Handel, Manufaktur, und Fabrik," *Geschichte*, Bd. II, 369.

[148] *Geschichte der Technischen Universität Dresden, 1828–1978* (Berlin: 1978), 24–6, hereafter cited as *Geschichte TH*; Kiesewetter, 674–6.

[149] Schulze, Teil III, 180; *Geschichte TH*, 26; Dietrich Conrad, "Technischer Fortschritt und industrielle Entwicklung," *Geschichte*, Bd. II, 577–604; Forberger Bd. I, 1, 220; http://de.wikipedia.org/windex.php?title=Wilhelm_Gotthelf_Lohrmann; http://de.wikipedia.org/wiki/Rudolf_Sigismund_Blochmann, both retrieved 1/27/2014.

[150] Conrad, *Geschichte*, Bd. II, 581; http://de.wikipedia.org/wiki/Johann_Andreas_ Schubert, retrieved 1/28/2014.

[151] Carl-Ludwig Paeschke and Dieter Zimmer, *Dresden: Geschichten einer Stadt* (Berlin: 1994), 65; "Zeitgenössischer Bericht," *Alte Dresden Bilder/Dokumente*, 295–6.

[152] "Zeitgenössischer Bericht," 296; Taggesell, 785.

[153] Conrad, *Geschichte*, Bd. II, 594; http://en.wikipedia.org/wiki/Royal_Saxon_State_Railways, retrieved 6/2/2014; Carus, Bd. II, 53; Förster, *Dresden Wort/Bild,* 101.

[154] Caris-Petra Heidel," Ärztliche Ausbildung in Dresden seit Mitte des 18. Jahrhunderts," *Dresdner Hefte* 113 (2013), 6–8; Carus, Bd. I, 160, 471, 478, 480, 483 and Elmar Jansen, "Nachwort," Bd. II, 355–7, 379–80, 385.

[155] Wolfgang Hädecke, *Dresden: Eine Geschichte von Glanz, Katastrophe und Aufbruch (*München: 2006), 111.

[156] Voss, 35–38–9, 66, 90, 98, 110, 281.

[157] Friedrich Christian August Hasse, *Das Leben Gerhards von Kügelgen* (Leipzig: 1824, SLUB Digitale Sammlung), 103, 125; Kügelgen, 28, 467; http://de.wikipedia.org/wiki/Gerhard_von_Kügelgen, retrieved 1/30/2014.

[158] Hans Joachim Neidhardt, "Bildhauerkunst und Malerei," *Geschichte*, Bd. II, 705

[159] Kügelgen, 113; Carus, Bd. I, 165–66, 498; https://en.wikipedia.org/wiki/List_of_works_by_caspar_david_friedrich, retrieved 10/31/2020.

[160] Ludwig Richter, *Lebenserinnerungen eines deutschen Malers* (Leipzig: 1950), 348, 365–8; Anke Fröhlich, "Malerei und Bildhauerkunst," *Geschichte, *Bd. II, 476–7; http://de.wikipedia.org/wiki/Karl_August_Böttiger; Günter Jäckel, *Dresden zwischen Wiener Kongress und Maiaufstand* (Berlin: 1989),

16, hereafter cited as *Kongress/Maiaufstand*; http://de.wikipedia.org/wiki/Sächsischen_Kunstverein, retrieved 1/31/2014.

[161] Carus, Bd. I, 567–8; https://en.wikipedia.org/wiki/Eduard_Bendemann, retrieved 10/17/2020.

[162] Harald Marx in Richter, ix–xxxviii and 1–2, 42, 53, 114–7, 408; http://de.wikipedia.org/wiki/Ludwig_Richter, retrieved 2/20/2014.

[163] Ernst Rietschel, *Jugenderinnerungen* (Leipzig: 1994), 7–8, 12, 58–60, 69; Neidhardt, *Geschichte*, Bd. II, 702–3; https://de.wikipedia.org/wiki/Ernst_Rietschel, retrieved 2/12/2014.

[164] Harry Francis Mallgrave, *Gottfried Semper: Architect of the Nineteenth Century* (New Haven: 1996), 8–9, 11–12, 14–21, 63–64, 75–6, 80–1, 92–7, 101.

[165] Fritz Löffler, *Das Alte Dresden: Geschichte seiner Bauten* (Leipzig: 1989), 374; Mallgrave, 100, 117–23; Hahn, *Geschichtsverein*, 145–6; Hädecke, 158–9.

[166] Löffler, *Das Alte Dresden*, 379–80; Mallgrave, 107–9, 112, 116.

[167] Hahn, *Geschichtsverein*, 147; Mallgrave, 100, 358.

[168] Hans John, *Der Dresdner Kreuzchor und seine Kantoren* (Berlin: 1982), 22, 55–6; Charles Burney, "Tagebuch seiner musikalischen Reisen," *Alte Dresden Bilder/Dokumente*, 16–8.

[169] Gina Pellegrino, "Robert Schumann and the Gesangverein: The Dresden Years (1844–1850)," *All Theses and Dissertations (ETDs), 2011*, https://openscholarship.wustl.edu/etd/276, 49; Karl Maria von Weber, "Die Anfänge der Dreyssigschen Singakademie," *Alte Dresden Bilder/Dokumente*, 192; Kügelgen, 457, 459, 466; https://de.wikipedia.org/wiki/ SingakademieDresden.

[170] Hans John "Musik und Oper," *Geschichte*, Bd. II, 425–30; Voss, 94, 99 113, 199; Hädecke, 111–6; Max von Weber," Karl Maria von Weber: Ein Lebensbild," and Karl von Holtei, "Vierzig Jahre," both in *Alte Dresden Bilder/Dokumente*. 211, 213, 217.

[171] Hans John "Musik und Oper," *Geschichte*, Bd. II, 425–30; Voss, 94, 99 113, 199; Hädecke, 111–6; Max von Weber," Karl Maria von Weber: Ein Lebensbild," and Karl von Holtei, "Vierzig Jahre," both in *Alte Dresden Bilder/Dokumente*. 211, 213, 217.

[172] Karl Gutzkow, "Rückblicke," *Alte Dresden Bilder/Dokumente*, 347; Eckland Roch, "Richard Wagners Reformpläne. Die Königliche Kapelle betreffend, oder Musikalische Schwierigkeiten mit der Demokratie," *Der Klang der Sächsischen Staatskapelle Dresden: Kontinuität und Wandelbarkeit eines Phänomens* (New York: 2001), 160, 164–66, hereafter cited as *Klangkapelle*.

[173] Roch, *Klangkapelle*, 159; Hans John, "Musikschaffen," *Geschichte*, Bd. II, 651, 665–6; Carus, Bd. I, 492, 530.

[174] Wagner, 258, 328–30.
[175] John, *Geschichte*, Bd. II, 657–8; Hädecke, 120–1; Wagner, 297–8.
[176] Carus, Bd. II, 140.
[177] Wagner, 363; John, *Geschichte,* Bd. II, 667, 679–81; Carus, Bd. I, 502–3.
[178] Eduard Devrient, *Aus seinen Tagebücher: Berlin-Dresden 1836–1851* (Weimar: 1964), 532; Gutzkow, *Alte Dresden Bilder/Dokumente*, 347; Hahn, *Geschichtsverein*, 142; http://de.wikipedia.org/wiki/Wolf_Adolf_August_von_Lüttichau,retrieved 2/26/2014
[179] http://de.wikipedia.org./wiki/Ludwig_Tieck, retrieved 2/3/2013.
[180] Voss, 28, 35, 43. 84–5, 115, 154, 165.
[181] Günter Jäckel, "Literatur der Goethezeit," *Geschichte,* Bd. II, 463–5; Simon Williams, The Romantic Spirit in German Theatre," *A History of German Theatre* (Cambridge: 2008), 137–8, hereafter cited as *German Theatre.*
[182] Eduard Devrient, xiv–xviii, 222–3, 228–9, 234, 239, 243, 298; http://de.wikipedia, org/wiki/Eduard_Devrient.
[183] Devrient, xvi, 138, 142, 244, 259–60, 311; Friedrich Kummer, *Dresden und Seine Theaterwelt* (Dresden: 1938), 146; Anthony Meech, "Classical theatre and the formation of a civil society, 1720–1832," *German Theatre*, 82–4; Alfred Meissner, "Im Vormärz," *Alte Dresden Bilder/Dokumente, 333–4.*
[184] Taggesell, 844, 866; Schmidt, 123–27; Karl Heinz Blaschke, "Bernhard von Lindenau, *Neue Deutsche Biografie* (Berlin: 1985), Bd. 14, 593; Jäckel, 37–8; Löffler, *Das Alte Dresden,* 377; Roch, *Klang Kapelle*, 167; John, *Geschichte*, Bd/ II, 658.
[185] Taggesell, 800, 844, 846, 849, 866; Jäckel, *Kongress/Maiaufstand*, 39; Kiesewetter, 336–7; Gustav Nieritz, *Selbstbiographie* (Leipzig: 1872), 389, 392, https://books.google.co.zw/books, retrieved 9/5/2024.
[186] Gross, *Geschichte*, Bd. II, 548; www.pirna.de, retrieved 5/13/2014: https://en.wikipedia.org/wiki/List_of_Ministers_President_of_Saxony, updated 3/2/20, retrieved 10/26/2020.
[187] Carus, Bd. II, 163; Wagner, 362.
[188] Wagner, 363–4; Nieritz, 401; Hahn, *Geschichtsverein*, 151; Zeise, *Geschichte Sachsens,* 356–61; Gross, *Geschichte*, Bd. II, 550.

[189] Wagner, 363–4; Taggesell, 889, 897; Nieritz, 401, 407, 411; Devrient, 429, 431; Gross, *Geschichte*, Bd. II, 553.

[190] Hajo Holborn, *A History of Modern Germany, 1840–1945* (New York: 1969), Vol. III, 72; Nieritz, 412; "Robert Blum," *Neue Deutsche Biografie*, Bd. 2, 322–3; Robin Oomkes, https://www.slowtravelberlin.com/ Nov_9_1848_the_execution_of_Robert_Blum. retrieved 7/24/2024.

[191] Taggesell, 908; Devrient, 456.

[192] Taggesell, 880, 890–92, 904; Richard J. Bazillion, *Modernizing Germany: Karl Biedermann's Career in the Kingdom of Saxony 1835–1901* (New York: 1990, 201; Carus, Bd. II, 170.

[193] Taggesell, 897, 906–7; Nieritz, 412–4; Gross, *Geschichte*, Bd. II, 550.

[194] Gustav Nieritz, "Der Maiaufstand 1849," *Alte Dresden Bilder/Dokumente*, 357; Hahn, *Geschichtsverein*, 151; Taggesell, 912–3.

[195] Holborn, Vol. III, 84–6.

[196] Taggesell, 917–26; Carus, Bd. II, 176; Bazillion, 186–7; Hahn, *Geschichtsverein*, 152; Nieritz, *Alte Dresden Bilder/Dokumente*, 358; Zeise, *Geschichte Sachsens*, 362.

[197] Taggesell, 927; Schöne, "Einzelbilder aus den Maitagen," *Alte Dresden Bilder/Dokumente*, 377.

[198] Hahn, *Geschichtsverein*, 152; Bazillion, 186–7; Wagner, 392; Carus, Bd. II, 176–7; Devrient, 478–9; Gross, *Geschichte*, Bd. II, 554.

[199] "Saxon Generalleutnant August von Schubert," *Alte Dresden Bilder/Dokumente*, 364; Ingo Zimmermann, *Sachsens Markgrafen, Kurfürsten und Könige: Die Wettiner in der Meissnisch-Sächsischen Geschichte* (Berlin: 1990), 108–9; Hahn, *Geschichtsverein*, 153; Carus, Bd. II, 178.

[200] Devrient, 480; Carus, Bd. II, 178–9; Hahn, *Geschichtsverein*, 154; Schöne, *Alte Dresden Bilder/Dokumente*, 378.

[201] Bazillion, 194; Hahn, *Geschichtsverein, 155;* Carus, Bd. II, 179–81; Nieritz, 419.

[202] Carus, Bd. II, 182; Devrient, 483; Schöne, *Alte Dresden Bilder/Dokumente*, 381, 383.

[203] Devrient, 484.

[204] Carus, Bd. II, 183–4; Devrient, 485; Zeise, *Geschichte Sachsens*, 366; Hahn, *Geschichtsverein*, 155; Gross, *Geschichte*, Bd. II, 505.

[205] Carus, Bd. II, 184; Devrient, 485; Jäckel, *Kongress und Maiaufstand*, 293.
[206] Jäckel, *Kongress und Maiaufstand*, 44, 305, 310–11; Mallgrave, 169.
[207] Zeise, *Geschichte Sachsens,* 366; Hahn, *Geschichtsverein*, 155–6; Carus, Bd. II, 185–6; Devrient, 486.
[208] Devrient, 491; Carus, Bd. II, 182; Nieritz, *Alte Dresden Bilder/Dokumente,* 360.
[209] Nieritz, *Alte Dresden Bilder/Dokumente*, 357–63; Mallgrave, 167.

Chapter VII

[210] Rudolf Förster, *Dresden: Geschichte der Stadt in Wort und Bild* (Berlin: 1984), 99, hereafter cited as *Dresden Wort/Bild*; Wilfrid Hahn, "Auf den Weg zur Grossstadt," *Dresden: Die Geschichte der Stadt von den Anfangen bis zur Gegenwart* (Dresden: 2002), 156, hereafter cited as *Geschichtsverein*.
[211] http://de.wikipedia.org/wiki/Marienbrücke_(Dresden), retrieved 6/2/14; https://en.wikipedia.org/wiki/Dresden-Friedrichstadt_station,edited 5/22/2020, retrieved 11/8/20; Hahn, *Geschichtsverein,* 157.
[212] Thomas Kantschew, *Die Städtebauliche Entwicklung Dresdens im 19. Jahrhundert: Von der Entfestigung bis zur Gründerzeit* (Magisterarbeit FU Berlin: 1996), Section 5.2.1, www.TOM-CONNECT.de/Städtebau-Dresden/Stadt.html; Gerhard Schmidt, *Die Staatsreform im Sachsen in der ersten Hälfte des 19. Jahrhunderts: Eine Parallele zu den Steinsche Reformen in Preussen* (Weimar: 1966), 314; Hahn, *Geschichtsverein*, 156.
[213] Hubert Kiesewetter, *Industrialisierung und Landwirtschaft: Sachsens Stellung im regionalen Industrialisierungsprozess Deutschlands im 19. Jahrhundert* (Köln: 1988), 501, 543, 546, 554–6; Rudolf Forberger, *Die Industrieller Revolution in Sachsen 1800–1861* (Berlin: 1982), Bd. I, 223, 353, 356, 360; Tilo Richter, *Industriearchitektur in Dresden* (Leipzig: 1997), 59, hereafter cited as *industriearchitektur*.
[214] http://de.wikipedia.org/wiki/Friedrich_Siemens, edited 3/16/14, retrieved 6/3/14; www.dresdner-stadtteile.de/Zentrum/Wilsdruffer_Vorstadt/Freiberger_Strasse/Glaswerk_Lobtau, html, retrieved 11/14/20.
[215] *Industriearchitektur*, 69;

http://dresden.stadtwiki/de/wiki/Gottlieb_Traugott_Bienert, edited 4/11/14, retrieved 6/2/14.

[216] http://Dresden.stadtwiki.de/wiki/Traugott_Jakob_Hermann_Seidel; Gerald Kolditz," In der Zeit des Kaiserreiches (1871–1918)," *Geschichtsverein*, 181; https://www.bsz-ae-dd.de/Index.php/schulgeschichte-des-bsz-agrarwirtschaft/37-schulgeschichte42.html,edited7/14/2019,retrieved 11/12/20.

[217] Kiesewetter, 517; https://wikipedia.org/wiki/Clemens_Müller, edited 4/19/19, retrieved 5/30/19; www.dresdner-stadtteile.de/Leipziger_Vorstadt/Grossenhainer_Strasse.html, retrieved 11/14/20; http://de.wikipedia.org/wiki/Seidel_Naumann, edited 3/30/14, retrieved 7/31/14.

[218] Wilhelm Jollet," Die Geschichte der Dresdner Steingutfabrik Villeroy & Boch von 1856–1906," www.Geschichte-der-Fliese.de/vbd_Geschichte. html, retrieved, 11/14/20.

[219] *Industriearchitektur*, 7–8, 64–5; http://www.wtbc.de/yenidze_en.html; www.dresdner-stadtteile.de/Ost/Striesen/Striesener_Zigarettenfabriken/html, retrieved 11/15/20.

[220] https://en.wikipedia.org/wiki/Zollverein, retrieved 1/20/15; Reiner Gross, "Dresden im zweiten Drittel des 19. Jahrhunderts—Zentrum des politischen Geschehens im Lande," *Geschichte der Stadt Dresden* (Stuttgart: 2006), Bd. II, 564–6, hereafter cited as *Geschichte*; Heinrich Friedjung, *The Struggle for Supremacy in Germany, 1859–1866* (New York: 1966) 206, 210, 225, 235, 285; James Retallack, "Why Can't a Saxon be More like a Prussian? Regional Identities and the Birth of Modern Political Culture," *Canadian Journal of History* 32 (1997): Sections 1 and 4.

[221] Otto Richter, "Die Heimkehr des siegreichen Heeres," *Das Alte Dresden: Bilder und Dokumente aus zwei Jahrhunderten* (Leipzig: 1934/Reprint: Frankfurt/Main: 1977) 429-30, hereafter cited as *Alte Dresden Bilder/Dokumente*.

[222] *Industriearchitektur*, 7; Holger Starke, "Das Werden der Grossstadt," *Geschichte*, Bd. III, 28, 30; Ernst Venus, *Amtshauptmann in Sachsen: Lebenserinnerungen des letzten Dresdner Amtshauptmanns und Landrats* (Bonn: 1970), 25.

[223] Heidrun Wozel, "Alltag, Freizeit, Festkultur," *Geschichte*, Bd. III, 225–6.
[224] Holger Starke, *Geschichte*, Bd. III, 31; Erwin Fink, "Symbolic Representations of the Nation: Baden, Bavaria, and Saxony, c. 1860–80," *Different Paths to the Nation: Regional and National Identities in Central Europe and Italy, 1830–70* (New York: 2007), 207–8, 211, 213; Kolditz, *Geschichtsverein*, 180.
[225] Rudolf Förster, *Dresden: Geschichte der Stadt in Wort und Bild (*Berlin: 1984), 108, hereafter cited as *Dresden Wort/Bild*.
[226] https://de.wikipedia.org/wiki/Friedrich_Enzmann, retrieved 6/4/14; https://de.wikipedia.org/wiki/Hermann_Krone, edited 4/10/18, retrieved 5/3/19; https://de.wikipedia.org/wiki/Richard_Hüttig, retrieved 11/16/20; https://de.wikipedia.org/wiki/Heinrich_Ernemann, retrieved 10/7/15; https://en.wikipedia.org/wiki/Praktica/Older_company_history,retrieved 11/16/20; *Industriearchitektur*, 72; also see https://www.Dresdner-kameras.de/firmengeschichte. html, retrieved 11/16/20.
[227] http://de.wikipedia.org/wiki/Carl_Friedrich_August_Kühnscherf, retrieved 1/26/15; http://de.wikipedia.org/wiki/Kelle_Hildebrandt, retrieved 9/2/14; http://blog.andic.org.uk/2014/10/the-real-life-grand-budapest-hotel.html, retrieved 1/28/15.
[228] http://de.wikipedia.org/wiki/Oskar_Ludwig_Kummer, retrieved 5/27/14; http://de.wikipedia.org/wiki/Sachsenwerk, retrieved 7/10.10; http://www.ig-kraftwerk-mitte.de/Geschichte-des-Standorts, retrieved 10/24/16.
[229] http://saebi.isgv.de/biografie/Carl_Eschebach_(1842–1905), retrieved 6/4/2014; http://de.wikipedia.org/wiki/Eschebachsche_Werke,edited10/27/13, retrieved 6/4/14.
[230] http://de.wikipedia.org/wiki/Kaffeesurrogatfabrik_Otto_E._Weber, edited 10/7/2011, retrieved 10/17/11; http://de.wikipedia.org/wiki/Teekanne_(Unternehmen), retrieved 7/31/14; http://de.wikipedia.org/wiki/Stengel_Co., edited 2/15/14, retrieved 9/4/14; Kolditz, *Geschichtsverein*, 194.
[231] *Industriearchitektur*, 66.

[232] www.dresdner stadtteille.de/Nordwest/Pieschen, retrieved 5/8/22. http://de.wikipedia.org/wiki/Konsum_Dresden, edited 1/5/14, retrieved 7/31/14.

[233] Carl-Ludwig Paeschke, Dieter Zimmer, *Dresden: Geschichten einer Stadt* (Berlin: 1994), 73–77; Wolfgang Hädecke, *Dresden: Eine Geschichte von Glanz. Katastrophe und Aufbruch* (München: 2006), 237–8.

[234] Frank Heidenreich, *Arbeiter Kulturbewegung und Sozialdemokratie in Sachsen vor 1933* (Weimar: 1995), 27; Eugen Kalkschmidt, "Die Grossstadt bis zur Jahrhundertwende," *Alte Dresden Bilder/Dokumente*, 147.

[235] Hahn, *Geschichtsverein*, 161; Kalkschmidt, *Alte Dresden Bilder/Dokumente*, 59–66.

[236] Kantschew, Section 5.2.2; Erich Kästner, *Als ich ein kleiner Junge war* in *Gesammelte Schriften* (Zürich: 1959), Bd. 6, 114; Matthias Lerm, Stefan Jarman, "Die bauliche Entwicklung Dresdens von 1871 bis 1918," *Bauen in Dresden im 19. Und 20. Jahrhundert* (Dresden: 1991), 43, hereafter cited as *Bauen*.

[237] Kantschew, Section 5.4.3; Jürgen Paul, "Stadtentwicklung und Architektur," *Geschichte*, Bd. III, 78; www.dresdner stadtteile.de/Neustadt/Albertstadt, retrieved 11/17/20. The German Kaserne translates as barracks., thus "barracksville."

[238] Kolditz, *Geschichtsverein*, 176–7; Förster, *Dresden Wort/Bild*, 108, 112, 222; www.dresdner stadtteile.de/Ost/Striesen, retrieved 2/8/15.

[239] www.dresdner stadtteile.de/Nordwest/Mickten/Trachenberge, retrieved 2/9/15; www.dresdner stadtteile.de/sudost/Reick/Strehlen, retrieved 2/9/15; apply also to note 29; Förster, *Dresden Wort/Bild*, 113; Kolditz, *Geschichtsverein*, 170; Starke, *Geschichte*, Bd. III, 33; Fritz Löffler, *Das Alte Dresden: Geschichte seiner Bauten* (Leipzig: 1989), 390.

[240] Heidi Kreibich, Annegret Thicken, "Coping with floods in the city of Dresden, Germany," *Natural Hazards* 51:3 (2009), 423–36, www.researchgate.net/publication/225641029; Kolditz, *Geschichtsverein*, 185.

[241] Lerm/Jarmen, *Bauen*, 44; Hans John, *Der Dresdner Kreuzchor und seine Kantoren* (Berlin: 1982), 88; Daniel, Hartwig, "Die Kreuzschule im Zeitenwandel," *Der Dresdner Kreuzchor: Geschichte und Gegenwart*,

Wirkungsstätten und Schule (Leipzig: 2006), 320–6; Ulrich Amlung, "Schulwesen," *Geschichte,* Bd. III, 170–3; https://de.wikipedia.org/wiki/Freiherrlich_von_Fletchersches_Lehrerseminar, edited 10/1/20, retrieved 11/18/20.

[242] *Geschichte der Technischer Universität Dresden 1828–1978* (Berlin: 1978), 37, 51, 57, 83, 86; Reiner Pommerin, *Geschichte der TU Dresden 1828–2003* (Köln: 2003), 57–60, 79–80, 123–4; Klaus Mauersberger, "Vom Polytechnikum zur Technischen Hochschule," *Geschichte,* Bd. III, 174–6, 180; Förster, *Dresden Wort/Bild,* 114–5; Thomas Hänseroth, *Wissenschaft und Technik: Studien zur Geschichte der TU Dresden* (Köln: 2003), 124–6.

[243] http://dresden.stadtwiki.de/wiki/Hochschule_für_Bildende_Künste, retrieved 2/9/15; Fritz Löffler, *Das alte Dresden: Geschichte seiner Bauten,* 9 ed. (Leipzig: 1989), 94; https://en.Wikipedia.org/Constantin_Lepsius, edited 1/26/22; retrieved 2/9/22.

[244] http://dresden.stadtwiki.de/wiki/Kunstgewerbeschule,edited12/4/14, retrieved 2/10/15; http://www.johanstadtarchiv.de/article_id=98, retrieved 2/10/15.

[245] Paul, *Geschichte,* Bd. III, 83–4, 91.

[246] Anka Böthig, "Hans Jakob Erlwein-Stadtbaurat in Dresden von 1905 bis 1914," *Bauen,* 75, 77, 78–84; Hädecke, 191–5.

Chapter VIII

[247] Friedrich Kummer, *Dresden und seine Theaterwelt* (Dresden: 1939), 219–21, 233–4; Harry Francis Mallgrave, *Gottfried Semper: Architect of the Nineteenth Century* (New Haven: 1996), 4–8, 321–2, 339–40; Carl-Ludwig Paeschke und Dieter Zimmer, *Dresden: Geschichten einer Stadt* (Berlin: 1994), 45.

[248] Kummer, 223, 264–7; Willi Apelt, *Jurist im Wandel der Staatsformen: Lebenserinnerungen* (Tübingen: 1965), 172–3; Fritz Löffler, *Dresden so wie es war* (Düsseldorf: 1979) 60; Wolfgang Hädecke, *Dresden: Eine Geschichte von Glanz, Katastophe und Aufbruch* (München: 2006), 214–20; Rudolf Förster, *Dresden: Geschichte der Stadt in Wort und Bild* (Berlin: 1984), 114, hereafter cited as *Wort/Bild*: https://wikipedia.org/wiki/Ernst_von_Schuch, edited 2/17/19, retrieved 6/7/19.

[249] Hans John, "Musik und Oper," *Geschichte der Stadt Dresden* (Stuttgart: 2006) Bd. II, 423, hereafter cited as *Geschichte;* and Hans John, "Musikstadt von Europäischen Rang," *Geschichte*, Bd. III, 131, 133–4; Förster, *Wort/Bild*, 114.

[250] Hans John, *Der Dresdner Kreuzchor und seine Kantoren* (Berlin: 1982), 102–4; and John, *Geschichte*, Bd. III, 138–9; Roland Zeise and Bernd Rüdiger, "Bundesstaat im deutschen Reich," *Geschichte Sachsens* (Weimar: 1989), 402.

[251] John, *Geschichte*, Bd. III, 131.

[252] Ernst Venus, *Amtshauptmann in Sachsen: Lebenserinnerungen des letzten Dresdner Amtshauptmanns und Landrats* (Bonn: 1970), 15; Erich Kästner, *Als ich ein kleiner Junge war* in *Gesammelte Schriften*, Bd. 6 (Zürich: 1959), 79–80; Kummer, 43, 196–8, 221, 231–3, 247–9, 255–7; Ernst Günther, *Sarrasani wie er wirklich war* (Berlin: 1984), 40.

[253] Carl Gustav Carus, *Lebenserinnerungen und Denkwürdigkeiten* (Dresden: 1865–6; Reprint Weimar: 1966), Bd. 2, 279; Gerald Heres, "Die Dresden Museen," *Geschichte*, Bd. III, 153–6; Iris Bundt, "Bildende Kunst," *Geschichte*, Bd. III, 143; Karl Woermann, *Lebenserinnerungen einer Achtzigjährigen* (Leipzig: 1924), Bd. 2, 1014, 58–9, 86.

[254] Woermann, Bd. 2, 120–1, 214.

[255] Jürgen Paul, *Cornelius Gurlitt: Ein Leben für Architektur, Kunstgeschichte, Denkmalpflege und Städtebau* (Dresden: 2003), 17–21, 30–3, 38–42, 75, 104–6; also Paul's short biography of Gurlitt, *175 Jahre TU Dresden* (Köln: 2003), Bd. III, 304–5. For son Hildebrand's commerce with modern art during the Third Reich, https://en.wikipedia.org/wiki/Hildebrand_Gurlitt, edited 12/11/20, retrieved 12/15/20; Jan Lubitz, www.architekten-portrait.de/Fritz_Schumacher, retrieved 12/16/20.

[256] Woermann, Bd. 2, 60, 119; Fritz Löffler, *Otto Dix: Leben und Werk* (Dresden: 1967), 9; Reinhold Heller, "Brücke in Dresden and Berlin," *Brücke: The Birth of Expressionism in Dresden and Berlin, 1905–1913* (New York: 2009), 18, hereafter cited as *Brücke*; Gerald Kolditz, "In der Zeit des Kaiserreiches (1871–1918)," *Dresden: die Geschichte der Stadt von den Anfängen bis zur Gegenwart* (Dresden: 2002), 193–4, hereafter cited as *Geschichtsverein*.

[257] Förster, *Wort/Bild*, 130; Heller, *Brücke*, 13, 16–8, 20, 22–3, 26–31, 35–7, 39; Jill Lloyd, "Brücke: National Identity and International Style," *Brücke*, 60–8, 70–1, 74; Christian Wiekop, "Brücke and Canonical Association," *Brücke*, 103–7, 117; Iris Barndt, "Bildende Kunst," *Geschichte*, Bd. III, 148–9; Matthew Jeffries, *Imperial Culture in Germany, 1871–1918* (New York: 2003), 236.

[258] Heidrun Wozel, "Alltag, Freizeit, Festkultur," *Geschichte*, Bd. III, 229; Woermann, Bd. 2, 34, 42–3; Apelt, 8.

[259] Woermann, Bd. 2, 310–11.

[260] Dirk Hempel, *Literarische Vereine in Dresden: Kulturelle Praxis und politische Orientierung des Bürgertums im 19. Jahrhundert* (Tübingen: 2008), 31, 228, 230–32; Woermann, Bd. 2, 34–5, 102–4; Gerald Kolditz, "Politische Vereine und Parteien," *Geschichte*. Bd. III, 51–2.

[261] Hempel, 234, Kolditz, *Geschichte*, Bd. III, 53; Roger Chickering, *We Men who Feel Most German: A Cultural Study of the Pan-German League* (Boston: 1984), 183–4, 188, 190.

[262] Michael Schmidt, *Dr. Lahmanns Sanatorium im Kurort Bad Weisser Hirsch, 1888–heute* (Dresden: 2015), 4–6, 28, 32-3, 38.

[263] Caris-Petra Heidel, "Medizin und Gesundsheitswesen," *Geschichte*, Bd. III, 189–90; "C.P. Heidel, "Grundung des Stadtkrankenhauses und Entwicklung bis 1918," *Vom Stadtkrankenhaus zum Universitätsklinikum: 100 Jahre Krankenhausgeschichte in Dresden* (Köln: 2001), 29–33, 36, 43, 57–63.

[264] Roland Zeise and Bernd Rüdiger, "Bundesstaat im deutschen Reich (1871–1917)," *Geschichte Sachsens* (Weimar: 1989), 397; Hermann Beck, "Working-Class Politics at the Crossroads of Conservatism, Liberalism and Socialism," *Between Reform and Revolution: German Socialism and Communism from 1840 to 1890 (New York: 1998), 65–7, 69, 73–80;* Reiner Gross, "Dresden im Zweiten Drittel des Jahrhunderts—Zentrum des politischen Geschehens im Lande," *Geschichte,* Bd. III, 562–3; Frank Heidenreich, "Arbeiter Kulturbewegung und Sozialdemokratie in proletarischen Parteibildung," *Geschichte Sachsens, 106–8, 379–80;* Franz Walter, "Freital: Das 'Rote Wien' Sachsens," *Die SPD in Sachsen und Thüringen zwischen Hochburg und Diaspora: Untersuchungen auf lokaler Ebene vom Kaiserreich bis zur Gegenwart* (Bonn: 1993), 56–7, 60;; Franz Walter et al., *Die SPD in Sachsen und Thüringen zwischen Hochburg und*

Diaspora: Untersuchungen auf lokaler Ebene vom Kaiserreich bis zur Gegenwart (Bonn: 1993), 56–7, 60; James Retallack, *Red Saxony: Election Battles and the Spectre of Democracy in Germany, 1860–1918* (Oxford: 2017), 37–8, 95–100, 103, 107; Förster, *Wort/Bild, 110.*

[265] Thomas Adam, "How Proletarian was Leipzig's Social Democratic Milieu," *Saxony in German History: Culture, Society, and Politics, 1830–1933* (Ann Arbor: 2000) 262, hereafter cited as *Saxony/Germany;* Heidenreich, 49; Wozel, *Geschichte,* Bd. III, 222; Rudolf Förster, *Damals in Dresden: Porträt einer Stadt um 1900* (Berlin: 1990), 132, 135, 157–9, hereafter cited as *Damals;* Kästner, 55–61, 84–5; Kolditz, *Geschichtsverein,* 186.

[266] Zeiss/Rüdiger, *Geschichte Sachsens*, 397, 413–4; Herbert Wehner, "Interview mit Bernhard Wördehoff und Karl Donat, 9.7.76 in Deutschlandfunk," *Zeugnis* (Köln: 1982), 353; Förster, *Wort/Bild,* 111–2; Swen Steinberg, "August Kaden," *Sächsische Biografie,* #162 (2007).

[267] Förster, *Welt/Bild,* 111–12; Heidenreich, 38, 40; Kersten Rudolph, *Die sächsische Sozialdemokratie vom Kaiserreich zur Republik, 1871–1923* (Weimar: 1995), 52–6.

[268] Gunda Ulbricht, "Kommunale Vertretung und Verwaltung", *Geschichte,* Bd. III, 41–5; Kolditz, *Geschichtsverein,* 173; Karl Heinrich Pohl, "Power in the City: Liberalism and Local Politics in Dresden and Munich," *Saxony/Germany*, 297–8.

[269] Rudolph, 56; Pohl, 299; Ulbricht, *Geschichte,* Bd. III, 49; Heidenreich, 38; Walter Fabian, "*Klassenkampf um Sachsen: Ein Stück Geschichte 1918–1930*" (Löbau: 1930; Reprint Berlin: 1972), 15–16.

[270] F.L. Kroll, "Friedrich August III," *Die Herrscher Sachsens* (München: 2004), 312; Walter Fellmann, *Sachsens letzter König: Friedrich August III* (Leipzig: 1992), 130–36; Rudolph, 58–60; Pohl, *Saxony/Germany,* 301.

[271] Venus, 44–46.

[272] Heidrum Wozel, *Die Dresdner Vogelwiese: Vom Armbrustschiessen zum Volksfest* (Dresden: 1993), 3–9, 12–3, 20–7, 30, 34; Ulrich Rosseaux, *Freiräume: Unterhaltung, Vergnügen, und Erholung in Dresden, 1694–1830* (Köln: 2007), 160–3.

[273] Rosseaux, 163–8; 170, 172; Carl von Voss, *Eine Reise nach Dresden 1822: Aufzeichnungen des Kammerherrn Carl von Voss* (Pfüllungen: 1986), 167–70; Wozel, 34, 55–6; Karl Otto Bucher, "Jugenderinnerungen eines alten

Sachsen," *Das Alte Dresden: Bilder und Dokumente aus zwei Jahrhunderten* (Leipzig: 1934, Reprint Frankfurt/Main: 1977), 408, 410.

[274] Reinhard Delau and Lothar Sprenger, *Schmidt's Erben: Die Deutschen Werkstätten Hellerau* (Dresden: 1998), 27–8; Klaus-Peter Arnold, *Vom Sofakissen zum Städtebau: Die Geschichte der deutschen Werkstätten und der Gartenstadt Hellerau* (Dresden: 1993), 18–9, 25.

[275] https://ask.com/wiki/Arts_and_Craftsmovement, retrieved 3/31/15; Arnold, 15–6, 21–2, 31, 38, 47–8, 75–6, 79–80, 104.

[276] Clemens Galonska and Frank Elstner, *Gartenstadt/Garden City of Hellerau: Einhundert Jahre erste deutsche Gartenstadt/One Hundred Years of Germany's First Garden City* (Chemnitz: 2007), 13; Arnold, 69, 330; Peter de Mendelssohn, *Hellerau: Mein Unverlierbares Europa* (Dresden: 1993), 7.

[277] Joan Campbell, *The German Werkbund: The Politics of Reform in the Applied Arts* (Princeton: 1978), 9–10, 20.

[278] Galonska/Elstner, 7–8; Arnold, 330–1; Jeffries, 213, Gerald Heres, "Kulturelle Reformbewegungen der Jahrhundertwende," *Geschichte,* Bd. III, 198–9.

[279] Jeffries, 214; Arnold, 332–4, 340, 345; Gablonska/Elstner, 22–26.

[280] http://www.ask.com/wiki/Wolf_Dohrn, retrieved 2/8/15; Campbell, 20; Arnold, 353–8; Gablonska/Elstner, 38–40, 43; Mendelssohn, 52.

[281] Nils Shinker, *Die Gartenstadt Hellerau 1909–1945: Stadtbaukunst, Kleinwohnungsbau, Sozial-und Bodenreform* (Dresden: 2013), 7–8, 47; Arnold, 335.

[282] Woermann, Bd. 2, 304.

[283] Apelt, 35; Woermann, Bd. 2, 320–3, 331–2.

[284] Gerald Kolditz, "Dresden im ersten Weltkrieg," *Geschichte,* Bd. III, 246–7, 249, 250–1; Woermann, Bd.2, 332–3; Rudolph, 131, 133.

[285] Woermann, Bd. 2, 324–7.

[286] Rudolph, 103–12, 119, 129–33, 135–40.

[287] Rudolph, 148; Zeise/Rüdiger, *Geschichte Sachsens*, 427; Woermann, Bd. 2, 348.

[288] Rudolph, 157–8, 166.

[289] Karl Dietrich Erdmann, *Die Zeit der Weltkriege,* 4th ed., *Handbuch der deutschen Geschichte,* Bd. 4 (Stuttgart: 1959), 74–7; Rudolph, 162, 166.

290 http://www.ask.com/wiki/Kiel_Mutiny, retrieved 5/11/15; Rudolph, 172–4; Zeise/Rüdiger, *Geschichte Sachsens*, 429; Heidenreich, 137–8; Förster, *Wort/Bild,* 139–140.
291 Friedrich Salzburg, *Mein Leben in Deutschland vor und nach dem 30. Januar. 1933: Lebensbericht eines jüdischen Rechtsanwaltes aus dem amerikanischen Exil im Jahr 1940* (Dresden: 2001), 41; Rudolph, 173–4; Heidenreich, 139, 143, 145; Zeise/Rüdiger, *Geschichte Sachsens*, 431–3; Kroll, *Herrscher Sachsens, 316.*
292 Hädecke, 198.

Chapter IX

293 Wolfgang Hädecke, *Dresden: Eine Geschichte von Glanz, Katastrophe und Aufbruch* (München: 2006), 201; Karsten Rudolph, *Die sächsische Sozialdemokratie vom Kaiserreich zur Republik, 1871–1923* (Weimar: 1995), 180–2; Friedrich Salzburg, *Mein Leben in Deutschland vor und nach dem 30. Januar 1933: Lebensbericht eines jüdischen Rechtsanwaltes aus dem amerikanischen Exil im Jahr 1940* (Dresden: 2001), 42–4; Karl Woermann, *Lebenserinnerungen eines Achtzigjährigen* (Leipzig: 1924), Bd. 2, 376, 378; Frank Heidenreich, *Arbeiterkulturbewegung und Sozialdemokratie* (Weimar: 1995), 149.
294 Heidenreich, 146–7; Rudolph, 199–201,
295 Heidenreich, 148–50.
296 Rudolf Förster, *Dresden: Geschichte der Stadt in Wort und Bild* (Berlin: 1984), 41, hereafter cited as *Wort/Bild*; Christel Hermann, http://saebi.isgv.de/biografie/Bernhard_Blücher(1864–1938), retrieved 5/11/2015.
297 Rudolph, 224–8.
298 http://en.wikipedia.org/wiki/Bavarian Council Republic, retrieved 5/12/2015.
299 Woermann, Bd. 2, 360–2.
300 Rudolph, 244–8; Ernst Günther, *Sarrasani wie er wirklich war* (Berlin: 1984), 297.
301 Förster, *Wort/Bild*, 142; Heidenreich, 151.
302 Eric D. Weitz, *Weimar Germany* (Princeton: 2007), 99–100.

[303] Benjamin Lapp, *Revolution from the Right: Politics, Class, and the Rise of Nazism in Saxony, 1919–1933* (Boston: 1997) 65, 68–9, hereafter cited as *Revolution*; Benjamin Lapp, "Remembering the Year 1923 in Saxon History," *Saxony in German History: Culture, Society and Politics, 1830–1933* (Ann Arbor: 2000), 324–5, hereafter cited as *Saxony/Germany*.

[304] Hajo Holborn, *A History of Modern Germany, 1840–1945* (New York: 1969), 595–99, 601, 607–08; Weitz, 135–7.

[305] Förster, *Wort/Bild*, 145; Salzburg, 45; Lapp, *Revolution*, 79.

[306] Lapp, *Revolution*, 83, 85; Rudolph, 352–8, 366–7, 371–2; Walter Fabian, *Klassenkampf um Sachsen. Ein Stück Geschichte 1918–1930* (Löbau: 1930, Reprint Berlin: 1972), 161; Donald Pryce, "The Reich Government versus Saxony, 1923: The Decision to Intervene," *Central European History* 10:2 (1997), 116, 120, 124, 126,

[307] Rudolph, 379; Henry Ashby Turner, *Stresemann and the Politics of the Weimar Republic* (Princeton: 1963), 135–6.

[308] Lapp, *Saxony/Germany*. 327–30; Lapp, *Revolution*, 89–91, 95, 98; Fabian, 166; Mike Schmeitzner, "Revolution und Republik: Die Bildung des Freistaates Sachsen 1918/19 bis 1923," *Der Gespaltene Freistaat: Neue Perspecktiven auf die sächsische Geschichte, 1918 bis 1933* (Dresden: 2019), 107; Claus-Christian Szejnmann, *Von Traum zum Alptraum: Sachsen in der Weimarer Republik* (Leipzig: 2000), 44–5, hereafter cited as *Traum*.

[309] Rudolph, 402, 405; Lapp, *Revolution*, 99–101; Fabian, 174–6: Szejnmann, *Traum*, 46.

[310] Rudolph, 396–9, 408–9; Heidenreich, 164–6; Lapp, *Saxony/Germany*, 331.

[311] Report of Consul Louis Dreyfus, Nov.2, 1923, U.S. National Archives, WA D.C., 862.00m 1361, quoted by Lapp, *Saxony/Germany* 332; Lapp, Revolution, 118, 125; Rudolph, 402, 409; Heidenreich, 165, 168.

[312] Holger Starke, "Hauptstadt des Freistaats Sachsen," *Geschichte der Stadt Dresden* (Stuttgart: 2006), Bd. III, 263, 270–2, hereafter cited as *Geschichte*; Förster, *Wort/Bild*, 222.

[313] Holger Starke, "Wirtschaft und Verkehr," *Geschichte*, Bd. III, 285–7, 289; Thomas Kübler, "Die Stadt in der Weimarer Republik und in der NS-Zeit, 1918–1945," *Dresden: Geschichte der Stadt von den Anfängen bis zur Gegenwart* (Dresden: 2002), 207–9, hereafter cited as *Geschichtsverein*; Förster, *Wort/Bild*, 141.

[314] Herbert Blumtritt, *Geschichte der Dresdner Fotoindustrie* (Stuttgart: 2000), 49–54, 83–101; for Dresden firms, http://www.dresdnerkameras.de/index.html.accessed7/31/2014; http://fischi-online.de/foto /museum_hersteller_2, accessed 6/4/16; http://de.wikipedia.org/wiki/Zeiss_Ikon, accessed 7/31/2014; chief competitor Ernst Leitz Werke, https://de.wikipedia.org/wiki/Leica_Camera#Geschichte, accessed 1/4/21; also https://www.wikiwand.com/de/Zeiss-Ikon, accessed 1/5/2021.

[315] Starke, *Geschichte,* Bd. III, 290; Kübler, *Geschichtsverein,* 209.

[316] Kübler, *Geschichtsverein,* 208–9; Förster, *Wort/Bild,* 141; http://history.praktika.de/index, accessed 6/4/2014.

[317] https://de.wikipedia.org/wiki/Alfred_Reucker, edited 9//20/2020, retrieved 1/5/21; http://www.staatsschauspiel-dresden.de/ensemble/mitarbeiter/ehrenmitglieder/paul_wiecke,retrieved 6/28/2015; Woermann, Bd. 2, 367.

[318] Hädecke, 244–6; Matthias Herrmann, "Musik und Musikleben, 1918–1945," *Geschichte, Bd. III,* 385; Willibalt Apelt, *Jurist im Wandel der Staatsformen: Lebenserinnerungen* (Tübingen: 1965), 172–3; Henny Brenner, *The Song is Over: Survival of a Jewish Girl in Dresden* (Tuscaloosa: 2010), 23–4; Hansjörg Schneider, "Schauspiel in Dresden, 1918–1945," *Geschichte,* Bd. III, 402–3.Heide Lazarus, "Anfänge eines modernen Bühnentanzes," *Geschichte,* Bd. III, 377–80; Mary Anne Newhall, *Mary Wigmann* (New York: 2009), 4–5, 27–8; Jack Anderson, "Who Was Gret Palucca? A Legend in her Time," *New York Times,* August 15, 1993.

[319] https://de.wikipedia.org/wiki/Gret_Palucca, retrieved 6/28/2015; https://de.wikipedia.org/wiki/Ida_Bienert, retrieved 6/28/2015; Heike Biedermann," Will Grohman_Freund und Berater der Dresdner Kunstsammlerin Ida Bienert," *Zwischen Intuition und Gewissheit: Will Grohmann und die Rezeption der Moderne in Deutschland und Europa 1918–1968* (Dresden: 2013), 228, 230–3, hereafter cited as *Intuition*; Jasmin Kossman, "Will Grohmann, Laser Segall und die Dresdner Sezession Gruppe 1919," *Intuition,* 127–9.

[320] *Intuition,* 129–30, 228, 231–2; Erhold Frommhold and Gerlint Söder, "Bildende Kunst," *Geschichte,* Bd. III, 364–5;

https://de.wikipedia.org/wiki/Ida_Bienert, retrieved 6/28/2015.

[321] Frank Whitford, *Oskar Kokoschka: A Life* (New York: 1996), 27–9, 78–9, 115, 122, 129, 132–3, 140, 145–6; Frank Whitford, "Chronology," *Oskar Kokoschka* (Munich: 1991), 218–20.

[322] https://de.wikipedia.org/wiki/Otto_Dix, retrieved 6/20/2015; Fritz Löffler, *Otto Dix: Leben und Werk* (Dresden: 1967), 17, 36–7, 76, 92–3; Keith Hartley, catalogue entries, *Otto Dix: 1891–1969* (London: 1992), 89, 91, 115–6.

[323] Kübler, *Geschichtsverein, 214–5;* Annegret Karge, "Mitstreiter oder Mitarbeiter? Will Grohmann und die Internationale Kunstausstellung, Dresden 1926," *Intuition*, 94–5; Günther, 70; Starke, *Geschichte*. Bd. III, 296–7.

[324] Claudia Rasche, "Planung und Bau von Lichtspieltheatern in den 20er Jahren in Dresden," *Bauen in Dresden im 19.und 20. Jahrhundert* (Dresden: 1991), 111, hereafter cited as *Bauen*; Holger Starke and Heidrun Wozel, "Freizeit, Alltagsleben und Sport," *Geschichte,* Bd. III, 298; Gilbert Lupfer, "Architektur und Stadtplanung," *Geschichte*, Bd. III, 311.

[325] Mischnick, 41.

[326] Kübler, *Geschichtsverein*, 204–6, 220; Kersten Hahn and Ines Marrin, "Die bauliche Entwicklung Dresdens von 1918 bis 1933," *Bauen*, 95, 100–1; Lupfer, *Geschichte,* Bd. III, 305, 308–9; Starke, *Geschichte,* Bd. III, 302; Caris Heidel and Maria Lienert, "Das Stadtkrankenhaus von 1919 bis 1932," *Von Stadtkrankenhaus zum Universitätsklinikum: 100 Jahre Krankenhausgeschichte in Dresden* (Köln: 2001), 90, 94–5.

[327] Lupfer, *Geschichte,* Bd. III, 311; Heinrich Magirius, "Stadtbild und Denkmalpflege," *Geschichte*, Bd. III, 322–26; Kübler, *Geschichtsverein*, 209–10.

[328] Lapp, *Revolution*, 133, 202.

Chapter X

[330] http://de.wikipedia.org/wiki/Wilhelm_Külz, retrieved 5/11/15: Benjamin Lapp, *Revolution from the Right: Politics, Class and the Rise of Nazism in Saxony, 1919–1933* (Boston: 1997), 188.

[331] Thomas Kübler, "Die Stadt in der Weimarer Republik und in der NS-Zeit, 1918–1945," *Dresden: die Geschichte der Stadt von den Anfängen bis zur Gegenwart* (Dresden: 2002), 222–3, hereafter cited as *Geschichtsverein;*

Rudolf Förster, *Dresden: Geschichte der Stadt in Wort und Bild,* 154, hereafter cited as *Wort/Bild*.

[332] Lapp, 162, 164, 174–6; Claus-Christian Szejnmann, *Nazism in Central Germany: The Brown Shirts in Red Saxony* (New York: 1999), 6–7, 17–20, 308, hereafter cited as *Nazism;* Frederick Taylor, *Dresden: Tuesday, February 13, 1945* (New York: 2004), 43; Otto Griebel, *Ich war ein Mann der Strasse: Lebenserinnerungen eines Dresdner Malers* (Frankfurt/Main: 1986), 317.

[333] Frank Heidenreich, *Arbeiterbewegung und Sozialdemokratie in Sachsen vor 1933* (Weimar: 1995), 204–5; https://de.wikipedia.org//Paul_Ferdinand_Schmidt, retrieved 6/29/15; Lapp, 145; Herbert Wehner, *Zeugnis* (Köln: 1982), 326; Claus-Christian Szejnmann, *Vom Traum zum Alptraum: Sachsen in der Weimarer Republik* (Leipzig: 2000), 99, hereafter cited as *Traum*.

[334] Szejnmann, *Nazism,* 18, 166; Lapp, 196; Mike Schmeitzer, "Dresden in der Weltwirtschaftskrise, 1919–1933," *Geschichte der Stadt Dresden* (Dresden: 2006), Bd. 3, 410–11, hereafter cited as *Geschichte*.

[335] Heidenreich, 217–19, Szejnmann, *Traum,* 100.

[336] Szejnmann. *Nazism,* 3–7, 12, 15 and *Traum,* 58.

[337] Lapp, 193, 197; Claus-Christian Szejnmann, "The Development of Nazism in the Landscape of Socialism and Nationalism: The Case of Saxony 1918–1933," *Saxony in German History: Culture, Society, and Politics, 1830–1933* (Ann Arbor: 2000), 368, hereafter cited as *Saxony;* Szejnmann, *Traum,* 49–54, 61–3.

[338] Szejnmann, *Nazism,* 26–9 and *Traum,* 105–6; https://en.wikipedia.org/wiki/National_Socialist_Program # German_Party_Program, edited 1/31/22, retrieved 4/21/22.

[339] Szejnmann, *Nazism,* 33; Lapp, 212–13; https://de.wikipedia.org/wiki/Ergebnisse_der_Landtagswahlen_in_Weimarer_Republik#Sachsen; retrieved 1/4/18; Gunda Ulbricht, "Kommunalpolitik und Stadtverwaltung," *Geschichte*, Bd. 3, 275.

[340] Szejnmann, *Nazism*, 32, 222; Gunda Ulbricht, "Die Wahlen in Dresden 1932/33," *Dresden unterm Hakenkreuz* (Köln: 1998), 25–9, 31, 34–5, 40–1, hereafter cited as *Dresden Hakenkreuz*.

[341] http://www.wahlen-in-deutschland.de/wrtwdresdenbautzen.htm, retrieved 1/4/18; Andreas Wagner, *"Machtergreifung" in Sachsen: NSDAP und Staatliche Verwaltung 1930–1935* (Köln: 2004), 129–33; Szejnmann, *Nazism*, 21 and *Traum*, 137.

[342] Andreas Wagner, "Martin Mutschmann: Der braune Gaufürst (1935–1945)," *Von Macht und Ohnmacht: Sächsische Ministerpräsidenten im Zeitalter der Extreme 1919–1952* (Beucha:2006), 290, 292, 385, hereafter cited as *Macht/Ohnmacht*; Ernst Venus, *Amtshauptmann in Sachsen: Lebenserinnerungen des letzten Dresdner Amtshauptmanns und Landrats* (Bonn: 1970), 95; Heidenreich, 414.

[343] Swen Steinberg and Willy Bushak, "Die frühe Besetzung der Sächsischen Gewerkschaftshäuser im März 1933 am Beispiel von Dresden," *Führerschule, Thingplatz," Judenhaus': Orte und Gebäude der nationalsozialistischen Diktatur in Sachsen* (Dresden: 2014), 57, hereafter cited as *Führerschule*.

[344] Heidenreich, 416–17.

[345] Ulbricht, *Geschichte*, Bd. 3, 416, 419–20, 422 and Ulbricht, "Dresdner Juden im Nationalsozialismus," *Geschichte*, Bd. 3, 489.

[346] Ulbricht, *Geschichte*, Bd. 3, 416; Szejnmann, *Nazism*, 22; Mike Schmeitzner, "Verfolgung und politischer Widerstand," *Geschichte*, Bd. 3, 426–7.

[347] Adolf Diamant, *Chronik der Juden in Dresden: Von der ersten Juden bis zur Blüte der Gemeinde und deren Ausrottung* (Frankfurt/Main: 1973), 288; Förster, *Wort/Bild,* 161; Christoph Zuschlag, "Neues Rathaus Dresden: Die Ausstellung 'Entartete Kunst' 1933," *Führerschule*, 155–8; Wolfgang Hädecke, *Dresden: Eine Geschichte von Glanz, Katastrophe und Aufbruch* (München: 2006), 209.

[348] Förster, *Wort/Bild*, 165; Henriette Kunz, "Zwei Bücherverbrennungen in Dresden," *Führerschule*, 79–80.

[349] Andreas Wagner, "Manfred von Killinger: Putschist und SA-Führer (1933–35)," *Macht/Ohnmacht*, 258–69, 275–6.

[350] Wagner, *Macht/Ohnmacht*, 282–89, 293; Szejnmann, *Nazism*, 23, 210; Simone Lässig, "Nationalsozialistische Judenpolitik und jüdische Selbstbehauptung vor dem Novemberpogrom. Das Beispiel der Dresdner Bankiersfamilie Arnhold," *Dresden Hakenkreuz*, 152; Mike Schmeitzner, "Dresden: Landtag und Staatskanzlei," *Führerschule*, 59.

[351] Wagner, *Macht/Ohnmacht,* 297–9, 300, 302, 304–5; Hädecke, 243; Venus, 95, 97.

[352] Gerhard Lindemann, "Das Landeskirchenamt Dresden," *Führerschule,* 144.

[353] Hugo Hahn, *Kämpfer wider Willen: Erinnerungen des Landesbischofs von Sachsen D. Hugo Hahn aus dem Kirchenkampf 1933–1945* (Metzingen: 1969), 17–18, 20, 32, 37, 39, 43, 72, 86–8; Sophie von Bechtolsheim, "Die staatstreue Opposition: Die bekennende Kirche und der Kirchenkampf in Dresden 1933–1939," *Dresden Hakenkreuz,* 72.

[354] Hahn, 30–1, 55, 79–80, 93–4, 109, 113–15, 155; Bechtolsheim, *Dresden/Hakenkreuz,* 77.

[355] Hahn, 162–5, 175–7, 188.

[356] Friedrich Delekat, *Lebenserinnerungen* (Bonn: 1971), 91; Bechtolsheim, *Hakenkreuz,* 85.

[357] Birgit Mitscherlich, "Römisch-Katholische Kirche," *Geschichte,* Bd. 3, 451–3; Winfried Halder, "Katholische Kirche und Nationalsozialismus in Sachsen—(K)ein Thema der Zeitgechichte," *Dresden/Hakenkreuz,* 125–6.

[358] Wolfgang Mischnick, *Von Dresden nach Bonn: Erlebnisse—jetzt aufgeschrieben* (Stuttgart: 1991), 92–3; Mike Schmeitzner and Andreas Wagner, "Ministerpräsident und Staatskanzlei in Freistaat Gau und Land: Ein sächsischer Vergleich 1919–1952," *Macht/Ohnmacht,* 33.

[359] Kübler, *Geschichtsverein,* 224; Holger Starke, "Alltagsleben und Kultur," *Geschichte,* Bd. 3, 472; Victor Klemperer, *Ich will Zeugnis ablegen bis zum letzten: Tagebücher 1933–1941* (Berlin: 1995), hereafter cited as *Zeugnis,* 323 (diary entry 10/30/1936); Taylor, 56; Gilbert Lupfer, "Architektur und Stadtplanung," *Geschichte,* Bd. 3, 313.

[360] Norbert Haase, "Umgang mit wieder aufgefunden NS-Relikten im Ortsbild," *Führerschule, 305;* Gunda Ulbricht, "Altstadtgesundung in Dresden und Leipzig 1935–1939—Städteplanung des Nationalsozialismus," *Führerschule,* 272.

[361] Hermann Magirius, "Stadtbild-und-Denkmalpflege," and Matthias Herrmann, "Musik und Musikleben, 1918–1945," both in *Geschichte,* Bd. 3, 323ff., 391.

[362] Linda von Keyserlingk, "Die Albertstadt, der Widerstand und General-Major Hans Oster-Ein Dresdner im Zentrum der Verschwörung," 232–3; Manfred Zeidler, "Luftkriegschule Dresden-Klotzsche," 286; Siegfried

Bannack, "Stadt der Flieger—Klotzsches Erhebung zur Stadt 1935," 195–6; Hanka Blesse, "Die Nationalpolitische Erziehungsanstalt in Dresden-Klotzsche," 118–19, all foregoing in *Führerschule;* Klemperer, *Zeugnis,* 310–13 (entry 10/4/1936).

[363] Joachim and Waltraud Petzold, *Ideale und Idole im Schatten Hitlers und Stalins: Dresden Oberschüler auf dem Wege aus dem Dritten Reich in die DDR* (Potsdam: 1997), 82; Starke, *Geschichte,* Bd. 3, 474; Thomas Widera, *Dresden, 1945–1948: Politik und Gesellschaft unter sowjetischer Besatzungsherrschaft* (Göttingen: 2004), 29–30.

[364] Friedrich Reichert, "Turnen, Sport und Spiel in Dresden seit 1844," *Dresdner Geschichtsbuch* 6 (2000), 154.

[365] Hädecke, 278–9, 284; https://de.wikipedia.org/wiki/Richard_Hofmann_Fussballspieler, edited 9/23/2015, accessed 1/15/16; https://de.wikipedia.org/wiki/Helmut_Schön, edited 12/26/15, retrieved 1/15/16.

[366] Kübler, *Geschichtsverein,* 228; Hansjörg Schneider, "Schauspiel in Dresden, 1918–1945," *Geschichte,* Bd. 3, 405–6.

[367] Glen W. Gladberry, "The First National Socialist Theatre Festival—Dresden 1934," *Theatre of the Third Reich, the Prewar Years: Essays on Theatre in Nazi Germany* (Westport, CT: 1995), 121–132; Konstantin Hermann, "Der Führerbesuch 1934 und die 'Treuekundgebung' 1944 in Dresden," *Führerschule,* 75–6; Mischnick, 94.

[368] Starke, *Geschichte,* Bd. 3, 476–7.

[369] Ernst Günther, *Sarrasani wie er wirklich war* (Berlin: 1984), 34–44, 57–79, 84–5, 88–95, 109–17, 129–30, 139–41, 144–6, 151–2, 169–72, 168–9, 174, 235.

[370] Günther, 94, 159, 189, 204–9, 215–16, 218–19, 228, 230.

[371] Klemperer, 49–51, 53–4, 55, 139, 204–5, 258, 272, 314.

[372] Fritz Löffler, *Dresden wie es war* (Düsseldorf: 1979), 98–9; Heidrun Wozel, "Der Dresdner Striezelmarkt—ein Weihnachtsmarkt mit Tradition.," and "Alltagsleben," both in *Geschichte der Stadt Dresden* (Stuttgart: 2006), Bd. 2, 333–4, 336, 739–40; https://en.wikipedia.org/wiki/Striezelmarkt, edited 2/10/22, retrieved 4/12/22.

[373] Mischnick, 34–6. https://en.wikipedia.org/wiki/stollen, edited 1/8/22, retrieved 4/12/22; www.regionales.sachsen.de/spezialitaeten/details/dresdner-stollen#~:text=GeschichteDresdnerChriststollen, retrieved 4/12/22; www.dresdnerstollen.com/de/schutzverband, retrieved 4/12/22

[374] Szejnmann, *Nazism*, 190, Paeschke, 77; Kübler, *Geschichtsverein, 230;* Peter Fässler, "Sozialhygiene-Rassenhygiene-Euthanasie: Volksgesundheitspflege im Raum Dresden," *Dresden Hakenkreuz*, 200–01.

[375] Fässler, *Hakenkreuz*, 204; Klemperer, *Zeugnis,* 594 (entry 5/21/1941); Marina Leinert, "Medizin und Gesundheitswesen," *Geschichte*, Bd. 3, 462–3, 469.

[376] Förster, *Wort/Bild*, 167.

[377] Klemperer, *Zeugnis,* 479–80 (entry 8/29/1939), 490 (entry 9/18/1939), 486 (entry 9/10/1939), 491 (entry 9/20/1939), 480 (8/29/1939); Mischnick, 102–4.

Chapter XI

[378] Victor Klemperer, Ich will Zeugnis ablegen bis zum letzten: Tagebücher 1933-1941 (Berlin: 1995), hereafter cited as Zeugnis, 479-80 (entry 8/29/39); Mischnick, 102–4.

[379] Alexandra-Katrin Stanislaw-Kemenah, "Kirche, geistliches Leben und Schulwesen im Mittelalter," *Geschichte der Stadt Dresden* (Stuttgart: 2005), Bd. 1, 241–6, hereafter cited as *Geschichte;* Christiane Donath, "Anfänge judischen Lebens in Sachsen im Mittelalter," *Juden in Sachsen* (Leipzig: 2013), 29, hereafter cited as *Juden/Sachsen*; Uwe Ullrich, *Zur Geschichte der Juden in Dresden* (Dresden: 2001), 9–10.

[380] Werner Bergmann, "Vom Antijüdaismus zum Antisemitismus. Zur Geschichte eines Vorurteils von der Frühen Neuzeut bis in die Gegenwart," *Anti-Semitismus in Sachsen im 19. und 20. Jahrhundert* (Dresden: 2004), 20, 22, hereafter cited as *Antisemitismus;* Jacob Katz, *Out of the Ghetto: The Social Background of Jewish Emancipation* (Cambridge, MA: 1973), 4, 26–7.

[381] Jewish policy/fiscalpolicy in Bergmann, *Antisemitismus*, 20; Daniel Ristau, "Jüdisches Leben in Sachsen vom 17. Jahrhundert bis 1840," *Juden/Sachsen, 41*.

[382] Ristau, *Juden/Sachsen,* 43–5, 46–8; Ullrich, *Juden/Dresden*, 13–14; Gunda Ulbricht, "Juden in Dresden," *Geschichte,* Bd. 2, 390; Diamant, 127–8;

Simone Lässig, *Jüdische Wege ins Bürgertum: Kulturelles Kapital und sozialer Aufstieg im 19. Jahrhundert* (Göttingen: 2004), 568–9, hereafter cited as *Jüdische Wege*.

[383] Lässig, *Jüdische Wege,* 570; Katz, 17; Alexander Altmann, *Moses Mendelssohn: A Biographical Study* (University, AL: 1973), 427–30.

[384] Herbert Kupferberg, *The Mendelssohns: Three Generations of Genius* (New York: 1972) 4–13, 15–18, 25–8, 41–3, 48–50; Lässig, *Antisemitismus*, 43; Altmann, 514–52.

[385] Ristau, *Juden/Sachsen*, 43–4, 53; Lässig, *Jüdische Wege,* 525, 527, 572; Diamant, 317.

[386] Lässig, *Jüdische Wege*, 43, 50–1, 198.

[387] Lässig, *Jüdische Wege,* 390, 405; http://www.deutsche-biographie.de/pnd 11809503X.html, retrieved 1/25/16.

[388] Lässig, *Jüdische Wege,* 205, 390, 399–400, 404, 406, 524.

[389] Ulbricht, *Geschichte*, Bd. 2, 623; Lässig, *Jüdische Wege*, 385, *Saxony/Germany*, 112, *Antisemitismus*. 57–8.

[390] Christopher Friedrichs, "Introduction" and "Afterword," *A Jewish Youth in Dresden: The Diary of Louis Lesser, 1833–1837* (Bethesda MD: 2011), 25, 27, 181–2, 185–6, 192–5, 205, diary entries 12, 15, 26, 40, 71, 78–80, 107–11, 133 and chapter 6; further analysis in Lässig, *Jüdische Wege*, 224–7, 416–18.

[391] Lässig, *Jüdische Wege,* 395–7 and *Saxony/Germany*, 113–17; Diamant, 129, 132, 134–5, 316–17.

[392] Lässig, *Jüdische Wege,* 395–7 and *Saxony/Germany*, 113–17; Diamant, 129, 132, 134–5, 316–17.

[393] Ullrich, 16.

[394] Lässig, *Antisemitismus,* 60–2, 64; Solveig Höppner, "Juden in Sachsen zwischen bürgerlichen Revolution und ersten Weltkrieg," *Juden in Sachsen,* 87–8.

[395] Lässig, *Jüdische Wege*, 597, 600, 605.

[396] Gunda Ulbricht, "Israelitische Religionsgemeinde," *Geschichte*. Bd. 3, 122–3.

[397] List of organizations in Diamant, 172, also 179–80; *Spurensuche: Juden in Dresden. Ein Begleiter durch die Stadt* (Hamburg: 1996), 52; Lässig, *Jüdische Wege*, 510–13.

[398] Ulrich, 26; Diamant, 255–6, 258, 260–3;

http://de.wikipedia.org/wiki/Carl_von_Kaskel,retrieved11/8/20; https://de.wikipedia.org/wiki/Dresdner_Bank#19.Jahrhundert_bis_zum Ersten_Weltkrieg, edited 1/4/21, retrieved 1/25/21.

[399] Simone Lässig, "Nationalsozialistische Judenpolitik und Jüdische Selbstbehauptung vor dem Novemberpogrom. Das Beispiel der Dresdner Bankiersfamilie Arnhold," *Dresden Hakenkreuz,* 133–136.

[400] Höppner, *Antisemitismus,* 139–40; Diamant, 231, 243.

[401]) Henny Brenner, *The Song is Over: Survival of a Jewish Girl in Dresden* (Tuscaloosa: 2010), 3–5.

[402] Höppner, *Juden/Sachsen,* 102, 104, 106; *Spurensuche,* 25; Ullrich, 24–5.

[403] Höppner, *Juden/Sachsen,* 112–3, 116; Ulbricht, *Geschichte,* Bd. 3, 124–5.

[404] Diamant, 87; Ullrich, 21; James Retallack, *Red Saxony: Election Battles and the Spectre of Democracy in Germany, 1860–1918* (Oxford: 2017), 200.

[405] Friedrich Salzburg, *Mein Leben in Deutschland vor und nach dem 20. Januar. 1933: Lebensbericht eines jüdischen Rechtsanwaltes aus dem amerikanischen Exil im Jahr 1940* (Dresden: 2001) 20, 22–7, 36, 38–9; Diamant, 44; Höppner, *Juden/Sachsen,* 117; https://en.wikipedia.org/wiki/Judenzählung, retrieved 2/1/2016; Ulbricht, *Geschichte,* Bd. 3, 123, 125; *Spurensuche,* 87.

[406] Salzburg, 44, 46; *Spurensuche,* 28, 31–2; 67, 86–7; Diamant, 243; Ullrich, 285.

[407] Diamant, 124; 244; *Internationale Kunst-Ausstellung 1926* (Dresden-A.: 1926), 6; Starke, *Geschichte,* Bd. 3, 302; Salzburg, 48.

[408] Höppner, *Antisemitismus,* 131; Diamant, 62, 105.

[409] Höppner, *Antisemitismus,* 131–5.

[410] Mike Schmeitzner, "Georg Gradnauer: Der Begründer des Freistaates Sachsen (1918–20)," *Von Macht und Ohnmacht: Sächsisches Ministerpräsidenten im Zeitalter der Extreme 1919–1952 (*Beucha: 2006), 54–66, 71, 77–8, 80–3, 86–7.

[411] Agata Schindler," Das Schauspielhaus Dresden—Vom Schicksal des Musikdirektors Arthur Chitz," *Führerschule, Thingplatz, "Judenhaus": Orte und Gebäude der nationalesozialistischen Diktatur in Sachsen* (Dresden: 2014), 178–9, hereafter cited as *Führerschule;* Ulbricht, *Geschichte,* Bd. 3, 489; Werner Bramke, " Unter der faschistischen Diktatur (1933–1945)," *Geschichte Sachsens* (Weimar: 1989), 501;

http://wikipedia.org/wiki/Kaffeesurrogat/fabrik_Otto_E._Weber,retrieved 10/17/2011.

[412] Klemperer, *Zeugnis*, 14 (3.22.33) 15–6 (3.30.33).

[413] Salzburg, 53; Klemperer, *Zeugnis*, 18 (4.3.33); Lässig, *Dresden/Hakenkreuz*, 148.

[414] Lässig, *Dresden/Hakenkreuz*, 162; Salzburg, 54–8.

[415] Lässig, *Dresden/Hakenkreuz*, 163; Salzburg, 58, 63–5, 67, 69.

[416] Lässig, *Dresden/Hakenkreuz*, 145, 147–8, 155–9, 164–73, 180; Diamant, 265; https://de.wikipedia.org/wiki/Dresdner_Bank#19_Jahrhundert_bis_zum_Eren_Weltkrieg, retrieved 1/25/2021.

[417] Diamant, 307; Ulbricht, *Geschichte*, Bd. 3, 489–90; Klemperer, *Zeugnis*, 82 (1/27/34), 382 (10/9/37), 467 (4/7/39); Ullrich, 32–3; *Spurensuche*, 60–1; Volker Stöhr, "Deutsche Wege der Rationalisierung im Nationalsozialismus- dargestellt am Beispiel der sächsischen Maschinenbauindustrie," Beiträge *zur Geschichte des sächsischen Werkzeugmaschinenbaus im Industriezeitalter* (Dresden: 2000), 118.

[418] Salzburg, 59, 72–5, 77.

[419] Lässig, *Dresden/Hakenkreuz*, 139, 142–4; Ulrich Amlung, "Schulwesen," *Geschichte*, Bd. 3, 460; Diamant, 151–2, 66; Ulbricht, *Geschichte*, Bd. 3, 491.

[420] Lässig, *Dresden/Hakenkreuz*, 143–4 164, 182–3. 185–7; Schindler, *Föherschule*, 180; Salzburg, 79; Diamant, 118. 344.

[421] Ulbricht, *Geschichte*, Bd. 3, 493; Brenner, 33–4; Klemperer, *Zeugnis*, 408–9 (5/23/38).

[422] Ullrich, 35; Brenner, 35; Klemperer, *Zeugnis*, 395 (1/31/38); Marina Lienert, "Medizin und Gesundheitswesen," *Geschichte*, Bd. 3, 462.

[423] Ullrich, 20, 35; Nora Goldenbogen, "Zur Chronologie des Alltags der Tyrannei—Die Verfolgung und Vernichtung der jüdischen Bevölkerung Dresdens 1933 bis 1945," *Leben in Zwei Diktaturen: Victor Klemperers Leben in der N-S Zeit und in der DDR* (Dresden: 1997) 43–4; Diamant, 404–11.

[424] Ulbricht, *Geschichte*, Bd. 3, 493; Klemperer, *Zeugnis*, 311 (10.9.38), 438–9 (12/3.38), 442 (12.6.38), 447 (12.15.38), 466 (3.28.39).

[425] Diamant, 415, 417; https://de.wikipedia.org/wiki/LeaGrundig, retrieved 2/4/2016.

[426] Klemperer, *Zeugnis*. 490 (9.30.39), 494 (10.6.39), 503 (12.9.39), 509 (1.13.40); Goldenbogen, 45; Victor Klemperer, *I Will Bear Witness: A Diary of the Nazi Years, 1942–45 (*New York: 1999), 12 (2.8–9.42), hereafter cited as *Diary*.

[427] Klemperer, *Zeugnis*. 503 (12.9.39), 545 (8.11.40), 549 (8.30.40), 669 (9.18.41), 696 (12.22.41); Klemperer, *Diary*, 12 (5.29.42), 29 (3.16.42), 34 (3.27.42), 37 (4.7.42), 50 (5.11.42), 80 (6.16.42); 86 (6.26.42), 153 (10.10.42); Diamant, 437 and letter of Heinz Mayer to Rudolf Apt 1945, 451; Brenner, 49.

[428] Brenner, 53–4.

[429] Klemperer, *Zeugnis*, 663 (9.8.41 & 9.15.41), 688 (11.24.41); Klemperer, *Diary* 241 (6.24.43); Brenner, 44; see Christopher Browning, *Ordinary Men* (New York: 1992).

[430] https://de.wikipedia.org/wiki/Goehle-Werk, retrieved 1/27/21; Klemperer, *Zeugnis*, 686 (11.18.41); Christine Pieper, "Das 'Judenlager Hellerberg'_Ein (un) vergessener Ort?" *Führerschule*, 278–80; Holger Starke, "Wirtschaft und Verkehr," *Geschichte*, Bd. 3, 495–6; Klemperer, *Diary*, 29 (3.16.42) 190 (1.17.43).

[431] Brenner, 47–8, 58; Martin Chalmers in preface to Klemperer, *Diary*, ix–x.

[432] Klemperer, *Diary*, xi, 288 (1.8.44 & 1.10.44)

Chapter XII

[433] Heinz Schulz, *Rustungsproducktion im Raum Dresden 1933–1945* (Dresden: 2005), 8, 12, 22, 27, 29, 109, 112–13; Frederick Taylor, *Dresden: Tuesday, February 13, 1945* (New York: 2004), 53; Thomas Widera, *Dresden 1945–1948: Politik und Gesellschaft unter sowjetischer Besatzungsherrschaft* (Göttingen: 2004), 34 and "Krieg, Zerstörung und Besetzung von Dresden," *Geschichte der Stadt Dresden* (Stuttgart: 2006), 505, hereafter cited as *Geschichte*; Victor Klemperer, *I Will Bear Witness: A Diary of the Nazi Years, 1942–1945* (New York: 1999), 115 (8.6.42), hereafter cited as *Diary*.

[434] Reiner Pommerin, *Geschichte der TU Dresden 1828–2003* (Köln: 2003), Bd. 1, 129, 161, 204–06, hereafter cited as *TU Dresden*; Volker Stöhr, "Zwischen Anpassung und Selbstmobilisierung: Die Mechanische Abteilung in der Zeit des Nationalsozialismus," *TU Dresden*, Bd. 2, 162–4, 166; Sven Steinberg and Uwe Frauenholz," Die reine Luft der Wissenschaft?—Rüstungs-

und-Autarkieforschung an sächsischen Hochschulen," *Führerschule, Thingplatz, 'Judenhaus': Orte und Gebäude der nationalsozialistischer Diktatur in Sachsen* (Dresden: 2004), 129–31, hereafter cited as *Führerschule*.

[435] Dieter Hölsken, *V-Missiles of the Third Reich: The V-1 and V-2* (Starbridge, MA: 1994), 11–12, 15, 28; Ralf Pulla, *Raketentechnik in Deutschland: Ein Netzwerk aus Militär, Industrie, und Hochschulen, 1930 bis 1945* (Frankfurt/Main: 2006), 116–7, 119, 214.

[436] Taylor, 161–3; Götz Bergander, *Dresden im Luftkrieg: Vorgeschichte, Zerstörung, Folgen* (Weimar: 1995) 9, 19, 112–13, 115, 121.

[437] Bergander, 9–25, 88, 92, 95–6, 97–8, 99–100, 108–9; Taylor, 137–8, 144–5, 225; Klemperer, *Diary*, 352 (9.4.44).

[438] Bergander, 56, 58–9, 358–9 notes 7 and 10.

[439] Bergander, 4, 65, 67, 71; Widera, *Geschichte*, Bd. 3, 503; Raymond Willcocks, *The Ethics of Bombing Dresden* (Carlisle Barracks, PA: 1998), 16.

[440] www.tenhumbergreinhard.de/taeter-und-mitlaeufer/kampf-um-breslau, retrieved 2/4/21; https://de.wikipedia.org/wiki/Schlacht_um_Breslau, edited 8/15/20, retrieved 2/4/21; Widera, *Geschichte*, Bd. 3, 502; Taylor, 188, 191–2, 228–32; Klemperer, *Diary*, 334 (7.17.44), 370 (10.16.44).

[441] Ernst Günther, *Sarrasani wie er wirklich war* (Berlin: 1884), 303; Max Seydewitz, *Die Unbesiegbare Stadt: Zerstörung und Wiederaufbau von Dresden*, 3. Auflage (Berlin: 1956), 71; https://en.wikipedia.org/wiki/Bombing_of_Dresden_in_World_War_II, edited 2/4/21, retrieved 2/4/21; Widera, *Geschichte*, Bd. 3, 506; Bergander, 148–50, 158, 169; Rudolf Förster, *Dresden: Geschichte der Stadt in Wort und Bild* (Berlin: 1984), 174, hereafter cited as *Dresden Wort/Bild*.

[442] Carl-Ludwig Paeschke and Dieter Zimmer, *Dresden: Geschichten einer Stadt* (Berlin: 1994) 130–2.

[443] Bergander, 166, 230–1; Willcocks, 18, Taylor, 131; https://en.wikipedia.org/wiki/Bombing_of_Dresden_in_World_War_II, retrieved 2/4/21.

[444] Taylor, 240, 252, 268, 278, 299, 323–4, 353.

[445] Günther, 245–7; Paeschke, 138.

[446] Widera, *Dresden*, 42; Paeschke, 141.

[447] Joachim and Waltraud Petzold, *Ideale und Idole im Schatten Hitlers und Stalins: Dresdner Oberschüler auf dem Wege aus dem Dritten Reich in die DDR* (Potsdam: 1997), 90; Taylor, 342.

[448] Paeschke, 149–51.

[449] Brenner, 59–66; Klemperer, *Diary*, 404 (2.13.45), 408–18 (2.22–24.45), 426–514 (March to June, 1945).

[450] Bergander, 237–9, 242, 244, 251, 259.

[451] Taylor, 355–9, 380–1; Bergander, 179–80; Widera, *Dresden*, 38.

[452] Widera, *Geschichte*, Bd. 3, 506; Bergander, 174–7; Taylor, 342, 350–1.

[453] Bergander, 229–30; https://de.wikipedia.org/wiki/Bombing_of_Dresden_in_World_War_II, retrieved 2/4/21; Taylor, 351, 443–8; http://www.dresden.de/en/02/07/03/historical.commission.php,_final_revision_6/15/15, retrieved 6/5/16.

[454] Bergander, 287, 312–3, 317, 320, 345–7, 349; Taylor, 413–15.

Chapter XIII

[455] Götz Bergander, *Dresden im Luftkrieg: Vorgeschichte, Zerstörung, Folgen* (Weimar: 1995), 251, 279; Thomas Widera, *Dresden 1945–1948: Politik und Gesellschaft unter sowjetischer Besatzungsherrschaft* (Göttingen: 2004), 47–9, 51–2, hereafter cited as *Dresden*; Heinz Quinger, *Dresden und Umgebung: Geschichte, Kunst und Kultur der sächsischen Hauptstadt* (Ostfildern: 2011), 216; https://de.wikipedia.org/wiki/ Werner_von_Gilsa, edited 8/10/20, retrieved 2/8/21; Thomas Widera, "Krieg, Zerstörung und Besetzung von Dresden," *Geschichte der Stadt Dresden* (Stuttgart: 2006), Bd. 3, 509–11, hereafter cited as *Geschichte*.

[456] Frederick Taylor, *Dresden: Tuesday, February 13, 1945* (New York: 2004), 283–5.

[457] Widera, *Dresden*, 287–9; Max Seydewitz, *Die unbesiegbare Stadt: Zerstörung, und Wiederaufbau von Dresden* (Berlin: 1956), 282–3; Rudolf Förster, *Dresden: Geschichte der Stadt in Wort und Bild* (Berlin: 1984), 186.

[458] Widera, *Dresden,* 246, 285, 290–2.

[459] Henry Ashby Turner, *Germany from Partition to Reunification* (New Haven: 1992), 9–13; Widera, *Dresden,* 296–304, 310–11 and *Geschichte*, Bd.

3, 538; Edward Peterson, *Russian Commands and German Resistance: The Soviet Occupation, 1945–1949* (New York: 1999), 10, 103.

[460] Förster, 185, 197; Peterson, 20–2, 110; Widera, *Dresden*, 101–2, 108, 110–14, 120–1, 127, 129, 131, 236–7, 240–2; http://de.wikipedia.org/wiki/Walter_Weidauer, edited 12/25/20, retrieved 2/9/21.

[461] Widera, *Dresden*, 151, 154, 157, 166–7, 169, 172, 199–201, 206, 209–10, 254, 305–7, 322 and *Geschichte*, Bd. 3, 538.

[462] Widera, *Dresden*, 188–90, 196, 199, 203–4, 211, 213–17, 223–8, 250, 252–5.

[463] Widera, *Dresden*, 169, 174, 179, 243–5, 259, 261, 263–4.

[464] Widera, *Dresden*, 261, 265–7, 269, 272–7 and *Geschichte*, Bd. 3, 536; Peterson, 40–2; Förster. 205; Anne Fuchs, *After the Dresden Bombing: Pathways of Memory, 1945 to the Present* (New York: 2012), 98.

[465] Widera, *Dresden*, 331, 342–3, 347–8, 350–4, 357, 360–1; Wolfgang Mischnick, *Von Dresden nach Bonn: Erlebnisse-jetzt aufgeschrieben* (Stuttgart: 1991), 216, 235, 247–8, 253, 257; https://de.wikipedia.org/wiki/Gustav_Leissner, edited 7/25/21, retrieved 8/20/21.

[466] Widera, *Dresden*, 360, 368–71, 386, 389–91, 394, 399, 406; Petzold, 120; Mischnick, 284–92, 294.

[467] Widera, *Dresden*, 382; Förster, 222–3; Mike Schmeitzner and Andreas Wagner, "Ministerpräsident und Staatskanzlei in Freistaat Gau und Land: Ein sächsischer Vergleich, 1919–1952," *Von Macht und Ohnmacht: Sächsische Ministerpräsidenten im Zeitalter der Extreme 1919–1952* (Beucha: 2006), 24–6, 40–1, 44.

[468] Widera, *Dresden*, 318, 326–30, 334, 336; Carl-Ludwig Paeschke and Dieter Zimmer, *Dresden: Geschichten einer Stadt* (Berlin: 1994), 78; https://en.wikipedia.org/wiki/nordmende, edited 6/30/20, retrieved 2/11/21; camera-wiki: org/wiki/Balda, edited 6/12/20, retrieved 2/11/21.

[469] Klaus-Peter Arnold, *Vom Sofakissen zum Städtebau: Die Geschichte der deutschen Werkstätten und der Gartenstadt Hellerau* (Dresden: 1993), 73, 117–18, 123–4.

[470] Patrick Major, *Behind the Berlin Wall: East Germany and the Frontiers of Power* (New York: 2010), 60; Petzold, 196–9; Gerhard Lindemann, "Kirchen

und Religionsgemeinschaften," *Geschichte*, Bd. 3, 585; Mary Fulbrook, *Anatomy of a Dictatorship: Inside the GDR, 1949–1989* (New York: 1995), 179, hereafter cited as *Anatomy*; Karl Wilhelm Fricke, "Zur Geschichte und historischen Deutung des Aufstands von 17. Juni," in: Heidi Roth, *Der 17. Juni in Sachsen* (Köln: 1999), 17, 21–2, 24, hereafter cited as *17. Juni*.

[471] Fricke, *17. Juni*, 26–7, 33–4, 36; Fulbrook, *Anatomy*, 181.

[472] Fricke, *17. Juni*, 37–8; Roth, *17. Juni*, 589–90.

[473] Roth, *17. Juni*, 186–7, 190, 205 ("Spitzbart, Bauch und Brille sind nicht des Volkes Wille"); Thomas Widera, "Zwischen Repression und Opposition," *Geschichte*, Bd. 3, 562.

[474] Roth, *17. Juni*, 192–4, 538; https://de.wikipedia.org/wiki/Wilhelm_Grothaus, retrieved 7/14/16.

[475] Roth, *17. Juni*, 195–7, 199, 200–3; https://de.wikipedia.org/wiki/Otto_Buckwitz, edited 8/05/16, retrieved 3/18/17.

[476] Roth, *17. Juni*, 183–5, 204, 207–8, 210–12, 213–16; Widera, *Geschichte*, Bd. 3, 563–4.

[477] Fricke, 66–7, 71–2 and Roth, *17. Juni*, 216–18, 221, 224, 486–7, 510–11, 514–15, 564.

[478] Fricke, 78 and Roth, *17. Juni*, 439–40, 442, 483–4; Major, 60–1.

[479] Hans-Peter Lühr, "Unter dem Zeichen von Hammer und Sichel (1945–1990)," *Dresden: Die Geschichte der Stadt von den Anfängen bis zum Gegenwart* (Dresden: 2002), 254–5; John Soane, "Dresden: its Destruction and Rebuilding 1945–85," *Dresden: A City Reborn* (New York: 1999), 84; Ingrid Wenzkat, "Fritz Löffler 'Das Alte Dresden'", *Geschichte*, Bd. 3, 631–4; http://de.wikipedia.org/wiki/Fritz_Löffler, edited 6/2/21, retrieved 8/20/21; Heike Bidermann, "Will Grohmann-Freund und Berater der Dresdner Kunstsammlerin Ida Bienert," *Zwischen Intuition und Gewissheit: Will Grohmann und die Rezeption der Moderne in Deutschland und Europa 1918–1968* (Dresden: 2013), 228 note 10.

Chapter XIV

[480] Matthias Herrmann, "Musik in Dresden," *Geschichte der Stadt Dresden* (Stuttgart: 2006), Bd. 3, 659, hereafter cited as *Geschichte*; Max Seydewitz, *Die Unbesiegbare Stadt: Zerstörung, und Wiederaufbau von Dresden* (Berlin:

1956), 340, 355, 358; April Eisman, "East German Art and the Permeability of the Berlin Wall," *German Studies Review* 38 (2015), 599.

[481] Rudolf Förster, *Dresden: Geschichte der Stadt in Wort und Bild* (Berlin: 1984), 232; Hans-Peter Lühr, "Unter dem Zeichen von Hammer und Sichel (1945–1990)," *Dresden: Die Geschichte der Stadt von den Anfängen bis zum Gegenwart* (Dresden: 2002), 254, hereafter cited as *Geschichtsverein;* Clare Ford-Wille, "The Art Collections of Dresden," *Dresden: A City Reborn* (New York: 1999), hereafter cited as *Dresden Reborn;* Werner Schmidt, "Die Wiedererstehen der Kunstsammlungen, 1955–1970," *Geschichte,* Bd. 3, 545–6; Harald Marx, "Dresden und die Wiedereröffnung der Gemäldegalerie, 1956," *Geschichte,* Bd. 3, 688.

[482] Anke Dietrich, "Rehabilitierung der Moderne: Will Grohmann und die 'Allgemeine Deutsche Kunstaustellung' 1946 in Dresden," *Zwischen Intuition und Gewissheit: Will Grohmann und die Rezeption der Moderne in Deutschland und Europa 1918–1968* (Dresden: 2013), 101–3, 107, hereafter cited as *Intuition;* Erhard Frommhold and Gerlint Söder, "Bildende Kunst," *Geschichte,* Bd. 3, 679–81; https://www.gerhard-richter.com/en/chronology, retrieved 2/18/21; Hans Modrow, *Ich wollte ein neues Deutschland* (Berlin: 1998), 206, hereafter cited as *Neues Deutschland;* Angelika Weissbach, *Frühstück im Freien—Freiräume im offiziellen Kunstbetrieb der DDR. Die Ausstellungen und Aktionen im Leonhardi Museum in Dresden 1963–1990* (Berlin: 2009), 122–3, 171–6, 241, 246, at https://library.oapen.org/handle/20.500.12657/34652, retrieved 2/21/21.

[483] Lühr, *Geschichtsverein,* 269–70; *The Splendor of Dresden: Five Centuries of Art Collecting* (New York: 1978); references to exhibitions outside the GDR in "Bibliography," *Dresden in the Ages of Splendor and Enlightenment: Eighteenth-Century Painting from the Old Masters' Picture Gallery* (Columbus, OH: 1999); Förster, 253; Holger Starke, "Zwischen Zwang und Anpassung," *Geschichte,* Bd. 3, 711.

[484] Anne Fuchs, *After the Dresden Bombing: Pathways of Memory, 1945 to the Present* (New York: 2012), 51–2, 54–5, 57–9; "50 Jahre Forschung in Rossendorf," at https://www.hzdr.de/db/Cms?pOid=38032, retrieved 8/20/21.

[485] Hans John, *Der Dresdner Kreuzchor und seine Kantoren* (Berlin: 1982), 109–113; Carl-Ludwig Paeschke and Dieter Zimmer, *Dresden: Geschichten einer Stadt* (Berlin: 1994), 134–5; Matthias Herrman, "Die Kreuzkantorate

1828–1971 von Otto bis Mauersberger," *Der Dresden Kreuzchor: Geschichte und Gegenwart, Wirkungsstätten und Schule* (Leipzig: 2006), 138–9, hereafter cited as *Kreuzchor Wirkungsstätten*.

[486] Seydewitz, 116–7; Herrman, *Kreuzchor Wirkungsstätten*, 146–7 and "Musik in Dresden," *Geschichte*, Bd. 3, 515; John, 114–15.

[487] John, 114–7.

[488] John, 119–20; Herrmann, *Geschichte*, Bd. 3, 664.

[489] Herrmann, *Kreuzchor Wirkungsstätten*, 154–6.

[490] Seydewitz, 340–1; Herrmann, *Geschichte*, Bd. 3, 660.

[491] Förster, 250; https://www.dw.com/en/50-years-ago-benjamin-brittens-war-protest-in-germany/a-16863533, retrieved 10/18/19.

[492] http://www.bach-cantatas.com/Bio/Adam-Theo.htm, retrieved 2/15/17, Neil Genzlinger, "Theo Adam, Acclaimed in Wagner Operas, Is Dead at 92," *New York Times*, 1/15/19; http://www.bach-cantatas.com/Bio/ Schreier-Peter.htm, accessed 2/15/17; Anthony Tommasini, "Peter Schreier, 84, Elegant German Tenor Who Also Conducted, Dies," *New York Times*, 12/31/19.

[493] Hermann, *Geschichte*, Bd. 3, 662; Lühr, *Geschichtsverein*, 269; https://peoplepill.com/people/rainier-kunad, retrieved 10/10/19; https://en.wikipedia.org/wiki/Udo_Zimmermann, retrieved 10/10/19; https://en.wikipedia.org/wiki/Der_Schuhu_und_die_fliegende_Prinzessin, retrieved 10/10/19.

[494] Dieter Härtung, *125 Jahre Dresdner Philharmonie: 1870–1995* (Altenburg: 1995), 35, 38–42, 45–8, 51–2, 54–7, 59–62, 65, 70, 76–7; Herrmann, *Geschichte*, Bd. 3, 662.

[495] https://de.wikipedia.org/wiki/Herkuleskeule_(Kabarett), edited 1/22/21, retrieved 2/22/21; Herrmann, *Geschichte*, Bd. 3, 668–71; Förster, 202.

[496] Hans-Peter Lühr, "Theater," *Geschichte*, Bd. 3, 691–5; Seydewitz, 349; Förster, 238; http://www.staatsschauspiel-dresden.de/ensemble/mitarbeiter/ehrenmitglieder/erich_ponto,retrieved 1/12/17.

[497] Lühr, *Geschichte*, Bd. 3, 697; Judith Purver, "Dresden's Literary and Theatrical Traditions," *Dresden Reborn*, 219; Michael Raab, *Patterns of Continuity in German Theatre: Interculturalism, Performance, and Cultural*

Mission (Cambridge, U.K.: 2008), 352–3; https://www.staatsschauspiel-dresden.de/ensemble/gerhard_wolfram, retrieved 10/8/19.

[498] Friedrich Reichert, "Turnen, Sport und Spiel in Dresden seit 1844," *Dresdner Geschichtsbuch* 6 (2000), 156–8; Ingolf Pleil, *Mielke, Macht und Meisterschaft: Die "Bearbeitung" der Sportgemeinschaft Dynamo Dresden durch das MFS 1978–1989* (Berlin: 2001), 264–5.

[499] http://de.wikipedia.org/wiki/SG Dresden-Friedrichstadt, edited 2/6/11, retrieved 2/18/11; Wolfgang Hädecke, *Dresden: Eine Geschichte von Glanz. Katastrophe und Aufbruch* (München: 2006), 285;

[500] Uwe Karte and Gert Zimmermann, *Dynamo Dresden: Das Buch zum Verein 1953–1993* (Leipzig: 1993) 11–12, 16, 19, 22–4, 28, 32–3, 41–2.

[501] Förster, 275; Karte/Zimmermann, 42–3, 47–8, 57, 65–6, 91, 195–6; Hädecke, 285: Alan McDougall, *Football, State and Society in East Germany* (Cambridge, U.K.: 2014), 73–4; https://www.dynamo-dresden.de/dynamogespräche/kreisel-interview-mit-Gerhard-Prautzsch, retrieved 1/31/22.

[502] Karte/Zimmermann, 67–72; https://en.wikipedia.org/wiki/Dynamo_Dresden#SV_Dynamo, retrieved 3/4/21.

[503] https://www.sächsische.dc/der_rivale_aus_berlin-3915035.html, retrieved 8/3/21; https://en.wikipedia.org/wiki/berliner_FC_Dynamo#SG_Dynamo_Dresden, retrieved 8/3/21.

[504] https://www.weltfussball.de/spieler_profil/walter-fritzsch, edited 11/24/20, retrieved 2/23/21; https://de.wikipedia.org/wiki/SG_Dresden_Friedrichstadt, edited 5/20/21, retrieved 1/28/22; McDougall, 3, 224–39, 241; Mike Dennis and Jonathan Grix, *Sport Under Communism: Behind the East German 'Miracle,'* (New York: 2013) 148–50, hereafter cited as *Sport/Communism*. Steven Ungerleider, *Faust's Gold: Inside the East German Doping Machine* (New York: 2001), 45–7; McDougall, 9, 95; Pleil, 234–5, 239; Mike Dennis, "Doping in East German Football since the Mid-1960," *Baltic worlds.com,* June 19, 2012, accessed 1/3/22; *Sport/Communism, 116, 155.*

[505] McDougall, 9, 95; 239; Pleil, 234–5, 239; Mike Dennis, "Doping in East German Football since the Mid-1960s," *Baltic Worlds.com,* June 19, 2012, retrieved 1/3/22; *Sport/Communism,* 116, 155.

Chapter XV

[506] Hans-Peter Lühr, "Unter dem Zeichen von Hammer und Sichel (1945–1990)," *Dresden: die Geschichte der Stadt von den Anfängen bis zur Gegenwart* (Dresden: 2002), 237, hereafter cited as *Geschichtsverein*; Frederick Taylor, *Dresden: Tuesday, February 13, 1945* (New York: 2004), 396; Max Seydewitz, *Die unsiegbare Stadt: Zerstörung und Wiederaufbau von Dresden* (Berlin: 1956), 298–9; Anne Fuchs, *After the Dresden Bombing: Pathways of Memory, 1945 to the Present* (New York: 2012), 57; David Crew, *Bodies and Ruins: Imagining he Bombing of Germany, 1945 to the Present* (Ann Arbor: 2017), 81; https.//www.warhistoryonline.com/war-articles/myth-of-the-trummerfrau.html, accessed 8/5/2020.

[507] Matthias Lerm, "Ein neues Dresden. Städtebau und Architektur," *Geschichte der Stadt Dresden* (Dresden: Stuttgart: 2006), Bd. III, 602, hereafter cited as *Geschichte*; Fuchs, 95; John Soane, "Dresden, its Destruction and Rebuilding, 1945–85," *Dresden: A City Reborn* (New York: 1999), 74–5.

[508] Matthias Lerm, "Ein neues Dresden. Städtebau und Architektur," *Geschichte*, Bd. III, 602, hereafter cited as *Geschichte*; Fuchs, 95; John Soane, "Dresden, its Destruction and Rebuilding, 1945–85," *Dresden: A City Reborn* (New York: 1999), 74–5.

[509] Lühr, *Geschichtsverein*, 241; Seydewitz, 335; Heinrich Magirius, "Denkmalpflege," *Geschichte*, Bd. III, 623–5.

[510] Magirius, *Geschichte*, Bd. III, 626–7; Seydewitz, 338.

[511] Taylor, 378; Matthias Lerm, *Abschied vom alten Dresden: Verluste historischen Bausubstanz nach 1945* (Rostock: 2000), 78–81, 95, hereafter cited as *Abschied*; Ronald Franke, "Zur Planungs-und-Baugeschichte Dresdens in den 50er Jahren," *Bauen im Dresden im 19.und 20. Jahrhundert* (Dresden: 1991) 116; Magirius, *Geschichte*, Bd, III, 625; Carl-Ludwig Paeschke und Dieter Zimmer, *Dresden: Geschichte einer Stadt* (Berlin: 1994), 182; https://de.wikipedia.org/wiki/Hans_Nadler_ (Denkmalpfleger), edited 4/29/13, retrieved 6/13/13; "Zum Denkmal gewordenen Denkmalschützer," *Dresdner Neueste Nachrichten*, 10/12/05.

[512] Fuchs, 101–2, 104–7, 111; Franke, 123–4, 126; Jürgen Paul, "Dresden: Suche nach der verlorenen Mitte," *Neue Städte aus Ruinen; Deutscher Städtebau der Nachkriegszeit* (München: 1992), 319–20, 324–5.

[513] Franke, 124; Fuchs, 114–5; Soane, 83.

[514] Lühr, *Geschichtsverein*, 259; Lerm, *Abschied*, 41–2, 83, 126, 202–3, 208–9, 224–5, 227–8.

[515] Magirius, *Geschichte,* Bd. III, 626–7.

[516] https://de.wikipedia.org/wiki/Luftangriffe_auf_Dresden, edited 1/1/16, retrieved 2/18/16; Holger Starke, "Bezirkstadt in der DDR," *Geschichte*, Bd. III, 554.

[517] Seydewitz, 301–2; Soane, 86; Lerm, *Geschichte*, Bd. III, 616–17; Gisela Radat, "Mein Vater," *Hans Nadler 1910–2005: Ein Leben in Fünf Staatsordnungen* (Dresden: 2016), 79–80; Anita Maass, "Wohnen Im Neubaugebiet—Prohlis und Gorbitz," *Geschichte*, Bd. III, 718–20; Förster, *Dresden Wort/Bild*, 285.

[518] Rudolf Förster, *Damals in Dresden: Porträt einer Stadt um 1900* (Berlin: 1990), 70–5, hereafter cited as *Damals;* Tanya Scheffler, "Fachbeitrag: Dresden, Prager Strasse*,"* *Modern Regional,* 15/2 (2015), 1–3, In: http://www.moderne_regional.de/fachbeitrag-dresdens-prager-strasse, retrieved 2/2/17; Fuchs, 116; https://de.wikipedia.org/wiki/Prager_Strasse_(Dresden), edited 1/19/17, accessed 2/2/17.

[519] Nora Goldenbogen, "Jüdisches Leben in Sachsen, 1945–1989," *Juden in Sachsen* (Leipzig: 2013), 177, 183, 193, 198, hereafter cited as *Juden/Sachsen;* Uwe Ullrich, *Zur Geschichte der Juden in Dresden* (Dresden: 2001), 41; Adolf Diamant, *Chronik der Juden in Dresden: Von den ersten Juden bis zur Blüte der Gemeinde und deren Ausrottung* (Frankfurt/Main: 1973), 459–61; *Spurensuche Juden in Dresden: Ein Begleiter durch die Stadt* (Hamburg: 1996), 56.

[520] Nora Goldenbogen, "Zum Zusammenhang zwischen Antisemitismus und spätstalinistischen Säuberungswellen in Sachsen zwischen 1949 und 1953," and Mario Kessler, "Kommunismus und Anti-Semitismus in Deutschland: Der 'Fall Merker,' seine Vorgeschichte und seine Folgen," both in *Antisemitismus in Sachsen im 19. und 20. Jahrhundert* (Dresden: 2004), 211–12, 215–19, 197–204, hereafter cited as *Antisemitismus;*

http://en.wikipedia.org/wiki/László_Rayk; and https://en.wikipedia.org/wiki/Rudolf_Slansky, both retrieved 2/14/17; Lühr, *Geschichtsverein*, 249.

521 Goldenbogen, *Juden/Sachsen*, 201; Olaf Glöckner, "Immigranten und Visionen—Juden in Sachsen seit 1990," *Juden/Sachsen*, 211, 215; Judith Kessler, "Fast 'unsicher'—Juden in der SBZ/DDR 1945–1989," https://www.hagafil.com/2014/11/juden-in-der-DDR, retrieved 8/3/21.

522 Goldenbogen, and Glöckner, *Juden/Sachsen*, 201–3, 205–6, 208, 211; Ullrich, 44. In September, 1990, a group of 150 "right-wing radicals" disrupted a rally of the Party of Democratic Socialism on the Elbe meadows by hurling stones, bottles, flashbangers and slurs of "Jewish swine"—directed at party chair Gregor Gysi. The police broke up the disturbance and brought charges against four of the group, https://taz.de/rechtsradikale_attackieren_PDS/1751045, retrieved 8/3/21; Alexander Walther, "Helmut Eschwege and Jewish Life in the German Democratic Republic," *Rebuilding Jewish Life in Germany* (New Brunswick: 2020), 108–13.

Chapter XVI

523 Herbert Blumtritt, *Geschichte der Dresdner Fotoindustrie* (Stuttgart: 2000), 115, 121–3, 162, 167, 185; https://www.dresdner-kameras.de (Go to Praktika, then Exportvarianten), retrieved 3/3/21; www.pentacon.six.com (Go to History of Pentacon.Six, then Praktiflix), retrieved 3/4/21; Lydia Jacobi, "Das Ende des DDR-Kamerabestellers Pentacon," MDR.de, retrieved 2/5/20. Dresden firms, including the German Workshops in Hellerau, employed both political and criminal prisoners, at reduced wages, https://www.deutschlandfunkkultur.de/ohne-die-häftlingsarbeit-hätte-den-plan-nicht-erfüllt.954.de.html, retrieved 5/7/21.

524 https://de.wikipedia.org/wiki/NAGEMA, edited 7/2/15, retrieved 6/14/16; http://www.kombinat-nagema.de/Geschichte/body_geschichte.html, retrieved 1/26/15; Mirko Buschmann, "Maschinen für den Konsum: Zur Wissenschaftskooperation zwischen der TU Dresden und dem VEB Nagema," *175* (Köln: 2003), Bd. 2, 217–19, 221–4, 228–30, hereafter cited as *TU Dresden*.

[525] https://de.wikipedia.org/wiki/VEBTransformatoren-und Röntgenwerk Overbeckstr 48, edited, 6/23/16, retrieved 11/10/16; www.dresdner-stadtteile.de/nordwest/ übigau.html, retrieved 2/15/17.

[526] https://de.wikipedia.org/wiki/VEBTransformatoren-und Röntgenwerk Overbeckstr 48, edited, 6/23/16, retrieved 11/10/16; www.dresdner-stadtteile.de/nordwest/ übigau.html, retrieved 2/15/17.

[527] https://www.elbeflugzeugwerke.com/en/our-company/our-history, retrieved 2/6/17.

[528] Gerhard Merkel, "Dresden-wissenschaftlich-technisches Zentrum der Computerentwicklung in der DDR," *Industriegeschichte der Stadt Dresden 1945–1990: Beiträge zum 800. Stadtjubiläum* (Leipzig: 2006), 52–6, 59; Petra Jacoby, *Leben in Dresden, 1920–1990* (Erfurt: 2000), 65; Gerhard Barkleit, "Kombinatsbildung und neue Industriestruktur in den 1960er Jahren," *Dresdner Hefte* 128:4(2016), 21, hereafter cited as *DH*; https://de.wikipedia.org/wiki/Kombinat_Robotron, edited 6/6/2016, retrieved 6/14/16; Hans Modrow, *Ich wollte ein neues Deutschland* (Berlin: 1998), 162.

[529] Gerhard Barkleit, "Von der Luxusgüterindustrie zur Hochtechnologie," *Geschichte der Stadt Dresden* (Stuttgart: 2006), Bd. 3, 642–3; *Geschichte der Technischen Universität Dresden, 1828–1978* (Berlin: 1978), 176, hereafter cited as *TU Geschichte*; Reiner Pommerin, *Geschichte der TU Dresden 1828-2003* (Köln: 2003), 222, 234–5, hereafter cited as TU Dresden. https://en.wikipedia.org/wiki/Werner_Hartmann_(physicist), edited 5/14/16, retrieved 2/19/17.

[530] Pommerin, *TU Dresden,* 291.

[531] Pommerin, *TU Dresden,* 291.

[532] *TU Geschichte*, 173–4, 176–7, 179; Pommerin, *TU Dresden* 215, 219–24, 232, 234, 236–9, 241, 249.

[533] Pommerin, *TU Dresden*, 243–9; *TU Geschichte*, 175.

[534] Pommerin, *TU Dresden,* 258; Thomas Widera, "Zwischen Repression und Opposition," *Geschichte*, Bd. 3, 564–6.

[535] Pommerin, *TU Dresden*, 256–8, 277, 281; *TU Geschichte*, 213–14, 234, 241, 245, 272, 274; http://de.wikipedia.org/wiki/Technische_Universität_Dresden; https://de.wikipedia.org/wiki/Urania_Gesellschaft_zur_Verbreitung_wissenschaftlicher_Kenntnisse, edited 9/21/19, accessed 8/9/21.

⁵³⁶ Pommerin, *TU Dresden,* 279; *TU Geschichte,* 278, 317.

⁵³⁷ *TU Geschichte,* 298, 326, 360, 364; Pommerin, *TU Dresden,* 308; http://www./de.wikipedia.org/wiki/ Gedenkstätte_Münchner_Platz_Dresden, accessed 10/31/19.

⁵³⁸ Förster, *Dresden Wort/Bild,* 230.

⁵³⁹ Hans John, "Musikstadt von Europäischen Rang," *Geschichte,* Bd. 3, 137–8; Hans John, "Musikschaffen," *Geschichte,* Bd. 2, 676; Matthias Herrmann, "Musik in Dresden," and "Musik und Musikleben," *Geschichte,* Bd. 3, 667, 395.

⁵⁴⁰ Erhard Frommhold and Gerlint Söder, "Bildende Kunst," *Geschichte,* Bd. 3, 676; https://stadtwikidd.de/wiki/HFBK_Dresden, retrieved 2/13/17; https://mart-stam.de/app/uploads/2020/07/Mart_Stam_Bio_H._Ebert.pdf

⁵⁴¹ Albrecht Scholz, "Gesundheits und Sozialwesen," *Geschichte,* Bd. 3, 651, 653–8; Albrecht Scholz, "Die medizinische Akademie 'Carl Gustav Carus' von 1954 bis 1992," *Vom Stadtkrankenhaus zum Universitätsklinikum: 100 Jahre Krankenhausgeschichte in Dresden* (Köln: 2001), 168–73, 177, 179, 184–6, 191–201.

⁵⁴² Holger Starke, "Bezirkstadt in der DDR," *Geschichte,* Bd. 3, 559; https://de.wikipedia.org/wiki/Militärakademie_"Friedrich_Engels," edited 2/16/21, retrieved 3/7/21.

⁵⁴³ https://de.wikipedia.org/wiki/Manfred_von_Ardenne, edited 11/2/19, retrieved 11/6/19; Gerhard Barkleit, *Manfred von Ardenne: Selbstverwirklichung im Jahrhundert der Diktaturen* (Berlin: 2006), 63, 66, 104, 108, 127–32, 158, 164–5, 167–8, 186–7, 199, 245–51; https://de.wikipedia.org/wiki/Forschungsinstitut_Manfred_von_Ardenne,edited 11/1/19, retrieved 11/6/19; https://en.wikipedia.org/wiki/Manfred_von_Ardenne, retrieved 8/7/20.

Chapter XVII

⁵⁴⁴ Hans Modrow, *Ich wollte ein neues Deutschland* (Berlin: 1998), 261, hereafter cited as *Neues Deutschland*; Hans Modrow, *Von Schwerin bis Strasbourg: Erinnerungen an ein halbes Jahrhundert Parlamentsarbeit* (Berlin: 2001), 79, hereafter cited as *Schwerin/Strasbourg*; Wolfgang Berghofer, *Meine Dresdner Jahre* (Berlin: 2001), 102–3, hereafter cited as

Dresdner Jahre; Holger Starke, "Zwischen Zwang und Anpassung," *Geschichte der Stadt Dresden* (Stuttgart: 2006), Bd. 3, 715, hereafter cited as *Geschichte*; https://en.wikipedia.org/wiki/Hans_Modrow, edited 2/16/17, retrieved 2/16/17.

[545] Modrow, *Neues Deutschland*, 184–5; Rudolf Förster, *Dresden: Geschichte der Stadt in Wort und Bild* (Berlin: 1984), 285, hereafter cited as *Dresden Wort/Bild*; Carl-Ludwig Paeschke and Dieter Zimmer, *Dresden: Geschichte einer Stadt* (Berlin: 1994), 188–90, 192; Hans-Peter Lühr, "Unter dem Zeichen von Hammer und Sichel", *Dresden: Die Geschichte der Stadt von den Anfängen bis zur Gegenwart* (Dresden: 2002), 275–6, hereafter cited as *Geschichtsverein*.

[546] Modrow, *Neues Deutschland*, 181–3; https://de.wikipedia.org/wiki/Blockhaus_ (Dresden), retrieved 1/16/23.

[547] Modrow, *Neues Deutschland,* 184–6; Paeschke and Zimmer, 190.

[548] Modrow, *Neues Deutschland,* 207.

[549] Thomas Widera, "Zwischen Repression und Opposition," *Geschichte*, Bd. 3, 568, 571–2; Gerhard Lindemann, "Kirchen und Religionsgemeinschaften," *Geschichte*, Bd. 3, 590, 596; Mary Fulbrook, *The Divided Nation: A History of Germany 1918–1990* (New York: 1992), 272–6.

[550] Widera, *Geschichte*, Bd. 3, 572–3; Modrow, *Neues Deutschland*, 199; Lindemann, *Geschichte*, Bd. 3, 594.

[551] Michael Beleites, "Die einzige osteuropäische Stadt. Dresden in der Auseinandersetzung mit der Umweltkrise," *Dresden Hefte* 128:4 (2016), 46; Lühr, *Geschichtsverein*, 273.

[552] Berghofer, *Dresdner Jahre*, 78, 148.

[553] Mary Fulbrook, *Anatomy of a Dictatorship: Inside the GDR, 1949–1989* (New York: 1995), 235; Lühr, *Geschichtsverein*, 274; Berghofer, *Dresdner Jahre,* 104–6; Herbert Wagner, *Zwanzig gegen die SED: Der Dresdner Weg in die Freiheit* (Leipzig: 2000), 145–8; Lindemann, *Geschichte,* Bd. 3, 596–7.

[554] Beleites, 49–50; Berghofer, *Dresdner Jahre, 97–9;* Patrick Major, *Behind the Berlin Wall: East Germany and the Frontiers of Power* (New York: 2010), 236; Heiko Weckbrodt, https://oiger.de/2011/09/25/dresden-1989-siliziumwerk-wird-zur-kraftprobe-zwischen-burger-und-stadt, retrieved 2/20/17;

https://www.stadtwikidd.de/wiki/reinstsiliziumwerk_Gittersee,edited 9/16/19, retrieved 3/9/21.

[555] Lindemann, *Geschichte*, Bd. 3, 597; Berghofer, *Dresdner Jahre,* 55–6; 58, 136, 138–9.

[556] Berghofer, *Dresdner Jahre, 127–33.*

Chapter XVIII

[557] Wolfgang Berghofer, *Meine Dresdner Jahre* (Berlin: 2001), 134; Henry Ashby Turner, *Germany from Partition to Reunification* (New Haven: *1992), 226–228;* Michael Meyer, *The Year that Changed the World (New York: 2009), 32–3, 43–4, 52–3, 58, 67,* 72–3, 79–81, 84, 97–104, 113–16.

[558] Turner, 228–9; Wolfgang Berghofer, *Keine Figur im Schachspiel: Wie ich die "Wende" erlebte* (Berlin: 2014) 70, hereafter cited as *Figur.*

[559] Berghofer, *Figur,* 70–1 and *Dresdner Jahre,* 154–5, 158–9; Hans Modrow, *Neues Deutschland,* 266, 269, 270, 286.

[560] https://de.wikipedia.org/Neues Forum, edited 8/27/20, retrieved 6/14/21; Berghofer, *Dresdner Jahre*. 150; Michael Richter and Erich Sobeslavsky, *Die Gruppe der 20: Gesellschaftlicher Aufbruch und politische Opposition in Dresden 1989/90* (Köln: 1999), 35–6; Modrow, *Neues Deutschland*, 286.

[561] Turner, 230; https://www.WNYCStudios.org/podcasts/OTM/segments/132560-tear-down-this-quote, retrieved 3/9/21; Modrow, *Neues Deutschland,* 264–5, 273; Berghofer, *Dresdner Jahre*, 157, 159.

[562] Berghofer, *Dresdner Jahre,* 159–64 and *Figur,* 76–82; Modrow, *Neues Deutschland*, 273; Gisela Radat, "Mein Vater*,"* Hans Nadler 1910–2005: Ein Leben in fünf Staatsordnungen. Ein Leben für die sächsische Kulturlandschaft –(Dresden: 2016), 115, hereafter cited as *Nadler*; Lindemann, *Geschichte*, Bd. 3, 598; Richter and Sobeslavsky, 46–7, 52–64.

[563] Karl-Ludwig Hoch, "Always in Dresden—A Personal Memoir," In: *Dresden: A City Reborn* (New York: 1999), 68. Hoch was pastor at the church in Plauen for thirty-five years and supported the Gittersee protestors. Uwe Tellkamp, *The Tower: Tales from a Lost Country* (London: 2016), 992–3.

[564] Turner, 230–1; Radat, *Nadler*, 115; https://www.dresden.de/meda/pdf/presseant/2024_09_02_pressekonferenz_landtagswahl_2024.pdf, retrieved 9/5/2024. https://de.wikipedia.org/wiki/Sechs_von_ Leipzig, edited 9/27/20, retrieved 3/7/21; https://de. Wikipedia.org/wiki/Christoph_ Wonneberger, retrieved 2/26/17; Lühr, *Geschichtsverein*, 278–9; Michael Brettin, "Plauen, 7. Oktober. 1989: Die Initialzündung der Friedlichen Revolution in der DDR," *Berliner Zeitung,* 7.10.19; Reiner Petzner, *Leipziger Ring: Aufzeichnungen eines Montagsdemonstranten, Oktober 1989 bis 1. Mai.1990* (Frankfurt/Main: 1990), 28.

[565] Berghofer, *Dresdner Jahre*, 170–2; Modrow, *Neues Deutschland*. 274; for mistreatment Wagner, 39–44.

[566] Richter and Sobeslavsky, 54, 60, 77–8, 94–97, 101–09; Berghofer, *Dresdner Jahre,* 173–6; Modrow, *Neues Deutschland*, 274–81; Wagner, 18, 31, 145.

[567] Richter and Sobeslavsky, 109–11, 114–18; 120, 123–4, 129–31, 135–7; Modrow, *Neues Deutschland,* 283–5; Turner, 231, Wagner, 36–8.

[568] Modrow, *Neues Deutschland*, 292–3; Berghofer, *Dresdner Jahre*, 179–80, 184–9.

[569] Turner, 232–9, 242–4; Konstantin Herrman, "Kohls Treffen mit Modrow: Ein Wegweiser zur deutschen Einheit," *Dresden—Schauplatz grosser Geschichte* (Dresden: 2006) 107–10; Richter and Sobeslavsky, 167–74, 181; Wagner, 52–3, 59–64, 69–73, 101–12, 172–5.

[570] Wagner, 119, 123, 176–9, 184; Richter and Sobeslavsky, 194, 200; Turner, 244–6.

Chapter XIX

[571] A. James McAdams, *Judging the Past in Unified Germany* (New York: 2001), 56–7, 60, 64–5, 72–6; Katy A. Crossley-Frolick, "Scales of Justice: The Vetting of Former East German Police and Teachers in Saxony," *German Studies Review*, 30 (2007), 152–4; Peter-André Alt, "Rasche Neugestaltung nach der Wende," *Berliner Zeitung, #258,* 6. November.2019.

[572] Stanislav Rosenberg, "Dresden's transition into the market economy and the impact on its business community," *Dresden Discussion Paper Series in*

Economics, No. 01/02, Technische Universität Dresden Fakultät Wirtschaftswissenschaften, http://hdl.handle.net/10401/48111; Henry Ashby Turner, *Germany from Partition to Reunification* (New Haven: 1992), 247–8; Holger Starke, "Dresden auf dem Weg ins 21. Jahrhundert," *Geschichte der Stadt Dresden* (Stuttgart: 2006), Bd. 3, 763–4, 773–77, hereafter cited as *Geschichte;* www.Dresden.de/dresden_in_zahlen_11_2015, retrieved 3/15/21; www.dresden.de/de/leben/stadtporträt/statistik/wirtschaft-finanzen/arbeitslose.php, retrieved 3/15/21.

[573] McAdams, 125, 136.

[574] Herbert Blumtritt, *Geschichte der Dresdner Fotoindustrie* (Stuttgart: 2000), 199–206; https://en.wiki.org/wiki/Pentacon,retrieved2/6/17;camera-wiki.org/wiki/Pentacon, retrieved 2/10/20; https://de.wikipedia.org/wiki/NAGEMA, edited 7/2/15, retrieved 6/14/16; http://www. HIGHVOLT.de, retrieved 2/6/17; https://www.-VEM-group.com/en/about-VEM/company-history/VEM-group.html, retrieved 3/10/21; https://de.wikipedia.org/wiki/Kombinat_Robotron, retrieved 4/20/16; https://de.wikipedia.org/wiki/Silicon_Saxony, retrieved 2/9/17; https://www.vonardenne.biz/de/kontkt/zentrale, retrieved 3/16/21; https://www.dr-quandt.de, retrieved 3/16/21; www.dr-doerr.de, retrieved 3/16/21; Reinhard Delau and Lothar Springer, *Schmidts Erben: Die deutschen Werkstätten Hellerau* (Dresden:1998), 40, 42–6, 57–8, 62, 64, 73, 92–3 96, 103–5; Nils M. Schinker, *Die Gartenstadt Hellerau 1909–1945:Stadtbaukunst, Kleinwohnungsbau, Sozial-und Bodenreform* (Dresden: 2013), 107; https://www.spiegel.de/wirtschaft/deutsche-werkstätten-hellerau-schrankwände-zu-luxusyachten-a-496919, html, retrieved 2/21/20; www.dwh.de/en/aktuell/details/article/richtfest-fuer-neubau-in-grossroehrsdorf, retrived 2/25/20; https://www.dresden.de/de/wirtschaft, Medieninformation 169/2020, retrieved 12/21/20; Statistisches Landesamt des Freistaates Sachsen, https://www.statistik.sachsen.de/html/presse.html, retrieved 3/17/21.

[575] http://de.wikipedia.org/wiki/Technische_Universität_Dresden, retrieved 4/30/15; https://www.Dresden.de/wirtschaft/wissenschaft/studentenstadt, php, retrieved 4/30/15.

[576] Starke, *Geschichte*, Bd. 3, 767–9; https://de.wikipedia.org/wiki/Liste_der_Oberbürgermeister_von_Dresden, retrieved 3/18/21.

[577] Hartmut Kowalke, "The Saxon Regional Capital Dresden: 20 Years after the German Reunification," *Quaestiones Geographical*, 28B/2 (2009), 23; Mattias Lerm, "Dresdner Städtebau 1989–2009 zwischen Anspruch und Wirklichkcit," *Dresdner Hefte.* 27:4 (2009), 55, 57, 59; Starke, *Geschichte*, Bd. 3, 764–5; 780.

[578] Lerm, 56–7; Starke, *Geschichte,* Bd. 3, 780–1; Tanya Scheffler, *modern regional,* 15/2, 4, http://www.moderne-regional.de/fachbeitrag-dresdens-pragerstrasse, retrieved 2/2/17; see wikipedia.de entries for Hauptstrasse and Altmarkt Dresden; https://de.wikipedia.org./wiki/Residenzschloss_Dresden, retrieved 8/15/21.

[579] *The Frauenkirche in Dresden: History and Rebuilding* (Dresden: 2005), 11–22, 35–7, 40, 42–3, 46–7, 69. 76, 80, 83, 124; H. Jäger, "The citizens' Initiative to promote the rebuilding of the Frauenkirche in Dresden" and W. Köcheritz, The Redevelopment of the Neumarkt", both in *The Revival of Dresden* (Boston: 2000), 149, 152, 117–25; Carl-Ludwig Paeschke and Dieter Zimmer, *Dresden: Geschichten einer Stadt* (Berlin: 1994), 209–11; Hans Nadler, "The Battle to Conserve—Securing the Ruins of the Frauenkirche," Carl-Ludwig Hoch, "Always in Dresden—A Personal Memoir," Alan Russell, "Dresden and the Dresden Trust," and Appendix 2, all in *Dresden: A City Reborn* (New York: 1999), 92, 69, 5–7, 232–3; Victoria Knebel, *Preserve and Rebuild: Dresden during the Transformations of 1989–90* (New York: 2007), 80, 101–3, 124, 126, 128, 132, 135;
https://en.wikipedia.org/wiki/Günter_Blobel, retrieved 8/15/21;
https://de.wikipedia.org/wiki/Frauenkirche_(Dresden), edited 2/24/21, retrieved 3/19/21; Kunsthalle im Lipsiusbau,"
https://www.skd.museum/en/besuch/lipsiusbau, retrieved 8/15/21.

[580] Olaf Glöckner, "Immigranten und Visionen—Juden in Sachsen seit 1990," *Juden in Sachsen* (Leipzig: 2013), 213, 215, 223, 225; Uwe Ullrich, *Zur Geschichte der Juden in Dresden* (Dresden: 2001), 45; Knebel, 42, 111 (note 54); Susanne Vees-Gulani, "The Politics of New Beginnings: The Continued Exclusion of the Nazi Past in Dresden's Cityscape," *Beyond Berlin: Twelve German Cities Confront the Nazi Past* (Ann Arbor: 2008), 26, 33–4, 38, 42–4; https://www.sachsen-online.de/land-leute/juden-in-mittelsachsen, retrieved

3/19/21; https://www.revosax.sachsen.de/ vorschrift/5350-Vertrag Sachsen-Landesverband-der-Jüdischen Gemeinden, retrieved 8/16/21;https://de.wikipedia.org/Neue_Synagogue_(Dresden), edited 12/10/20, retrieved 3/20/21;
https://www.dresden.de/en/tourism/attractions/sights/old-town/new-synagogue php, retrieved from official city Website, 3/20/21;
https:// en.wikipedia.org/wiki/Bescht_Yeshiva_Dresden, edited 3/19/21, retrieved 3/19/21.

[581] https://en.wikipedia.org/wiki/Neo-Nazism, edited 3/20/21, retrieved 3/23/21; www. JTA.org/1990/10/23/archive, Neo-nazi March in Dresden Outrages Jewish Community, retrieved 4/19/20;
https://en.wikipedia.org/wiki/Neo-Nazi_marches_in-Dresden, edited 3/14/21, retrieved3/21/21;
https://dresden1302.noblogs.org/post/2011/01/21/aktuellen-stand-und-sich-überschlagende-ereignisse-zum-13-und-19-februar-2011-in-dresden, retrieved 5/7/20;
https://dresden1302.noblogs.org/post/2011/02/18/verwaltungsgericht-dresden-erlaubt-drei-naziveranstaltungen-am-19-2-in-Dresden,retrieved 5/11/20; www.antifainfoblatt.de/artikel/keine-neonazidemonstration-dresden, retrieved 5/11/20; Moritz Wichmann, "Dresden, Nazi-Free: The New Politics of German Civil Disobedience," *Dissent*, 3/8/13,
https://www.dissentmagazine.org/online/articles/dresden-nazi-free,retrieved 2/18/20.

[582] https://de.wikipedia.org/wiki/Pegida, edited 3/23/21, retrieved 3/23/21; Karl-Heinz Reuband, "Wer demonstriert in Dresden für Pegida? Ergebnisse empirischer Studien, methodische Grundlagen und offene Fragen," *Mitteilungen des Instituts für Deutsches und Internationales Parteienrecht und Parteiforschung* 21 (2015), 133-147.

[583] https://de.wikipedia.org/wiki/Alternative-für-Deutschland, edited 3/23/21, retrieved 3/23/21;
https://en.wikipedia.org/wiki/2017_German-federalelection#Parties_and_ leaders, edited 3/16/21, retrieved 3/24/21;
https://www.haz.de/Nachrichten/Politik/Deutschland-Welt/Landtagswahlin-Sachsen-2019-Erst-Hochrechnung-und-Ergebnisse, retrieved 3/24/21;

https://news.yahoo.com/ww2-bombing-commemorated-for-stronghold145702904. html, retrieved 3/23/21; https://www.mz.de/deutschland-undwelt/politik/bjorn-hocke-spricht-bei-demo-in-dresden-1648873, accessed 5/6/22; https://www.dw.com/en/Germany-dresden-declares-naziemergency/a-51085539, retrieved 1/23/20; "So war der 13. Februar in Dresden," Sächsische Zeitung, 13.2.2021, sächsische.de, retrieved 8/17/22; Neo-Nazi March mars remembrance of World War II bombing," Deutsche Welle, 13. Februar. 2022, dw.de, retrieved 8/17/22; "Menschenkette am Sonntag, 13. Februar. 2022 in Dresden," Pressemitteilungen der Stadt Dresden, 10.02.2022, retrieved 8/20/22; https://2n.wikipedia.org/wiki/Björn_Höcke, retrieved 7/1/24; Polizeieinsatz zum Versammlungsgeschehen am 13.Februar 2023, https://www.polizei.sachsen.de/de/MI_2023_96132.html, retrieved 7/1/24; Polizeieinsatz am 11. und 13. Februar 2024, https://www.polizei.sachsen.de/de/MI_2024_104151.html, retrieved 6/30/24: www.dw.com/en/german-city-of-dresden-commemorates-wwII-bombing/1-68250052, retrieved 6/30/24; https://wahlen.dresden.de/2024/srw/index/.html, retrieved 7/1/24; Claudia Jerzak, "Der 13.Februar 1945 im kollektiven Gedächtnis Dresden," https://www.bpb.de/themen/deutschlandarchiv/518214/der 13.februar/1945, retrieved 6/30/24; www.mdr.de/nachrichten/sachsen/dresden-radebeul/gedenken-erinnerungen-bombardierung-menschenkette-100.html, retrieved 7/1/24; https://www.vorwaerts.de/inland/studie-der-uni-leipzig-darum-ist-die-afd-in-ostdeutschland-so-stark, retrieved 7/2/24; https://www.augsburger-allgemeine.de/politik/darum-ist-die-afd-im-osten-besonders stark, retrieved 7/21/24; https://www.dresden.de/media/pdf/presseamt/2024_09_02_pressekonferenz_landtagswahl_2024.pdf, retrieved 9/5/24.

[584] https://de.wikipedia.org/wiki/Bundesautobahn_17#Konflikte_um_den_Bau, edited 1/26/20, retrieved 2/27/20.

[585] Bénédicte Gaillard and Dennis Rodwell, "A Failure of Process? Comprehending the Issues Fostering Heritage Conflict in Dresden Elbe Valley and Liverpool-Maritime Mercantile City World Heritage Sites," *The Historic Environment* 6:1 (2015), 17–19, 21–2, 28–9, 35–6, 38–9 (notes 10/16);

www.engageliverpool.com/wp-content/uploads/2017/03/2015-05-HEN-61-Dresden-Liverpool-BG-DR-pdf, retrieved 5/3/20; Waldschlösschen_Bridge, retrieved 3/5/20; "Ruckblick: Der Streit um die Waldschlösschenbrücke in Dresden," *Dresdner Neueste Nachrichten* 7/14/2016; Peter Schilder, "Auch die Kleine Hufeisennase bleibt glücklich," http://www.faz.net/aktuell/kpolitik/inland/waldschlösschenbrücke-in-dresden-eröffnet, retrieved 8/25/13; Knebel, 144–7, 149–50.

[586] Bettina Klemm, *Der Dresdner Kulturpalast: Eine Zeitreise von 1969 bis heute* (Berlin: 2016), 12–15, 25–6, 38, 40–1, 43, 58, 63–4, 74, 81–2, 93–4, 100, 104–5, 113–17, 121–7, 135–6, 139, 158–60, 173; Frauke Roth, "Eine neue Heimat für die Dresdner Philharmonie," *Kulturpalast Dresden* (Berlin: 2018), 17; for George Arnhold and the Philharmonic, https://de.wikipedia.org/wiki/George_Gerard_Arnhold, retrieved 12/29/2024.

Epilogue

[587] *Mythos Dresden: Eine kulturhistorische Revue* (Köln: 2006), 99, 132, 101–14, 135–40. The Deutsches Hygiene-Museum, Dresden sponsored this work. Sigrid Walther summarized the exhibit's interpretations.